Power and Primacy

Power and Primacy:

A Recent History of Western Intervention in the Asia-Pacific

A. B. Abrams

PETER LANG
Oxford • Bern • Berlin • Bruxelles • New York • Wien

Bibliographic information published by Die Deutsche Nationalbibliothek.
Die Deutsche Nationalbibliothek lists this publication in the Deutsche National-bibliografie; detailed bibliographic data is available on the Internet at http://dnb.d-nb.de.

A catalogue record for this book is available from the British Library.

Library of Congress Cataloging-in-Publication Data
Names: A. B. Abrams, author.
Title: Power and primacy: A Recent History of Western Intervention in the Asia-Pacific / A. B. Abrams.
Description: Oxford ; New York : Peter Lang, [2019] | Includes bibliographical references and index.
Identifiers: LCCN 2018057323 | ISBN 9781788746120 (alk. paper)
Subjects: LCSH: Asia--Foreign relations--1945- | Asia--Foreign relations--Western countries. | Western countries--Foreign relations--Asia. | Intervention (International law)--Asia.
Classification: LCC DS33.3 .A36 2019 | DDC 303.48/2501821--dc23 LC record available at https://lccn.loc.gov/2018057323

Cover image: http://www.apimages.com/metadata/Index/North-Korea-Succession/001a1709f98f40e790ddc6f12f3484c0/12/0

ISBN 978-1-78874-612-0 (Hardback) • ISBN 978-1-78997-623-6 (Paperback)
ISBN 978-1-78874-613-7 (ePDF) • ISBN 978-1-78874-614-4 (ePub)
ISBN 978-1-78874-615-1 (mobi)

Published by Peter Lang Ltd, International Academic Publishers,
52 St Giles, Oxford, OX1 3LU, United Kingdom
oxford@peterlang.com, www.peterlang.com

This publication has been peer reviewed.

Contents

Abbreviations

A2AD	Anti Access Area Denial
ABCC	Atomic Bomb Casualty Commission
ABMI	Asian Bond Market Initiative
AEC	(United States) Atomic Energy Commission
AFOSI	(United States) Air Force Office of Special Investigations
AIG	American International Group
AIIB	Asia Infrastructure Investment Bank
AMF	Asian Monetary Fund
ATP	ASEAN Plus Three
ASEAN	Association of South East Asian Nations
BPHPJ Axis	Beijing-Pyongyang-Hanoi-Phnom Penh-Jakarta Axis
CAT	Civil Air Transport
CCP	Chinese Communist Party
CFR	Council on Foreign Relations
CIA	Central Intelligence Agency
CIS	Commonwealth of Independent States
CMI	Chiang Mai Initiative
CONEFO	Conference of the New Emerging Forces
DARPA	Defence Advanced Research Projects Agency
DCPSCS	Declaration on the Conduct of Parties in the South China Sea
DPRK	Democratic People's Republic of Korea
EAEC	East Asian Economic Caucus
EAEG	East Asian Economic Group
EAS	East Asian Summit
ECOSOC	United Nations Economic and Social Council
EU	European Union
GANEFO	Games of New Emerging Forces
GDP	Gross Domestic Product
GMD	Guomindang

GNP	Gross National Product
HUK	Hukabalahap (People's Army Against Japan)
ICBM	Intercontinental Ballistic Missile
IISS	International Institute for Strategic Studies
IMF	International Monetary Fund
IS	Islamic State (alternative name for ISIS)
ISIS	Islamic State of Iraq and Syria
JCS	(United States) Joint Chiefs of Staff
JGR	(Routledge) *Journal of Genocide Research*
KGB	Komitet gosudarstvennoy bezopasnost (Soviet Union's State Security Agency)
KMAG	Korean Military Advisory Group
KPA	Korean People's Army
MAD	Mutually Assured Destruction
MAP	(United States) Military Assistance Program
MENA	Middle East and North Africa
MGR	Mere Gook Rule
MIT	Massachusetts Institute of Technology
NAFTA	North American Free Trade Agreement
NATO	North Atlantic Treaty Organization
NPT	Treaty on the Non-Proliferation of Nuclear Weapons
NSC	(United States Government's) National Security Council
OSS	Office of Strategic Services
PKI	Partai Komunis Indonesia (Indonesian Communist Party)
PKP	Partido Komunista ng Pilipinas (Communist Party of the Philippines)
PLA	(Chinese) People's Liberation Army
PNAC	Project for the New American Century
PNI	Partai Nasional Indonesia (Indonesian Nationalist Party)
POGO	Project on Government Oversight
POW	Prisoner of War
PPKI	Panitia Persiapan Kemerdekaan Indonesia (Preparatory Committee for Indonesian Independence)
PPP	Purchasing Power Parity
PRC	People's Republic of China

PRK	People's Republic of Korea
RAA	Recreation and Amusement Association
RAF	(British) Royal Air Force
RAS	Russian Academy of Sciences
RCEP	Regional Comprehensive Economic Partnership
ROK	Republic of Korea
ROC	Republic of China
SCO	Shanghai Cooperation Organization
SEATO	South East Asian Treaty Organization
STRATCOM	United States Strategic Command
TCDD	2,3,7,8-Tetrachlorodibenzo-p-dioxin
TPP	Trans Pacific Partnership
UK	United Kingdom
UN	United Nations
UNCOK	United Nations Commission on Korea
UNESCO	United Nations Educational, Scientific and Cultural Organization
UNICEF	United Nations Children's Fund
UNSC	United Nations Security Council
U.S.	United States (of America)
USA	United States of America
USSR	Union of Soviet Socialist Republics
VC	Viet Cong
WIDF	Women's International Democratic Federation
WMD	Weapons of Mass Destruction
WTO	World Trade Organization

Introduction

Since the expansion of the Portuguese Empire to the Asia-Pacific in the early sixteenth century the West has long been intrinsically involved in the region through the projection of its military power. By the beginning of the Second World War regional maps demonstrated the near complete dominance of Western empires over the peoples of the Asia-Pacific. The entire region, except for the Japanese Imperial territories including the home islands, Manchuria, Taiwan and Korea, was comprised of territories either subservient to the interests of Western powers or, in most cases, ruled by them directly. Much of Indonesia was known as the Dutch East Indies while Vietnam, Laos and Cambodia were known as French Indochina. British Malaya, British Borneo, Hong Kong and a number of strategic islands were among other extensive British owned territories – not to mention Oceania which had almost entirely been forcefully depopulated and repopulated by European settlers. Thailand was divided between British and French spheres of influence and made a client state under the Anglo-Siamese treaty which granted Britain extensive one-sided concessions. China was similarly long subjected to 'unequal treaties' with and forced to grant extensive territorial concessions to Western imperial powers. The Americans ruled the Philippines and Guam as colonies, as the Portuguese ruled Macau, the Maluku Islands and East Timor among their 'possessions.' Germany and Spain had also formerly held extensive colonial possessions in the region – one where Asian self-determination was suppressed by the dominant military might of the West.

Direct European rule and near absolute Western dominance could change only with the end of the West's longstanding monopoly on modern industrial and military capabilities, which came with the modernization of Japan in the late nineteenth century and the Soviet Union's rapid Stalinist industrialization program in the 1930s. Both of these developments challenged the Western centric world order and put significant pressure on the Western empires, which had otherwise sought an indefinite colonial administration over their Pacific territories.[1] The emergence of two major Eastern nations as military and industrial powers caused a momentous shift in the global balance of power. Imperial Japan and the USSR were key to facilitating the independence of numerous Asia-Pacific states – providing arms, ideologies and inspiration, which allowed Asian peoples to challenge the Western empires. The result was the postwar emergence of independent Asian Pacific nations capable of opposing Western regional designs after centuries of subjugation, all of which were largely facilitated by either Japanese pan-Asianism or Soviet communism – in several cases by a combination of both.

This book explores the recent history of Western intervention in the Asia-Pacific region and its impacts – from the waging of the Pacific War against Japan to the extensive continued Western involvement in the twenty-first century. The means consistently used by the Western Bloc to maintain their extensive regional influence and their primacy, both as the center of power globally and as the dominant force in Asia, are covered extensively. The Pacific War marked a point of no return for the centuries old Western colonial structures, with the Japanese Empire's string of early military victories expelling the Western empires from their colonial possessions across the region – many of which had been held continuously for several centuries. The example set by Japan's successes inspired nationalists across the region by demonstrating that the West could be confronted and defeated. In the words of Dutch Prime Minister Gebrandy, the Japanese had undermined both 'white prestige' and the 'racial instincts and inferiority complexes' which had for so long facilitated Western dominance – posing an existential threat to the status quo.[2] Though Japan was eventually brought to its knees, with what U.S. President Harry Truman referred to as 'a rain of ruin from the air, the like of which has never been seen on this Earth' devastating 69 of its cities in a nuclear and firebombing campaign killing millions, the legacy of its victories could not be reversed. The end of the Pacific War marked the beginning of a new era for the Asia-Pacific, and challenges to Western dominance emerged across the region from insurgencies in Malaysia and the Philippines to successful armed struggles against Western military forces in Korea, Indonesia and Vietnam – twice in the case of the latter two. The overthrow of the U.S. client government in China in

1949 and establishment of the People's Republic of China furthered this trend towards genuine sovereignty and a decline in Western influence.

The Western powers have since 1945 undertaken extensive efforts to maintain their regional dominance, and this struggle has continued into the twenty-first century. Armed interventions in the immediate aftermath of the Pacific War ranged from the British, French, American and Dutch military efforts to re-obtain their overseas colonial possessions following Japan's defeat to the United States' abolition of the People's Republic of Korea by military decree and imposition of a military government run by leaders hand-picked by the U.S. military itself. The U.S. deployment of vast fleets and over 1,000 nuclear warheads across East Asia in the 1950s to maintain a favorable balance of power against then non-nuclear China and North Korea was another example of an attempt to maintain regional dominance by deploying overwhelming force when challenged by the capabilities of emerging independent regional powers. More recently the announcement of the 'Obama doctrine' and 'Pivot to Asia' in 2010 marked the beginning of a redeployment of substantial American, British, French and other European forces to Asia under a single banner. The Western Bloc, since the Second World War led by the United States, has thus remained both consistent and resolute in its attempts to maintain its position as the dominant power in this critical region. An analysis of the means by which Western powers have waged wars on, overthrown or otherwise undermined independent and post-colonial states and installed client governments in their place across the Asia-Pacific to cement their dominance, and the impacts of all of these efforts on the region and its peoples, is thus critical to evaluating the overall impacts of Western interventionism in the region.

From the dismantling of the Japanese Empire and the country's subsequent remaking under an American military government to the wars that formed China, Indonesia and Vietnam as independent nations and the deals made by Western powers to grant independence to states such as the Philippines in exchange for continued concessions to their former rulers, the circumstances of state formation have tangible implications to this day. These are explored in the first two sections of this work – with each chapter focusing on different aspects of Western intervention in the region. The legacy of decolonization and the independence struggles of the twentieth century continue to shape the Asia-Pacific in the twenty-first century, an understanding of which is crucial to comprehending the region today. Contemporary inter-Korean and Korean-American relations for example can only be fully understood with a knowledge of the major events that occurred on the peninsula after the Japanese occupation ended in 1945, with the background of the Korean War, the differing cultural and social influences on each of the Koreas and the factors which shaped modern North Korean ideology and identity and led to a perceived need for a nuclear deterrent.

The Korean Peninsula has been a site of paramount importance regarding Western involvement and attempts to maintain dominance over the Asia-Pacific region, and was the site of the only major modern conventional land war the Western Bloc has fought in Asia. The Korean War represented the most direct confrontation between Western and Asian powers since Japan's fall, and the peninsula has ever since been at the center of several key conflicts including the Western Bloc's confrontation with Asian nationalism, the People's Republic of China, Soviet communism, and more recently the 'Axis of Evil.' A great deal regarding the conduct of Western powers in the Asia-Pacific, both in wartime against an Asian adversary and in peacetime towards a population under their power, as well as the means used by the Western Bloc to wage war on Asia-Pacific nations and the effects on populations, both allied and otherwise, can best be explored in the Korean conflict. This makes Korea the most suitable exemplar of a number of phenomena regarding the nature of Western intervention in the region. As a result of these factors and the ongoing nature of the conflict, which has lasted for almost three quarters of a century, the second of three sections is devoted entirely to a detailed coverage of Western intervention on the Korean Peninsula.

The third section of this work analyzes contemporary relations and factors affecting the balances of powers in the Asia-Pacific. Economic warfare and its implementation in the region are explored, with particular attention being paid to the 1997 Asian financial crisis and its continuing implications. Changes to the military balance of power in the region and Western attempts to maintain a longstanding dominant position are also analyzed, drawing on critical studies carried out by military analysts, governments and think tanks. The exploitation of divisions amongst Asian powers, the suppression of regional economic initiatives and promotion of those which strongly favor Western interests, and the nature of the Western Bloc's relations with and means of exerting influence over its client states as a vital means of furthering its goals, are also explored.

The recurring and primary cause for conflict in the Asia-Pacific region between the West and those states which have asserted their independence and opposed Western dominance and intervention has been a stark conflict in their worldviews. This is a factor consistent in almost all such conflicts in the region. It does not refer to a clash of capitalist and socialist ideologies, often perceived to be the cause of most regional conflicts during the Cold War, but rather refers to nations' perceptions of the nature of international relations, the Asian regional order and states' right to self-determination. Several independent Asian states which emerged in the aftermath of the Pacific War have sought an international regional order comprised of sovereign states equal in their rights to their sovereignty, including self-defense and self-determination and prohibiting forced external interference into any state's domestic affairs – the same order enshrined in the United Nations charter. The Western Bloc on the other hand has consistently sought a framework of international relations under which both the world and regional orders are centered on its own dominance – allowing Western powers to influence the affairs of all other states and retain indefinite dominion over the Asia-Pacific. This essential clash of word views, which largely dates back to the 1940s when the popular slogan 'Asia for the Asiatics' was seen as a critical threat to the status quo of Western regional dominance, has continued in various forms ever since. It has been the underlying cause of most major conflicts in the Asia-Pacific region in the modern era, from Indonesia and Vietnam's wars of independence to the United States' ongoing tensions with both China and North Korea today.

After reading this work the nature of contemporary relations in the Asia-Pacific and their historical and contemporary determinants can be better understood, as can Western intentions towards the Asia-Pacific. The British paper the *The Economist* was among the Western sources which claimed: 'Outside China, every Asian country bar North Korea welcomes America's presence in the region and wants it to remain.'[3] Then

U.S. Secretary of State Hillary Clinton, a key architect behind the expansion of the American military presence in Asia, stated similarly though more bluntly in 2011: 'An engaged America is vital to Asia's future. The region is eager for our leadership and our business.'[4] Whether, based on the United States and its Western partners' intentions, their historical conduct in the region and the impacts of their previous interventions, this 'desire for American leadership' – if it truly exists – is well deserved can be ascertained.

As then U.S. President Barack Obama declared in May 2016 regarding the future the United States intended for the Asia-Pacific region: 'America should write the rules. America should call the shots. Other countries should play by the rules that America and our partners set, and not the other way around.'[5] Whether this vision will be attained and the primary means used by state actors on all sides to either bring about a continued Western dominated regional order or to prevent it will be elaborated. Understanding of vital historical background, the goals of major state actors and the means used to obtain these goals over many years are all key to comprehending the ongoing and decades long conflict being waged ideologically, militarily, economically and otherwise for the future of the Asia-Pacific – the outcome of which, given the region's vital importance, is set to determine the fate of the entire world in the twenty-first century.

Terms

Asia-Pacific: Collective term for East and Southeast Asia.

China: Unless otherwise specified will from 1949 in political contexts refer to the Beijing-based *People's Republic of China* rather than the Taipei-based *Republic of China*. The *Republic of China* will from 1949 be referred to as Taiwan.

East Asia: The region encompassing China – including Taiwan, the Koreas and Japan. Geographically also includes the Russian Far East.

Pacific War: Otherwise known as the Pacific theater of the Second World War.

Southeast Asia: Members and observers in the ASEAN including Brunei, Cambodia, East Timor, Indonesia, Laos, Malaysia, Myanmar, Papua New Guinea, the Philippines, Singapore, Thailand and Vietnam.

Western Bloc: Alliance of leading Western powers established in the early Cold War and led by the United States, since incorporating East Germany, including Belgium, Britain, Canada, Denmark, France, Germany, Italy, Norway, the Netherlands, Luxembourg, Portugal and the United States. All but Canada, Luxemburg and Norway were major colonial powers – with these three having spent extended periods incorporated into larger European empires. Often abbreviated to 'the West.'

Notes

1 Frey, Marc and Pruessen Ronald W., *The Transformation of Southeast Asia: International Perspectives on Decolonization*, Armonk, NY, M. E. Sharpe, 2003 (p. 11).

2 Hotta, Eri., *Pan Asianism and Japan's War 1931–1945*, New York, Palgrave Macmillan, 2007 (p. 217).
3 '"Disorder Under Heaven," Special Report,' *The Economist*, April 22, 2017 (p. 9).
4 Clinton, Hillary, 'America's Pacific Century,' *Foreign Policy*, October 11, 2011.
5 Obama, Barack, 'President Obama: The TPP would let America, not China, lead the way on global trade,' *The Washington Post*, May 2, 2016.

PART I

War with Japan and its Aftermath: How Western Powers Met New Challenges to their Dominance in the Pacific

CHAPTER I

Japanese Empire: The Rise and Fall of Asia's First Independent Industrial Power and How It Undermined Western Hegemony in the Pacific

> Eastern peoples were, for the greater part, still subject to racial instincts and inferiority complexes. The Japanese slogan 'Asia for the Asiatics,' might easily destroy the carefully constructed basis of our cultural synthesis ... Japanese injuries and insults to the White population – and these were already being perpetrated by the detestable Asiatic Huns- would irreparably damage white prestige unless severely punished within a short time.[1]
>
> — PIETER SJOERDS GERBRANDY, Dutch Prime Minister

> So far and wide have the roots of Japanese victory spread that we cannot now visualize all the fruit it will put forth. The people of the East seem to be waking up from their lethargy.[2]
>
> — MOHANDAS GHANDI on the impact of Japan's military successes

Imperial Japan in a Western Dominated Regional Order

Since Western powers first came to dominate the Asia-Pacific region in the sixteenth century, racial stereotyping and perceptions among Westerners of Asian races as inferiors came hand in hand with military occupation and colonial rule. The British Empire in its occupation of Singapore, Myanmar, Malaysia and parts of China, condescendingly referred to Asian peoples as the 'little yellow men.' Their attitude to the so called 'yellow race' was in many ways similar to that of other Western imperial powers in their own military involvement in the region. A great deal of the pride of Western imperial powers was based on their perceived racial and civilizational superiority relative to others, and particularly to the ancient Asian civilizations which they had conquered. The West's leading powers between them maintained an effective monopoly of both modern economies and industrial technologies, and the disparity between these and their resulting modern militaries relative to those of the rest of the world were the cornerstones which facilitated the indefinite continuation of their empires and sustained the West's global primacy for several centuries. This would come to be challenged only with the industrialization and military modernization of Japan and the Soviet Union in the twentieth century – marking a major turning point in the history of the region and the wider world.

Japan had initially been a partner of Western powers in Asia. The country's economic modernization was accomplished using Western models, a process initiated as a defensive response following the United States Navy's forceful opening of Japan to trade in 1854 under the Treaty of Kanagawa.[3] The country went on to adopt all that was Western, from ballroom dancing in Western dress to the modern capitalist economy and military. Japan had initially been subject to the 'Unequal Treaties' with Western powers which categorized it, as with the rest of Asia, as an 'uncivilized nation' inferior to those of Europe. While Western powers militarily threatened Japan, Western citizens were granted extraterritorial rights putting them above the laws of Japanese courts, and terms of trade highly favoring Western economic interests were also imposed. Such treaties were signed with the United States, Britain, France, the Netherlands, Germany (then Prussia) and Spain from 1858 to 1868. Many Western cultural practices were adopted at this time because it was crucial for the Japanese to prove to the Western powers that they were a 'civilized nation.' The only way to be considered 'civilized' under the Western-centric world order of the time was not to adhere to one's own culture – but rather to adopt prominent aspects of Western culture.

Over time Japan gained the approval of the Western powers and threats to its independence largely subsided. The government succeeded in negotiating revisions of the unequal treaties, primarily through a combination of military and industrial modernization and adoption of 'civilized' Western practices. Japan's armed forces were heavily modeled on emulation of those of the Western powers, from the weapons used and uniforms worn to the command structures. Following a rapid modernization program, the Imperial Japanese Army and Navy proceeded to claim victory over the Russian Empire in 1905. Although Russia was only partially considered a Western nation at the time, it had adopted some limited industrialization along Western lines and become, largely by virtue of its size, one of the world's largest economies and greatest powers. The defeat of this Christian world power by a small Asian nation was a shock to Western imperial nations, which began to perceive Japan's rise as a potential threat. There was much fear and speculation of a coming 'Yellow Peril' – under which Japan would lead Asia to overcome the West and 'civilization' would be lost. Fear of this emerging 'Yellow Peril' was widely used by European scholars and leadership to encourage a heavier hand and more interventionist policies in Asia and a more complete subjugation and occupation of China to eliminate the potential for an alliance of Asian peoples to rise to challenge Western primacy.[4]

By the 1930s Japan's armed forces were among the most modern and capable in the world and could rival those of the greatest Western empires, in many fields surpassing them technologically. The country had increasingly developed an Asian nationalist ideology, and many in Japan were appalled at the state of their East and Southeast Asian neighbors subjugated under Western imperial rule. Several Japanese intellectuals sought to support other Asian nations to become independent from the Western empires. One of these was Duke Konoe Atsumaro, who established the Pan-Asian East Asian Common Culture Society and sought to boost China's economic development through mutually beneficial educational and cultural ties. He played a central role in overseeing the creation of pan-Asian ideology at the turn of the century (Konoe died in 1905). Due to European occupation of almost all neighboring countries and instability in China, however, early efforts were met with limited success.

In the scholarly field the pan-Asian movement in Japan, manifested most profoundly through the famous Kyoto school and its renowned associated historians such as Naitō Konan, sought to challenge the West's extremely Eurocentric definition of modernity and depiction of history. The Kyoto school constructed a Sinocentric East Asian region as a historical universe with unique dynamics of modernity. They sought to determine the social and cultural characteristics of an 'East Asian modern age,' and to define modernity themselves rather than have it defined for them by Western powers. It was critical for the future of Asia to compete with rather than acquiesce to the Western definition of modernity, which tied Westernization inextricably with modernization. With China's civilization long predating that of Japan, and with Chinese thought and history profoundly influencing that of Japan over centuries, it was not surprising that they would choose China as the center of their pan-Asian narratives.[5] Indeed, the Japanese long saw themselves as the true cultural representatives of ancient Chinese and Confucian thought – a far cry in their eyes from China's own highly corrupt and militaristic Guomindang government Japan would soon engage in war.

Pan-Asian ideology advocated regional co-operation and unity against foreign exploitative forces, aiming to end Western imperialism which had brutally subjugated Asian peoples for over three centuries. The Asia-Pacific region would co-operate in economic development and defense to bring about regional co-prosperity. Leading pan-Asian figure Naniwa Kawashima described the ideology and Japan's responsibility as the only modern and free Asian nation: 'We will liberate various Asian peoples from their enslaved state, placing them under the management of first-class national governments. Rallying them all into a unified bloc, we will free them from the unjust, aggressive chokehold … we will curb the unjust, inhumane, thoroughly evil actions, which have been undertaken by the Europeans.'[6]

Under the influence of pan-Asian thought, the Japanese government had sent agents and support to various nationalist movements throughout the Asia-Pacific. Indonesia was one example, where nationalists were sponsored to visit Japan and discuss the future of their country's independence after centuries of Dutch occupation.[7] Many individuals were also inspired to act themselves, such as Captain Hara Tei of the Imperial Army who renounced his service to fight alongside the First Philippine Republic against the American invasion; Yoshida Yamada who, after working for the School of Sino-Japanese Trade Study in Shanghai, who joined Sun Yat-sen's anti-imperialist revolutionary movement and was lost in action;[8] and the many Japanese educators such as Kawahara Misako who, seeking to aid China's emergence as a modern economic partner in Asia, endured great hardship to teach a new generation of Chinese leadership throughout the country at the behest of the Chinese government. All of these were inspired by the idea of seeing Asia develop freely from their subservience to Western imperial interests.

By the 1940s Japan's pan-Asian ideology had changed significantly from its origins. Though still advocating Asian co-prosperity, assertion of Japanese primacy and regional dominance became increasingly prominent themes. Imperial Japan's ideology increasingly became a Japanese nationalism disguised as pan-Asianism, which the conduct of the Japanese military in neighboring Asian nations quickly proved. The softer tones of peaceful co-prosperity from the early 1900s of Duke Konoe and others like him had been drowned out by the calls for iron fisted imperialism in the manner practiced by European states.

Kawashima himself observed the dangerous changes which took place in this regard as Japanese forces conducted themselves as conquerors rather than as liberators. He stated: 'our military authorities now stationed in Manchuria must ease up on the excessively interventionist approach they have assumed in the affairs of Manchukuo and restore cooperation as the operating mode in Japanese-Manchurian relations.' He warned: 'If in our zeal to capitalize on patriotic passions to effect an immediate territorial settlement we turn our backs on the enduring ideals of Imperial Japan and do nothing more than reenact the evil deeds of the European and American powers, there will be repercussions. We will not see the day when we can make definitely clear to Asians and other peoples of the world Japan's true spirit and gain their heartfelt allegiance and trust.'[9]

Japan's previous perceptions of neighboring Asian nations had changed significantly, from fraternity and a sense of injustice, felt by many Japanese intellectuals and elites who had witnessed the subjugation of the region to Western imperial interests, to a perception of superiority over other Asian peoples. Following the significant cultural and philosophical influence Western powers had on Japan, this perception was extremely similar to that which had dominated Western thought in regard to the Asia-Pacific for centuries. This was described by Tamura Yoshio, a member of Japan's biological warfare unit, who stated: 'I had already gotten to [a point] where I lacked pity. After all, we were already implanted with a narrow racism, in the form of a belief in the superiority of the so-called "Yamato Race." We disparaged all other races. … If we didn't have a feeling of racial superiority, we couldn't have done it."[10] Japan's actions in Asia had grown to resemble the very powers from which they had sought to liberate it.

In September 1940 Japan invaded French-occupied Vietnam and ended the brutal French occupation which had lasted over half a century. Although Vichy France was if anything their enemy at the time, the British, Americans, Australians and Dutch nevertheless all found it unacceptable for an Asian power to intervene to end Western rule over an Asian colonial possession. The potential for the formation of an alliance of Asian powers, regardless of whether by force or consent, as per the Japanese proposed Asian Co-Prosperity Sphere that was beginning to take shape, was a considerable threat to their continued regional dominance. A unified Asia independent of external influence, with its large population and considerable resources combined with Japan's institutional system and advanced industrialization techniques, was furthermore a very potent threat to the West's primacy and continued position as a global center of power.

Signs that Japan would implement a rapid regional modernization program throughout the Asia-Pacific were it to replace the Western imperial powers as the dominant power in the region were already manifold. Examples included the Empire's extensive industrialization and infrastructure development in Japanese controlled territories such as in Taiwan, where agricultural development was also substantial,[11] and in northern Korea. Korean economic output had increased tenfold after thirty years of Japanese rule.[12] If similar growth occurred throughout the region it would have been the most significant threat yet to Western economic and military primacy by ending the critical disparity between the developed West and the subjugated, dependent and industrially backward Asian nations. Small and resource poor Japan had itself been able to challenge the West economically and militarily, and had it implemented a modernization program across the region based on lessons from its own rapid industrialization the military and economic clout of the resulting Japanese led Asia-Pacific power bloc would very likely have surpassed that of the Western powers. While the Koreans and other subjects themselves were not the primary beneficiaries of this economic development, the modernization of the Asia-Pacific under a united Asian Empire was an imminent threat to the West's position.

As well as its potential to modernize Asia and end Western economic and industrial primacy, Japan also challenged the centuries-old and strategically critical Western military primacy in the Pacific. Western imperial powers were particularly threatened because Japan had withdrawn from the American and British drafted Washington Naval Treaty and London Naval Treaty. These treaties had been written to ensure Western military dominance in the Asia-Pacific region continued. The Washington treaty stated that the United States Navy had to equal the Japanese Navy by a ratio of at least 10:7.[13] The London treaty meanwhile restricted the Japanese Navy to 12 heavy cruisers, where the United States and Britain were permitted 18 and 15 respectively. Similar restrictions were placed on other warship types, with the combined tonnage of Japan's light cruiser fleet restricted to 100,450 tons where Britain and the United States were permitted fleets of over 335,00 tons between them.[14] Even before its withdrawal however, Japan had focused on developing a better trained and technologically superior warships, fielding more advanced carrier aircraft, battleships and submarines – something which they were able to achieve to compensate for their considerable quantitative disadvantage.[15,16]

To prevent the emergence of a unified, modern and militarily powerful Asia the Allied Western powers initiated a trade embargo on Japan and cut off 90 percent of the country's oil supplies. This embargo was effectively an act of war. Under the United States' Export Control Act steel exports to Japan were also cut. Cutting off Japan from its oil supplies was seen by many in the United States leadership to be a guarantee that war would break out. As a modern industrialized nation Japan needed oil to be able to operate its economy and military, otherwise both would be crippled. Oil in the region was controlled by the British and Dutch in the territories they occupied, while Japan also relied heavily on imports from the United States. Japan's leadership thus perceived military action as a necessary measure to ensure the coutnry's survival.

The United States' own *Eight Action Memo*, an intelligence report on the Second World War from October 7, 1940, strongly indicated that Washington sought to take measures to provoke Japan into committing an 'overt act of war.' This was supported by several members of the Office of Naval Intelligence. Similar strategies had often been implemented by Western powers, where non-violent provocation was used to goad an adversary into war – allowing the Western Bloc to depict itself as responding to rather than initiating aggression. Indeed, the *Eight Action Memo* and Western embargoes on Japan are until today scantly mentioned in relation to the causes of the outbreak of the Pacific War. The memo stated that public opinion in the United States would not support a war of aggression, it was thus seen as highly desirable to provoke Japan into starting a war itself. This would increase public support for the war. The memo read: 'It is not believed that in the present state of political opinion the United States government is capable of declaring war against Japan without more ado … If by [the eight-point plan] Japan could be led to commit an overt act of war, so much the better.' These measures included military escalation in the region, but most crucially an oil embargo and economic warfare against Japan.[17]

In 1941 the Western powers' economic warfare efforts against Japan escalated, as dictated by the memo. In July a full oil embargo was imposed and all Japanese assets in the United States were frozen. Japan's oil reserves were set to run out, and although the country had been hesitant to start a war with the major Western military powers the oil embargo necessitated such action. (The United States itself has similarly used protecting its oil supplies as a just pretext for military intervention since then.)[18] It was essential for the United States to enter the war against Japan with its public onside. If Japan were to successfully create a pan-Asian Co-Prosperity Sphere it would mean an end to Western imperial dominance in the region, and this could seriously threaten the future global primacy of the Western world. To allow the Asian nations including China to be united under a single economic, military and political bloc led by a modern and demonstratively highly efficient world power such as Japan was an unacceptable outcome.

When in December 1941 Japan engaged itself in a war with the leading Western powers in the Asia-Pacific region, including Britain, Australia, the Netherlands and the United States, it was initially victorious over all of them. Japan won every major battle for the first six months of the war. From the battles of Guam and Wake Island, Bataan and Corregidor in the

American occupied Philippines, to taking British occupied Hong Kong and Singapore, and battles from Borneo to Java in Indonesia to name but a few, the Japanese won victory after victory against Western military forces. For the Western powers defeat at the hands of these 'racial inferiors' was a great humiliation. Their belief in racial superiority had been a cornerstone of Western society and empire for well over a century. As British Prime Minister Winston Churchill had several times reiterated: 'The Aryan stock is bound to triumph.'[19] This belief held by the Western imperial nations had been so suddenly challenged with the swift destruction of their armies and sinking of their navies by the first and only modern Asian nation, a very small one no less, which had singlehandedly defeated all of them.

The Western imperial powers were deeply humiliated by their defeat at the hands of a small Japanese force, as clearly shown in British historian Professor Angus Calder's account of the British military defeat in Singapore and the devastating impact of this in undermining the psychology and world view of the West. Singapore had been the leading overseas British military site in the world and the center of the Empire's control of the Asia-Pacific, Oceania and its vital South Asian colonies, with more personnel stationed there than in Britain itself in peacetime. Calder wrote:

> Most British officials, soldiers, planters and businessmen in Asia had underestimated Asiatic peoples in general. Their racialist contempt for 'little yellow men,' against whom their clubs maintained a color bar, was unlikely to foster loyalty to the British Empire among Chinese and Malay subjects. Their power depended not on their subjects' love, but ultimately on the Royal Navy. Whites had faith in the great Singapore naval base ... It symbolized the UK's will to remain a great power in the East and to guarantee the safety of kith and kin in Australia and New Zealand ... British behavior in Penang [in northwest Malaya] was symptomatic. Even after the Japanese, on Pearl Harbor day, invaded the Malayan Peninsula, British inhabitants complacently flocked to the bar of the Eastern Oriental Hotel. But soon air raids brought terror and chaos. Whites – and whites only – were evacuated in haste. Almost all British officials, doctors and nurses withdrew, leaving Malay and Indian subordinates to make terms with conquerors and serve the sick.[20]

Calder goes on to conclude:

> Next day the commanding officer, General Arthur F. Percival, surrendered. The largest army ever assembled by Britain in the Far East, 130,000 British, Empire and

> Commonwealth troops, became prisoners of war of 50,000 'little yellow men' ... the façade of Western imperialism had been blown away like balsa wood. A high U.S. official had recently warned that if Singapore fell it would 'lower immeasurably the prestige among Eastern peoples of the "white race", and particularly of the British Empire and the United States.' So it proved.[21]

Military defeat at the hands of the Japanese not only undermined the West's view of themselves as superior powers, but it also changed the perception of the West by Asians and subjugated peoples at the time – who had for so long seen the imperial powers that ruled them as an undefeatable superior force in the world. Japan's 1905 victory against Russia had previously inspired those under European imperial rule throughout the Asia-Pacific and beyond, showing that a European Christian empire could be defeated by an Asian power. As Indian political analyst Pankaj Mishra had noted: 'For the first time since the middle ages, a non-European country had vanquished a European power in a major war. And Japan's victory sparked a hundred fantasies – of national freedom, racial dignity, or simple vengefulness – in the minds of those who had sullenly endured European authority over their lands.'[22] Mohandas Ghandi, later to become India's renowned independence leader, observed the profound psychological impact of Japan's victory, stating: 'so far and wide have the roots of Japanese victory spread that we cannot now visualize all the fruit it will put forth. The people of the East seem to be waking up from their lethargy.'[23]

Japan's string of victories from 1941 swept European imperial rule out of much of Asia where it had been entrenched for several centuries, in many cases for over 300 years. This if anything had a greater effect on the Asian populations' perception of the West than their victory in 1905. American historian John Dower referred to Japan's success in 'forever destroying the myth of white omnipotence,' one which had prevailed for centuries across the Asia-Pacific and been a key facilitator of Western imperial rule.[24] The loss of this substantial psychological asset, and evidence that European rule over the Asia-Pacific could not be justified by ideas of racial supremacy, was met with much apprehension by Western leaders. Dutch Prime Minister Pieter Gerbrandy expressed in a meeting with Winston Churchill and other Western leaders the need for immediate retaliation, not to 'defeat fascism' or 'liberate' Asian peoples, but because Japan threatened to undo the work of centuries of European imperialism by undermining the image of Western supremacy.

Underlining the true importance of this Western prestige to imperial domination of the Pacific region, Gerbrandy stated:

> Eastern peoples were, for the greater part, still subject to racial instincts and inferiority complexes. The Japanese slogan 'Asia for the Asiatics,' might easily destroy the carefully constructed basis of our cultural synthesis ... Though a lengthy Japanese occupation of important parts of the Pacific Territories might not necessarily turn the final victory of the Western powers into virtual defeat, it would at least prove a formidable obstacle to a real peace in the Far East. Japanese injuries and insults to the White population – and these were already being perpetrated by the detestable Asiatic Huns – would irreparably damage white prestige unless severely punished within a short time.[25]

Gerbrandy's fears were shared by German leader Adolf Hitler. While Germany was then in a frugal alliance with Japan, its Nazi leadership was notably distressed by the rapid victories of their Asian ally over their European adversaries for fear that the prestige and supremacy of the Western races and empires be undermined by an Asian power.[26] While the punishment Gerbrandy had called for would come swiftly and terribly, the psychological impacts of Japan's victory were nonetheless substantial. As Oxford University Professor E. Hotta concluded: 'Southeast Asia stood at the point of no return after the Japanese occupation.' She attributed the subsequent independence of Vietnam, Indonesia, Malaysia, Singapore, the Philippines, Cambodia and Myanmar all being largely due to the psychological impact of Japanese victories over European imperialism. While Japan was ultimately defeated, they had themselves defeated the idea of Western supremacy and so delegitimized European imperialism in the eyes of the Asian peoples.[27]

Japanese victories had a profound psychological impact on the people of the Asia Pacific and even of India, to the strong detriment of the ideal of Western supremacy. An example was the *The Bombay Chronicle* which, having previously suggested that the Western powers would punish Japan, changed its tone in 1942 to talk for the first time of Western 'blunders and inefficiency' in the defense of Singapore. It instead hailed the 'heroic' China as Asia's new hope for the future. Lee Kuan Yew, the founding father of

Singapore, similarly attested to the psychological impact of the Japanese victory, stating:

> My colleagues and I are of the generation of young men who went through the Second World War and the Japanese Occupation and emerged determined that no one – neither the Japanese nor the British – had the right to push and kick us around. We are determined that we could govern ourselves and bring out children in a country where we can be proud to be self-representing people (having previously been under foreign rule). When the war came to an end in 1945, there was never a chance of the old type of British colonial system ever being re-created. The scales had fallen from our eyes and we saw for ourselves that the local people could run the country.[28]

This was true across Southeast Asia, and several countries owed their independence largely to the legacy of the Japanese Empire.

Though Japan had effectively learned how to build a modern economy by following the West's example to the letter, the cultural and ideological influences of the West on the country went far deeper than dresses and ballroom dances. Japan was inspired by Western medicine, arts, technology but also ideology. Japan's elites were deeply influenced by European theories of racial superiority and 'exceptionalism,' which they also applied to their own nation as they had done with other Western behaviors and ideas.

Japan had always particularly admired Germany's own achievements and culture. When Germany, alongside Belgium, France, Britain, Italy and others, committed holocausts and genocide in Africa decades before the well-known killing of minorities in Europe the Japanese observed this as well. It was the German conduct in southern Africa in particular which Japan emulated – though the brutalities of the Japanese Empire even at its height arguably fell far short of those of the European powers. German military forces used their own military strength to facilitate the extermination of indigenous peoples,[29] committing widespread sexual violence in the process against African women which was condoned by imperial authorities.[30] In German occupied Namibia sexual slavery of women was widespread as much of the male population was exterminated and land fell under German control.[31] Many of these 'racially inferior' Africans were shipped to Europe for experimentation to prove the racial superiority of the European race, and medical experiments on live prisoners were also carried out on a considerable scale.[32,33] Japan observed this also.

Brutal conduct towards occupied populations was far from unique to Germany but could be observed as endemic to European imperialism due to its consistency. British imperial forces committed acts often termed as genocide, which if anything surpassed those of the Germans in baseness and brutality. In Australia for example native peoples were according to a British Central Independent Television report: 'hunted and raped and massacred, and few doubted at the time that genocide was the official policy.' Babies' heads were kicked off in contests between British colonizers, who raped and sexually tortured women to death, commonly 'by sticking sharp things like spears up their vaginas until they died.' Men were commonly castrated for amusement and left to die.[34] This was but one case of British imperial conduct, and other Western imperial powers were little different. In East Asia the Bandanese Massacre carried out by the Dutch Empire[35,36] and the conduct of U.S. forces during the conquest of the Philippines,[37] as covered respectively in Chapter 4 and Chapter 5, serve as two examples of such conduct which have widely been termed by experts to be acts of genocide. Genocide and war crimes consistently accompanied the successful appropriation of territory and wealth crucial to Europe's economic prosperity. It was in this manner that the populations and civilizations of three of the world's six inhabited continents were effectively erased from history by European conquest – those of the Americas and Oceania. As leading European imperial nations such as Britain, France, the Netherlands and Belgium were never defeated in the manner that Imperial Japan was they could to some degree maintain control of their historical narratives and prevent the crimes of their past from surfacing and being as well publicized – something defeated nations such as Germany and Japan were unable to do.[38]

Japan had been strictly conditioned to emulate the West, which was largely the source of its own success in industrialization and military development. Following the 'fine example' set by Western imperial powers had gained Japan the respect of the Western world and a military capable of matching its Western counterparts. The Japanese therefore saw no reason to cease copying Europeans, and so adopted not only their technology but also their inhumanity and their barbarism which manifested itself in their conduct in the Second World War.

Gross misconduct notably did not occur in Japan's previous wars, such as during the First World War and Russo-Japanese War, where Japanese forces conducted themselves with distinction. Japanese soldiers had in fact previously been considered to have the most admirable conduct of all the great powers. In their co-occupation of Beijing alongside Western nations in 1900 a period of 'splendid looting' by the occupying forces ensued. British and American sources cited the notable restraint of Japanese soldiers, far from the excesses of all the Western nations.[39] Japan only engaged in such 'excesses' in later years, following the example consistently set by the 'civilized' Western nations. It was clear that beside emulating military economic and social development, the source of Western nations' power was empire – and empire in turn had been built on brutality. Having suffered from economic downturns and facing a fast growing population and highly limited resources in the early 1930s, the Japanese leadership saw the need for an empire of their own to emulate those which had for so long supported high living standards in Europe. Japan set about creating an empire as European powers had, a logical next step in its emulation of the West.

During the Pacific War Asian peoples suffered terribly under European brutality, although unlike in previous wars it was the Japanese soldiers who were applying European methods. Chinese civilians were experimented on while still alive, young Chinese girls were raped by soldiers using bayonets – conduct which was hardly unique to Japan. Western powers conducted themselves in much the same way in Asia and would continue to do so in their later wars across the Asia-Pacific region (as covered in the following chapters).

The fact that Japan's brutal wartime conduct was an emulation of that of Western powers was alluded to by renowned Japanese historian and philosopher Okakura Kakuzo who wrote: 'The average Westerner, in his sleek complacency, will see in the tea-ceremony but another instance of the thousand-and-one oddities which constitute the quaintness and childishness of the East to him. He was wont to regard Japan as barbarous while she indulged in the gentle arts of peace: he calls her civilized since she began to commit wholesale slaughter on Manchurian battlefields.'[40] Essentially the Japanese had been conditioned by Western powers to conduct themselves as the West did in all aspects of life including their behavior towards subjugated races, and from this came the barbarism of their conduct in much of Asia.

While Western influence does not extol Japan of its responsibility for its crimes, and nor does it necessarily mean war crimes would not have been committed otherwise, it shows that the Western 'civilizing' influence was always an important factor in the way Japan conducted itself and war crimes were no exception to this. The severity of the crimes committed and the techniques used both to dehumanize the enemy and to torture civilians, particularly women, closely mirror those long used by the Western empires which Japan came to emulate. These influences and the pressure exerted on Japan for over a century to conduct itself as a 'civilized nation,' which led to the remaking of the country, are therefore also largely responsible for Japanese atrocities during the Pacific War.

Japan's initial military successes against Western powers were to be short lived. While they had proven to be a highly effective fighting force, they could not fight simultaneously against the major European, North American and Oceanic military powers and the whole of China, later joined by the USSR, with their far more limited industrial capacity, resource base and manpower. In a war with the United States, a resource rich nation which could replenish its losses and had several times the population of Japan, the U.S. had a critical advantage which ultimately led to Japan's defeat. American Military sociologist Roger Thompson, a former member of the U.S. Navy and expert on the history of the organization, himself attributed Japan's defeat in several pivotal battles such as Midway to 'plain old dumb luck.' Thompson made a strong case that despite Japan's relatively limited industrial base its considerable technological superiority in several key fields and the better training and preparedness of its navy, particularly its aircraft carrier groups, did much to compensate for its numerical and resource disadvantages. Indeed, Japan had proven its ability to achieve a great deal with very little, as demonstrated in the country's early overwhelming victories against far more numerous Western forces despite committing only a fraction of its own forces – with the majority still occupied at war in China.[41]

Japan was well aware of its severe disadvantage in resources and industrial capacity, only engaging in a war when given no other option. Only through war could Japan secure its own access to oil, rubber, iron and other critical industrial materials rather than rely on hostile Western nations. It was a choice between either war with a far larger military force while already committed to the costly Chinese front or running out of resources, namely oil, and facing inevitable economic and military collapse as a result. The war with China exacerbated the strains of Japan's smaller manpower and economy, meaning the country could only ever spare 18 percent of its forces for war in the Pacific against the combined forces of the US, Australia, New Zealand, the Netherlands and Britain. Entering such a war was highly undesirable and risky, and according to many analysts a near suicidal task, but one in which the small but elite Japanese forces came very close to success. The remaining 82 percent of Japan's military could not be spared as it was spread between the Japanese mainland, Manchuria, Korea and China.[42] Indeed, the forces of China's Western-backed ruling Guomindang party alone were on paper far larger and in many respects more heavily armed than those of Japan, while the Chinese economy was also considerably larger. The Guomindang's army outnumbered the Japanese almost five to one,[43,44] but endemic corruption among its leadership, low morale and lack of effective military planning meant that these forces were consistently routed by a more efficient and better organized, though much smaller, Japanese force. To defeat both China and the combined forces of the Western powers simultaneously was not to ask a miracle of the Japanese military, but to ask for two miracles at once – two simultaneous victories each against overwhelming odds.

Due to the United States' considerable industrial advantage, the Japanese military strategy had to rely on destroying the U.S. Navy's aircraft carriers in the Pacific and thereby crippling its power projection capabilities in a first strike, something which due to the unfortunate timing of their first attacks on American naval facilities at Pearl Harbor in December 1941 could not be achieved. In fact, having expected a Japanese attack, not only were the critical U.S. aircraft carriers not present but the American battleships left within range of an enemy strike were all near obsolete First World War-era ships – the loss of which had little impact on America's ability to wage war. Ships attacked at Pearl Harbor included the *Arizona*,

California, *Maryland*, *Oklahoma*, *Tennessee*, *West Virginia*, *Nevada* and *Pennsylvania* – none of which were a match for modern U.S. and Japanese warships such as the Iowa class and Kagero class. Having failed to incapacitate the U.S. Navy's key power projection assets, Japan would be unable to sustain a war on all fronts and against nations with far greater industrial capacities, manpower and resources. By 1944 it was clear that Japan was set to lose the war.

Japan's lack of resources and a relatively small industrial capacity relative its adversaries meant that even efficient military campaigns and victories in battle, of which Japan had many, were insufficient to ensure the war would be won. A key example of this was following the Battle of Sana Cruz in October 1942, when the Japanese Navy won decisively against the United States and inflicted heavy losses. Japan itself also suffered moderate losses however, including damage to two of its carrier warships. As a result, Japan's Admiral Nagumo, observing the terrible odds against a Japanese victory in a wider war, considered Sana Cruz a pyrrhic victory noting: 'The battle was a tactical win, but a shattering strategic loss to Japan. Considering the great superiority of our enemy's industrial capacity, we must win every battle overwhelmingly in order to win this war. This last one, although a victory, was not an overwhelming victory.'[45]

Poor resource endowment could not be circumvented because it was impossible to make positive relations with neighboring countries which could guarantee supplies, as almost all these countries were occupied by the Western empires. Admiral Harold Stark, American Chief of Naval Operations, had – based on this decisive factor – predicted Japan's eventual defeat at a time when the Empire had yet to suffer a single major battlefield loss. Stark had said to Kichisaburō Nomura, Japanese ambassador to the United States, in 1941: 'You will not only be unable to make up your losses but you will grow weaker as time goes on ... we will not only make up our losses but will grow stronger as time goes on. It is inevitable that we shall crush you before we are through with you.'[46] The United States' highly effective war economy and Japan's lack of resources thus ensured an overwhelming advantage for the allied Western powers in the Pacific.

Conduct in the Pacific War

The retribution of the Western powers against an Asian nation which had sought to defy them and challenge their right to regional dominance was great indeed. Calls for a harsh response exceeded anything widely expressed towards Nazi Germany, fascist Italy or other European Axis powers in their ferocity, and the war against Japan would very quickly come to be seen as a race war against a 'Yellow Menace.' John A. Wahlquist, a faculty member in the School of Intelligence Studies at the National Defense Intelligence College, James A. Stone, a military Special Agent with the U.S. Air Force Office of Special Investigations (AFOSI) and David P. Shoemaker, a civilian Special Agent with AFOSI, co-published a study regarding the conduct of the United States military during the war. They concluded based on their study of the United States' war with Japan that conduct was influenced significantly by the fact that they were fighting an Asian power, which was seen as a threat to Western values and culture and to Western global primacy. They wrote: 'Conflict in Asia differed greatly from that in Europe, for Japan was considered to be a "racial menace" as well as a cultural and religious one. If Japan proved victorious in the Pacific, there would be "perpetual war between the Oriental ideas and the Occidental." At the time, the conflict was perceived as a clash of civilizations.'[47]

In their history of interactions with Asia-Pacific nations, Western powers have notably been highly consistent in the harshness of their retribution towards those which have pursued policies independent of or opposed to their regional designs. The response to Imperial Japan's defiance, though it had long been expected as evidenced by the Eight Action Memo, was a case in point. Conduct was considerably more brutal than in any other theatre of the war, and the Japanese were portrayed and widely viewed as a subhuman race over which Western dominance had to be asserted. The dehumanization and demonization of the Japanese people fueled hatred towards Japan, and so fueled the atrocities committed against the 'yellow vermin' – as they were commonly referred to. Despite their technological advancements, modernization and literacy rates the Japanese were still, as with all East Asians, patronizingly and derogatively called 'the little yellow men' before the war. After the breakout of the war, the Japanese were depicted in state sponsored art in the United States as all manner of creatures. They were shown as cockroaches, monkeys, venomous snakes and vampire bats among other creatures associated with small stature and biting danger. An official film by the U.S. Navy described the Japanese soldiers as 'living snarling rats.' American wartime propaganda scripts showing an enemy population deceived by evil ideology and militaristic leaders, as Nazi Germany was commonly depicted, were not approved. Unlike the Western fascist powers, in Japan's case the entire population was target for demonization and dehumanization, rather than its political ideology or leadership.[48]

Respected Western magazines such as *Science Digest* and *Time* published articles examining whether and how the Japanese were racially inferior to Western peoples. U.S. President Roosevelt himself commissioned a study of the 'scientific evidence' of the inferiority of Asian races, including but not limited to the Japanese. As an Asian adversary the Japanese were hated by the Americans in a way the Germans and their European allies never came close to. *Science Digest* even ran an article titled: *Why Americans Hate Japs More than Nazis*. American historian Paul Ham observed that Hollywood never cast a good Japanese, but often a good German. The Germans were considered enemies for ideological reasons, while hatred for the Japanese was motivated by race. Ham noted: 'to the press this was a racial war in all but name [...] The Germans were [considered] a bit "like us", if deceived by an evil doctrine,' whereas the Japanese were considered racially and irredeemably evil.[49] The forcible internment of approximately 120,000 American citizens of Japanese origin and 22,000 Canadian citizens of Japanese origin into concentration camps without charge, where no remotely similar measures were taken against citizens of Italian or German origin, was a consequence which exemplified this phenomenon.

The actions of the U.S. leadership served to reinforce the dehumanization of the Japanese. Commander of U.S. military operations in the South Pacific Admiral William Halsey urged his men: 'Kill Japs! Kill Japs! Kill more Japs! Remember Pearl Harbor – keep 'em dying!'[50] The message from the leadership in the United States was unofficial but effective. All American servicemen were induced to show no mercy to the 'yellow vermin' in combat. A Marine colonel yelled to his men: 'you will take no prisoners, you will kill every yellow son-of-a-bitch, and that's it.' The tacit understanding was that the Japanese were subhuman, as were all Asian races to some extent, and that they were to be eradicated without mercy.[51] Another U.S. General, Sir Thomas Blamey, told Australian troops under his command in 1943: 'Your enemy is a curious race – a cross between the human being and the ape ... he is inferior to you ... and that knowledge will help you to victory. ... We must go on to the end if civilization is to survive. We must exterminate the Japanese.' Soon after, in an interview with the *The New York Times*, Blamey opined that the 'civilized' Western world was 'not dealing with human beings as we know them. We are dealing with something primitive. Our troops have the right view of the Japs. They regard them as vermin.' He referred to them as 'these things.'[52]

American Professor Jesse Glenn Gray, philosopher and writer, noted the highly prevalent dehumanization of the Japanese as an Asian race by Western powers and its critical implications, stating: 'On first reflection, the enemy conceived as beasts might be thought to be morally the most satisfactory of any image, since it avoids feelings of guilt. Granted the fact of war, the pursuit of killing without compunction could be considered the most healthy and rational.'[53] Dehumanization proved highly effective, as evidenced by the numerous atrocities committed against the Japanese, the desecration of their dead and the abuse of civilians and prisoners. The hatred Western powers incited in their militaries was directed not at Japanese imperialism and the Japanese military, the country's ideology or even at soldiers, but at all Japanese as an Asian race. The dehumanization was indiscriminate, leading to the targeting and abuse of Asian civilians – both Japanese and otherwise.

It was not only the Japanese who were subjected to acts of brutality at the hands of Western soldiers, but Asian populations in general. In India when en route to fight Japanese force in Burma, Americans took 'pot shots' at Indian cows and their owners, or what they called 'the wogs.' Historian Peter Schrijvers noted that Korean women were often made targets for sexual violence alongside the Japanese, stating: 'Remarkably, to be of Oriental appearance in Kanagawa was sufficient reason for women on Okinawa to run the risk of rape. When, for example, Korean "comfort women", brought to the island by Japanese forces before the battle, fell into American hands, some of them, too, were forced to succumb to the GIs.'[54] Americans were warned when operating in China not to assume 'an air of white superiority,' but this did not stop their violence and provocations of the local Chinese community. Incidents of violence increased throughout the war, with stabbings and shootings taking place by 1945. The American forces in supposedly allied territory to fight the Japanese enemy acted like hooligans and bandits rather than as respectful partners. *The Official Army History of the China Theater* noted of the relationship of the Americans and their Chinese allies: 'There was lacking the sense of fraternity with and close support by one's own people.'[55] The conduct of U.S. forces following landings in Japanese occupied southern Korea shortly after the Empire's surrender, as covered in Chapter 11, was considerably worse still.

Western coverage of the Pacific War often portrays Japanese soldiers so fanatically devoted to their emperor and country that they preferred death to the dishonor of surrender – an image which both justified the extremely low number of war prisoners taken by the Western powers and further served to portray the Japanese military as a radical organization. Accounts from the time however portray a very different reality to this convenient explanation. While it is true that Japanese military personnel often showed extreme devotion and bravery, exemplified by the kamikaze bombers, they were still human soldiers with lives and homes to return to who in most cases sought to survive the war. It was most often not the case that soldiers refused to surrender, but rather that their capitulations were rarely accepted. The Japanese had been demonized and dehumanized to an extent that Western soldiers would often kill them on site. This deterred Japanese soldiers from surrendering, lest they be gunned down unarmed. James A. Stone, an American military Special Agent with the Air Force Office of Special Investigations, noted in his study of American interrogation techniques: 'Japanese were known to come out of the jungle unarmed with their hands raised above their heads, crying, "Mercy, mercy", only to be mowed down by machine-gun fire. U.S. Marines took no prisoners. American forces justified this behavior on the basis of stories of Japanese treachery.' American officers commented on the small number of Japanese prisoners taken: 'Oh, we could take more if we wanted to, but our boys don't like to take prisoners. It doesn't encourage the rest to surrender when they hear of their buddies being marched out on the flying field and machine-guns turned loose on them.'[56]

Encouraging the view of the Japanese as subhumans facilitated the committing of war crimes by the American military. This repeated itself in all subsequent major wars in Asia involving Western powers in the region, including U.S. interventions in China, the Philippines, Korea and Vietnam. A lieutenant's letter to his mother effectively shows the attitude of the Americans to the Japanese as a race and people: 'Nothing can describe the hate we feel for the Nips [Japanese]. The destruction, the torture, burning and death of countless civilians, the savage fight without purpose – to us they are dogs and rats – we love to kill them – to me and all of us killing Nips is the greatest sport known – it causes no sensation of killing a human being but we really get a kick out of hearing the bastards scream.'[57] This attitude and the sadism expressed eclipses perhaps even the worst of Nazi Germany's brutal perceptions of and excesses committed against the Slavic peoples and Jews, or the Japanese brutality towards the Chinese. The pleasure in causing suffering among those seen to be inferior, and writing home taking pride in sadistic conduct in such a way, did not occur on other fronts of the war. Even when the Japanese committed atrocities in China or the Nazi Germans massacred civilians in Eastern Europe, it was always ensured that the populations at home never found out.

More accounts from American soldiers detailed the sadistic treatment of the Japanese. A veteran recalled:

> When a Japanese soldier was 'flushed' from his hiding place … the unit … was resting and joking … But they seized their rifles and began using him as a live target while he dashed frantically around the clearing in search of safety. The soldiers found his movements uproariously funny. Finally, however, they succeeded in killing him, and the incident cheered the whole platoon, giving them something to talk and joke about for days afterward.

The veteran emphasized that none of the soldiers considered that the victim may have had human feelings or the wish to be spared – noting the similarity between the way the soldiers viewed him and the way they would view an animal.[58]

American soldiers were shown to have taken a great deal of pleasure in carrying out sadistic actions to torture the Japanese. One U.S. observer noted that flamethrowers were a particularly sadistic way to 'roast rats' (rats being a term for Japanese soldiers). He noted: 'we regulated flamethrowers in such a way that enemy soldiers were set afire, to die slowly and painfully, rather than killed outright with a fully blast of the burning oil.' This was apparently not out of any military necessity, but rather was a common way for U.S. soldiers to take out their frustration.[59] Such attitudes permeated to the highest levels of command, with U.S. Navy Admiral William Halsey himself showing some level of sadistic pleasure in the destruction wrought by his forces. 'We are drowning and burning them all over the Pacific, and it is just as much pleasure to burn them as to drown them,'[60] the Admiral reported.

Generally considered the acts of only the most savage of nations, American soldiers would often desecrate the bodies of the Japanese from the beginning of ground operations. On the Guadalcanal several Japanese heads were mounted on pikes facing the main army across the river. The dead and even the dying were tossed into open latrines with the sewage by U.S. Marines, while others urinated in the open mouths of the wounded soldiers. Had any other nation committed such crimes, or had the Japanese committed such actions against the American forces or their European or Australian allies, they would have been well publicized to mark the Japanese as cruel savages. As it was, the United States and other Western nations were able to conduct such war crimes with impunity.

A pastime of many U.S. Marines during the war was the collecting of human body parts from dead Japanese soldiers. Many Marines wore them as trophy necklaces, a collection of ears, noses, fingers and other parts. American serviceman Charles Lindbergh reported of the barbaric practice: 'They often bring back the thigh bones from the Japs they kill and make pen holders and paper knives and such things out of them.' Another time he wrote: 'The officer said he had seen a number of Japanese bodies from which an ear or a nose had been cut off. Our boys cut them off to show to their friends in fun, or to dry and take back to the States when they go. We found one marine with a Japanese head. He was trying to get the ants to clean the flesh off the skull, but the odor got so bad we had to take it away from him. It's the same story everywhere I go.'[61]

Commenting on what he observed at the front, Lindbergh further stated: 'It seemed impossible that men – civilized men – could degenerate to such a level. Yet they had. It was we, Americans, who had done such things, we who claimed to stand for something different. We, who claimed that the German was defiling humanity in his treatment of the Jew, were doing the same thing in our treatment of the Jap.'[62]

The skulls of the Japanese dead were considered valuable trophies for U.S. forces. Some were sent back to America to friends, families or lovers. The heads were first 'cured' by ravenous ants or by boiling in kettles. Most were then sold to other members of the military. Bones collected were carved into letters and other shapes, and many were sent to America as gifts. *Life* magazine's 'picture of the week' in May 1944 showed a woman with a Japanese skull that her boyfriend had sent her. It was autographed by him and thirteen others, inscribed: 'this is a good Jap – a dead one picked up on the New Guinea beach.'[63] President Roosevelt, highly respected and esteemed to this day for his leadership, said of one such gift sent to the White House: 'This is the sort of gift I like to get.' 'There will be plenty more such gifts,' he went on.[64] Roosevelt not only received a Japanese skull but was also presented with a letter opener made with the arm bone of a Japanese soldier by a member of Congress.

One of the most coveted of trophies were gold-capped teeth. In a similar way to the Nazis in the European holocaust,[65] the Americans ripped these valuables from the mouths of the dead. This was done with the same disrespect for the dead that the Nazis showed the holocaust victims in Europe – where the same practice was commonplace. U.S. Marines were known to dig up the corpses of buried Japanese soldiers to look for gold teeth.[66] In one case a Marine felt he had got lucky finding a fallen Japanese soldier whose teeth he could steal. However, as a witness, U.S. Marine Eugene Sledge, recalled of the event:

> the Japanese wasn't dead. He had been wounded severely in the back and couldn't move his arms; otherwise he would have resisted to his last breath. The Japanese's mouth glowed with huge gold-crowned teeth, and his captor wanted them. He put the point of his knife on the vase of a tooth and hit the handle with the palm of his

> hand. Because the Japanese was kicking his feet and thrashing about, the knifepoint glanced off the tooth and sank deeply into the victim's mouth. The marine cursed him and with a slash cut his cheeks open to each ear. He put his foot on the sufferer's lower jaw and tried again. Blood poured out of the soldier's mouth. He made a gurgling noise and thrashed wildly. I shouted 'put the man out of his misery.' All I got for an answer was a cussing out. Another Marine ran up, put a bullet in the enemy soldier's brain, and ended his agony. The scavenger grumbled and continued extracting his prize undisturbed.[67]

Dr Victoria Munro, an American expert, noted in her study of racially motivated war crimes by United States forces:

> The treatment of this particular enemy as less than human widened what was acceptable to collect from the dead. Trophy-taking during the Pacific War needs to be interpreted in a similar way: not merely as an effect of the powerfully radicalized wartime imagery of the Japanese as subhuman, but as one of the symbolic practices by which these conceptualizations were reproduced and sustained – in opposition to a contrasting default recognition of the Japanese as human. With the media full of metaphors of the hunt and the depiction of the Japanese as any number of subhuman species, it is hardly surprising that these carried over into actions during the war.[68]

Munro further noted that the it was the dehumanization of the Japanese as an Asian race which had allowed American soldiers to desecrate their bodies – as it had allowed them to abuse and torture those under their power before. She stated: 'There was no comparable pattern of abuse of enemy dead in the battles between U.S. forces and troops of the European Axis, but the constructed images of the Japanese, on which rested these practices, were far different than those of the Germans or Italians.' She noted that collecting skulls was only practiced by American personnel in wars with Asian races – and that Asian peoples, unlike the other races the United States has fought, were associated with game animals from which trophies could be taken rather than with human soldiers, as was the case with European and other non-Asian soldiers.[69]

Aware of the grim fate that awaited them, if indeed they were captured alive, many Japanese chose to kill themselves rather than surrender. One American eyewitness recalled:

> The northern tip of Saipan is a cliff with a sheer drop into the sea. At high tide the sharp coral rocks are almost covered with swirling surf. The Japanese civilians and

> the surviving soldiers were all crowded into this area. Now one of the worst horrors of the war occurred. In spite of loudspeaker messages asking them to surrender, and assurances that they would be well treated, they began killing themselves. Soldiers clutched hand grenades to their bellies and pulled the pins. Through our spotting scopes from our observation post I witnessed this sickening spectacle. One of the worst experiences of my life.[70]

There were almost no survivors among the 30,000-man Japanese garrison on Saipan. Two thirds of the 22,000 civilians were murdered or killed themselves – it was considered better to take one's own life and be spared the humiliation and suffering.

An Australian soldier, Eddie Stanton, said of the campaign: 'Japanese are still being shot all over the place. The necessity for capturing them has ceased to worry anyone. Nippo soldiers are just so much machine gun practice.'[71] At some stages a few Japanese prisoners were taken, though not in significant numbers. They were used for the information they could provide. 'When they flew Japanese prisoners back for questioning on a C-47, they kept the freight door at the side of the plane open, and when the questioning of each man was concluded, they'd be kicked overboard before they reached their destination.'[72] In October 1944, after three years of fighting, the Allies were holding only 604 Japanese in prisoner of war camps.[73] Compared to numbers in other nations, the most being 2.7–3 million Germans held in the USSR after surrendering, the paucity of Japanese in American custody was highly abnormal.

The U.S. Navy was similarly merciless in its conduct towards its Japanese counterparts. The Navy would routinely target lifeboats and machine gun unarmed survivors in the water. In the air many Japanese pilots were also killed while parachuting out of their planes or still in their harnesses. Rescue boats were frequently targeted to ensure maximum casualties even after a battle was over – all these actions being severe war crimes.[74] Although survivors of naval encounters are to be rescued at sea as prisoners according to international law, and the shooting of downed pilots was strictly forbidden, the law was not applied to adversaries perceived as subhuman.

Japanese sailors were often left in the water to drown. After the Battle of Leyte Gulf Admiral William Halsey told his destroyers not to be over-zealous about rescuing Japanese survivors. He advised them to bring in a few survivors only for intelligence, and said that the rest 'would probably like to join their ancestors and should be accommodated [in this wish].' This is a reference to the Confucian practice of ancestor worship, which was used as justification for committing war crimes.[75] Halsey's intentions, like those of many in the U.S. military leadership, appeared to border on genocidal and these sentiments were strongly reflected in their condoning and at times encouragement of atrocities in battle. 'When this war is over, the Japanese language will be spoken only in hell,' the Admiral had said, and he was hardly alone in expressing such a sentiment.[76]

In the United States the gross misconduct of the military was widely sanctioned, from a highly respected president to the civilian population to the admirals and the soldiers and sailors themselves – as exemplified by the skull on President Roosevelt's desk and that on the cover of *Life*. This was a key difference between American and Japanese war crimes – the American public and leadership were widely aware of the conduct of their forces where Japan's military and civilian leadership was consistently found to have had no knowledge of their forces misconduct. Japanese civilians would have been horrified by the massacres carried out in their name – of which they had no knowledge. There were no similar displays by the country's own heads of state or even its military leaders, and certainly no bones or skulls sent back to Japanese sweethearts at home.

The Nanjing Massacre, the most notorious incident of misconduct perpetrated by the Japanese military, demonstrated a considerable contrast between the Japanese response to the incident and the American response to their own war crimes in the region. Not only where Japanese journalists shocked at the misconduct they observed, but Prince Asaka, General Yanagawa and General Iwane Matsui where themselves horrified at the conduct of their own army upon entering the city and immediately took measures to withdraw their looting forces and restore order. This was confirmed by Chinese sources.[77] The atrocious exploits of the Japanese armed forces in Nanjing were never proudly displayed to the population back home, and when word reached Japanese command of what had transpired not only did they not endorse it, much unlike the United States leadership when informed of its own forces' war crimes, but Japan also took swift measures to send officers and troops involved back home to prevent recurrences of such incidents.[78]

War crimes and by Western forces targeted not only Japanese soldiers, but also civilians in the limited encounters they had. The first heavily populated Japanese territory the United States attempted to capture with ground forces was Okinawa, where after isolating the heavily outnumbered Japanese garrison of the island the whole of four Army and two Marine divisions supported by naval, amphibious and air forces waged a grueling 82-day campaign to defeat them. The Americans suffered over 14,000 deaths and 82,000 other casualties, and the resolve of the island's defense led the U.S. military leadership to seriously reconsider plans for an invasion of other populated islands or the Japanese mainland. Japanese forces were well dug in and fought to the last, knowing that there were no other options. An estimated quarter to a third of the population were killed, while over 90 percent of the building structures were destroyed during the campaign.[79]

When U.S. forces landed on the island, even before the fighting had ended, they began mass sexual assaults against the women of Okinawa. In just one prefecture over 1,000 women reported having been raped. Sexual assaults by American soldiers were so pervasive that hundreds of Okinawan women reportedly swallowed poison or leapt to their deaths to end their lives. In one incident personnel from the 4th Marines passed a group of some ten American Marines bunched together in a tight circle next to the road. A Marine corporal wrote: They were 'quite animated,' and he assumed they were playing a game of craps. 'Then as we passed them,' said the shocked Marine, 'I could see they were taking turns raping an oriental woman. I was furious, but our outfit kept marching by as though nothing unusual was going on.'[80]

Okinawan historian Oshiro Masayu, director of the Okinawa Prefectural Archives, described American soldiers' conduct in Okinawa: 'Soon after the U.S. marines landed, all the women of a village on Motobu Peninsula fell into the hands of American soldiers. At the time, there were only women, children and old people in the village, as all the young men had been mobilized for the war. Soon after landing, the Marines "mopped up" the entire village, but found no signs of Japanese forces. Taking advantage of the situation, they started "hunting for women" in broad daylight and those who were hiding in the village or nearby air raid shelters were dragged out one after another.'[81]

According to a report by the *New York Times* multiple elderly Okinawans recounted that after the Battle of Okinawa was over, three armed American Marines would come to the village every week and force the villagers to gather all local women. They were then taken to the hills and raped by the soldiers. Veterans from that campaign refused the *New York Times'* request for an interview. Ultimately both the Okinawans and the Americans preferred not to acknowledge the past, as it tarnished the image of both parties. Japanese Professor Masaie Ishihara noted in relation to this: 'There is a lot of historical amnesia out there, many people don't want to acknowledge what really happened.'[82]

In his book *Bloody Pacific, American Soldiers at War with Japan*, historian Peter Schrijvers wrote:

> Many women in Okinawa came to wish the Americans had just killed them and dumped them in a hole. Instead, the enemy brutally violated them, showing not even the least mercy [...] Wartime rape serves to sharpen the aggressiveness of soldiers [...] But rape just as much reflects a burning need to establish total dominance over the other. That is why enemy women are quite commonly sexually abused in front of fathers, husbands, or brothers with the express purpose of increasing also the humiliation of the male foe. That drive for indisputable control, to be accomplished in part through demeaning, was undoubtedly what moved U.S. Marines, for example, to rape almost all women of one of the villages of the Motobu Peninsula. Exactly how many Okinawan women were raped by American troops will never be known, as the victims were either too ashamed – or too frightened to report the crime. The estimate of one Okinawan historian for the entire three-month period of the campaign exceeds 10,000 [note this is not the number of rapes that occurred, but the number of women targeted. It is most common for women to be raped multiple times and repeatedly.] A figure that does not seem unlikely when one realizes that during the first 10 days of the occupation of Japan there were 1,336 reported cases of rape of Japanese women by American soldiers in Kanagawa prefecture alone. Again the emphasis is the word *reported*; likely the vast majority of rapes went unreported.[83]

Despite the history of brutal conduct on both sides of the war Japan today is widely perceived as being far more brutal than the Western powers. This however remains far from the truth. Although the Japanese imperial soldiers are remembered for their brutality in conduct in China and against

American soldiers, this brutality appears to have been exceeded by American soldiers' conduct towards Japanese soldiers and civilians. An unnamed American soldier of the 592nd Engineers himself concluded, based on the atrocities of both his own side and his enemies: 'I found that any atrocity the Japanese commit can be matched by Americans.' This engineer experienced firsthand the slaughter and conduct of the Americans in Asia. Six months later he stated: 'There is but one law here, KILL, KILL, KILL.'[84]

The association of Imperial Japan with war crimes today, in contrast to Western powers which hold far fewer such associations even in the Asia-Pacific, is due to the potency of the West's position as both the victor and the dominant global power, which combined with its considerable soft power allows it to effectively control historical narratives. American journalist Edgar L. Jones, the war's contemporary, noted that the Americans had no moral high ground regarding their conduct in the war. He stated:

> We Americans have the dangerous tendency in our international thinking to take a holier-than-thou attitude toward other nations. We consider ourselves to be more noble and decent than other peoples, and consequently in a better position to decide what is right and wrong in the world. What kind of war do civilians suppose we fought, anyway? We shot prisoners in cold blood, wiped out hospitals, strafed lifeboats, killed or mistreated enemy civilians, finished off the enemy wounded, tossed the dying into a hole with the dead, and in the Pacific boiled the flesh off enemy skulls to make table ornaments for sweethearts, or carved their bones into letter openers ... We mutilated the bodies of enemy dead, cutting off their ears and kicking out their gold teeth for souvenirs, and buried them with their testicles in their mouths. ... We topped off our saturation bombing and burning of enemy civilians by dropping atomic bombs on two nearly defenseless cities, thereby setting an all-time record for instantaneous mass slaughter. As victors we are privileged to try our defeated opponents for their crimes against humanity; but we should be realistic enough to appreciate that if we were on trial for breaking international laws, we should be found guilty on a dozen counts.[85]

Jones went on to note that America's war crimes were well concealed while Japan's crimes were highly publicized, stating regarding the strongly Western favoring narratives which emerged following the war's end: 'we publicized every inhuman act of our opponents and censored any recognition of our own moral frailty in moments of desperation.'[86] Essentially the image of the war today magnifies the crimes of Japanese forces while ignoring or otherwise granting minimal attention to the crimes of Western powers including the United States. These double standards of Western powers are perhaps best exemplified at the trial of former Japanese Prime Minister Hideki Tojo under an International Military Tribunal. When Tojo's lawyers asked why crimes he was accused of were any worse than the American crimes including the atomic bombing of Japanese population centers, the prosecutors interrupted the Japanese translation and ordered that the remarks be removed from the official trial record and the press.[87] The allegation of double standards seemed to have struck a chord with them.

Notes

1 Hotta, Eri., *Pan Asianism and Japan's War 1931–1945*, New York, Palgrave Macmillan, 2007 (p. 217).

2 Getz, Marshall J., *Subhas Chandra Bose: A Biography*, Jefferson, NC, McFarland, 2002 (p. 76).

3 'The United States and the Opening to Japan, 1853,' Office of the Historian, Milestones 1830–1860, United States of America Department of State.

4 Röhl, John, *The Kaiser and His Court: Wilhelm II and the Government of Germany*, Cambridge, Cambridge University Press, 1994 (p. 203).

5 Wang, Hui, *China From Empire to Nation State*, Cambridge, MA, Harvard University Press, 2014 (p. 6–10).

6 Harrel, Paula S., *Asia for the Asians, China in the Lives of Five Meiji Japanese*, Portland, ME, MerwinAsia, 2012 (p. 226).

7 Vickers, Adrain, *A History Modern of Indonesia*, Cambridge, Cambridge University Press, 2005 (pp. 83–84).

8 Ikeo, Aiko, *Economic Development in Twentieth-Century East Asia: The International Context*, Abingdon, Routledge, 2015 (p. 24).

9 Harrel, Paula S., *Asia for the Asians, China in the Lives of Five Meiji Japanese*, Portland, ME, MerwinAsia, 2012 (p. 229).

10 Cook, Haruko Taya and Cook, Theodore F., *Japan at War: An Oral History*, New York, The New Press, 1993.

11 Hsiao, Mei-Chu W., and Hsiao, Frank S. T., *Taiwan in the Global Economy – Past, Present and Future*, Section V., *Taiwan in the Global Economy During the Japanese Period*, University of Colorado at Boulder, University of Colorado at Denver.

12 '朝鮮総督府統計年報 昭和１７年 [Governor-General of Korea Statistical Yearbook 1942].' Governor-General of Korea, March 1944.
13 Andrade Jr., Ernest, 'The United States Navy and the Washington Conference,' *The Historian*, Vol. 31, No. 3, May 1969 (p. 345–363).
14 'The London Naval Conference, 1930,' Office of the Historian, Milestones 1921–1936, United States of America Department of State.
15 Murdoch, James, *A History of Japan*, Abingdon, Routledge, 2004 (p. 648).
16 Thompson, Roger, *Lessons Not Learned; The U.S. Navy's Status Quo Culture*, Annapolis, MD, Naval Institute Press, 2007, Chapter 5: ('A Lucky Break at Midway and the Big Carrier Navy').
17 Stinnett, Robert B., *Day of Deceit: The Truth About FDR and Pearl Harbor*, New York, Free Press, 2000 (p. 14).
18 Bush, George H. W., *Address to the Nation Announcing the Deployment of United States Armed Forces to Saudi Arabia*, August 8, 1990.
19 Tharoor, Ishaan, 'The dark side of Winston Churchill's legacy no one should forget,' *Washington Post,* February 3, 2015.
20 *World War II, The Experience*, Sheffield, Angus Books Ltd, 2006 (p. 51).
21 Ibid. (p. 51).
22 Mishra, Pankaj, 'The Ruins Of Empire: Asia's Emergence From Western Imperialism' *The Guardian*, April 13, 2017.
23 Getz, Marshall J., *Subhas Chandra Bose: A Biography*, Jefferson, NC, McFarland and Company, 2002 (p. 76).
24 Dower, John, *War Without Mercy: Race and Power in the Pacific War*, New York, Panthoen, 1986 (p. 175).
25 Hotta, Eri., *Pan Asianism and Japan's War 1931–1945*, New York, Palgrave Macmillan, 2007 (p. 217).
26 Dower, John, *War Without Mercy: Race and Power in the Pacific War*, New York, Panthoen, 1986 (p. 207).
27 Hotta, Eri., *Pan Asianism and Japan's War 1931–1945*, New York, Palgrave Macmillan, 2007 (p. 217–218).
28 Kim, Wah Yeo, *Political Development in Singapore, 1945–1955*, Singapore, Singapore University Press, 1973 (p. 87).
29 Hull, Izabel, *Absolute Destruction: Military Culture and the Practices of War in Imperial Germany*, Ithaca, NY, Cornell University Press, 2005.
30 Klotz, Marcia, *White women and the dark continent: gender and sexuality in German colonial discourse from the sentimental novel to the fascist film*, Thesis (Ph.D.), Stanford University, 2010 (p. 72).
31 Grobler, John, 'The tribe Germany wants to forget,' *Mail & Guardian*, March 13, 1998.

32 Conrad, Sebastian, *German Colonialism: A Short History*, Cambridge, Cambridge University Press, 2008 (p. 129).
33 Olusoga, David, and Erichsen, Casper W., *The Kaiser's Holocaust: Germany's Forgotten Genocide and the Colonial Roots of Nazism*, London, Faber & Faber Ltd, 2011.
34 'The Secret Country: The First Australians Fight Back,' British Central Independent Television, (Documentary), 1985.
35 Pisani, Elizabeth, *Indonesia Etc.: Exploring the Improbable Nation*, London, Granta Books, 2014 (p. 17).
36 Hanna, Willard A., *Indonesian Banda: Colonialism and its Aftermath in the Nutmeg Islands*, Philadelphia, PA, Institute for the Study of Human Issues, 1991 (p. 55).
37 Boot, Max, *The Savage Wars Of Peace: Small Wars And The Rise Of American Power*, New York, Basic Books, 2002 (p. 125).
38 Parry, Marc, 'Uncovering The Brutal Truth About The British Empire,' *The Guardian*, August 18, 2016.
39 Harrel, Paula S., *Asia for the Asians, China in the Lives of Five Meiji Japanese*, Portland, ME, MerwinAsia, 2012 (p. 186).
40 Okakura, Kakuzo, *The Book of Tea*, Duffield and Company, 1906.
41 Thompson, Roger, *Lessons Not Learned; The U.S. Navy's Status Quo Culture*, Annapolis, MD, Naval Institute Press, 2007.
42 *World War II, The Experience*, Sheffield, Angus Books Ltd, 2006 (p. 82).
43 Murray Horner, David, *The Second World War: The Pacific*, Abingdon, Routledge, 2003 (pp. 14–15).
44 Australia-Japan Research Project, *Dispositions and Deaths* (based on data compiled by the Relief Bureau of the Ministry of Health and Welfare in March 1964).
45 McCormack, David, *Japan At War 1931–1945; As the Cherry Blossom Falls*, Stroud, Fonthill Media, 2016 (pp. 59–60).
46 Baer, George W., *One Hundred Years of Sea Power: The U.S. Navy, 1890–1990*, Stanford, CA, Stanford University Press, 1996.
47 Stone, James A. and Shoemaker, David P. and Dotti, Nicholas R., *Interrogation: World War II, Vietnam, and Iraq*, Washington D.C., National Defence Intelligence College, September 2008 (p. 34).
48 Dower, John, *War Without Mercy: Race and Power in the Pacific War*, New York, Panthoen, 1986 (p. 18).
49 Ham, Paul, *Hiroshima Nagasaki: The Real Story of the Atomic Bombings and their Aftermath*, New York, Doubleday, 2012 (p. 14).

50 Wright, James, *Those Who Have Borne the Battle: A History of America's Wars and Those Who Fought Them*, New York, PublicAffairs, 2012 (p. 114).
51 Hastings, Max, *Nemesis: The Battle for Japan*, New York, Harper Perennial, 2008 (p. 39, 200–201).
52 Dower, John, *War Without Mercy: Race and Power in the Pacific War*, New York, Panthoen, 1986 (p. 71).
53 Glenn Gray, Jesse, *The Warriors, Reflections of Men in Battle*, Winnipeg, Bison Books, 1998 (p. 150).
54 Schrijvers, Peter, *The GI War Against Japan: American Soldiers in Asia and the Pacific During World War II*, New York, New York University Press, 2005 (p. 212).
55 Ibid. (p. 217).
56 Fenton, Ben, 'American Troops Murdered Japanese Pows,' *The Telegraph* August 6, 2005.
57 Schrijvers, Peter, *The GI War Against Japan: American Soldiers in Asia and the Pacific During World War II*, New York, New York University Press, 2005 (p. 207).
58 Glenn Gray, Jesse, *The Warriors, Reflections of Men in Battle*, Winnipeg, Bison Books, 1998 (p. 150).
59 Jones, Edgar L., 'One War is Enough,' *The Atlantic Monthly*, February 1946.
60 Will, George F., 'Iwo Jima's Lesson in Empathy,' *Washington Post*, February 25, 2007.
61 Harrison, Simon, *Dark Trophies: Hunting and the Enemy Body in Modern War*, New York, Berghahn Books, 2012 (p. 133).
62 Munro, Victoria, *Hate Crime in the Media, A History*, Santa Barbara, CA, Praeger 2014 (p. 43).
63 Wright, James, *Those Who Have Borne the Battle: A History of America's Wars and Those Who Fought Them*, New York, PublicAffairs, 2012 (p. 115).
64 *Nevada Daily Mail*, June 13, 1944.
65 Wroe, David, 'Hitler had fillings made from gold torn from mouths of Jews,' *The Telegraph*, October 8, 2009.
66 Dower, John, *War Without Mercy: Race and Power in the Pacific War*, New York, Pantheon, 1986 (p. 71).
67 Sledge, Eugene Bondurant, *With the Old Breed: At Peleliu and Okinawa*, Oxford, Oxford University Press, 1990 (p. 120).
68 Munro, Victoria, *Hate Crime in the Media, A History*, Santa Barbara, CA, Praeger, 2014 (p. 44).
69 Ibid. (pp. 42–43).

70 Paul, William T., *From Butte to Iwo Jima, The Memoirs of William T. Paul*, 1996 (available at <http://www.sihope.com/~tipi/marine.html>).
71 Fenton, Ben, 'American Troops Murdered Japanese Pows,' *The Telegraph*, August 6, 2005.
72 Munro, Victoria, *Hate Crime in the Media, A History*, Santa Barbara, CA, Praeger 2014 (p. 44).
73 Krammer, Arnold, 'Japanese Prisoners of War in America,' *Pacific Historical Review*, Vol. 52, No. 1, 1983 (p. 70).
74 Gillson, Douglas, *Royal Australian Air Force 1939–1942*, Canberra: Australian War Memorial, 1962.
75 Hastings, Max, *Nemesis: The Battle for Japan*, New York, Harper Perennial, 2008 (p. 173–174).
76 Marston, Daniel, *The Pacific War: From Pearl Harbor to Hiroshima*, Oxford, Osprey Publishing, 2011 (p. 29).
77 Chang, Iris, *The Rape of Nanjing: The Forgotten Holocaust of World War II*, New York, Basic Books, 2012 (pp. 50–52).
78 Storry, Richard, *Japan and the Decline of the West in Asia, 1894–1943*, London, Macmillan, 1979 (p. 153).
79 Koikari, Mire, *Cold War Encounters in US-Occupied Okinawa*, Cambridge, Cambridge University Press, 2015 (p. 29).
80 Schrijvers, Peter, *Bloody Pacific: American Soldiers at War with Japan*, London, Palgrave Macmillan, 2010 (p. 211).
81 Tanaka, Yuki and Tanaka, Toshiyuki, *Japan's Comfort Women: Sexual Slavery and Prostitution During World War II*, Abingdon, Routledge, 2003 (pp. 110–11).
82 Ibid.
83 Schrijvers, Peter, *Bloody Pacific: American Soldiers at War with Japan*, London, Palgrave Macmillan, 2010 (p. 211).
84 Schrijvers, Peter, *The GI War Against Japan: American Soldiers in Asia and the Pacific During World War II*, New York, New York University Press, 2005 (p. 208).
85 Jones, Edgar L., 'One War is Enough,' *The Atlantic Monthly*, February 1946.
86 Ibid.
87 *Washington Post*, May 25, 1998, (p. B4).

CHAPTER 2

The War Against a Defeated Japan: Elimination of a Threat to Western Hegemony in Asia

> The entire population of Japan is a proper Military Target ... There are no civilians in Japan ... We intend to seek out and destroy the enemy wherever he or she is, in the greatest possible numbers, in the shortest possible time.[1]
>
> — U.S. Military report during firebombing campaign against Japan

> We, who claimed that the German was defiling humanity in his treatment of the Jew, were doing the same thing in our treatment of the Jap.[2]
>
> — American Soldier CHARLES LINDBERGH

> This is most emphatically not a war [but rather an] attempt at the terrorization of the civilian population through the most horrible means ever conceived by a fiendish mind ... Against such enemies of decency and humanity, the civilized world must rise in protest and back up that protest with punitive force. Only through the complete chastisement of such barbarians can the world be made safe for civilization.[3]
>
> — Japanese media on the U.S. Air Force's firebombing of Tokyo and the killing of over 100,000 civilians in a single night

Concluding the Pacific War: Firebombing of 67 Cities and Massacring a Defeated Population

By mid-1945 it was overwhelmingly clear that Japan had lost the Pacific War. Though the Western powers had yet to take back most of their overseas colonies, they had moved to directly attack the Japanese mainland

and surrounding islands. Following this development and the beginning and intensifying of Western bombing raids on the mainland, the Japanese Empire offered to surrender to the Western powers on terms almost identical to those on which the final surrender would come to be premised. However before the war could end, the Western powers led by the United States engaged in a deadly, months long bombing campaign, unprecedented in world history and specifically targeting Japanese population centers.

To destroy Japanese cities the United States military launched an intense firebombing campaign from the air. This involved using incendiaries such as napalm combined with regular explosives dropped from dozens, often hundreds, of colossal B-29 Superfortress heavy bombers. These indiscriminate weapons, deployed against population centers, would ignite and suck in all surrounding oxygen, growing as they consumed the city and its inhabitants. The fire would expand with tremendous force – killing tens of thousands at a time and leaving dozens of cities in ruins. The destruction wrought by firebombing was unmatched by any conventional weapons. Such attacks were only carried out by British and American forces in the Second World War, and would less than five years afterwards be carried out again by these same parties against Korean population centers.

The firebombing campaign in Japan targeted civilian population centers, and was a highly effective means of inflicting maximum damage and maximum casualties where the density of civilian targets was highest. Now that victory was assured the Western powers' strategy was not based on destroying Japan's capacity to wage war, but rather on racking up a body count large enough to force Tokyo to surrender unconditionally. American Army Air Force General Curtis LeMay led the bombing attacks on the Japanese mainland and surrounding islands. He was instructed by his superior, General Hap Arnold, Commanding General of the U.S. Army Air Forces, to prioritize targeting cities – not factories.[4,5]

The first firebombing of Tokyo, the most densely populated city in the world,[6] was scheduled for the night of March 9, 1945. The date remains to this day by far the bloodiest in the history of warfare. The attack plan involved flying over 300 B-29 heavy bombers low over the city, at altitudes of just 500 to 800 feet and firebombing the population there. Although the bombers would be highly vulnerable, this operation was possible because the Japanese mainland had few remaining effective anti-aircraft defenses – leaving even the capital itself unguarded.

334 B-29 Superfortress bombers were packed with incendiaries to strike Tokyo in a bombing raid unmatched in its carnage in history until today. Their mission was to burn the city's most congested residential areas. The U.S. Air Force was well aware that Japan's air defense capacity on the mainland was severely depleted, and bomber crews were told to jettison guns and ammunition, thus risking flying over enemy territory unable to lay down retaliatory fire, in order to accommodate more M69 cylinders or jellied petroleum bombs. Command was certain that this would not be a fight, but a massacre of one party which had little to no capacity for retaliation. Only this assuredness in the lack of Japanese defensive capabilities allowed them to carry out such an attack.

Each Superfortress carried 1,520 incendiary bombs. Pilots themselves, unaware of how worn out Japan's air defenses were, feared this would be a suicide mission. At such low altitudes they would be cut to pieces by anti-aircraft fire if they were facing an even remotely capable adversary. General LeMay recalled that if the mission horrified U.S. pilots who feared for their own lives – how would the Japanese themselves react to a low altitude incendiary raid? The attack was gargantuan in its scale and unprecedented in its destructive potential – an attempt to shock the Japanese. This was an early example of the U.S. application of what would later come to be known as 'shock tactics.' LeMay knew the unsuspecting Japanese had no experience of a low-level mass incendiary strike. They would not know how to react – it would be something they had never experienced before.

At 10:30 pm Tokyo residents heard the air raid sirens. A city of 4.3 million, one of the largest in the world at the time, had lost around 1000 people to air raids thus far. The Superfortresses reached the city shortly after midnight. They first approached east of Tokyo, the primary target, as it was the city's most densely populated area. Australian historian Paul Ham presents a vivid account of the firebombing of Tokyo and the circumstances under which it took place based on his extensive research of the incident and the bombing of Japan. His writing also presents an effective description of the effects of firebombing on population centers – later employed by the United States against other Japanese cities and eventually against those of Vietnam and Korea. He writes of East Tokyo:

> Its scattering of small factories and cottage industries confirmed – in U.S. Air Force public relations' parlance – its designation as a 'military target.' Hundreds of thousands of people scurried from their homes; some wore air raid hoods and lugged buckets and wet towels; fathers carried sleeping mats and food; mothers bore children in their arms or on their backs. They ran towards the few concrete shelters ... expecting high explosives, they hoped to shield themselves from shrapnel and flying debris. Then, above the roar of the planes came a strange, new whizzing sound unknown to the people of Joto, the first targeted area of Tokyo's eastern plain, and the most densely populated area of the world.
>
> Weather conditions were perfect for igniting a paper city: a cold, moonlit night with fierce northerly gales that would act as a giant bellows to the storm. The incendiary canisters burst on impact. The four-pound bounced across the parks and rooftops, spewing flaming jellied petroleum onto homes, attics, alleys, schools, hospitals, temples and factories. The high winds fanned these spot fires into a fireball that sucked in the surrounding oxygen. What followed was a firestorm more terrible than anything seen in Germany.
>
> The flat plain of Tokyo's Shitamachi [downtown] residential area, where up to 84,000 people per square kilometer lived in a crush of little paper-and-wood dwellings, was the kindling for a hurricane of flames: 'the scattered fires came together into a single huge flame and 40% of the capital was burned to the ground,' the Japanese Home Affairs Ministry blankly reported. In his memoirs LeMay chose a biblical metaphor: 'it was as though Tokyo had dropped through the floor of the world and into the mouth of hell.'[7]

The 334 American heavy bombers dropped almost half a million incendiary cylinders onto the world's most densely populated city, destroying the homes of an estimated 372,000 families alongside hospitals, temples, shrines and all manner of other civilian targets. Figures for the death doll of the firebombing attack put the number of dead at approximately 120,000,[8] though some sources' estimates are considerably higher. The historian Mark Selden concluded in his own study of the attack that the death toll very likely numbered in the hundreds of thousands given Tokyo's population density, 'ludicrously inadequate' firefighting and the hurricane-force winds – noting that it was in the interests of both U.S. and Japanese authorities to cite a considerably lower death toll. The majority of deaths occurred through burning or asphyxiation, and General LeMay's insistence that Tokyo be 'burned down, wiped off the map' appeared to have yielded the results desired – creating well over a million refugees in a single night.[9]

U.S. pilots likened the scale of the conflagration to 'a glow on the horizon like the sun rising,' with pilot Robart Ramer recalling: 'The whole city of Tokyo was below us ... ablaze in one enormous fire with yet more fountains of flame pouring down. ...' Clouds of black smoke and huge updrafts that buffeted the planes 'like embers over a campfire,' and throwing up 'the horrible smell of human flesh.'[10] Describing the impact of the firebombing attack on the civilian population of Tokyo, Paul Ham wrote:

> Millions chose to flee the flames that chased them through the city like furies. The firestorm flung ahead gigantic cinders – burning beams, joists, palings – which smashed to the ground, or into buildings, lighting new spot fires that fed the advancing inferno. Homes and people, like trees in the paths of a bushfire, burst into flames; families, the elderly, mothers and children went mad with pain and terror; victims rolled about on the molten streets unable to douse the jelly that burned to their bone. The people headed for the parks or along the train lines or rushed to the river and hurled themselves in. Coils of flame surrounded and ensnared the weak or slow or overburdened, who caught fire and fell, unhelped by the fleeing populace; others gave up and knelt at prayer in the direction of the Imperial Palace as the conflagration swept over them. No structures were safe or sacred: hospitals crashed down, their patients incinerated where they lay; temples collapsed on the bowed heads inside; schools, mercifully deserted at night, were ash by dawn [...]
>
> The U.S. Air Force judged the first firebombing of Tokyo – several raids would follow – a great success, as measured by the scale of destruction and loss of life. General Arnold praised LeMay's brilliant planning and execution, and the courage of his crews. 'Under reasonably favorable conditions,' Arnold added, the U.S. Air Force 'should have the capacity to destroy whole industrial cities.'
>
> That is what they did. LeMay meant to take the war to the Japanese people with every weapon in his arsenal: 'Bomb and burn them until they quit,' was the general's guiding principle. In the following weeks LeMay's XXI Bomber Command firebombed the urban areas of every major Japanese city, dropping almost five million incendiaries (98,466 tons/89,327 tonnes) – one third which fell in July 1945 – burning more than two million properties. Tokyo, Nogoya, Yokohama, Osaka, Koba and Kawasaki were

> the worse hit, sustaining 315,922 casualties (of whom 126,762 were killed) and the loss of 1,439,115 properties covering 270 square kilometers.[11]

The United States Strategic Bombing Survey stated that the goal of bombing Japan's cities was to destroy 'the basic economic and social fabric of the country.' The survey concluded that 'probably more persons lost their lives by fire at Tokyo in a six-hour period than at any time in the history of man. People died from extreme heat, from oxygen deficiency, from carbon monoxide asphyxiation, from being trampled beneath the feet of stampeding crowds, and from drowning. The largest number of victims were the most vulnerable: women, children and the elderly.'[12]

Japanese media reported on the firebombing of Tokyo and other cities, events unprecedented in the history of war: 'this is most emphatically not a war.' It was rather an 'attempt at the terrorization of the civilian population through the most horrible means ever conceived by a fiendish mind.' By these acts, the United States had shown themselves to be 'utterly lacking in any ability to understand the principles of humanity. Whatever may be the state of their material civilization, they are nothing but lawless savages in spirit who are ruled by fiendish passions and unrestrained lust for blood. Against such enemies of decency and humanity, the civilized world must rise in protest and back up that protest with punitive force. Only through the complete chastisement of such barbarians can the world be made safe for civilization.'[13]

American press, with very few exceptions, hailed this new strategy of burning Japanese population centers as a brilliant policy that would win the war. *Time* magazine described the Tokyo air raid as a 'dream come true ... properly kindled, Japanese cities will burn like autumn leaves.'[14] The media in general demanded more bombing of civilian targets and criticized the earlier policy which had restricted U.S. aircraft to targeting military and industrial facilities. LeMay, at a press conference on May 30, 1945, had boasted that firebombing had killed a million Japanese so far.

The military publicly claimed to be attacking only military targets, a claim difficult to substantiate, but privately had abandoned any pretense to be doing so. A military report authored by intelligence officer Colonel Harry F. Cunninghan stated: 'The entire population of Japan is a proper Military Target ... There are no civilians in Japan ... We intend to seek out and destroy the enemy wherever he or she is, in the greatest possible numbers, in the shortest possible time.'[15] Was this not an official authorization to commit war crimes? There was little to nothing gained strategically by Western powers from slaughtering Japanese civilians in such a way. More favorable surrender terms or a significant degradation in the country's remaining limited capability to wage war were not achieved. It was abundantly clear that these attacks on Japan were not intended to achieve military objectives. While the U.S. bomber fleet was burning population centers, several armament factories and facilities for wartime production, which would otherwise have been priority targets, were allowed to survive until the end of the war.

America's Nuclear Experiment: Strategic Benefits of Deploying Nuclear Weapons Against a Civilian Population

When atomic strikes hit Hiroshima and Nagasaki on August 6 and 9, 1945, respectively, the response from the American public was much the same as it had been for the firebombing campaign. The two cities were chosen largely due to the fact that the vast majority of other population centers were ruled out as viable targets, with little left intact to destroy due to the intensity of the firebombing campaign. U.S. media glorified the atomic bomb as the savior of mankind, and under two percent of the 595 newspaper editorials criticized the weapon's use. Though there were slight differences of opinion and continuing claims to impartiality, the media had long acted mouthpieces for the nations' agendas in accordance with national interests.[16] 85 percent of Americans supported use of the bomb, which was widely seen to be a spectacular new weapon that could bring a cleaner and quicker end to the Japanese menace. Many felt it avenged attacks against the United States Navy's base at Pearl Harbor, despite this attack having been against a military installation while the bombs were used against civilian population centers.[17]

While the deployment of nuclear force against two Japanese cities is widely credited until today by Western sources for ending the Pacific

War, a justification for what was in fact a severe war crime, analysis of the strikes' impact on Japan's willingness to accept an unconditional surrender strongly indicates otherwise. This has increasingly become a consensus among analysts of the Pacific War. Firebombing had failed to break the Japanese people's will to resist or to move the Japanese militarist leaders to alter their terms of surrender. All those who expected the Japanese Empire to be bombed to submission had underestimated its resilience. Japan's decision to surrender was influenced overwhelmingly by other factors during the war. The bombings of Hiroshima and Nagasaki, with similar death tolls to those of the firebombings of other population centers, equally failed to break the leadership's will to resist. Both the nuclear and firebombing campaigns killed hundreds of thousands and destroyed targets overwhelmingly civilian in nature across 69 devastated Japanese cities, but had little effect on the outcome of the war.

Ward Wilson, senior fellow at the British American Security Information Council, gave an insightful analysis into the situation facing the Japanese leadership and how, in the context of the destruction wrought by firebombings, the use of nuclear weapons would have had little to no impact on their decision to surrender. Wilson noted the regularity with which the Japanese leadership received reports of cities being devastated by American bombing raids and suffering colossal civilian casualties, each in the tens of thousands, in the three weeks preceding the atomic attacks. As a result, the destruction of just two more cities to a similar extent – the only difference being the use of new and seemingly more efficient weapon of mass destruction – would have had little impact on their strategic thinking or willingness to surrender.

Wilson noted:

> In the three weeks prior to Hiroshima, 26 cities were attacked by the U.S. Army Air Force [the U.S. Air Force was not yet a separate branch of the military]. Of these, eight – or almost a third – were as completely or more completely destroyed than Hiroshima. The fact that Japan had 68 cities destroyed in the summer of 1945 poses a serious challenge for people who want to make the bombing of Hiroshima the cause of Japan's surrender. The question is: If they surrendered because a city was destroyed, why didn't they surrender when those other 66 cities were destroyed? ... Given that Japan had already had major bombing damage done to 68 cities, and had, for the most part, shrugged it off, it is perhaps not surprising that Japan's

> leaders were unimpressed with the threat of further bombing. It was not strategically compelling.[18]

Evidence strongly indicates that the United States was aware that dropping the bomb for military purposes was entirely unnecessary. Walter Brown, assistant to U.S. Secretary of State James Byrnes, gave an account that President Truman, who had replaced Roosevelt upon his death in April 1945, had agreed to hold a meeting three days before the first bomb was dropped, and that he was fully aware that Japan was 'looking for peace' and willing to surrender. Truman was told by Generals Douglas Macarthur and Dwight Eisenhower and Naval Chief of Staff William Leahy that there was no military need to use the bomb. Japan was defeated already.

It was clear that Japan was willing to surrender well before the nuclear attack. In April and May 1945 alone Japan had made three attempts to surrender through the neutral states of Portugal and Sweden. On April 7, acting Foreign Minister Mamoru Shigemitsu met with Swedish ambassador Widon Bagge in Tokyo and requested he 'ascertain what peace terms the United States and Britain had in mind.' Bagge relayed the message to the United States, but Secretary of State Stettinius told the U.S. Ambassador in Sweden to 'show no interest or take any initiative in pursuit of the matter.'[19] Similar Japanese peace signals through Portugal, on May 7, and again through Sweden, on the May 10, proved equally fruitless. On July 12, a month before the nuclear attacks, Emperor Hirohito summoned Prince Fumimaro Konoe (son of Atsumaro Konoe) who had served as Prime Minister in 1940–1941. 'It will be necessary to terminate the war without delay,' the Emperor said. He wished Konoe to secure peace with the Americans and British through the Soviets. As the Prince later recalled, the Emperor instructed him 'to secure peace at any price, notwithstanding its severity.'[20]

The presidentially assigned U.S. Strategic Bombing Survey group's report on the air campaign against Japan made it clear that the dropping of atomic bombs was wholly unnecessary to bring the war to an end. They wrote: 'Based on a detailed investigation of all the facts and supported by the testimony of the surviving Japanese leaders involved, it is the Survey's opinion that certainly prior to 31 December 1945 and in all probability prior to 1 November 1945, Japan would have surrendered even if the atomic bombs had not been dropped, even if Russia had not entered the war, and even if no invasion had been planned or contemplated.'[21]

Supreme Commander of all Allied Forces General Eisenhower said of the use of the bomb: 'The Japanese were ready to surrender and it wasn't necessary to hit them with that awful thing.'[22] He went on to recall that before the bomb was used: 'I had been conscious of a feeling of depression and so I voiced to him my grave misgivings, first on the basis of my belief that Japan was already defeated and that dropping the bomb was completely unnecessary, and secondly because I thought that our country should avoid shocking world opinion by the use of a weapon whose employment was, I thought, no longer mandatory as a measure to save American lives. It was my belief that Japan was, at that very moment, seeking some way to surrender with a minimum loss of "face."'[23]

Even Admiral William Halsey, a war hero renowned for his aggressive and often brutal tactics, dismissed the weapon as 'a "toy" the scientists wanted to try out.' He stated regarding the nuclear attack: 'the first atomic bomb was an unnecessary *experiment* ... It was a mistake ever to drop it.'[24] Brigadier General Bonner Fellers, then aide to General Douglas MacArthur, described America's strategic air offensive's firebombing and atomic attacks as 'one of the most ruthless and barbaric killings of non-combatants in all history.'[25]

General Kurtis LeMay dismissed the bomb, believing conventional explosives and the firebombing campaign would have eventually forced Japan to surrender. He proudly portrayed the bombing campaign against the Japanese civilian population in terms of a body count scorecard, one which he would later apply to his campaign in Vietnam. 'We scorched and boiled and baked to death more people in Tokyo on that night of 9–10 March than went up in vapor at Hiroshima and Nagasaki combined.'[26] In this he was indeed correct – with the death toll from the firebombing of Tokyo five months prior on the night of March 9 potentially numbering in the hundreds of thousands and surpassing that of both nuclear strikes combined. While the atomic bombings were devastating, they paled in comparison to the damage wrought by a several months long firebombing campaign against Japanese population centers.

In his extensive study of the use of nuclear weapons and its implications historian Gar Alperovitz writes: 'Although Japanese peace feelers had been sent out as early as September 1944 (and China's Chiang Kai-shek had been approached regarding surrender possibilities in December 1944), the real effort to end the war began in the spring of 1945. This effort stressed the role of the Soviet Union [...] In mid-April [1945] the [US] Joint Intelligence Committee reported that Japanese leaders were looking for a way to modify the surrender terms to end the war. The State Department was convinced the Emperor was actively seeking a way to stop the fighting.'[27]

Western accounts overwhelmingly continue to justify the use of nuclear weapons against Japanese cities, justifications which are widely accepted rather than being acknowledged as a severe war crime, possibly a crime against humanity, which was strategically unnecessary in the context of bringing about the defeated nation's surrender. Accustomed to crude propagandistic portrayals of the 'Japs' as virtually subhuman beasts, most Americans in 1945 heartily welcomed any new weapon that would wipe out more of the detested Asiatic race and help avenge the dead American soldiers. For the young Americans who were fighting the Japanese in bitter combat, the attitude was 'Thank God for the atom bomb.' Almost to a man, they were grateful for a weapon whose deployment seemed to end the war and allow them to return home. It was only after the war that the American public learned about Japan's efforts to bring the conflict to an end. *Chicago Tribune* reporter Walter Trohan, for example, was obliged by wartime censorship to withhold for seven months one of the most important stories of the war regarding Japan's leadership's willingness to surrender. This stated:

Japanese were offering surrender terms virtually identical to the ones ultimately accepted by the Americans at the formal surrender ceremony on September 2 – that is, complete surrender of everything but the person of the Emperor. Specifically, the terms of these peace overtures included:

- Complete surrender of all Japanese forces and arms, at home, on island possessions, and in occupied countries.
- Occupation of Japan and its possessions by Allied troops under American direction.
- Japanese relinquishment of all territory seized during the war, as well as Manchuria, Korea and Taiwan.

- Regulation of Japanese industry to halt production of any weapons and other tools of war.
- Release of all prisoners of war and internees.
- Surrender of designated war criminals.

The authenticity of Trohan's article was never challenged by the White House or the State Department, but he was nevertheless ordered to delay its release to avoid such information becoming publicly known. After General MacArthur returned from Korea in 1951, his neighbor in the Waldorf Towers, former President Herbert Hoover, took the Trohan article to the General and the latter confirmed its accuracy in every detail and without qualification.[28]

The Japanese leadership's ever growing willingness to bring the war to a swift end and accept American terms was influenced not by the suffering of their population inflicted by bombing raids, but rather the military reality of the situation. The threat of Soviet invasion was a decisive factor. As Prime Minister Suzuki stated upon hearing of the swift Soviet victory in Manchuria, 'the game is up.'[29] Having been overwhelmingly defeated by the USSR in previous military clashes, the Japanese government and military had always remained highly wary of this enemy and had since taken extensive measures to avoid any future conflict.[30] Unlike Western powers, the Soviets were certain not to allow the Japanese hierarchical social order to continue. There would be no emperors and aristocrats under Soviet rule, whereas under the Western powers it was likely that such elements in power would prevail – as indeed they did. As demonstrated in their occupation of Manchuria and northern Korea, Soviet courts showed little mercy to war criminals or the imperial leadership – a sharp contrast to the United States which pardoned many of these figures and placed them in prominent positions of power. A surrender to the West was therefore seen as far more favorable by the Japanese leadership to avert the risk of an imminent Soviet invasion.

Russian Prince Vladimir Obolensky, an exile living in London at the time, challenged the general conception that the bomb had ended the war. 'The belief that it has saved millions of the Allies' lives is a misconception. … In reality, Japan has been brought down by the interruption of her sea communications by Anglo-American air and sea power, and a danger of a Soviet thrust across Manchuria, cutting Japanese armies in Asia from home.'[31] Several Western historians and experts continue to assert that the bombs were wholly unnecessary. The threat of a Soviet invasion of the Japanese mainland after their swift victory over the elite Kwantung Army in Manchuria, as well as the extensive American and British blockade of the Japanese mainland which had reduced most of the population to hunger or starvation and made chances of winning the war impossible, had made the Japanese all the more willing to surrender.[32]

American press helped portray Japan as a nation which had surrendered as a direct result of the nuclear attacks after the war had ended. In the months before its surrender Japan was portrayed as a starving and vanquished nation reduced to sending out desperate peace feelers. After the war the retrospective portrayal of Japan made it appear as a resilient and threatening nation whose surrender required a land invasion and the loss of American lives. Depictions of a defeated country were far closer to the truth. The press were obliged to present the facts as President Truman's administration wanted, to depict Japan in the way that best suited its wartime aims. The nuclear strikes on Japanese cities had to be made to appear a moral and justifiable decision.

While nuclear strikes were not necessary to bring about an end to the Pacific War, they did serve other purposes which would benefit the United States' position in the war's aftermath. These were to demonstrate the effectiveness of these weapons in a show of force to the Soviet Union, itself set to imminently launch an invasion of Japan as of August 1945, and to test the impact of the atomic bomb on live human subjects – from which American scientists would obtain valuable data key to preparations for a potential nuclear war with the USSR in the early stages of the Cold War.

Although it is still widely believed in the West today that the decision to drop the atomic bombs was the decisive event that led to Japan's surrender, the circumstances indicate an alternative and more viable explanation.[33] Long before the end of the Pacific War the United States leadership was well aware that in the postwar world they would lead the sole remaining major power – challenged in their hegemony only by the USSR. They were correct to a large extent, as the industrial centers of Japan, Germany, Britain and other Western imperial nations had been bombed and destroyed – while the limited industrial development that China had embarked on had been severely impeded by years of war with Japan. Though the USSR had been thoroughly ravaged by the German, Romanian, Hungarian, Italian, Bulgarian and other invading forces from Europe since 1941, they had the largest standing army in the world and retained many major industrial centers in the far east of Russia beyond Stalingrad which were near untouched.

The Western Bloc had long been hostile to the USSR despite their common enmity towards Nazi Germany and the Axis powers, and as the Second World War neared its end relations again started to deteriorate between the two powers. There was much concern among the U.S. leadership regarding the balance of power between the United States and the USSR after the war. Responding to this emerging threat was at times prioritized above bringing about the swift defeat of the Axis powers. President Truman had himself stated in 1941, before assuming the presidency: 'If we see that Germany is winning we ought to help Russia, and if Russia is winning we ought to help Germany, and that way let them kill as many as possible.'[34] The Soviet threat was far more dire in his eyes than it was in those of his predecessor President Roosevelt, and America's new leader believed that the USSR posed as much of a threat to the United States and its allies as the Axis powers did. This seriously influenced policymaking as the war neared its end and the defeat of Imperial Japan appeared inevitable.

Henry Stimson, U.S. Secretary of War (his office is now called Secretary of Defense), told President Truman he was highly 'fearful' that American air attacks would leave Japan so 'bombed out' that there would be no opportunity to test the new atomic weapon and allow it to 'to show its strength.' Stimson admitted 'no effort was made, and none was seriously considered, to achieve surrender merely in order not to have to use the bomb.' He and his colleagues were keen to deploy the weapon against a Japanese city, despite the lack of a military need, 'to browbeat the Russians with the bomb held rather ostentatiously on our hip.' The day after Hiroshima was obliterated, President Truman voiced his satisfaction with the 'overwhelming success' of what he revealingly referred to as 'the experiment.' General Leslie Groves, director of the Manhattan Project that made the bomb, himself testified: 'There was never any illusion on my part that Russia was our enemy, and that the project was conducted on that basis.'[35]

The United States rushed to use two atomic bombs at almost exactly the time that a Soviet attack on Japan had originally been scheduled – August 9. It was in the interests not only of the Japanese ruling elites that the Soviets should not invade, but also of the United States which wanted to place Japan under its own influence and so needed to preempt both the landing of Soviet troops on Japanese shores and the Japanese surrender. The Presidency, which directly ordered the nuclear attacks, thus timed attacks on Hiroshima on August 6 and Nagasaki on August 9. Circumstances surrounding the strike, the timing of the attack, the lack of military necessity and the nature of relations with the USSR point to the fact that the United States dropped the bombs both to demonstrate its capabilities to the USSR and to prevent a Soviet invasion of Japan. Studies of the US, Japanese and Soviet diplomatic archives all strongly indicate that this was the true motive of the nuclear attacks.[36]

Not only was the U.S. leadership well aware that nuclear weapons were not needed to end the Pacific War, but their conduct in the early months of the occupation strongly gave the impression that they perceived the attack as a scientific experiment which, far from alleviating conditions for survivors, exacerbated them significantly. Survivors of the attacks at Hiroshima and Nagasaki and those suffering from the resulting radiation and contamination hoped to receive government support as casualties of war, as all casualties had under Japanese rule. The American military government which took control of Japan in the war's aftermath however not only ended the guaranteed compensation for war casualties, stripping millions of wounded of income, but it also refused to acknowledge the existence of radiological contamination or of any unusual conditions arising in civilians exposed to nuclear bombs. All mention of the subject was strictly censored throughout the seven year occupation period.[37]

Several teams of specialists from the United States visited Japan to study the effects of the nuclear attacks, gathering invaluable information for a potential future nuclear war. This was largely done under General

MacArthur's Atomic Bomb Casualty Commission (ABCC) which collected a wide range of data on the bomb victims, in the process gaining a reputation for harvesting Japanese cemeteries for remains. Specialists including American doctors were strictly forbidden from treating victims or providing information on their findings which could have aided the treatment of the survivors.[38] The way they sought data on the effects of the bomb while being totally uninvolved in aiding the affected population, even by providing basic information on the impacts of this otherwise wholly unknown scientific phenomenon which Japanese doctors struggled to understand, strongly gave the impression of an experiment being carried out on live subjects.

Paul Ham noted in his study of the nuclear attack:

> The directive did not mention treatment: prolonging life, easing pain, were neither the intentions nor the by-products of the job. Whether the patients – or more accurately the exhibits – lived or died was immaterial to the foreign doctors' charter. *How* the victims lived or died, *whether* their conditions improved or deteriorated; *whether* they suffered from cancer at some distant date or reproduced it in their children; such were the questions of cold scientific enquiry. In short, irradiated Japanese civilians were to serve as American laboratory rats. Herein lay a benefit – future rationalists would argue – of dropping the bomb on a city: to harvest scientific data about gamma radiation.[39]

Surrender on the Home Islands: Conduct of Occupying Forces

While it would be untrue to say that American military rule over Japan had only negative consequences, Western nations' depictions of this occupation generally tend to ignore the negative impacts and are overly positive to the point of being caricature-like. American newsreels from the 1940s and 1950s show U.S. soldiers being greeted by cheering crowds of grateful Japanese citizens in the streets. They show women bowing and handing bouquets of flowers to each soldier, and describe how Americans offer a helping hand to Japan and to rebuild it into a prosperous nation.

Much of this was true. Through imposition of a very different value system to Japan's previous militarist rulers, the American occupation did have many impacts on the Japanese society which can be considered positive. Women were given equal rights to men by law, including the rights to vote, own property, obtain a higher education, enter government and work in the police department. Under Chapter 3 of the new constitution drafted under occupation Japanese citizens were given inalienable individual rights, that is rights upon which the government could not infringe. This included the unprecedented right of peasants to own property. Land owning rights for the poor and legal equality of women and of working classes were notably prominent elements of the communist ideology the Japanese and Americans had both so feared – though when imposed on Japan from the West rather than by the Soviets these reforms were perceived positively.

There was a far darker side to the U.S. and allied occupation of Japan, one which is little mentioned in the vast majority of histories – American or otherwise. When Japan surrendered in August 1945, mass rapes by occupying forces were expected. Based on the behavior of American soldiers in Okinawa, Japanese officials were certain of this. To protect the chastity of their own daughters the Japanese leadership and elites took measures to prevent mass rapes by Western military forces. The United States, while to a large extent turning a blind eye to the sexual crimes of their military personnel, took precautions to ensure that their soldiers would not alienate the Japanese elites by raping their daughters, the 'chaste women' of *ippan katei* – daughters of middle- or upper-class families – and to minimize the negative perceptions of Americans among the population.

Compared to in Okinawa and later American wars in Asia, such as Korea and Vietnam, sexual assaults by occupying personnel were relatively few – particularly given the size of the occupying forces. Instead the U.S. military alongside ruling elements in Japan had the local police force set up 'comfort stations' for the Western soldiers, namely Americans and Australians. These stations provided occupation forces sexual access to Japanese women at negligible prices, approximately half the price of a pack of cigarettes.[40,41] Comfort stations primarily employed young girls and women who had many dependents, particularly those with parents or young children. Hunger was still endemic in cities following a months-long blockade by the Western powers, as it would remain for years under the occupation, and this was an important motivator. Comfort stations have been referred to by historians as 'rape stations,' which perhaps better represents their nature. In a society where chastity was highly valued, supporting these establishments was seen as the better alternative in the eyes of Japan's leadership to allowing Western soldiers to abuse any women they pleased. As sexual crimes by U.S. forces were seen as an inevitability, the establishment of comfort stations was essentially a concentration of rape among a segment of the population's women in order to spare the others.[42]

The official history of the Ibaraki Prefectural Police Department states: 'The comfort women ... had some resistance to selling themselves to men who just yesterday were the enemy, and because of differences in language and race, there were a great deal of apprehensions at first.' Police were ordered to set up these comfort stations for American personnel, something they were not pleased to do. 'Sadly, we police had to set up sexual comfort stations for the occupation troops ... to create a breakwater to protect regular women and girls.'[43]

From their opening the brothels were in extremely high demand. The chief of public relations for the RAA (Recreation and Amusement Association), the organization run by police officials and Japanese businessmen under supervision of the occupation government which organized comfort stations for American soldiers, said that on the day of opening he 'was surprised to see 500 or 600 soldiers standing in line on the street.' He said the Americans themselves could hardly keep their troops under control. Demand forced the RAA to recruit more and more women, each of which had to take up to 60 clients a day. In the field of sex work ten clients a day would be considered highly strenuous even for experienced women, and for inexperienced young girls to accommodate such high numbers of foreign clients would be considered an inhuman endeavor.[44]

Adverts for the RAA called for 'Women of the New Japan,' and did not specify the kind of work involved. They targeted young women left destitute by war. An example was Natsue Takita, who was a 19-year-old worker left with no relatives after the war. Although reluctant, she needed the income to survive and was persuaded by authorities to accept the offer.

She jumped in front of a train a few days after the brothel started operating, as the working conditions were intolerable and both psychologically and physically extremely strenuous. Takita, like many other women, had no other options to survive at a time when many were dying of hunger.

The RAA chief noted that the victims who suffered most were the many women who had no experience of such work and unknowingly answered the adverts. By the end of 1945 the RAA employed 70,000 women in this line of work. By 1946 this number had increased to 150,000 due to the very high sexual demands of the occupation troops. There was no shortage of war widows after the war. Despite these high figures it is highly likely that this number is far lower than the true figure. Toshiyuki Tanaka, a history professor at the Hiroshima Peace Institute, indicated that due to the significant number of private brothels operating and the number of undocumented destitute women who sold sex the numbers of Japanese comfort women serving the Western soldiers were likely to be far greater.

A significant degree of coercion was used to persuade Japanese women to serve occupation forces. Despite the fact that many were hungry and the country was on the brink of starvation, more incentives were at times needed due to the considerable demand and the undesirability of such work. A memorandum from American Lieutenant Colonel Hugh McDonald shows that it was clear to U.S. forces that the Japanese comfort women were very often not working consensually. McDonald admitted in his writing: 'The girl is impressed into contracting by the desperate financial straits of her parents and their urging, occasionally supplemented by her willingness to make such a sacrifice to help her family. It is the belief of our informants, however, that in urban districts the practice of enslaving girls, while much less prevalent than in the past, still exists.'[45]

Where financial incentives failed, recruitment of women to provide sexual services for occupation forces against their will also took place. Independent brokers, many associated with organized crime and the Japanese Yakuza, were relied on to provide women in such ways. The Women's Volunteer Corps, a government organization which mobilized girls and young women aged 14–25 to work in factories in wartime was used in particular. Groups of these women would be deceived and delivered not to factories, but to brothels serving occupation forces where they would be forced to work.[46]

The RAA ceased to operate in 1946 when over one quarter of U.S. personnel had contracted sexually transmitted diseases. This left 150,000 Japanese women, many of whom themselves had contracted such diseases, as social outcasts in destitute circumstances. Most continued to work as comfort women illegally, as there were few other options for them.[47] Even when Western soldiers had sexual access to Japanese women at low prices through the comfort stations however, widespread sexual crimes still occurred. Following the closure of comfort stations, incidences of sexual crime increased significantly. Historian John Dower noted in his own study of the occupation period: 'According to one calculation the number of rapes and assaults on Japanese women amounted to around 40 daily while the R. A. A. was in operation, and then rose to an average of 330 a day after the service was terminated in early 1946.'[48] Due to the value of chastity in traditional Japanese society, the number of rapes was significantly underreported, with a report from Japanese police stating in regards to this: 'victimized women feel too ashamed to make it public.'[49]

Though measures such as the creation of the RAA reportedly reduced incidences of sexual attacks by occupation soldiers, such crimes were still common and several of them were extremely brutal and resulted in the deaths of the victims. Political science professor Eiji Takemae wrote regarding the conduct of American soldiers occupying Japan:

> U.S. troops comported themselves like conquerors, especially in the early weeks and months of occupation. Misbehavior ranged from black-marketeering, petty theft, reckless driving and disorderly conduct to vandalism, assault, arson, murder and rape. Much of the violence was directed against women, the first attacks beginning within hours after the landing of advanced units. In Yokohama, China and elsewhere, soldiers and sailors broke the law with impunity, and incidents of robbery, rape and occasionally murder were widely reported in the press [which had not yet been censored by the U.S. military government]. When U.S. paratroopers landed in Sapporo an orgy of looting, sexual violence and drunken brawling ensued. Gang rapes and other sex atrocities were not infrequent [...] Military courts arrested relatively few soldiers for their offences and convicted even fewer, and restitution for the victims was rare. Japanese attempts at self-defense were punished severely. In the sole instance

> of self-help that General Eichberger records in his memoirs, when local residents formed a vigilante group and retaliated against off-duty GIs, the Eighth Army ordered armored vehicles in battle array into the streets and arrested the ringleaders, who received lengthy prison terms.[50]

The U.S. and Australian militaries did not maintain rule of law when it came to violations of Japanese women by their own forces, neither were the Japanese population allowed to do so themselves. Occupation forces could loot and rape as they pleased and were effectively above the law.

An example of such an incident was in April 1946, when approximately 50 U.S. personnel in three trucks attacked the Nakamura Hospital in Omori district. The soldiers raped over 40 patients and 37 female staff. One woman who had given birth just two days prior had her child thrown on the floor and killed, and she was then raped as well. Male patients trying to protect the women were also killed.[51] The following week several dozen U.S. military personnel cut the phone lines to a housing block in Nagoya and raped all the women they could capture there – including girls as young as ten years old and women as old as fifty-five.[52]

Such behavior was far from unique to American soldiers. Australian forces conducted themselves in much the same way during their own deployment in Japan. A member of the occupation force testified: 'As soon as Australian troops arrived in Kure in early 1946, they 'dragged young women into their jeeps, took them to the mountain, and then raped them. I heard them screaming for help nearly every night.' Such behavior was commonplace, but news of criminal activity by Occupation forces was quickly suppressed.[53]

Australian officer Allan Clifton recalled his own experience of the sexual violence committed in Japan:

> I stood beside a bed in hospital. On it lay a girl, unconscious, her long, black hair in wild tumult on the pillow. A doctor and two nurses were working to revive her. An hour before she had been raped by twenty soldiers. We found her where they had left her, on a piece of waste land. The hospital was in Hiroshima. The girl was Japanese. The soldiers were Australians. The moaning and wailing had ceased and she was quiet now. The tortured tension on her face had slipped away, and the soft brown skin was smooth and unwrinkled, stained with tears like the face of a child that has cried herself to sleep.[54]

Australians committing such crimes in Japan were, when discovered, given very minor sentences. Even these were most often later mitigated or quashed by Australian courts. Clifton recounted one such event himself, when an Australian court quashed a sentence given by a military court martial citing 'insufficient evidence,' despite the incident having several witnesses. It was clear that courts overseeing Western occupation forces took measures to protect their own from crimes committed against the Japanese – crimes which were largely regarded as just access to 'spoils of war' at the time by the Western occupiers.[55]

As had been the case during the war, underreporting of rapes in peacetime due to the associated shame in a traditional society and inaction on the part of authorities (rapes in both cases occurred when Western militaries were themselves in power) would lower the figures significantly. In order to prevent ill feeling towards their occupation from increasing, the United States military government implemented very strict censorship of the media. Mention of crimes committed by Western military personnel against Japanese civilians was strictly forbidden. The occupying forces 'issued press and pre-censorship codes outlawing the publication of all reports and statistics "inimical to the objectives of the Occupation."'[56] When a few weeks into the occupation Japanese press mentioned the rape and widespread looting by American soldiers, the occupying forces quickly responded by censoring all media and imposing a zero tolerance policy against the reporting of such crimes.[57] It was not only the crimes committed by Western forces, but any criticism of the Western allied powers whatsoever which was strictly forbidden during the occupation period – for over six years. This left the U.S. military government, the supreme authority in the country, beyond accountability. Topics such as the establishment of comfort stations and encouragement of vulnerable women into the sex trade, critical analysis of the black market, the population's starvation level calorie intakes and even references to the Great Depression's impact on Western economies, anti-colonialism, pan-Asianism and emerging Cold War tensions were all off limits.[58]

What was particularly notable about the censorship imposed under American occupation was that it was intended to conceal its own existence. This meant that not only were certain subjects strictly off limits, but the mention of censorship was also forbidden. As Columbia University Professor Donald Keene noted: 'the Occupation censorship was even more exasperating than Japanese military censorship had been because it insisted that all traces of censorship be concealed. This meant that articles had to be rewritten in full, rather than merely submitting XXs for the offending phrases.'[59] For the U.S. military government it was essential not only to control information – but also to give the illusion of a free press when the press was in fact more restricted than it had been even in wartime under imperial rule.

By going one step further to censor even the mention of censorship itself, the United States could claim to stand for freedom of press and freedom of expression. By controlling the media the American military government could attempt to foster goodwill among the Japanese people while making crimes committed by their personnel and those of their allies appear as isolated incidents. While the brutality of American and Australian militaries against Japanese civilians was evident during the war and in its immediate aftermath, it did not end with occupation. The United States has maintained a significant military presence in Japan ever since and crimes including sexual violence and murder against Japanese civilians continue to occur.

Remaking of Japan: Redirecting a Nation

The American and allied attitude towards Japan changed considerably after the war, as the former enemy was reshaped into a Western client state and its depiction in Western media was adjusted to accommodate this. What had been the greatest challenge to Western hegemony over the Asia-Pacific region would become a key facilitator of the new Western dominated regional order. The Japanese were as before perceived as subservient and beneath Westerner races – but they were no longer the rats and monsters they had previously been made out to be. Portrayals of the Japanese as monstrous, bestial and outright evil were replaced with a depiction as primitive and culturally immature dependents. This attitude was highly prevalent among Western nations in their dealings with Japan in the postwar period.[60]

General Douglas MacArthur, who as Supreme Commander of all U.S. forces in the Asia-Pacific region would go on to run the U.S. military occupation from his command center in Tokyo, revealed through his comments how attitudes to Japan and its people and had changed in peacetime. He was asked whether the Japanese could be counted on to defend the freedoms they had gained following the occupation. It was implicit in this question, and in the widespread fears in the United States at the time, that there was much concern that Japan would revert to being a fully independent Asian power and potentially again challenge Western regional dominance following the end of American military rule. MacArthur responded, however, that he was fully assured that this would not occur, stating: 'If the Anglo-Saxon was say 45 years of age in his development, in the sciences, the arts, divinity, culture, the Germans were quite as mature. The Japanese, however, in spite of their antiquity measured by time, were in a very tuitionary condition. Measured by the standards of modern civilization, they would be like a boy of twelve as compared with our development of 45 years ... they were working on a different level.'[61]

American historian John Dower wrote regarding the attitude to the Japanese and MacArthur's views of the backwardness of the Japanese as an Asian civilization, and Japan's 'place' in America's future order in Asia:

> The general's disquisition on the evolutionary backwardness of Japan fit perfectly with the patronizing and dismissive appraisals others were offering of the country's economic immaturity [...] The issue he [MacArthur] had unwittingly brought so floridly to the fore would not and could not be dispelled. After all, the Japanese had routinely spoken of themselves as MacArthur's children ... The entire occupation had been premised on acquiescing to America's overwhelming paternalistic authority; and even as sovereignty drew near, even as the nations was being rehabilitated as a Cold War partner, the Americans never had any real expectation that an equitable relationship would be the result. The new military was a 'little American army,' obviously destined to remain under U.S. control. The new economy was inordinately dependent on American support and indulgence.[62]

Extending the general's metaphor, the United States would reeducate and shape this 'boy of twelve' to become an adopted son America could count on to support its initiatives in the Pacific. Now that the Japanese Empire had been bombed, 69 of its cities destroyed, millions killed, forced to accept an unconditional surrender and left with a population living below starvation levels, they could be brought down to the level of a young boy. They were indeed at the mercy of the United States as a boy of twelve would be to a master. The United States controlled the oil and the food, and thereby controlled the nation and its people. Japan was in the ideal position to be manipulated and remade in the image the United States saw fit. The pan-Asian power would become an American client and help the United States and its Western partners maintain their newfound and now undisputed hegemony in the Pacific.

General MacArthur's faith that Japan would continue to follow the path laid out for it by the United States in the war's aftermath was far from without reason – given the considerable power America now had over the East Asian state. Since the 1930s the Japanese people had been told that they were fighting from the purest and noblest of causes – the overthrow of Western imperialism in the Asia-Pacific to lead the region into modernity under the 'Greater East Asia Co-Prosperity Sphere.' After eight years of war all their efforts and sacrifices appeared to have amounted to nothing. What could they say to the war dead? The nation needed to redefine itself, suffering from a state of exhaustion and defeat which came to be known in Japanese as *kyodatsu*. British historian Richard Storry, the war's contemporary, referred to the result as: 'destruction of traditional beliefs that amounted to a moral revolution,' in which the status of the country's feudal system and its armed forces were discredited – providing the new occupation forces with significant room to remake the country.[63] The population had endured great hardship and made major sacrifices to support the war effort, with everyone from schoolchildren to the elderly being mobilized to provide assistance, and so the impact of a military defeat and humiliating surrender was particularly considerable.

During the war there had been significant food shortages both at home and for soldiers fighting abroad. The average calorie intake had by the end of the war declined tremendously, stunting the growth of children during this period. Elementary school children in 1945 were significantly smaller on average than in 1937 for example. Infant mortality was also much higher.

Japan's defeat occurred in midsummer when the harvests of the previous year had run out. The harvest of 1945 was meek, with the U.S. military having directly targeted crops to starve the country of food and resources under the appropriately named 'Operation Starvation.' A combination of manpower shortages, adverse weather and insufficient tools exacerbated the situation. In early October Tokyo had only a 'three day' rice supply (mixed with soybeans and *mamekasu*, the residuum from processed soybeans). This estimate was based on rations barely sufficient to keep a non-active adult alive. To make matters worse, upon its defeat Japan was forcibly cut off from the food supplies it had been receiving from Asia and prevented from purchasing food from abroad. Many in Japan expected that a resulting famine would kill millions.

In late October, shortly after the country's surrender and the cutting of food supplies by the Western powers, the first deaths from malnutrition were recorded. These began to occur in all the country's major cities. 'The Peoples' Association for a Policy Against Starvation' announced that as many as six individuals from among Tokyo's Ueno Station's homeless were dying every day due to malnutrition. The minister of finance informed the United Press that as many as ten million citizens might starve to death if food imports were not immediately forthcoming. In the midst of this fear of an imminent famine the United States had begun food shipments to Japan, averting the anticipated disaster. The Japanese population was still hungry, but they would no longer starve. The U.S. thus on the one hand continued to prevent Japan from importing the food it needed, but on the other provided some food themselves. By positioning itself as the sole source of food for the starving nation, the United States could portray itself as a generous benefactor. A yearbook from the time described such shipments from America as coming to Japan 'like a merciful rain during a drought.' Holding back the rain for months, then allowing a trickle to return did much for the Americans' image. In the words of a Japanese history, they 'kindled a light of hope in the hearts of depressed residents.' These food rations were nevertheless well below the starvation level, poorer than even the negligible wartime food supplies the country had received from its government during the war when under blockade.[64]

The second effect was one of control. The United States ensured that the Japanese did not starve, but for many years the population was not far from starvation. Control over a food supply has long been an effective means of exerting control over a population – hence the statement of renowned national security advisor of the Nixon administration, Secretary of State Henry Kissinger: 'Control oil and you control nations; control food and you control people.'[65] The United States and its Western allies had undertaken significant measures to ensure they controlled Japan – leveraging control over its access to oil and other raw materials such as iron and rubber to threaten the country's economy at the time of the oil embargo. Their ability to bring the entire empire to a halt through control of the resources it needed had been a crucial factor that forced Japan to war. Now that Japan was occupied and the Japanese had lost their independent government, the Western powers led by the United States increased their influence by effectively controlling the food supply, with 90 percent of the country's staples provided by the U.S. – thus allowing them to exercise control over both the nation and its people.

With prospects for a resurgent Japanese threat to Western dominance in the Pacific apparently quashed indefinitely, the American press, now extensively covering the new threat of communism, emphasized repeatedly that to rebuild a strong safe Japan and maintain it as an ally with substantial American influence and anti-communist foreign policy was a crucial asset against the spread of communism in Asia. U.S. policymakers concluded that having a strong Japan onside was essential to managing the region.[66] The American special relationship with Japan lent it significantly more influence in East and Southeast Asia. Japan would go on to be used extensively as a base from which the United States would conduct military operations against other Asian nations including Indonesia, Vietnam, Korea and China, and the U.S. retains 113 military bases in the country today.[67] It was on this basis that Japanese Prime Minister Yasuhiro Nakasone would in 1983 refer to his own country as the United States' 'unsinkable aircraft carrier in the Pacific.'[68] The country would go on to aid the United States militarily both through provision for its armies and through direct personnel contributions. Japan's biological warfare research and many members of the infamous biological warfare Unit 731 were also incorporated into the United States' own biological weapons program where their experience proved 'absolutely invaluable.'[69] They too were reportedly sent to Korea during the Korean War to supervise the waging of biological warfare against Chinese and Korean forces. (Use of the Japanese armed forces to support the United States in its wars is covered in Chapter 13. For details on biological warfare and the integration of Unit 731 see Chapter 9.)

While American influence over Japan was an invaluable asset, control over Okinawa in particular was essential to allowing the United States to project power throughout the Asia-Pacific. The island enjoyed a special status as an American territory, or as U.S. Ambassador Edwin Reischauer called it 'a colony of 1 million Japanese.'[70] Okinawa would be used as a base for American bombers to launch strikes against Indonesia, Vietnam and Korea. In a 'legal limbo' subject to neither Japanese nor American laws it was an ideal storehouse for weapons of mass destruction, both nuclear and chemical, aimed squarely at the Soviet Union, China and North Korea for much of the Cold War. The territory was militarized to such an extent that investigative journalist and expert on Okinawan human rights Jon Mitchell stated: 'Okinawa didn't just have bases – the *entire island* was a base.'[71] Military facilities on Okinawa were such an essential asset in war efforts against other Asian nations that Admiral Grant Sharp, the commander of U.S. Pacific Forces, stated in 1965: 'Without Okinawa, we couldn't continue fighting the Vietnam War.'[72] The territory was only returned to Japan 27 years later in 1972, when its military importance dwindled as the Vietnam War de-escalated.

Use of Okinawa was far from the only way Japan would go on to benefit the United States' designs in the region, but it was one of the most significant. Okinawans themselves were heavily involved in supporting the American War efforts, particularly during the Vietnam War. Approximately 50,000 worked as employees of the United States military. They packed explosives, processed munitions, printed Vietnamese language war propaganda for American psychological operations forces, dressed as Vietnamese to participate in war-games for the training of U.S. personnel, and even drove buses and transported supplies in Vietnam itself.[73] As Okinawans were under American military rule, it followed that they would come to work for America's war efforts. Extensive military facilities employing

Okinawans remain on the island to this day, over 70 years after the United States first captured the territory. The United States has continued to benefit from use of the island since its return to Japanese sovereignty. Okinawans themselves have even in recent years suffered numerous rapes including child rapes,[74] killings, and severe damage to the island's environment.[75,76] Despite their express wishes to the contrary conveyed through numerous protests, lawsuits,[77] and through elected officials[78] however, the American military presence has been non-negotiable due to its strategic importance. (Japan and Okinawa's critical roles in supporting the new US-led regional order are covered further in Chapter 13.)

The government the United States set up in Japan was largely compromised of the same figures which had preceded the occupation – now made subordinate to the United States in governing the country. Despite their initial ideological rhetoric regarding democratization, what the United States really needed was a reliable apparatus through which to run the country – for which Japan's imperial system remained highly practical. As John Dower went on to write regarding the United States maintaining keeping much of Japan's old order in place: 'Much of the rest of the world – on both sides of the Cold War divide – was in fact, appalled and alarmed by the haste with which the democratization agenda had been abandoned, the old guard resurrected, and remilitarization promoted. In such circumstances, it was still difficult to imagine a sovereign Japan as anything other than dependent on and subordinate to the United States – a client state in all but name.'[79]

With an effective government willing to co-operate with Western interests, the United States had in a relatively short period reshaped the leading threat to Western dominance in the Pacific into the Western Bloc's most critical and reliable regional partner. Japan went from opposing Western dominance of Asia to facilitating it long after the Cold War's end, and from the 1990s would begin to more actively deploy military force overseas in support of Western war efforts (as covered in Chapter 13). As General MacArthur proclaimed following the defeat of Japan: 'the Pacific is now an Anglo Saxon lake' – with the only Asian power which was capable of challenging Western primacy brought to its knees.[80] This would leave the West in a dominant position in the Asia-Pacific for decades to come.

Notes

1 Weintraub, Stanley, *The Last Great Victory: The End of World War II, July/August 1945*, New York, Dutton Adult, 1995, (p. 205).
2 Munro, Victoria, *Hate Crime in the Media, A History*, Santa Barbara, CA, Praeger, 2014 (p. 43).
3 Dower, John, *War Without Mercy: Race and Power in the Pacific War*, New York, Panthoen, 1986 (p. 72).
4 Kennedy, Michael Dana, *The Flowers of Edo*, New York, Vertical, 2010 (Chapter 23).
5 Karsten, Peter, *Encyclopedia of War and American Society*, Thousand Oaks, CA, SAGE Publications, 2005 (p. 418).
6 Ham, Paul, *Hiroshima Nagasaki: The Real Story of the Atomic Bombings and their Aftermath*, New York, Doubleday, 2012 (p. 59).
7 Ibid. (pp. 59–60).
8 Wiilson, Ward, 'The Bomb Didn't Beat Japan … Stalin Did,' *Foreign Policy*, May 30, 2017.
9 Selden, Mark, 'A Forgotten Holocaust: U.S. Bombing Strategy, the Destruction of Japanese Cities & the American Way of War from World War II to Iraq,' *The Asia-Pacific Journal*, Vol. 5, Issue 5.
10 Ham, Paul, *Hiroshima Nagasaki: The Real Story of the Atomic Bombings and their Aftermath*, New York, Doubleday, 2012 (p. 60).
11 Ibid. (pp. 60–62).
12 'United States Strategic Bombing Survey, Summary Report (Pacific War),' Washington, DC, U.S. GPO, 1946, Vol. 1 (p. 16).
13 Dower, John, *War Without Mercy: Race and Power in the Pacific War*, New York, Panthoen, 1986 (p. 72).
14 Toland, John, 'Beyond the Brink of Destruction,' *New York Time*, August 4, 1985.
15 Toland, John, *The Last Great Victory: The End of World War II, July/August 1945*, Boston, MA, Dutton Adult, 1995 (p. 205).
16 Ham, Paul, *Hiroshima Nagasaki: The Real Story of the Atomic Bombings and their Aftermath*, New York, Doubleday, 2012 (p. 459).
17 Ibid.
18 Wilson, Ward, 'The Bomb Didn't Beat Japan … Stalin Did,' *Foreign Policy*, May 30, 2017.
19 Wainstock, Dennis D., *The Decision to Drop the Atomic Bomb*, Santa Barbara, CA, Praeger, 1996 (p. 22).

20 Ibid. (p. 22, 31).
21 Truman Library: United States Strategic Bombing Survey, July 1, 1946. Truman Papers, President's Secretary's File. Atomic Bomb.
22 *Bulletin of Atomic Scientists*, December 1975 (p. 40).
23 Alperovitz, Gal, 'We didn't need to drop the bomb – and even our WWII military icons knew it,' *Salon*, May 11, 2016.
24 Alperovitz, Gar, 'The War Was Won Before Hiroshima – And the Generals Who Dropped the Bomb Knew It,' *The Nation*, August 6, 2015.
25 Sato, Kiroaki, 'Great Tokyo Air Raid was a war crime,' *Japan Times*, September 30, 2002.
26 Kristof, Nicholas D., 'Tokyo Journal: Stoically, Japan Looks Back on the Flames of War,' *New York Times*, March 9, 1995.
27 Alperovitz, Gar, *Atomic Diplomacy: Hiroshima and Potsdam – The Use of the Atomic Bomb and the American Confrontation with Soviet Power*, London, Pluto Press, 1994 (p. 107, 108).
28 Engdahl, Sylvia, *The Atomic Bombings of Hiroshima and Nagasaki*, Farmington Hills, MI, Greenhaven Press, 2011 (p. 117).
29 Ham, Paul, *Hiroshima Nagasaki: The Real Story of the Atomic Bombings and their Aftermath*, New York, Doubleday, 2012 (p. 339).
30 McCormack, David, *Japan At War 1931–1945; As the Cherry Blossom Falls*, Stroud, Fonthill Media, 2016 (p. 19).
31 Ham, Paul, *Hiroshima Nagasaki: The Real Story of the Atomic Bombings and their Aftermath*, New York, Doubleday, 2012 (p. 460).
32 Stone, Oliver, and Kuznick, Peter, 'Bombing Hiroshima changed the world, but it didn't end WWII,' *Los Angeles Times*, May 26, 2016.
33 'Atomic Diplomacy,' Office of the Historian, Milestones 1945–1952, United States of America Department of State.
34 McCullough, David, *Truman*, New York, Simon & Schuster, June 15, 1992 (p. 262).
35 Pilger, John, 'The lies of Hiroshima live on, props in the war crimes of the 20th century,' *The Guardian*, August 6, 2008.
36 Edwards, Rob, 'Hiroshima bomb may have carried hidden agenda,' *New Scientist*, July 21, 2005.
37 Ham, Paul, *Hiroshima Nagasaki: The Real Story of the Atomic Bombings and their Aftermath*, New York, Doubleday, 2012 (p. 447).
38 Ibid. (p. 435, 437).
39 Ibid. (p. 436).
40 Talmadge, Eric, 'GIs Frequented Japan's "Comfort Women",' *Washington Post*, April 25, 2007.
41 Ibid.

42 Orbaugh, Sharalyn, *Japanese Fiction of the Allied Occupation: Vision, Embodiment, Identity*, Boston, MA, Leiden, 2007 (p. 348).
43 Talmadge, Eric, 'GIs Frequented Japan's "Comfort Women",' *Washington Post*, April 25, 2007.
44 Ibid.
45 Ibid.
46 Tanaka, Yuki, *Japan's Comfort Women: Sexual Slavery and Prostitution During World War II and the U.S. Occupation*, Abingdon, Routledge, 2002 (pp. 138–147).
47 'U.S. troops used Japanese brothels after WWII,' *NBC News*, April 27, 2007.
48 Dower, John, *Embracing Defeat, Japan in the Wake of World War II*, New York, W. W. Norton & Company, 2000 (p. 579).
49 Sims, Calvin, '3 Dead Marines and a Secret of Wartime Okinawa,' *The New York Times*, June 1, 2000.
50 Takemae, Eiji, *Allied Occupation of Japan*, New York, Continuum International Publishing Group, 2002 (p. 67).
51 Tanaka, Yuki and Tanaka, Toshiyuki, *Japan's Comfort Women: Sexual Slavery and Prostitution During World War II*, Abingdon, Routledge, 2003 (p. 163).
52 Ibid.
53 Takemae, Eiji, *Inside GHQ: The Allied Occupation of Japan and Its Legacy*, New York, Continuum International, 2003 (p. 67).
54 Ibid. (pp. 126–127).
55 Tanaka, Yuki; Tanaka, Toshiyuki, *Japan's Comfort Women: Sexual Slavery and Prostitution During World War II*, Abingdon, Routledge, 2003 (pp. 110–111).
56 Takemae, Eiji, *Inside GHQ: The Allied Occupation of Japan and Its Legacy*, New York, Continuum International, 2003 (p. 67).
57 Svoboda, Terese, 'U.S. Courts-Martial in Occupation Japan: Rape, Race, and Censorship,' May 23, 2009, *The Asia-Pacific Journal*, January 21, 2009.
58 Dower, John, *Embracing Defeat, Japan in the Wake of World War II*, New York, W. W. Norton & Company, 2000 (p. 412).
59 Rosenfeld, David M., *Unhappy Soldier: Hino Ashihei and Japanese World War II Literature*, Lanham, MD, Lexington Books, 2002 (p. 86).
60 Sato, Hiroaki, 'Irony of being in the company of "12-year-olds",' *The Japan Times*, June 25, 2012.
61 Billian, George Athan, *American Constitutionalism Heard Round the World, 1776–1989: A Global Perspective*, New York, New York University Press, 2009 (p. 295).
62 Dower, John, *Embracing Defeat, Japan in the Wake of World War II*, New York, W. W. Norton & Company, 2000.

63 Storry, Richard, *Japan and the Decline of the West in Asia, 1894–1943*, London, Macmillan, 1979 (p. 11).
64 Westad, Odd Arne, *The Cold War; A World History*, London, Allen Lane, 2017 (p. 134).
65 Zhao, Hongfu, *The Economics and Politics of China's Energy Security Transition*, London, Academic Press, 2019 (p. 48).
66 Stone, I. F., *Hidden History of the Korean War*, Amazon Media, 2014 (Chapter 6, 'Time Was Short').
67 Vine, David, 'How U.S. Military Bases Abroad Undermine National Security and Harm Us All,' *Huffington Post*, September 13, 2015.
68 Smith, William E. and McGeary, Johanna and Reingold, Edwin M., 'Beef and Bitter Lemons,' *Time*, January 31, 1983.
69 Taylor, Jeremy, 'Biology at War: A Plague in the Wind,' *BBC Horizon*, October 29, 1984.
70 Mitchell, Jon, 'Battle scars: Okinawa and the Vietnam War,' *The Japan Times*, March 7, 2015.
71 Ibid.
72 Havens, Thomas R. H., *Fire Across the Sea: The Vietnam War and Japan 1965–1975*, Princeton, NJ, Princeton University Press 1987 (p. 85).
73 Mitchell, Jon, 'Battle scars: Okinawa and the Vietnam War,' *The Japan Times*, March 7, 2015.
74 Lev, Michael A., '3 Gis Convicted in Okinawa Rape,' *Chicago Tribune*, March 7, 1996.
75 'Endangered Okinawa dugong's habitat to be bulldozed for the sake of U.S. military base,' *RT*, April 29, 2015.
76 Mitchell, Jon, 'Contamination: Documents reveal hundreds of unreported environmental accidents at three U.S. Marine Corps bases on Okinawa,' *The Japan Times*, November 19, 2016.
77 'Okinawa villagers sue authorities for construction of "unlivably loud" U.S. helipads,' *RT*, September 27, 2016.
78 Wanklyn, Alastair, 'Onaga takes base argument to U.N. human rights panel,' *Japan Times*, September 22, 2015.
79 Dower, John, *Embracing Defeat, Japan in the Wake of World War II*, New York, W. W. Norton & Company, 2000 (p. 408).
80 Futrell, Robert Frank, *Ideas concepts doctrine: basic thinking in the United States Air Force 1907–1960*, Volume 1, Alabama, Maxwell Air Force Base, Air University Press, 1989 (p. 292).

CHAPTER 3

Emergence of a People's Republic in China: Efforts to Undermine the Rise of an Independent Asian Power

China ... looms as a major power threatening to undercut our importance and effectiveness in the world and, more remotely but more menacingly, to organize all of Asia against us.[1]

— 1969 Pentagon Papers

Our hope of solving the problem of the mainland of China was not through attack on the mainland but rather by actions which would promote disintegration from within.[2]

— Assistant Secretary of State for Far Eastern Affairs
WALTER ROBINSON

The United States and the Chinese Civil War

By the time of the Japanese Empire's surrender in 1945 China had been in a state of civil war for 18 years. This period was itself preceded by years of factionalism and instability in which the country was governed by several rival warlords – somewhat resembling Afghanistan in the 1990s. The civil war had primarily been fought by two factions, the nationalist Guomindang (GMD) led by Chiang Kai-shek, and the communist forces led by Mao Zedong and Zhou Enlai. Hostilities between the formerly unified factions broke out in 1927 when Chiang Kai-shek, following the death of nationalist leader Sun Yat-sen, had taken power and sought to purge communist elements of the nationalist movement – which he perceived to be a threat to his own position. Japan's occupation of Manchuria in China's far east in 1931 and the outbreak of open hostilities with Guomindang forces 1937 interrupted but did not bring a complete end to the struggle for power between the two Chinese factions. Despite the emergence of a common enemy, the Guomindang's forces continued to target the communists, and though Chiang opposed the Japanese he often avoided direct confrontation with them and prioritized fighting communist forces. Believing that enemies within the country were a greater danger than invasion by external powers, he had said: 'Communism is a disease of the heart, the Japanese are but a disease of the skin.'[3]

The U.S. Office of Strategic Services (OSS), predecessor of the CIA, estimated that during the war the Guomindang had directed most of their war effort against the communists rather than the Japanese. After the war several Japanese collaborators would go on to serve in the Guomindang government, much as they would in the American backed South Korean government.[4,5] The Guomindang's forces were, according to U.S. reports, crippled by their own corruption and saw many of their own defect to join either the Japanese or the communists as a result. An example was Wang Jingwei who, disillusioned with Chiang's government, defected and formed his own Japanese aligned government.[6] Nevertheless, following the outbreak of US-Japanese hostilities in 1941, both communist and nationalist forces worked with the United States against their common enemy. The communist People's Liberation Army (PLA) had been willing to work very closely with U.S. forces, rescuing and caring for downed U.S. airmen and returning them to U.S. bases.[7] The *New York Times* noted regarding the extent of this co-operation: 'The Communists did not lose one airman taken under their protection. They made a point of never accepting rewards for saving American airmen.'[8,9]

Despite prior co-operation, the United States almost immediately turned against the Chinese communists following Japan's surrender – seeking to gain an absolute victory for its Guomindang partners. Chiang's government's close co-operation with and ties to the West and his reliance on the United States made him the ideal client leader, whereas the communists appeared entirely independent, with negligible ties even to the Soviet Union, and as a result could not be guaranteed to govern in line with American interests. Shortly after the Japanese surrender in August 1945 the U.S. had begun to rearm Japanese soldiers, now subordinate to American officers, to fight alongside Guomindang forces and their own

Marine Corps. At this point the now subdued Japan was no longer a threat to U.S. interests in Asia and their forces could be co-opted to fight alongside the Americans. To justify rearming Japanese troops who had just weeks before been the United States' most loathed adversary, President Harry S. Truman stated: 'It was perfectly clear to us that if we told the Japanese to lay down their arms immediately and march to the seaboard, the entire country would be taken over by the communists. We therefore had to take the unusual step of using the enemy as a garrison until we could airlift Chinese National troops to South China and send the Marines to guard the seaports.' He described this strategy as 'using the Japanese to hold off the communists.'[10] It was clear that the swift defeat of China's independent communist movement was a priority for both the Guomindang and the U.S. – regardless of their feelings towards the Japanese. With the deployment of the U.S. Marines in their tens of thousands, these three major forces all fought in unison against the far smaller and relatively poorly armed PLA.

Following Tokyo's sudden surrender in September 1945 there was a power vacuum in many of the Japanese occupied territories in China, leading to a race among competing local forces to reach key strategic locations such as major ports and cities. The United States undertook extensive measures to ensure that these did not fall under communist control. American air and naval assets were used to facilitate a massive and rapid strategic redeployment of 400,000–500,000 nationalist military personnel across the country to seize key locations – many of which would otherwise have quickly fallen to the communist PLA. Two weeks after the end of the war Beijing was surrounded and about to be captured by the People's Liberation Army, and only the swift deployment of the U.S. Marines prevented this.[11] Communist troops were pushing into Shanghai at speed until U.S. transport planes were used to transport some of the Nationalists' elite ground units into the city to secure it.[12] U.S. aircraft also made regular reconnaissance flights over communist territory to scout the position of their forces, providing vital intelligence to their Guomindang allies and compounding their already considerable advantage. U.S. forces were also directly involved in combat on the side of the Guomindang, which alongside an air campaign included the deployment of substantial ground forces. 50,000 U.S.

Marines were sent to guard railway lines, coal mines, ports, bridges and other strategic locations. There was little doubt therefore that the United States military was actively involved in the civil war against the Chinese communists. Reports from the communist leadership indicate that U.S. forces also actively took to the offensive, attacking areas under their control and bombarding PLA positions.[13,14] The United States, though war weary in the Pacific War's aftermath, was using all means at its disposal to ensure a communist defeat.

Faced with a vastly larger and better armed adversary, the People's Liberation Army waged a guerrilla war – relying heavily on aid and shelter from the population. This led to the saying among Chinese communists: 'Guerrillas are fish swimming in the water of the people.' The result was severe reprisals by American and Guomindang forces against population centers suspected of aiding their enemies. A rare report surfaced from a U.S. Marine deployed in China to his congressman stating that in at least one incident the Marines had blasted a small Chinese village 'unmercifully' without knowing 'how many innocent people were slaughtered.' The destruction wrought by 50,000 fully armed U.S. Marines deployed in China, often operating in an offensive capacity, served only to worsen conditions for Chinese civilians.[15] The communists claimed U.S. combat aircraft continuously strafed and bombed their troops and in at least one instance massacred the population of a communist held town by machine gun.[16,17] As the PLA enjoyed widespread support particularly from rural communities into which they so often integrated themselves, entire populations could easily be perceived as 'the enemy' and were targeted indiscriminately as a result. Such occurrences would later become commonplace on a far larger scale during U.S. interventions in Korea and Vietnam.

By 1946 100,000 American military personnel had been deployed to China, under the pretext of disarming and repatriating the Japanese. While this was eventually carried out, it was often secondary to their more immediate objective – providing the support needed to ensure a Guomindang victory. A Marine lieutenant in China in December 1945, Christmas time, said: 'They ask me, too, why they're here. As an officer I am supposed to tell them, but you can't tell a man that he's here to disarm Japanese when he's guarding the same railway with (armed) Japanese.'[18] Many U.S. military personnel around the world, the Marines in China included, started to protest against not being sent home after the end of the war. Many were kept overseas for anti-communist operations.[19]

The United States attempted to mediate in the civil war between the communist and Nationalist forces, under the guise of being an impartial actor, despite its active involvement on the side of the Guomindang. General George Marshall, who would months later become Secretary of State, was sent to arrange a ceasefire and a coalition government which would include the Guomindang as the dominant party. Neither the communists nor the Guomindang however were seriously committed to sharing power, as the former would not accept a junior position in a coalition while the latter felt the communist threat, the 'cancer of the heart,' was too great to allow them into government – preferring a military solution which at the time appeared likely to succeed. As historian D. F. Fleming wrote: 'One cannot unite a dying oligarchy with a rising revolution.'[20] Each side was confident in its ability to achieve an absolute victory, the Guomindang due to their overwhelming military superiority and U.S. backing and the PLA due to their widespread popular support and the ineffectiveness of their adversaries in combat.

Despite fighting against the combined Japanese, American and Nationalist forces, the PLA managed to regroup from their initial series of losses and went on to gain the upper hand. By 1947 a communist victory, considered near impossible by all major powers in 1945, appeared imminent. In early 1947 the U.S. began the withdrawal of its ground forces from China. At around the same time they deployed a new asset against the communist forces, the renowned Flying Tigers Air Force squadron that had fought against Japan. The Tigers had interlocked with the newly formed Central Intelligence Agency (CIA) to become the agency's first ever air unit. They flew supply missions to besieged nationalist cities and transported supplies, food and munitions.[21,22] Generous American military and financial assistance, from arms to intelligence and airlifts, continued to flow to the Guomindang.

By 1949 the U.S. aid going to the Guomindang forces since the war had begun had almost reached $2 billion in cash and a further $1 billion worth of military hardware. These were tremendous sums at the time, tens of billions of dollars in in the 2010s, given at a time when the United States itself was undergoing a serious postwar economic recession. The provision of aid on such a scale represented the importance of retaining China in the Western sphere of influence at all costs. A full 39 Guomindang divisions had been fully trained and equipped by the Americans to fight communist forces.[23] The PLA on the other hand had received negligible foreign support, and their only major foreign backer had been North Korea – as the Japanese imperial era Korean resistance which had gone on to form the new North Korean leadership had formed close ties with the PLA during their joint struggle for independence. The main contribution the Koreans provided however was manpower, as the small state did not have the funds or the industrial capacity to support the PLA.

Despite their overwhelming material and manpower advantages the Guomindang quickly saw their position deteriorate, leading to their eventual defeat. Chiang Kai-shek had hardly proven himself an effective commander in the war with Japan, and he was known to set his generals impossible tasks while his scorched earth polices caused far more damage to rural communities than the Japanese themselves. This was exemplified at the Battle of Nanjing in 1937, when a small Japanese force subjugated a far more numerous and well-armed Chinese garrison within days due to failures in its command, organization and leadership which led to low morale and a chaotic retreat, while Japanese forces themselves suffered negligible losses.[24,25] Another was Chiang's personal decision to destroy the dams on the Yellow River in 1938 in a desperate attempt to slow the Japanese advance. This directly caused the deaths of 1 million of China's rural population, flooding 500 square miles of land (an area today larger than all but the world's 18 largest countries, well over three times the landmass of Japan itself) and causing both plague and famine.[26] The flooding meanwhile had a negligible impact on the Japanese advance.[27,28] These failures continued into the civil war, where scorched earth policies alienated and impoverished much of the population and inefficient tactics and poor leadership undermined the enormous advantages in manpower and equipment the Guomindang had enjoyed over Japan.

The communists were seen to lead by example and took great care to portray themselves to the impoverished population as paragons of honesty, progressiveness and fairness. As a result, the people voted with their support, and not only did the rural populations support the PLA, but disillusioned Guomindang forces transferred entire divisions and their weapons to the PLA through mass defections. As former U.S. State Department employee William Blum observed: 'The Chiang dynasty was collapsing all around in bits and pieces. It had not been only the onslaught of Chiang's communist foes, but the hostility of the Chinese people at large to his tyranny, his wanton cruelty, and the extraordinary corruption and decadence of his entire bureaucratic and social system.'[29] As U.S. General David Barr, head of the U.S. Military Mission in China, had said, the Guomindang were under 'the world's worst leadership,' noting 'widespread corruption and dishonesty throughout the armed forces.' There was a broad consensus among U.S. analysts at the time supporting Barr's views regarding the cause of the Guomindang's failure despite generous American support.[30]

American delegations which had visited Chinese communist territory noted the stark discrepancy with areas under the Guomindang. It was these differences which can be largely credited for the latter's ultimate defeat. Reports on the communists by an American delegation sent in 1944 were immensely positive, with a sense that they had 'come into a different country and are meeting different people.' The leader of the delegation, political analyst John Service, noted that 'bodyguards, gendarmes and the clap-trap of Chungking officialdom are ... completely lacking.' By contrast he noted of the Chinese communist leadership: 'Mao and the other leaders are universally spoken of with respect ... these men are approachable and subservience toward them is completely lacking.' He observed the lack of censorship which had been prevalent in Guomindang areas, and the sense of freedom in communist areas. 'To the casual eye there are no police in Yenan,' he reported of the communist controlled region by contrast to the nationalist police state. 'Morale is very high ... there is no defeatism but rather confidence.' Service and others in his delegation reported that communist troops were better disciplined, their government and military did not face the widespread corruption their adversaries did, and policies were more economically just – which won a great deal of support from the population. It was these factors which likely decided the outcome of the war despite American and Japanese military support and far larger forces and territories at the disposal of Chiang's government.[31]

Chiang Kai-shek had himself written in his personal diary in late 1948, by which time a communist victory appeared inevitable, that the Guomindang had failed primarily due to the corruption and 'rot' within its leadership.[32] While the U.S. was under no illusions as to the nature of their client government, they nevertheless wished such leadership upon China and undertook extensive measures to impose it.[33] Short of a full-scale invasion with hundreds of thousands of troops, something which would have been impossible in such a large country as China in the post-war international and domestic political climate, all methods possible to sustain Chiang's government were attempted.[34] For the United States a dependent client dictatorship, even 'the world's worst leadership,' was far preferable to their interests than to a genuinely independent and popular communist government.

Following the communist victory, British journalist and China scholar Felix Greene noted: 'Americans simply could not bring themselves to believe that the Chinese, however rotten their leadership [under the Guomindang], could have preferred a communist government.'[35] Many in the U.S. justified this with the illusion that the Chinese communists must have been supported by the USSR. This was despite the USSR openly refusing to side with the communists against the nationalists, and advising Mao Zedong to dissolve the PLA and join the GMD government as a junior partner. American sources reported repeated attempts by the USSR to distance themselves from Chinese the communists, who firmly believed that the communist military struggle was unwinnable.[36] The Soviets had simultaneously signed a Treaty of Friendship and Alliance with the Guomindang and were far from supportive of the communist cause. The USSR was facing the hard task of rebuilding after the war, and in any case was not willing to help aid a Chinese war effort against such overwhelming odds.[37] The Soviet leadership believed the Nationalist forces represented stability, and stability on their borders was a priority.[38,39] In 1947 Secretary of State George Marshall publicly stated that there was no evidence that the Chinese communists were being supported by the USSR.[40] In fact it was known that the USSR had sent military aid to Guomindang forces to fight the Japanese Empire in 1941 – while refusing to aid the communists.[41,42,43] Nevertheless, the myth of Soviet support for Chinese reds persisted.

The communist victory came as much as a surprise to the Soviet Union as it did to the United States. The forces arrayed against the communists had been so much greater that prospects for victory had seemed impossible. In 1948 Soviet leader Joseph Stalin admitted that he had advised the CCP against fighting a revolutionary war, and now it was clear that he had been mistaken to do so. He stated:

> It is true, we also have made mistakes ... we considered the development of the uprising in China had no prospects, that the Chinese comrades should join the Chiang Kaishek government and dissolve their army. The Chinese comrades agreed here in Moscow with the views of the Soviet comrades, but went back to China and acted quite otherwise. They mustered their forces, organized their armies and now, as we see, they are beating Chiang Kaishek's army. Now, in the case of China, we admit we were wrong. It has proved that the Chinese comrades and not the Soviet comrades were right.[44,45]

Guomindang forces were forced to flee to Taiwan, taking with them numerous national and artistic treasures and the country's entire gold reserve – the former which remain on Taiwan to this day.[46] They had prepared Taiwan two years beforehand by terrorizing its native population using military force to assert their authority and establish their leadership. The massacres are estimated to have killed up to 28,000 of Taiwan's indigenous population.[47] The Guomindang themselves admitted to killing 18,000–28,000 native-born Taiwanese in a single 1947 massacre alone.[48] With Taiwan held by a U.S. aligned government the territory would become a key staging ground for the United States to wage a concerted campaign to undermine the Chinese government on the mainland, and would come to host American nuclear weapons and 30,000 military personnel. As the flags of the Guomindang's Republic of China were lowered on the mainland, the new People's Republic of China (PRC) was declared on September 21, 1949.

Sabotage and Terrorism: The U.S. Campaign to Bleed China Out After Independence and Undermine National Development

The communist victory, in the United States widely termed the 'Loss of China,' came as the greatest blow to America's foreign policy designs in the postwar era. The new People's Republic of China (PRC) was thus met with unrelenting hostility by Washington, and while the Chinese communist movement had not been distinctly anti-American throughout the civil war it would very soon become so. Despite U.S. involvement in the civil war, Chinese Foreign Minister Zhou Enlai made repeated overtures to the United States seeking friendship and a strengthening of bilateral relations. These were flatly rejected by the United States, and rather than accepting his offers of friendship the U.S. would undertake several attempts to assassinate Zhou.[49]

The CIA and its predecessor the OSS had been involved extensively in the Chinese Civil War, and they continued to operate extensively against the newly formed PRC. While the Guomindang had relocated their capital to Taiwan off the eastern coast, much of their forces had fled to Myanmar in the east following the end of the war, and the CIA quickly moved to regroup these remnants into a fighting force which it could direct against the PRC. These forces were directed in their combat operations by the CIA – allowing the agency to wage a continued war by proxy against the newly formed Chinese republic. In the early 1950s forces based in Myanmar carried out a number incursions, some of them on a large scale, into Chinese territory. In April 1951, a time when the United States was directly engaged in battle with Chinese forces on the Korean Peninsula, a few thousand troops accompanied by CIA advisers who were running the operation, supplied by airdrops from American C-46s and C-47 military transport aircraft, crossed into Yunnan province. This was an effective attempt to open a smaller second front against the PLA, thus further stretching the new republic's already scarce resources. The incursion force was defeated and driven back by communist forces in a matter of days and sustained heavy casualties, while several CIA advisers were killed in the fighting.[50]

Later in 1951 a similar force penetrated 65 miles into Chinese territory where they held a 100-mile strip of territory. It would be hard to entertain the illusion that these forces were realistically meant to overthrow the Chinese government. Rather they were there to cause destruction and hinder China's development and rebuilding efforts while diverting the PLA's attention from the Korean front. Raids by these CIA proxy forces appeared to have no objective other than sabotage and maximum destruction to disrupt postwar reconstruction.[51]

Attacks on China by CIA proxies continued intermittently, while the agency went to much effort and expense to upgrade the capabilities of its assets. American engineers were flown to Myanmar to construct and expand airstrips invaluable for military operations against China. CIA air squadrons were brought in for logistical services, and huge quantities of American heavy arms were flown into the country. Much of these supplies were brought in via Thailand. The force was expanded through recruitment of men from the Myanmar hill tribes, while more and more troops were flown in from Taiwan. The CIA army in Myanmar soon numbered over 10,000 men.

Such a well-armed CIA trained force backed by American weapons and air power was a major thorn in the side of the Chinese government. By the end of 1952 the Guomindang government in Taiwan claimed 41,000 communist soldiers were killed, and over 3,000 were wounded by these forces – although these were almost certainly gross exaggerations. By this time not one but two other wars were raging on China's borders, with Korea and Vietnam, the former which led to U.S. troops approaching the Chinese borders and threatening on numerous occasions to expand the war into Chinese territory from the Korean Peninsula (see Chapters 8 and 9). The new state was undergoing harsh trials – and its internal development was being shaped for the worse as a result.

Having been ravaged by war over several decades China's economy was extremely weak when civil war ended in 1949. The key for the United States and its partners was to divert the new republic's efforts and resources away from rebuilding and modernization, lest the independent power became a modern and capable rival like the USSR had. The Soviet Union had in little over a decade (1928–1941) industrialized itself and developed from a backward state facing regular famine to a major world military and economic power. Constant threats on its borders and the need to divert resources to war was an effective means to prevent the PRC from undertaking the same course – with the Korean War alone absorbing half of the state budget and engagements with forces backed by Washington collectively seriously hindering the country's postwar industrialization plans.

As U.S. reporter Hugh Deane, former Coordinator of Information and naval intelligence officer on General MacArthur's staff and an expert on the Korean War and Sino-U.S. relations, concluded regarding the drain that China's responses to military threats on its borders put on its finances: 'The young People's Republic of China spent 6.2 billion Yuan it could hardly afford on the intervention, forgoing much expenditure on economic development and social remedies.' By their own count almost 150,000 Chinese soldiers were killed, with significant additional casualties, and 5.6 million tons of war materials were consumed in the Korean war effort alone. All of the manpower and these significant resources were required for defense almost immediately after the country gained independence, and this significantly stifled social and economic development and growth at a time when it was most essential.[52]

Shortly after the outbreak of the Korean War in 1950, before Chinese forces had become involved in the conflict, the U.S. command had repeatedly threatened attacks on critical Manchurian infrastructure facilities near the Korean border – providing the PRC with no assurances of its security as a vast American force approached its territory. At a time when rebuilding the nation was essential, the United States turned the Korean War into a critical threat to China's own military and economic security. As a result, the country had little choice but to enter the war, though it would go to great lengths to prevent its escalation. The U.S. economy on the other hand could not only afford a major war in Korea, but actually benefited and emerged from a severe recession as a result. Due to the large military industrial base developed in the Second World War, the American economy was in an excellent position to take advantage of the situation (see Chapter 7).

Along China's second front in Myanmar U.S. proxy forces continued to harass the PLA for over a decade. The CIA supplied these assets up to 1961, at which point the agency phased out direct involvement. Heavily armed former Guomindang forces were deployed against the will of the government of Myanmar, and between raids into China they would frequently clash with Myanmar's own military – an unwelcome presence extensively backed by the United States and wreaking much havoc in both Asian nations. These forces would frequently indulge in banditry and trade in drugs, with many of their leaders becoming opium barons. They operated in the Golden Triangle, a term coined by the CIA for a slice of land encompassing parts of Myanmar, Laos and Thailand – the world's largest source of opium and heroin. It was one of the many incidents of Western intelligence agencies' involvement in the drug trade in Asia. CIA pilots flew the drugs to their destinations to secure the co-operation of those in Thailand who were assisting the military operation.[53]

The government of Myanmar protested the presence of the proxy forces, their criminal activities, and the substantial American support they were receiving, to both the United States and the United Nations. The CIA responded to this potential embarrassment by trying to put pressure on their assets to leave Myanmar. Chiang Kai-shek however, who maintained ties to these forces which were primarily comprised of his former troops, had been happy to allow them to bleed the new Chinese republic on his behalf. Unwilling to lose an armed group of his supporters which he viewed as a valuable asset, and still entertaining hopes of a reconquest of the Chinese mainland with their support, Chiang responded by threatening to expose the CIA's covert support for these forces. This reflected poorly on his leadership and priorities, as he revealed himself to be so eager to prolong the civil war over a decade after his defeat and use foreign backed forces to disrupt the development of and terrorize his own people – rather than working to end hostilities for the greater good of the country.

The CIA had at some point hoped the China's People's Liberation Army could be provoked into attacking Myanmar to root out the hostile forces based there, forcing the neutral government in Yangon to make closer partnerships with the West in response to a perceived Chinese threat – and so strengthen the Western Bloc's presence in the region. In January 1961 the Chinese PLA launched an attack into Myanmar's territory to root out the CIA proxy forces – but they did so as part of a combined effort co-ordinated with Myanmar's own military. The two parties jointly overwhelmed the main base of the hostile forces, ending their operations permanently.[54]

This result was very much the opposite of what the American agency had intended, and Myanmar soon after renounced U.S. aid and moved to improve relations with China.[55] Many of the former Guomindang forces who had worked for the CIA in Myanmar soon after found work as part of another CIA army being built in Laos. Western aligned Guomindang linked forces had also participated in a CIA war by proxy to undermine the newly formed Indonesian government in early 1958 (as covered in Chapter 4).

Alongside operations from Myanmar, several islands within 5 miles of the Chinese mainland, particularly Quemoy and Matsu, were used as staging grounds for the CIA and their proxy forces to conduct raids into China. These operations enjoyed generous U.S. financial and logistical support. Such hit and run attacks again could not possibly hope to overthrow the PRC but were intended to weaken and spread terror in the nation and bleed it out. Again, the goal was to divert attention and funds from national reconstruction – a peaceful China allowed to focus on economic development was the greatest threat to the Western Bloc's interests. Proxy forces based on these islands carried out frequent attacks at battalion strength, and bombing forays were also launched against mainland targets. According to American reports, Chiang Kai-shek was himself 'brutally pressured' by the U.S. to build up military forces on these islands in around 1953, as Washington sought to 'unleash' him against China.[56] The islands were also used to disrupt trade with minor attacks and sabotage and to launch incursions by small commando-type teams to gather intelligence and destroy Chinese infrastructure. These teams were often dropped in by air.

The CIA regularly trained teams of Nationalist Chinese combatants on Taiwan before dropping them into the mainland to conduct sabotage, gather intelligence and otherwise undermine the government. As CIA case officer Ralph McGhee who had formerly been stationed in Taiwan stated, the CIA was working with the Western aligned Taiwanese forces 'to train and drop teams of Chinese onto the mainland to develop resistance movements and gather intelligence.'[57] Destabilization for its own sake appeared to be the goal.

The Chinese PLA was portrayed in Western reports as having acted sporadically and attacked islands surrounding the mainland unprovoked. However attacks on these islands were in fact measured responses to the little mentioned incursions carried out by U.S. backed forces which used them as staging grounds for miltiary operations. Heavy artillery attacks on the Quemoy islands, just 2 kilometers east of the mainland, killed American officers stationed there on at least one occasion. These officers were heavily involved in continued postwar military harassment operations against the PRC. In November 1952 Richard Fecteau and John Downey, who were part of the operations to fly teams into Chinese territory and drop them supplies, were shot down. Beijing announced their capture and sentencing two years later. The U.S. State Department in turn claimed that the two men had been civilian employees of the U.S. Department of the Army in Japan who were presumed lost on a flight from Korea to Japan. They responded: 'How these two men came into the hands of the Chinese Communists is unknown to the United States ... the continued wrongful detention of these American citizens furnishes further proof the Chinese Communist regime's disregard for accepted practices of international conduct.'[58]

In December 1971 Fecteau was released shortly before President Nixon's trip to China. Downey was freed in March 1973, soon after the president publicly acknowledged him to be a CIA officer.[59] The CIA later themselves confirmed that Fecteau and Downey had been paramilitary officers working for them.[60,61] According to the CIA, they had been 'promoting domestic anti-government guerrilla operations. This was to be accomplished by small teams of Chinese agents, generally inserted through airdrops, who were to link up with local guerrilla forces, collect intelligence and possibly engage in sabotage and psychological warfare, and report back by radio.'[62] The U.S. itself was engaging in aggressive acts of war against China while blaming the country which had wanted peace for 'disregard for accepted practices of international conduct,' bombing China and carrying out killings and acts of sabotage while taking an active role in the drug trade in neighboring countries for good measure. While China was regularly attacked by Western forces and their proxies, seriously threatened through the Korean Peninsula and even made subject to biological weapons attacks (see Chapter 9),[63,64] the country is depicted by the West as an aggressor and an irrational actor.

Despite the substantial evidence supporting the PRC's claims to have been the victim of aggression, in March 1966 U.S. Secretary of State Dean

Rusk stated in response: 'At times the Communist Chinese leaders seem to be obsessed with the notion that they are being threatened and encircled.' He spoke of China's 'imaginary almost pathological, notion that the United States and other countries around its borders are seeking an opportunity to invade Mainland China and destroy the Peiping [Peking] regime.' He went on to say: 'How much Peiping's "fear" of the United States is genuine and how much it is artificially induced for domestic political purposes only the Chinese Communist leaders themselves know. I am convinced, however, that their desire to expel our influence and activity from the western Pacific and Southeast Asia is not motivated by fears that we are threatening them.'[65] An analysis of American operations against the PRC however does much to undermine Rusks' refutation of the PRC's allegations regarding U.S. hostility.

Continued U.S. credibility, despite having repeatedly committed acts of aggression and committing lies to the record regarding operations against the PRC, was largely facilitated by to the United States and its partners' far greater international prestige and soft power relative to the newly formed Chinese republic. Had China, as an independent or 'rogue' state and enemy of the West, committed these same acts themselves, they would not be some obscure little known facet of history. Such 'acts of terrorism,' as they would likely be called would be considered highly relevant to understanding the nature of the PRC's government until today. Committing lies directly to record would have tarnished their credibility for years to come, but the United States was never held accountable for these very same actions.

The Chinese government announced in 1954 that 11 Americans had been shot down over China in January 1953 on a mission which was the 'air drop of special agents into China and the Soviet Union.' They were freed after two and a half years. The Chinese went on to say that they had killed 106 American and Taiwanese agents who had parachuted into China between 1951 and 1954, and had captured 124 others. The CIA maintained its commando program until at least 1960. The agency flew many other flights over China, using high altitude U-2 spy planes, pilotless drones and other aircraft – a practice which continued until 1971. During this period several U-2 planes and 19 drones were shot down by Chinese fighters and air defenses.[66,67]

Military provocations were far from the only efforts undertaken to undermine China's new government, with the country subject to a harsh U.S. trade embargo for over two decades almost immediately after the civil war's end. American partners such as Japan were also strictly prohibited from forming economic ties with or recognizing the PRC. In the immediate aftermath of the PRC's formation the U.S. government also moved to spark an international campaign against the country by raising and making an issue of Tibet's autonomy from China. Chinese governments had claimed Tibet as part of the country for over two centuries, and had the U.S. aligned Guomindang won the civil war an issue of the matter would not have been made. Before the communist takeover the United States made their position on Tibet's autonomy clear: 'The Government of the United States has borne in mind the fact that the Chinese Government has long claimed sovereignty over Tibet and that the Chinese constitution lists Tibet among areas constituting the territory of the Republic of China [The state's name under GMD rule before declaration of the PRC]. This Government has at no time raised a question regarding either of these claims.'[68,69] After an independent government took power in 1949 this quickly changed.

Having previously refused requests from the Tibetan separatist leadership for assistance in obtaining independence from the Guomindang government, the United States would within weeks of the civil war's end move to capitalize on a potential asset. On November 1, 1949, President Truman called for 'modern weapons and sufficient advisors' to be sent to separatist forces.[70] Just days before the outbreak of the Korean War in June the following year, Secretary of State Dean Acheson stated that Britain and the United States were jointly exploring means to 'encourage Tibetan resistance to Commie control.'[71] Efforts would escalate from the mid-1950s, in an attempt to keep pressure on China following the Korean War's end, as part of a broader policy effectively summarized by Assistant Secretary of State for Far Eastern Affairs Walter Robinson, who stated: 'our hope of solving the problem of the mainland of China was not through attack on the mainland but rather by actions which would promote disintegration from within.' Plans laid out at a four-day conference between U.S. intelligence and the Tibetan separatist leadership in 1955 saw a ten-year joint plan laid out to end Chinese rule over Tibet – with the fragmentation of the new People's Republic strongly in line with Western interests.[72]

Alongside pledges of material assistance, Truman also began a program which would make extensive use of the United States' considerable control of information and status globally – namely 'to organize the moral forces of the world against the immoral' – stated in reference to the extensive support the Western Bloc would go on to give the separatist movement in response to the change in government in Beijing. John F. Avedon, a high level American associate of the Tibetan separatist leadership, stated regarding this support: 'for its part the United Stated pledged to support [the Dalai Lama] and his government abroad, reintroduce Tibet's cause in the United Nations and finance its struggle against China including, if it developed, a military option.'[73] Media organizations serving to promote U.S. interests were instrumental in supporting the campaign, key examples being the CIA financed and staffed Congress of Cultural Freedom which had established both the London based *China Quarterly* and *Quest* – both of which played a central role in supporting the Tibetan separatist movement and demonizing the Chinese republic. The CIA and European intelligence agencies later jointly set up the International Commission of Jurists, whose claim to represent objective findings of reputable jurists and respectable names provided a great deal of credibility to articles condemning the actions of the Chinese republic in the harshest possible language. The commission's reports were heavily based on interviews with the CIA funded Tibetan separatist leadership, and would go on to form the basis of the international support campaign for Tibetan separatism.[74,75]

In the mid-1950s the CIA began a program to recruit and train Tibetan exiles in neighboring countries such as India and Nepal. Among them were members of the Dalai Lama's guard and others who had already engaged in guerilla activity against the Chinese government. They were flown to the United States to an unused military base in Colorado's mountains, where the high altitude simulated that of their homeland, to be trained in the fine points of paramilitary warfare. After training they were flown to friendly Asian countries to then be infiltrated back into China. As Harvard's *Journal of Cold War Studies* stated: 'The first group of Tibetan rebels was secretly brought to Saipan for training in December 1956. The trainees were then sent back to Tibet in 1957 to help the Tibetan rebels to establish contacts with the CIA and to join the resistance themselves. Available Chinese sources give no indication that the Chinese Communists were aware of America's secret involvement in promoting the rebellion in Tibet during this period.'[76] Through Tibetan guerillas, the CIA had another proxy force with which to bleed China out.

Once in China the infiltrators would sabotage infrastructure, mine roads, cut communications lines and ambush PLA forces – a stark contrast to the image of pacifist Tibetans widely promoted by Western media. Their actions were supported by CIA aircraft and at times led by CIA contracted mercenaries. Extensive support facilities for these infiltrators were constructed in Northeast India. The training program continued until the 1960s. The number of infiltrators remains unknown, but the CIA did continue to support them.[77]

Along with clandestine operations under the cover names of St Circus and St Barnum, one for training Tibetan guerillas and one for airlifting CIA agents and military supplies to Tibet respectively, operation St Bailey was undertaken as an extensive classified propaganda campaign among Tibetan communities to foster anti-Chinese, anti-communist and separatist thinking.[78] The U.S. Department of State described the objectives of its propaganda in Tibet as follows: 'In the political action and propaganda field, Tibetan program objectives are aimed toward lessening the influence and capabilities of the Chinese regime through support, among Tibetans and among foreign nations, of the concept of an autonomous Tibet under the leadership of the Dalai Lama; toward the creation of a capability for resistance against possible political developments inside Tibet; and the containment of Chinese Communist expansion – in pursuance of U.S. policy objectives.'[79]

The United States could, via such programs, manipulate potential Tibetan recruits by demonizing the Chinese government and nurturing their unlikely dream of 'freeing' their homeland. The great irony was that rule by the Chinese Communist Party freed many in Tibet in a far more direct way. Tibet had previously had widespread serfdom and slavery which the Chinese government abolished. Women were also liberated, in that for the first time they could no longer be bought and sold as property, and were given equal rights. As was often the case, the Western Bloc sided against progressive forces in Asia to further its own regional interests.

In 1961 the *New York Times* found out about the secretive Colorado training operation. It acceded to a Pentagon request not to investigate the matter however, as it was a particularly sensitive issue. The CIA's 1947 charter and the U.S. Congress' interpretation of it had limited the agency's domestic operations to information collection, but they had overstepped this line on several counts – of which this was but one case.[80] Only because the media collaborated with the government by failing to report on the CIA overstepping its mandate, as was often the case in sensitive foreign operations, could this remain a secret.

American intelligence documents published in 1998 revealed much regarding the country's operations against China in the 1950s as well as the Dalai Lama's close co-operation with the CIA. Tibetan separatist combatants were revealed to have received generous funding to carry out anti-Chinese activities. A 1964 memorandum gave the precise sums: $500,000 to support 2,100 fighters based in Nepal, $400,000 in expenses for a covert training site in Colorado and $185,000 in black air transportation of trainees from Colorado in India, for later infiltration into China. The Dalai Lama was also given a personal subsidy of $180,000 annually. Use of Tibetan separatists to establish a spy network to gain information on Chinese government activities, possibly on the coinciding Chinese nuclear program, was also detailed.[81] Other reports indicated that the CIA had armed a sizeable force of 14,000 Tibetan militiamen against the PRC, providing both training and a wide variety of armaments from silencers to rocket propelled grenades and mortars, while regularly dropping supplies from bases in Thailand using C-130 and C-54 transports.[82]

Funding Tibetan fighters and saboteurs against China benefited only those powers which sought to weaken the Chinese state. Both China and its Tibetan minority suffered as a result of the conflict from which neither reaped any benefits. As the fourteenth Dalai Lama recalled, co-operation with the CIA against China 'only resulted in more suffering for the people of Tibet.'[83] The United States could achieve its objectives of further draining the resources of the Chinese state by waging war by proxy, thereby itself incurring minimal costs and minimal losses. The campaign, while potentially promising and a considerable drain on Chinese resources, ultimately floundered due to lack of support from the vast majority of the Tibetan population. Armed uprisings against Chinese authorities tended to flounder for this reason, and often led to figures in the separatist leadership being quickly evacuated by the CIA,[84] while U.S. trained agents were regularly turned in to Chinese authorities by the Tibetans themselves.[85,86]

The longstanding Western campaign for 'freeing Tibet' has been cover for interventions to weaken an independent China and tarnish its image internationally. It has always been a point the Western Bloc has used whenever it needed to demonize and discredit the PRC in the eyes of the world and stir up anti-Chinese sentiment. Even in 2008 when Beijing hosted the Olympic games, several Western cities through which the Olympic torch passed were filled with crowds of 'free Tibet' protestors. Many tried to attack the Olympic torchbearer, particularly in London[87] and Paris.[88] Xinjiang independence protests and several protests against other alleged 'Chinese human rights abuses' also took place. As a result media attention was largely directed towards the human rights campaign targeting China and the several alleged abuses the country committed, casting a shadow over the sporting event.

It is worthy of note that support for separatist movements in China began immediately after China became an independent People's Republic in 1949 – not before. The 14th Dalai Lama himself wrote that the West supported Tibetan separatism 'not because they cared about Tibetan independence, but as part of their worldwide efforts to destabilize all communist governments.'[89] Policy regarding Tibetan separatism is itself highly indicative of the reality of Western morality and concern regarding Asian populations – that 'human rights' only become an issue raised against states which pursue independent policy contrary to Western interests, which at the time were mostly communist or communist aligned states. Indeed, all states which have been at least somewhat antagonistic to the United States have without exception been accused of committing human rights abuses and oppressing their people – most often proportionally to their level of opposition to Western policy. This has remained a widely observable pattern into the twenty-first century.

While the Chinese Civil War supposedly concluded in 1949, the United States and its partners never accepted peace and would continue to subject China to aggression and provocation. For the CIA the war against China never ended. The continuation of this war had significant effects on Chinese political and social development. The war-weary nation was never truly allowed peace, not only due to the Korean War breaking out less than a year after the end of the Civil War, but also numerous other military provocations for decades afterwards. This combined with threats of nuclear and biological weapons attacks (see Chapter 9), infiltration by saboteurs and hostile paramilitary forces meant that the country was always in a state of war. The free and open society and approachable leadership described by political analyst John Service when he led the American delegation to the Chinese communists in 1944 could never last under such circumstances. Why would anyone who approached the PRC's leaders, which Service had noted were remarkably approachable in the 1940s, not be a CIA mercenary or Formosan assassin? Would government critics truly be acting in the nation's interest, or were they promoting subversion in the interests of a foreign power? The immense scale of the security threat thus necessitated precautions which compromised the freedom of the Chinese people.

Civil society was similarly increasingly restricted due to threats from 'enemies of the people,' in ways the communist government had never previously found to be necessary. It is clear that China under threat could never develop to its full potential, and into the free society which could have been an attractive model to much of Asia, due to the continuing war waged against it. To most who mistook the People's Republic of China in its early years to be a country at peace, it could easily be portrayed by the West as needlessly repressive and paranoid. Without the context of the military incursions and threats as persistent as they were dire which the state faced ever since its formation, as well as the extreme hostility China's communists faced from the United States during the civil war, the development of Chinese civil society and government can never be properly understood and can be easily misrepresented.

Notes

1 Draft Memorandum From Secretary of Defense McNamara to President Johnson, Washington, November 3, 1965.

2 Deane, Hugh, *Good Deeds & Gunboats*, San Francisco, CA, China Books & Periodicals, 1990 (p. 179).

3 Kantowicz, Edward R., *The Rage of Nations*, Grand Rapids, MI, Wm. B. Eerdmans Publishing Company, 1999 (p. 358).

4 Harris Smith, Richard, *OSS: The Secret History of America's First CIA*, University of California Press, 1972 (pp. 259–282).
5 *New York Times*, December 19, 1945 (p. 2).
6 Mitter, Rana, *China's War With Japan 1937–1945; The Struggle for Survival*, London, Allen Lane, 2013 (p. 207).
7 Barrett, David, *Dixie Mission: The United States Army Observer Group in Yenan, 1944*. Oakland, University of California Centre for Chinese Studies, 1970.
8 *New York Times*, December 9, 1945 (p. 24).
9 *New York Times*, December 26, 1945 (p. 5).
10 Truman, Harry S., *Memoirs, Vol. Two: Years of Trial and Hope, 1946–1953*, New York, Doubleday & Company Inc., 1956 (p. 66).
11 Harris Smith, Richard, *OSS: The Secret History of America's First CIA*, University of California Press, 1972 (pp. 259–282).
12 Fleming, Denna Frank, *The Cold War and its Origins, 1917–1960*, Crows Nest, Allen and Unwin, 1961 (p. 570).
13 *New York Times*, September-December 1945.
14 Tuchman, Barbra W., *Sitwell and the American Experience in China 1911–1945*, London, MacMillan Publishers, 1970 (pp. 666–677).
15 'Letter to Congressman Hugh de Lacy of State of Washington,' *Congressional Record*, January 24, 1946, Appendix, Vol. 92, Part 9 (p. A225).
16 *New York Times*, November 6, 1945 (p. 1).
17 *New York Times*, December 19, 1945 (p. 2).
18 *New York Times*, December 26, 1945 (p. 5).
19 Lee, R. Alton, 'The Army "Mutiny" of 1946,' *The Journal of American History*, Vol. 53, No. 3, December 1966 (pp. 562–571).
20 Fleming, Denna Frank, *The Cold War and its Origins, 1917–1960*, Crows Nest, Allen and Unwin, 1961 (p. 587).
21 Robbins, Christopher, *Air America*, New York, Avon Books, 1985 (pp. 46–57).
22 Marchetti, Victor, and Marks, John, *The Cia and the Cult of Intelligence*, New York, Alfred A. Knopf, 1974 (p. 149).
23 Testimony of Dean Acheson, Hearings held in executive session before the U.S. Senate Foreign Relations Committee during 1949–1950 (p. 23).
24 Mitter, Rana, *China's War With Japan 1937–1945; The Struggle for Survival*, London, Allen Lane, 2013 (p. 128).
25 Ikuhiko Hata, 'The Nanjing Atrocities: Fact and Fable,' *Japan Echo*, August 1998, (p. 51).
26 'Japan's Sorrow,' *Time*, June 27, 1938.
27 Lary, Diana, *Drowned Earth: The Strategic Breaching of the Yellow River Dyke, 1938*, War in History, Vol. 8, No. 2, April 1, 2001 (pp. 191–207).

28 Ma Zhonglian, 'Huayuankou Jueti de Junshi Yiyi (The Military Significance of the Breaking of the Yellow River Dike at Huayuankou),' *Kang Ri Zhanzheng Yanjiu (Studies on the War to Resist Japan)*, Vol. 4, 1999 (p. 207).
29 Blum, William, *Killing Hope: U.S. Military and C.I.A. Interventions Since World War II*, London, Zed Books, 2003 (p. 21).
30 Conn, Peter, *Pearl S. Buck: A Cultural Biography*, Cambridge, Cambridge University Press, 2010 (p. 316).
31 Mitter, Rana, *China's War With Japan 1937–1945; The Struggle for Survival*, London, Allen Lane, 2013 (pp. 331–333).
32 Bethell, Tom, 'Chiang Kai-shek and the Struggle for China,' *Hoover Digest*, January 30, 2007.
33 Tuchman, Barbra W., *Sitwell and the American Experience in China 1911–1945*, London, MacMillan, 1970 (p. 676).
34 Blum, William, *Killing Hope: U.S. Military and C.I.A. Interventions Since World War II*, London, Zed Books, 2003 (p. 21).
35 Greene, Felix, *A Curtain of Ignorance*, London, Cape, 1965.
36 Henzig, Deiter, *The Soviet Union and Communist China 1945–1950, the Arduous Road to the Alliance*, Abingdon, Routledge, 2003 (p. 22).
37 Mitter, Rana, *China's War With Japan 1937–1945; The Struggle for Survival*, London, Allen Lane, 2013 (p. 372).
38 Tuchman, Barbra, *Sitwell and the American Experience in China 1911–1945*, London, MacMillan, 1970 (p. 676).
39 Djilas, Milovan, *Conversations with Stalin*, London, Penguin, 2014 (p. 164).
40 *New York Times*, January 12, 1947 (p. 44).
41 Jowett, Philip, *China's Wars: Rousing the Dragon 1894–1949*, Oxford, Osprey Publishing, 2013.
42 Henzig, Deiter, *The Soviet Union and Communist China 1945–1950, the Arduous Road to the Alliance*, Abingdon, Routledge, 2003 (p. 24).
43 Rappaport, Helen, *Joseph Stalin: A Biographical Companion*, Santa Barbara, CA, ABC-CLIO, 1999 (p. 36).
44 Dedijer, Vladimir, *Tito Speaks*, London, Weidenfeld & Nicolson, 1953 (p. 331).
45 Henzig, Deiter, *The Soviet Union and Communist China 1945–1950, the Arduous Road to the Alliance*, Abingdon, Routledge, 2003 (Chapter 2, 'Moscow's Two-Faced Policy Toward China'; Part Three, 'The Sino-Soviet Treaty of Alliance of August 14, 1945: Moscow's Betrayal of the Chinese Communists').
46 Hutchings, Graham, *Modern China, A Guide to a Century of Change*, Cambridge, MA, Harvard University Press, 2003 (p. 259).
47 Anderson, Scott and Anderson, Jon Lee, *Inside the League: The Shocking Expose of How Terrorists, Nazis, and Latin American Death Squads Have Infiltrated the World Anti-Communist League*, New York, Dodd Mead, 1986 (pp. 47–49).
48 *Los Angeles Times*, February 24, 1992.

49 Blum, William, *Killing Hope: U.S. Military and C.I.A. Interventions Since World War II*, London, Zed Books, 2003 (p. 21).
50 Ibid. (pp. 24–25).
51 Mitchell, Arthur H., *Understanding the Korean War: The Participants, the Tactics, and the Course of Conflict*, Jefferson, NC, McFarland, 2013 (p. 177).
52 Deane, Hugh, *The Korean War, 1945–1953*, San Francisco, CA, China Books & Periodicals, 1999 (p. 192).
53 Blum, William, *Killing Hope: U.S. Military and C.I.A. Interventions Since World War II*, London, Zed Books, 2003 (p. 24).
54 *New York Times*, April 25, 1966 (p. 20).
55 Burkholder Smith, Joseph, *Portrait of a Cold Warrior*, New York, Putnam, 1976 (pp. 77–78).
56 *Washington Post*, August 20, 1958.
57 McGhee, Ralph W., *Deadly Deceits: My 25 Years in the CIA*, New York, Sheridan Square Press, 1983.
58 Wise, David, and Ross, Thomas, *The Invisible Government*, New York, Random House, 1965 (p. 114).
59 'The People of the CIA ... John Downey & Richard Fecteau,' Website of the Central Intelligence Agency, News & Information, November 14, 2007.
60 Ibid.
61 'Two CIA Prisoners in China, 1952–1973,' Website of the Central Intelligence Agency, News & Information, April 5, 2007.
62 Ibid.
63 Blum, William, *Killing Hope: U.S. Military and C.I.A. Interventions Since World War II*, London, Zed Books, 2003 (p. 26).
64 McCormack, Gavan, 'Korea: Wilfred Burchett's Thirty Year's War' in Ben Kiernan (ed.), *Burchett: Reporting the Other Side of the World, 1939–1983*, London, Quartet Books, 1986 (p. 204).
65 Department of State Bulletin, May 2, 1966.
66 Marchetti, Victor, and Marks, John, *The Cia and the Cult of Intelligence*, New York, Alfred A. Knopf, 1974 (p. 150).
67 *New York Times*, March 28, 1969 (p. 40).
68 Aide-memoire from U.S. State Department to the British Embassy, July 13, FO371/35756, British Foreign Office Records, The National Archives of the United Kingdom (UKNA).
69 'The United States, Tibet and the Cold War,' *Journal of Cold War Studies*, Massachusetts Institute of Technology, Vol. 8, Issue 3, Summer 2006 (pp. 145–164).
70 Deane, Hugh, *Good Deeds & Gunboats*, San Francisco, CA, China Books & Periodicals, 1990 (p. 177).
71 Grunfeld, A. Tom, *The Making of Modern Tibet*, Armonk, NY, M. E. Sharpe, 1987 (p. 95).

72 Deane, Hugh, *Good Deeds & Gunboats*, San Francisco, CA, China Books & Periodicals, 1990 (p. 179).
73 Avedon, John F., *In Exile From the Land of the Snows*, New York, Knopf, 1984 (p. 36).
74 Grunfield, Tom, *The Making of Modern Tibet*, Armok, M. E. Sharpe, 1987. (p. 141–144).
75 Deane, Hugh, *Good Deeds & Gunboats*, San Francisco, CA, China Books & Periodicals, 1990 (pp. 180–181).
76 Chen, Jian, 'The Tibetan Rebellion of 1959 and China's Changing Relations with India and the Soviet Union,' *Journal of Cold War Studies*, Volume 8, Issue 3, Summer 2006 (p. 68).
77 Blum, William, *Killing Hope: U.S. Military and C.I.A. Interventions Since World War II*, London, Zed Books, 2003 (p. 26).
78 Roberts, John B., and Roberts II, Elizabeth A, *Freeing Tibet 50 years of struggle, resilience, and hope*, New York, AMACOM, 2009 (p. 82).
79 'Memorandum for the 303 Committee,' Office of the Historian, Historical Documents, Foreign Relations of the United States, 1964–1968, Volume XXX, China, United States of America Department of State, January 26, 1968.
80 Wise, David, *The Politics of Lying*, New York, Random House, 1973 (pp. 239–254).
81 United States of America Department of State, Office of the Historian, Historical Documents, Foreign Relations of the United States, 1964–1968, Volume XXX, China, *337. Memorandum for the Special Group*, Washington, DC, January 9, 1964.
82 Deane, Hugh, *Good Deeds & Gunboats*, San Francisco, CA, China Books & Periodicals, 1990 (pp. 181–182).
83 Mann, Jim, 'CIA Gave Aid to Tibetan Exiles in '60s, Files Show,' *Los Angeles Times*, September 15, 1998.
84 Prouty, Leroy Fletcher, *The Secret Team: The CIA and its Allies in Control of the United States and the World*, Englewood Cliffs, NJ, Pretense Hall, 1973 (p. 395).
85 Epstein, Israel, *Tibet Transformed*, Beijing, Foreign Languages Press, 1983 (pp. 224–225).
86 Deane, Hugh, *Good Deeds & Gunboats*, San Francisco, CA, China Books & Periodicals, 1990 (p. 180, 183).
87 Edwards, Richard, 'Tibet protests disrupt Olympic torch parade,' *Telegraph*, April 6, 2008.
88 Ward Anderson, John, and Moore, Molly, 'Paris Protests Disrupt Torch Relay,' *Washington Post*, April 8, 2008.
89 Mann, Jim, 'CIA Gave Aid to Tibetan Exiles in '60s, Files Show,' *Los Angeles Times*, September 15, 1998.

CHAPTER 4

Sukarnoism and the Rise and Fall of an Independent Indonesia: Wars both Overt and Covert to Return an Asian Power to Western Clienthood

> It is necessary to expose the false propaganda of the imperialists and thoroughly dispel the illusion that the imperialists will give up their colonies and dependent countries with good will.
>
> — KIM IL SUNG

> To me, both the [American] Declaration of Independence and the Communist Manifesto contain underlying truths, but the West doesn't permit a middle road.[1]
>
> — SUKARNO

Fighting for Independence: A European Possession No Longer

The Pacific War and the victories of the Imperial Japanese military over European colonial empires brought about profound and irreversible changes throughout Southeast Asia. Japan's expulsion of European colonial forces throughout the region ended centuries of Western dominance, with Indonesia, Malaysia and Singapore having endured over 350 years of Dutch and British rule. The resource rich colonies of the region had proved to be valuable economic assets for both European empires, with Indonesia at one stage accounting for half of the Netherlands' national income. The Indonesian people had suffered immensely under Dutch rule, with farmers forcibly enlisted en masse to grow cash crops at fixed prices to enrich the Empire while themselves barely subsisting. Harsh Dutch retribution against rebellion ensured that their rule lasted for centuries, with the Empire ethnically cleansing entire island civilizations – acts of genocide – to suppress dissent and ensure continued profits. One early example of such conduct was the 1621 Bandanese Massacre under Dutch Governor-General Jan Pieterszoon Cohen, what would today be called genocide of the peoples of the Banda islands, to enforce the Dutch monopoly over their lucrative spice trade. Cohen's men 'killed anyone that they didn't think would make a good slave, then exported the rest, reducing the islands' population of 15,000 to a few hundred souls.' The islands were subsequently resettled by slaves and convicts, while Cohen was rewarded with 3,000 guilders for his success in ensuring a Dutch monopoly through elimination of the entire Bandanese people.[2,3]

Without the emergence of Imperial Japan as a modern Asian economic and military power, the status quo of European domination of and direct rule over Southeast Asia may well have continued indefinitely. By co-operating with the Japanese Empire, Indonesian nationalists gained the support necessary to strengthen their movement and form an independent government and parliament – something which had been strictly forbidden under European governance. Indonesian nationalist movements such as Budi Utomo, the Indonesian National Party (PNI), Sarekat Islam, and the Indonesian Communist Party (PKI) had all long sought autonomy from Dutch colonial rule. Japan's three-and-a-half-year occupation broke the tight and longstanding European hold over the country after centuries and gave independence groups a chance to gather their forces and organize wider public support.

Indonesian nationalists were struggling against and had experienced the brutalities of European Imperialism and many saw the pan-Asian Japanese Empire as a potential ally. The Japanese in turn, unlike in Manchuria, Korea and elsewhere in the Pacific, did not seek to establish large settler communities in Indonesia. It would not be integrated to the same extent or indefinitely placed under direct Japanese rule, but expelling Western imperial forces and ensuring a supply of raw materials such as rubber and oil were prioritized. As a result the conduct of Japanese forces in much of Indonesia was starkly different and often very lenient towards its people, and many nationalist groups went on to co-operate closely with the Japanese. Though the population suffered under Japanese occupation, it helped the movement for independence from Western imperialism tremendously.

While the conduct of Japanese Imperial forces varied, they were welcomed as liberators in much of the country. In many of the central islands the coming of the Japanese was seen as the fulfillment of an ancient prophecy of Jayabaya, which predicted a brutal and lengthy occupation by outsiders ending only with the coming of Polynesian saviors descended from Indonesians themselves to liberate them.[4] The Japanese were believed to have originated from Indonesia centuries before and crossed the ocean to inhabit Japan – which remains a plausible theory considering their common Polynesian linguistic and early architectural influences and shared cultural concepts, such as that of the sacral monarchy descended from the sun. Japanese soldiers were at times greeted with fruit and addressed with great reverence. Japanese General Hitoshi Imamura would later recall the sweet taste of coconut water and his affection for Indonesia's people and their culture.

Leading Indonesian Nationalist figures Mohammad Hatta and Sukarno had foreseen that an expanding Japanese Empire could aid them in freeing their country.[5] As Sukarno had said after being approached by the Japanese for help in organizing and governing the country: 'Yes, Independent Indonesia can only be achieved with Dai Nippon.'[6] Japan supported nationalist sentiment in Java and Sumatra, largely for their own political gain, which elevated nationalist leaders such as Sukarno. Under Japanese occupation new Indonesian run state institutions were created along with the economic and political infrastructure – a departure from the previous system where the bureaucracy was overwhelmingly run by Europeans,. Often highly educated, nationalist figures who had been political prisoners under the Dutch were employed in large numbers as administrators by Japan. The Japanese were effectively fostering Indonesian independence, while in Korea and China they were at the same time brutally suppressing such movements. Indonesian independence movements were not seen as a threat to Japanese dominance in East Asia, but rather as assets directed against European Imperial interests. With Japan seeking to remake Indonesia as a friendly self-governing peripheral member of the East Asian Co-Prosperity Sphere, one relied on to provide vital resources, the goals of the nationalists strongly aligned with their own.

Though there was little resistance to Japanese rule, some leftist elements led by Amir Sjarifuddin attempted to organize an underground resistance movement. Sjarifuddin and his co-operators were quickly discovered and captured by the Japanese, though Sukarno was able to intervene and successfully appealed to the Japanese to prevent their execution.[7] Other resistance to the Japanese came from Islamist elements which saw the end of Dutch rule as an opportunity to establish a Sharia based Islamic state.

On September 7, 1944, eleven months before the end of the war, Japanese Prime Minister General Kuniaki Koiso promised Indonesia its independence in the near future – though there was no set date announced. This allowed Indonesian nationalists to work more closely with the Japanese. On April 29, 1945, Japan allowed for the establishment of an Indonesian parliament which represented most of the vast territory's many ethnic groups. Sukarno was appointed as its head and discussions regarding the future formation of an Indonesian state were encouraged. Sukarno spoke out strongly against fascism, particularly as practiced by Japan's ally Nazi Germany, and ideas of racial purity – stating that all humanity had equal rights to contribute to world peace. This too was tolerated by Japanese occupation forces. So long as Indonesia maintained its stance against Western imperialism and supplied Japan with the materials it needed for the war the direction of the new Indonesian state mattered little.

In August 1945 the Japanese granted Indonesia further powers for self-government, allowing the formation of the PPKI (Preparatory Committee for Indonesian Independence), a committee tasked with creating the governmental structure of a future Indonesian State on August 7. Two days later Sukarno, Hatta and Wediodiningrat, the leading Nationalist members of the PPKI, met with Hisaichi Terauchi, Commander-in-Chief of Japan's Southern Expeditionary Forces, in Vietnam. There he gave them the freedom to proceed with preparation for Indonesian independence and guaranteed no Japanese interference.

On August 15, 1945, the Japanese Empire announced its surrender to the United States and its Western allies, bringing the Second World War to an end. Two days later, on the 17th, Sukarno and Mohammad Hatta, the two foremost independence leaders, declared Indonesia an independent state. On the 18th, the Central Indonesian National Committee elected Sukarno as the first president, and Hatta as vice president. Many in the Japanese military leadership such as Admiral Tadashi Maeda had been highly sympathetic to Indonesia's Nationalist cause and supported this development. As news of independence spread to the outer islands, nationalist pro-republican sentiment increased throughout the country and the independence declaration was largely regarded positively. Centuries of humiliating and repressive European rule was seen to have come to an end.

While the Japanese forces were required to hand over their weapons and governance over their territories to European colonial forces under their surrender terms, they often instead handed them to the Indonesians. Having expected a wartime Western counter-invasion the Japanese military had trained and armed Indonesian forces for modern warfare, such as the Giyugun and Heiho forces. As Japan had surrendered before a Western invasion of Indonesia could be launched, there were substantial Japanese weapons and equipment available for use throughout the ensuing independence war – a major asset for the nationalists against the European imperial powers. Independence forces also had their own air force comprised of Japanese fighters, as well as captured Dutch fighters abandoned before 1941. The Republican Pemuda (youth organization) took control of the major infrastructure and installations and set up radio stations and newspapers to help spread messages of nationalism and independence.

The Republicans gained the approval of the population, and of several local leaders such as the King of Bona and many of the Balinese Rajas (rulers). Several Rajas from outer islands, who had acquired vast personal fortunes under Dutch rule, opposed the independence movement however. Parts of eastern Indonesia formed the short-lived State of East Indonesia which sought compromise with Holland and the formation of a new state under the Dutch monarchy. The vast majority of the country, including the central islands of Java and Sumatra, almost unanimously supported the formation of an independent republic. A combination of centuries of exploitation under Dutch occupation and the Republicans' successful campaign to spread nationalist ideology throughout the country during the Japanese occupation period and represent members from all major ethnic groups in the parliament meant that the population overwhelmingly supported the Republicans and their war effort. Nationalist newspapers and journals were widespread and particularly well established in Jakarta, Yogyakarta and Surakarta – fueling public support for the establishment of an independent Indonesian Republic.

The British and Dutch Empires dismissed the nationalist republican government as a creation of Japanese fascism and attempted to re-aquire their 'possession' – as Indonesia had long been viewed under European rule – by force. The United States provided the Netherlands with a $10 million loan to finance its war effort to recapture and again subjugate Indonesia.[8] The U.S. forces in the region were at this point preoccupied with their own occupation of the Japanese mainland and South Korea, fighting the Chinese civil war and suppressing the Philippines' own independence movement. France meanwhile was attempting to reoccupy its imperial territories in Southeast Asia, having lost them to the Japanese and, much like the Dutch, forced to contend with local nationalist independence forces which emerged in the aftermath with Japanese support.[9] Indonesia was therefore put under the jurisdiction of the British Admiral Earl Louis Mountbatten, the Supreme Allied Commander of the South East Asia Command. The purpose of the British military intervention was explicitly to restore Dutch sovereignty over Indonesia and the pre-war Dutch colonial administration.[10] The Netherlands own armed forces took months to restore even limited expeditionary capabilities, and Britain and Australia were to manage their former colony in the interim. Western forces landed in Indonesia in late September of 1945 and left only 13 months later, by which time the Dutch had deployed over 55,000 troops and taken over the war effort. The Western powers had split the task of re-imposing, or in the case of Japan and Korea imposing, their administration over the Asian peoples, suppressing independence movements, and restoring their regional dominance briefly lost to them under the Japanese, among themselves.

As Western forces moved into Indonesia, Dutch administrators quickly returned to enclaves of Western control in Kalimantan, Morotai and Irian Jaya. Australian and Dutch troops and administrators met the surrendering Japanese in several areas of east Indonesia. Britain delayed landing troops in Java, prioritizing freeing prisoners of war and repatriating around 300,000 Japanese stationed in the area.

Indian troops fought on the frontlines of the British army in their wars across much of Asia, and the majority of British casualties in the war effort in Indonesia were Indian soldiers.[11] Gurkha troops from Sri Lanka were also heavily relied on for operations against the Indonesian Republican forces. Entering Java and Sumatra in September 1945, British troops began to engage Republican forces in October. To minimize casualties among their own forces, surrendered Japanese Imperial troops were enlisted under British command to recapture territory in the hands of the Republicans and return it to European rule. The Japanese Empire was obliged under its terms of surrender to ensure the transfer of Indonesian sovereignty back to European colonial rule, which forces deployed to Indonesia were reluctantly pressed into seeing through.

Japanese troops drove Indonesian Republican forces out of the West Javanese capital of Bandung and handed the city to the British in early October. Five hundred Japanese soldiers and over 2,000 Indonesians lost their lives, and the British went on to claim the city with no losses. The Japanese were soon afterwards repatriated, but not before many of their leadership were put on trial – 93.4 percent of whom were condemned by the European courts and 24.4 percent of whom were then executed.[12] Hundreds of Japanese chose to remain in the country and assimilated into the Republican forces fighting against the Europeans. Many were influenced by pan-Asian ideals and supported the cause of Asian independence and self-determination. Japanese civilian Ichiki Tatsuo, who changed his name to Abdul Rahman, was but one example and became a national hero in Indonesia. He was deeply ashamed that Japan had failed to safeguard Indonesian sovereignty from European imperialism when the war ended, and surrendered his Japanese nationality to fight and die in Indonesia's independence war.[13] The British tried to frame Indonesian resistance to European colonial efforts as a Japanese fascist plot, though privately admitting that aside from the few recovered bodies of Japanese soldiers who had fought alongside the Republican forces there was no evidence of any official Japanese involvement after its surrender.[14]

The British and Dutch forces notably conducted themselves very poorly and did little to gain the good will of the Indonesian population. The reports of British officers who served in Indonesia accused their own forces of committing 'unprofessional' and crude torture and other war crimes. Officers reportedly bragged of beating women to death, while other personnel reportedly tortured civilians for pleasure – rather than information or military necessity. Firsthand British sources strongly indicate that racial contempt appeared to be a critical factor which caused the mistreatment of civilians.[15]

One British Sergeant, Jackie Tertis, a member of the PEA (Prevention of Enemy Activity) force, recalled several incidents of torture and beatings to death of captured Indonesian prisoners and civilians. Regarding his unit's treatment of a captured woman he recalled receiving the following report: 'We questioned the girl all morning. She was guilty all right – confused in her answers. We stripped her off and tied her to the table with her legs open. Fought like a tiger, she did. We tore every strip of clothes off her and then raped her, all four of us, and then we mashed her tits [breasts] and head in with golf clubs.'[16]

Britain's armed forces evacuated 10,000 Indo-Europeans and European internees from Japanese captivity in central Java. Aerial assets were to gain a significant advantage over the Republican forces, who lacked trained pilots and had negligible aerial warfare capabilities of their own, inflicting heavy casualties. Sukarno tried to arrange a ceasefire on November 2, but by the end of the month the fighting had fully resumed and British forces, encountering fierce resistance, withdrew to the coast. Republican forces retaliated by attacking Western civilians, as well as those perceived to be 'pro-Dutch.' As the Netherlands rebuilt its armed forces Dutch troops increasingly became involved in the war. By the end of November 1946, over a year after the Republican declaration of independence, Britain withdrew its forces from Indonesia. By then the Netherlands had deployed 55,000 troops in Java alone. Amsterdam had prioritized rebuilding its fighting capacity at a time when its country was in the midst of postwar reconstruction. It was critical for the Netherlands to quickly re-occupy Indonesia – which was perceived to be a prize possession of the Dutch crown and the source of the Empire's wealth. Once re-acquired, Indonesia's resource wealth was set to be used to pay for the European state's reconstruction – with the archipelago having long subsidized the European state's living standards.

The war between the Republicans and the Netherlands continued until 1949, with the Dutch diverting considerable resources to the war effort. Though Dutch forces did manage a tenuous control of towns and cities in Java and Sumatra, Indonesia was still a primarily rural society and the European armies struggled to control the villages and countryside. Republican forces refused to surrender their cause and waged a protracted guerilla war. Control of major cities was also far from absolute and several cities such as Yogyakarta changed hands many times, making it difficult for European forces to consolidate their gains.

The conduct of Dutch forces was if anything more brutal than that of the British, who were reportedly appalled by the barbarism of the Dutch military. The Dutch would regularly massacre civilians and loot and raid Indonesian houses. A British intelligence summary noted that its Dutch troops would fire 'indiscriminately and unnecessarily at inoffensive Indonesians. As an immediate consequence of such incidents, they have sometimes suffered themselves from the irritated population.'[17] Dutch commander Raymond Westerling was particularly known for his reign of terror, and he prized public executions of those who opposed European rule as a means of cowing the population.[18] Indonesian Republican forces were themselves also known to execute prisoners of war in retribution.

Failing to secure a victory, Dutch forces increasingly turned to brutalizing the civilian population. Severe war crimes were committed which the Netherlands fails to acknowledge to this day. Analysts who have compared the actions of the Dutch in Indonesia to those of the Nazi occupation in the Netherlands have found that the Dutch were if anything far more brutal in their methods. Individuals who have made such claims have been persecuted by the Dutch government and faced criminal charges decades later for accurately comparing the conduct of supposedly 'civilized' Dutch colonial forces to the notorious Nazi Waffen-SS. The British newspaper the *The Independent* noted regarding this:

> In the Netherlands there is a memory hole about this period, while volume after volume has been produced describing the horrors of life under the German occupation or the savagery of the Japanese forces in Dutch colonies in the Far East. The Dutch, quick to moralize about human rights abuses by other nations, have never properly examined or debated the unpleasant history of their own experience in the colonial war. Dutch society seems to suffer from collective amnesia when it comes

> to the murderous behavior of the soldiers who tried unsuccessfully to suppress the Indonesian independence movement in the jungles of Java and other islands almost 50 years ago. Young conscript soldiers, acting under orders, put numerous hamlets to the torch and butchered men, women and children.

The British paper further stated that the Dutch knowingly committed war crimes and have extensively harassed those who have raised the issue, including banning its own citizens from entering the Netherlands.[19] The country until today goes to great lengths to maintain its image as a progressive and civilized nation and to disguise its history of severe war crimes in imperial territories overseas – which if known would seriously undermine its much valued soft power.

After a long and protracted period of fighting it became clear that a Dutch victory was effectively impossible and the Indonesians would never again accept subjugation. As Dutch Prime Minister Pieter Gerbrandy had predicted, the Japanese Empire and their pan-Asian ideological influence had destroyed the 'racial instincts and inferiority complexes,' which he referred to as the 'carefully constructed basis of our cultural synthesis.' They had set an example that the West could be defeated by an Asian force, and this had brought about a change in the Indonesian people's mentality from which there was no going back.[20] Western governments started to turn against the war to reinstate Dutch colonial rule in Indonesia as it was increasingly seen as unwinnable. In the Cold War era the war reinforced the image of Western powers as colonialists and oppressors – something it was crucial to avoid now that their global power was challenged by a near peer economic and military force seeking to win the sympathies of colonized peoples and third world nations. Though the United States had initially supported Dutch and British attempts to occupy Indonesia, America altered its stance as the war drew out and prospects for a swift reinstating of colonial rule faded.

While the United States called on the Netherlands to bring an end to the war and limit its colonial ambitions, the Dutch chose to continue regardless – they could not accept the loss of their empire's most prized 'possession.' American aid to the European country under the Marshall Plan, vital to rebuilding after the Second World War, was therefore reconsidered. Aid had so far totaled $1 billion and an amount equivalent to half of this, supposedly for postwar recovery, had been used to finance the colonial war in Indonesia. The Dutch had apparently perceived reconstruction and recovery to mean reconstruction and recovery of their empire, not only their own war-ravaged country. In the United States many in the Republican Party and other organizations began to support Indonesian independence. They were not willing to back a losing struggle to reassert what the U.S. Congress termed 'a senile and ineffectual imperialism.'[21,22] In 1949 the United Nations, then firmly under the influence of the United States, passed a resolution demanding the reinstatement of Indonesia's Republican government.

Support for the Indonesian independence movement notably only came four years into the war, when the Dutch had already proven themselves incapable of winning the decisive victory they had expected. While the U.S. promoted itself as anti-imperialist, its motives for switching support from the Dutch to the independence movement lay elsewhere. The United States was itself in the process of fighting the Philippines' own independence movement, and would soon after lend the French support for a similar operation in their own Southeast Asian colonies. The idea therefore that Washington opposed the Dutch doing essentially the same thing out of principle would make little sense. As the outcome of the conflict became clear, it was best for the United States to support the winning side and thus form good relations with the new Indonesian government. This was not due to some perceived 'anti-imperialist' conscience, but a strategic move to allow them influence and friendship with a new nation and inevitable key player on the international stage. Upon the formal postwar declaration of independence, the United States moved immediately to recognize the Indonesian state.

Under pressure from the American-led international community, the Netherlands agreed to peace talks in August 1949. Through these negotiations the Indonesian Republicans gained independence. The new state was however burdened with billions of dollars in war reparations. Though no targets in the Netherlands were struck, and much of Indonesia had been devastated by the war – with tens of thousands killed by Dutch forces and their allies, not to mention the considerable wealth transferred to Europe over hundreds of years of colonial rule, it was still Indonesia which was arbitrarily saddled with this debt. This was a price the Republican government was willing to pay to end the war, and sovereignty was formally transferred on December 27, 1949, four years after the people had first declared their own independence. Under the Western dominated international system however, the Dutch had to consent for this to be considered a 'formal independence' and be internationally recognized.

Upon attaining independence and ending the war, Sukarno recalled: 'Millions upon millions flooded the sidewalks, the roads. They were crying, cheering, screaming "... Long live Bung Karno ..." They clung to the sides of the car, the hood, the running boards. They grabbed at me to kiss my fingers. Soldiers beat a path for me to the topmost step of the big white palace. There I raised both hands high. A stillness swept over the millions. "Alhamdulillah – Thank God", I cried. "We are free."'[23] It was only due to the unrelenting zeal for confronting the Western imperial powers and demonstrations of force, particularly among nationalist youth groups, which had placed the Republicans in a strong negotiating position and thus facilitated their diplomatic efforts to gain independence. Had the Indonesian population not shown willingness to fight for independence and resist a European invasion through armed struggle, the Dutch would not have accepted anything less than the reinstatement of their imperial rule.

The Rajas who had governed under the European imperial powers and supported the return of Dutch rule lost much of their power and authority, and the Western colonial administration was dismantled entirely. Indonesia's people had genuine independence for the first time in centuries. Indonesian deaths were estimated at between 45,000 and 100,000 during the war. The Dutch lost an estimated 5,000 soldiers, while Britain lost 1,200 – the majority of them Indians and Sri Lankan Gurkhas fighting for the Empire. Japanese forces are estimated to have lost several thousand themselves, though the exact number is unknown. This meant that around 95 percent of casualties on either side of this war to establish European colonial rule were of Asian origin. This was a key example of the longstanding European imperial practice of co-opting local forces to further one's own objectives and bear the brunt of casualties – thus minimizing losses among one's own forces.

Holding Sukarno's Feet to the Fire: The Non-Aligned Movement and the CIA's Little-Known War Against Indonesia

Though the United States had hoped to count Indonesia as an ally in Southeast Asia, the new Republican government under President Sukarno soon fell out of favor with Washington. With the beginning of the Cold War, Sukarno was one of five founding members of the Non-Aligned Movement – a stated goal of which was to 'struggle against imperialism, colonialism, neo-colonialism, racism, and all forms of foreign aggression, occupation, domination, interference or hegemony as well as against great power and bloc politics.'[24] As arguably the most influential leader of the movement, Sukarno hosted the Bandung Conference in 1955 and drew together non-aligned leaders from across Asia and Africa, as well as Yugoslavia. The movement gained a great deal of influence and was based on the concept that countries had the right to independence from the Western Bloc and from the communist USSR. The aim was to thwart attempts at hegemony by either side.

As a result of the Western Bloc's imperialist history and its designs on hegemony and control over other nations, including non-aligned countries, the formation of the Non-Aligned Movement of independent states was far more a threat to Western imperial designs than to those of the USSR. Non-aligned leaders consistently came to have better relations with the Soviet Union than with Western nations, largely because the latter made far more attempts to undermine their sovereignty than the former, and these leaders therefore more often found their interests at odds with the interventionist Western powers. Particularly in the early stages of the Cold War the USSR did not seek to overthrow non-aligned governments as many of the Western powers so often did, and the Western Bloc alone instigated 'regime change' operations in several countries whose policy did not reflect the interests of Western hegemony. Of the five founding members of Sukarno's Non-Aligned Movement, Indonesia, Yugoslavia, India, Egypt and Ghana, all came under attack by the Western Bloc. This came either through extensive support for coups by the CIA (Ghana,[25,26,27] Indonesia), by direct Western military intervention (Yugoslavia, Egypt, Indonesia), or by assassination attempts against their leaders (India in 1955, Indonesia in the 1950s and 1962, Egypt in 1957).[28,29]

The USSR by contrast was only ever perceived as a potential threat by its immediate neighbors such as Iran and Yugoslavia, though fears of invasion never materialized. The Soviet Union had no history of colonialism or of military intervention further afield as the Western powers did, and engaged in far fewer military interventions during the course of the war – with the only large scale military intervention comparable to those of the Western Bloc in scale being that in neighboring Afghanistan in the 1980s. As a result the Soviets were not perceived as a threat by the majority of non-aligned states, and went on to form close relations with most of them. The only exception was Yugoslavia which did fear an attack by the USSR – though this never occurred and it was, in fact, the Western rather than the Soviet Bloc which would go on to attack and dismember the state in the 1990s.

The new Indonesian republic's relations with the United States notably deteriorated after Jakarta purchased arms from communist Eastern European countries, despite having only done so after being turned down by the U.S. itself beforehand – which had been the first choice for arms imports. The nationalization of several private holdings of Dutch colonialists further colored Sukarno's image red in the eyes of the West – though this nationalization represented a nationalist oriented attempt to reverse the acquisitions made under imperial rule rather than a communist oriented attempt to bring private holdings under state control. The United States did not distinguish nationalism and neutrality from pro-communism. Sukarno had visited the White House, the Kremlin and communist China, but far more attention was paid to his visits to the latter two as proof that he was a communist sympathizer. With the Western Bloc adopting a Cold War mentality and dealing with a polarized world in which every developing nation was either a Western client or a communist puppet, they could not comprehend a genuinely independent foreign policy such as that of Indonesia which sought non-alignment. The fact that Sukarno had visited the major powers as equals, and the United States had been his country's first choice for arms imports, and had nevertheless been labeled a communist client, was but one indicator of this. The polarized Cold War perceptions in the U.S. however were an earlier iteration of the 'if you're not with us, you are against us' foreign policy – as expressed by the Bush administration in 2002. Instead of being 'with the terrorists' as in the post-9/11 era, independent states which were not aligned with the Western Bloc were considered to be 'with the communists' – Indonesia being but one example.

U.S. Secretary of State John Foster Dulles stated to regarding American perceptions of and resulting policy towards those newly independent nations which did not join the Western led alliance against the communist powers: 'neutrality ... has increasingly become an obsolete conception, and, except under very exceptional circumstances, it is an immoral and shortsighted conception.'[30,31] The Western Bloc's far less tolerant approach to neutral or non-aligned states relative to the Soviet Bloc meant that nationalist Indonesia faced considerable threats from the former, but not from the latter. President Sukarno had commented on what he perceived to be the highly intolerant stance of the Western Bloc towards genuine neutrality in the third world: 'To me, both the [American] Declaration of Independence and the Communist Manifesto contain underlying truths, but the West doesn't permit a middle road.' Indonesia's domestic political developments only strengthened American hostility, in particular when the Indonesian Communist Party (PKI) made significant electoral gains and succeeded in unionizing much of the workforce. Though they had not played a major role in the independence war, the PKI emerged as key players in Indonesian politics and in the republic's coalition government. Sukarno however held the power. He was a nationalist, or as some said a 'Sukarnoist,' who ran the country largely by balancing the power of the PKI and the military against one other. After the Indonesian independence war, he had led nationalist forces to swiftly crush the PKI communist factions which had sought power by force. Sukarno was far from a communist himself. The PKI gained over 1 million members by the mid-1950s. However, as to excluding them from government, Sukarno had said: 'I can't and won't ride a three-legged horse.'[32]

Though many countries excluded or suppressed communist parties from the democratic process, the majority of Western clients among them, it seemed Sukarno was the more genuine democrat in this regard as communists and other potentially undesirable but popular political groups were allowed to participate in elections. Indonesia appeared to enjoy a great deal of stability, and there was no likelihood at the time of the country taking a side in the Cold War of its own accord. In the eyes of the United States however Sukarno's independence made the country a threat. If he was not entirely with them, if he supported policy independent of Western control, it was a threat to Western designs. Branding Sukarno a communist was therefore critical to facilitating taking further hostile actions.

In the autumn of 1956, the Central Intelligence Agency's Deputy Director of Plans Frank Wisner said, 'I think it's time we held Sukarno's feet to the fire.'[33] In 1975 the Senate committee, which was investigating the CIA, heard testimony that CIA officers were stationed in East Asia and suggested that a certain East Asian leader be assassinated. The purpose of this assassination was 'to disrupt an impending Communist Conference in 1955.'[34] While the Non-Aligned Movement which held the prolific Bandung Conference that year was far from communist, the 'communist' label could be applied to almost any individual or organization, particularly those with leftist or anti-imperialist leanings, to condone actions against them. This was common practice during the Cold War, and allowed the CIA to operate in many such countries under the often unfounded claim that they would otherwise turn to communism.

The Senate committee elsewhere reported that it had 'received some evidence of CIA involvement in plans to assassinate President Sukarno of Indonesia' and that this planning had proceeded to the point of identifying an agent whom it was believed might be recruited for the job. Those in the CIA who were concerned with possible assassinations were known internally as the 'Health Alteration Committee.'[35]

In 1955 before Indonesia's first national election the CIA had given a million dollars to the Masjumi Party, a centrist coalition of Indonesian Islamist organizations, to aid their election campaign and thwart Sukarno's nationalists and the PKI. Their finances were highly dubious however, and former CIA officer Joseph Burkholder Smith said that the project to fund the Masjumi Party 'provided for complete write-off of the funds, that is, no demand for a detailed accounting of how the funds were spent was required.

I could find no clue as to what the Masjumi did with the million dollars.' The Masjumi Party performed poorly in the elections and the investment failed to yield the results Washington desired.[36]

Two years later in 1957 the CIA decided that the Indonesian political situation warranted more direct intervention. The Agency made contact with several officers in the military and others who wanted to oust the Nationalist Sukarno government – valuable contacts who supported regime change either to expel the central government's authority from their specific regions so as to take power themselves or because they opposed its tolerance of the PKI. The CIA sought to use these anti-government figures to take military action to oust Sukarno's government and install a more compliant one – failing this to undermine and fragment the new Indonesian state and thereby expand the Western Bloc's influence in the country. Such dissenters had designs which would have significantly undermined and likely fragmented the new country, leaving it both vulnerable to and dependent on external forces, and were thus ideal partners for the CIA. To conduct an operation on this scale the agency needed to gain the Pentagon's support through the National Security Council's (NSC) 'Special Group.' This 'Special Group,' at other times called the 5412 Committee, the 303 Committee, the 40 Committee or the Operations Advisory Group, was a small group of NSC officials who acted in the name of the president. Their role was to evaluate proposed covert actions and monitor the CIA's operations.

Joseph Burkholder Smith, in charge of the CIA's Indonesian desk from 1956 to 1958, described the series of steps the CIA took to gain approval for intervention. He said that instead of proposing the plan to Washington for approval first, as there was the risk that 'premature mention [...] might get it shot down' the CIA adopted a different strategy:

> We began to feed the State and Defense departments intelligence that no one could deny was a useful contribution to understanding Indonesia. When they had read enough alarming reports, we planned to spring the suggestion we should support the colonels' plans to reduce Sukarno's power. This was a method of operation which became the basis of many of the political action adventures of the 1960s and 1970s. In other words, the statement is false that the CIA undertook to intervene in the affairs of countries like Chile only after being ordered to do so by [...] the Special

> Group [...] In many instances, we made the action programs up ourselves after we had collected enough intelligence to make them appear required by the circumstances. Our activity in Indonesia in 1957–1958 was one such instance.[37]

When the communist PKI did well in Indonesian elections in July, the CIA viewed it as 'a great help to us in convincing the Washington authorities how serious the Indonesian situation was. The only person who did not seem terribly alarmed at PKI victories was ambassador Allison. This was all we needed to convince [Secretary of State] John Foster Dulles finally that he had the wrong man in Indonesia. The wheels began to turn to remove this last stumbling block in the way of our operation.'[38] According to Smith, U.S. ambassador to Indonesia John Allison did not approve of the CIA's actions. In early 1958, after less than a year in the post, he was replaced by Howard Jones. This new choice of ambassador 'pleased' the CIA Indonesia staff.[39]

CIA case officer Ralph McGhee alleged that the agency acted far beyond its intelligence gathering role and would manipulate its own intelligence to support foreign policy goals, including regime change operations. He stated: 'The CIA is not now nor has it ever been a Central Intelligence Agency. It is the covert action arm of the president's foreign policy advisers. In that capacity it overthrows or supports foreign governments while reporting "intelligence" justifying those activities. It shapes its intelligence, even in such critical areas as Soviet nuclear weapons capability, to support presidential policy. Disinformation is a large part of its covert action responsibility, and the American people are the primary target audience of its lies.'[40] The events in Indonesia essentially demonstrated how the CIA, through manipulating intelligence it gave Washington, could effectively direct American foreign policy to a large extent.

The CIA continued to work against the Nationalist Sukarno government rather than target the communist PKI directly. Had Indonesia's communist opposition party truly been their sole target, an attempt to overthrow the entire government in which the PKI were but a minority likely would not have been necessary. U.S. foreign policy objectives however appeared to seek not only to contain communism, but also to undermine any and all independent Asian governments which either opposed or conducted foreign policy independently of the Western Bloc's designs. The fact that Sukarno allowed the PKI to grow and participate in elections was however a useful pretext for military action against him due to the strong anti-communist sentiment in the United States. The CIA helped spread reports pertaining to the Sukarno government's close relationship with the communists. They made reports of a seductive blonde-haired Soviet stewardess accompanying Sukarno everywhere he went during his trip to the USSR. The reports stated that this same woman had come to Indonesia during Soviet Presidium Chairman Voroshilov's visit to Indonesia and was seen with Sukarno several times. Sukarno himself was a known womanizer, and this CIA used his reputation to propagate the idea that he had been seduced by a Soviet agent who had placed him under communist control – such were the fantastic stories about the 'international communist conspiracy' that were widely believed in the United States at the time.

CIA case officer Smith wrote in his memoirs: 'This formed the foundation of our flights of fancy ... We had as a matter of fact considerable success with this theme. It appeared in the press around the world, and when *Round Table*, the serious British quarterly of international affairs, came to analyze the Indonesian revolt in its March 1958 issue, it listed Sukarno's being blackmailed by a Soviet female spy as one of the reasons that caused the uprising.'[41] This success of the disinformation campaign led to efforts by the CIA to come up with a pornographic film or pornographic photos of Sukarno and his Russian girlfriend. Available pornographic films at the time failed to come up with a pair who could pass for the dark skinned and balding Sukarno and a blonde Russian. The CIA resorted to producing its own films, to act as 'the very films with which the Soviets were blackmailing Sukarno.' A full-face mask of Sukarno was made, and the police were to pay pornography actors to stage out the scene – with one wearing the mask. This resulted in the production of at least some photographs, though this stage of the plan was never implemented and they were never used. Former FBI agent Robert Maheu was involved in the project and produced a film entitled *Happy Days*, starring an actor resembling Sukarno. What became of this film remains unknown.[42]

In the 1960 edition of *Reader's Digest*, U.S. Army Ret. Colonel Truman Smith wrote on the KGB (Soviet security agency): 'It is difficult for most of us to appreciate its menace, as its methods are so debased as to be all but beyond the comprehension of any normal person with a sense of right and wrong.' The colonel wrote of the KGB's production of sex films to be used as blackmail: 'People depraved enough to employ such methods [...] find nothing distasteful in more violent methods.'[43] This proved to be highly ironic, not only because of the lack of evidence of his claims but also because of the extensive evidence of the CIA doing precisely what the Soviets were being accused of.

In November 1957 the 'Special Group' gave its approval to the CIA's military action in Indonesia.[44] The CIA was able to use the United States' vast network of military bases for their operations to destabilize the Sukarno government. An army of Indonesian dissidents and mercenaries of Chinese, Filipino, Taiwanese and American descent among others, the 'soldiers of fortune,' were assembled in Okinawa and the Philippines with full logistical support and a vast arsenal of weapons and equipment. Headquarters were established in British occupied Singapore with London's permission. Training bases were set up in the Philippines. Airstrips were prepared across the Pacific to transport the CIA's new proxy army, and for use by the heavy bombers under the CIA paramilitary wing that would target Indonesia.

This was one of the CIA's largest military operations to date, eclipsing even the arming of proxy armies to target China in the 1950s. Their army numbered in the tens of thousands – all equipped and trained by the CIA. The U.S. Navy's submarines were used to deploy parties on the Sumatran coast with their supplies and equipment. The U.S. Air Force was enlisted to airdrop thousands of weapons deep into Indonesian territory. Fifteen B-26 Marauder bombers were made available for the operation – though they had to be 'sanitized' to ensure that their origin could not be proved if them fell into enemy hands. All airborne equipment had to be 'deniable.' This was essentially a large-scale CIA military operation, what would otherwise have been called an act of war, against the newly independent Indonesian Republic.

In early 1958, armed conflicts started to spread throughout the country. CIA pilots from Pacific bases carried out bombing and strafing missions against government forces to support their proxies on the ground. Colonel Alex Kawilarang, the Indonesian military attaché in Washington, was persuaded to defect and was soon helping to co-ordinate the military campaign. CIA operated bombers exacted a heavy toll on Indonesian forces and targeted civilians, causing massive casualties. Sukarno would later claim that on an April Sunday morning in 1958 a CIA plane, in a single bombing run, bombed a ship in the harbor of Ambon killing all those aboard, as well as hitting a church and killing all those inside. He alleged that this one bombing run killed 700 civilians – a claim which was later supported by American sources.[45]

On May 15, 1958, the CIA's air units bombed Ambon marketplace killing many civilians on their way to Church on Ascension Thursday. This was part of a wider air campaign against the Indonesian government in support of their proxies on the ground, but it led to a significant public backlash and large demonstrations.[46] Three days later the CIA conducted another bombing run over Ambon. This time however CIA pilot Allen Lawrence Pope was shot down and captured. He had flown for the CIA tens of times in Vietnam, supporting the French in their attempt to restore their colony, and in Korea. Pope carried with him a set of incriminating documents, some of which established him as a U.S. Air Force pilot flying under a CIA airline. Pope had apparently smuggled papers onboard for fear for his own safety – because to have been captured as an unknown stateless civilian bomber would have granted him few legal rights. A captured U.S. agent however could be valuable to his captors. Pope's identification upon capture, much to the chagrin of the CIA, proved their involvement in the disastrous operation to the world.[47,48,49]

On May 27 Pope and his documents were presented at a news conference for the world to see. This contradicted several statements recently made by American officials. President Eisenhower had notably said just days before on April 30 regarding Indonesia 'Our policy is one of careful neutrality and proper deportment all the way through so as not to be taking sides where it is none of our business.' On May 9 a *New York Times* editorial stated: 'It is unfortunate that high officials of the Indonesian Government have given further circulation to the false report that the United States Government was sanctioning aid to Indonesia's rebels. The position of the United States Government has been made plain, again and again. Our Secretary of State was emphatic in his declaration that this country would not deviate from a correct neutrality … the United States is not ready … to step in to help overthrow a constituted government. Those are the hard facts. Jakarta does not help its case, here, by ignoring them.' Despite the usual condescending tone the U.S. took in response to Indonesia's claims regarding attacks on their country, these claims were later proven to be entirely correct while President Eisenhower's statement was not. Pope spent four years as a prisoner before Sukarno accepted Robert Kennedy's request to release him in exchange for extensive U.S. concessions.[50,51]

The war ended in June that year. The CIA's proxy dissident and mercenary forces had been decisively defeated by the Indonesian military, while the agency itself suffered much international embarrassment after its support for the insurgency and the mass killings of civilians was revealed. Despite the formidable firepower deployed and the support of an extensive U.S. and British military apparatus including cutting edge air and naval capabilities, the CIA could not influence the tide of battle sufficiently in favor of its proxies. The failure of their forces to win victories or launch a successful offensive, and the exposure of one of their pilots, forced the CIA to roll back their war effort. Many Indonesians had lost their lives needlessly in this conflict, and the newly formed Republic had been forced to pledge significant resources and attention to fighting – resources it diverted away from economic development and postwar recovery. Again, Asian lives mattered little so long as the objectives of Western policymakers could be achieved. This war against Indonesia was unnecessary in the context of the Cold War and containing communism – but it was essential to the West's agenda of dominating the Asia-Pacific region. Though the new Republic had triumphed, the U.S. and CIA had in relative terms lost very little themselves. Casualties were overwhelmingly Indonesian dissidents or mercenaries, while the CIA had meanwhile sustained negligible losses itself while doing great damage to the emerging Asian power. The failure of the proxy war to gain any tangible results hardly meant an end to CIA actions against Indonesia. The nationalist Republic would see other means brought to bear in the future to undermine it and bring a government more favorable to Western interests into power.

Hostile Policy and Indonesia's Pivot Away from the West

Following the CIA's failed attempt to use military force to destabilize and partition the nationalist government in Indonesia, President Sukarno and his government fell further out of favor in the West. Sukarno kept the country heavily involved in the Non-Aligned Movement as a leading member and continued to allow the communist PKI to act as part of the ruling coalition government by popular vote – in contrast to the Asian 'democracies' the United States considered most exemplary such as the Philippines, the Republic of Korea and the Republic of China which outlawed the popular movement. In response to Western hostility, Jakarta aligned its foreign policy more closely with independent powers such as China. Sukarno personally took more power over the state, and in March 1960 changed the parliamentary structure so that he as president would appoint half of its members. Several Islamist elements which the United States had aided, either in political campaigns or armed rebellion, faced a crackdown by the government.

The United States has a long history of aiding Islamist groups to destabilize independent states – more recent examples including the Mujahideen in Afghanistan and various extremist militant groups in Syria and Chechnya (see Chapter 18). Their alliance with the Islamists in Indonesia in the 1950s was an earlier iteration of this same strategy for destabilization, and came at the same time as close ties were being formed with similar groups in Egypt – then another leading member of Sukarno's Non-Aligned Movement. Islamist groups, like the US, opposed the secular Indonesian government and their tolerance of the 'godless' communist PKI. Several Islamist leaders had been invited to the United States by a program run covertly by the U.S. Information Agency in 1953, under which relations were cemented and communist, secular nationalist and other such 'atheistic' governments opposed to the United States were portrayed as the common enemy of both the U.S. led Western Bloc and of political Islam.[52] This common enemy allowed for the formation of a strong and lasting partnership between the two. In the early 1960s there were many attempts on President Sukarno's life by Islamist groups. This included an attempt by Indonesian Air Force lieutenant Daniel Maukar, an Islamist sympathizer, to kill the president by strafing the Bogor presidential palace on March 9, 1960, with a MiG-17 fighter. Sukarno escaped these attempts on his life unharmed. Islamist rebel forces faced several defeats at the hands of the military, and the leader of Darul Islam, the most prominent Islamist movement, was captured and executed in 1962.

Britain, Australia and New Zealand also went to great lengths to destabilize the country and forcefully bring about political change in line with their own interests. They in some cases sought to provoke the breakup of Indonesia as a viable state through provision of arms and funding to separatist groups, radio broadcasts advocating autonomy or independence for certain regions, and conducting a psychological warfare campaign intended to "aid and encourage dissident movements inside Indonesia."[53,54] There was a strong trend towards newly independent non-aligned countries, after repeatedly facing aggression from various Western powers, consistently shifting their foreign policies to more closely align with the USSR or China in order to better ensure their security. The actions of the United States and its allies had made their positions clear and forcibly pushed Indonesia away from neutrality. Indonesia needed to defend itself against the Western Bloc's demonstratively aggressive designs, and closer alignment with communist powers was thus seen to be necessary. Absolute neutrality was no longer an option. Similar policies were taken by other initially non-aligned states including Egypt, Ghana and India. As a result, by the early 1960s the USSR provided more aid to Indonesia than it did any other non-communist country. Soviet military aid to Indonesia was equaled only by its aid to Cuba (hence the aforementioned Soviet MiG-17 fighter operated by the Indonesian Air Force). As a large nation and key player in world affairs, Indonesia's alliance was a key prize for both Cold War blocs.

In an attempt to amend the souring of relations following the CIA's proxy war, President Kennedy's new administration invited Sukarno to Washington D.C. and increased aid to Indonesia, which amounted to billions in both the civilian and military fields. The United States' provision of Indonesia with aid however proved an invaluable investment which did much to further American interests, including the undermining of the Indonesian state. One example was the American training of Indonesian policemen under the aid program, which led many policemen to study in the United States where they were recruited to provide information on the activities of Soviets, Chinese and the PKI communists in their country. Some of these policemen with good prospects were sent to Washington for special training, where they formed close ties with U.S. intelligence agencies.[55] The development of close ties with the military under the military aid program would later prove an invaluable asset to the United States – and the key to Sukarno's eventual overthrow.

Indonesia's foreign relations showed it to be an influential player in international affairs. The country led calls to form an alliance of Asia-Pacific states independent of the Western Bloc, which came to be known as the Beijing-Pyongyang-Hanoi-Phnom Penh-Jakarta (BPHPJ Axis. The country was a leading supporter of several international initiatives which threatened Western alternatives, such as the Games of New Emerging Forces (GANEFO) – an alternative to the 'imperialist' Western-dominated Olympic Games, and crucially the Conference of the New Emerging Forces (CONEFO) – an alternative to the heavily Western dominated United Nations. Formation of such blocs with the potential to facilitate co-operation between Asian states, or to unite states which challenged Western domination worldwide in the case of CONEFO, were a significant threat to the Western Bloc's position of power.

The nationalist government's domestic policies were also very much non-compliant with what the United States wished for Indonesia. Sukarno continued to balance power between the PKI communists and the military. When the military's power appeared to increase, Sukarno declared in 1960 that Indonesia's government was based on the union of three ideological strands in the society. These were: nationalism, religions (Indonesia long prided itself on its tolerance for religious diversity) and, crucially, communism. This was an unprecedented step and a divergence away from the country's initial non-aligned stance. The CIA's hostile actions had led to Indonesia moving towards the communist powers, China, North Korea and North Vietnam in particular, and this in turn had triggered Western powers to more urgently seek to overthrow the government. Branding Sukarno a communist was to some degree a self-fulfilling prophecy, as it was the hostile actions taken against the 'communist' Sukarno which led him to turn towards and cement ties with communist powers. There was a prevailing fear in the United States that as Sukarno moved closer to communist China abroad and to the PKI at home, communists would take outright power in Indonesia – a significant loss in the Cold War context and particularly in the context of isolating China from the rest of the Asia-Pacific region. The CIA and clandestine allied elements within the Indonesian military therefore felt it necessary to take swift action.

Ending Sukarno's Non-Aligned Republic: Making a Western Client State Out of Indonesia

In the early hours of October 1, 1965, a small force of junior military officers from the Indonesian army seized key strategic points in the capital Jakarta. They abducted and killed six generals, afterwards going on air to announce that they had taken action to forestall a coup by a 'Generals' Council' scheduled for October 5, Army Day. They said this coup was supported by the CIA aimed at capturing power from President Sukarno – and they were intervening to preempt it. The military subsequently intervened and crushed the junior officers' movement across several cities within a few days. Control of Jakarta was seized from the officers by the military within hours.

Major General Suharto, Commander of the 1st Armed Force and Strategic Reserve and one of the most influential figures in the Indonesian military, and his colleagues charged the communist PKI with being behind what they alleged was the junior officers' 'coup attempt,' claiming that behind the actions of this large and influential communist party stood communist China. There had long been antagonism between the military and the communists, hence why President Sukarno had worked to balance the power of the two against one another. The military would now take the offensive to eliminate the PKI, and the actions of the young officers gave them the pretext they needed, whether communist involvement could be proven or not, to legitimize their attack. The offensive received strong support from Islamist and Catholic groups, both of which maintained strong ties to the Western powers. The result was a mass slaughter on a scale with few equals in modern history as the military moved to cement their power and eliminate associates of the PKI and other leftist movements. Estimates of the number of Indonesian civilians killed in the military's purge range from 500,000 to over 3 million.[56,57] The communist movement was widespread, and anyone even suspected of being communist was a target – as were their families. Stories were spread of the atrocities the communists committed and much of the public was worked up into a frenzy, leading to the targeting of ethnic Chinese who were portrayed as proxies of a Chinese communist conspiracy. The *New York Times* called the resulting carnage led by the military 'one of the most savage mass slaughters of modern political history.'[58]

Islamist groups in particular were encouraged to join the bloodbath and attack anyone suspected of sympathizing with the PKI – spurred on by warnings from religious leaders of the evils of 'atheistic' communist menace. Imams instructed their followers that it was a religious obligation to kill any suspected communists. Suspected PKI members and their associates were said to be the lowest order of infidels, 'the shedding of whose blood is comparable to killing chicken.'[59] The badly decomposed bodies of the generals who had been killed by the young officers were shown on television to further work up anti-communist sentiment. Though the generals were victims of the junior officers' coup, which was pro-Republican and had no proven ties to communism or the PKI whatsoever, their deaths were portrayed as part of the communist conspiracy to inflame public opinion. The public was told by the army that the generals had been castrated and had their eyes gouged out by communist women – depicting them as savages to incite hatred and legitimize their purge and mass murder. The military later made the mistake of allowing official medical autopsies to be included as evidence in some of the trials. The extremely detailed reports showed their claims to have been entirely fabricated to stir up the public. They mentioned only bullet wounds and bruising – no eye gouging or castration on any of the generals' bodies.[60]

Time magazine wrote in December 1965: 'Armed with wide-bladed knives called *parangs*, Moslem [Muslim] bands crept at night into the homes of the communists, killing entire families [...] Travelers [...] tell of small rivers and streams that have been literally clogged with bodies. River transportation has at places been seriously impeded.'[61] The *Life* magazine described the violence as being 'tinged not only with fanaticism but with blood-lust and something like witchcraft.'[62] The *New York Times* wrote in May 1966: 'Nearly 100 communists, or suspected Communists, were herded into the town's botanical garden and mowed down with a machine gun [...] the head that had belonged to the school principal, a P.K.I. [Communist Party] member, was stuck on a pole and paraded among his former pupils, convened in special assembly.'[63] CIA officer Edward Masters sent a cable from the U.S. Embassy in 1966 noting the 'problem' the authorities faced in dealing with communist prisoners. He stated: 'Both in the provinces and Djakarta [Jakarta], repression of the PKI continued, with the main problem that of what to feed and where to house the prisoners. Many provinces appear to be successfully meeting this problem by executing their prisoners, or killing them before they are captured, a task in which Muslim youth groups are providing assistance.'[64]

While Western involvement in the slaughter had long been suspected, with a purge of the PKI, the ousting of Sukarno and the realignment of Indonesian foreign policy all having been key goals of the Western Bloc which the actions of the military and the Islamists accomplished, it was proven only 25 years later. Later declassified U.S. government documents revealed that the country had carried out black operations in Indonesia throughout the early 1960s, which played a key role in laying the ground for the later massacre. These operations had been carried out with the express intention of exacerbating tensions between the military and the PKI, and if possible causing a direct conflict between the two to facilitate a forceful move against Indonesia's communists – exactly the result which was achieved in 1965.[65] U.S. officials had met with figures in the Indonesian military leadership, and noted 'receptiveness' within the high command for a coup which would enjoy full American support. General Siswondo Parman, the head of Indonesia's military intelligence who had previously studied in the United States, had reported in January 1965 that there was a 'strong sentiment' within the 'top military command' for a 'takeover of government' – for which specific plans were being developed.[66]

Specifically, it was repeatedly alluded to that engineering a PKI coup could provide precisely the pretext the military needed to carry out its own coup – removing Sukarno and eliminating the communist movement. A CIA strategy outlined in a US-Indonesian relations memorandum in September 1964 stated that the military would be more capable of acting forcefully if it were responding to some provocative action on the part of the PKI. It read: 'An abrupt or aggressive move on the latter's [PKI's] part would surely evoke Amy reaction.'[67] Ambassador Howard Jones concurred, stating at a closed meeting of State Department officials in March 1965: 'from our viewpoint, of course, an unsuccessful coup attempt by the PKI might be the most effective development to start a reversal of political trends in Indonesia.'[68] The assistant secretary of state in the British Foreign Office Edward Peck similarly noted in a memorandum from late November 1964: 'there might therefore be much to be said for encouraging a premature PKI coup during Sukarno's lifetime.'[69] Another British official commented the following month: 'a premature PKI coup may be the most helpful solution for the West – provided the coup failed.'[70] New Zealand's legation to Jakarta came to much the same conclusion regarding the benefit of a failed premature PKI coup to Western interests.[71,72]

As American Professor Geoffrey B. Robinson concluded in his extensive study of the massacre: 'We have here clear evidence that in the year before the purported coup of October 1965, U.S. officials were seriously contemplating – and indeed starting to implement – strategies designed to encourage the army and its civilian allies [Islamist groups in particular] to act against the PKI, without leaving U.S. or other foreign fingerprints.'[73] The United States continued to be involved long after the killings had started, and American diplomats disclosed that they had systematically compiled comprehensive lists of 'communist operatives,' from top echelons down to village cadres, and turned over thousands of names to the Indonesian military. The military in turn located and eliminated these individuals, while Americans would then check off the names. Mary Vance Trent, the Embassy's First Secretary, reported the elimination of the PKI and mass killings of civilians to Washington as a 'fantastic switch which has occurred over 10 short weeks.'[74] Robert Martens, who had been a member of the embassy's political section in Jakarta, said in 1990 regarding the information the embassy had provided: 'It really was a big help to the army. They probably killed a lot of people, and I probably have a lot of blood on my hands, but that's not all bad. There's a time when you have to strike hard at a decisive moment.' Again, the loss of Asian civilians, even in the hundreds of thousands, were acceptable losses for the Western Bloc in its attempts to assert its interests in the region.[75]

Martens viewed the fall of the Indonesian government as a crucial step towards the collapse of the international communist movement, including the eventual fall of the USSR and communist states in Europe. He stated: 'Indonesia was a major step in destroying the myth of communist momentum, the image of its supposed inevitable triumph.'[76] The importance of having prevented the country from potentially having become a communist state was emphasized as a pivotal moment in the Cold War in his later publication titled: *The Indonesian Turning Point*. Allowing the country to join the communist bloc in full was something the United States was willing to prevent at all costs after their failure to do so in China. While the claim that Sukarno was about to go fully communist was doubtful, the successful toppling of his nationalist and highly influential anti-imperialist government was arguably far more meaningful to Western efforts to dominate the Asia-Pacific than the loss of a small, war-ravaged and resource-scarce South Vietnam ten years later.

Marshall Green, U.S. Ambassador to Indonesia during the purge, said: 'I know we had a lot more information [about the PKI] than the Indonesians themselves.' He said that Robert Martens 'told me on a number of occasions that [...] the government did not have very good information on the communist setup, and he gave me the impression that this information was superior to anything they had.' Intelligence long gathered through American-friendly police officers and army members trained in the United States under the U.S. aid programs were among the means that was put to use in the hands of the new Western backed establishment against the PKI. Howard Federspiel, an Indonesia expert at the State Department's Bureau of Intelligence and Research at the time of the incident, said: 'No one cared, as long as they were Communists, that they were being butchered ... No one was getting very worked up about it.'[77,78] Had they been communists in a Western country such comments could not have been so easily made. 'No one cared [...] that they were being butchered' not only because they were communists, but primarily because the deaths of Asian peoples were far more easily dismissed in the West.

Rape and torture were common, and Indonesia's large Chinese community was singled out for targeting. Mass killings and sexual abuse against women and children, all in the frenzy encouraged by several Western powers and their proxies, were widespread. Methods of torture included forcing victims to drink urine, cutting off their ears and forcing them to consume them, burning body parts, electric shocks and pulling out fingernails.[79] Those considered not to support Suharto's new government with 'sufficient fervor' were also targeted.[80] It was a war against Indonesia itself, purging its largest political groups, its minorities which had been key to economic success, and anyone the New Order perceived as a potential threat to their power.

The massacre ended the PKI. What had once been the world's largest communist opposition party, the third largest worldwide, was brutally uprooted overnight. The circumstances under which this took place and leading up to the massacre somewhat undermine the official story. Former U.S. State Department analyst and historian William Blum noted:

> What was the role, if any, of the CIA? Was the coup attempt instigated by an agent provocateur who spread the story of the Generals' Council and its imminent putsch? (The killing, or even the abduction, of six generals probably could not have been foreseen – three of them were actually slain resisting abduction.) Was PKI participation induced to provide the excuse for its destruction? There are, in fact, indications of an agent provocateur in the unfolding drama, one Kamarusaman bin-Ahmed Mubaidah, known as 'Sjam.' According to the later testimony of some of the arrested officers, it was Sjam who pushed the idea of the hostile Generals' Council and for the need to counteract it. At the trials and in the CIA Study, the attempt is made to establish that, in so doing, Sjam was acting on behalf of the PKI leader Aidit. Presentation of this premise may explain why the CIA took the unique step of publishing such a book; that is, to assign responsibility for the coup attempt to the PKI so as to 'justify' the horror which followed. But Sjam could just as easily have been acting for the CIA and/or the generals in the same manner. He apparently was a trusted aide of Aidit and could have induced the PKI leader into the plot instead of the other way around. Sjam had a politically checkered and mysterious background, and his testimony at one of the trials, in which he appeared as a defendant, was aimed at establishing Aidit as the sole director of the coup attempt. The CIA, in its intimate involvement in Indonesian political affairs since at least the mid-1950s [...] had undoubtedly infiltrated the PKI at various levels, and the military even more so, and was thus in a good position to disseminate disinformation and plant the ideas for certain actions, whether through Sjam or others.

The Western Bloc was the greatest beneficiary of the fall of Sukarno's independent nationalist government and the PKI, removing Indonesia as a thorn in the side of their regional designs. As William Blum concluded:

'It could not have worked out better for the United States and the new military junta if it had been planned.'[81]

CIA case officer Ralph McGhee, having been assigned to East and Southeast Asia for 19 years and heavily involved in a number of operations, also alleged that the CIA was heavily involved in the massacre of civilians in Indonesia from 1965 to 1966. His allegations were at the time censored by the CIA. Mcghee described Suharto's Western backed takeover as a 'model operation' for similar regime change effects later conducted elsewhere. He reported that the CIA had falsified information to implicate the PKI, which led to the military reacting as they had wanted, stating: 'The CIA forged a document purporting to reveal a leftist plot [...] in 1965.'[82]

In 2016 an international tribunal in The Hague released a verdict which shed new light on the massacres of 1965. It called upon over 20 witnesses to give their testimony. It found that Australia, the United Kingdom and the United States were all complicit in the mass killings that took place. The report released also stated: 'it has also been demonstrated that sexual violence, particularly against women, was systematic and routine, especially during the period 1965 to 1967.' The tribunal accused Australia, the U.S. and Britain of using their considerable influence over information to manipulate world public opinion in favor of the military, Suharto and the new Indonesian government they supported. Australia and the UK were said to have participated because they 'shared the U.S. aim of seeking to bring about the overthrow of President Sukarno. They continued with this policy even after it had become abundantly clear that killings were taking place on a mass and indiscriminate basis. On balance, this appears to justify the charge of complicity.'[83]

The United States had long been building closer links with the Indonesian military, which was key to facilitating the overthrow of the Sukarno led republic. Roger Hilsman, who worked in the CIA and the State Department during his career, wrote in 1963: 'One third of Indonesian general staff had had some sort of training from Americans and almost half of the officer corps. As a result of both the civic action project and the training program, the American and Indonesian military had come to know each other well. Bonds of personal respect and even affection existed.'[84] Reports by the United States' House Committee on Foreign Affairs stated:

> At the time of the attempted Communist coup and military counter-coup of October 1965, more that 1,200 Indonesian officers including senior military figures, had been trained in the United States. As a result of this experience, numerous friendships and contacts existed between the Indonesian and American military establishments, particularly between members of the two armies. In the post-coup period, when the political situation was still unsettled, the United States, using these existing channels of communication, was able to provide the anti-Communist forces with moral and token material support. When the average MAP (Military Assistance Program) trainee returns home he may well have some American acquaintances and a fair appreciation of the United States. This impact may provide some valuable future opportunity for communication as occurred in Indonesia during and immediately after the attempted Communist-backed coup of October 1965.[85]

The *New York Times* wrote that the CIA had: 'been so successful at infiltrating the top of the Indonesian government and army that the United States was reluctant to disrupt CIA covering operations by withdrawing aid and information programs in 1964 and 1965. What was presented officially in Washington as toleration of President Sukarno's insults and provocations [he was well known for his rhetoric against 'Western imperialism'] was in much larger measure a desire to keep the CIA fronts in businesses as long as possible.'[86] Aid had been an essential means by which the CIA could infiltrate the government to further U.S. interests and ultimately undermine Sukarno. Aid therefore continued despite Indonesia's increasingly anti-American stances and its several steps to undermine U.S. influence in the region, such as formation of CONEFO and the BPHPJ Axis. Defense Secretary Robert McNamara gave testimony before the Senate Committee in 1966 further indicating that U.S. aid to Indonesia was crucial to furthering American designs in the country and yielded results. This was the reason why aid continued despite Indonesia's anti-American policies. Based on the timing of the testimony, it appears he is alluding to the fact that the aid in someway facilitated the change in government which had so recently occurred:

> Senator Sparkman: At a time when Indonesia was kicking up pretty badly – when we were getting a lot of criticism for continuing military aid – at that time we could not say what the military aid was for. It is a secret any more?
>
> McNamara: I think it retrospect, that the aid was well justified.

Sparkman: You think it paid dividends?
McNamara: I do, sir.[87]

The New York Times wrote in 1966:

> Washington is being careful not to claim any credit for this change [in government, from Sukarno's Republic to Suharto's New Order] [...] but this does not mean that Washington had nothing to do with it. There was a great deal more contact between the anti-Communist forces in that country and at least one very high official in Washington before and during the Indonesian massacre than is generally realized. General Suharto's forces, at times severely short of food and munitions, have been getting aid from here through various third countries, and it is doubtful if the (Suharto) coup would ever had been attempted without the American show of strength in Vietnam or been sustained without the clandestine aid it had received indirectly from here.[88]

Neville Maxwell, a Senior Research Officer at the Institute of Commonwealth Studies in Oxford University, similarly reported significant Western involvement in the coup against Indonesia's government. He wrote:

> A few years ago I was researching in Pakistan into the diplomatic background of the 1965 Indo-Pakistan conflict, and in foreign ministry papers to which I had been given access came across a letter to the then foreign minister, Mr Bhutto, from one of his ambassadors in Europe (I believe Mr J. A. Rahim, in Paris) reporting a conversation with a Dutch intelligence officer with NATO. According to my note of that letter, the officer had remarked to the Pakistani diplomat that Indonesia 'was ready to fall into the Western lap like a rotten apple.' Western intelligence agencies, he said, would organize a 'premature communist coup ... [which would be] foredoomed to fail, providing a legitimate and welcome opportunity to the army to crush the communists and make Soekarno [Sukarno] a prisoner of the army's goodwill.' The ambassador's report was dated December 1964.[89]

The Dutch still maintained special links within the country, as the former colonizing power, and so were able to provide valuable support to Western regime change efforts. The two Western powers worked towards the same agenda against both Asian nationalist and communist movements.

Former U.S. ambassador to Australia Marshall Green, speaking in from his posting, said: 'In 1965 I remember, Indonesia was poised at the razor's edge. I remember people arguing from here that Indonesia wouldn't go communist. But when Sukarno announced in his August 17 speech that

Indonesia would have a communist government within a year [there are no records of him having said this in fact – but again such hearsay gave a valuable pretext for action to be taken against his government] then I was almost certain ... What we did we had to do, and you'd better be glad we did because if we hadn't Asia would be a different place today.'[90,91] In this statement Green effectively admitted that the United States had masterminded, if not had at least been heavily involved in overthrowing the Sukarno government and destroying the PKI. This was one of the bloodiest coups in recent history – all 'worth it' for the objectives of the Western Bloc to be attained.

General Suharto became Indonesia's next president and would remain in power for over three decades until 1998. His government declared itself the 'New Order,' and was essentially imposed on the country by the United States and its Western allies after their intervention to destroy the previous republic. Corruption was rampant and military rule was harsh. In the province of Aceh for example it was reported by the *Los Angeles Times*: 'An army officer fires a single shot in the air, at which point all young males must run to the central square before the soldier fires a second shot. Then, anyone arriving late – or not leaving his home – is shot on the spot.'[92] The Suharto 'New Order' government also strongly reflected Western interests in the conduct of its foreign policy. The CONEFO, set to materialize the years of the purge and be hosted in Jakarta, ceased to exist and Indonesia's support for GANEFO was also withdrawn. The Beijing-Pyongyang-Hanoi-Phnom Penh-Jakarta Axis was also dissolved after 1965. One of the New Order's first acts was to cut all diplomatic relations with China after taking power in 1967. The close relations between the two independent Asian powers had long been a threat to the West. Relations between the two would remain poor for over 20 years, and have yet to recover to what they were previously under Sukarno's presidency. This served the interests of the Western Bloc, which following its efforts to drive a rift between the USSR and China (see Chapter 16) took further measures to ensure that Japan and Indonesia would not have positive relations with the government in Beijing. This essentially destroyed any chance of a united independent Asian front of major powers. A divided Asia could be more easily exploited and could never threaten the Western powers' united front, their place as a global center of power, or their dominance of the Asia-Pacific region.

Notes

1 Kinzer, Stephen, *The Brothers: John Foster Dulles, Allen Dulles, and Their Secret World War*, New York, Henry Holt, 2013 (p. 219).
2 Pisani, Elizabeth, *Indonesia Etc.: Exploring the Improbable Nation*, London, Granta Books, 2014 (p. 17).
3 Hanna, Willard A., *Indonesian Banda: Colonialism and its Aftermath in the Nutmeg Islands*, Philadelphia, PA, Institute for the Study of Human Issues, 1991 (p. 55).
4 Cribb, R. B. and Kahin, Audrey, *Historical dictionary of Indonesia*, Vol. 51 of *Historical dictionaries of Asia, Oceania, and the Middle East*, Lanham, Scarecrow Press, 2004 (p. 210)
5 Sukarno, *Sukarno, An Autobiography as Told to Cindy Adams*, Indianapolis, IN, Bobbs-Merrill, 1965 (p. 92).
6 Friend, Theodore, *The Blue-Eyed Enemy: Japan Against the West in Java and Luzon 1942–1945*, Princeton, NJ, Princeton University Press, 1988 (pp. 82–84).
7 Reid, Anthony, *The Indonesian National Revolution 1945–1950*, Melbourne, Longman Pty., 1973 (p. 12).
8 Bidien, Charles, 'Independence the Issue,' *Far Eastern Survey*, December 5, 1945.
9 Goscha, Christopher E., *Belated Asian Allies: The Technical and Military Contributions of Japanese Deserters*, in Young, Marilyn B., and Buzzanco, Robert A., *A Companion to the Vietnam War*, Hoboken, Wiley-Blackwell, 2002 (pp. 46–55).
10 Vickers, Adrian, *A History of Modern Indonesia*, Cambridge, Cambridge University Press, 2005 (p. 97).
11 McMillan, Richard, *The British Occupation of Indonesia: 1945–1946: Britain, The Netherlands and the Indonesian Revolution*, London, Royal Asiatic Society Books, 2005 (p. 73).
12 Piccigallo, Philip R., *The Japanese on Trial: Allied War Crimes Operations in the East, 1945–1951*, Austin, University of Texas Press, 2011.
13 Goto, Ken'ichi, *Tensions of Empire: Japan and Southeast Asia in the Colonial and Postcolonial World*, Athens, Ohio University Press, 2003 (pp. 197–209).
14 Bayly, Christopher Alan, and Norman Harper, Timothy, *Forgotten Wars: Freedom and Revolution in Southeast Asia*, Cambridge, MA, Belknap Press, 2007 (p. 180).
15 McMillan, Richard, *The British Occupation of Indonesia: 1945–1946: Britain, The Netherlands and the Indonesian Revolution*, London, Royal Asiatic Society Books, 2005 (p. 75).
16 Ibid. (pp. 73–75).

17 McMillan, Richard, *The British Occupation of Indonesia: 1945–1946: Britain, The Netherlands and the Indonesian Revolution*, London, Royal Asiatic Society Books, 2005 (pp. 86–87).

18 Bayly, Christopher Alan, and Norman Harper, Timothy, *Forgotten Wars: Freedom and Revolution in Southeast Asia*, Cambridge, MA, Belknap Press, 2007 (pp. 182–183).

19 Doyle, Leonard, 'Colonial atrocities explode myth of Dutch tolerance,' *The Independent*, May 29, 1994.

20 Hotta, Eri., *Pan Asianism and Japan's War 1931–1945*, New York, Palgrave Macmillan, 2007 (p. 217).

21 Burleigh, Michael, *Small Wars, Far Away Places: The Genesis of the Modern World 1945–1965*, London, MacMillan, 2013 (p. 66).

22 Friend, Theodore, *Indonesian Destinies*, Cambridge, MA, Belknap Press, 2003 (p. 38).

23 Sukarno, *Sukarno, An Autobiography as Told to Cindy Adams*, Indianapolis, IN, Bobbs-Merrill, 1965 (pp. 262–263).

24 Canterbury, Dennis C., *European Bloc Imperialism*, Leiden, Brill, 2010 (p. 79).

25 Stockwell, John, *In Search of Enemies: A CIA Story*, New York, W. W. Norton & Company, 1978 (p. 201).

26 Prados, John, Safe For Democracy: The Secret Wars of the CIA, Chicago, Ivan R. Dee, 2006 (p. 329).

27 Hersh, Seymour, 'CIA Said to Have Aided Plotters Who Overthrew Nkrumah in Ghana,' New York Times, May 9, 1978.

28 Cockburn, Andrew, *Kill Chain, Drones and the Rise of High-Tech Assassins*, London, Picador, 2016 (p. 84).

29 Blum, William, *Killing Hope: U.S. Military and C.I.A. Interventions Since World War II*, London, Zed Books, 2003 (Appendix III).

30 Nashel, Jonathan, *Edward Lansdale's Cold War*, Boston, University of Massachusetts Press, 2005 (p. 96).

31 Gabriel, Jürg Martin, *The American Conception of Neutrality After 1941*, London, Palgrave MacMillan, 2002 (p. 175).

32 Wise, David, and Ross, Thomas, *The Invisible Government*, New York, New York Random House, 1965 (p. 148).

33 Burkholder Smith, Joseph, *Portrait of a Cold Warrior*, New York, Putnam, 1976 (p. 205).

34 Supplementary Detailed Staff Reports on Foreign and Military Intelligence, Book 4, Final Report of the Select Committee to Study Governmental Operations with Respect to Intelligence Activities (U.S. Senate), April 1976.

35 Interim Report: Alleged Assassination Plots Involving Foreign Leaders, The Select Committee to Study Governmental Operations with Respect to Intelligence Activities (U.S. Senate), November 20, 1975 (p. 4).
36 Burkholder Smith, Joseph, *Portrait of a Cold Warrior*, New York, Putnam, 1976 (p. 210–211).
37 Ibid. (pp. 228–229).
38 Ibid. (p. 240).
39 Ibid. (p. 229, 246).
40 McGehee, Ralph, *Deadly Deceits: My 25 Years in the CIA*, New York, Open Road Media, 2015 (Chapter 14, 'Conclusion').
41 Burkholder Smith, Joseph, *Portrait of a Cold Warrior*, New York, Putnam, 1976 (p. 238–240, 248).
42 *New York Times*, January 26, 1970.
43 Smith, Truman, 'The Infamous Record of Soviet Espionage,' *Reader's Digest*, August 1960.
44 Memorandum from Alan Dulles to White House, April 7, 1961, Declassified Documents Reference System (Arlington, Va.) released December 18, 1974.
45 Kahin, Audrey, and Kahin, George McT., *Subversion as Foreign Policy*, New York, New Press, 1995 (pp. 179–184).
46 Blum, William, *Killing Hope: U.S. Military and C.I.A. Interventions Since World War II*, London, Zed Books, 2003 (p. 103).
47 Wise, David, and Ross, Thomas, *The Invisible Government*, New York, Random House, 1965 (pp. 145–156).
48 Sukarno, *Sukarno, An Autobiography as Told to Cindy Adams*, Indianapolis, IN, Bobbs-Merrill, 1965 (pp. 267–271).
49 Burkholder Smith, Joseph, *Portrait of a Cold Warrior*, New York, Putnam, 1976 (pp. 220–221).
50 Wise, David, and Ross, Thomas, *The Invisible Government*, New York, Random House, 1965 (pp. 145).
51 Hyde, Ed, *Air America – The CIA's Secret Air Force*, Approved For Release 2003/12/02 obtained from <http://www.cia.gov/library/readingroom/docs/CIA-RDP75-00001R000300130013000 4-7.pdf>.
52 Johnson, Ian, 'Washington's Secret History with the Muslim Brotherhood,' *The New York Review of Books*, February 5, 2011.
53 Easter, David, British and Malaysia Covert Support for Rebel Movements in Indonesia during the 'Confrontation,' 1963–1966, *Intelligence and National Security* 14, no. 4, Winter 1999 (pp. 195–208).
54 Robinson, Geoffrey B., *The Killing Season, A History of the Indonesian Massacres, 1965–66*, Princeton, NJ, Princeton University Press, 2018 (p. 107).

55 Burkholder Smith, Joseph, *Portrait of a Cold Warrior*, New York City, Putnam, 1976 (pp. 246–247).
56 'Looking into the massacres of Indonesia's past,' *BBC*, June 2, 2016.
57 'Indonesia's killing fields,' *Al Jazeera*, December 21, 2012.
58 *New York Times*, March 12, 1966 (p. 6).
59 Henschke, Rebecca, 'Indonesia massacres: Declassified U.S. files shed new light,' *BBC News*, October 17, 2017.
60 Chomsky, Noam, and Herman, Edward, *The Washington Connection and Third World Fascism*, Boston, University of Toronto Press, 1979 (p. 207).
61 *Time*, December 17, 1965.
62 *Life*, July 11, 1966.
63 *New York Times Magazine*, May 8, 1966 (p. 89).
64 Robinson, Geoffrey B., *The Killing Season, A History of the Indonesian Massacres, 1965–66*, Princeton, NJ, Princeton University Press, 2018 (pp. 106–107).
65 Ibid. (p. 105).
66 CIA Intelligence Info Cable #TDCS-315-00846-64, *U.S. Indonesian Relations*, September 19, 1964, DDC, 1981, #273B.
67 Jones, Howard P., *American-Indonesian Relations*, presentation at Chiefs of Mission Conference, Baguio, Philippines, Howard P. Jones Papers, box 21, Hoover Institution Archives, 12, cited in Roosa, John, *Pretext for Mass Murder*, Madison, University of Wisconsin Press, 2006 (p. 193).
68 Cited in Roosa, John, *Pretext for Mass Murder*, Madison, University of Wisconsin Press, 2006 (p. 190).
69 British Foreign Office note on Mr. M. J. C. Templeton, New Zealand High Commission in London to Mr. Peck, *The Succession to Sukarno*, December 18, 1964, FO 371/175251, UKNA.
70 Reports from the New Zealand Legation, Jakarta to Secretary of External Affairs, Wellington, *Sukarno and the Succession*, December 1, 1964, FO371/175251, UKNA.
71 Robinson, Geoffrey B., *The Killing Season, A History of the Indonesian Massacres, 1965–66*, Princeton, NJ, Princeton University Press, 2018 (p. 337).
72 Ibid (p. 106).
73 'U.S. "actively supported" Indonesia mass killings in 1960s, documents reveal,' *RT*, October 19, 2017.
74 'U.S. Role in 1960s Indonesia Anti-Communist Massacre Revealed,' *Sputnik*, October 18, 2017.
75 Martens, Robert, *The Indonesian Turning Point*, Amazon Digital Services, 2012 ('Preface').
76 Ibid.

77 *Covert Action Information Bulletin*, No. 35, Fall 1990 (p. 59).
78 Kadane, Kath, 'CIA lists,' *San Francisco Examiner*, May 20, 1990.
79 Hawley, Samantha, 'Australia, UK, U.S. all complicit in Indonesian 1965 massacres, international judges say,' *ABC News*, July 20, 2016.
80 Perry, Juliet, 'Tribunal finds Indonesia guilty of 1965 genocide; US, UK complicit,' *CNN*, July 22, 2016.
81 Blum, William, *Killing Hope: U.S. Military and C.I.A. Interventions Since World War II*, London, Zed Books, 2003 (p. 195).
82 Pilger, John, 'Our model dictator,' *The Guardian*, January 28, 2008.
83 Hawley, Samantha, 'Australia, UK, U.S. all complicit in Indonesian 1965 massacres, international judges say,' *ABC News*, July 20, 2016.
84 Hilsman, Roger, *To Move a Nation: The Politics of Foreign Policy in the Administration of John F. Kennedy*, New York, Doubleday, 1967 (p. 377).
85 Military assistance Training in East and Southeast Asia, a Staff Report for the Subcommittee on National Security Policy and Scientific Developments of the House Committee on Foreign Affairs, February 16, 1971 (p. 18).
86 *New York Times*, April 27, 1966, (p. 28).
87 Hearings on Foreign Assistance, 1966, before the Senate Committee on Foreign Relations, May 11, 1966 (p. 693).
88 *New York Times*, June 19, 1966, (p. 12E).
89 *Journal of Contemporary Asia*, Vol. 9, No. 2, 1979 (p. 252).
90 Freney, Denis, *The CIA's Australian Connection*, Sydney, D. Freney, 1977 (p. 17).
91 Britton, Peter, 'Indonesia's Neo-colonial Armed Forces,' *Bulletin of Concerned Asian Scholars*, July-September 1975.
92 *Los Angeles Times*, June 15, 1991 (p. 10).

CHAPTER 5

America in the Philippines: How the United States Established a Colony and Later Neo-Colony in the Pacific

> The Americans found it hard to realize that in the eyes of Asia they had become almost a spearhead of imperialism.[1]
>
> — CLEMENT ATLEE

> A state in the grip of neo-colonialism is not master of its own destiny.[2]
>
> — KWAME NKRUMAH

Genocide? The Philippine-American War and How the United States Joined Europe in Staking an Imperial Claim to Asia

The Philippines was among the earliest countries in the Asia-Pacific to suffer from occupation and subjugation to Western interests. From 1521 to 1898 Spain imposed an imperial government over the country for over 350 years. This occupation came to an end only following Spain's defeat at the hands of the United States at the end of the nineteenth century, after which the Filipinos proclaimed their own independent republic. Almost all Asia-Pacific nations were Western 'possessions' at the time however and, as Spain withdrew, they sought to pass what they viewed as their territory onto another Western imperial power. The Spanish Empire thus sold the territory of the Philippines to the United States for $20 million, and the U.S. then sent over 50,000 troops to establish their rule and crush the country's independence movement in its infancy. The Spanish had not trained or armed a Filipino fighting force during their centuries-long occupation, and only the Japanese Empire, guided by pan-Asian principles at the time, helped the republican movement with limited funding and arms. While this was a valuable asset to the independence struggle, it was negligible compared to the forces which would be brought against the Philippines by the new Western power which laid claim to its territory.

U.S. President William McKinley moved to intervene to subjugate the Philippines under what he felt was the will of the Christian God. In 1899, he wrote:

> I went down on my knees and prayed to the Almighty God for light and guidance more than one night. And one night late it came to me this way – I don't know how it was, but it came: (1) That we could not give them [The Philippines] back to Spain – that would be cowardly and dishonorable; (2) that we could not turn them over to France or Germany – our commercial rivals in the Orient – that would be bad business and discreditable; (3) that we could not leave them to themselves – they were unfit for self-government – and they would soon have anarchy and misrule over there worse than Spain's was; and (4) that there was nothing left for us to do but to take them all, and to educate the Filipinos, and uplift and civilize then Christianize them, and by God's grace do the very best we could by them, as our fellow-men for whom Christ also died.[3]

The president thus launched a war which would devastate the Philippines, and to do 'the very best we could by them' and fulfill a 'moral duty' to God entailed the killing of hundreds of thousands, torture of dissidents, the destruction of population centers, construction of concentration camps and economic exploitation for the enrichment of the United States. Leading American statesmen proudly referred to subjugating of the Philippines as 'imperialism' – though this was at a time when the United States portrayed itself as 'anti-imperialist' and a protector of oppressed nations.

Emilio Aguinaldo, leader of the Philippines independence forces and later in January 1899 elected the first country's first president, proclaimed following the opening of hostilities by the American invasion forces: 'My government cannot remain indifferent in view of such a violent and aggressive seizure of a portion of its territory by a nation which arrogated to itself the title champion of oppressed nations. Thus it is that my government is disposed to open hostilities if the American troops attempt to take forcible possession of the Visayan Islands. I denounce these acts before the world, in order that the conscience of mankind may pronounce its infallible verdict as to who are the true oppressors of nations and the tormentors of human kind.'[4] The United States, self-proclaimed champion of democracy, did not respect the people's right to self-determination – deeming them 'unfit' to rule themselves just as European colonial powers did across their own overseas possessions. As U.S. Senator Albert J. Beveridge, a much renowned historian and intellectual leader, had said: 'The Philippines are ours forever. They are not capable of self-government. How could they be? They are not a self-governing race [...] We will not abandon our opportunity in the Orient. We will not renounce our part in the mission of our race.'[5] The U.S. thus continued to land their troops without the permission of the elected government or its president – as it did not suit their interests to recognize this infant democracy. Hostilities soon broke and escalated into a three-year war between the United States military and First Philippine Republic.

As had been the general case with Western military interventions in the Asia-Pacific, the war targeted the entire population indiscriminately. The U.S. State Department estimated 220,000 Filipinos died in the war, of which 200,000 were civilians.[6] Other sources however strongly disputed these claims, with the People's History of the United States claiming a death toll of 300,000 in the small province of Bantangas alone – potentially indicating a death toll of several million across the entire country. U.S. Brigadier General J. Franklin Bell estimated a death toll of 600,000 on Luzon island alone,[7,8] while a number of studies, such as that of political scientist Eqbal Ahmad, put the death toll even higher at around 3 million Filipinos – though this claim remains unverified.[9] A study by Filipina historian Luzviminda Francisco came to 1.4 million dead from 1899 to 1905 alone – though this date did not mark the end of the fighting.[10] Filipino historian E. San Juan also reached a figure of 1.4 million Filipinos killed, arguing that this constituted an act of genocide by the United States against the Philippines.[11] The population at the time was estimated to be between 6 and 8 million.[12]

Facing a highly capable U.S. military contingent, which by several estimates outnumbered Filipino forces and was armed with modern firearms which their adversaries largely lacked, the tide of the conventional war initially waged was strongly in favor of the Americans. As a result,

Filipino forces altered their strategy and began to engage in a guerilla war, a strategy more suited to their asymmetrical capabilities which took full advantage of their familiarity with the archipelago's terrain. Guerilla warfare was widely adopted from November 1899. On November 13, Emilio Aguinaldo, who was by that time leading the war effort of the Philippine Republic against the Americans, declared that his forces would thenceforth use guerilla tactics.[13]

Guerrilla warfare proved significantly more successful against American forces than open engagement had been. The U.S. military was vulnerable to such attacks, and in turn responded with scorched earth tactics and the targeting of civilian population centers in areas suspected of sheltering or otherwise aiding guerillas. These tactics took a heavy toll on the Republican forces, but an even greater one on the civilian population.[14] According to the testimonies of U.S. Marines, they were under orders to turn the island of Samar into a 'howling wilderness' and maximize casualties, which led to the targeting of civilians and their property on a large scale. The age limit for targeting civilians was reportedly 'everything over ten [years old].'[15] A letter from a U.S. captain from Kansas regarding the conduct of American forces during the scorched earth campaign: '[the regional capital of] Caloocan was supposed to contain 17,000 inhabitants. The Twentieth Kansas [division] swept through it, and now Caloocan contains not one living native.' A private from the same unit wrote that he had 'with my own hand set fire to over fifty houses of Filipinos after the victory at Caloocan. Women and children were wounded by our fire.'[16]

Scorched earth campaigns destroyed entire villages and the use of torture against Republicans was widespread. This included the infamous 'water cure.' American Lieutenant Grover Flint described the process regularly used to torture Filipino suspects during counterinsurgency operations:

> A man is thrown down on his back and three or four men sit or stand on his arms and legs and hold him down; and either a gun barrel or a rifle barrel or a carbine barrel or a stick as big as a belaying pin, – that is, with an inch circumference, – is simply thrust into his jaws and his jaws are thrust back, and, if possible, a wooden log or stone is put under his head or neck, so he can be held more firmly. In the case of very old men I have seen their teeth fall out, – I mean when it was done a little roughly. He is simply held down and then water is poured onto his face down

> his throat and nose from a jar; and that is kept up until the man gives some sign or becomes unconscious. And, when he becomes unconscious, he is simply rolled aside and he is allowed to come to. In almost every case the men have been a little roughly handled. They were rolled aside rudely, so that water was expelled. A man suffers tremendously, there is no doubt about it. His sufferings must be that of a man who is drowning, but cannot drown.[17]

President Theodore Roosevelt referred to the water cure as 'an old Filipino method of mild torture.' Its application in the Philippines was far from mild, however. A report from the time stated: 'soldier who was with General Funston had stated that he helped to administer the water cure to one hundred and sixty natives, all but twenty six of whom died.'[18] In his book *The Forging of the American Empire* Sidney Lens noted: 'If the prisoner tries to keep his mouth closed, his nose is pinched to cut off the air and force him to open his mouth, or a bamboo stick is put in the opening. In this way water is steadily poured in, one, two, three, four, five gallons, until the body becomes "an object frightful to contemplate". In this condition, of course, speech is impossible, so the water is squeezed out of the victim, sometimes naturally, and sometimes – as a young soldier with a smile told the correspondent – "we jump on them to get it out quick." One or two such treatments and the prisoner either talks or dies.'[19]

As would come to be the case in the United States' future wars in the region, the peoples of the target Asian state, in this case the Filipinos were, extensively dehumanized. In November 1901 the Manila correspondent of the Philadelphia Ledger wrote: 'The present war is no bloodless, opera bouffe engagement; our [American] men have been relentless, have killed to exterminate men, women, children, prisoners and captives, active insurgents and suspected people from lads of ten up, the idea prevailing that the Filipino as such was little better than a dog.' The report noted regarding the resulting conduct of U.S. forces towards the Filipino population: 'Our soldiers have pumped salt water into men to make them talk, and have taken prisoners people who held up their hands and peacefully surrendered, and an hour later, without an atom of evidence to show that they were even insurrectos [insurgents], stood them on a bridge and shot them down one by one, to drop into the water below and float down, as examples to those who found their bullet loaded corpses.'[20]

British writer Geoff Simons described the conditioning of American soldiers and the way this led to atrocities. He wrote:

> America's onslaught on the Philippines in 1898 was characterized by familiar racist slogans. Thus the American whites claimed that the native peoples engaged in 'base treachery, revolting cruelty'; a U.S. general depicted the Filipinos as 'gorillas' who hid in the bush; and Theodore Roosevelt saw the conquest of the Philippines as a triumph of Christian civilization over 'the black chaos of savagery and barbarism.' In this racist climate, the native Filipinos were 'niggers,' 'savages,' 'gugus'; a U.S. private, talking of the 'goo-goo' hunt, commented that 'no cruelty is too severe for these brainless monkeys, who can appreciate no sense of honor, kindness or justice'; and yet again American soldiers saw themselves as involved in 'Injun warfare,' a war with an honorless indigenous force. The perennial slogans were dusted off and adapted to the new situation: 'the only good Filipino is a dead one. Take no prisoners. Lead is cheaper than rice.'[21]

General Arthur MacArthur reckoned that 'inferior races' succumbed to wounds more easily than Anglo-Saxons. His son Douglas was to become Field Marshal of the Philippine Army and later the Supreme Commander of the Allied Forces in the Asia-Pacific and Commander in Chief of the United Nations Command, and was to wage wars against the Japanese, Chinese and the Koreans – overseeing war crimes committed against all of them (as covered in their respective chapters). He would display similar attitudes to his father with statements such as that 'Chinamen can't fight' – shortly before his career ended in a string of defeats by the Chinese and North Korean militaries. Such concepts were common, with British author Rudyard Kipling, writing *The White Man's Burden* in 1899 as a response to the American war in the Philippines, portraying the Asians as a 'fluttered folk and wild ... sullen people, half devil and half child.'[22]

Letters written by the American soldiers give valuable insights as to their conduct and mentalities in the war. One volunteer from Washington wrote: 'Our fighting blood was up, and well all wanted to kill "niggers." ... This shooting human beings beats rabbit hunting all to pieces.'[23] An unknown soldier from New York wrote: 'The town of Titatia was surrendered to us a few days ago, and two companies occupy the same. Last night one of our boys was found shot and his stomach cut open. Immediately orders were received from General Wheaton to burn the town and kill every native in sight; which was done to a finish. About 1,000 men, women and children were reported killed. I am probably growing hard-hearted, for I am in my glory when I can sight my gun on some dark skin and pull the trigger.'[24] As was often the case, retribution was indiscriminate and the entire population was targeted. Corporal Sam Gillis recalled: 'We make everyone get into his house by seven p.m., and we only tell a man once. If he refuses, we shoot him. We killed over 300 natives the first night. They tried to set the town on fire. If they fire a shot from the house we burn the house down and every house near it, and shoot the natives, so they are pretty quiet in town now.'[25]

In many areas, Filipinos were forced into concentration camps, used to isolate them from the guerilla fighters they were often suspected of supporting. These were often overcrowded which led to the spread of disease and often resulted in the deaths of their inhabitants. In some camps death rates were as high as 20 percent. Filipino historian Arnaldo Dumindin wrote, 'One camp was two miles by one mile [3.2 by 1.6 km] in area and home to some 8,000 Filipinos. Men were rounded up for questioning, tortured, and summarily executed.'[26] In Batangas Province the operation under General Franklin Bell was described as 'relentless.' The general ordered that the populations of Batangas and Laguna Provinces be put in concentration camps. Anyone found outside these camps was to be shot. The families had to bring all they could carry, and all the land, houses and other valuables would be burned by the U.S. Army. One of these camps was referred to by commanders as the 'suburbs of Hell.' General Bell insisted however that these camps were built to 'protect friendly natives from insurgents, assure them an adequate food supply' as well as to teach them 'proper sanitary standards.' These camps in fact had extremely poor sanitation if any at all and were rife with disease.[27]

The United States military repeatedly proved to be a far greater danger to the Filipino population than Republican fighters.[28] The majority of civilian deaths in the war were due to disease caused by poor sanitation in concentration camps. Massacres and atrocities against the population were widespread but cutting off their means of supporting guerilla forces, through a concentration of the population, ultimately proved successful and was key to America's eventual victory. The Republicans' ties to their support base was severed and the movement thus failed to sustain itself. The United States claimed the Philippines as its own territory – an Asian nation made subservient to a new Western colonial master.

Second War in the Philippines, Quashing Popular Resistance and the United States' Victory

Following the subjugation of the First Philippine Republic American colonial administration of the Philippines saw few serious challenges until December 1941, when the Japanese Empire launched a swift campaign to drive the United States out of their colony. Breaking the United States' hold over the territory led to the reemergence of the nationalist independence movement, which began an active resistance to the Japanese themselves. This led to formation of the Hukbalahap movement, or 'Huks,' meaning 'People's Army Against Japan' in the Tagalog language. When American forces landed in October 1944 to retake the Philippines from Japan, they notably often prioritized targeting Huk forces over the Japanese themselves. Though Huk units fought against the same enemy, they operated independently of the U.S. and had grown into a powerful, organized and popular movement. By the time U.S. forces returned in late 1944 it was clear that the Pacific War with Japan was already won, and ensuring that the Huks could not become a powerful pro-independence force which could challenge American sovereignty over the country in the aftermath of the war, became a priority.

Huk forces had been organized as an armed resistance to the Japanese invasion, and the Communist Party of the Philippines (PKP) had played a key role in organizing them. Many in the United States considered the Huks to be a tool of the what was termed the 'International Communist Conspiracy,' which proved a valuable pretext for action to be taken against them. Labeling any movement or adversary as communist became a useful means for policymakers to justify taking a hard line against them, often involving military force, due to the strength of anti-communist sentiment in the United States. The threat the Huks posed however was not a result of their tenuous links to communist ideology, but rather the fact that they were an organized and armed force striving for national independence and genuine sovereignty just as the First Philippine Republic had before them. The US, with good reason, believed that after the Japanese were gone the Huks would not accept either a return to colonial status under U.S. rule or a position of subservience as an American client state.

Much like the preceding war against the Philippine Republic, the Filipino population were widely targeted indiscriminately on suspicion of aiding the Huk movement. American officers led units of U.S. and Filipino soldiers in a reign of terror against suspected supporters. Local governments the Huks had helped to establish, through which communities had begun to rule themselves as Japanese forces had withdrawn, were quickly dismantled through American intervention. Many high-ranking members of the Huk movement were imprisoned, while the capture and imprisonment of the leaders of the PKP which had resisted the Japanese occupation had been made a priority for U.S. forces long before the Japanese had surrendered. Huk forces on the other hand frequently came to the aid of American soldiers, showing solidarity against Japanese forces, while American forces often allowed the Japanese to attack Huk forces and took no action to stop these attacks or counter the Japanese. It was clear where their priorities lay.[29]

After over 400 years of Spanish then American rule, the Philippines suffered from grinding poverty, illiteracy and poverty-caused illnesses such as tuberculosis and beriberi. The Huks supported land reform, something so popular that even the U.S. colonial administration had been forced to pay lip service to the idea – despite not having carried out any such reform during their 40-year occupation. The Huks were also keen to industrialize the Philippines, which was strongly opposed by the United States. Industrialization and land reform were considered by the Huks to be key to raising the country from poverty – much as these policies had so recently been implemented under a Stalinist program in the USSR to great effect – turning a peasant society experiencing frequent famines into a global superpower within 15 years. Preventing such a process from occurring in the Asia Pacific was central to the United States' strategy towards the region, as outlined by the chair and founder of the State Department's Policy

Planning Staff George Kennan who stressed the importance of maintaining the 'position of disparity' between the modernity of the United States and Western Europe and the underdeveloped state of Asia.[30] This policy long predated Kennan's tenure in the State Department, and had previously been widely practiced by European imperial powers such as France and the Netherlands in the Asian possessions – referred to by scholars as 'colonial non-industrialisation' or the 'development of underdevelopment.' This was considered to be the crux of American and Western primacy in the Asia-Pacific region.[31] Leaving the nation backward and dependent without a modern economy gave American industries what has been called a 'veritable playground in the Philippines.'[32] Indeed, American President McKinley's Postmaster General, Charles Emory, had stated shortly after the U.S. first intervened in the Philippines regarding designs for the country: 'what we want is a market for our surplus.'[33] For this it was critical that the Philippines remain poor and anything resembling the Huk movement's industrialization drive never be implemented – while the U.S. would push through agreements which would provide their industries with priority access to the country's markets without meaningful competition from abroad. A lack of education, industry or any substantial research or development ensured the country was perfectly suited to become a dependency of the United States, granting the U.S. substantial economic benefits to trade with a resource rich country which could not produce for itself.

By the end of 1945, immediately after the end of the Second World War, the United States was equipping a force of 50,000 Filipino soldiers. Militarization was taking place across several countries, as it was an asset for the Western Bloc to have armed clients ready to aid it in the Cold War at a time when there was potential for it to break out into an open hot conflict.[34] Filipinos would soon join the American-led war efforts in Korea and Vietnam. Another critical reason for rearmament was the need to suppress pro-independence forces domestically. Major General William Arnold of the U.S. Army said in a testimony before congress that this program was 'essential for the maintenance of internal order, not for external difficulties at all.' This policy was unopposed by congress.[35]

The aftermath of Imperial Japan's defeat saw a continuation of the military campaign against the Huks. Combat training was reestablished for at least one U.S. division, which led to protests by the soldiers themselves who wanted to return home. According to the *New York Times* the start of combat training was 'interpreted by soldiers and certain Filipino newspapers as the preparation for the repression of possible uprisings in the Philippines by disgruntled farm tenant groups.' The article added that the soldiers also had much to say 'on the subject of armed intervention in China and the Netherlands Indies [Indonesia].'[36] These were occurring simultaneously. Before one war had ended, another global conflict appeared to have begun.

The Philippines was granted a token independence under the Treaty of General Relations in July 1946, under which American sovereignty over the territory was relinquished. The terms of independence strongly favored the United States, while the elites put in power were loyal to Washington – many of them American educated. U.S. forces also worked closely with Filipinos who had collaborated with the Japanese, much as they did in at the same time in Korea, and many collaborators were restored to power. Under the terms of the Philippines' independence the United States was guaranteed a substantial permanent military deployment in the country. An agreement between the United States and the Philippines provided sites for 23 U.S. military bases – and this was set to last for 99 years. Much like the arrangement under previous Western colonial systems in Asia, Americans were granted extraterritoriality and could not be held accountable by Filipino courts for their crimes.

The European colonial powers had previously established exclusive trading rights with occupied nations, allowing the powers to dictate prices for imported goods and ban all rival imports. It had earned colonial powers substantial profits at the expense of occupied nations. The Companion Military Assistance Pact similarly stripped the Philippines of self-determination in military affairs to benefit U.S. interests. The Filipino government was prohibited from purchasing weapons, from small arms to heavy equipment, without the approval of the United States. This also left the country's armed forces heavily dependent on the U.S. for the maintenance of its equipment.

Under the Companion Military Assistance Pact, no foreigners other than Americans were permitted to perform any function for or with the

Philippine military without the approval of the United States. Within only a few years, by 1950, the United States had provided the Philippines with over $200 million of military equipment and supplies (several billion in today's currency). The Philippines military was reorganized under an American selected leadership and trained and organized to do what the United States wanted – to fight a counterinsurgency and purge the Huk movement – and later to assist them in projecting power elsewhere in Asia.[37] The Joint U.S. Military Advisory Group reorganized the Philippine intelligence capability and defense department and chose Ramon Magsaysay as its head. They formed the Philippine army into battalion combat teams trained specifically for counter-insurgency warfare. This was an experiment for this type of warfare, and terminology coined here such as 'pacification' and 'search and destroy' was used later in Vietnam to counter the Viet Minh independence movement there.[38]

The Huks did not trust the United States but nevertheless took part in the April 1946 national elections as part of the Democratic Alliance of socialist and liberal political groups. Elections were being held and Philippine independence was scheduled for three months later. Luis Taruc, the commander in chief of the Huks, and several others were elected to congress. Three were elected to the senate and seven to the house. Their appointment contravened with the interests of the United States however – which sought a parliamentary majority for then President of the Commonwealth of the Philippines Manuel Roxas, the candidate Washington favored to become the first president following the granting of independence. As a result, the Democratic Alliance members were not allowed to take their seats based on unproven charges of election fraud. The electoral tribunal never carried out a review of the cases.[39,40]

Without the Democratic Alliance represented in the senate, President Roxas' majority could push the Philippine-U.S. Trade Act – which passed only narrowly. It yielded the U.S. bountiful privileges and concessions in the Philippine economy including 'equal rights [...] in the development of the nation's natural resources and the operation of its public utilities.'[41] These 'equal rights' were then extended to every sector of the economy.[42] The United States granted independence two days after this act was passed, and had strongly supported its passage. It was critical for Washington to ensure, as many colonial powers did when granting their former possessions any form of token independence, that the groundwork was laid to ensure a continuing economic relationship which would strongly favor the interests of the former occupying power at the expense of the formerly occupied. Critics called the act's passage an inexcusable surrender of national sovereignty.[43]

American historian George E. Taylor wrote that the Philippines' independence: 'was marked by lavish expression of mutual good will, by partly fulfilled promises, and by a restoration of the old relationship in almost everything except in name [...] Many demands were made of the Filipinos for the commercial advantage of the United States, but none for the social and political advantage of the Philippines.'[44] Following the elections the military and police began a wave of violence in rural areas, with the support of hit men in the employ of many of the country's landlords who opposed the Huks due to their pledge to instate land reform. Hundreds of farmers and their community leaders were killed, jailed, tortured, maimed, or disappeared based on often unproven allegations of support for the Huks. This was an attempt to undermine the movement by destroying its popular support base – a strategy which had previously proven highly successful against the Republican guerilla forces. Unlike the previous war which had taken place at the turn of the century in the colonial era however, it was no longer feasible to put the country's rural population into concentration camps.

Lt. Col. Edward G. Lansdale, head of the CIA clandestine paramilitary operations in the Philippines, was also struck by the repressive and brutal nature of the government the U.S. was supporting. He relates his surprise at hearing informed Filipino civilian friends tell him how oppressive the practices of the very government he was working to support were. Government atrocities in reality matched those they were falsely attributing to the Huks. The government was 'rotten with corruption,' which Lansdale himself observed was from the highest levels down to the policemen in the street. He wrote that President Quirino himself, who had taken power in 1948 following President Roxas' heart attack and death, had been elected through 'extensive fraud' and that 'the Huks were right,' they were the 'wave of the future.' He went on to note that violence was the only way people could get a government of their own. The oppression of the

Filipinos' aspirations under a corrupt American client regime was apparent for all to see, even recognized by their American sponsors.[45] Others reacted to the unjustness of their cause with action – such as American airman William J. Pomeroy of the 5th Air Force, who after fighting against the Huks was utterly disillusioned with the American cause and returned to the Philippines to fight alongside them.

Lansdale was undeterred by the immorality he observed in the American cause. He had little choice than to persuade himself that if the Huks took over there would only be another privileged elite running another form of unjust government. The alternative would have ended his career. By the next chapter in his reminiscences he seemed to have convinced himself that he was working with those committed to 'defend human liberty in the Philippines.'[46] Lansdale created the Civil Affairs Office and used psychological warfare to gain an advantage in the war against the insurgents. By the time of his deployment, the war had become a drawn out affair with no end in sight. His Civil Affairs Office's activities were based on the premise that such popular insurgency could not be defeated by use of force alone.

With the concentration camps that had previously proven strategically successful, though incurring a great human cost, now ruled out in the postcolonial era due primarily to a combination of associations with Nazi German practices and the risk of alienating third world allies with such direct methods, other means of cutting the popular guerillas from their support base were explored. This led to radical and often ingenious solutions on the part of the CIA's paramilitary forces. Lansdale's Psychological Warfare team carefully studied the superstitions of the peasant populations living in areas which supported the Huks. They learned their lore, taboos, myths and other such information to gain an understanding of what would motivate them and how their support for the Huks could be eroded. Lansdale's team often played on the superstitions of the peasants to achieve their desired outcomes, which proved to be extremely effective. The Huk fighters, themselves mostly peasants who had taken up arms, were also susceptible to these 'psywar' operations. The following are examples of psywar operations and other programs conducted by the CIA's Psychological Warfare team to undermine the Huks' and their results:

- Lansdale's men flew over Huk supporting areas in a small plane hidden by cloud cover and broadcast mysterious curses on any villagers who would provide the Huks with food or shelter. This is reported as having terrified locals and starved many of the Huk units into surrender, as they relied heavily on local support to operate.[47]
- One psywar operation played on the fear of the *ausang*, a mythical vampire of legend. A psywar team entered a town and planted rumors that the neighboring hills where the Huks were based were home to an *ausang* vampire. The Huk forces were entrenched in these hills and the government forces were eager to get them out. Two nights later, after giving these rumors time to circulate and themselves time to get up the hill, the psywar team ambushed a Huk patrol and took the last man silently as they passed. They punctured his neck with two holes, as a vampire would, and held him upside down until the blood drained out. They then put the corpse back on the trail. When the Huks, having heard the rumors themselves, saw their comrade struck by an *ausang*, they fled the region and it fell to government forces.[48]
- The Economic Development Corps was created to adopt one of the Huks' most attractive pledges – land redistribution – which to an impoverished peasant society facing centuries of colonial rule under both foreign and collaborationist landowners meant a great deal. The corps would lure Huks with a program of resettlement on their own patch of farmland, with cash, seeds and loans as well. This was never a genuine undertaking, and was a wholly inadequate solution to the land problem and the peasants' grievances. Though very few responded, the aim was to undermine the appeal of the Huks to the peasant population.
- Lansdale's team began to produce films and radio broadcasts which would justify the government's actions to the population.
- Government agents were infiltrated into the ranks of the Huks to provide information and sow dissent.
- There were genuine attempts to modify the behavior of the government soldiers to curtail their abuse of the peasant population. The Huks had long followed an explicit code of conduct which had gained them widespread support, and this was particularly apparent when contrasted with the abominable behavior of the government forces.

A correspondent from the *Saturday Evening Post* had written that the police in the Philippines were 'bands of uniformed thieves and rapists, more feared than bandits ... the army was little better.'[49]

- As well as an attempt to improve the conduct of government forces, efforts were made to defame the Huks themselves. Government forces disguised as Huk forces were allowed to pillage villages and wreak havoc. L. Fletcher Prouty, a retired U.S. Air Force officer, said this technique was 'developed to a high art in the Philippines.' Soldiers were 'set upon the unwary village in the grand manner of a Cecil B. DeMille production.'[50]

Retired U.S. Air Force Colonel L. Fletcher Prouty was the focal point officer for contacts between the Pentagon and the CIA for nine years. He described another strategy by which the reputation of the Huks was tarnished and the true nature of the conflict obscured. The Huks largely lost the moral high ground in the eyes of the people, losing them the popular support that had been key to their success. Prouty also noted how the Philippine government used the Huks as an explanation for social unrest caused by its own corrupt policies and by U.S. interests:

> In the Philippines, lumbering interests and major sugar interests have forced tens of thousands of simple, backward villagers to leave areas where they have lived for centuries. When these poor people flee to other areas, it should be quite obvious that they in turn then infringe upon the territorial rights of other villagers or landowners. This creates violent rioting or at least sporadic outbreaks of banditry, that last lowly recourse of dying and terrorized people. Then when the distant government learns of the banditry and rioting, it must offer some safe explanation. The last thing that regional government would want to do would be to say that the huge lumbering or paper interests had driven the people out of their ancestral homeland. In the Philippines it is customary for the local/regional government to get a 10 percent rake-off on all such enterprise and for national politicians to get another 10 percent. So the safe explanation becomes 'Communist-inspired subversive insurgency.' The word for this in the Philippines is Huk.[51]

As the *New York Times* reported 'The Communist Hukbalahap rebellion is generally regarded as an outgrowth of the misery and discontent among the peasants of Central Luzon.' A later U.S. Army study reported the Huks' 'main impetus was peasant grievances, not Leninist [communist] designs.'[52]

The Huks' ranks swelled with peasants as a response to their mistreatment and to the corruption and brutality of the U.S. backed Philippines government, rather than to the ideals of communism.

The CIA was highly successful in its efforts to manipulate the country's political life and manage public opinion. There were stage-managed elections and widespread disinformation campaigns, turning the people against those who fought to free them from occupation and poverty and brutal government rule 'rotten with corruption' – in Col. Lansdale's words. In 1953 Ramon Magsaysay, the former American-selected defense department head, was elected president. Again corruption and misconduct in Philippine elections was highly prevalent. It was said that Lansdale, working for the CIA, had 'invented Magsaysay.'[53] The National Movement for Free Elections was among others a CIA front organization running Magsaysay's election campaign. Behind it was the funding and impunity that U.S. candidates would have had, unmatched by any rivals. Elpidio Quirino who ran against Magsaysay had his drinks drugged by the CIA on one occasion before he gave a speech, in which he would thereby appear incoherent.[54] Magsaysay did win the elections, but the CIA had smuggled in guns for use in a coup in case he lost.[55] They were taking no chances – the Philippines was to be under U.S. control regardless of the outcome.

Magsaysay was managed by the CIA so that he would in turn manage the Philippines in accordance with U.S. interests. His speeches were always written by Lansdale's teams. On one occasion he reportedly insisted he be allowed to read a speech written by a Filipino, to which Lansdale reacted in such a rage that he knocked the Filipino politician unconscious.[56] The relationship between the American colonel and the Filipino politician was highly symbolic of that between the Western superpower and Asian client state – in which one party's dominance over the other was evidently clear. Once in office, President Magsaysay's policy was guided according to the interests of the United States. The illusion of genuine independence and democracy were essential to make continued U.S. control over the country sustainable, effectively silencing pro-independence movements and maintaining the American image abroad as an anti-colonialist power and friend of the third world – critical at a time of Cold War competition. A CIA-managed puppet government acting as an illusory democracy was an essential means to achieve this without compromising American interests or influence in their former colony. As U.S. Senator Albert J. Beveridge had proclaimed half a century prior: 'The Philippines are ours forever.'[57] Similar strategies were undertaken in other 'possessions' of Western powers which were granted an illusory independence – hailing a shift in the postwar era from direct colonial rule to neocolonialism for which the Philippines would serve as a template.

The CIA used several paid editors and journalists to provide support for the president's domestic programs, which were essentially their domestic programs – in that they had overwhelmingly been drafted to suit American interests, and to manipulate public opinion to consent to taking part in the U.S. led anti-communist crusade. CIA assets in the press were also paid to defame anti-U.S. newspaper columnists.[58] Magsaysay was a puppet president in every sense of the word, exactly what the U.S. wanted. Presidential assistant Sherman Adams wrote that the Philippines' president 'sent word to Eisenhower that he would do anything the United States wanted him to do – even though his own foreign minister took the opposite view.'[59] With such a government in place, direct occupation was no longer necessary. It was because of this that the Philippines was referred to as 'democracy's showcase in Asia'[60] – it truly was the ideal 'democratic' Western client state. Ultimately the Western imperial powers were strongly inclined to term such client states 'democracies' and claim that those states which asserted their interests against the West lacked democracy – regardless of the actual nature of their governance. 'Democracy' became a label for Western allies and client states in the postcolonial era. Almost all Western allies, from those managed from abroad such as the Philippines to military dictatorships such as Taiwan, other than the few absolute monarchies such as Brunei, could thus be termed 'democratic.'

By 1953 the Huks had largely lost support and were scattered and demoralized. The impoverishment of the peasantry as a whole also likely played a part, and may have led to malnutrition and disease among Huk fighters at a time when many of the rural peoples were struggling to feed themselves. The Huks were also lacking in weapons and equipment, forced to rely on whatever they could salvage from the Japanese occupation period, while the government forces had the full backing of the United States and were heavily armed. The lack of arms among Huk fighters significantly undermines claims that the Huks were armed by and acting at the behest of the USSR and the Chinese communists as proxies of an 'International Communist Conspiracy,' and were not simply an oppressed people fighting for their sovereignty, rights and dignity.[61,62,63] Depicting them as the former rather than the latter however played well into the hands of their adversaries.

Perhaps, as Col. Lansdale had said when he first arrived on his mission, the Huks were once the 'wave of the future.' Now the course of the Philippines' history had been altered dramatically, and the suffering and subjugation of the Filipinos was set to continue for years. A people eager to develop and determine their future had twice had their ambitions crushed by an external power. This was all done under the guise of altruism and democratization, or in the words of President McKinley to 'uplift and civilize then Christianize them.' Following the fall of the Huks most of the social programs made by the government to compete with the movement's appeal were terminated. They were never intended to support or benefit the population, but rather to win support. As historian George Taylor noted: 'since the destruction of Huk military power the social and political program that made the accomplishment possible has to a large extent fallen by the wayside.'[64] The land reform and industrialization promised by the movement and intended to modernize the country was never implemented – with lasting consequences to this day.

By the end of the uprising political life was heavily under the influence of the Washington, which exerted a great deal of control through the CIA. One example was the character assassination of Senator Claro M. Recto, President Magsaysay's chief political opponent and a stern critic of American policy. The CIA planted stories that he was a communist Chinese agent and prepared packages of condoms labeled 'Courtesy of Claro M. Recto – the People's Friend.' The condoms all had holes in them, suggesting Recto's involvement in sexual malpractice to harm his image.[65] When the Senator continued to pose a threat to Magsaysay's position, thus to American interests, the agency also planned to kill him. A substance was prepared to poison him, but the agency in the end decided against it.

According to the analysis of former U.S. Marine, *New York Times* writer and Pulitzer Prize winner Raymond Bonner, this was entirely 'for pragmatic considerations rather than moral scruples.'[66]

After Magsaysay himself died in a plane crash in 1957, a new candidate was sought out by the CIA who could be relied on to oblige American demands while in office. Diosdado Macapagal offered himself as a client and became president in 1961. He had provided the CIA with political information for years, and in return received extensive financial support for his campaign as Magsaysay had before him. The CIA's support was itself against Philippine law, which stated under Article X, Section 81 of the election code that no foreigner was permitted: 'to aid any candidate or political party, directly or indirectly, or take part in or influence in any manner any election, or to contribute or make any expenditure in connection with any election campaign or partisan political activity.'[67] Providing extensive support to favorable political candidates was found to be common practice for the United States in the Asia-Pacific region to ensure client governments would remain in power. Perhaps the most prominent other example was in Japan, where much like the Philippines the CIA intervened extensively in the country's elections to support client candidates who would carry forward American interests after the end of direct military rule.[68]

In 1957 the Philippine government passed a law which outlawed the Communist Party and the Huks entirely. Ironically the reason given for this was that the Huks aimed to place the nation 'under the control and domination of an alien power.'[69] America's *Reader's Digest* however called Macapagal's campaign 'certainly a demonstration of democracy in action.'[70] It truly was in line with the Western vision for 'democracy' in Asia, with extensive economic and military reliance on the West, extensive foreign influence over the electoral process, and suppression or banning of political parties unfavorable to the interests of Western powers – namely communists, nationalists and those who demanded an equitable rather than subservient status in their partnership.

With the Philippines secure, the United States had an excellent second staging ground for its operations throughout the Asia-Pacific, and the country would come to house extensive American military facilities for decades to come. This came alongside all the material benefits of controlling the country through a client government and gaining access to its resources on highly favorable terms. From the Philippines the United States would launch military interventions against Vietnam, North Korea, China and Indonesia, all of which were waging similar struggles against Western subjugation as the Huks had. The Philippine government itself would send American trained and armed forces, 'little American armies' as they were so often known, to fight in Vietnam and Korea alongside the United States. The Filipino people funded these war efforts through their taxes – and the acquisition and operation of state of the art U.S. made equipment in major wars overseas put an immense budgetary strain on the already impoverished nation.[71] The art of counterinsurgency that Edward G. Lansdale had worked toward perfecting would be further developed and widely employed, while Lansdale himself would go on to apply the invaluable lessons he had learned in the Philippines to conduct operations against Vietnam and Cuba.[72]

Notes

1 Deane, Hugh, *The Korean War, 1945–1953*, San Francisco, CA, China Books and Periodicals, 1999 (p. 112).

2 Rosskam, Ellen, and Hill, Dave, *The Development World and State Education: Neoliberal Depredation and Egalitarian Alternatives*, Abingdon, Routledge, 2009 (p. 203).

3 Olcott, Charles S., *The Life of William McKinley*, Vol. 2, Charleston, SC, Nabu Press, 2010 (pp. 110–111).

4 Wolff, Leon, *Little Brown Brother: How the United States Purchased and Pacified the Philippine Islands at the Century's Turn*, New York, History Book Club, 2006 (p. 201).

5 Senator Albert J. Beveridge Speaks On The Philippine Question, U.S. Senate, Washington, DC, January 9, 1900.

6 'The Philippine-American War, 1899–1902,' Office of the Historian, Milestones 1899–1902, United States of America Department of State.

7 Jummel, Rudolph J., *Statistics of Democide: Genocide and Mass Murder Since 1900*, Münster, LIT Verlag, 1998.

8 Gates, John M., 'War-Related Deaths in the Philippines, 1898–1902.' *Pacific Historical Review*, 1983.

9 Ahmed, Eqbal, 'The Theory and Fallacies of Counter-Insurgency,' *The Nation*, August 2, 1971.

10 Francisco, Luzviminda, *The End of an Illusion*, London, AREAS, 1973.

11 San Juan, Epifanio, 'U.S. Genocide in the Philippines: A Case of Guilt, Shame, or Amnesia?,' *Medium*, March 22, 2005.

12 Boot, Max, *The Savage Wars Of Peace: Small Wars And The Rise Of American Power*, New York, Basic Books, 2002 (p. 125).

13 Linn, Brian McAllister, *The U.S. Army and counterinsurgency in the Philippine war, 1899–1902*, Chapel Hill, The University of North Carolina Press, 2000 (pp. 186–187).

14 Schirmer, Daniel B. and Shalom, Stephen Rosskamm, *The Philippines Reader: A History of Colonialism, Neocolonialism, Dictatorship, and Resistance*, New York, South End Press, 1987.

15 Zinn, Howard, *A People's History of the United States: 1492-Present*, New York, Harper Perennial, 2005 (p. 316).

16 Ibid. (p. 315).

17 Tucker, Spencer, *Almanac of American Military History, Vol. 1*, Santa Barbara, CA, ABC-CLIO, 2012 (p. 1248).

18 Palitto, Robert M., *Torture and State Violence in the United States: A Short Documentary History*, 3.12 Letter from Secretary of War Elihu Root to Henry Cabot Lodge, February 27, 1906.

19 Lens, Sydney, and Zinn, Howard, *The Forging of the American Empire: From the Revolution to Vietnam: A History of American Imperialism*, London, Pluto Press, 2003 (p. 189).

20 Saito, Natsu Taylor, *Meeting the Enemy: American Exceptionalism and International Law*, New York, New York University Press, 2010 (p. 153).

21 Simons, Geoff, *The Vietnam Syndrome: Impact on U.S. Foreign Policy*, Abingdon, Palgrave Macmillan, 1998 (p. 125).

22 Ibid.

23 Zinn, Howard, *A People's History of the United States: 1492-Present*, New York, Harper Perennial, 2005 (p. 315).

24 Ash, Chris, *Kruger, Kommandos & Kak: Debunking the Myths of The Boer War*, Pinetown, 30 Degrees South Publishers, 2014 (p. 321).

25 Welman, Frans, *Face of the New Peoples Army of the Philippines: Volume Two*, Bangkok, Booksmango, 2012 (p. 137).

26 Ibid. (p. 138).

27 Ibid. (p. 139).

28 Ibid. (p. 139).

29 Blum, William, *Killing Hope: U.S. Military and C.I.A. Interventions Since World War II*, London, Zed Books, 2003 (p. 37).
30 Chomsky, Noam, *Who Rules the World?*, London, Hamish Hamilton, 2016 (p. 73).
31 Howe, Stephen, *Empire; A Very Short Introduction*, Oxford, Oxford University Press, 2002 (p. 78).
32 Blum, William, *Killing Hope: U.S. Military and C.I.A. Interventions Since World War II*, London, Zed Books, 2003 (p. 40).
33 Zinn, Howard, *A People's History of the United States: 1492-Present*, New York, Harper Perennial, 2005 (p. 314).
34 *New York Times*, January 5, 1946 (p. 26).
35 Hearings before the House Committee on Foreign Affairs in executive session, June 7, 1946 (p. 31).
36 *New York Times*, January 8, 1946, (p. 3).
37 *New York Times*, February 11, 1950 (p. 6).
38 Lansdale, Edward G., *In the Midst of Wars: An American Mission to Southeast Asia*, New York, Harper & Row, 1972.
39 *New York Times*, May 20, 1946 (p. 8).
40 *New York Times*, June 2, 1946 (p. 26).
41 *New York Times*, March 12, 1947 (p. 15).
42 Pomeroy, William J., *An American Made Tragedy: Neo-Colonialism & Dictatorship in the Philippines*, New York, International Publishers, 1974 (p. 28).
43 Dolan, Ronald E., ed., *Philippines: A Country Study*, Washington, D.C., GPO for the Library of Congress, 1991.
44 Taylor, George E., *The Philippines and the United States: Problems of Partnership*, New York, Praeger, 1964 (pp. 114–115).
45 Blum, William, *Killing Hope: U.S. Military and C.I.A. Interventions Since World War II*, London, Zed Books, 2003 (p. 42).
46 Lansdale, Edward G., *In the Midst of Wars: An American Mission to Southeast Asia*, New York, Harper & Row, 1972 (pp. 24–30, 47).
47 Burkholder Smith, Joseph, *Portrait of a Cold Warrior*, New York, Putnam, 1976 (p. 95).
48 Lansdale, Edward G., *In the Midst of Wars: An American Mission to Southeast Asia*, New York, Harper & Row, 1972 (pp. 72–73).
49 Worden, William, 'Robin Hood of the Islands,' *Saturday Evening Post*, January 12, 1952 (p. 76).
50 Prouty, L. Fletcher, *The Secret Team: The CIA and its Allies in Control of the World*, New York, Ballantine Books, 1974, (pp. 38–39).
51 Ibid. (pp. 102–103).
52 *New York Times*, December 19, 1952 (p. 13).

53 Burkholder Smith, Joseph, *Portrait of a Cold Warrior*, New York, Putnam, 1976 (p. 95).
54 Blum, William, *Killing Hope: U.S. Military and C.I.A. Interventions Since World War II*, London, Zed Books, 2003 (p. 43).
55 Bonner, Raymond, *Waltzing With a Dictator: The Marcoses and the Making of American Policy*, New York, Times Books, 1987 (p. 41).
56 Ibid. (pp. 39–40).
57 Senator Albert J. Beveridge Speaks On The Philippine Question, U.S. Senate, Washington, DC, January 9, 1900.
58 Blum, William, *Killing Hope: U.S. Military and C.I.A. Interventions Since World War II*, London, Zed Books, 2003 (p. 41).
59 Adams, Sherman, *Firsthand Report; The Story of the Eisenhower Administration*, New York, Harper and Brothers, 1961 (p. 123).
60 *New York Times*, October 16, 1953 (p. 26).
61 *New York Times*, April 3, 1949 (p. 20).
62 *New York Times*, June 30, 1950 (p. 4).
63 Lachicha, Eduardo, *Huk: Philippine Agrarian Society in Revolt*, Santa Barbara, CA, Praeger, 1971 (p. 131).
64 Taylor, George E., *The Philippines and the United States: Problems of Partnership*, New York, Praeger, 1964 (p. 192).
65 Burkholder Smith, Joseph, *Portrait of a Cold Warrior*, New York, Putnam, 1976 (p. 280).
66 Bonner, Raymond, *Waltzing With a Dictator: The Marcoses and the Making of American Policy*, New York, Times Books, 1987 (p. 42).
67 Election Code of the Philippines, Article X, Campaign and Election Propaganda, Section 81.
68 Weiner, Tim, 'C.I.A. Spent Millions to Support Japanese Right in 50's and 60's,' *New York Times*, October 9, 1994.
69 House Bill No. 6584, Republic Act No. 1700, approved June 20, 1957.
70 'Democracy Triumphs in the Philippines,' *Reader's Digest*, April 1963.
71 Hastings, Max, *Korean War*, London, Michael Joseph, 1988 (p. 238).
72 'Our Best-Known Covert Operative,' *New York Times*, February 26, 1989.

CHAPTER 6

Vietnam's Thirty Years of War

> The trouble is no one sees the Vietnamese people. They're not people. Therefore it doesn't matter what you do to them.[1]
>
> — TELFORD TAYLOR, American war crimes expert, on the prevailing attitudes within the U.S. military during the war

> The war in Vietnam is but a symptom of a far deeper malady within the American spirit.[2]
>
> — MARTIN LUTHER KING JR.

The Emergence of the Viet Minh and End of the French Colonial Era

Following the surrender of the Japanese Empire in 1945, Vietnam experienced three decades of war with Western imperial powers which sought to assert their dominance over its territory. While the outcome and several highly publicized events from the war are widely known, the underlying reality of the war, the Western powers' motives for fighting and the conduct of Western militaries during their intervention are critical facts which remain little known.

Having been a French colonial possession along with Laos and Cambodia, collectively termed French Indochina, the Vietnamese had long suffered under foreign rule. It is highly indicative of the overall conduct of the French colonial administration that there were more educators in Vietnam before French rule was instated than after it left – with well under 10 percent of children having access to even a basic primary education (perhaps the lowest in the region – particularly when compared to Korea, Taiwan and the Chinese mainland). Any hopes for

Vietnam's industrialization, modernization or an improvement in living standards were quashed by the French administration, which benefitted from sustaining poverty and a subsistence living among its Asian subjects to better exploit their resources and thus enrich the Empire's European subjects in France itself.[3,4] Under French rule European culture had been fiercely promoted at the expense of Vietnam's own ancient civilization, which the French undertook great efforts to whitewash. An example was the enforced adoption of the Latin script and the motives behind it. One primary reason was that France had been involved in extensive repression of Buddhism and fierce promotion of Catholicism – to the extent that the Asian scripts, seen by the French as an obstacle to the people's mass conversion to Catholicism, were outlawed in favor of the imposition of the more Church friendly Latin script. The change in script was also seen as an invaluable means by France of cutting the Vietnamese people off from their traditional literature and neutralizing the country's established scholarly elite – forcibly alienating the country from its own history and culture while increasing its reliance on those of France and Europe.[5,6] The country's ancient Confucian education was also suppressed for the same reason, increasing the country's elites' reliance on the French education system in an attempt to create a 'Francophone Asia' as had been done in Africa.

France had openly declared its intention to keep French Indochina as a colonial possession indefinitely. As the colonial commissioner of the renowned General Charles De Gaulle declared in 1944 regarding of the country's intentions towards 'French Indochina': 'the aims of France in her civilizing work in the colonies exclude any idea of self-government, any possibility of development outside the French Empire; the formation of independent governments in the colonies, however distant, cannot be contemplated.'[7] As had been the case with the Dutch in Indonesia however, it was near impossible to reassert European colonial authority after it had been so seriously undermined by the swift Japanese string of victories there, while the Japanese imperial period gave local nationalist elements time and space to organize themselves. Though France had been overwhelmingly defeated and itself occupied during the Second World War, the country still perceived itself as a major world power with a right to reassert its imperial claims. The result was an extensive campaign to 'require' former colonial possessions and the deployment of 200,000 French soldiers, aided by a further 200,000 local troops, to 'exclude any idea of self-government, any possibility of development outside the French Empire' for Vietnam.

Despite France's overwhelming military advantage, the Vietnamese people, much like the Indonesians, were unwilling to accept colonial rule again once the facade of European superiority and invulnerability had been lifted. The Viet Minh nationalist movement, which had grown significantly in strength since the eviction of the French colonial administration in 1941 and gained widespread public support, proved to France through their staunch resistance that a return to the pre-Japanese status quo was impossible. Several thousand Imperial Japanese military personnel also chose to stay in Vietnam after their Empire's defeat and trained the Viet Minh in warfare and administration, with several serving at the Quang Ngai Military Academy. Japanese officers were even known to lead Vietnamese nationalist forces into battle against the French,[8] while others provided invaluable training in fields such as night fighting and communications. Many were given Vietnamese citizenship and several are commemorated in Japan's Yasukuni Shrine for the war dead today.[9] The Japanese contribution to the war was critical as they provided the military knowhow and experience necessary to engage a modern army, something which the Viet Minh themselves almost entirely lacked.

While Paris saw the return of its overseas colonial possessions as a symbol to restore its much wounded postwar national pride and prestige, leading France to persist in its war effort for almost nine years, in 1954 the Empire eventually withdrew – having lost over 20,000 soldiers and 55,000 local auxiliary fighters.[10] The Battle of Dien Bien Phu that year, which cost French forces heavily and demonstrated the growing offensive capabilities of the Viet Minh against French positions, was critical in bringing about this result and had a significant influence on the signing of the 1954 Geneva Accords – under which imperial forces withdrew and Vietnam was partitioned into a northern and a southern state. Unifying elections were scheduled for the following year, but France's withdrawal hardly spelt the end of Western military involvement in the country. With the Cold War escalating in the Asia-Pacific in the aftermath of the Korean War, what had been one country's simple struggle for independence became a central part of a major regional strategic effort undertaken by the Western Bloc – the result of which would have implications far beyond Vietnam's borders.

U.S. Involvement in Vietnam

While the United States was initially unsupportive of the French effort to reacquire its Asian colonial possessions, the 'Loss of China' in 1949 made containing Chinese influence in the Asia-Pacific and prevention of the emergence of a new independent regional bloc that could challenge Western regional dominance a priority for American policymakers. The outbreak of the Korean War and the unexpectedly successful performance of both North Korean and Chinese forces against those of the United States and their Western allies only exacerbated the perceived threat posed by this emerging 'Yellow Peril' – demonstrating the true potency of Asian armies which for over a century had been, with the partial exception of Japan, considered incapable of engaging Western forces or posing any threat to Western regional designs.

From June 1950, in the immediate aftermath of the outbreak of the Korean War, the U.S. began to openly endorse the French colonial war and provided extensive financial support. Facing a series of humiliating defeats spanning several months in its initial confrontations with North Korean forces, the United States became actively militarily involved in Vietnam, providing extensive logistical and political support to French forces from September 1950. Though the use of military force was not authorized, CIA airline CAT flew support missions for French forces – something long suspected but only confirmed in documents declassified 50 years later. The CIA were involved in airlifting paratroopers, artillery, ammunition and other military materials to support the French War effort.[11] The French forces in Vietnam were also provided with much-needed warships and combat aircraft, and in 1954 U.S. President Eisenhower seriously considered carrying out nuclear strikes against Viet Minh forces to support a besieged French garrison at Dien Bien Phu.[12,13]

The United States remained heavily involved in Vietnam after the French withdrawal, and it was only with U.S. support that the Western aligned state of South Vietnam could unilaterally cancel unifying elections in defiance of the Geneva Accords and remain a separate Western client state. The CIA in particular was involved in assisting South Vietnamese efforts to undermine the Viet Minh in the north and backing crackdowns on popular uprising and guerilla movements among the southern population – as well as collecting vital intelligence on the enemy. Colonel Edward Lansdale, who had directed CIA operations in the Philippines against the popular Huk insurgent forces there and whose psychological warfare team had produced outstanding results, deployed with his team to Vietnam both to train the South Vietnamese in psychological warfare and to conduct covert paramilitary operations.[14] American assistance was key to propping up the southern government, ruled by a small Francophone elite and facing growing internal discontent, against overthrow by Viet Minh aligned insurgent groups. The Military Advisory Group were deployed in the aftermath of the cancellation of the elections, from November 1955, to train the South Vietnamese military. In 1961 400 further U.S. Special Forces were deployed for training purposes. That same year President Kennedy authorized 'a program for covert actions to be carried out by the Central Intelligence Agency which would precede and remain in force after any commitment of U.S. forces to South Vietnam.'[15,16] This program effectively paved the way for a full U.S. military intervention three years later, which was at that point under preparation.

Involvement in Vietnam was on the part of the United States a response to the new 'Yellow Peril which was emerging in the aftermath the Pacific War – both an attempt to maintain subservient governments in the region as well as an attempt to contain China's influence. As the United States' Pentagon Papers stated: 'the February decision to bomb North Vietnam and the July approval of Phase I deployments make sense only if they are in support of a long-run United States policy to contain China.'[17]

Though the United States waged wars throughout Asia to 'contain communism,' the true motive for these military actions was more often to 'contain China' and ensure the region remained in the Western sphere of influence. Anti-communist sentiment among the populations of many leading Western nations however remained a far greater motivator than anti-Chinese sentiment. It was easier to justify a war to save Asians from an 'evil' and 'atheist materialist' ideology than it was to save Asians from falling out of the sphere of influence of the Western Bloc and into that of a major regional power. Indeed at the height of the Cold War, the term 'communist' could be applied to any figure who threatened the interests of the United States government – from nationalist leaders such as Indonesian President Sukarno who had actively fought against communist insurgencies in his country to Martin Luther King and the African American Civil Rights Movement which were accused by American media of being under communist control to undermine the United States from within.

The need to 'contain China' was not due to a fear of China itself specifically, but rather of its independence and its power, which gave it the potential to reduce other Asian nations' dependence on the West by forming close economic, political and military ties. By doing so Asian nations could develop and modernize interdependently and independently of external powers – thus potentially emerging as a major center of power as the West had long feared. As the Pentagon Papers stated:

> China ... looms as a major power threatening to undercut our importance and effectiveness in the world and, more remotely but more menacingly, to organize all of Asia against us. The long-run U.S. policy is based upon an instinctive understanding in our country that the peoples and resources of Asia could effectively be mobilized against us by China or by a Chinese coalition and that the potential weight of such a coalition could throw us on the defensive ... Our ends cannot be achieved and our leadership role cannot be played if some powerful and virulent nation is allowed to organize their part of the world according to a philosophy contrary to ours.[18]

China and Imperial Japan have been the primary forces which have had the potential do to so – both vehemently opposed by the Western Bloc as a result.

Despite having written several letters to President Truman asking for help in obtaining a peaceful independence for his country from the French occupation and modeling Vietnam's Declaration of Independence on that of the United States, Viet Minh leader Ho Chi Minh was labeled with little basis as a 'communist' and the U.S. set itself against him. As an independent nationalist leader of an Asian nation who promised to unify and modernise his nation, which could potentially in turn become a successful model for Asian development under an independent and nationalist leadership, Vietnam under Ho Chi Minh was a threat to the status quo of Western dominance in the region – communist or not.

The initial ideology of the Vietnamese independence movement was influenced far more by the American revolution than the Soviet one, and Ho reportedly had a picture of George Washington and a copy of the United States' declaration of independence on his desk – not a picture of Stalin or a communist manifesto. Reflecting this influence, the opening of Vietnam's 1945 independence declaration is almost identical to that of the United States: 'All men are created equal. They are endowed by their Creator with certain inalienable rights, among these are Life, Liberty and the pursuit of Happiness.' As reported by an officer from the Office of Strategic Services (predecessor of the CIA) Ho had even sought American advice on how to frame Vietnam's independence declaration.[19]

The United States chose to oppose the independent Vietnamese government of the Viet Minh despite the fact that this government was not distinctly communist in its foundation. In this respect Ho Chi Minh was much like Indonesia's Nationalist leader Sukarno, who had said: 'To me, both the [American] Declaration of Independence and the Communist Manifesto contain underlying truths, but the West doesn't permit a middle road.' The Viet Minh had formed as a coalition of nationalist and anti-imperialist parties, its name literally translating to 'League for the Independence of Vietnam.' The driving idea behind Vietnam's struggle was to win national dignity and independence – with communist ideology later being adopted in the Cold War context as a means by which this could be achieved. This being the case, the Vietnamese people were unwilling to surrender their cause, since it was not just a political or economic model that was at stake, but their nation's very independence – an inalienable part of them.

Due to the threat an independent Vietnam posed to Western imperial interests the elections set to reunify North and South Vietnam under the Geneva Accords of July 1954,[20] in which all Vietnamese, northern and southern, would have voted for the future of the country, were prevented from taking place. The United States was instrumental in cancelling the elections in 1955, the year after the French withdrawal, giving its full support to the pro-Western South Vietnamese government which, expecting to lose a national election, cancelled them unilaterally and thereby prevented reunification for the next two decades. This decision would come to cost millions of lives. Both the Americans and the South Vietnamese were certain that should fair elections take place Ho Chi Minh and the Viet Minh would win a landslide victory. Cancelling the elections and preventing reunification was therefore key to avoiding this outcome. U.S. President Eisenhower had himself concluded based on the intelligence available that 'had elections been held as of the time of the fighting, a possible 80 per cent of the population would have voted for the communist Ho Chi Minh as their leader.'[21] The CIA had predicted in their own report: 'if scheduled national elections are held in July 1956 ... the Viet Minh will almost certainly win.'[22] This closely reflected the situation in Korea in 1948, when scheduled nationwide elections were cancelled by the pro-Western south with American approval because U.S. intelligence was near certain that they would produce a victory for the communist northern government and an end to American influence (see following chapter).[23,24]

The South Vietnamese government itself proved to be highly unpopular and repressive, enacting policies which appeared to be a continuation of the practices of the French colonial era. South Vietnamese Prime Minister Ngo Dinh Diem came to power with strong U.S. support in elections which are widely accepted by even American sources to have been heavily rigged.[25] Having been educated in Catholic institutions, Diem's policies reflected those of a religious extremist and strongly discriminated against the country's Buddhist majority in favor of its Francophone Catholic minority. The result was something of a religious dictatorship. While the South Vietnamese government conscripted its citizens to hard corvée labor, Catholics were treated as a privileged class and were de facto exempt from this labor. American Professor Spencer C. Tucker found based on his research that Diem's government had been very heavily biased towards the Catholic elite in many aspects including public service, military promotions, business favors, and allocation of land and tax concessions.[26] Exemplifying this policy Diem had himself told a high ranking army officer: 'Put your Catholic officers in sensitive places. They can be trusted.'[27] The officer turned out to in fact be a Buddhist, but this preferential treatment forced many officers in the military to convert to Catholicism for the sake of their careers.[28] The Roman Catholic Church, by far the largest landowner in the country, was also exempt from the harsh land reforms imposed nationwide which targeted Vietnamese rural communities.[29] State funds were meanwhile used for projects such as the construction of the Catholic universities of Hue and Da Lat – both of which were built specifically to train a new elite with Catholic allegiance. These state universities were placed under the authority of the Vatican to foster an environment they deemed suitable.[30]

Vietnamese Buddhists had had a 'private' status imposed on them under French rule, which meant that they required official permission to conduct religious activities publicly, while Christians were allowed to practice religion freely and publicly. This French policy was maintained under Diem.[31] Diem himself openly dedicated his entire country to the Virgin Mary in 1959.[32] He regularly flew the flag of the Vatican at public events, and it was no secret that this was where his allegiance belonged.[33] Buddhists were forbidden from flying religious flags during Vesak religious celebrations meanwhile, leading to widespread protests. Several Vietnamese Catholic priests were themselves allowed to run private armies, which were known to force conversions and engage in looting and shelling of pagodas – relics of Vietnam's cultural history associated with Buddhism.[34] Protests led by the country's Buddhist leaders against religious discrimination were met with raids by special forces. Holy sites were destroyed and dozens of civilians were killed, with hundreds more wounded and 1,400 monks arrested. The revered statue of Gautama Buddha was also demolished.[35] Government forces were known to pour chemicals over the heads of praying Buddhist protestors, which in one case hospitalized 67 of them. The brutality of the Catholic elite in its repression of the Buddhist majority was so great that even Diem's U.S. allies voiced their disapproval.[36]

As a result of its repressive policies the South Vietnamese government faced a growing popular insurgency, the Viet Cong, which were aligned with the Viet Minh and received extensive support from North Vietnam. Despite the United States' provision of extensive financial and military aid, deployment of special operations forces and training programs for the South Vietnamese military, the strength of the Viet Cong was only growing, while the north was eager to reunify the country and displace the failing southern government. It appeared only a matter of time before the Viet Minh would gain control and the United States would lose a critical client state. While the United States had provided similar assistance to the Chiang Kai-shek's government in China in the 1940s during the civil war as it did to South Vietnam, it was clear in both cases that no amount of aid could save a corrupt and unpopular regime from collapse. The U.S. therefore took action in Vietnam which they had failed to do, and ever since regretted, in China. A full-scale military intervention of several million U.S. personnel was undertaken to save the ailing South Vietnamese state.

Fourteen years after their first military involvement, the United States began its first official participation in Vietnam's war in 1964 by staging a naval incident blamed on North Vietnamese forces in the Gulf of Tonkin. The Vietnamese were accused of provoking aggression based on highly dubious reports, which gave the United States and its allies the pretext needed to escalate the war. This was attested to several members of the United States military after the war had begun, such as Naval Officer John White who stated in 1967: 'I maintain that President Johnson, Secretary McNamara and the Joint Chiefs of Staff gave false information to Congress in their report about U.S. destroyers being attacked in the Gulf of Tonkin.' Captain Herrick of the USS *Maddox*, the destroyer allegedly attacked, himself refuted reports of North Vietnamese provocation.[37] U.S. Congressman Ron Paul, who had been serving in the military at the time of the incident, stated years later regarding its true purpose as a false flag attack to allow the U.S. military to intervene militarily: 'Just look at the Gulf of Tonkin. We staged all that. 68,000 Americans died over this because we got into that war based on a lie.'[38]

The Gulf of Tonkin incident served its purpose in giving the United States a pretext to further intervene in Vietnam. The war would go on for over a decade, during which severe war crimes and atrocities would be widely committed and an estimated 3.8 million Vietnamese people would die – the vast majority of them civilians.[39] As victory continued to elude United States forces in the face of unyielding Vietnamese resistance they resorted to increasingly radical methods of fighting to break the will of the Viet Minh.

The United States largely lacked tangible objectives, and as a result turned to a strategy of attrition. This essentially involved doing as much damage to Vietnamese resistance forces and their supporters as possible – very often translating into indiscriminate attacks on the country's population. The purpose was to kill enough of the enemy – the North Vietnamese, Viet Cong and the civilians on which they relied for support – so that they would be unable to continue the war. This was intended to make fighting a war of resistance against the United States and its allies such a terrible ordeal that the population would cease to support it. This strategy can be summed up in a statement by U.S. Air Force General Curtis LeMay, who replied when asked how to overcome a determined and ruthless adversary: 'if you kill enough of them, they will stop fighting.'[40] LeMay was an advocate of waging a massive and indiscriminate bombing campaign against North Vietnam, similar to that he had directed against Tokyo in March 1945. The influential general had threatened a campaign against the Viet Minh to 'shove them back to the Stone Age with Air power or Naval power,' one which would come to target major population centers.[41] The American campaign thus harshly tested the resolve of the Vietnamese population and its willingness to resist subjugation – a trial withstood due to the fundamental importance of what was in their eyes at stake – the right to sovereignty, national dignity and the independence to determine their country's own future.

My Lai Massacre: A Unique Incident or a Revelation of Common Practice?

On March 16, 1968, U.S. Army soldiers of the 1st Battalion, 20th Infantry Regiment, 11th Brigade of the 23rd Infantry Division moved into the small Vietnamese village of My Lai. Approaching the village the soldiers shot and killed villagers in the rice fields without warning. They went on to kill over 500 Vietnamese civilians who lived there. Men, women, children and infants were all massacred, while many women and young girls were gang raped.[42] The bodies of the dead were then mutilated by the soldiers.[43]

The attack was entirely unprovoked and no shots were fired at the U.S. soldiers. The BBC reported of the incident: 'Soldiers went berserk, gunning down unarmed men, women, children and babies. Families which huddled together for safety in huts or bunkers were shown no mercy. Those who emerged with hands held high were murdered […] Elsewhere in the village, other atrocities were in progress. Women were gang raped; Vietnamese who had bowed to greet the Americans were beaten with fists and tortured, clubbed with rifle butts and stabbed with bayonets. Some victims were mutilated with the signature "C Company" carved into the chest.'[44]

Private First Class Michael Bernhardt recalled the events which occurred at My Lai:

> I walked up and saw these guys doing strange things … Setting fire to the hootches and huts and waiting for people to come out and then shooting them … going into the hootches and shooting them up … gathering people in groups and shooting them … As I walked in you could see piles of people all through the village … all over. They were gathered up into large groups. I saw them shoot an M79 [grenade launcher] into a group of people who were still alive. But it was mostly done with a machine gun. They were shooting women and children just like anybody else. We met no resistance and I only saw three captured weapons. We had no casualties. It was just like any other Vietnamese village – old papa-sans, women and kids. As a matter of fact, I don't remember seeing one military-age male in the entire place, dead or alive.[45]

Larry Colburn, a helicopter gunner who witnessed the event reported: 'These were elders, mothers, children and babies … They come into a town and rape the women, kill the babies, kill everyone … And it wasn't just murdering civilians. They were butchering people. The only thing they didn't do is cook 'em and eat 'em. How do you get that far over the edge?'[46]

What is notable about the conduct of the American military in My Lai was that this particular incident was well publicized in the media – not that such conduct was uncommon. For over a year the event had been well covered up, and it was only later that, due to the testimonies of some honest soldiers, the U.S. military admitted that the events took place. Ron Ridenhour, an American GI in Vietnam, was largely responsible for exposing the massacre to the public. He had collected information about the massacre from a number of witnesses while in Vietnam. Afterwards he sent letters detailing the exact events that occurred, including names and locations, to a number of leading political figures. Despite the media being widely uninterested[47] in portraying the atrocities of their own military, as such reports could easily be written off as communist propaganda and tarnish the credibility of the publisher, Ridenhour's perseverance eventually bore fruit.

Though it took a full year, news of the massacre reached the public outside Vietnam in a way it had not for other such atrocities. Public opinion against the Vietnam War increased significantly internationally as a result of the events in My Lai being better publicized. This gave the United States and particularly the U.S. military a significant public relations problem, as the revelation had exposed the true nature of their conduct towards the Vietnamese people to the world.

The response of the United States military to the massacre was revealing as to its effectiveness in managing public relations. As the event was uniquely well publicized, it was portrayed as a one-off 'freak accident.' The military went on to court martial several soldiers responsible and put the blame solely on them, so as to avoid criticism of the military and war effort as a whole. The blame for the massacre was placed almost on entirely Lieutenant William Calley who had commanded U.S. forces at My Lai, a low-level commander, which did a great deal to protect the image of the United States and its military. Atrocities could, if publicized, be attributed to the actions of a few low-level personnel. Calley and some other soldiers were sentenced, and it was widely believed that the military had carried out justice in response to the public outrage which had ensued when details of the massacre were revealed to the world.

In fact Lieutenant Calley and the soldiers under his command had conducted themselves quite typically of U.S. military personnel in Vietnam, and their punishment was an attempt to scapegoat them after their actions in My Lai were publicized. In doing so, the United States military indicated that the incident was a one-off case of misconduct, thus avoiding the revelation that massacres such as that at My Lai were in fact extremely frequent and the conduct of the soldiers was far from irregular. The conduct of the soldiers who were indicted was common and in fact encouraged by the United States military throughout the war, and My Lai was one of many massacres that was a result of the military's policy.

U.S. Colonel David H. Hackworth commented on the United States' depiction of My Lai as a unique one-off event, stating that massacres such as My Lai were typical of the military's conduct and of the entire war. He said: 'Vietnam was an atrocity from the get-go ... There were hundreds of My Lais. You got your card punched by the numbers of bodies you counted.'[48]

American investigative journalist and historian Nick Turse noted on the scapegoating of Calley by the United States military forced the military leadership to take action against its own soldiers to protect its reputation. Turse wrote:

> Ridenhour's letter, filled with names, locations, and description of the mass killing, soon had Washington buzzing. Looking for a suitably low-level fall guy on whom to hang responsibility, the army settled on Lieutenant William 'Rusty' Calley, who had commanded Charlie Company's 1st Platoon at My Lai and had no shortage of blood on his hands. Conveniently enough, Calley was no West Pointer, but a product of the Officer Candidate School at Fort Benning, which churned out low-level commanders for Vietnam after just months of training; placing the blame entirely on him would avoid sullying the reputation of the army's academy-trained top ranks, thus protecting the public image of the army as a whole. In September, Calley was charged with the murder of 109 'Oriental human beings' and quietly hidden away at Fort Benning.[49]

What all of this indicates was that My Lai was crucially depicted as a one-off atrocity of the United States military committed only by a few. By doing so the wider issue of the conduct of the military would not be brought to light. Had My Lai been exposed as one of many massacres endemic to the United States' military operations in Vietnam, and in the Asia-Pacific in general, then perceptions of the United States military would have been significantly more negative. American public perceptions of their own government and particularly its policies pertaining to intervention in Southeast Asia would also have been affected far more significantly than they already were.

What was perhaps the best indicator that My Lai was far from a freak accident was the very similar massacre that occurred on the same day at My Khe, under an entirely different American unit. This was highly indicative of the fact that such events were so extremely common that two totally unrelated such events occurred in one day – possibly more. The Pentagon notably undertook significant measures to hide the My Khe massacre, as it effectively undermined their portrayal of My Lai as a unique and rare incident. The emergence of My Khe, though it was never well publicized like My Lai, strongly indicates that such conduct, mass killings, rapes and war crimes were endemic to the United States military itself – not to a Lieutenant Calley or a particular unit.

Nick Turse, in his study of American cover-ups of war crimes in Vietnam, also noted how the My Khe massacre effectively undermined the United States' military's attempt to scapegoat the soldiers responsible for My Lai, and proved that such behavior was indeed typical of the conduct of the United States military and indeed occurred more than daily in Vietnam. He wrote:

> The Pentagon was especially dismayed that Peers had chronicled not only the slaughter at My Lai by Charlie Company, 1st Battalion, 20th Infantry, but also the killings carried out on the same day in the nearby village of My Khe by the men of Bravo Company, 4th Battalion, 3rd Infantry. The whole Pentagon strategy centered on portraying My Lai as a one-off aberration, rather than part of a consistent pattern of criminality resulting from policies set at the top. Having two different massacres carried out within hours of each other by two entirely different army united in two separate villages was hardly compatible with that message.[50]

The Pentagon undertook significant efforts to deny responsibility for the massacre at My Khe. It was crucial to maintaining their image to do so. Lieutenant General William Peers, when questioned by reporters about the events at My Khe, sidestepped and avoided the questions. The Pentagon briefers meanwhile simply lied, blaming the massacre on South Vietnamese troops.[51,52,53]

Colonel Henry Tufts, the head of the army criminal investigative command, commented years later about Chief of Staff's handling of the affair and manipulation of the truth that 'He did what he had to do to sort of preserve the system.'[54,55]

My Lai was indicative not only of what was happening throughout Vietnam, but the way the United States, and most often their Western military partners as well, conducted themselves throughout the war in Vietnam – and by extension throughout their wars in the Asia-Pacific region. Similar conduct was observed by the forces of the United States and Australia in

Japan, those of Britain and the Netherlands in Indonesia and a broad coalition of Western powers in Korea, among other cases. Misconduct was far from unique to Vietnam, but what happened in the Vietnamese village was a microcosm of a wider phenomenon present throughout Western military interventions in the country and the wider region. As U.S. General Willoughby responded to the 'fuss' being made about the My Lai massacre: 'In Korea we had My Lais all the time.'[56] He pointed to it being far from an exceptional case to receive the media attention that it did – and in this regard he was entirely correct.

Facilitators of Terror

A key factor influencing the of the conduct of U.S. forces in the Vietnam War, an understanding of which is key to comprehending the true nature of the American intervention, was the drug abuse which had become endemic to the military. The Vietnam War came to be known as the first 'pharmacological war' because, more so than in Korea, prescribed and self-prescribed consumption of psychoactive substances by American military personnel took place on a scale unprecedented in history. This led British philosopher Nick Land to describe the Vietnam War as 'a decisive point of intersection between pharmacology and the technology of violence.'[57]

In 1973, 70 percent of U.S. military personnel in Vietnam used intoxicants. In 1971, 28 percent of personnel in Vietnam took hard drugs, namely heroin. These statistics among others justified the claim that American military personnel in Vietnam were largely drug takers.[58] During a trip to Vietnam Egil Krogh, President Nixon's liaison to the Bureau of Narcotics and Dangerous Drugs, reported: 'Mr. President, you don't have a drug problem in Vietnam; you have a condition. Problems are things we can get right on and solve. Conditions we have to ameliorate as best we can. I don't think we can solve this short of bringing everybody home.'[59] This was highly indicative of the extent to which drug abuse was endemic in the military.

American military personnel were heavily drugged for combat, and this was in part responsible for their aggressive and often sadistic behavior in Vietnam and gross mistreatment of its population. Many of these drugs were prescribed by the military itself, while others were tolerated as necessary supports to allow soldiers to perform in the war and cope with its hardships. Use of drugs notably increased significantly after the Viet Cong launched the Tet Offensive in 1968, which increased the pressure on American soldiers considerably. Drugs were considered an effective means to help soldiers handle such pressures amid flagging morale.[60]

An example of drug use and the way it increased the aggression of American personnel was the consumption of amphetamine. A navy commando said that this drug was 'routinely consumed. They gave you a sense of bravado as well as keeping you awake. Every sight and sound was heightened. You were wired into it all and at times you felt really invulnerable.' Lukasz Kamienski, Associate Professor at the Faculty of International and Political Studies, concluded based on his research of the use of drugs in Vietnam: 'In short, the administration of stimulants by the military contributed to the spread of drug habits that sometimes had tragic consequences, because, as many veterans claimed, next to alertness amphetamine increased aggression. Some remembered that when the effect of speed faded away, they were so irritated that they felt like shooting "children in the streets" ... Amphetamine was to blame for ... unjustified violence against the civilian population.' Among other stimulants reportedly given out 'like candies,' amphetamine was distributed to soldiers by the military on a large scale. A 1971 report by the United States House Select Committee revealed that from 1966 to 1969 the military had used 225 million tablets of these stimulants.[61]

Drugs were not the only facilitator of atrocities carried out against the Vietnamese people. In addition to drugging their soldiers the United States military also took measures to dehumanize the Asian peoples in the eyes of their soldiers, as they had done in the Philippines, Japan and Korea beforehand. The Viet Cong were likened to a disease spreading through the country. This too was largely responsible for the soldiers' sadistic behavior and for the ease with which they killed, tortured and otherwise mistreated the Vietnamese, whether civilians, Viet Cong, children or infants. The attitude towards Asian peoples as subhumans is best exemplified by the 'Mere Gook Rule.' This was a code of conduct in the American military to dehumanize Vietnamese people and so make it easier for U.S. military personnel to target them. In this way killings of 'mere Gooks' could be justified – it's only a 'mere Gook' you're killing after all. American soldiers were told when stationed in Vietnam, contrary to all rules of war, 'Gooks are gooks [...] The rule in Viet-Nam was the M.G.R – the "mere gook rule": that it was no crime to kill or torture or rob or maim a Vietnamese because he was a mere gook.'[62] Telford Taylor, renowned American lawyer specializing in war crimes, commented on the American's attitude to the Vietnamese as an Asian race and the resulting war crimes: 'The trouble is no one sees the Vietnamese people. They're not people. Therefore it doesn't matter what you do to them.'[63]

Drugged, and often seemingly insane,[64] soldiers who saw their enemies as subhumans due to the extensive dehumanization that was encouraged by the military, also had a third major reason for committing atrocities against the Vietnamese, specifically for massacring Vietnamese people in large numbers. This was the U.S. military's encouraging and incentivizing of soldiers to 'rack up' the highest body counts as possible, largely due to a lack of tangible objectives in the campaign. This was attested to by Colonel David Hackworth who stated: 'You got your card punched by the numbers of bodies you counted.'[65] Body counts included Vietnamese civilians suspected of aiding the Viet Cong forces, which included essentially all Vietnamese people living in the north, near combat zones or anywhere the Viet Cong were thought to be operating. The BBC reported:

> Unable to deal with an enemy that dictated the time and place of combat, U.S. forces took to destroying whatever they could manage. If the Americans could kill more enemies – known as Viet Cong or VC – than the Vietnamese could replace, the thinking went, they would naturally give up the fight. To motivate troops to aim for a high body count, competitions were held between units to see who could kill the most. Rewards for the highest tally, displayed on 'kill boards' included days off or an extra case of beer. Their commanders meanwhile stood to win rapid promotion. Very quickly the phrase – 'If it's dead and Vietnamese, it's VC' – became a defining dictum of the war and civilian corpses were regularly tallied as slain enemies or Viet Cong. Civilians, including women and children, were killed for running from soldiers or helicopter gunships that had fired warning shots, or being in a village suspected of sheltering Viet Cong.[66]

Based on all of these factors, U.S. military personnel in Vietnam were set up by their government and military to fight an extremely brutal war and commit war crimes. The majority of American soldiers were very young men, often between 18 and 20, and they were easily influenced by the culture of their country's military to commit atrocities. A combination of rewards for maximum casualties, drugs which influenced their minds, a gross lack of accountability for crimes against civilians, and a perception of the enemy as being less than human were a terrible and effective combination which facilitated this. The Vietnamese people would suffer the consequences.

Recalling his interview with a Vietnam War veteran, Nick Turse revealed much about the psychology of American soldiers to the Vietnamese during the war. The interview strongly indicates that soldiers' behavior was often entirely out of character, and this poor conduct was influenced by the military itself. In this way men were taught to hate the Vietnamese people as a subhuman Asian race, and thereby act in an inhuman way themselves. Turse recalled:

> He [a Vietnam war veteran] talked about how they were going through a village and burning it down, which was standard operating procedure. And in the midst of this, this woman runs up and grabs this GI by the sleeve, and is tugging at him and yelling at him – obviously because her home is being burned down, all her possessions are going up in flames. And she's angry, scared, upset. And he said this GI just pushed her off, and then took his rifle and hit her squarely in the nose with the butt. And he said her face just erupted in blood. She was screaming. And the GI just turned around and walked away laughing. And he paused a second and said, 'Do you know that GI was me?' He had such a tough time figuring out how he could have done it. All these years later. At the time he didn't think anything of it, and in the years since, he couldn't help but think of it on a constant basis. And it really haunted him. And I had the same problem trying to match up the man that I was talking to with his 19-year-old self. He told me about how the training that he went through dehumanized the Vietnamese to the point where they didn't think of them as human. They thought of them as – they had a whole bunch of slurs that were used: dinks, slopes, slants, gooks. And he talked about how 'I didn't become exactly like a robot but it was like that.' You're trained to kill, you chant 'Kill, kill kill.' It psychologically readies you for this.[67]

Turse further testified to this based on his research and how it led to mass killings of Vietnamese people:

> The idea is that the Vietnamese weren't real people. They were sub-humans. Mere gooks who could be abused or even killed at will. And this is something that was inculcated in troops from the earliest days of training. I talked to a lot of veterans

> who told me that as soon as they arrived at boot camp, they were told you never call them *Vietnamese*. You call them gooks, dinks, slants, slopes. Anything to take away their humanity. Anything to make it easier to kill them. They were told by their superiors that all Vietnamese were likely the enemy. That children might carry grenades, women were probably the wives or girlfriends of guerillas, and they were probably making booby traps. And even if there were rules of engagement on paper, or little cards handed out saying to treat the Vietnamese properly, the message that they were really given was that it was a lot safer to shoot first because no one was going to ask questions later [...]

> The troops in the field, they were pressed for bodies [due to the demand for body counts]. Their commanders were leaning on them heavily. You were told to produce Vietnamese bodies, and if you didn't you were going to stay out in the field longer. They learned pretty quickly that the command wasn't discerning about what bodies were turned in, that just about any Vietnamese bodies would do. This pushed American troops toward at least calling in all Vietnamese who were killed as enemies, and also to the killing of detainees and prisoners and civilians, and calling them in as enemy dead. This coupled with the much higher level of strategic thinking like the use of 'free fire zones,' which was basically a legal fiction that the U.S. came up with to open wide swaths of the countryside to unrestrained bombing and artillery shelling. This caused tremendous amounts of death and destruction in the countryside. And it opened it up to all this heavy firepower and made it inevitable that large numbers of civilians would be killed or wounded.[68]

American soldiers, conditioned to behave as they did, went on to commit further sadistic acts beyond killings. An investigation found for example that not only was it common for civilian prisoners to be slaughtered, but also tortured. This was done using fists, sticks, bats, water and electric shocks.[69] Rape of Vietnamese women and children was highly common, and was carried out sadistically – symbolizing the assertion of dominance over the Vietnamese race where military victory remained elusive. Women were often raped using bottles and rifles.[70] An example of such conduct and of the prevalent attitudes among U.S. personnel was recalled by former GI John Ketwig, who witnessed a 'ceremony,' what he referred to as a 'revenge type of thing: hate against the Vietnamese, the "gooks"', when three young Vietnamese women were captured. He recalled: 'everybody circled around and they tortured these women with lit cigarettes [...] the one girl, they held her down and put the hose from the fire truck between her legs and turned on the water and exploded her. And the explosion of body fluids splashed across our faces.'[71]

Rape was such a common occurrence that it was considered standard procedure in Vietnam. Many U.S. personnel recalled being told by instructors from the Marine Corps: 'we could rape the women,' 'spread them open' and 'drive pointed sticks or bayonets into their vaginas.' As a squad leader in the 34d platoon attested: 'That's an everyday affair ... you can nail just about everybody on that – at least once.' While the military officially disapproved of such practices, in practice they turned a blind eye to it, accepting it as necessary for morale and effective performance in combat. Rape and threat of rape were widely used strategically as well as recreationally – an effective way of 'enforcing submission' as well as obtaining information from both prisoners and civilians.[72,73]

It is clear that American soldiers' atrocities were influenced significantly by the conditioning they had. The crimes and slaughter committed against the Vietnamese people was facilitated largely by the military and government policy. This encouraged perceptions of the Vietnamese, including civilians, as 'mere gooks,' allowed a large proportion of the military to become drug abusers and actively encouraged and incentivized soldiers to rack up high body counts – with rewards rather than punishments for causing civilian deaths. Attitudes to rape meanwhile ranged from normalization to active encouragement. This had a great deal in common with the conditioning of soldiers of Western nations involved in the wars against Japan and Korea beforehand.

Chemical Weapons and the Lingering 'Orange Pain'

The extensive use of chemical weapons in the Vietnam War by U.S. forces will continue to scar the country for generations. Though official American military involvement in Vietnam began only in 1964, the United States had been using chemical weapons in the country since 1962.[74] During the war the U.S. military sprayed around 75 million liters of chemical herbicides and defoliants under the area defoliation program, Operation Ranch Hand. This strategy was based on the successful British defoliation of Malaysia's forests to combat independence fighters there, and its implementation in Vietnam destroyed over 30 million acres of farmland and forest (an area larger than the whole of North Korea or three times the area of Switzerland).[75] It was part of the United States' strategy of Forced Draft Urbanization, which entailed the destruction of the livelihoods of rural population centers by destroying their environment with chemical defoliants – thereby leaving them unable to provide for themselves. This would in turn force the country's rural population to move to cities under the control of the United States, and so deprive independence fighters of their support base.[76,77] The strategy mirrored the successful employment of concentration camps and the scorched earth policy in the Philippines, which in much the same way sought to destroy the livelihoods of the rural population and concentrate them in more densely populated and better supervised areas to strip resistance fighters of their support.

Operation Ranch Hand was both extensive and devastating, leaving concentrations of chemicals in soil and water hundreds of times greater than those considered safe in several parts of the country.[78] By 1971, 12 percent of South Vietnam had a concentration of defoliating chemicals at 13 times the concentration recommended by the U.S. Department of Agriculture. Ten million hectares of agricultural land were destroyed.[79] The purpose was destruction of the livelihoods of the Vietnamese rural population. A report to the U.S. Congress in 1965 regarding the spraying of chemicals in Vietnam stated: 'crop destruction is understood to be the more important purpose ... but the emphasis is usually given to the jungle defoliation in public mention of the program.'[80]

The targeting of crops was widely supported by many elements within the United States. The RAND Corporation think tank advocated the targeting of crops in Vietnam, stating in a 1967 memorandum: 'the fact that the VC obtain most of their food from the neutral rural population dictates the destruction of civilian crops ... if they [the VC] are to be hampered by the crop destruction program, it will be necessary to destroy large portions of the rural economy – probably 50% or more.' Targeting of the Vietnamese people's crops, considering the prevalence of subsistence farming, invariably had a devastating effect on the population. The strategy is highly indicative of the United States' perception of Vietnam and disregard for the wellbeing of a supposedly allied population. Soldiers destroying crops were told that it was because they were feeding the enemy, and this was the consistently given reason for doing so. As crops were targeted indiscriminately, and the Viet Cong combatants were a small minority among those affected, it was the Vietnamese civilians who bore the brunt of the targeting of their livelihoods. Was the entire Vietnamese rural population perceived as 'the enemy'?

Destruction of crops led to malnourishment and starvation throughout targeted areas. In Quang Ngai province 85 percent of arable land was scheduled for destruction in 1970 alone, and this was not an exceptional case. This drove people to desperation, and as in Korea before, into the hands of the American military. Villages were forced to migrate to cities, as per the American strategy of Forced Draft Urbanization. From 1958 to 1971 the urban population increased from 2.8 million to 8 million as a result, with many living in poverty and 1.5 million living in slums. This migration was not done willingly, but rather out of desperation in response to the United States' deliberate targeting of rural peoples' livelihoods.[81]

Vietnamese families forced into cities were very often starving and had no ways of providing for themselves. As a result many women and young girls were forced by circumstances to sell their bodies to American soldiers for sex – with little choice but to sell themselves to the very same military that had destroyed their livelihoods. As soldiers were very often drug abusers and viewed the Vietnamese as subhumans,[82] this led to widespread and severe abuses of Vietnamese women not only in the villages where they were raped, but in the camps of the U.S. military where they were forced to work. As American historian Nick Turse reported regarding the forced sexual relations between Americans and Vietnamese women: 'I felt I didn't have the language to describe exactly what I found in the cases, because rape or even gang rape didn't seem to convey the level of sexual sadism.'[83]

The Vietnam War not only forced Vietnamese women to resort to prostitution, but also led to the growth of a large sex trade catering to foreigners in neighboring Thailand which remains prominent until today.[84] American military personnel in Thailand had a high demand for comfort women, and as a result the number of prostitutes in Thailand grew from 20,000 to between 500,000 and 700,000 during the war. As a result 6.2–8.7 percent of Thai women aged between 15 and 34 were working as prostitutes by the end of the Vietnam War.[85] The U.S. military presence and their practice of buying Thai women introduced a new word into the Thai language, *mia chao* meaning 'rented wife.'[86] The Thai government, itself a close partner of the United States at the time, was contracted to provide 'rest and relaxation' for the American military. The seat of ancient Buddhist civilization came to be known as 'America's Brothel,' a term coined by an American senator.[87]

When the war ended these women continued to service sex tourists, a practice which continues to this day and is a direct result of the Vietnam War. As Bradley R. Simpson, American Professor of History and Asian studies, noted: 'The U.S. presence profoundly affected Thai society, fueling a massive temporary service economy geared to meeting the economic and sexual needs of American troops, as well as an explosion in the regional trafficking of drugs and women's bodies that long outlasted the war.'[88,89] The Vietnam War had been injecting $16 million per year into the then tiny Thai economy, and GI spending accounted for 40 percent of the country's export earnings. As a result, sex tourism was resorted to as a replacement for this major earner of foreign currency, and would remain the largest source of foreign exchange.[90]

The United States' military's need for comfort women has been extremely consistent. As American scholar Cynthia Enloe noted regarding the U.S. military presence in Asia and its commitments to its regional client states: 'None of these institutions – multilateral alliances, bilateral alliances, foreign military assistance programs – can achieve their militarizing objectives without controlling women for the sake of militarizing men.'[91] In the Vietnam War this was again the case, and it had severe repercussions for the Vietnamese and Thai societies. Okinawa, the Japanese territory that remained under American military governance until 1972, was similarly affected as high numbers of American personnel deployed in Vietnam were sent there for 'rest and recreation' and it remained a hub of American supplies for the war.

As part of the U.S. Forced Draft Urbanization program, one of the defoliants used to destroy crops was Agent Orange. This was a combination of various chemicals and contaminated with TCDD

(2,3,7,8-Tetrachlorodibenzo-p-dioxin), the most poisonous form of dioxin which has been proven to cause cancer among other serious illnesses. It remains one of the most toxic chemicals ever used on such a scale in populated areas. The first precedent for the use of Agent Orange was set by British Imperial forces in Malaysia, which had used it against independence fighters who had sought an end to British rule – though it was used on a far smaller scale.[92] Approximately 11 million gallons of Agent Orange were poured over Vietnam in a ten-year period. The United States military has consistently denied that TCDD and other chemicals used have effects on humans. This denial has continued despite overwhelming evidence, and despite offering its own war veterans compensation for a number of diseases they suffered when handling dioxin.[93]

Several investigations launched have all reached the same conclusion regarding the effects of Agent Orange on humans. One research team from Canada studied levels of dioxin in an area that had been targeted by the United States decades later. They concluded: 'We should not think of this as a historical problem. This is a present-day contamination issue. The dioxins that are present are entering the food chain today, and also being taken up by the people living in the area today.' The impacts persist in contaminated land itself, and pose a significant danger to the Vietnamese people. As the United States sprayed 10 percent of the country, and particularly targeted farmland, much of the land contaminated remains inhabited today.[94]

Vietnamese doctor Nguyen Viet Nhan, based on his investigation into the impacts of American chemical weapons in Vietnam, alleges that in areas where Agent Orange was used children suffer from multiple serious health issues. Nhan compared the health of children in an area which had been sprayed with an area that had not. He found that in areas that had been sprayed children were more than three times as likely to have cleft palates, more than three times as likely to suffer from mental retardation, more than three times as likely to have extra fingers or toes and nearly eight times as likely to suffer hernias.[95] The legacy of the war continues to strain the country's health services, imposing a significant and continuing burden on Vietnam.

Dr James R. Clay, former senior scientist at the Chemical Weapons Branch of the Air Force Armament Development Lab in Florida, attested to the fact that the United States were knowingly using defoliants which would poison the Vietnamese population. He stated: 'When we initiated the herbicide program in the 1960s, we were aware of the potential for damage due to dioxin contamination [...] We were even aware that the military formulation had a higher dioxin concentration than the civilian version due to the lower cost and speed of manufacture. However, because the material was to be used on the enemy, none of us were overly concerned.'[96] The 'enemy' referred to was the rural population of Vietnam.

The United States had been challenged by United Nations resolutions due to the war crimes it committed by illegally using chemical weapons. While these did not seek to punish the United States in any way, General Assembly Resolution 2162 B and 2603 did indicate that conduct of the U.S. was illegal.[97] The U.S. denied these allegations and refuted the charges on the basis that chemicals targeted the environment rather that the population. Ultimately due to the considerable influence of the United States in the organization, it was highly unlikely that a resolution could force a change in policy.

Chemicals such as dioxin used by the U.S. military caused considerable environmental contamination, and its entry into food chains caused further adverse effects on the environment and the population. It can cause serious skin diseases and a number of cancers. Dioxin levels have been found to persist throughout the environment, causing severe adverse effects. It has been found in high levels in the breast milk of Vietnamese women. It has also severely impacted the country's wildlife, and areas of the country which were targeted have a far lower diversity of birds and mammals than those which were not.[98]

Perhaps the most serious effect of the chemicals sprayed over Vietnam's countryside however is the number of severe genetic diseases they cause. 4.8 million Vietnamese were exposed to Agent Orange, while 3 million of these suffer illnesses as a result according to the Vietnamese Red Cross.[99,100] Those who suffer from exposure to the chemical are said to suffer from the 'orange pain,' an affliction which causes severe genetic mutations which are passed down several generations by those originally exposed to the chemical. Several claims put this figure far higher. Nguyen Thi Phuong Tan, director of a rehabilitation center for children with chemical weapons induced genetic abnormalities, stated that 5 million Vietnamese 'have incurable chronic diseases due to Agent Orange. They can't lead normal lives or find jobs [...] When, after the war, people started having kids with abnormalities, they realized what "orange pain" means [...] If the poison gets into a person's body, it stays there forever. People who have been affected by the poison have developed cancer and diabetes. They also suffer from brain cell degeneration, leading to muscular dystrophy and mental problems. These conditions stem from gene mutations which can be passed on for generations.'[101] The government has as a result been forced to set up special schools, known as 'peace villages,' for all the children born with severe birth defects.

Second and third generations of Vietnamese continue to be born with genetic deformities due to their parents or grandparents' exposure to American chemical weapons. A former Vietnamese independence fighter, Nguen Than, recounted in 2014 the war's lasting impacts on the population: 'The Americans tried to frighten us. We prayed the bombs would avoid us as we ourselves couldn't avoid them. I hated them with all my heart and passed this hatred onto my child. He hates them with all his heart, too. They completely destroyed this province. This area was poisoned but we didn't know it. We just went on with our lives. We only realized when we started having kids. Then we hated them more. What's there to talk about now?' Than's son was born deformed and suffers from disabilities which have affected him his whole life.[102]

Due to the indiscriminate nature of chemical attacks by U.S. forces and their extremely widespread use, a number of American personnel were also exposed to dioxin. The U.S. Veterans Administration lists prostate cancer, respiratory cancers, multiple myeloma, diabetes mellitus Type 2, B-cell lymphomas, soft-tissue sarcoma, chloracne, porphyria, cutanea tarda, peripheral neuropathy and spina bifida as being highly common in the children of veterans exposed to dioxin poison. These same diseases are highly common in Vietnamese children, though they are not acknowledged by the United States in the case of the Vietnamese, despite them having been the primary targets of the defoliants.[103]

Mike Hastie, former U.S. Army medic in Vietnam who has since then studied the effects of chemical weapons used by the United States, commented:

> The spraying of 70 million liters of Agent Orange on the Vietnamese people by the United States Government, is one of the worst war crimes ever committed in modern warfare. It is the war crime that is born again with every new generation. Children die from cancer, they are born without arms and legs, they are born with twisted bodies, mental illness, or no eyes, to name a few birth defects. Their parents and society have an enormous burden to try and make their lives as meaningful as possible. The U.S. Government and the American people share no responsibility in humanitarian justice. Whenever national shame is at stake, the truth is against the law …
>
> What the United States Government did in Vietnam is beyond the human mind to comprehend. How can you possibly grasp the great suffering the Vietnamese people went through in a barbaric war that lasted 10,000 days. Maybe you could just pick one day and multiply it by 10,000. The Vietnamese people defeated the most powerful military force the world has ever seen, because they were willing to lose everything … All you have to look at is the millions of civilians who sacrificed their lives for the cause of independence. The United States could have never won the war in Vietnam, because the vast majority of the civilian population living in what was then South Vietnam, never supported the puppet governments the U.S. put in power. For the Vietnamese, the United States was just another foreign invader trying to conquer their homeland.[104]

Chemical weapons were not the only lasting legacy of the Vietnam War which continue to harm its people today. During the war 15 million tons of explosive ordinance were dropped on Vietnam from the air. The Pentagon estimates around 10 percent did not explode. This ordinance remains a threat to the Vietnamese throughout the country, a threat which persists until today. Over 100,000 Vietnamese people have been injured by unexploded ordinance since the war ended. Vietnam war veteran Chuck Searcy commented in an interview in 2014 that based on the continuing effects of the war on the Vietnamese people and the weapons used by the United States: 'For America the war ended in 1975. For the Vietnamese the war has still not ended.'[105] During the United States' bombing campaign against neighboring Laos and Cambodia to prevent supplies from reaching Vietnam along the 'Ho Chi Minh trail,' Secretary of State Henry Kissinger had ordered the U.S. Air Force to target the population indiscriminately using all assets at its disposal – 'anything that flies on anything that moves.'[106] The result was the dropping of a further 5 million tons of munitions, killing hundreds of thousands in both countries and leaving thousands of unexploded shells which continue to endanger their populations until today.[107]

As was the case in Korea, the war left its scars of trauma on the population – scars which will continue to affect the population well into the future. Millions of Vietnamese still suffer from serious physical injuries during the war, as well as mental scars. Many veterans suffer from undiagnosed mental disorders and cannot access therapy or treatment. One veteran interviewed, Le Van Nam, suffers in a way typical to many survivors of the war. A 2013 report titled '*The Mental Scars of Vietnam's War Veterans*' portrayed the continuing ordeal faced by many of Vietnam's veterans, stating:

> Le Van Nam still sees the soldiers who died while fighting alongside him in the 1960s. Most nights he lies awake in bed, gripped by visions of his fallen comrades beckoning him to join them in heaven. He cries out, trembling with fear, until his wife wakes him and calms him down. Nam, who fought for the North Vietnamese army, was partially paralyzed after a mortar pierced his skull during a 1969 battle. The 76-year-old now has no function in his left arm or leg. And about once a month, he has a panic attack that requires hospitalization in the mental ward of a local hospital. His doctors typically give him an anticonvulsant sedative that helps break his mood.[108]

Denied reparations and under a decades long U.S. embargo following the war's end, Vietnam would struggle to provide those affected by the war with the care they needed.

In 1975 the war finally came to an end with a victory for the Viet Minh as North Vietnamese forces captured Saigon, renaming it Ho Chi Minh City. All Western military personnel – French, American, Australian and New Zealander – were forced to withdraw along with their regional military partners from Thailand, the Philippines and South Korea. The official end of a war however would not mean the Vietnamese people were free to know peace. The scars left by the Vietnam War continue to have profound impacts on the country, much as they do in neighbouring Laos and Cambodia to which the United States extended its military and bombing campaigns. The U.S. bombing campaign against Vietnamese population centers was so severe as to be criticized even by American allies. The extent of the attacks was compared by Swedish Prime Minister Olof Palme to the Nazi German genocide against the Jewish people, while media in West Germany noted that 'even allies must call this a crime against humanity.'[109]

While the war is considered a defeat for the United States, it is notable that its most crucial objectives in Vietnam were achieved. The threat of

Vietnam emerging as a vibrant independent Asian nationalist power under Ho Chi Minh effectively died during the war. Not only was the country forced into a reliance on the Soviet Union by American and French interventions, but its population and environment were devastated beyond recovery. The gene pool for generations remains poisoned, something which exerts serious costs on the state. Those who experienced the war continue to suffer from trauma, which research has shown can potentially continue to seriously affect future generations.[110] The land itself is tainted as well, not only with the countless American shells which continue to kill Vietnamese children decades later, but also with the poisoned earth and water which seriously impedes the lives of the population today. With these handicaps and the weariness of war, and having been dragged into the Cold War which would further take its toll on the country, Vietnam could never rise to fulfill its potential as it could have had France, the United States and their partners not intervened as they did to undermine its drive towards independence three decades prior. The United States may have failed to preserve their client state in South Vietnam, but in achieving their primary and most crucial objective of preventing Vietnam's emergence as a strong and independent Asian nation, a potential model to others across the region, they succeeded. The Viet Minh independence movement could not be crushed, but the nation as a whole could be crippled. When the nation, its people's minds, their health and the country's environment, will ever fully recover is yet to be seen – but given the extent of the damage it is set to be a very long recovery.

Notes

1 Solis, G. D., *Son Thang. An American War Crime*, New York Bantam Books, 1997, (p. 115).
2 Martin Luther King, Jr., Speech at Riverside Church, April 4, 1967.
3 Ngô, Vĩnh Long, *Before the Revolution: The Vietnamese Peasants under the French*, Cambridge, MA, The MIT Press, 1973, (pp. 73–74).
4 Cumings, Bruce, *Parallax Visions: Making Sense of American-East Asian Relations*, Chapel Hill, NC, Duke University Press, 2002 (pp. 83–86).

5 Anderson, Benedict, *Imagined Communities: Reflections on the Origin and Spread of Nationalism*, New York, Verso, 1991 (p. 126).

6 Pears, Pamela A., *Remnants of Empire in Algeria and Vietnam: Women, Words and War*, Lanham, MD, Lexington Books, 2006 (p. 18).

7 Frey, Marc, and Pruessen Ronald W., *The Transformation of Southeast Asia: International Perspectives on Decolonization*, Abingdon, Routledge, 2003 (p. 11).

8 Goscha, Christopher E., *Belated Asian Allies: The Technical and Military Contributions of Japanese Deserters*, in Young, Marilyn B., and Buzzanco, Robert A., *A Companion to the Vietnam War*, Hoboken, Wiley-Blackwell, 2002 (pp. 46–55).

9 Igawa, Sei, *Japan-Vietnam relations were passed on the performance of Japanese Volunteers in the Vietnam Independence War*, Tokyo Foundation, October 10, 2005.

10 Dalloz, Jacquez, *La Guerre d'Indochine 1945–1954*, Paris, Seuil, 1987 (pp. 129–130).

11 *U.S. Pilots Honored For Indochina Service*, Embassy of France in the U.S., February 24, 2005.

12 Whitfield, Stephen J., *The Culture of the Cold War*, Baltimore, MD, The Johns Hopkins University Press, 1996 (p. 6–7).

13 Marder, Murrey, 'When Ike Was Asked to Nuke Vietnam,' *Washington Post*, August 22, 1982.

14 'Document 95, Lansdale Team's Report on Covert Saigon Mission in 1954 and 1955,' *The Pentagon Papers, Gravel Edition*, Volume 1 (pp. 573–583).

15 Herring, George C., *America's Longest War: The United States and Vietnam, 1950–1975*, Philadelphia, PA, Temple University Press, 1986 (pp. 80–81).

16 Ahern, Thomas L., Jr., *CIA and Rural Pacification in South Vietnam*, Center for the Study of Intelligence, NSA Archive.

17 Conrad Gibbons, William, *The U.S. Government and the Vietnam War: Executive and Legislative Roles and Relationships, Part IV: July 1965–January 1968*, Princeton, NJ, Princeton University Press, 1995 (p. 84).

18 Ibid. (p. 84).

19 Blum, William, *Killing Hope: U.S. Military and C.I.A. Interventions Since World War II*, London, Zed Books, 2003 (p. 123).

20 Geneva Accords, Agreement on the Cessation of Hostilities in Vietnam, July 20, 1954.

21 Eisenhower, Dwight, *Mandate for Change, 1953–1956; The White House Years*, New York, Doubleday, 1963 (p. 372).

22 Kolko, Gabriel, *Vietnam: Anatomy of a War, 1940–1975*, New York, HarperCollins, 1987 (p. 85).

23 Hanley, Charles J., and Choe, Sang Hun and Mendoza, Martha, *The Bridge at No Gun Ri: A Hidden Nightmare from the Korean War*, New York, Henry Holt and Company, 2002 (p. 170).

24 Weathersby, Kathryn, '"Should We Fear This?" Stalin and the Danger of War with America,' Cold War International History Project: Working Paper No. 39, 2002.

25 Karnow, Stanley, *Vietnam: A History*, New York, Penguin, 1997 (pp. 223–224).

26 Tucker, Spencer C., *Encyclopedia of the Vietnam War: A Political, Social and Military History*, Oxford, Oxford University Press, 2000 (p. 291).

27 Gettleman, Marvin E., *Vietnam: History, documents and opinions on a major world crisis*, Robbinsdale, MN, Fawcett, 1966 (pp. 280–282).

28 'South Vietnam: Whose funeral pyre?' *The New Republic*, June 29, 1963 (p. 9).

29 Buttinger, Joseph, *Vietnam: A Dragon Embattled*, Santa Barbara, CA, Praeger, 1967 (p. 993).

30 Halberstam, David, 'Diệm and the Buddhists,' *New York Times*, June 17, 1963.

31 Karnow, Stanley, *Vietnam: A History*, New York, Penguin, 1997 (p. 294).

32 Jacobs, Seth, *Cold War Mandarin: Ngo Dinh Diem and the Origins of America's War in Vietnam, 1950–1963*, Lanham, MD, Rowman and Littlefield, 2006 (p. 91).

33 'Diệm's other crusade,' *The New Republic*, June 22, 1963 (p. 5–6).

34 Fall, Bernard B., *The Two Viet-Nams*, Santa Barbara, CA, Praeger, 1963 (p. 199).

35 Jacobs, Seth, *Cold War Mandarin: Ngo Dinh Diem and the Origins of America's War in Vietnam, 1950–1963*, Lanham, MD, Rowman and Littlefield, 2006 (pp. 147–154).

36 Ibid. (p. 100).

37 Burham, Robert, 'False Flags, Covert Operations and Propaganda,' *lulu.com*, 2014 (p. 86).

38 Paul, Ronald, and McAdams, Daniel, *U.S. Practices 'Taking Out' Kim Jong Un – What Will Be the Consequences*, Ron Paul Institute for Peace and Prosperity, Ron Paul Liberty Report, March 14, 2017.

39 Rummel, Rudolph Joseph, *Statistics of Democide*, University of Hawaii, 1997, (Table 6.1A 'Vietnam Democide: Estimates, Sources, and Calculations').

40 Fujimoto, Masaru, 'The Executioner of Tokyo,' *The Japan Times*, March 13, 2005.

41 Kozak, Warren, *LeMay: The Life War Wars of General Curtis LeMay*, Washington, DC, Regnery Publishing, 2009 (p. 341).

42 Brownmiller, Susan, *Against Our Will: Men, Women and Rape*, London, Simon & Schuster, 1975 (pp. 103–105).

43 'Murder in the name of war – My Lai,' *BBC*, July 20, 1998.

44 Ibid.

45 Hersh, Seymour M., 'Eyewitness accounts of the My Lai massacre; story by Seymour Hersh,' *The Plain Dealer*, November 20, 1969.

46 Kuznick, Peter, and Stone, Oliver, *The Untold History of the United States*, London, Elbury Press, 2012 (p. 368).

47 Turse, Nick, *Kill Everything That Moves: The Real American War in Vietnam*, London, Picador, 2014 (p. 226).
48 Kifner, John, 'Report on Brutal Vietnam Campaign Stirs Memories,' *New York Times*, December 28, 2003.
49 Turse, Nick, *Kill Everything That Moves: The Real American War in Vietnam*, London, Picador, 2014 (p. 226).
50 Ibid. (p. 229–230).
51 United Press, 'The Army's My Lai Report Is Released,' *San Francisco Chronicle*, November 14, 1974.'
52 Bilton, Michael, and Sim, Kevin, *Four Hours in My Lai*, New York, Penguin, 1996 (pp. 308–309).
53 Beecher, William, 'Songmy Data Lag Laid to 2 Groups,' *New York Times*, March 19, 1970.
54 Bilton, Michael, and Sim, Kevin, *Four Hours in My Lai*, New York, Penguin, 1996 (p. 309).
55 Tufts, Henry, 'Transcript of Interview With Dwight Oland,' University of Michigan, December 11, 1995 (p. 36, 38).
56 Deane, Hugh, *The Korean War, 1945–1953*, San Francisco, CA, China Books & Periodicals, 1999 (p. 143).
57 Kamienski, Lukasz, 'The Drugs That Built a Super Soldier,' *The Atlantic*, April 8, 2016.
58 Kamienski, Lukasz, *Shooting Up; A History of Drugs in Warfare*, London, C. Hurst & Co. Publishers Ltd, 2016 (p. 188).
59 Ibid. (p. 189).
60 Ibid. (p. 189).
61 Ibid. (pp. 189–190).
62 Gabrial Mestrovic, Sejepan, *Rules of Engagement?: A Social Anatomy of an American War Crime – Operation Iron Triangle, Iraq*, New York, Algora Publishing, 2008 (p. 159).
63 Taylor, Telford, *Nuremberg and Vietnam*, New York, Quadrangle Books, 1970 (p. 103).
64 Marlantes, Karl, *What It Is Like To Go To War*, London, Corvus, 2012.
65 Kifner, John, 'Report on Brutal Vietnam Campaign Stirs Memories,' *New York Times* December 28, 2003.
66 'Was My Lai just one of many massacres in Vietnam War?,' *BBC*, August 28, 2014.
67 Denvir, Daniel, 'The Secret History of the Vietnam War' (Interview with Nick Turse), *Vice News*, April 17, 2015.
68 Ibid.

69 Turse, Nick, and Nelson, Deborah, 'Civilian Killings Went Unpunished,' *Los Angeles Times* August 6, 2006.
70 Denvir, Daniel, 'The Secret History of the Vietnam War' (Interview with Nick Turse), *Vice News*, April 17, 2015.
71 Kendall, Bridget, *The Cold War; A New Oral History of Life Between East and West*, London, BBC Books, 2017 (p. 305).
72 Meger, Sarah, *Rape Loot Pillage: The Political Economy of Sexual Violence in Armed Conflict*, Oxford, Oxford University Press, 2016 (pp. 60–61).
73 Askin, Kelley Dawn, *War Crimes Against Women: Prosecution in International War Crimes Tribunals*, The Hague, Kluwar Law International, 1997 (p. 50).
74 Buckingham, William A., Jr., *Operation Ranch Hand: The Air Force and Herbicides in Southeast Asia 1961–1971*, Scotts Valley, CA, CreateSpace Independent Publishing Platform, 1982 (Chapter 5).
75 McMahon, Robert J., and Simpson, Bradley R., *The Cold War in the Third World*, Oxford, Oxford University Press, 2013 (p. 54).
76 Stellman, Jeanne, et al., 'The extent and patterns of usage of Agent Orange and other Herbicides in Vietnam,' *Nature*, April 17, 2003.
77 Kolko, Gabriel, *Anatomy of a War: Vietnam, the United States, and the Modern Historical Experience*, New York, Pantheon, 1985 (pp. 144–145).
78 Fawthrop, Tom, 'Vietnam's war against Agent Orange,' *BBC News*, June 14, 2004.
79 Luong, Hy V, *Postwar Vietnam: dynamics of a transforming society*, Lanham, MD, Rowman & Littlefield, 2003 (p. 3).
80 Verwey, Wil D., *Riot control agents and herbicides in war: their humanitarian, toxicological, ecological, military, polemological, and legal aspects*, Leiden, A. W. Sijthoff, 1977 (p. 113).
81 Luong, Hy V, *Postwar Vietnam: dynamics of a transforming society*, Lanham, MD, Rowman & Littlefield, 2003 (p. 3).
82 Denvir, Daniel, 'The Secret History of the Vietnam War' (Interview with Nick Turse), *Vice News*, April 17, 2015.
83 Ibid.
84 Bishop, Ryan, Robinson, Lilian, *Night Market*, New York, Routledge, 1998 (p. 98).
85 Holcomb, Briavel, and Turshen, Meredeth, *Women's Lives and Public Policy: The International Experience*, Westport, Connecticut, Greenwood Press, 1993 (p. 134).
86 Ibid. (p. 134)
87 Gay, Jill, 'The "Patriotic Prostitute",' *The Progressive*, February 1985 (p. 34).
88 McMahon, Robert J., and Simpson, Bradley R., *The Cold War in the Third World*, Oxford, Oxford University Press, 2013.

89 Osornprasop, Sutayut, 'Amidst the Heat of the Cold War in Asia: Thailand and the American Secret War in Indochina (1960–1974),' Journal of Cold War History 7, no. 3, July 12, 2007 (pp. 349–371).
90 Rhodes, Richard, 'Death in the Candy Store,' *Rolling Stone*, November 28, 1991 (p. 65–67).
91 Enloe, Cynthia, *Beyond 'Rambo': Women and the Varieties of Militarized Masculinity*, Brighton, Wheatsheaf, 1988 (p. 85).
92 Haberman, Clyde, 'Agent Orange's Long Legacy, for Vietnam and Veterans,' *New York Times*, May 12, 2014.
93 'Agent Orange blights Vietnam,' *BBC*, December 3, 1998.
94 Ibid.
95 Ibid.
96 Grotto, Jason, and Jones, Tim, 'Agent Orange's lethal legacy: Defoliants more dangerous than they had to be,' *Chicago Tribune*, December 17, 2009.
97 Zierler, David, *Inventing Ecocide: Agent Orange, Antiwar Protest, and Environmental Destruction in Vietnam*, Charleston, SC, BiblioBazaar, 2011 (p. 246).
98 Chiras, Daniel D., *Environmental science*, 2010, 8th edn, Jones & Bartlett (p. 499).
99 Hughes, Richard, 'The Forgotten Victims of Agent Orange,' *New York Times*, September 15, 2017.
100 Steward, Phil, 'U.S. prepares for biggest-ever Agent Orange cleanup in Vietnam,' *Reuters*, October 17, 2018.
101 'Vietnam: My Orange Pain,' *RT*, (Documentary), September 21, 2014.
102 Ibid.
103 U.S. Department of Veterans Affairs, Public Health, Veterans' Diseases Associated with Agent Orange.
104 Hastie, Mark, 'Photo Essay: Agent Orange Children Vietnam 2016 by Mark Hastie,' Vietnam Full Disclosure, May 13, 2016.
105 'Vietnam: My Orange Pain,' *RT*, (Documentary), September 21, 2014.
106 Becker, Elizabeth, 'Kissinger Tapes Describe Crises, War and Stark Photos of Abuse,' *New York Times*, May 27, 2004.
107 McMahon, Robert J., and Simpson, Bradley R., *The Cold War in the Third World*, Oxford, Oxford University Press, 2013 (p. 54).
108 Ives, Mike, and Nguyen, Na Son, 'The mental scars of Vietnam's war veterans,' *Aljazeera*, January 22, 2016.
109 Herring, George C., *Why the North Won the Vietnam War*, Abingdon, Palgrave Macmillan, 2002 (p. 92).
110 Thomson, Helen, 'Study of Holocaust survivors finds trauma passed on to children's genes,' *The Guardian*, August 21, 2015.

PART II

Intervention and Conflict in Korea

CHAPTER 7

The Outbreak of War in Korea

> When one side only of a story is heard and often repeated, the human mind becomes impressed with it insensibly.[1]
>
> — GEORGE WASHINGTON

> Korea has been a blessing. There had to be a Korea whether here or some place in the world.[2]
>
> — U.S. General JAMES VAN FLEET in 1952 on the benefits of the Korean War for the American position in the Cold War

Competing Narratives

The Korean War began on June 25, 1950, less than five years after the end of the Second World War. It was very likely the most brutal war fought since Japan's surrender in 1945, and according to the testimony of the Supreme Commander of U.S. and UN forces General MacArthur was more brutal than the Second World War itself or any other war fought in his lifetime.[3] The impacts of the Korean War continue to have significant effects today, ranging from the permanent shift it caused in the United States' foreign policy to the shaping of the modern state identities of both Koreas. It served as a critical pretext and facilitator for the string of U.S. military bases and maintenance of military partnerships throughout the Asia-Pacific region and worldwide, setting a trend which is set to continue well into the twenty-first century, as well as continuing to define inter-Korean and Korean-American relations.

Regarding the continuing relevance of the Korean War in the twenty-first century, the conflict reshaped the nature of international relations with consequences lasting long after the Cold War's end. The foreign policy of the United States was irrevocably changed as a direct result of the Korean War, with the emergence of the 'National Security State,' the country's first ever peacetime standing army, and a new reliance on high military spending as an economic stimulus – all of which remain to this day. Doctrine for the deployment of nuclear weapons would change dramatically, as would the ways war would be fought, which marked a dramatic change from the Second World War. The possibility for a removal of U.S. military bases from Germany and Japan, the latter which faced considerable pressure from the local population to see American forces leave, was crushed by the outbreak of a hot war against Asian communist powers – which would shape the remainder of the Cold War. The emergence of Japan and much of Europe as effective defense dependencies of the US, and the vast and historically unprecedented system of officially self-ruling but in practice semi sovereign states hosting American military contingents, is itself also a direct legacy of the Korean War. This goes without mentioning the continued division of the strategically located Korean Peninsula, ongoing tensions between North Korea and the Western Bloc, and the shaping of modern North Korean identity – which in turn has been a major determinant of the country's foreign policy including its eventual pursuit of a nuclear deterrent.

At its outbreak the Korean War was waged primarily between the Democratic People's Republic of Korea (DPRK) – North Korea, and both the Republic of Korea (ROK) – South Korea and the United States. Despite its fear reaching implications, or perhaps because of them, the war is little mentioned and even less well understood in most Western accounts of the Cold War and of American intervention in East Asia. As American professor Bruce Cumings, historian of East Asia and Korea specialist holding South Korea's honorable Kim Dae Jung Academic Award for Outstanding Achievements and Scholarly Contributions to Democracy, Human Rights and Peace, wrote regarding the West's limited interpretation of the conflict: 'If people do know the Korean War, they usually know the official story. This presents the war as a simple sequence: in June 1950 the North Koreans, at [Soviet leader Joseph] Stalin's order, suddenly attacked an innocent and defenseless Republic of Korea; the Truman administration responded by invoking the collective security procedures of the United Nations in a "police action" designed to restore the *status quo ante*, the thirty-eighth parallel that divided North and South. General Douglas MacArthur accomplished that task by the end of September, after a brilliant amphibious landing in the port of Inch'on. Thereafter things went awry, as MacArthur sought to unify Korea through a march into the North, soon bringing Chinese "hordes" into the fighting; [U.S. President Harry] Truman attempted to limit the war and ultimately was forced to dismiss his recalcitrant field commander in April 1951. Ceasefire talks soon began, but seemingly minor issues, like prisoner of war exchanges, kept the war going until July 1953. It ended in a stalemate that left Korea divided into two states, as it had been before the war began.'[4] While this effectively summarizes the story of the Korean War as purported by the West, an analysis of the events leading up to and in the early stages of the war put many of Western claims and the entire narrative into serious question.

Regarding how the war started, an understanding of the circumstances in which the governments of the DPRK, ROK and United States found themselves during the months leading up to its outbreak and the possible incentives each may have had for sparking conflict gives a valuable indication as to which party would be the prime beneficiary. There were significant incentives both in the ROK and the United States to start a large-scale war with the Democratic People's Republic of Korea at this time, as shown by an analysis of both the political situation on the Korean peninsula and the political and economic situation in the United States itself. While the cause of the war's outbreak is until today disputed, an understanding of which party was most threatened by a continuing peace and which benefited from war gives a strong indication as to which party was likely responsible for starting it – *cui bono.*

Syngman Rhee's Government

Regarding how the war started, each side to this day continues to claim that the other was the sole aggressor responsible for initiating the conflict. An analysis of the circumstances facing the governments of the DPRK, ROK and United States in the months leading up to the war's outbreak and the possible incentives each side may have had for initiating conflict give strong indications as to which party could have been responsible. An understanding of which party was most threatened by a continuing peace and which, for political or economic reasons, could have sought to strengthen its position by starting a war, is thus essential.

In South Korea the Liberal Party of President Syngman Rhee had attempted but failed to win the country's first parliamentary elections on May 30, 1950, less than a month before the war's outbreak. The results had been a disaster for Rhee's government, with 128 of the 210 seats won by independents and Rhee's own party sure of only 45 seats. Meanwhile there was increasing pressure from the public to begin the process of peaceful reunification with the north, which at that time had been separate for less than five years. With the division of Korea initiated on a temporary basis by the United States and the Soviet Union in the aftermath of the Japanese Empire's expulsion from the peninsula, the DPRK was proposing a coalition government representing both north and south to jointly rule Korea. This was however against express wishes of the United States, which threatened to withdraw critical aid to the ROK should the two Koreas agree to a peaceful unification. Rhee himself viewed any such co-operation as 'concessions' to the north and 'a road to disaster,' and favored bringing about unification unilaterally and by force rather that by compromise and dialogue. Support for peaceful reunification nevertheless continued to grow in the ROK, with the country's elected assembly itself strongly in support of reunification, even if on North Korean terms, and a peaceful resolution to the conflict through dialogue and compromise. Such an outcome, against the interests of both Rhee and the United States, appeared inevitable.[5]

Rhee had been selected by the United States' Office for Strategic Services for the South Korean presidency, and enjoyed the full support of the American military government which ruled the country until 1948. He was considered an ideal candidate by General MacArthur, head of the United States' Pacific command. Rhee was a strongly pro-American Princeton educated exile politician, a devout Christian and a staunch anti-communist. He left his home in Washington D.C. and was flown to Japan to meet with General MacArthur in person. He was then flown to Seoul on the General's personal plane in mid-October 1945, from which time he proceeded to rule South Korea under American auspices. America's chosen president would years later leave the country in much the same way as he came to rule it. After altering the country's constitution in 1956 to extend his presidency, Rhee's repressive government was overthrown and the new South Korean leadership sought his arrest. He was extracted covertly by a CIA DC-4 plane in April 1961 as protestors converged on his presidential residence. Rhee and his wife would afterwards return to live in the United States.[6]

While Rhee had won the 1948 presidential elections, these could hardly be considered free or fair. This was not only due to the intimidation of political opposition reported by U.S. sources, but also more importantly because no one was able to run against Rhee. The only contender was Korean Independence Party candidate Kim Koo, who was targeted for assassination by the CIA and killed less than a month before the election.[7] Koo had vehemently opposed the joint Soviet-American trusteeship of Korea and had met with the North Korean leadership and its president, Kim Il Sung, to discuss a peaceful reunification. Unlike Rhee he was not an anti-communist, but a staunch nationalist who prioritized Korean reunification and opposed foreign intervention in Korean affairs. Rhee's victory in the presidential elections was therefore highly dubious as the only alternative candidate was dead when the votes were cast.

Rhee relied heavily on intimidation of his political opponents. When later putting forth constitutional amendments to increase the powers of his presidency he would detain those representatives who opposed the motion, charging them with 'communist connections.'[8] Two United Nations Commissions reflected poorly on the way Rhee's government handled political elections and used threats to gain votes. Threats to confiscate rice ration cards, on which much of the population relied, was a milder form of coercion, according to the UN which had observed the 1948 elections that established Rhee's government.[9] The CIA had a similar view of Rhee, and the agency stated in 1950: 'Syngman Rhee and his regime are unpopular among many if not the majority of non-communist Koreans.'[10]

On June 7, 1950, North Korean President Kim Il Sung called for Korea-wide elections to be held in August, and for a consultative conference in Haeju from June 15 to 17. Four days later the DPRK sent three diplomats to the south in a peace overture to begin talks on reunification. Rhee rejected this outright. This was not a result of his hardline anticommunist views alone, but his awareness that peaceful reunification would inevitably lead to his loss of power due to his government's unpopularity and the widespread appeal of North Korean communism at the time.[11] The interests of the United States, much like those of Rhee, were severely threatened by the potential for nationwide elections across both Koreas in which the communist Korean Workers' Party of Kim Il Sung would be allowed to run. American sources predicted that a reunified Korea with free elections would almost certainly lead to communist rule under a government similar to that in place in the north. The DPRK had in five years since the end of Japanese rule advanced its economy considerably, and living standards were far higher than those in the ROK – as they would remain for decades. The ROK meanwhile had one of the lowest living standards in the world, and saw little development under the Rhee government. *Time* magazine referred to it as 'an economic wasteland [...] really one of the poorest places in the world.'[12] The economy, calorie intake and education all lagged far behind the north, and South Koreans were thus expected to favor a government based on the apparently more successful North Korean model. The personal charisma of the communists' leader, a renowned anti-Japanese resistance fighter who had alongside his family fought the Japanese Empire for decades, formed a stark contrast to Rhee's own background as an exile who had spent decades outside the country, and further increased the appeal of the northern government.

Rhee's government had prioritized militarization and strongly advocated for reunification by force and initiating military action against the DPRK. This was combined with a reign of terror domestically in which members political organizations with communist or socialist leanings were arrested and often killed. In the five years since Japanese occupation ended the ROK government forces were estimated to have killed 100,000 civilians in South Korea – 2 percent of the population at the time.[13] These figures were, according to the government-funded Truth and Reconciliation Commission report made decades later, 'highly conservative.' Kim Dong Choon, commissioner of the South Korean government's Truth and Reconciliation Commission, who had investigated these killings for two years stated that he estimated the death toll was at minimum half of the 300,000 South Koreans who were imprisoned in concentration camps by the Rhee government.[14]

An example of the Rhee government's conduct towards its people was on Cheju island, where extreme political repression and massacres of political protestors at the hands of government sponsored rightist youth groups and police forces sparked a rebellion among its rural population.[15,16] The brutality of the response against the civilian population led the U.S. military to refer to it as the Cheju Civil War. American public sources claimed 15,000–20,000 islanders were massacred in the thirteen-month conflict, which ended in May 1949. The ROK's own official figure was 27,719. The DPRK said that over 30,000 islanders had been 'butchered' in the suppression. The military governor of Cheju himself had privately told American intelligence, according to declassified intelligence reports, that 60,000 islanders had died and up to 40,000 had fled to Japan. South Korean scholarly sources put the death toll at 38,000. Officially 39,285 homes had been demolished and, according to the governor, 'most of the houses on the hills' were gone. Of 400 villages only 170 remained. According to this previously classified report therefore, around a fifth of the population of Cheju had been killed and the majority of villages had been destroyed.[17,18,19,20]

New York Times correspondent Walter Sullivan wrote in early 1950 that large parts of southern Korea 'are darkened today by a cloud of terror that is probably unparalleled in the world.' The persistence of guerrillas 'puzzles many Americans here,' as does 'the extreme brutality' of the conflict. He went on to argue that 'there is a great divergence of wealth' in the country leaving both middle and poor peasants living 'a marginal existence.' Exactions from the peasants, not only on Cheju but throughout the ROK, from both the government and the landlords was up to 70 percent of the annual crop. Sullivan believed that it was this oppression and exploitation of the majority of the population that was the primary cause of unrest, not only on Cheju but throughout the country.[21]

While Rhee ran a reign of terror against his people and threatened war with the DPRK, electoral results indicated he was highly unlikely to remain in power and the country was set undergo peaceful reunification with the

DPRK – as the parliamentary majorities of both countries desired. The outbreak of the Korean War however meant that Rhee and his government would survive, their war-mongering and far-right positions strengthened, while calls for peaceful reunification became impossible. Less than a month after the May 30 elections were held, which had seriously compromised the positions of both Rhee and of the United States, war broke out on the Korean Peninsula which saved the ailing government and thus ensured the U.S. would maintain its strategically valuable client state.

Beneficiaries of the Korean War's Outbreak

After the outbreak of the Korean War and intervention by an American led UN force to support the ROK, the *New York Times* correspondent, in discussing prospects for mediation between the two Koreas, reported: 'Some saw the possibility that the Kremlin may also suggest that elections be held afterwards in both North and South Korea to set up a government for the entire country – in the expectation of course, that this would produce a communist majority, thus bringing about the same result as if the United Nations had not intervened.' A communist government was widely expected to emerge should the Korean people be given the right to choose freely, and it was this that the both the U.S. and the ROK government sought to prevent.[22]

It was in the interests of America, the 'beacon of democracy' and 'leader of the free world,' to directly intervene against the democratic will of the Korean people to reunite to protect its own interests in East Asia. Those in the ROK who opposed inter-Korean negotiations to achieve reunification had become a small and marginalized minority since the parliamentary elections. Regardless of this, if democracy would be contrary to American strategic interests and potentially lead to a communist government then there would be no democracy. If there was to be reunification it would be on U.S. terms and under their influence, not on terms favored by the Korean people. As one of America's most renowned strategists, presidential national security adviser Henry Kissinger, would later remark: 'I don't see why we need to stand by and watch a country go communist due to the irresponsibility of its own people.' This very much applied to the situation in Korea, where the feared 'communist takeover' by democratic means had to be prevented.[23] The fear wasn't necessarily of communism itself as an economic system, but rather that communism represented a divergence away from the United States and the entire Western sphere of influence – and should this occur in Korea it would represent a considerable strategic loss at a time of Cold War competition.

American journalist I. F. Stone, who won numerous awards as one of the most renowned men of his profession in twentieth-century America and who conducted an intensive study of the Korean War as it unfolded, concluded – based on the circumstances surrounding the outbreak of war – that it was likely Syngman Rhee's government had collaborated with hardline anticommunist elements in the United States leadership to provoke a war. Many in the U.S. military leadership, General MacArthur included, were eager to launch a war against communism[24] while for Rhee such a war was essential to retaining power. Stone wrote: 'Could it be that Rhee received advice that it would be wiser to invite or provoke attack, and then trust to the impact on American public opinion to change American policy [to force America to commit to an offensive war against the north]? Rhee was apparently content to let that basic American strategic decision go unchallenged, to draw up his troops into defensive positions, to give them orders to withdraw in event of attack, and to arrange for United Nations observers to see how defensive all his military dispositions were. The observers brought in their reports on the 24th. That night, in their absence, the war began. Rhee announced that it began with an unprovoked invasion from the North. The North Korean government, on the contrary, reported that South Korean forces crossed the Parallel in three different places, were hurled back, and the North Korean forces then went over to the offensive.' The use of such strategies would be far from unprecedented. The United States had just nine years earlier openly sought to provoke Japan into launching an attack on the U.S. military and thereby gain public support both to launch a war in Asia and to intervene in the European theatre – as revealed in the *Eight Action Memo* intelligence report (see Chapter 1).[25]

While a continued peace almost guaranteed that the south would willingly turn communist, launching a war would at once empower Rhee, indefinitely postpone peaceful reunification against U.S. interests, and give the United States a vital pretext for military intervention – not only preventing a 'loss' of the south just a year after the 'loss of China' to communism, but also bringing the strategically placed north of Korea into its sphere of influence and providing a key staging ground for further operations against neighboring China.

Implications a new conflict against a communist power would have went well beyond the Korean Peninsula, and served to make war highly attractive from the perspective of a number of anticommunist hardliners in the US. Open hostilities against the communist world war would provide ample pretext to establish a worldwide network of military bases to contain communism – which was seen to be spreading rapidly particularly in Asia. These bases remain a critical source of American power to this day. The United States' military involvement throughout the region escalated, and within two days of hostilities breaking out remnants of Chiang Kai-shek's government in Taiwan were given American military protection from an impending Chinese invasion, indefinitely postponing the final end of China's civil war and thereby maintaining American influence in the strategically critical Taiwan Strait – also an asset which the country retains until this day. Taiwan would by the end of the decade house American nuclear weapons little over 130 km from the coast of mainland China. In Japan too, where public pressure to eject U.S. military bases had been growing, the withdrawal of U.S. forces could be postponed indefinitely. American troops never left Japan as a result.[26]

The outbreak of the Korean War also substantially benefited the U.S. position in the European theatre, to the detriment of the USSR. The war began just months after the Soviet Union had tested its first nuclear device, and the country was still far from achieving nuclear parity with the United States. According to a report from the *Project for the New American Century* neoconservative think tank, the pretext of a communist threat based on events in Korea was instrumental in allowing the United States to press its nuclear advantage to the fullest – changing the balance of power in the European theatre dramatically by deploying large numbers of nuclear weapons at a rate which the Soviets could not match at the time.[27]

The outbreak of the Korean War did much to strengthen the United States' position vis-à-vis the Soviet Union following the disastrous 'loss of China' a year prior to the communist bloc. U.S. Secretary of State Dean Acheson noted in this regard that the Korean War was the crisis that 'came along and saved us.' It allowed for the drafting of NSC 68, the key National Security Council report that became one of the most important statements of American foreign policy, and 'provided the blueprint for the militarization of the Cold War from 1950 to the collapse of the Soviet Union at the beginning of the 1990s.'[28] NSC 68 advocated the development of the hydrogen bomb and a significant expansion in U.S. military spending, which would quadruple after the war's outbreak. A peacetime military draft was established, along with a permanent standing army of three million American personnel deployed across the world. West Germany and Japan could also be rearmed under the pretext of fighting communism as part of this initiative sparked by the Korean War. The United States correspondingly escalated its involvement in Vietnam in support of French colonialist forces, sowing the seeds for another conflict yet to come.[29] NATO was established as a formal U.S. led military alliance which unified the Western Bloc as a direct result of the war in Korea. The legacies of these military structures and organizations remain prominent today.

In December 1950 President Truman declared an indefinite national state of emergency, mobilizing the United States for a permanent state of Cold War. In the president's words, he summoned 'our farmers, our workers in industry, and our businessmen to make a mighty production effort to meet the defence requirements of the Nation [...] every person and every community to make, with a spirit of neighbourliness, whatever sacrifices are necessary for the welfare of the Nation [...] all State and local leaders and officials to cooperate fully with the military and civilian defence agencies of the United States in the national defence program.'[30] With what itself sounded much like communist rhetoric, the United States, and by extension the entire Western Bloc, devoted itself wholeheartedly to its crusade against communism.

Those who sought a harder line against communism for political reasons were hardly the only ones who benefited from the outbreak of war in Korea, and the formerly struggling U.S. economy also saw a marked improvement following the opening of hostilities. While the U.S. economy had thrived and doubled in size during the Second World War,[31] the U.S. leadership feared the potentially catastrophic consequences peace could have on the war-oriented economy that had developed in the early 1940s to fight the Axis powers. The dominant trend in American economic and military thinking, according to a number of highly placed sources, had become a fear of genuine peace. The threat of war had to be ever present as the nature of the economy meant that it relied heavily on stimulation from military expenditure. General MacArthur himself attested to the United States' government's fear of peace and overreliance on its war economy, stating: 'It is part of the general pattern of misguided policy that our country is now geared to an arms economy which was bred in an artificially induced psychosis of war hysteria and nurtured upon an incessant propaganda of fear. While such an economy may produce a sense of seeming prosperity for the moment, it rests on an illusionary foundation of complete unreliability and renders among our political leaders almost a greater fear of peace than is their fear of war.'[32]

The U.S. economy had grown overwhelmingly as a result of war, and the new orientation towards war production that resulted meant that it relied on military spending far more than others to prevent a recession. This remains the case until today where wars or even threats of wars will often boost the U.S. economy due to its high reliance on its military industries.[33] This phenomenon, which first emerged in the aftermath of the Second World War, was attested to by U.S. President Eisenhower, who replaced Truman in 1953. He stated: 'Our military organization today bears little relation to that known by any of my predecessors in peacetime [...] We have been compelled to create a permanent armaments industry of vast proportions. Added to this, three and a half million men and women are directly engaged in the defense establishment. We annually spend on military security more than the net income of all United States corporations. This conjunction of an immense military establishment and a large arms industry is new in the American experience. The total influence – economic, political, even spiritual – is felt in every city, every Statehouse, every office of the Federal government.'

Eisenhower, himself a former general, warned that economic reliance on military industries was so great as to potentially compromise democratic processes. Policy could be substantially influenced by the need to produce arms.[34] With the outbreak of the Korean War America's vast military economy could again begin to work and would continue to work indefinitely to arm the United States and its allies – all made to fear 'communist aggression' and driven into the arms of American military industrialists as a result.

The Korean War gave the pretext for a permanent large-scale military industrial complex for the first time in American history, something highly desirable for militarists, hardline anticommunists and military industrialists alike. This also served to inevitably postpone the post war recession which seemed inevitable with a contraction in defense spending. Several large-scale defense projects which were imminently about to lose funding were saved. In Southern California alone projects developing 'strategic bombers, supercarriers, and [...] a previously cancelled Convair contract to develop an intercontinental rocket for the Air Force' were resumed. The colossal wartime aircraft production industry was again booming in 1952, saved by the outbreak of the war. These defense industries were, and remain today, central to the United States economy. Los Angeles County for example had 160,000 people employed in aircraft production. Defense and aerospace accounted for 55 percent of employment in the county – in San Diego this figure was nearly 80 percent. Defense industries, reliant on war to stimulate demand, kept hundreds of thousands of factories working throughout the United States.

While in 1949 the American economy had been in recession, from 1950 to 1953 it saw significant economic expansion with growth rates at 8.7 percent in 1950.[35] The key change was the boost to military expenditure, which acted as a highly potent stimulant. Vastly increased arms exports to a number of defense clients, from the Philippines and South Korea to Germany and Japan, were also a considerable factor. As I. F. Stone noted at the time: 'With the arms race and the rampant inflation and costs piling up, American leadership was still gripped by dread of the consequences of peace upon the economy. This dread was dictating the actions of the politicians and mega business leaders. An economy accustomed to injections of inflationary narcotic trembled at the thought that its deadly stimulant might be shut off [...] The dominant trend in American political, economic and military thinking was, and is, a fear of peace.'[36]

Effects of the Korean War's Outbreak on the Communist Powers

While the Rhee government and several key interest groups in the United States had much to gain from the outbreak of war, open hostilities created immense difficulties for the communist powers. The new Chinese communist government could not take back Taiwan to bring the civil war to its final conclusion and recover either the strategic outlying islands held by the U.S. backed Guomindang, or their national treasures and gold reserves held in Taipei – funds much needed to modernize the country's economy. What British and American intelligence termed 'the last battle' of the Chinese Civil War, the final defeat of Chiang Kai-shek's government, was expected to occur within weeks. This was indefinitely postponed by American intervention in Taiwan, which was justified by 'communist aggression' in Korea.[37] Had there been no Korean War, Taiwan would have been lost as an asset to the Western Bloc. Chiang's government, the 'Republic of China,' was granted the United Nations Security Council's China seat – one of five permeant seats – and this would not be restored to Beijing until 1971. The existence of the Taiwan based ROC was thus crucial to U.S. efforts to isolate the new People's Republic on the mainland both politically and economically, while Washington could press many of its client states across the world, from South America to Japan, not to recognize the PRC due to the existence of the alternative ROC. Had there been no Chinese government in Taipei to rival that in Beijing for legitimacy then the U.S. would have lacked a pretext upon which to deny the PRC recognition.

In a private report to the Senate Foreign Relations Committee Republican Senator H. Alexander Smith dealt with the intelligence information available to the American government concerning Soviet and Chinese intentions for Korea and their relations with the north. When reporting North Korea's requests for assistance from China he wrote: 'the Chinese turned them down on the grounds that they had too many responsibilities in other parts of China.' This would make sense considering China was still recovering from decades of war and faced regular incursions from U.S. backed forces based in Myanmar and the surrounding islands.[38] The journalist and reporter John Gunther also reported from Tokyo on the Chinese attitude to the outbreak of the Korean War and what he claimed was a North Korean attack: 'they deplored it – strange as it may seem now. For the North Korean aggression had, for the moment at least, cost Mao Tsetung a prize he coveted above all – Formosa.' Essentially, according to U.S. intelligence, the Chinese did not endorse and had little to gain from war – regardless of who started it.[39]

Soviet interests also suffered as a result of the war's outbreak. Senator Smith's report to the Senate also covered the state of Soviet–North Korean relations. Regarding the USSR's desire to maintain parity and prevent conflict on the peninsula the Senate report stated: 'they did not wish to initiate World War 3 by creating an incident in a minor area like Korea.' Soviet Chief of General Staff Marshal Matvei Zakharov had addressed the Soviet military mission in Korea, telling them that while it was easy to organize an air force of 1,000 planes or so, and there were no shortages of trained North Korean pilots, it was necessary for political reasons not to do so. He feared that should North Korea have a potent air force this would escalate regional tensions and lead to an arms race, which could in turn 'bring war with the United States, and we are not interested in provoking such a war.' The USSR for this reason ensured that they supplied North Korea with only what was necessary for defense, to retain a balance of power with the south, and not more.[40]

Further compromising Soviet interests, the outbreak of the war gave the United States the pretext it needed to retain their bomber bases indefinitely in Japan near Vladivostok – a highly advantageous strategic position – as well as to expand its nuclear forces in Europe. Calls for peace treaties in Japan, including a peace treaty with the USSR, were postponed indefinitely, hindering relations until today (the Russian Federation still does not have a peace treaty with Japan, and the two have yet to resolve their territorial disputes).

The USSR had at the time been seeking peace with the United States and General Secretary Stalin had indicated that he wished to personally meet President Truman. Soviet foreign policy designs at the time did not require war but rather would have been served far better by peace. With more and more nations gaining independence from European empires and the widespread appeal of its ideology at the time, the Soviet Union was in a strong position to win a soft war in which its ideas and its model for rapid industrialization would win over more developing nations as allies.[41] John Foster Dulles, author of the influential American containment policy analysis *War and Peace* and soon after Secretary of State, dismissed Russian 'Peace Offensives' as 'deceptive Cold War strategy' which posed an imminent threat to U.S. interests. The United States was not interested in peace, but needed war. Dulles declared: 'as things are going now ... we must develop better techniques ... They [the USSR] can win everything by the cold war they could win by a hot war.' As a lasting peace was in the Soviet Union's interests, these were far from served by the outbreak of the Korean War and the resulting military escalations against communism worldwide. The USSR would go on to take significant measures throughout the war to prevent its escalation and limit the conflict to the Korean Peninsula.[42]

North Korean interests were also hindered, as war was wholly unnecessary for them to reunify the Korean peninsula. The weakening of Rhee's government and growing calls for reunification within the ROK, both among the population and within the new parliamentary majority, led analysts from the *New York Times* to the State Department, the CIA and the Soviet Union to unanimously predict with near certainty that peaceful reunification was imminent and that country would go on to elect a communist government. Korea was set to imminently be reunified under the communist Korean Workers' Party, which was far more popular among southerners at the time. The DPRK was thus set to achieve far more by peace than it could by war. North Korean peace overtures were increasingly being met with success, something the CIA assassination of Kim Koo had stalled but not derailed. The election of an assembly in the south strongly in favor of co-operation and peaceful reunification which the DPRK made a highly favorable bloodless reunification appear imminent – a far more desirable outcome than what could ever be achieved by force. This occurred just days before the war started. As U.S. President John F. Kennedy would state twelve years later: 'those who make peaceful revolution impossible will make violent revolution inevitable.'[43] Applied to the Korean Peninsula, it appeared that a peaceful but revolutionary change in the south was well underway – in that the failings of the Rhee government domestically had let it to lose popularity and a peaceful reunification which would lead to its end was imminent. 'Violent revolution,' or any use of force, was therefore wholly unnecessary. For the north to initiate hostilities to derail this peace process at a time when the south appeared ripe to fall into their hands peacefully would have made no strategic sense.

Applying one of the oldest principles in determining the perpetrators of a crime, *cui bono*, an analysis of how the outbreak of war affected the interests of each party, there is a strong indication that the United States and ROK were responsible for initiating hostilities. Considering the great benefits to the United States and the Rhee government gained from starting the war, saving both parties from their otherwise fast deteriorating positions, and contrasting these with the considerable losses faced by the North Koreans, the Chinese and the Soviets, whose 'peace offensives' were yielding considerable results, the Western claim that the war was indisputably started by North Korean aggression at the behest of the USSR and communist China is largely discredited.

How the War Begun

Though the exact events that took place on the 38th parallel in 1950 are uncertain, American sources clearly show that the ROK had been escalating border tensions unilaterally leading up to the war. Months before the war's outbreak South Korean military expanded to 100,000 troops, a strength the North responded to by matching only the following year.[44,45] South Korea then again enlarged its military, which when the war started outnumbered the North Koreans by 18,000 personnel.[46] Syngman Rhee had not only been pushing for a more direct American military commitment, but had strongly advocated a joint attack on the north in his meetings with the U.S. representatives. William Mathews, a reporter accompanying John Foster Dulles to a meeting with Rhee, wrote a report immediately afterwards. He recalled that Rhee was 'militantly for the unification of Korea. Openly says it must be brought about soon ... Rhee pleads justice of going into North country. Thinks it could succeed in a few days ... if he can do it with our help he will do it.' Mathews noted that Rhee was willing to attack even if 'it brought on a general war.'[47] He had made open threats to march on the north many times before, something known to the leaders in the DPRK.

There were several skirmishes along the 38th parallel from May to December 1949, which according to internal American accounts were almost all initiated by the southern forces. UN military observers were posted to the border for this reason, to monitor both sides. Unlike retrospective Western portrayals of events would indicate, the south by far was the more belligerent party. The head of United States' Korean Military Advisory Group (KMAG), General William L. Roberts, observed of the border clashes: 'almost every incident has been provoked by the South Korean security forces.'[48] North Korean sources claim that thousands of South Korean troops led by Kim Suk Won, a former officer in northern Korea under the Japanese Imperial forces and now close confidant of Syngman Rhee, led ROK forces in attacks across the border. This initiated six months of border fighting. These claims seem substantiated by the officer's calls for war with the North and reunification of the country under southern rule. He said: 'We should have a program to recover our lost land, North Korea, by breaking through the 38th border which has existed since 1945.' Kim told the United Nations Commission on Korea shortly before the outbreak of the war that the moment of major battles was 'rapidly approaching.'[49] This not only somewhat substantiates the claims made by DPRK sources, but also indicates that many in power in the ROK anticipated the outbreak of war – calling for an invasion of the DPRK and initiating skirmishes on the border. There were no similar such calls for war from the DPRK.

Kim Suk Won was far from alone in the ROK in calling for attacks on North Korea to forcefully reunify the country under the Rhee government. British sources reported just weeks before the outbreak of the war that KMAG advisers were concerned that the South Korean military's 'over-aggressive officers in command positions along the parallel' presented a significant risk that 'a border incident [...] could precipitate civil war.'[50] As American General W. L. Roberts had noted of attacks on border villages in the DPRK by military and paramilitary units that 'each was in our opinion brought on by the presence of a small South Korean salient north of the parallel […] The South Koreans wish to invade the North.'[51] Other British intelligence sources similarly concluded that the leadership of the south was willing to initiate a war of aggression, with one stating that South Korean commanders' heads 'are full of ideas of recovering the North by conquest.'[52,53]

A key expert from the United Nations Commission on Korea (UNCOK), Egon Ranshofen-Wertheimer, also saw the dangers on the peninsula and high potential for aggressive war to be initiated specifically by South Korea. He wrote in September 1949: 'the ROK might feel that its chances of absorbing the North are diminished from month to month in view of the growing strength of Kim Il Sung's armies […] The temptation for Rhee to invade the North and the pressure exerted upon him to do so might, therefore, become irresistible. The top military authorities of the Republic … are exerting continual pressure upon Rhee to take the initiative and cross the parallel.'[54]

The U.S. Ambassador to the ROK John Muccio gave a report to similar effect shortly before the outbreak of the war. He observed of the South Korean military leadership:

> There is increasing confidence in the army. An aggressive, offensive spirit is emerging. Nerves that were frayed and jittery the past few months may now give way to this new spirit. A good portion of the Army is eager to get going. More and more people feel that the only way unification can be brought about is by moving north by force […] Chiang Kaishek told Rhee that the Nationalist [Guomindang] air force could support a move North and that they discussed the possibility of the Nationalists starting an offensive move against Manchuria through Korea! There is some feeling that now is the time to move north while the Chinese communists are preoccupied. I doubt whether Rhee would actually order a move North in his saner moments […] However, should we have another Kaesong or Ongjin flare-up, a counter-attack might lead to all sorts of unpredictable developments.[55]

M. Preston Goodfellow, a Captain in the United States military during the Korean War, had previously paid many visits to Syngman Rhee in Seoul. In his discussion with the Chinese Nationalist [Guomindang] ambassador it was made clear that there was an outcome favorable to both the United States and to the Rhee government. He told the ambassador that the momentum for attack had shifted, and the ambassador reported from their meeting: 'it was the South Koreans anxious to go into N. K., because they were feeling sharp with their army of well-trained 100,000 strong. But U.S. Govt was most anxious to restrain any provocation by the S. K. and Goodfellow had gone there lately to do just that. I asked how great was the possibility or danger of war breaking out in Korea. Goodfellow said U.S. Govt. position is this: avoid any initiative on S. Korea's part in attacking N. K., but if N. K. should invade S. K. then S. K. should resist and march right into N. K [...] in such a case, the aggression came from N. K. and the American people would understand it.'[56,57]

The analyses of both Goodfellow and Muccio may well have been particularly prophetic. Goodfellow's report was highly reminiscent of U.S. policy preceding the outbreak of war with Imperial Japan. It was not altogether opposed to war but it needed to ensure that it could not be perceived both by the world and by its own people as an aggressor or supporting an aggressor. American policy made clear that should the north invade the south, the ROK could go ahead with its plans to occupy the north under this pretext and the United States would be able to support them in full. The Rhee government which sought war was therefore incentivized to continue border provocations and attempt to provoke a counterattack.

Gaining United Nations Support and Determining the Aggressor

Following the outbreak of hostilities on the border on June 25, 1950, North Korean forces claimed that South Korean troops had attacked and captured their assets on the border and seized the small city of Haeju near the border. These claims were initially substantiated by South Korea sources, with the South Korean Office of Public Information announcing the capture of the northern city by its forces. According to North Korean sources, northern forces moved to reclaim the city and repel other attacks which had occurred simultaneously on the border, and proceeded to launch a counterattack. With the capture of Haeju undermining the South Korean narrative of an unprovoked northern attack, Seoul later denied that the successful attack on the city had ever taken place – refuting the earlier report by the Office of Public Information which had supported the northern narrative.[58,59]

Almost immediately after the outbreak of the war the United States moved to form a military coalition through the United Nations with the purpose of launching an armed intervention against North Korea. The American representative declared the 'unprovoked assault' by North Korea to be an attack on 'the vital interest which all members of the United Nations have in the organization.' The United Nations Security Council's permanent members were at the time the United States, the United Kingdom, France and the Republic of China, all anticommunist states and close U.S. partners heavily reliant on American aid. The USSR had boycotted the council and the United Nations in protest at the organization's refusal to recognize the People's Republic of China, meaning there were no states able to veto the motion. Deploying armed force was strongly in the interests of the Western powers and certainly in the interests of Chiang Kai-shek's government. For the remnants of the Guomindang, involving the United States and its Western allies in a war on the Asian mainland was perceived to be the only potential means of returning to power in Beijing.

The UN was far from a neutral or politically balanced organization in 1950, with the vast majority of its members highly dependent on the United States for economic recovery or development assistance. There were no political blocs representing 'Non-Aligned' or 'Third World' nations and only four Soviet Bloc nations were members at the time – none of them Security Council members.[60] UN Secretary General Trygve Lie made very clear in his later memoirs that he too was no neutral outsider but a staunch anti-communist. His memoirs also reveal his maneuvering in the UN to best assure the interests of the Western Bloc were met against those of the USSR and North Korea.[61] It was later revealed that in 1949 Lie had entered into an agreement with the U.S. State Department to dismiss those from employment at the UN whose political leanings were not favored by Washington.[62,63] As a result the United States was able to dominate and effectively set the agenda at the UN.

Despite the United States' overwhelming influence, the United Nations investigative team could not bring itself to condemn North Korea as the aggressor. The cable from the United Nations mission in Seoul confirmed that observers on the spot were unable to decide which of the Koreas had initiated hostilities. The UN commission merely reported that the South Koreans alleged they had been attacked and they denied the North Korean radio account that claimed the South had attacked first and that Northern forces had repelled the invaders and then gone over on to launch a counteroffensive. The commission itself expressed no opinion as to who had started the war.[64]

The U.S. State Department notably withheld evidence from the UN Security Council when calling for a military intervention on the Korean Peninsula. The 171-word cable from Seoul received by the U.S. was very different from the 38-word and highly paraphrased sentence the State Department presented to the council. The full text of the cable the State Department received from Seoul and the early reports which could have further elaborated on how hostilities broke out were all withheld without explanation. Meanwhile U.S. ambassador Muccio said from Seoul that he could only 'partly confirm' South Korea's accusation of North Korean aggression. Weeks into the war Muccio never gave evidence or even claimed that the DPRK had been responsible for the opening of hostilities, let alone that they were the sole initiator of aggression as the U.S. was claiming before the Security Council. The U.S. military advisers serving alongside the South Korean forces on the border themselves were not cited as sources to confirm the ROK government's claims.[65]

The United States not only asked the Security Council to brand North Korea the sole aggressor while wholly lacking evidence, but the resolution they had introduced, UNSC resolution 82, also asked for a ceasefire directed solely at North Korea. The Yugoslav delegation at the UN, representing a country which at the time had hostile relations with the USSR and was highly dependent on American aid and support, nevertheless insisted that though the United States asked for North Korea to be declared the aggressor, 'there seemed to be lack of precise information that could enable the council to pin responsibility.'[66] Yugoslavia instead proposed that North Korea be invited to present its side of the story, though this was strongly opposed by the council's permanent members as it would have undermined their ability to dictate the narrative of the war's outbreak in line with their own interests. When the USSR did return to the UNSC three months later its Foreign Minister, Vyacheslav Molotov, put forward a motion for representatives from both sides to be heard at the UN. This was met with the same staunch opposition, and the Western dominated Security Council decided to invite representatives from South Korea alone.[67] The Western Bloc would therefore ultimately maintain a monopoly on the narratives put forth at the United Nations.

Many cables and documents in U.S. possession were denied as evidence to the Security Council – likely because they did not point to North Korea as the sole aggressor.[68] Though UN investigators had no proof that North Korea was the aggressor, and had never made such a claim, 'peacekeeping' actions were initiated exclusively targeting the East Asian state. Upon the deployment of a joint UN force to the peninsula, they fell under the command of U.S. General Douglas MacArthur. He made efforts to persuade the United Nations that the war was with all communist powers, not just the DPRK, and thereby give a pretext for escalation against China and possibly the USSR. MacArthur informed the United Nations: 'From the continuing appearance on the battlefield of large numbers of enemy personnel and equipment it is now apparent that the North Korean aggressors have available to them resources far in excess of their internal capabilities.' He claimed the North Koreans were without a doubt drawing personnel and supplies from beyond their borders and that the USSR and/or China were waging a covert war against the United Nations itself. This being the case, should not MacArthur's Unified Command of UN forces be allowed to retaliate?[69] MacArthur would increasingly stress this final question in later reports, strongly implying that military action should be taken against communist China and the USSR.

It began to appear that MacArthur was the only one at Tokyo Headquarters, the United States' command center which oversaw military operations in the Asia-Pacific, who believed that the war involved either the USSR or China. Either the General had failed to pass his information on to his own intelligence or he was fabricating these accusations himself. At a Tokyo Headquarters Korean War briefing the speaker for the military's Far East Command explained that North Korean forces were suffering shortages of men and equipment, which would not have been the case had they been receiving support from two great powers on their border. The speaker also explained that 'there was no indication that the North Korean tank losses were being replaced by further supplies from the Soviet Union, which furnished the original armor and lent instructors who taught the North Koreans how to use it.'[70] Tokyo headquarters later reported on the same day that 'the weapons captured from the North Koreans have been a wide assortment, even including some World War 1 rifles [...] The latest estimates [...] are that neither the North Korean army nor the air force has any post war Soviet weapons.' They said the recent report 'that Communist-flown jet planes have been sighted over South Korea now is evaluated as an error in identification.' Verifying these findings, intelligence sources later reported to the *New York Times* that they had 'no knowledge that the North Korea invaders actually received new supplies from the Soviet Union since the war began.' Not only were the Soviets not sending weapons, but none of their military advisers assisted the Korean People's Army (North Korean military, KPA) in their advance.[71] North Korean forces were fighting the war, and winning, with very limited means, and received little if any support from the USSR or China. This also discredits the notion that the USSR was backing North Korea to occupy the ROK, as the very absence of any evidence of material support was a very significant statement in and of itself. In falsely indicting the USSR and China in war at the time MacArthur was purposefully misleading the United Nations to bring about a greater war against communism in Asia – in line with his own hardline anti-communist views.

Notes

1 Zall, Paul M., *Washington on Washington*, Lexington, University Press of Kentucky, 2003 (pp. 118–119).

2 Grausam, Daniel, and Belletto, Steven, *American Literature and Culture in an Age of Cold War: A Critical Reassessment*, Iowa City, University of Iowa Press, 2012 (p. 138).

3 Neer, Robert M., *Napalm: An American Biography*, Cambridge, MA, Harvard University Press, 2013 (p. 100).
4 Stone, I. F., *Hidden History of the Korean War*, Amazon Media, 2014 (Foreword by Bruce Cumings).
5 Ambrose, Stephen E., and Brinkley, Douglas G., *Rise to Globalism: American Foreign Policy Since 1938*, London, Penguin, 2010 (p. 115).
6 Farivar, Cyrus, *The Internet of Elsewhere: The Emergent Effects of a Wired World*, New Brunswick, NJ, Rutgers University Press, 2011 (p 26).
7 Blum, William, *Killing Hope: U.S. Military and C.I.A. Interventions Since World War II*, London, Zed Books, 2003 (Appendix III).
8 Heo, Uk, and Roehrig, Terence, *South Korea Since 1980*, Cambridge, Cambridge University Press, 2010 (p. 17).
9 Stone, I. F., *Hidden History of the Korean War*, Amazon Media, 2014 (Chapter 17, 'Free Elections?').
10 Hanley, Charles J. and Choe, Sang Hun and Mendoza, Martha, *The Bridge at No Gun Ri: A Hidden Nightmare from the Korean War*, New York, Henry Holt and Company, 2001 (p. 170).
11 Weathersby, Kathryn (2002), *'Should We Fear This?' Stalin and the Danger of War with America*, Cold War International History Project: Working Paper No. 39.
12 'Is South Korea the greatest success story of the last century,' *Time*, December 6, 2012.
13 Cumings, Bruce, *The Korean War: A History*, New York, Modern Library, 2010 (p. 189).
14 Hanley, Charles J., and Change, Jae-Soon, 'Summer of Terror: At least 100,000 said executed by Korean ally of U.S. in 1950,' *The Asia-Pacific Journal*, Volume 7, Issue 7, July 2, 2008.
15 U.S. Forces in Korea, G-2 Intelligence Summaries nos. 134–142, April 2–June 4, 1948; *Seoul Times*, April 7 and April 8, 1948.
16 Office of the Chief of Military History, History of the U.S. Armed Forces in Korea, vol. II, part 2, 'Police and National Events, 1947–1948.'
17 'The Background of the Present War in Korea,' *Far Eastern Economic Review*, 31 August 1950 (pp. 233–237).
18 Cumings, Bruce, *Korea's Place in the Sun: A Modern History*, New York, W. W. Norton & Company, 1997 (p. 221).
19 'The Background of the Present War in Korea,' *Far Eastern Economic Review*, 31 August 1950 (pp. 233–237).
20 Hwang, Su Kyoung, *Korea's Grievous War*, Philadelphia, University of Pennsylvania Press, 2016 (p. 29).
21 Sullivan, Walter, *New York Times*, March 6, 1950.

22 Stone, I. F., *Hidden History of the Korean War*, Amazon Media, 2014 (Chapter 17, 'Free Elections?').
23 Hersh, Seymour M., 'The Price of Power,' *The Atlantic*, December 1982.
24 Ridgway, Matthew B., *The Korean War*, New York, Doubleday, 1967 (pp. 143–145).
25 Stinnett, Robert B., *Day of Deceit: The Truth About FDR and Pearl Harbor*, New York, Free Press, 2000 (p. 14).
26 Stone, I. F., *Hidden History of the Korean War*, Amazon Media, 2014 (Chapter 6, 'Time Was Short').
27 Donnelly Thomas, *Rebuilding America's Defenses, A Report of The Project for the New American Century*, A report of the Project for the New American Century, September 2000 (p. 20).
28 Heale, Michael, *The United States in the Long Twentieth Century: Politics and Society Since 1900*, London, Bloomsbury Academic, 2015 (p. 174).
29 Hanley, Charles J. and Choe, Sang Hun and Mendoza, Martha, *The Bridge at No Gun Ri: A Hidden Nightmare from the Korean War*, New York, Henry Holt and Company, 2001 (p. 222).
30 Truman, Harry S., 304 – 'Proclaiming the Existence of a National Emergency,' December 16, 1950.
31 Harrison, Mark, *The Economics of World War II: Six Great Powers in International Comparison*, Cambridge, Cambridge University Press, 2000 (p. 1–42).
32 Speech to the Michigan legislature, in Lansing, Michigan, May 15, 1952, published in *General MacArthur Speeches and Reports 1908–1964* (2000) by Edward T. Imparato, (p. 206). Much of this was used in speeches of 1951, as quoted in *The Twenty-year Revolution from Roosevelt to Eisenhower* (1954) by Chesly Manly (p. 3), and *Total Insecurity: The Myth Of American Omnipotence* (2004) by Carol Brightman (p. 182).
33 Barro, Robert J., 'Why the War against Terror Will Boost the Economy,' *Bloomberg*, November 5, 2001.
34 Farewell Address of President Dwight D. Eisenhower, January 17, 1961.
35 'Unemployment Rate by Year Since 1929 Compared to Inflation and GDP, U.S. Unemployment Rate,' *The Balance*.
36 Stone, I. F., Hidden History of the Korean War, Amazon Media, 2014 (Chapter 48, 'Van Fleet Sums Up').
37 FO317, piece no. 83297, comment or 'minute' on Gascoigne to FO, Jan. 13, 1950; piece no. 83243, memo on invasion of Formosa, Jan. 25, 1950, minute by Burgess; piece no. 83247, report on Formosa, April 14, 1950, minute by Burgess.
38 Blum, William, *Killing Hope: U.S. Military and C.I.A. Interventions Since World War II*, London, Zed Books, 2003 (pp. 24–25).

39 Stone, I. F., *Hidden History of the Korean War*, Amazon Media, 2014 (Chapter 10, 'The Best Army in Asia').
40 Ibid. (Chapter 7, 'The Stage Was Set').
41 Levine, Alan J., Stalin's Last War; Korea and the Approach to World War III, Jefferson, McFarland & Company, 2005 (p. 10–11).
42 Stone, I. F., *Hidden History of the Korean War*, Amazon Media, 2014, (Chapter 4, 'The Role of John Foster Dulles').
43 Kennedy, John F., *Address on the first Anniversary of the Alliance for Progress*, March 13, 1962.
44 Cumings, Bruce, *Korea's Place in the Sun: A Modern History*, New York, W. W. Norton & Company, 1997 (p. 247).
45 Boose, Donald W., Jr., and Matray, James I., *The Ashgate Research Companion to the Korean War*, Farnham Ashgate, 2015 (p. 28).
46 Government of Canada, Veterans Affairs Canada, The Korean War, Land of the Morning Calm, Did You Know.
47 Mathews Papers, box 90, *Korea with the John Foster Dulles Mission*, June 14–29, 1950.
48 National Records Center, USFIK 11071 file, box 62/96, G-2 'Staff Study,' February 1949, signed by Lieutenant Colonel B. W. Heckemeyer of Army G-2.
49 UN Archives, BOX DAG-1/2.1.2, box 3, account of briefing on June 15, 1949.
50 Cumings, Bruce, *Korea's Place in the Sun: A Modern History*, New York, W. W. Norton & Company, 1997 (p. 257).
51 Ibid. (Chapter 5).
52 Washington to Canberra, memorandum 953, August 17, 1949.
53 British Foreign Office (FO 317), piece no. 76259, Holt to FO, Sept. 2, 1949.
54 National Archives, 895.00 file, box 7127, Ranshofen-Wertheimer to Jessup, September 22, 1949.
55 National Archives, 895.00 file, box 946, Muccio to Butterworth, August 27, 1949.
56 Wellington Koo Papers, Colombia University, box 217, Koo Diaries, entry for Jan. 4, 1950.
57 Cumings, Bruce, *The Korean War: A History*, New York City, Modern Library, 2010 (p. 140).
58 Blum, William, *Killing Hope: U.S. Military and C.I.A. Interventions Since World War II*, London, Zed Books, 2003 (pp. 46–48).
59 *New York Times*, June 25, 1950 (page 1 for South Korean Announcement, page 3 for North Korean Announcement).
60 Baldwin, Frank, *Without Parallel: The American-Korean Relationship Since 1945*, New York, Panthoen Books, 1974 (pp. 109–142).

61 Lie, Trygve, *In the cause of peace: seven years with the United Nations*, New York, The MacMillan Company, 1954 (Chapters 18 and 19).
62 Hazzard, Shirley, *Countenance of Truth: The United Nations and the Waldheim Case*, New York, Viking Penguin, 1990 (pp. 13–22).
63 Lie, Trygve, *In the cause of peace: seven years with the United Nations*, New York, The MacMillan Company, 1954 (p. 389).
64 Stone, I. F., Hidden History of the Korean War, Amazon Media, 2014 (Chapter 7, 'The Stage Was Set').
65 Ibid. (Chapter 7, 'The Stage Was Set').
66 *New York Times*, June 26, 1950.
67 Ibid. October 1, 1950, p. 4.
68 Stone, I. F., *Hidden History of the Korean War*, Amazon Media, 2014, (Chapter 7, 'The Stage Was Set').
69 Stone, I. F., *Hidden History of the Korean War*, Amazon Media, 2014, (Chapter 13, 'MacArthur's Blank Check').
70 Ibid.
71 Cumings, Bruce, *Korea's Place in the Sun: A Modern History*, New York, W. W. Norton & Company, 1997 (p. 266).

CHAPTER 8

The Korean War: Part I – Meeting a New Challenge to Western Regional Primacy

The evils of tyranny are rarely seen but by him who resists it.[1] — JOHN HAY

I had seen the war-battered cities of Europe; but I had not seen devastation until I had seen Korea.[2]

— American Chief Justice WILLIAM O. DOUGLAS

Sweeping South: The Early Stages of the War

Following the outbreak of the Korean War, ROK forces were soon pressed into a rapid retreat southwards by advancing North Korean divisions. U.S. personnel were rushed to their aid from neighboring Japan, and within days were engaging the KPA on the front. Initial American reinforcements proved wholly inadequate however, and these troops were almost immediately forced to retreat alongside the South Koreans. The U.S. forces appeared to have wholly underestimated the capabilities of the North Koreans, their advanced training and extensive prior combat experience in particular, which led to American forces initially deployed being overwhelmingly outmatched. As one British report stated regarding U.S. troops: 'In their very first contact with the North Koreans they were outmaneuvered and soundly defeated. Retreat was the only option.'[3]

Pulitzer prize winning American journalist David Halberstam noted the attitude of the American military towards the North Koreans, expecting them to flee and surrender at the very sight of Western soldiers. He wrote: 'almost everyone, from top to bottom, seemed to share the view that the moment the North Koreans saw they were fighting Americans rather than the ROKs they would cut and run. It was arrogance born of racial prejudice.'[4] Even at the top levels of the United States military the North Koreans were seriously underestimated. On the day of the outbreak of the war General MacArthur demonstrated complacency and overconfidence, stating regarding the North Korean forces: 'I can handle it with one arm tied behind my back.' The following day he told John Foster Dulles that if he only put the U.S. 1st Cavalry Division into Korea, 'why, heavens, you'd see these fellows scuttle up to the Manchurian border so quick, you would see no more of them.'[5]

MacArthur had more of an intuitive approach to military intelligence, mingling hard facts with the enemy's presumed racial qualities. 'Chinamen can't fight,' he had once said, and he didn't expect Koreans to fight much better. As the war continued however MacArthur was faced with the reality that Koreans could indeed fight – perhaps better than his own men. At first he wanted an American regimental combat team in Korea, then two divisions. Within a week he cabled Washington that only a quarter of South Korean troops could even be located, and that the north's Korean People's Army was 'operating under excellent top level guidance and had demonstrated superior command of strategic and tactical principles.' By the beginning of July MacArthur wanted a minimum of 30,000 American combat personnel, meaning more than four infantry divisions, three tank battalions and assorted artillery. A week later his asked for eight whole divisions.[6]

South Korean forces, trained and armed by the United States, proved even less competent at fighting the North Koreans than the Americans did despite their considerable numerical superiority. Much like the first U.S. forces deployed to the peninsula, they too fell into disorder. Within days of the outbreak of the conflict masses of soldiers were defecting. Those that weren't were retreating.[7] They faced similar issues and proved similarly incapable of fighting North Korean forces as the Chinese Guomindang forces had when fighting against the Chinese communists – both were American client forces in disorder, under corrupt leadership, facing mass defections and with low morale. A month after the outbreak of the war fully half of the South Korean soldiers were dead, captured or missing.

Only two divisions maintained their equipment while the rest of the army, around 70 percent, had lost or abandoned their equipment.

An American Colonel in the war told British journalist Philip Knightly of his observations regarding the performance of the ROK military. He said: 'South Koreans and North Koreans are identical. Why then do North Koreans fight like tigers and South Koreans run like sheep?' The key difference was the morale and leadership of the two armies, the perceived legitimacy of their governments and the viability of their causes. The Morse code 'HA' was used all over the front to indicate South Korean forces 'hauling ass' – that is, retreating. Even in later stages of the war South Korean troops would continue to prove unreliable. American General Matthew B. Ridgeway noted in 1951 his dismay at the unwillingness of the South Koreans to fight a war supposedly being waged for their own freedom. He wrote: 'I drove out north of Seoul and into a dismaying spectacle. ROK soldiers by truckloads were streaming south, without orders, without arms, without leaders, in full retreat [...] They had thrown away their rifles and pistols and had abandoned all artillery, mortars, machine guns, every crew-serviced weapon.'[8]

Dr Gary Sous, Chief of the Oral History Unit at the Marine Corps Historical Center said of the U.S. forces first deployed to Korea from Japan: 'It was the very first days of the war. They were in full retreat. Their awareness of the tactical situation was minimal.'[9] Superior forces, the U.S. 7th Cavalry, were deployed to Korea within days to support the failing troops already deployed. These elite reinforcements also proved incapable of pushing back North Korean forces. Allied wartime reports revealed that within two days the 7th Cavalry had shot several of their own men by accident. 'On the next (3rd) night, July the 25th, elements were positioned on a hillside a few miles behind the front line. Rumors went around that the North Koreans had made a breakthrough causing mass panic. In the morning 119 cavalrymen were unaccounted for, along with many of the unit's heavy weapons.' A soldier interviewed said: 'It was just nothing but mass confusion. You didn't. You stop here. You dig in. You just wait. You're gonna have to leave. Nobody knew what was going on. Matter of fact I didn't even know if we had a platoon leader, majority of the time. I didn't know if we had a platoon sergeant. There was nobody in charge.'[10]

While the South Korean military had effectively ceased to fight, the American military reportedly 'did no fighting worthy of the name,' they just broke and ran. Disordered, retreating and often fearful, U.S. forces on many occasions turned to massacring South Korean civilians (as covered extensively in Chapter 10). Bruce Cumings gave a summary of the initial months of the war and American and South Korean initial military failures. He wrote: 'In the summer months of 1950 the Korean People's Army pushed southward with dramatic success, with one humiliating defeat after another for American forces. An army that had bested Germany and Japan found its back pressed to the wall by what it thought was a hastily assembled peasant military, ill-equipped and, worse, said to be doing the bidding of a foreign imperial power [as per the American perception of the KPA at the time, who were portrayed as doing the bidding of Stalin].'[11]

The retreating U.S. forces significantly underestimated the potency and efficiency of the North Korean fighting man, and assumed that the military which continued to best them must have had a significant numerical advantage. In fact, by the end of July 1950, with U.S. reinforcements continuing to pour into the country, American and ROK forces significantly outnumbered the KPA along the front, 140,000 to 70,000. Not only were the North Koreans outnumbered 2 to 1 on the front, but the United States also had complete and uncontested air and naval superiority and an overwhelming superiority in firepower. North Korean intelligence was also overwhelmingly outmatched, and they lacked the sophisticated logistical and technical support of the U.S. military. The fact that the U.S. forces continued to retreat in spite of every possible advantage, aside from that of morale and possibly training, attested to both the disorder within their own ranks and the effectiveness of the North Korean military. It seemed the quality and morale of the North Korean soldier and the organized efficiency with which their military was using its limited resources was more than capable of compensating for significant disadvantages in firepower, air superiority, naval capabilities, intelligence and numbers.[12]

It took some months for the majority of the United States' fully equipped fighting force, and whatever elements of the South Korean military remained, to finally halt the advanced of the relatively poorly armed Korean People's Army. While the former received a massive flow of supplies from food to artillery shells, North Korean forces engaging the U.S. military did not receive logistical support from the USSR or China which proved a significant disadvantage.[13] The fighting stabilized at what came to be called the Pusan Perimeter, an 80 by 50 mile right-angled front. Kim Il Sung later said that the plan was to win the war for the south in one month, and by the end of July he had nearly done so.[14] The formation of a 'Pusan Perimeter' and a halt to the North Korean advance in July 1950 were a direct result of the extremely limited logistics and lack of supplies North Korean forces had to contend with. Had this not been the case the entire peninsula would have been under North Korean control by the end of July 1950, and the calculus for any further landings of U.S. troops would have been entirely different.[15] Though the West depicted the 'Kim Il Sung regime' as proxies of the 'International Communist Conspiracy,' major communist powers were unwilling to support Korean communist forces fighting against the United States – much as they had neglected to supply the Huks in the Philippines or the PKI in Indonesia before them which were also engaged in wars against the Western powers.

Henry Luce's *Time* magazine indicated that the Chinese and Soviets had not given support to the North Korean military after the outbreak of the war and throughout its initial stages. The publication noted on October 6, 1950: 'If Russia [USSR] or China intended to intervene in Korea, they should have done so earlier when they could have pushed U.N. forces into the sea.' It was clear from the state of their supplies and the nature of their armaments that the KPA did not enjoy support from what was then the second largest military industrial economy in the world. The outgunned and relatively ill-equipped North Korean forces had come close to victory with little to no support. Had the KPA been rearmed and supplied by the communist powers, even with no personnel contributions, it would very likely have taken the entire peninsula and prevented the U.S. led alliance from landing their forces in Korea and gaining a foothold. Such was Beijing and Moscow's desire to avoid a confrontation however, that neither provided their communist neighbor with this much needed support.

With a population well over ten times that of North Korea and with support from British and South Korean forces, the numerical advantage certainly overwhelmingly favored the Americans. All of the United States' combat ready divisions worldwide, except for the 82nd airborne division deployed in Germany but including all divisions on the American mainland itself, would be deployed against North Korean forces – an unprecedented measure necessitated by the dire nature of the situation on the ground.[16,17] British forces were also swiftly deployed to the front. It is critical to note that the United States was challenged by a small and vastly outnumbered 'peasant army' which was outnumbered and outgunned, and yet despite the alleged unmatched military capabilities of the U.S. it was nearly defeated. Were it not for the several waves of reinforcements brought from across the world, something which added to their already considerable superiority in numbers, technology and firepower, the Korean campaign would have concluded by the end of 1950 with a U.S. defeat. These were assets which the small North Korean state could not itself call upon – without which the United States was set to suffer a decisive defeat.

While the KPA was significantly undersupplied – increasingly so as the front moved southwards – lacking basic necessities such as fuel to wage war, not only was the United States' unparalleled military industrial base working provide its forces with any equipment they could possibly need, but significant military support and personnel from Britain, France, the Philippines, Turkey, Australia, New Zealand, Canada, Thailand, Greece, Luxembourg, the Netherlands, Colombia and Belgium among others was also quickly forthcoming. A vast coalition of Western imperial powers and their partners and client nations were thus united against the KPA.[18] This was done using the authority of the United Nations, which though it found no evidence of North Korean aggression, had been pressured by the United States to intervene on its behalf and thereby grant further legitimacy to military action against the DPRK.[19]While there was a coalition, the United States' dominance of the other parties and of the UN was strongly reflected in the command structures. All United Nations forces were, under a UN resolution passed on July 7, 1950, subject to U.S. Supreme Commander MacArthur's command – while MacArthur himself was not made subject to the commands of the United Nations Security Council.[20] The resolution commanded 'that all members providing military forces and other assistance [...] make sure such forces and other assistance available to a unified command under the United States.' It further stated that the

United States was itself free 'to designate the commander of such forces,' for which MacArthur was chosen.[21] It was clear from this point that it was primarily an American war effort. U.S. President Eisenhower himself stated the true purpose of the coalition and why it was preferable for the United States to wage war in this way rather than intervening unilaterally. He stated: 'the *token forces* supplied by other nations, as in Korea, would lend real moral standing to a venture that otherwise could be made to appear as a brutal example of imperialism.'[22]Two months after the war's outbreak the U.S. and their allies were continuing to retreat and struggling to counter North Korean forces. In late August the KPA reportedly made 'startling gains' for two consecutive weeks which seriously strained UN coalition forces. UN forces were pressed at three points at once, Kyongju, Masan and Taegu, and their perimeter was 'near breaking point.' DPRK forces crossed the Naktong River and took Pohang and Chinju, and the more numerous, better armed and fresh UN forces were hard pressed on the defensive. On September 9 Kim Il Sung, who was directing the war effort, said the war had reached an 'extremely harsh, decisive stage' with the enemy now being pressed on three fronts. Two days later Commander of the U.S. Eighth Army General Walton Walker reported the frontline situation was the most dangerous since their perimeter had been established.

Renowned American historian Roy Appleman covered the United States' military involvement in Asia closely. 'After two weeks of the heaviest fighting of the war' he wrote, UN forces 'had just barely turned back the great North Korean offensive.' By September 15 the United States forces, who were doing the bulk of the fighting, had alone suffered 20,000 casualties.[23]The ability of the relatively poorly armed Korean People's Army, despite being vastly outnumbered and outgunned, to fight the United States military to a standstill did not go unnoticed by American command. Major General William F. Dean reported to MacArthur: 'I am convinced that the North Korean Army, the North Korean solider and his status and training and the quality of his equipment have been underestimated.'[24] General Mathew Ridgeway too was taken aback by the North Korean military, stating: 'we had never ... imagined that the NKPA [North Korean People's Army, same as KPA] was a force so well-trained, so superbly disciplined, so battle-ready.'[25] Even General MacArthur, after having done so himself, warned of the dangers of underestimating the capabilities of the North Korean soldiers and military leaders.[26]

The lack of weapons and support needed to sustain a war against the fast growing UN forces led to an eventual halt in the KPA's advance. An amphibious landing at Inchon in mid-September 1950 placed more U.S. forces in position to retake Seoul and was the beginning of the UN counter-offensive. Almost all the United States' global military forces were focused on turning back the small Korean People's Army. At Inchon 80,000 elite U.S. Marines landed on a fleet of 270 ships, further compounding American numerical superiority. The North Koreans began to see the tide of war turn against them. Many weapons lacked ammunition and their country's air and naval capabilities were negligible to begin with. North Korean divisions were often forced to abandon their tanks due to fuel shortages, as the DPRK had no domestic energy resources and lacked the fuel to maintain them or foreign sponsors to provide such essential resources.

After the Inchon landings the KPA began a strategic withdrawal, avoiding suffering significant casualties as they certainly would have if facing the now colossal UN forces head-on so far south. The majority of KPA forces escaped into the north, while many guerilla forces including the entire KPA 10th Division, withdrew into the mountains in the south. They would continue to cause significant problems for U.S. forces for much of the war. Leading the coalition, the United States military managed to push the KPA back over the 38th parallel. Whether the Korean withdrawal was a strategic necessity or a ploy to lure the UN forces into the north and overstretch their supply lines remains disputed today. There is still some evidence however indicating that many in the KPA's command may have planned to lure the far more numerous UN forces further north, thinking they would overstretch their overconfident adversary. Pak Ki Song, chief of political intelligence for the KPA's 8th division, stated: 'The main force of the enemy still remained intact, not having been fully damaged. When they were not fully aware of the power of our forces, they pushed their infantry far forward [...] to the Yalu River. This indicated that they underestimated us. All these conditions were favorable to lure them near.'[27]

A KPA officer captured later in the war explained what he alleged was the true nature of the North Korean strategy of continuous withdrawal, stating: 'One may think that going down all the way to the Pusan perimeter and then withdrawing all the way to the Yalu River was a complete defeat. But that is not so. That was a planned withdrawal. We withdrew because we knew that UN troops would follow us up here, and that they would spread their troops thinly all over the vast area. Now, the time has come for us to envelop these troops and annihilate them.'[28]

DPRK military officials' claims that their retreat was in fact an organized strategic withdrawal following its rapid string of hard earned victories could well have been made in order to avoid admitting defeat or demoralizing its forces. The North Korean claims of a strategic withdrawal were however tacitly supported by Western reporters at the time. Reginald Thompson, a British reporter present at Inchon at the time, wrote of the nature of the United States' military victory there. 2000 North Koreans had defended the position against 80,000 elite U.S. Marines, and were quickly defeated and taken captive. These troops had turned out to be young wholly inexperienced decoys, while the actual Korean People's Army 'had disappeared like wraiths into the hills.' MacArthur's trap 'had closed, and it was empty.' The North Koreans seemed to have mastered strategic withdrawal, escaping a colossal U.S. offensive with negligible losses.[29]

Over three divisions of North Koreans had fought in the Chinese civil war, while Kim Il Sung's own guerilla forces had before then maintained close connections with their counterparts in China fighting against the Japanese Empire. As a result of their shared experiences, KPA military doctrine shared many concepts with the Chinese People's Liberation Army (PLA). One such strategy was that of 'luring the enemy in deep,' described in 1938 by Mao Zedong as follows: 'We have always advocated the policy of "luring the enemy in deep", precisely because it is the most effective military policy for a weak army strategically on the defensive to employ against a strong army.'[30] So it came to be that when DPRK forces would choose to at last turn and fight at their northern border, the speed and effectiveness with which they did so astonished not only their enemies, but the Chinese as well. British correspondent and writer Russel Spurr himself observed that 'The North Koreans had in fact astonished the Chinese by the speed at which they had reconstituted their shattered forces.'[31] American pilots themselves observed large and intact North Korean forces in October (a month after Inchon), at a time when their fighting capability was considered spent. As reporter Hugh Deane, former Coordinator of Information and naval intelligence officer on General MacArthur's staff, reported, General MacArthur 'announced that the Korean People's Army had been destroyed when in fact a number of reconstituted divisions were about to take the field against him.' By early 1951 it was clear that the KPA was far larger than expected, estimated at around 200,000 personnel, indicating a strategic withdrawal from the south had taken place rather than a retreat.[32] While only partially mobilized in the war's initial months, the threat posed by a far greater adversary led the KPA to begin recruiting larger numbers of personnel, often with far less combat experience than the hardened units which had fought in the first battles, to increase their numbers and better confront their enemy.

The Terms of Surrender: What America's Peace Terms Would Have Meant for North Korea and Why this Guaranteed the War Would Continue

The United Nations forces under the command and leadership of the United States Far East Command, having received hundreds of thousands of fresh troops and outflanked the KPA by landing forces at Inchon, pushed North Korean forces northwards and up to the 38th parallel – then beyond. UN forces had no mandate to continue the war north of the parallel and into North Korean territory under the July 7 UN resolution, but this was entirely ignored. The mandate of restoring peace and security did not include provisions for an invasion and the destruction of one Korean government to impose the power of another – only the repelling of North Korean forces to the 38th parallel. The UN had not given a mandate for regime change in the DPRK, only to restore the territorial integrity of the ROK. Nevertheless General MacArthur ordered the vast forces under his command to continue north into the DPRK's territory. As the UN prepared to offer terms for peace and to re-establish the 38th parallel as a border between the two Koreas, the general pre-empted and thus prevented such a settlement by both sending his forces into the DPRK and by dictating his own surrender terms – offering only an 'unconditional surrender' which it was almost impossible for the North Koreans to accept.

The demand for 'unconditional surrender' and the provocative advance towards the Soviet and Chinese borders, when read in the context of America's fear of peace and of MacArthur's calls for a major war against international communism – in particular the 'rolling back' of Chinese communism to reverse the outcome of the Guomindang's defeat, have significant connotations regarding his intentions. The United Nations could have offered to negotiate with the North Korean government directly at this point and asked for surrender on specific terms. It could have even sought to promise regime change and countrywide elections with supervision of the communist powers, and even this was more likely to be accepted than the terms they offered which placed the future of the North Korean people in MacArthur's and Rhee's hands.

While several far more reasonable surrender or armistice terms could have been offered, all of which were more likely to end the war soon and save millions of lives, any possibility of such a settlement was made impossible when General MacArthur acted on his own initiative and demanded unconditional surrender. For the North Koreans to accept this would have been to accept an American occupation under a client dictatorship known to massacre its own people en masse,[33,34] one which the United States had installed in the south under Syngman Rhee. Unconditional surrender could mean absolutely anything – including the sexual enslavement of the Korean women,[35] organized mass extermination of dissenters,[36] and an indefinite Western occupation[37,38] – incidentally exactly what happened under the Rhee government in the south. It would mean an industrialized and fast modernizing country falling under the administration of government which had left its people destitute and was so inept it would never draft an economic policy in 12 years in office.[39,40]

General MacArthur proclaimed: 'I [...] call upon you [the North Korean commander] and the forces under your command, in whatever part of Korea situated, forthwith to lay down your arms and cease hostilities *under such military supervisions as I may direct*.' Rhee's government would claim sovereignty over the whole of Korea, and his soldiers were openly known to massacre possible communist sympathizers – let alone communists themselves. Rhee had made his intentions in occupying the North very clear, stating: 'I can handle the Communists. The Reds can bury their guns and burn their uniforms, but we know how to find them. With bulldozers we will dig huge excavations and trenches, and fill them with Communists. Then cover them over. And they will be really underground.'[41,42] Rhee was not bluffing – he had in fact killed and buried suspected communists and dissenters and their families, including children, in their thousands in mass graves in South Korea exactly as he described during peacetime.[43,44] These killings escalated after the outbreak of the war, with a Reuters' dispatch reporting shortly after the war began: 'Twelve hundred Communists and suspected Communists have been executed by South Korean police since the outbreak of the hostilities, Kim Tai Sun, chief of National South Korean police, said today.'[45]

Several U.S. sources attested to the Rhee government's frequent practice of burying suspected communists and their families in mass graves. The U.S. 3rd Engineers Company witnessed such an incident, with private Donald Lloyd recalling: 'We heard the machine-gun fire and saw them burying them in this big pit. There were women in that pit holding babies. I'd say one hundred people.'[46] CIA Operative Col. Donald Nichols detailed in his book the systematic slaughter of political prisoners in South Korea near Suwon in the first week of July 1950. He wrote: 'I stood by helplessly, witnessing the entire affair. Two big bulldozers worked constantly. One made the ditch-type grave. Trucks loaded with the condemned arrived. Their hands were already tied behind them. They were hastily pushed into a big line along the edge of the newly opened grave. They were quickly shot in the head and pushed into the grave.'[47] The South Korean government's Truth and Reconciliation Commission conducted a thorough investigation after the establishment of democratic rule in the country, and long after the overthrown of the Rhee government. Though the United States had knowingly falsely attributed many of the mass graves and massacres to the North Koreans, the South Korean commission proved using declassified records that it was in fact the Rhee government, with the compliance of the US, which was responsible for these extermination programs targeting suspected dissidents and their families. The mass burial sites uncovered contained thousands of bodies including children.[48] The victims among South Korea's civilian population numbered in the hundreds of thousands in the weeks following the outbreak of the Korean War.[49]

Even Britain and France, both close allies of the United States and strongly anti-communist, expressed major doubts as to whether the Rhee government was a suitable administrator for Korea should it be unified by military force. They claimed the ROK government had shown itself to be weak, corrupt and highly repressive and would in all likelihood 'provoke a widespread terror.' They questioned not only whether the Rhee government should be given control over the north, but whether it should even be allowed to retain control over the south after the war's end.[50]

Rhee's government did not recognize the DPRK, so would the communist forces be treated honorably as a defeated enemy, or as treasonous seditionists attempting to overthrow the 'true government of Korea?' Almost certainly the latter. Considering that an unconditional surrender would leave North Koreans at the mercy of such a leader, who had demonstrated even according to his allies gross and inhumane mistreatment of suspected dissidents and their families, it seemed that there was little if nothing to lose in fighting on – not merely out of pride but due to a basic need to survive. It was clear that General MacArthur's surrender terms could never be accepted, and that they therefore guaranteed the war would continue. North Koreans had nothing to lose by continuing to fight to the bitter end.

As previously mentioned, it was expected that if elections were conducted in Korea a communist party would me most likely to come to power. The *New York Times* wrote that free elections in Korea 'would produce a Communist majority, thus bringing about the same result as if the United Nations had not intervened.'[51] The United States was well aware of this, and was not willing to allow for reunification and free elections to take place. Warren Austin, U.S. ambassador to the UN, made a speech on August 17, around the time the UN forces were demanding a North Korean absolute surrender. This speech 'revealed that the United States wants them [the elections] to be held on the basis that the Republic of Korea's jurisdiction would be extended over North Korea automatically.'[52] This meant that the Rhee government, which had killed hundreds of thousands of communist suspects and dissenters, was to supervise elections in the north. The CIA had strongly advised the White House against an invasion of North Korea, and particularly against imposing the Syngman Rhee led government of the south on the North Korean people. It warned that if instead of imposing the ROK's government however, free elections were to be held then it would likely bring about a communist government for the whole of Korea.[53] While Western leaders, South Korean officials and others spoke of reunification following an unconditional surrender, but all seemed aware that a genuine democratic process which allowed the communists to contend for power would lead to their victory – and so could not be allowed for.

Such harsh surrender terms may well have been put forward by MacArthur with the expectation that they would not be accepted. An unconditional surrender was not fitting for the military situation at the time, as the North Korean forces had mostly retreated rather than having been destroyed. If the terms were accepted it would give the United States free reign and the North Koreans would lose all say in determining their own future. MacArthur's desire for an expanded campaign which took the fight to China's borders was a significant incentive for him to issue unacceptable terms to ensure that the war would continue and UN forces would push on past the 38th parallel. A statement by MacArthur, though addressing the ROK rather than the DPRK, is remarkably true when applied to the latter considering the surrender terms offered: 'They have chosen to risk death rather than slavery.'[54] The war would go on, the risk of war drawing in other communist powers would continue to increase as the fighting approached their borders, and millions more Koreans would suffer and die over the next three years.

Avoiding Peace

As the U.S. and its allies continued to push further into North Korean territory the threat of conflict arising on the Chinese or Soviet borders grew. Chinese premier Zhou Enlai, in an address at the first anniversary of the founding of the People's Republic of China, warned that his country would not 'supinely tolerate' an invasion of North Korea. China was reluctant to risk a war with the United States by intervening however, and only did so when its own territorial integrity was directly threatened. Nevertheless, MacArthur's Tokyo Command which oversaw the campaign did not heed Beijing's warning. Despite the United States' initial defeats against the small North Korean force, the military leadership appeared confident of their forces' supremacy over those of China. As one U.S. official said regarding the prospects for the East Asian power entering the war: 'I don't think China wants to be chopped up.' Despite the 'important economic as well as political and military stakes of the Peiping [Peking] regime in North Korea,'[55] China was expected to either tolerate its neighbor's destruction or face destruction itself for its defiance.

UN forces swept through northern Korea and approached the Chinese border while the KPA continued to withdraw north. With the approach of U.S. led forces openly hostile to the new Chinese republic and their leaders pledging to 'roll back' communism, China feared for the security of its Manchurian industrial centers on the Korean border – including the key power plants the two countries used jointly. Having spent 13 years under the Japanese Empire, which had prioritized industrial development in its East Asian territories with impressive results, Manchuria was by far the most industrialized and developed area of China and a vital part of the nation's economy. A *New York Times* correspondent at the time pointed out that the Yalu River power plant on the border with Korea 'has been supplying electrical power for the Manchurian industrialization program,' which the Chinese regarded as their 'pilot zone' for nationwide industrialization. This industrial zone was therefore of great importance to the Chinese government. China's People's Liberation Army (PLA) had thus deployed a small detachment of troops to form a thin buffer zone to protect their key industrial interests. UN forces continued to advance towards these Chinese forces however, and undertook no measures to avoid hostilities. China's concerns regarding the security of its industrial zone were ignored, and U.S. and South Korean troops which were spearheading the advance proceeded to engage Chinese forces deployed to protect these border investments. The initial Chinese deployment south of the power plants were censored from American media – so when it emerged that Chinese forces had been engaged by UN forces in Korea it made it seem an act of Chinese aggression. This was made possible only because U.S. media during the war operated under strict censorship. British reporter and author Reginald Thompson, the war's contemporary, wrote in regards to this: 'There are few who dared to write the truth of things as they saw them ... correspondents were placed under the jurisdiction of the army' and criticism of U.S. and allied troops was strictly prohibited. The concoction of false reports was far from uncommon, with UN Command widely perceived by journalists to be consistently committing 'lies, half-truths and serious distortions.'[56] While MacArthur's headquarters pushed for war, the United Nations itself undertook measures to preempt and prevent any expansion of the conflict to involve China. On November 7, the United Nations Interim Committee on Korea issued a statement 'to reassure the Chinese Communists regarding their interests on the Korean-Manchurian border.' China quickly responded, and on the same day Tokyo HQ released that: 'Chinese and North Korean troops in a surprise maneuver broke contact with United Nations forces on the defense line north of Anju this morning.' Tokyo HQ for their part did not seem to welcome the ending of hostilities, and asserted that a withdrawal must be taking place with the intention to 'regroup large concentrations of ... communist troops for a new onslaught rather than retreat.' The withdrawal from combat had to be depicted as having aggressive intent.[57]

With the PLA and KPA having withdrawn, the United Nations Security Council was set to meet on November 8. The Chinese delegation was to arrive at the peace talks on November 15, and they were strongly interested in making peace and in preventing any conflict while these talks took place. Everything seemed in place for the war to end, as the UN and the Chinese wished. MacArthur and the U.S. command however could take no chances of peace breaking out. If there was a cessation in the fighting it had to be reignited and quickly, lest their war against communism end prematurely.

On November 8, just hours before the peace talks began, it was suddenly announced by a U.S. Air Force spokesman in Washington that 'an earlier ban against flights within three miles of Manchuria' put in place to avoid provocation of China, had been lifted and that 'United States pilots in Korea are operating right up to the Chinese border along the Yalu River.' The actions of the U.S. Air Force soon made it clear why they had chosen the words 'are operating' rather than 'may operate' as would normally be the case when lifting regulations. The 'danger spot,' Sinuiju, was a Korean city across the river from Antung next to the Chinese border. That day 79 B-29 Superfortress bombers and three fighter planes from the U.S. Air Force attacked this city. This massive attack formation dropped 630 tons of bombs and were 'said to have destroyed ninety percent of the city' having used 'rockets, demolition bombs, and 85,000 incendiaries.'[58] The scenes were reminiscent of the firebombing of Tokyo five years beforehand, with the very same weapons again being used en masse to target an Asian population center.

The *New York Times* reported that 'the attack came almost simultaneously with an announcement by an Air Force spokesman in Washington that United States fliers had received permission to bomb right up to the Manchurian border instead of remaining three miles south in an attempt to avoid possible frontier violations.'[59] Considering the preparation such a large strike force would need and the timing and circumstances of the bombing, it would seem that the attack had been planned and prepared before authorization had been given, if not that the attack forces had already been dispatched. It was a *fait accompli* by Tokyo Command put in motion long before the lifting of the flight ban was announced. Just when there was a chance for peace, to which Chinese and North Korean forces had responded with withdrawal and de-escalation, a massive attack in a particularly sensitive area was staged to disrupt the process.

American Journalist I. F. Stone commented at the time on the policy MacArthur's Tokyo Command pursued and their attempts to avoid peace and draw China into an open and full scale war. He analyzed the actions of the American military leadership and the effects these had on the Korean civilians, and on prospects of peace in Korea:

> Just when there was a lull in the fighting and it looked as if peace were possible, MacArthur staged a gigantic and murderous raid directly across from the Chinese frontier, destroying most of a city in an area where bombings had been forbidden to prevent border violations. He had gotten the Air Force to lift the bombing

restriction – how, when or why nobody knows. Perhaps he did it by starting the raid first and asking permission afterwards [...] this is what he is reported to have done the very first week of the war, in forcing the President to 'allow' him to bomb north of the 38th parallel. 'There were reports,' the *New York Times* said, 'that General MacArthur had ordered the first bombings of North Korean cities without authorization from Washington.'

The pretext for the raid was 'to eliminate Sinuiju as a future stronghold for supplies and communications.' This was stated in the announcement later issued by Lieutenant General George E. Stratemeyer, commander of the Far East Air Forces. The description based on the briefing in Tokyo is not pleasant reading. The attack began in the morning 'when fighter planes swept the area with machine guns, rockets and jellied gasoline bombs.' They were followed by 'ten of the superforts' which 'dropped 1000-pound high-explosive bombs on railroad and highway bridges across the Yalu River and on the bridge approaches' (if dropped on the bridges as well as the approaches, the bombers were obviously operating right up to the boundary line on the river itself). After this, 'the remaining planes used incendiaries exclusively on a two and one-half mile built-up area along the southeast bank of the Yalu.' General Stratemeyer maintained that all targets were of a military nature and bomb runs 'had kept away from the city's hospital areas.' At the same time the Air Force claimed ninety percent of the city had been destroyed. How these statements can be reconciled I do not know. There is an indifference to human suffering to be read between those lines which makes me as an American deeply ashamed of what was done that day at Sinuiju.

Tokyo Headquarters, with or without connivance by Washington, ravaged a city when a truce was in prospect. It deliberately took action which might have provoked a third world war – when the Chinese, of whose intervention it complained, were withdrawing. That the military knew what they were doing is indicated by a short Associated Press dispatch from Seoul which was printed the same day as the news of the mass raid on Sinuiju. A United States Eighth Army spokesman said that 'Chinese Communist troops might be avoiding fighting in North Korea pending high level diplomatic moves that would affect the course of the Korean War.' This spokesman stated that the withdrawal of the Chinese in the northwest 'has been gradual over a four-day period' while in the northeast 'a Tenth Corps spokesman said the Chinese 184th Division was 'in retreat' from the giant Changjin hydroelectric complex.' If the Chinese were even abandoning their dams, they must have wanted peace badly. Was the mass raid intended to goad them to war?

The mass bombing raid on Sinuiju November 8 was the beginning of a race between peace and provocation. A terrible retribution threatened the peoples of the Western world who so feebly permitted such acts to be done in their name. For it was by such means that the pyromaniacs hoped to set the world afire.[60]

Firebombing a population center on the Chinese border had severe implications on the peace process, and ultimately ensured that despite the efforts of the Chinese government and many in the United Nations the war would continue. As China increasingly became involved in the war and its forces proved themselves to be a formidable presence on the battlefield, MacArthur's willingness to engage them in a total war only increased. As Chairman of the U.S. Joint Chiefs of Staff General Omar Bradley observed: 'the only possible means left to MacArthur to regain his lost pride and military reputation was now to inflict an overwhelming defeat on those Red Chinese generals who had made a fool of him. In order to do this, he was perfectly willing to propel us into an all-out war with Red China and possibly the Soviet Union.'[61] As U.S. forces pushed north, declaring their intention to 'roll back communism,' conducting bombing raids on the Chinese border threatening key infrastructure, China had little choice but to enter the war. With General MacArthur prophesizing a 'final victory against communism' and holding meetings with Chiang Kai-shek, who himself sought to co-operate with the Americans to launch a war against the Chinese mainland using his own sizeable forces on Taiwan, the threat to Chinese sovereignty appeared both great and imminent.[62,63] Had China actively sought to fight the United States in Korea they could have easily intervened in the opening months when U.S. forces were on the verge of being driven off the peninsula entirely and any small assistance to the North Koreans could well have tipped the balance. As it was China sought to avoid war at all costs, and did so only when it faced a serious threat and attacks from a relentless hostile force.

Race and War: The Field Performance of China's Armed Forces

The military effectiveness of the Korean People's Army was covered in the West with strong racial themes typical of reporting on the successes of 'non-compliant' Asian nations. Following their rapid successive victories over

U.S. forces the *New York Times'* military editor Hanson Baldwin wrote of the North Koreans: 'We are facing an army of barbarians in Korea, but they are barbarians as trained, as relentless, as reckless of life, and as skilled in the tactics of the kind of war they fight as the hordes of Genghis Khan [...] They have taken a leaf from the Nazi book of blitzkrieg and are employing all the weapons of fear and terror.' Baldwin mentioned 'the most primitive of peoples,' referring to Chinese, 'Mongolians, Soviet Asiatics and a variety of races' who he claimed were involved in a conspiracy against the Western world of which the Korean War was a major part. He later likened Koreans to invading locusts,[64] referring to the Korean people as 'these simple primitive and barbaric peoples.'[65] Again the attitude of the West towards Asian races, particularly when they dared to 'step out of line' and exact military defeats upon a Western power were clear to see. Like Japan before and Vietnam afterwards however, 'stepping out of line' and defying the West's power and designs on Asian nations would cost the Koreans dearly. The United States would go on to commit severe war crimes, indiscriminately targeting civilian population centers, much as they had in Japan, to punish these 'most primitive of peoples' for their defiance. The West's perceptions of the Asian races profoundly influenced its conduct in the Korean War – as it has in all major wars in the region to date.

Racial stereotyping and perceptions of Asian racial inferiority were common in the West and reflected in both the statements of military officials and their brutal actions against the population. Reporter and author Reginald Thompson wrote that war correspondents found the U.S. military campaign in the south 'strangely disturbing' – very different in nature from the conflicts in the Second World War against European adversaries. He wrote: U.S. troops 'never spoke of the enemy as though they were people, but as one might speak of apes.' He said that even among correspondents 'every man's dearest wish was to kill a Korean. "Today ... I'll get me a gook."' Thompson believed that this dehumanization of Koreans based on their ethnicity was crucial to enabling American military personnel to commit atrocities against the Korean people, 'otherwise these essentially kind and generous Americans would not have been able to kill them indiscriminately or smash up their homes and poor belongings.'[66] American Professor H. Patricia Hynes noted that this dehumanization and the terms used to describe Koreans as subhuman was 'a linguistic device that numbs one's humanity and enables torture, killing of POWs and civilians, free-fire zones, and use of napalm and carpet-bombing.'[67] Racial hatred and dehumanization went hand in hand with the destruction the American forces would bring the Korean people. Koreans were otherwise referred to as 'communist monsters,' 'primitive North Koreans,' and a number of other terms widely used by Western media to gain public support for the continuation of the war. At the dawn of the postcolonial era the reference to a supposedly racially inferior enemy as 'primitives' resonated with Westerners who had for centuries been engaged in wars across the world against various 'primitives' and 'savages' in Asia, Africa and beyond. Indeed, it had long been generally accepted among Western powers that different rules applied when fighting 'savages' than in warfare between 'civilized' Western nations. 'Immense savagery' and often genocide were consistently the results of this under European empires,[68] and the labeling of Koreans as primitives and savages led to similarly brutal treatment at the hands of the United States and their Western allies during the Korean War. Such terms were scarcely if ever applied to European adversaries during the Second World War, but were applied to the Japanese imperial forces. This closely reflected the discrepancy between the severe abuses committed against the Chinese, North Koreans and the Japanese before them at the hands of Western militaries as opposed to the relatively humane treatment shown to European adversaries. American Lieutenant Uzal Ent attested to the effect of racialist perceptions of the Korean people on his soldiers' conduct towards them: 'Many men fought with a visceral hatred of the enemy. Maybe the fact that they were Orientals had something to do with it. "Gooks" was the standard term for them, and it was easier to think of them as not quite human, as something beneath us.'[69]

The repercussions of the racial demonization of Koreans extended to supposedly allied South Koreans as well. Walter Sullivan wrote that following the military victories of North Korean forces American personnel began to suspect South Korean civilians and associate them with the hostile forces. 'The American G. I. is now beginning to eye with suspicion any Korean civilian in the cities or countryside [...] "Watch the guys in white" – the customary peasant dress – is the cry often heard near the front.' This led to war crimes and massacres being carried out against South Korean civilians as well as North Koreans. All Koreans, from South Korean civilians to North Korea soldiers were to some degree seen as the enemy, and this was reflected in the orders of American commanders who on many occasions ordered the targeting and massacre of South Korean civilians (see Chapter 10).[70]

British Journalist Reginald Thompson, the war's contemporary, noted that the mistreatment of Koreans was based on racial hatred and the dehumanization of the Korean people. When General MacArthur triumphed at Inchon in landing 270 ships of U.S. Marines, U.S. forces celebrated by parading Korean prisoners of war stark naked to humiliate them. The dehumanization of 'the gooks' was palpable both in defeat in Taejon and in victory in Inchon. This slur, Thompson wrote, 'could not rob the slain or the living of their human kinship, nor the naked procession of prisoners, with their hands folded upon their heads – as though they might conceal weapons even in their bodies – of an uncouth and tragic dignity.'[71] Few correspondents commented on this.

A feeling of racial superiority over the enemy meant that when Western forces were engaged by highly capable North Korean and later Chinese troops, the reality of their capabilities was hard to reconcile with the racial stereotypes of Asian inferiority. While 'Chinamen can't fight,' a saying of MacArthur's, was widely believed in the West, the Chinese military quickly routed the UN forces and this dealt a particularly hard blow to their pride. To reconcile the belief that the U.S. and their partners were in fact fighting 'gooks' and racial inferiors with the reality of successive military defeats and failures, several mistruths were spread by the U.S. and allied Western powers.

The most prominent justification for defeat at the hands of the Koreans, and particularly the Chinese, was that they were 'barbaric hordes' who won battles only by outnumbering their 'superior' enemy many times over. This remains the predominant portrayal of Chinese victories and justification for Western defeats in the Korean War to this day.[72] An analysis of many battles of the war, the number of fighters involved and the weapons used indicates that this justification for defeat at the hands of 'the most primitive of peoples' is largely untrue.

Contrary to the notion that victories against the U.S. military were won only through strength in numbers, in several battles Chinese or North Korean forces, themselves outnumbered, were victorious. After North Korean forces pushed South, it was only after U.S. and British reinforcements were deployed which outnumbered the KPA by around 2 to 1 that the advance southwards could be stopped and a stalemate emerged at Pusan. Only the deployment of tens of thousands more U.S. troops could finally tip the balance against the already outnumbered KPA. Reporter Reginald Thompson who was present in Korea during the conflict noted in late 1950 that long after Chinese intervention UN forces continued to outnumber communist forces in Korea. The Chinese however did often make use of night maneuvers, feints, bugles and whistles to intimidate their enemies and give the impression of a larger force.[73,74]

In November 1950, shortly after the Chinese entry into the war, Chinese and North Korean forces equipped with only small arms and grenades attacked South Korean, Turkish and American forces including the elite X Corps, 2nd Division, 1st Cavalry and Eighth Army. Chinese and Korean forces lacked any form of air support or even anti-aircraft weapons, and the U.S. Air Force took a great toll on their numbers, but they were nevertheless able to route a far better armed force. Numbers on each side were roughly equal. U.S. forces were forced into a disorderly retreat, taking such fire as they did so. The Eighth Army sustained 11,000 casualties in the process. Despite superiority in weapons, equal numbers and the presence of air support to which Chinese forces were 'exceptionally vulnerable' according to American reports,[75] the poorly armed 'primitives' were nevertheless victorious.

As British military historian Max Hastings wrote in detail of the psychological impact of Chinese victory on the U.S. forces:

> Most of the Eighth Army fell apart as a fighting force in a fashion resembling the collapse of the French in 1940, the British in Singapore in 1942 [...] Rumor of every kind, the more dramatic the better, held sway over the minds of thousands of men [...] Most Americans expected Chinamen to be dwarves, but they found themselves assaulted by units which included men six feet and over. Yet the enemy wreaking such havoc with the Eighth Army was still, essentially, fighting a large-scale guerilla war [in that it was] devoid of all the heavy firepower every Western army considered

> essential. It was a triumph not merely for the prestige of Communism, but for that of an Asian army [...]
>
> From [General Walton] Walker's headquarters to Tokyo [command center] and on to the Joint Chiefs' offices in the Pentagon, there was bewilderment and deep dismay about the collapse of the Eighth Army. For public consumption, the sheer surprise and weight of the Chinese offensive were emphasized. But professional soldiers knew that these were not enough to explain the headlong rout of an army that still possessed absolute command of sea and air, and firepower on a scale the communists could not dream of. The Chinese victories were being gained by infantry bearing small arms and regimental support weapons – above all mortars. The Americans had been subjected to very little artillery fire, and no air attack whatsoever.[76]

The U.S. military had a significant advantage in military equipment, particularly in the first year of the war. Not only had the country's economy doubled in size during the Second World War primarily as a result of growing military industries and war provisions, but the U.S. mainland had not suffered a major attack in over a century and was working at full capacity. The Chinese by contrast were emerging devastated from a war with Japan, a civil war, and preceding decades of conflict with Western powers, the Japanese, and internal conflict among warlords. Decades of war in China had ended only the preceding year, and the country's manufacturing and military industrial bases were negligible. As a result the Chinese not only lacked sufficient heavy weapons, an air force or navy, but even small arms matching the caliber of the Americans could not be indigenously produced. Weapons used were either those left by the Japanese imperial forces or those American weapons which had been sent as aid to Chiang Kai-shek's forces during the Civil War.[77] Even basic equipment such as armored vests gave U.S. forces a distinct advantage, reducing casualties by 30 percent. The Chinese had no such luxury.[78]The ability of the Chinese forces to push back the near full might of the American military and their allies despite an overwhelming technological disadvantage had a devastating effect on morale among the Western armies. This retreat came to be known as 'The Big Bugout,' and seriously challenged the postwar consensus that the Asia-Pacific, following the downfall of the Japanese Empire, was again a region where Western dominance would reign unchallenged. It was the first time in well over a century that the Chinese had performed successfully against Western military powers – and this success only exacerbated fears of a 'Yellow Peril' that had grown in the West since the 'loss' of China in 1949. Indeed, the image of the 'Yellow Peril' which had characterized Japan in the Second World War would now transfer to China – a country which demonstrated in the Civil War, and more so in Korea, that it could pose a threat to absolute Western regional dominance just as the Japanese had – in some respects more so.

Renowned American journalist David Halberstam noted regarding the rapid retreat of U.S. forces from the Chinese border and its impacts on morale: 'Particularly upsetting was the fact that these [U.S. forces] [...] were the best the country had, and yet they had been hammered badly; and now the Americans were fighting [an enemy] [...] whose under armed forces suddenly seemed invincible. It was a horrendous equation: the war was much bigger, the enemy more powerful.'[79]

With the entry of Chinese People's Liberation Army (PLA) the U.S. led UN forces lost their frontline numerical advantage. Though there were more UN troops deployed to Korea than communist forces, the Chinese army still outnumbered them in more battles than the other way around. This was because the number of soldiers committed to the frontline did not wholly reflect which side held the overall numerical advantage. Every solider on the frontline would require supporting personnel behind the lines. These included those who transported them, cooked their food, repaired their weapons and performed many more essential functions. The ratio of supporting personnel to each man at the front differed vastly between the American and the Chinese forces. For each U.S. soldier on the front there were eight to nine personnel behind the lines providing support, whereas the Chinese each had only one – a porter who would bring food and ammunition over the mountains on foot.[80] The average Chinese division required just 50 tons of supplies per day, according to American reports, while their U.S. counterpart required over twelve times as much.[81] Therefore not only were the Chinese able to fight more efficiently and commit a far greater proportion of their manpower to the front, operating with far less food and weapons and without luxuries such as toiletries, but had the Americans committed a similar ratio of personnel to the front – they would have significantly outnumbered the Chinese in battle as they had the North Koreans before them. China's superior numbers were therefore not primarily a result of 'Asiatic breeding' and the like as widely claimed by Western reports, but of a more efficient military and soldiers who could do more with less.

British military historian Max Hastings noted regarding the way Chinese used their tactical and combat skills to compensate for their vast material disadvantages: 'The undoubted Chinese skills as tacticians, night-fighters, navigators, masters of fieldcraft and camouflage, caused even many senior [UN] officers to forget the enemy's huge disadvantages in resources and firepower. Worse, the leaders of the UN forces in Korea found themselves facing the stark fact that, man for man, most of their troops were proving nowhere near as hardy, skillful, and determined upon the battlefield as their communist opponents. It is difficult to overestimate the psychological effects of this conclusion upon strategic and tactical decision-making.'[82]

The U.S. Army Second Division published the following regarding the strengths of the Chinese soldier, and his ability to operate with far less firepower and supplies: 'He is well and courageously led at the small unit level and the results of actions at this level offer definite proof that he is thoroughly disciplined. His conduct of the defense is accomplished in spite of UN air superiority, UN liaison aircraft and inferior communications equipment. He is operating on a shoestring basis as is evidenced by the hodge-podge of equipment piled up on the battlefield after every encounter.'[83]

By contrast to the Chinese forces' ability to make do with very little, General Matthew Ridgeway, who would succeed MacArthur as U.S. and UN Supreme Commander, referred to the U.S. military as 'pampered troops.'[84] He noted 'the unwillingness of the army to forgo certain creature comforts, its timidity about getting off the scanty roads, its reluctance to move without radio and telephone contact, and its lack of imagination in dealing with a foe whom they so outmatched in firepower and dominated in the air and on the surrounding seas.'[85,86]

Lack of logistical support often critically hindered the Chinese war effort and slowed military advances.[87] This was true particularly when fighting in sub-freezing temperatures, for which Chinese forces were often ill equipped and suffered far more that the Americans. As Hastings reported:

> The men of the UN complained of the difficulty of fighting the ferocious cold as well as the enemy. But the winter was neutral. The Chinese were far less well-equipped to face the conditions that their opponents, possessing only canvas shoes and lacking such indulgences as sleeping bags. Marshal Peng's casualties from frostbite dwarfed those of the Americans. And the Chinese could expect no ready evacuation or medical care […]
>
> Chinese veterans later declared that 90 percent of the 'Volunteers' in Korea suffered from some degree of frostbite in the winter of 1950. Their Twenty-seventh Army suffered 10,000 noncombat casualties: 'a shortage of transportation and escort personnel makes it impossible to accomplish the mission of supplying the troops,' declared a Twenty-sixth Army document of November 1950, later captured by the UN. 'As a result, our soldiers frequently starve … they ate cold food and some had only a few potatoes in two days. They were unable to maintain their physical strength for combat; the wounded could not be evacuated … The firepower of our entire army was basically inadequate.'[88]

Despite these conditions, the Chinese forces were able to defeat elite American forces at sub-freezing temperatures which not only were better armed, better fed and better equipped for the weather, but which also outnumbered the Chinese significantly and had support from the air. At Chosin River nine Chinese divisions between them had a strength of 67,500. They routed a hostile force of around 105,000, of which 80,000 were from the elite X corps. The remaining 25,000 were largely ROK troops. While U.S. forces inflicted heavy casualties with artillery and air power, they were eventually forced to retreat from the strategic position.

Following this routing of U.S. forces, American Lt. Col. Roy E. Appleman wrote an analysis of the ability of the Chinese to win battles despite their lack of supplies. He wrote:

> Looking at the other side of the hill […] one cannot withhold some admiration, and humanitarian sympathy, for the Chinese peasants who made such great effort and sacrifice in trying to carry out their orders. One must say of them that Sung's IX Army Group did some spectacular things. It fought without air support, it had no tanks or artillery and almost no heavy mortars, it had poor and almost nonexistent ammunition after the first day or two of battle and no food or ammunition resupply once it crossed the Yalu River […] and it possessed no adequate footgear for the feet or mitten for the hands of its soldiers in an arctic clime […]

> In fact, the operations were a mismatch of a fine modern, mechanized body of soldiery against a peasant army of light infantry – but one that was highly mobile and expert at night fighting. The best weapons the Chinese possessed were the American Thompson submachine guns, 81mm mortars, grenades, and rifles they had captured from Chiang Kaishek's armies [...] Yet they did drive the X Corps completely out of northeast Korea and occupied and held henceforth that part of the country. No American troops ever returned there.[89]

The Chinese military's lack of logistical support, and their battlefield successes despite this gave rise to fantastical rumors and often absurd reporting among U.S. forces. One American intelligence report announced that, though the Chinese had far fewer men behind the lines supporting them, they were employing large numbers of monkeys as porters.[90] A more fantastical rumor used among UN forces to explain the effectiveness of Chinese soldiers' night-fighting abilities was the rumor of mysterious Dragon Ladies, women in black with superhuman abilities bordering on supernatural, who led the Chinese into battle in the dark.[91]

Another rumor used to explain not only the effectiveness and perceived fearlessness of the Chinese military, but also to further demonize them, was that Chinese soldiers could only fight so effectively because they were on drugs. Their ability to face death fearlessly was something the highly demoralized UN forces could hardly comprehend. As Lukasz Kamienski, Associate Professor at the Faculty of International and Political Studies, wrote in his own study: 'Within the allied [UN] forces rumor was rife that the Chinese went into battle intoxicated with opium. Major Real Liboiron, the commanding officer of Dog Company of the 2nd Battalion of the Canadian Royal 22nd Regiment, recalled that most of his men truly believed that "the Chinese were doped before they were committed to battle."' Kaminski noted that such beliefs were not only entirely unproven, but that they were also highly unlikely based on the nature of the Chinese leadership. To this end he wrote: 'Mao launched a decisive and victorious campaign to eradicate the opium habit amongst the military and civilian population. In February 1950 the Communist authorities banned the cultivation of the poppy plant and prohibited the production, import, and sale of opium and other intoxicating drugs. Opium stocks were burned in public, and dope peddlers were sent to work camps [...] Drugs, in a word, were equated with imperialist subversion. [...] Paradoxically, however, it was not the Chinese but the American forces that were regularly and extensively popping pills for combat.' Kaminski gave extensive details of widespread drug addiction throughout the U.S. military in Korea, and the work of South Korean police as drug traffickers.[92]

Chinese forces' lack of supplies was only worsened by the U.S. Air Force's complete control of the air in the early stages of the war, allowing it to attack supply routes and forcing the PLA to take extensive precautions to avoid being targeted. The disruption of supply routes and Chinese forces' lack of adequate equipment at the front lines arguably was critical to preventing an utter defeat for U.S. forces and their allies. With the little they had the Chinese were able to push their enemies to the 38th Parallel, but they could not move quickly and were often slowed by logistical issues and having to avoid overstretching supply lines.

According the General MacArthur, at their border the PLA could support 1 million troops; at Pyongyang this fell to 600,000; at the 38th parallel it fell to 300,000; by the time they reached 40 miles south of Seoul this fell to just 200,000 – leaving them hopelessly outnumbered.[93] His assertions were supported by statements from the Chinese military leadership. Hu Seng, a member of PLA Marshal Peng Dehuai's staff, had stated to similar effect: 'while we wished to continue to push the enemy, we could not open our mouth too wide [...] China was unprepared for the new military situation created by the deep advance. We were now in a position where we could not continue to reinforce our army in Korea.'[94] The restrictions China's poor postwar economy placed on its logistical capabilities was the primary reason why pushing further south and winning a decisive victory against the U.S. military and their allies was impossible. Had the PLA been backed by greater industrial capabilities allowing them supply forces at full strength across the Korean Peninsula, rather than a stalemate at the 38th parallel China's military would likely have pushed much further south and won a decisive victory within the war's first year. Logistical difficulties resulting from strained supply, according to Hastings, 'prevented the Chinese from converting the defeat of the UN forces into their destruction.'[95]

Notes

1 Desal, Meghnad, and Redfern, Paul, *Global Governance: Ethics and Economics of the World Order*, London, Pinter, 1995 (P. 129).
2 Boggs, Carl, *Masters of War: Militarism and Blowback in the Era of American Empire*, Abingdon, Routledge, 2003 (p. 205).
3 '"Kill 'Em All": American War Crimes in Korea,' *Timewatch*, (Documentary), February 1, 2002.
4 Halberstam, David, *The Fifties*, New York, Ballantine Books, 2012 (p. 71).
5 Cumings, Bruce, *The Korean War: A History*, New York, Modern Library, 2010 (p. 27).
6 Interview with John M. Allison, New York, April 20, 1969, conducted by Richard D. Challenger, John Foster Dulles Oral History, Seely G. Mudd Manuscript Library, Princeton University Archives.
7 Stokesbury, James L., *A Short History of the Korean War*, New York, William Morrow and Company, 1988 (p. 39, 42–43).
8 Gould, Dudley C., *Follow Me UP Fool's Mountain: Korea, 1951,'* Southfarm Press, Middletown, Conneticut, 2002 (p. 76).
9 '"Kill 'Em All": American War Crimes in Korea,' *Timewatch*, (Documentary), February 1, 2002.
10 '"Kill 'Em All": American War Crimes in Korea,' *Timewatch*, (Documentary), February 1, 2002.
11 Cumings, Bruce, *The Korean War: A History*, New York, Modern Library, 2010 (p. 29).
12 Hastings, Max, *Korean War*, London, Michael Joseph, 1988 (p. 103).
13 Cumings, Bruce, *Korea's Place in the Sun: A Modern History*, W. W. Norton & Company, 1997 (p. 266).
14 Cumings, Bruce, *The Korean War: A History*, New York City, Modern Library, 2010 (p. 29).
15 Hastings, Max, *Korean War*, London, Michael Joseph, 1988 (p. 98).
16 Cumings, Bruce, *The Korean War: A History*, New York, Modern Library, 2010 (p. 30).
17 Schnabel, James F., *United States Army in the Korean War, Volume 4, Policy and Direction in the First Year*, Washington, DC, United States Army Center of Military History, 1990 (p. 132).
18 United States Forces Korea, United Nations Command, About (<http://www.usfk.mil/About/United-Nations-Command/>).

19 Stone, I. F., *Hidden History of the Korean War*, Amazon Media, 2014 (Chapter 7, 'The Stage Was Set').
20 Ibid. (pp. 77–78).
21 UN Security Council Resolution 84, July 7, 1950 (in *New York Times*, July 8, 1950, p. 4).
22 Eisenhower, Dwight, *The White House Years: Mandate for Change, 1953–1956*, New York, Doubleday, 1963 (p. 340).
23 Cumings, Bruce, *The Korean War: A History*, New York, Modern Library, 2010 (p. 31).
24 Schnabel, James F., *United States Army in the Korean War, Volume 4, Policy and Direction in the First Year*, Washington, DC, United States Army Center of Military History, 1990 (p. 84).
25 Hastings, Max, *Korean War* London, Michael Joseph, 1988 (p. 22).
26 Cumings, Bruce, *Origins of the Korean War: The Roaring of the Cataract, 1947–1950*, Volume 2, Princeton, NJ, Princeton University Press, 2004 (p. 693).
27 Cumings, Bruce, *The Korean War: A History*, New York, Modern Library, 2010 (p. 32).
28 Ibid.
29 Thompson, Reginald, *Cry Korea*. London, Macdonald & Company, London, McDonald & Company, 1951 (p. 39, 72).
30 Mao, Zedong, Schram, Stuart, *Mao's Road to Power: Revolutionary Writings, 1912–1949, Volume 4: The Rise and Fall of the Chinese Soviet Republic*, Abingdon, Routledge, 1997 (p. 374).
31 Spurr, Russel, *Enter the Dragon: China's Undeclared War Against the U.S. in Korea, 1950–1951*, New York, William Morrow and Company, 2011 (p. 284).
32 Deane, Hugh, *The Korean War, 1945–1953*, San Francisco, CA, China Books and Periodicals, 1999 (p. 118, 112).
33 'The Background of the Present War in Korea,' *Far Eastern Economic Review*, 31 August 1950 (pp. 233–237).
34 'The Background of the Present War in Korea,' *Far Eastern Economic Review*, August 31, 1950.
35 Moon, Katherine H. S., *Sex Among Allies*, New York, Colombia University Press, 1997.
36 Cumings, Bruce, *The Korean War: A History*, New York, Modern Library, 2010, (p. 189).
37 Bandow, Doug, 'Why Are U. S. Troops Still in Korea?' *Forbes*, May 3, 2011.
38 Donnelly Thomas, *Rebuilding America's Defenses, A Report of The Project for the New American Century*, A report of the Project for the New American Century, September 2000 (p. 18).

(See for U.S. intention to maintain forces on the Korean Peninsula even after reunification to project power on the Asian mainland).

39 Heo, Uk, and Roehrig, Terence, *South Korea Since 1980*, Cambridge, Cambridge University Press, 2010 (p. 18).

40 Henderson, G., *The Politics of the Vortex*, Cambridge, MA, Harvard University Press, 1968 (pp. 348–349).

41 Baillie, Hugh, *High Tension: the Recollections of Hugh Baillies*, London, Harper, 1960 (p. 267–268).

42 Carter, Dale, and Clifton, Robin, *War and Cold War in American Foreign Policy, 1942–62*, New York, Palgrave, 2002 (p. 165).

43 Cumings, Bruce, *The Korean War: A History*, New York, Modern Library, 2010 (pp. 168, 181).

44 *The Times* (UK), December 18, 21 and 22, 1950.

45 Stone, I. F., *Hidden History of the Korean War*, Amazon Media, 2014, (Chapter 16, 'Reversal on the Parallel').

46 Hanley, Charles J. and Choe, Sang Hun and Mendoza, Martha, *The Bridge at No Gun Ri: A Hidden Nightmare from the Korean War*, New York, Henry Holt and Company, 2001 (p. 169).

47 Nichols, Donald, *How Many Times Can I Die?* Brooksville, FL, Brownsville Printing Co., 1981.

48 Spencer, Richard, 'More than 100,000 massacred by allies during Korean War,' *The Telegraph*, December 29, 2008.

49 Shaines, Robert A., *Command Influence: A story of Korea and the politics of injustice*, Denver, CO, Outskirts Press, 2010 (p. 54).

50 Cumings, Bruce, *The Korean War: A History*, New York, Modern Library, 2010 (p. 179).

51 Stone, I. F., *Hidden History of the Korean War*, Amazon Media, 2014 (Chapter 17, 'Free Elections?').

52 Stone, I. F., *Hidden History of the Korean War*, Amazon Media, 2014 (Chapter 17, 'Free Elections?').

53 Hanley, Charles J. and Choe, Sang Hun and Mendoza, Martha, *The Bridge at No Gun Ri: A Hidden Nightmare from the Korean War*, New York, Henry Holt and Company, 2001 (p. 170).

54 Douglas MacArthur Farewell Address to Congress, April 19, 1951.

55 Stone, I. F., *Hidden History of the Korean War*, Amazon Media, 2014, (Chapter 18, 'First Warnings').

56 Cumings, Bruce, *The Korean War: A History*, New York, Modern Library, 2010 (p. 84).

57 Stone, I. F., *Hidden History of the Korean War*, Amazon Media, 2014, (Chapter 24, 'The China Lobby Responds').

58 Ibid. (Chapter 24, 'The China Lobby Responds').

59 Stone, I. F., *Hidden History of the Korean War*, Amazon Media, 2014 (Chapter 24, 'The China Lobby Responds').
60 Ibid. (Chapter 24, 'The China Lobby Responds').
61 Halberstam, David, *The Fifties*, New York, Ballantine Books, 2012 (p. 113).
62 Rovere, Richard H., *General MacArthur and President Truman: The Struggle for Control of American Foreign Policy*, Piscataway, NJ, Transaction Publishers, 1997 (p. 127).
63 Wainstock, Dennis, *Truman, MacArthur, and the Korean War*, Santa Barbara, CA, Greenwood Publishing Group, 1999 (p. 40).
64 Cumings, Bruce, *The Korean War: A History*, New York, Modern Library, 2010 (p. 28).
65 *New York Times*, August 21, 1950.
66 Thompson, Reginald, *Cry Korea*. London, McDonald & Company, 1951 (p. 39, 44, 84, 114).
67 Hynes, Patricia, 'The Korean War: Forgotten, Unknown and Unfinished,' *Truthout*, July 12, 2013.
68 Howe, Stephen, *Empire; A Very Short Introduction*, Oxford, Oxford University Press, 2002 (p. 95).
69 Tomedi, Rudy, *No Bugles, No Drums: An Oral History of the Korean War*, New York, John Wiley & Sons, 1993, 1994 (p. 18).
70 Williams, Jeremny, "Kill 'Em All": The American Military in Korea,' *BBC*, February 17, 2011.
71 Cumings, Bruce, *The Korean War: A History*, New York, Modern Library, 2010 (p. 84).
72 Salmon, Andrew, *To The Last Round: The Epic British Stand on the Imjin River, Korea 1951*, London, Aurum Press, 2010.
73 Wainstock, Dennis, *Truman, MacArthur, and the Korean War*, Santa Barbara, CA, Greenwood Publishing Group, 1999 (p. 76).
74 Thompson, Reginald, *Cry Korea*. London, Macdonald & Company, 1951 (p. 247, 265).
75 Armstrong, Frank H., *The First Cavalry Division and Their 8th Engineers in Korea, America's Silent Generation at War*, Burlington, VT, Queen City Printers, 1997 (p. 111).
76 Hastings, Max, *Korean War*, London, Michael Joseph, 1988 (p. 170).
77 Deane, Hugh, *The Korean War, 1945–1953*, San Francisco, CA, China Books and Periodicals, 1999 (p. 128).
78 Veterans Affairs Canada, *Remembrance, History, Korean War, Land of the Morning Calm, Did You Know?* (http://www.veterans.gc.ca/eng/remembrance/history/korean-war/land-morning-calm/didyouknow).

79 Gady, Franz-Stefan, 'Military Stalemate: How North Korea Could Win a War With the US,' *The Diplomat*, October 10, 2017.
80 Deane, Hugh, *The Korean War, 1945–1953*, San Francisco, CA, China Books and Periodicals, 1999 (p. 141).
81 MacDonald, Callum A, 'Korea: The War Before Vietnam,' London, Macmillan, 1986, (p. 239).
82 Hastings, Max, *Korean War* London, Michael Joseph, 1988 (p. 171).
83 Hermes, Walter G., *Truce Tent and the Fighting Front*, Washington, DC, Center of Military History, 1992 (p. 511).
84 Hastings, Max, *Korean War*, London, Michael Joseph, 1988 (p. 190).
85 Malkasian, Carter, *The Korean War*, New York, Rosen, 2009 (p. 36).
86 Ridgeway, Matthew B., *The Korean War*, New York, Doubleday, 1967 (p. 86).
87 Dehuai, Peng, *Memoirs*, Forest Grove, OR, University Press of the Pacific, 2005 (p. 478).
88 Hastings, Max, *Korean War*, London, Michael Joseph, 1988 (p. 171).
89 Appleman, Roy E., *Escaping the Trap: The U.S. Army X Corps in Northeast Korea, 1950*, College Station, TX, A. & M. University Press, 1990 (pp. 367–368).
90 Hastings, Max, *Korean War*, London, Michael Joseph, 1988 (p. 170).
91 Kamienski, Lukasz, *Shooting Up; A History of Drugs in Warfare, London,* C. Hurst & Co. Publishers Ltd, 2016 (p. 151).
92 Ibid. (pp. 150–151).
93 Hastings, Max, *Korean War*, London, Michael Joseph, 1988 (p. 190).
94 Ibid. (pp. 190–191).
95 Ibid. (p. 172).

CHAPTER 9

The Korean War: Part II – Mass Destruction

> If we keep on tearing the place apart, we can make it a most unpopular affair for the North Koreans. We ought to go right ahead.[1,2]
>
> — U.S. Secretary of Defense ROBERT LOVETT

> As for the allegation that the U.S. used germ warfare in the Korean War, I can only say with some shame that what I dismissed as incredible then seems altogether credible to me now.[3]
>
> — GEORGE WALD, American expert from the Harvard Biological Laboratories and Nobel Prize Winner

The Bombing and Desolation of North Korea

As the Korean War escalated China was drawn into a full confrontation with the United States and its Western partners. During the war Chinese territory near the Korean border was bombed on numerous occasions, in which the Chinese reported that American planes destroyed homes and infrastructure and killed many civilians. The unprovoked bombing of Sinuiju on the Chinese border was targeting a civilian population center, and the United States was under no illusion otherwise. In July 1950 the city had 126,000 inhabitants and 14,000 buildings. The town had no industries that contributed to war production, but rather produced civilian goods according to an international commission's report. There were only light industries producing soya, tofu, shoes, matches, salt and chopsticks when the town was firebombed by dozens of B-29 bombers in 1950. The result was that in a few hours 2,100 state and municipal buildings out of a total of 3,017 were destroyed. Of the 11,000 houses 6,800 were destroyed. Thousands of inhabitants were killed, 80 percent of which were women and children. Sixteen of the town's 17 primary schools were destroyed as well as 15 of the 17 places of worship. In hospitals patients were burned to death in their beds by incendiary bombs. The attack was planned to maximize casualties, and following the dropping of incendiaries civilians who went outdoors either to escape or to put out the fires were machine gunned by low flying aircraft. Young children were also targeted in this way. The United States had refined its firebombing technique following the destruction of several dozen Japanese population centers in this manner, and the effect on the Chinese and Korean people was truly devastating. The attack on Sinuiju came wholly without warning to an area previously unaffected by war, and wrought tremendous destruction in a matter of hours.[4] Considering the destruction and suffering this caused in a few hours, it is notable that such attacks were carried out frequently all across North Korea for three years.

The United States' propensity to target Asian population centers of little strategic value was previously demonstrated in the firebombing of Japanese cities, and would later repeat itself during the Vietnam War. U.S. bombers had for example targeted population centers in Laos in November 1968 after they were prevented from targeting North Vietnam. Though there was no strategic value in doing so, the U.S. Deputy Chief of Mission Monteagle Stearns testified to the U.S. Senate Committee on Foreign Relations the following year regarding the Air Force's reason for doing so: 'Well, we had all those planes sitting around and couldn't just let them stay there with nothing to do.'[5] During the Korean War pilots were similarly ordered to target South Korean population centers with rockets not for any strategic benefit, but because it was better to use the rockets on a target 'rather than carry them home.'[6] It was forces commanded under a similar mindset with the same value for the lives of Asian peoples to which the North Koreans were subjected.

Contrary to the United States, which wrecked untold collateral damage, and committed atrocities against both soldiers and civilians, the Chinese and North Korea forces conducted themselves well and gained a higher standing in the eyes of the Korean people. On November 16, 1950, the London *Times* published an article showing that the North Korean leadership rejected a scorched earth program, one retreating armies very often employ to deny an advancing enemy vital supplies and strain their logistics. This would entail burning or destroying housing, crops and food supplies of the local population while retreating. Though it would have denied UN forces valuable supplies, the North Koreans left the countryside almost untouched. By contrast the United States and their partners fighting in Korea under UN command had ravaged the country and almost entirely destroyed it. This was through a combination of their own harsh scorched earth policy imposed on the Korean people and through the extensive bombing campaigns against civilian areas. A *New York Times* correspondent noted that 'when the Koreans saw that the Communists had left their homes and schools standing in retreat while the United Nations troops, fighting with much more destructive tools, left only blackened spots where towns once stood, the Communists even in retreat chalked up moral victories.'[7] This approach was much to the credit of the North Koreans, and indicated who had the best interests of the Korean people at heart.

An example of the United States enacting a scorched earth policy was in Pyongyang. The city had a large number of factories manufacturing primarily textiles, shoes, food products, tobacco, wine, beer and fertilizers. There was an opera house, nine theaters, 20 cinemas, seven universities and over 100 schools. When the city was retaken from United States forces almost all of it had been destroyed. This destruction was primarily not due to fighting, as U.S. forces evacuated before the KPA or PLA arrived, but instead was intentionally carried out systematically as the American military left the city as part of a scorched earth policy to destroy what the North Koreans had built – despite the buildings themselves being of little military value. All the city's tram cars, the water system, bridges and schools were destroyed beyond repair, while several time-bombs were left behind.[8] In spite of the thoroughness of the destruction, further bombings of Pyongyang would continue throughout the war.

Retreating U.S. forces had similarly laid waste to the city of Yongdong. An Associated Press reporter said following the departure of the U.S. military that the South Korean city 'no longer exists as a city. It looks like Nagasaki after the atom bomb [...] Yongdong has probably been here for 4,000 years – and never known such silence.' Those South Koreans from Yongdong who had not fled as refugees died with their city.[9] The *United*

Press similarly reported in Wonju, a South Korean city destroyed by the retreating U.S. 2nd Division: 'before the retreat, every house in Wonju was set afire, every bridge demolished, every morsel of food destroyed. Patrols were sent into the countryside to set fire to huts and haystacks [...] Then the artillery and aviation entered the picture.' The London *Times* reported on the same incident that on January 15 alone, 22 villages and 300 haystacks were burned.[10]

Even in the cold winter months scorched earth was applied to Korean population centers. Ralph Bernotas, an American serviceman from F Company, recalled of the application of this strategy: 'Food – whatever the hell – they left nothing. It was just like the [American] Civil War, the same as the Russians and Germans in the Ukraine.' Bernotas noted the absurdity of the disregard with which South Koreans were treated, stating: 'I used to sit over at the farm at my fireplace, and I'd think, boy, in our country nothing like that could happen – somebody come in here and tell me to move out, they're going to burn my house!' Koreans had all they owned destroyed and were left without food or shelter to face the country's harsh winter.[11] In December 1950, when Lt General Matthew B. Ridgeway was flown to Korea to take command of the U.S. 8th army he criticized the policy of scorched earth as yielding no strategic benefit – 'destruction for destruction's sake.'[12] As affirmed by General Kurtis LeMay: 'we burned down just about every city in North Korea and South Korea *both*.'[13,14]

Yet far more destructive than scorched earth policies were the fire-bombings. Bombings would begin with incendiaries followed by explosives followed by a combination of incendiaries and time bombs. This specific combination and series of bombings was designed to prevent inhabitants from going out onto the streets or doing any rescue work, thereby maximizing casualties among a civilian population. As a result, many of those who were buried alive could not be reached and died of suffocation. Hospitals which were properly marked to be visible from 6,000–8,000 meters were intentionally targeted, according to the findings of an international commission.[15] Several were targeted specifically by dive-bombers at only 30 meters.[16] It was clear that when fighting against 'subhumans' and 'the most primitive of peoples' in Asia the rules of war and humane conduct did not apply.

When the Chinese People's Liberation Army entered the war, Western powers escalated the racial demonization of the Chinese. They were most often referred to as 'Chinese hordes' attacking in 'endless waves.' Secretary of State Acheson assured that with firepower and organizational strength the Americans 'can hold back all sorts of hordes.'[17] Despite being depicted as brutal invaders the Chinese conducted themselves well – to a far higher standard than the Western forces under UN command.[18] Under U.S. and ROK forces all of North Korea from the industrial potential of every city, to the poorest possessions in the countryside was ravaged. Journalist and author Robert Jackson stated that when the Chinese entered the war: 'there was to be no attempt at ultra-precise bombing to avoid high civilian casualties. The B-29s were to carry full loads of incendiaries and their task was to burn the selected cities from end to end.'[19]

I. F. Stone reported on the bombings of civilian targets, both those in northern Korea and those in the south suspected of harboring a KPA presence:

> September, 1950, Far East Air Forces Headquarters announced that the first stage of its bombing program, aimed at industrial installations, was complete, and that there was now a 'paucity' of industrial targets for bombers. One of the problems which began to trouble the Air Force in Korea, judging by the communiqués, was that there was nothing left to destroy. These communiqué's must be read by anyone who wants a complete history of the Korean War. They are literally horrifying.
>
> 'Crews on the B-26 light bombers of the 452nd Bomb Wing,' said the Fifth Air Force operational summary at 5 P.M. Tokyo time, January 31, 'reported a scarcity of targets at Hamhung today.' According to Staff Sergeant Clark V. Watson of Hutchinson, Kansas, 'It's hard to find good targets, for we have burned out almost everything.'
>
> Other Air Force unites were still managing. 'The Eighth Fighter Bomber Wing F-80 jets,' said the same communiqué, 'reported large fires in the villages in the western sector following attacks with rockets, napalm, and machine guns. A village was hard hit south of Chorwon.' Why was not explained. Whether the village represented some military objective was not stated. Sometimes a possible military objective seemed to have been hit by accident. In the same communiqué it was announced that the navigator of one of the light bombers that attacked Pongung near Hamhung reported: 'One of our napalms must have hit a gas or oil dump. It landed and there was a big belch of orange flame and black smoke.' Peasants do not detonate so colorfully.

> Sometimes the reason offered for bombing a defenseless village was that it was 'enemy-occupied.' The same communiqué said, 'One flight dive-bombed the enemy occupied village of Takchong and then rocketed and strafed the area, reporting several buildings destroyed and large fires started.' Were all villages in enemy territory regarded as enemy-occupied? The ratio of civilian to soldier dead in these raids must have been very large. This same communiqué said the 'largest claim of troops casualties inflicted' in the day's raids were 100 enemy troops killed or wounded by one group of planes. Even in a small village more civilians than that could be killed in one raid. A complete indifference to the noncombatants was reflected in the way villages were given 'saturation treatment' with napalm to dislodge a few soldiers.[20]

The British military publication *Brassey's Annual* reported on the situation in South Korea in 1951 following the destruction wrought by the fire bombings and the U.S. military's scorched earth policy: 'The war was fought without regard for the South Koreans, and their unfortunate country was regarded as an arena rather than a country to be liberated. As a consequence, fighting was quite ruthless, and it is no exaggeration to state the South Korea no longer exists as a country. Its towns have been destroyed, much of its means of livelihood eradicated, and its people reduced to a sullen mass depending upon charity.'[21] South Koreans' loss of livelihoods and resulting inability to subsist led to its own tragic consequences.

Describing the nature and impacts of the U.S. firebombing campaign against Korean population centers, Stone stated:

> in Fifth Air Force operational summary February 4: 'Other F-80s from the Eighth reported excellent results in attacks on villages near Chorwon, Kumchon, Chunchon, and Chunchon-ni. The villages were hit with bombs as well as rockets and napalm.' The results were 'excellent.' Not all the reports were so brisk. There were some passages about these raids on villages which reflected, not the pity which human feeling called for, but a kind of gay moral imbecility, utterly devoid of imagination – as if the fliers were playing in a bowling alley, with villages for pins. An example was the Fifth Air Force operational summary 5 P.M. Tokyo time Friday, February 2. This told how the two man crew of a downed Mosquito patrol plane was rescued by helicopter 'from the midst of an enemy troop concentration near Hongchon.' Some fifty enemy troops had been sighted and between 300 and 400 foxholes reported so it was decided to give the whole area 'saturation' treatment.
>
> A mass flight of twenty-four F-51 mustangs poured 5000 gallons of napalm over the area. The flight leader, Lieutenant Colonel James Kirkendall, of Duluth, Minnesota –

> the Air Force communiqué's gave names, as if to foster individual pride in such handiwork – reported that 'his flight hit every village and building in the area.' Perhaps it was some uneasy qualm which led him to add, 'There was plenty of evidence of troops living in the houses there.' The evidence itself was not disclosed. It might have been hard to find, for Colonel Kirkendall added that 'smoke blanketed the area, rising to over 4000 feet when they left.' His subordinates were cheerful. Captain Everett L. Hundley of Kansas City, Kansas, who led one group of four planes, as quoted by the communiqué as saying, 'You can kiss that group of villages good-bye.' Captain Hugh Boniford of Montgomery, Alabama, said he saw 'tracks and other evidence of enemy activity in the area.' He added, 'That place can really be called devastated now.' Captain Boniford's remark applies to all Korea.[22]

The U.S. bombing campaign against the small East Asian nation was so intensive that within three months of the outbreak of the war the shortage of targets threatened to leave the U.S. fleet idle.[23,24] General Emmett O'Donnell, who had commanded the firebombing of Tokyo, was head of the Bomber Command in Asia. He testified that within three months 'almost all the Korean peninsula' was 'just a terrible mess.' As a result of the air campaign 'everything is destroyed. There is nothing standing worthy of the name [...] There were no more targets in Korea.'[25]

The destruction of the livelihoods of so many Koreans on both sides of the 38th parallel, destroying their farms through burning and bombing down to the smallest village in a mainly rural society left many in desperation. It was at this time that Koreans in the south flocked to UN forces to provide services, including many Korean women were forced en masse into prostitution for U.S. and other UN forces. The majority of these women were war widows, often with children depending on them. Many others were orphaned girls. This expanded the already prevalent prostitution of Korean women to American soldiers, a practice which the South Korean government had strongly encouraged and would expand further with time (as covered in Chapter 11). By August 11, 1950, the ROK's municipal authorities announced they had 'already issued the approval for establishing UN comfort stations in return for the Allied Forces' toil. In a few days five stations will be set up in the downtown areas of new and old Masan. The authorities are asking citizens to give much cooperation in the coming days.'[26,27] Ms Kim, a former prostitute, recalled: 'They urged us to sell as much as possible to the G. I.'s, praising us as "dollar earning patriots."'[28]

Destruction of livelihoods to leave women destitute proved a more effective way of acquiring comfort women for an occupying military force than forced enlistment and rape, although the latter also occurred on a large scale.

It became clear that in Korea, as in Vietnam later on, Asian civilians were seen as enemy combatants – including civilians of the supposedly allied ROK who were often deliberately targeted. U.S. bombings succeeded in wiping out a significant percentage of the population on a scale with no precedents in recent history or equals until today. Again the disregard for lives of Asian peoples by the United States and their military partners was extreme. North Korea suffered greatly under the U.S. bombing campaign, which killed the majority of the 4 million North Koreans estimated to have died in the war.[29] Some estimates by Western academia have put the North Korean casualties alone at near 30 percent of the population.[30,31] Air Force General LeMay, who had been so heavily involved in the firebombing of Japanese cities, said of the bombing of North Korea: 'Over a period of three years or so we killed off – what – twenty percent of the population.'[32] Even this relatively low estimate would make the losses North Korea suffered relative to the size of its population greater than any nation suffered during the Second World War. This death toll is extraordinarily high, not only as a percentage of the population, but as a figure unto itself. This figure does not account for the inevitable hundreds of thousands if not millions more wounded or maimed in the bombings and the fighting, or the tremendous economic losses the country suffered.* The North Korean government was forced to file a complaint to the United Nations as a result of these bombings of cities – though inevitably this had no impact.

By late 1950 the U.S. Air Force was dropping some 800 tons of bombs on North Korea every day, much of it pure napalm.[33] The goal of these bombing

* While there are no statistics for the number of Koreans wounded, considering that the death toll was in the millions and statistics from other conflicts where modern weapons such as incendiaries were used severe injuries have consistently significantly outnumbered the number of deaths. Hundreds of thousands injured in a war where several million were killed is therefore an extremely conservative estimate, with the number of wounded exceeding the numbers killed, several million, being statistically far more likely.

campaigns was to destroy the morale of the people (and so their support for the independent government) and to destroy the infrastructure of the country, both to leave it unable to wage war and destroy its potential to develop as an industrial power. Dean Rusk, assistant secretary of state at the time and strong supporter of the war, said of the intensity of the U.S. bombing that it would target 'everything that moved in North Korea, every brick standing on top of another.'[34] During the Korean War the United States Air Force dropped 635,000–698,000 tons of bombs on North Korea, a tremendous amount for such a small country.[35,36] In the Pacific theatre of the Second World War, in a conflict against the entire Japanese Empire which was itself devastated, the United States dropped 503,000 tons of bombs. This shows the extent of the destruction wrought on North Korea by the United States. 32,557 tons of napalm were used against North Korea.[37] Every building in the country was a target, whether a school, a hospital or a government office. The North Korean government instructed the population to build dugouts and mud huts and dig underground tunnels to solve the homelessness problem that had ensued. They had little other choice. Any building would be targeted from the air. No quarter was shown not only to the KPA, but to the North Korean people themselves. Air Force General LeMay said: 'we went over there and fought the war and eventually burned down every town in North Korea anyway, some way or another, and some in South Korea too.'[38]

The use of napalm on Korean settlements against civilians caused immense and terrible suffering. Such substantial quantities of napalm were very silently dropped on Korea in greater quantities and with far more devastating effects than they would in Vietnam. As the DPRK was a modern industrialized nation with concentrated population centers, urban industrial installations and other concentrated civilian targets it was far more vulnerable to such attacks than Vietnam would be.[39] The U.S. Air Force saw this infernal jelly as a 'wonder weapon,' one that wrecked maximum casualties as it had done in Japan five years before.[40,41,42] A report on the effects of napalm on humans surfaced when American Pfc. James Ransome Jr.'s unit suffered a 'friendly' hit of napalm. This 'wonder weapon' fired by their own forces had the same impact on these military personnel as it did on countless thousands of Korean civilians. The American soldiers hit reportedly rolled in the snow in agony and begged him to shoot them, as their skin burned to a crisp and peeled back 'like fried potato chips.' These hits were only partial – reporters in Korea saw countless cases of civilians drenched in napalm – their whole bodies, 'covered with a hard, black crust sprinkled with yellow pus.'[43] When the *New York Times* described the effects of napalm on the North Korean civilian population center Secretary of State Acheson called for such 'sensational reporting' to be censored.[44]

Physician Richard Perry, having spent years treating its victims, would write regarding napalm's horrific effects on civilian targets years later: 'I have been an orthopedic surgeon for a good number of years, with a rather wide range of medical experience. But nothing could have prepared me for my encounters with [...] women and children burned by napalm. It was shocking and sickening, even for a physician, to see and smell the blackened flesh. One continues for days afterward getting sick when he looks at a piece of meat on his plate because the odor of burning flesh lingers so long in the memory. And one never forgets the bewildered eyes of the silent, suffering, napalm-burned child. What could anyone possibly say to such a child?'[45,46]

Even British Prime Minister Winston Churchill who had had shown no qualms about bombing population centers and declared himself 'strongly in favor'[47] of the use of chemical weapons, which he ordered the use of many times, and who had personally approved the development of biological weapons for use against enemy population centers,[48] opposed the inhuman use of napalm on civilian targets on moral grounds – referring to it as 'a very cruel form of warfare.' He stated in reference to the excessive use of napalm in the Korean War against civilian targets: 'I do not like this napalm bombing at all. A fearful lot of people must be burned, not by ordinary fire, but by the contents of the bomb[...] Napalm in the war was devised by us and used by fighting men in action [...] No one ever thought of splashing it all over the civilian population. I will take no share in the responsibility for this.'[49,50,51]

A napalm survivor further attested to the terrible impacts of the weapons which were so liberally applied to Korean population centers. He stated: 'Napalm is the most terrible pain you can imagine. Water boils at 100 degrees Celsius. Napalm generates temperatures of 800 to 1,200 degrees Celsius.'[52] Napalm sticks to human skin and there is no way of removing the burning substance. Burns are severe and can be subdermal. Napalm fires can create an atmosphere of over 20 percent carbon monoxide and firestorms with self-perpetuating winds of up to 110 km per hour – as was the case during the firebombing of Tokyo.

The United States, as they had done in Japan and would do in Vietnam, claimed that firebombing population centers would erode morale and thus end the war sooner. This notably failed in Japan, and would fail in Korea, but was repeated again in Vietnam. While this was the pretext for the bombing, it proved a failed strategy which U.S. forces nonetheless continued to repeat in the region. Repetition of the same failed strategy by competent strategists, such those in the United States military, could well indicate an ulterior motive other than the pretext given. The aim was perhaps the devastation of a previously successful and modernizing Asian nations which had proven defiant – extermination by fire. U.S. General Ridgeway demanded that bigger and better napalm bombs be developed for use in Korea, 1,000 pound versions of these bombs which could be dropped from B-29s, thus to 'wipe out all life in the tactical locality.' 'If we keep on tearing the place apart, we can make it a most unpopular affair for the North Koreans. We ought to go right ahead,' said U.S. Secretary of Defense Robert Lovett.[53]

The United States also used chemical weapons during the war, as documented by several international observers. According to a report made by the International Association of Democratic Lawyers the evidence for the extensive use of chemical weapons by U.S. forces was overwhelming, enough to 'prove beyond question that the American Forces in Korea have in their possession chemical weapons of various kinds and that these have been used on many occasions against the civilian population, causing numerous casualties.' Their accounts of the effects of these weapons on Korean civilians are truly horrific.[54]

The *Armed Forces Chemical Journal* stated during the Korean War: 'our enemies now control or may eventually control countries whose populations add up to a total of almost one billion persons. Such an astronomical number of people can furnish virtually great hordes of military manpower.' It continued: 'if we are to [...] survive, we must employ weapons of mass destruction,' making a case for the use of chemical weapons in particular.[55] It was in the same vein that *Time* magazine's cover portrayed Chinese leader Mao Zedong leading swarms of red locusts on the front of their December 1950 issue to represent the coming hordes of Asiatic armies.[56] The depiction of perceived racial inferiors as pests, be they rats, locusts or spiders, had recently been widely employed by the United States in their depiction of the Japanese during the Pacific War and Nazi Germany's depiction Soviet peoples and ethnic minorities. The solution was to employ weapons of mass destruction (WMD) – the development and heavy use of incendiaries and the rapid development of a chemical weapons program with the goal of killing as many people indiscriminately as efficiently as possible. Indeed, based on common Western depictions and perceptions of communist China and North Korea and the way this translated into a relentless campaign against them making extensive use of WMD, it seemed that the United States viewed its air campaign against the 'Asiatic hordes' more as pest control than as war against human beings. The Chemical Corps was as a direct result tasked with developing napalm mines and more advanced incendiary weapons to burn enemies in larger numbers at once.[57] The targets were overwhelmingly civilian population centers.

Experts from the Chemical Corps alleged that chemical weapons were the most efficient means of exterminating all life in a target area. Renowned American war writer Cornelius Ryan, who was given unprecedented journalistic access to the Chemical Corps' facilities, reported: 'In World War II, it cost between $10,000,000 and $35,000,000 to eradicate people and buildings in one square mile of enemy territory by bombing. Nerve gas could do the same job for one twentieth the amount and leave buildings and industrial plants intact for an occupying force to take over.' The second measure of efficiency was in the area in which each warplane could eradicate people. Using a map comparing the effects of a nuclear bomb and GB (otherwise known as Sarin nerve gas) on a map of a city, the result was that 'fumes loosed by seven tons of GB bombs would drift 50 miles, killing everyone in their path. Atom bomb is lethal over only three-mile radius.'[58] Indeed, the inefficiency of nuclear weapons relative to other types of weapons such as nerve gas and napalm, largely due to the cumbersome nature and long response time of early nuclear bombs, was a key reason why nuclear weapons were never used in Korea, while chemical, biological and incendiary weapons were.

The *New York Times* would report 20 years after the Korean War that the U.S. military, facing numerous defeats in Korea, 'dug into captured Nazi chemical warfare documents describing Sarin, a nerve gas so lethal that a few pounds could kill thousands of people in minutes.' While the Sarin could not be mass produced as prescribed by the Nazi documents in time for use in the Korean War, 'by the mid-nineteen-fifties, the [U.S.] Army was manufacturing thousands of gallons of Sarin.'[59] This was a direct response to the military situation in the Korean War and the need for a weapon to engage 'Asiatic hordes' and kill large numbers efficiently.

Numerous correspondents and other observers, many of them Western, testified to the extent of the destruction wrought on North Korea by the United States. Tibor Meray, a Hungarian writer, had been a correspondent in the DPRK during the war. Meray was himself an anti-communist who later defected from Hungary after rebelling against its communist government. Despite his strong anti-communist views he was far more sympathetic towards the DPRK, saying afterwards when interviewed in Paris: 'I saw destruction and horrible things committed by the American forces [...] Everything which moved in North Korea was a military target, peasants in the fields were machine gunned by pilots who, this was my impression, amused themselves to shoot the targets which moved.' He said he had witnessed 'a complete devastation between the Yalu River [Chinese border] and the capital [Pyongyang].' There were simply 'no more cities in North Korea.' The bombing was incessant and wholly indiscriminate, restricting Meray to traveling only under cover of night: 'We travelled in moonlight, so my impression was that I am travelling on the moon, because there was only devastation [...] every city was a collection of chimneys. I don't know why houses collapsed and chimneys did not, but I went through a city of 200,000 inhabitants and I saw thousands of chimneys and that – that was all.'[60]

U.S. General William F. Dean, who had been captured by Korean forces, wrote of the destruction he witnessed after his release. 'The town of Huichon amazed me' he wrote. 'The city I'd seen before – two storied buildings, a prominent main street – wasn't there anymore.' Dean encountered only 'unoccupied shells' of town after town. Villages were reduced to rubble or 'snowy open spaces,' nothing more remained.[61] American professor Patricia Hynes noted regarding the bombings of the DPRK:

> The destruction within North Korean cities and towns ranged from 40 percent to nearly 100 percent. War commander General Ridgway wanted to 'wipe out all life in tactical sites,' sites which became, in the merciless momentum of air war, every city, town and village. North Korea's large dams, which provided irrigation water and generated electricity, were bombed, some at the onset of the rice-growing season. General MacArthur had boasted of a plan to win the war in 10 days: Drop 30 atomic bombs across the neck of Korea from sea to sea, leaving a belt of radiation between China and North Korea. The U.S. air war in Korea was so extreme as to be genocidal.[62]

North Korea had made considerable economic achievements and undergone effective industrialization since its independence. According to their own figures, the war destroyed 8,700 factories, 5,000 schools, 1,000 hospitals and 600,000 homes.[63] To escape the ravages of the bombing, entire factories, schools and hospitals were moved underground. The *Rodong Sinmun* newspaper referred to 1951 as 'the year of unbearable trials,' as such great suffering was imposed on a people whose entire country was destroyed. Due to the bombings, peasants would hide underground during the daytime and come out to farm under the cover of night. Agricultural output was reduced to near bare subsistence, as livestock was destroyed and shortages of everything from farm tools to fertilizers ensued. Industry and agriculture essentially ceased to function, bringing the people near famine.[64] American Chief Justice William O. Douglas attested to the unprecedented scale of destruction wrought by Western powers in Korea. He stated: 'I had seen the war-battered cities of Europe; but I had not seen devastation until I had seen Korea.'[65]

When President Truman's administration was replaced by that of Eisenhower in 1953 the new president reviewed the United States' strategy in Korea to enact what he referred to as the 'new and dynamic U.S. Far Eastern military strategy.' Subsequently there were significant proposals to extend the war and the bombing campaigns into China. In May 1953 the U.S. National Security Council were discussing memorandum NSC 147 outlining six options to end restraints on the U.S. military in Korea, a response to the stalemate which numerous American offensives northwards had been unable to break. Several of these options outlined expanding the war to China and ending the ban on bombing raids against Chinese population centers, as well as intensifying the already extensive air attacks against North Korea. The *New York Times* noted that the goal was not to achieve tactical military objectives. On May 21, Secretary Dulles warned that should armistice negotiations fail, 'the United States would probably make a stronger, rather than a lesser military exertion, and that this might well extend the area of conflict.' Dulles simultaneously proposed a blockade of China and seizure of its offshore islands.[66] In this case Eisenhower would signal Chiang Kai-shek to attack to Chinese mainland while the British and French would help enforce 'an effective blockade' of China.[67] These plans were almost put into place but ultimately, largely due to the military protection and nuclear umbrella of the USSR and the risk of Soviet involvement, they never came to fruition and the United States and its partners were thus deterred from expanding the war.

In the spring of 1953, having bombed every possible target in North Korea for three years and still failed to break its resolve, the United States Air Force targeted the crucial Yalu River irrigation dams – flooding whole towns and destroying North Korea's rice crop which the already dangerously malnourished nation needed to subsist. Five reservoirs were hit, flooding thousands of acres of farmland.[68] This would have condemned the population to a brutal famine and killed untold numbers of North Koreans. Millions were barely subsisting and relied on the crops from this farmland. A terrible widespread famine was only prevented by China increasing its food aid. This further put pressure on the already strained Chinese economy, which the United States and its partners were simultaneously attempting to bleed out and deplete.[69] Many Koreans died of hunger during the war as a direct result of the destruction of their food supplies.[70,71]

North Korean agriculture relied heavily on damming, which accounted for 75 percent of the country's rice crop.[72] The U.S. Air Force envisioned destroying 250,000 tons of rice by targeting this infrastructure. This included attacks on the Sui-ho dam, the second largest in the world at the time.[73] U.S. military reports appeared almost gleeful when reporting on the huge floods wiping out rice crops which 'the Asian' relied on for survival. Targeting dams to starve an enemy population was a severe war crime, one for which somewhat ironically an American-led tribunal at Nuremburg had recently hung Nazi German military leaders. Due to the United States' status as the dominant global power however, they inevitably escaped any such recriminations.[74] U.S. military journals at the time covered, with a strong tone of excitement, how excellent it was to see water pouring down and 'the Asians' scurrying around trying to survive. The result was mass starvation.[75] A U.S. military report at the time stated regarding the destruction of North Korea's rice crops by targeting the country's dams: 'The Westerner can little conceive the awesome meaning which the loss of this staple commodity has for the Asian – starvation and slow death.' This was a clear admission that the United States was willingly committing war crimes.[76] While destroying Koreans' source of food, the U.S. Air Force also initiated the fittingly named Operation Strangle which was set to destroy relief supplies coming into and crossing Korea at night. Despite claims to have destroyed many trucks, the operation ultimately failed to halt supplies and cause famine among the North Korean population on the scale intended. The North Koreans claim to this day that this bombing campaign indiscriminately targeting their food supplies and population centers was the greatest crime committed against their people.[77]

Biological Warfare

During the Korean War there were widespread reports indicating that the United States used biological weapons to target the populations of China and North Korea. During the Sino-Japanese war Japanese Imperial forces had carried out several experiments in bacteriological warfare, often on live human subjects.[78] Following the Empire's surrender a number of Japanese scientists responsible for this program were given full immunity from prosecution for their crimes by the United States, which thwarted efforts by the USSR to try them for war crimes. Soviet trials of those found to have experimented on live human subjects were dismissed as 'propaganda' and ignored in the West.[79] According to a BBC report the U.S. military meanwhile found the information of Japanese biological warfare scientists, 'absolutely invaluable.' It 'could never have been obtained in the United States because of scruples attached to experiments on humans,' and 'the information was obtained fairly cheaply.'[80] The scientists, many from the notorious biological weapons Unit 731, provided extensive technical information about their findings regarding biological warfare, based on tests on live subjects, to American scientists from the Army biological research center at Fort Detrick, Maryland, based on which the U.S. advanced its own biological warfare program.

China claimed that the United States had dropped quantities of bacteria and bacteria laden insects over Korea and northeast China during the war.[81] The U.S. had by this stage begun to see its formerly undisputed air superiority seriously challenged over Korea, seriously undermining one of its most crucial advantages. Resorting to germ warfare could be seen as an attempt to inflict as much damage as possible on the enemy population and thereby seriously undermine their war effort. The use of such weapons was an escalation to a new level of depravity.

Of all the war crimes committed by U.S. forces in Korea, the use of biological weapons was perhaps the most severe. The U.S. dropped insects and feathers carrying anthrax, cholera, encephalitis and bubonic plague. This was a well-kept secret at the time, but members of the U.S. military taken prisoner during the war confessed to what U.S. forces had been doing, and attested to it publicly when they later returned to the United States. These confessions could never be disproved and were backed up by independent scientific reviews.[82] The fact that the United States was carrying out such attacks against civilians would have shocked their own population and greatly tarnished the image of their government and military. The military's response to their soldiers' confessions was to claim that they had been 'brainwashed' by the communists, an entirely unfounded theory which the Western media strongly supported to save the government and military's image. The term 'brainwashing' was in fact coined in 1950 by Edward Hunter, an outspoken anti-communist and CIA agent who was working undercover as a journalist to discredit the testimonies of returning or captured U.S. personnel whose accounts threatened the official American narrative of the war.[83] The military personnel who detailed the biological weapons uses were associated with Fort Detrick in Maryland – the biological weapons facility. While there is no evidence against China's claims, the fact that those U.S. personnel accused of waging biological warfare later turned out to have come from a biological weapons facility would, if it were a coincidence as those who refute China's claims assert, be a remarkable and highly unlikely one.[84]

The Chinese devoted much effort to publicizing their claim that the United States was conducting germ warfare against them. They presented the testimonies of 38 captured American airmen who they claimed had flown the planes carrying these weapons. Many of these men went into precise and substantial details of the types of insects being carried, the types of containers dropped and the diseases used. The Chinese government published photographs of the germ bombs and the insects.[85]

Amid numerous reports of biological weapons being used against the Korean and Chinese populations, the World Peace Council established the International Scientific Commission for the Facts Concerning Bacterial Warfare in China and Korea in Oslo, Norway, on March 29, 1952. It was comprised of scientists from Sweden, France, Great Britain, Italy, Brazil and the Soviet Union and verified these findings. After over two months of investigation in China they produced a report comprising of some 600 pages and many photos that concluded: 'The peoples of Korea and China have indeed been the objectives of bacteriological weapons. These have been employed by units of the U.S.A. armed forces, using a great variety of different methods for the purpose, some which seem to be developments of those applied by the Japanese during the Second World War.'[86]

Conclusions were based on highly rigorous methodology, interrogation of Chinese and Korean witnesses, scientific testing of material evidence, careful checks on the collected specimens, and elaborate statistical calculations. Four of the investigators were renowned scientists at world leading universities, two were laboratory directors and the other was Dr Joseph Needham. Dr Needham, a professor at Cambridge University, represented one of the most esteemed British scientists of his time – a fellow of the Royal Society who would become a much renowned fellow of the British Academy and personally conferred the Companionship of Honor by Queen Elizabeth – the only living person to hold all three titles. Except for a single professor from the Soviet Academy of Medicine, Dr N. N. Zukov-Verzhnikov, all members of the commission were Westerners, unlikely to hold biases supporting North Korea or China. No Chinese or Koreans were involved.

Despite this, as the findings implicated the United States in such severe crimes, the commission was vilified and its conclusions were dismissed by the United States and Britain. Those organizations and commissions which collected evidence of biological weapons use were dismissed as 'communist' based on little more that their findings which implicated the United States in waging germ warfare, in an attempt to discredit their investigations.[87] Those who were not 'with us' or who were considered remotely critical of the U.S. intervention were widely labeled 'with the communists' in the United States at the time, and international commissions carrying out scientific research, no matter how impartial, were no exception.

Among the commission's report were the following findings: Evidence of a swarm of voles being dropped on several villages in Kan-Nan, Northeast China, on April 4, 1952, following the flight overhead of an American F-82 Twin Mustang fighter. 717 rodents, many evidently sick, were found. Most of the rodents were buried deep underground by the frightened villagers. Plague bacilli were found on the few rodents which were not buried. Kan-Nan had never known a plague in its entire history, and its appearance on the rodents was spontaneous and inexplicable unless introduced artificially. A telling detail was that all the voles without exception were adults, not a natural distribution of ages. The commission concluded: 'there remains no doubt that a large number of voles suffering from plague were delivered to the district of Kan-Nan during the night of 4–5 April, 1952 by [...] an American F-82 double-fuselage night-fighter.' Japan's Unit 731 had, reportedly, themselves devised means of landing plague rats from planes in much the same way.

In Liaotung and Liaoshi, Northeast China, the commission found beetles, houseflies and feathers contaminated with anthrax had been artificially introduced after American flights overhead. Five people, four of whom had been hunting for the insects, died of respiratory anthrax and hemorrhagic anthrax, exceedingly rare diseases in the area. Near Pyongyang the commission found evidence of cholera vibrio being artificially introduced, appearing in food dropped from the air on May 16, 1952, by a plane circling overhead. Cholera had never been prevalent in Korea before.[88]

Many Western experts who investigated claims of biological warfare against Chinese and Korean civilians went on to verify them, despite the often significant pressure from both state and non-state entities in the home countries not to do so. Dr Gene Weltfish, an anthropologist at Colombia University, was fired for reaching the scientific but unpopular conclusion that the U.S. was engaged in biological warfare against the North Korans and Chinese.[89] Dr Joseph Needham stated he remained '95–97 percent convinced' that the Chinese and North Korean charges that the United States was waging germ warfare against them were true. James Endicott, a Canadian peace activist, launched his own investigation into the biological warfare allegedly waged by the United States and verified the Chinese and Korean charges in his conclusion. He faced harassment from his government, as Canada was heavily involved in the war alongside the United States, and had his papers seized at the airport. He was tailed by the Canadian Mounted Police and strongly criticized by his Church, but despite this pressure stood by his claims.[90] (Many Christian religious organizations including the Vatican took strong political stances against the 'atheist' communist powers,[91,92,93] and many of them where advocates for the war in Korea.[94])

American journalist John W. Powell reported in 1952 that the United States was engaged in biological warfare in Korea, and as a result was tried for a dozen counts of sedition by the U.S. Department of Justice along with his wife – a charge punishable with a $10,000 fine and up to 20 years in prison. The editors of Powell's magazine, *China Monthly Review*, were charged with conspiracy. These charges were eventually dropped in 1959. Powell was able to publish additional evidence supporting his earlier reports only decades later in 1981 in *The Bulletin of the Atomic Scientists*, by which time the Korean War was but a distant memory and the report could have little impact on public opinion.

These findings by impartial international scientists and investigators have been supported by other evidence of the use of unconventional weapons by U.S. forces. North Korea continues to display what it alleges are biological warfare agents including preserved voles and insects at Korean War related museums. The descriptions of the means by which the United States waged biological warfare against them are fully consistent with the reports of the international commissions. Based on other numerous uses of biological and other unconventional weapons by the United States, including extensive use of such weapons against Cuba in the 1960s,[95] Chinese and North Korean claims to have been subjected to biological warfare cannot be so easily dismissed. Allegations of biological weapons use were supported by professor Jacob G. Hornberger, founder and president of the Future of Freedom Foundation who concluded: 'Given that the U.S. military had just a few years before dropped atomic bombs on Hiroshima and Nagasaki, why would they have any compunctions about bombing North Koreans with napalm and fleas with bubonic plague? Don't forget, after all, the mindset of the U.S. national-security state [...] A commie is a commie and a gook is gook; no big deal to send any and all of them to the hereafter.'[96]

Hugh Deane, reporter and former Coordinator of Information and naval intelligence officer on General MacArthur's staff, extensively researched his country's waging of biological warfare in Korea, as well as its incorporation of Japanese war criminals into its program, and concluded on the matter: 'The charge that the U.S. was indeed guilty of germ warfare can hardly be dismissed on the grounds that Americans would not consider such criminality. That persuaded great numbers at the time, but since then evidence of ongoing American development of bacteriological warfare capabilities and the actual use of chemical weapons in Vietnam have come to light. Several American military high-ups, including General Charles E. Loucks of the Army Chemical Corps, on January 22, 1951, made statements unequivocally giving their support to resorting to germ warfare.'[97]

One notable more recent case of censorship of evidence regarding American use of biological weapons in Korea was the publishing of the book *Unit 731: Japan's Secret Biological Warfare in World War II* by British professor Peter Williams and American professor David Wallace. The book was published in Britain in 1989, but American publishers refused to publish the book unless special editing for an 'American edition' was made.[98] This essentially involved the removal of Chapter 17, which covered the legacy of Unit 731 in relation to the Korean War, giving substantial evidence of U.S. involvement in biological warfare against the Korean and Chinese populations. Prominent among the evidence was that collected by the International Scientific Commission for the Facts Concerning Bacterial Warfare in China and Korea, the evidence of which Wallace and Williams claimed was 'generally accepted today as being of high quality.'

The Commission of International Association of Democratic Lawyers released their own report of war crimes committed by the United States in Korea.[†] The Commission sent an observer mission to Korea in 1952 to investigate claims that the United States was guilty of genocide based on the framework of the 1948 genocide convention. The observers found overwhelming evidence indicating that the United States was conducting biological warfare against North Korea and China. They carefully documented the types of insects which were being dropped from American planes and referred these to experts. Observing the insects, they made many notable discoveries. The commission noted:

> In many cases special kinds of flies, fleas, spiders, beetles, bugs, crickets, mosquitoes and other insects were found, many of which were hitherto unknown in Korea. Insects were found in different cases far from human habitation, on snow, on the ice of rivers, on grass and among stones. Considering the very low temperatures prevailing at the time [in January the maximum was 10C and in February 50C, but for a few hours, the average temperatures were far below freezing] which normally prevent the appearance of insects, and also considering that the insects were often found in great quantities and even in mixed groups of clusters consisting of different varieties of insects which would normally never be found together, like flies and spiders, the appearance of these insects roused suspicion. The results of expert examination showed that great quantities of insects were infected. In many cases it was also found that the insects were carrying eggs [not a natural occurrence in such weather and at such a time of year]. In the opinion of experts it could be safely assumed that these insects were bred artificially.

The commission details finding half rotten fish infected with cholera in great quantities near mountain settlements far from where such fish would naturally be found. It also listed the bacteria found: 'Vibrio cholera, pasteurella pestis, Eberthella typhosa, Bacillus paratyphi A and B, Rickettsia prowazeki and shigella dysenteriae.' The findings of the commission were published in 1952. They concluded that the United States was employing

† The International Association of Democratic Lawyers is an international NGO which researches legal issues affecting human, political and economic rights worldwide. It works as a consultative organization with the UN, UNESCO, UNICEF and ECOSOC, and has headquarters in Brussels and Tokyo.

biological warfare in Korea and China, and that it had committed war crimes and well as crimes against humanity. They went on to state that 'taking into account that the employment of bacteriological and chemical weapons over extensive areas of the country must constitute an attempt to destroy a whole people or part of a people, the Commission is of the opinion that the American forces are guilty of the crime of Genocide as defined by the Genocide Convention of 1948.'[99]

The details of the United States' biological warfare operations against North Korea and China were given and Chinese allegations were analyzed thoroughly by researcher Dave Chaddock in his book *This Must Be the Place: How the U.S. Waged Germ Warfare in the Korean War and Denied It Ever Since*, whose conclusion strongly supported these claims. It built on earlier evidence and an investigation by American researchers Stephen Endicott and Edward Hagerman, who arrived at the same conclusion that the United States had used such weapons extensively. Members of Imperial Japan's infamous Unit 731 who had extensively researched biological warfare weapons were reportedly carried along with their equipment to South Korea in 1951. Dr Shiro Ishii and Dr Masaji Kitano, 2nd commander of Unit 731, were among those involved in biological warfare operations in Korea.[100]

China's government responded to these attacks with a campaign of mass vaccinations and organized insect eradication, and as a result the biological weapons program ultimately failed. Chinese authorities requested immediate assistance from the USSR for disease prevention. Four anti-bacteriological warfare research centers were set up quickly on the Korean front while 5.8 million doses of vaccine and 200,000 gas masks were delivered. The Chinese government initiated the Patriotic Health and Epidemic Prevention Campaign which directed citizens to kill flies, mosquitoes and fleas.[101] Anti-communist Hungarian journalist Tibor Méray attested to seeing the North Koreans carrying out 'an unprecedented campaign of public health' during the war to prevent American biological weapons efforts from causing a widespread epidemic.[102]

Whatever the United States claimed, it was clear that the Chinese and North Koreans themselves certainly believed that they had been targeted by biological weapons due to the great expense they undertook to carry out their public health campaign despite the extreme scarcity of resources at their disposal. In March 1952 there were 129 teams, over 20,000 people, establishing 66 quarantine zones. Nearly 5 million people in China's northeast in regions closest to Korea were inoculated against plague.[103] These measures successfully improved the health of Chinese and Korean soldiers and civilians and prevented the outbreak of a large-scale epidemic, which had been the intention of the program.[104] Though the diseases killed thousands, they had the potential to cause a nationwide epidemic and kill many millions. This would have weakened China for decades – one of many measures taken to slow the new republic's postwar development and prevent it from emerging as a major independent power capable of challenging Western primacy in the Asia-Pacific (as previously detailed in Chapter 3).

The fact that the world's leading power could be involved in such operations was difficult for many to accept, and denial came naturally. Indeed, the tone used to refute Chinese claims was the same as that used to flatly deny the operations of CIA agents on Chinese territory in the same period – despite the CIA later declassifying information which fully verified Chinese claims.[105,106] Only an analysis of hard evidence could overcome inclinations to deny the uncomfortable truth of U.S. intentions towards China and North Korea and the means they were willing to employ against them. As George Wald, an expert from the Harvard Biological Laboratories and Nobel Prize Winner concluded after studying the evidence: 'As for the allegation that the U.S. used germ warfare in the Korean War, I can only say with some shame that what I dismissed as incredible then seems altogether credible to me now.'[107] America's position as the world's dominant power and its formidable soft power made it extremely difficult to accuse it of committing such crimes despite overwhelming evidence.

American Calls for the Use of Nuclear Weapons

The failure of U.S. military forces and their allies to win an outright military victory and obtain an unconditional surrender frustrated many in the United States leadership. Several American commanders, congressmen and other prominent figures voiced their strong support for the deployment of nuclear arms to subdue the Korean and Chinese forces. Christian leaders and their parishioners were among the loudest exponents of a nuclear solution to the war. A notable example was Reverend Kenneth Eyler of the Wesleyan Methodist Church addressing President Truman. 'Your excellency [...] As a minister of the Gospel and a Bible-believing Christian [...] there is much that has been bothering me lately. This war in Korea. Why is it we fuss around at the fringe instead of getting at the heart of the matter? [...] You know as well as I do where this whole matter lies. That is in MOSCOW. I would rather see Moscow destroyed than our boys die in Korea at the hands of the Chinese Red ... You can use the Atom bomb.'[108]

Albert Gore, United States Senator, made a strong suggestion to President Truman after the outbreak of the Korean War: 'Dehumanize a belt across the Korean Peninsula by surface radiological contamination [...] broadcast the fact to the enemy [...] that entrance into the belt would mean certain death or slow deformity to all foot soldiers [...] And further, that the belt would be regularly re-contaminated until such time as a satisfactory solution to the whole Korean problem shall have been reached.'[109] This was a creative idea for the use of nuclear weapons, again an attempt by the United States to solve an issue through force – to turn a lost conventional war around through employment of unconventional means, in this case by contaminating and regularly re-contaminating an Asian country with nuclear waste. The implications of this proposal on the Korean peninsula would have been devastating as once contaminated, even if not 're-contaminated,' the effects of the repeated use of nuclear weapons is very long lasting. One need only look at Bikini Island and the Algerian desert today.[110] Similar such 'solutions' to the conflict based on the use of nuclear weapons were popular with much of the American and Western public, and the majority supported nuclear strikes against North Korea[111,112] just as they had supported them against Hiroshima and Nagasaki.[113,114] Gore's son would become vice president from 1993 to 2001 and a leading presidential candidate running for election in 2000 on a similarly hawkish platform.

After the use of nuclear weapons against Japan it was largely believed that nuclear weapons would allow Western powers to avoid fighting major wars in the near future and guarantee their military supremacy for years to come. Many had therefore expected nuclear weapons to be used to 'resolve' the Korean War quickly. The power of these bombs would be used put an end to all challenges to American might – something which policymakers in Washington proved to their credit to be at least somewhat more aware was not feasible.

There were significant moves taken by the United States government and military to enable and prepare for the use of nuclear weapons in Korea. General MacArthur had proposed, similarly to Senator Gore, 34 nuclear strikes to create a radioactive belt – but across Manchuria to disrupt Chinese forces rather than across Korea. This plan did not materialize.[115] An alternative plan submitted by MacArthur in December 1950, following China's string of military victories against U.S. forces, called for 'retaliation targets' in China and the DPRK to be struck by 26 nuclear bombs. Eight of these would be used against enemy troop concentrations and airbases, while the other 18 would be used against industrial targets – likely population centers.[116] British historian Max Hastings referred to the General as 'instilled with a yearning for crude revenge upon the people who had brought all his hopes and triumphs in Korea to nothing' in his attitude towards the People's Republic of China following its military intervention, and this very likely had an impact on his willingness to deploy nuclear force against the Chinese.[117]

The United States came closest to using nuclear weapons in 1950 when the Chinese entered the war. The following year on March 10, 1951, MacArthur asked for 'D-Day atomic capability' in the Korean theatre after the Chinese PLA massed assets near the Korean border. He later demanded that up to 50 nuclear weapons be dropped on Manchuria to thwart the attacks of 'Chinese hordes' on his positions. At the end of March atomic bomb loading pits at Kadena Air Base on Okinawa were operational. The bombs were carried to the base and assembled there. Only the capsules, the essential nuclear cores, were missing from these bombs.[118]

On April 5, the United States came close to using nuclear weapons. Though this date is little known, it nears the Cuban Missile Crisis in its significance and its potential to have instigated nuclear war. The U.S. Joint

Chiefs of Staff (JCS) ordered immediate retaliation against Chinese bases in Manchuria using nuclear weapons if large numbers of new troops entered the fighting or if bombers were launched against American assets from there. For the Chinese to have taken such actions was far from unlikely. On the same day the chairman of the U.S. Atomic Energy Commission (AEC) Gordon Dean began arrangements to transfer nine Mark 4 nuclear capsules to the Air Force's 9th Bomb Group, the group designated to carry nuclear weapons. General Omar Bradley, the JCS chairman, got President Truman's approval for this transfer of Mark 4 bombs 'from AEC to military custody' on April 6. President Truman then signed an order to use these weapons against Chinese and North Korean targets. The nuclear-armed 9th Bomb Group then deployed to Guam.[119]

The Chinese for their part fought with highly limited means and avoided taking steps which could escalate the war. It was often the case that the oncoming 'Chinese hordes' were nowhere to be found on the front, at one moment fighting and the next withdrawing. Escalation and conflict were never in their interests – nor was any sort of conflict in the first place for that matter. The PLA therefore remained very conservative in committing its forces to the Korean front in order to avoid escalation. In this way, what could have easily been a nuclear holocaust in Manchuria, which the United States for their part had a finger ready on the button to unleash and orders to be ready to do so, was averted. There was no guarantee however that Chinese forces would not have operated more offensively when pressed near their own borders, and nuclear attacks could well have taken place had the Chinese military leadership only adopted a more offensive strategy.

Following the inauguration of President Eisenhower in 1953 the United States' nuclear policy regarding Korea was put under review. On March 27, two months into the administration, President Eisenhower and Secretary Dulles agreed 'that somehow or other the taboo which surrounds the use of atomic weapons would have to be destroyed.' Dulles stated that 'in the present state of world opinion, we could not use an A-bomb, we should make every effort now to dissipate this feeling.' If public perceptions towards nuclear weapons were to soften, the United States could employ them against North Korean and Chinese forces, or even population centers, as

Eisenhower wished. The following year the administration would consider use of nuclear weapons in Vietnam to aid French colonial forces besieged there.[120,121]

Eisenhower, himself a former General, stated in May that he 'thought it might be cheaper, dollar-wise, to use atomic weapons in Korea than to continue to use conventional weapons against the dugouts which honeycombed the hills along which the enemy forces were presently deployed.' He hoped to thereby break the stalemate that had emerged on the 38th Parallel which had prevented U.S. forces from advancing into northern Korea. The nuclear threats were later extended under the Eisenhower administration to China and Chinese population centers. The president 'expressed with great emphasis the opinion that if the Chinese Communists attacked us again, we should certainly respond by hitting them hard and wherever it would hurt most, including Peiping [old Romanization of Peking, today known as Beijing] itself.' The implication was that nuclear strikes were a possibility, and a key part of plans for what Eisenhower referred to as 'all-out war against Communist China.'[122,123]

Though April 1951 was the closest the United States had come to using nuclear weapons, it was by no means the last time the 'nuclear solution' was considered. Two months later in June the JCS again considered the use of nuclear weapons in tactical battlefield circumstances, and this occurred many more times throughout the war. Robert Oppenheimer, a scientist who had been crucial to helping develop the United States' Manhattan Project, went to Korea to gauge the feasibility of tactical use of atomic weapons against Korean and Chinese forces there.[124]

The U.S. also carried out Operation Hudson Harbor in Korea, a project to establish the capability to use nuclear weapons on the battlefield. To test this lone B-29 bombers were sent over North Korea on simulated atomic bombing runs, dropping 'dummy' bombs or heavy conventional bombs. The project called for 'actual functioning of all activities which would be involved in an atomic strike, including weapons assembly and testing and more.' The project indicated however that bombs were not technically useful in Korea. 'Timely identification of large masses of enemy troops was extremely rare,' military reports from the operation concluded. Korean and Chinese military forces were far from ideal targets, always operating either in fluid and constantly changing formations or dug into mountains.[125] Meanwhile, by the time Chinese forces intervened in Korea all major population centers in the DPRK had been destroyed and there were no remaining feasible targets for a nuclear strike. General J. Lawton Collins, the U.S. Army Chief of Staff at the time, stated regarding the limited military value of nuclear weapons in Korea: 'Personally, I am very skeptical about the value of using atomic weapons tactically in Korea. The Communists are dug into positions in depth over a front of 150 miles.' He believed that nuclear weapons would not be effective in targeting fortified positions based on the findings of American nuclear tests, stating that these tests 'proved that men can be very close to the explosion and not be hurt if they are well dug in.' Many other U.S. military leaders similarly perceived nuclear attacks to be of limited use given the situation.[126] While the advent of 'bunker buster' tactical nuclear weapons ideal for targeting fortified positions has today made nuclear arms the weapon of choice for the United States should it seek to attack North Korean fortified positions, with a central role in America's twenty-first-century war plans for military intervention on the Korean Peninsula, nuclear weapons of the Korean War era were ill suited to such a role.[127]

As for the North Korean and Chinese leadership, to see nuclear bombings simulated over one's territory never knowing which 'simulation' was a dud and which may be the weapon that had devastated Japan only a few years prior must have caused considerable trepidation. In Japan the United States had also flown lone B-29 bombers over potential targets for nuclear strikes in the weeks leading up to the attacks, and two of these routine bombers had destroyed two cities, taking around 200,000 lives – with estimates ranging from 150,000 to 230,000. In the eyes of the North Koreans and Chinese, why would these simulated flights over Korea necessarily be any different?[128]

The Korean War hardly saw the end of American nuclear threats against China and North Korea, and by the end of the decade 950 U.S. nuclear weapons were deployed to South Korea[129,130] with hundreds more deployed to Taiwan and Japan primarily to target the two non-nuclear Asian states. The United States came close to using these weapons on several occasions throughout the Cold War in conflicts with China over Taiwan and against

North Korea – one case of which was President Nixon's operation plan Freedom Drop to 'conduct strikes against military targets in North Korea employing one nuclear weapon on each target.'[131,132] Over a dozen tactical nuclear weapons were to be used to destroy Korean command centers and airfields in retaliation for the country downing a U.S. EC-121 spy plane in 1969 – though the fear of North Korean retaliation and all out war when the U.S. was already preoccupied in Vietnam, as well as the potential for Chinese and Soviet intervention, made such plans unfeasible. North Korea was safe from U.S. nuclear strikes largely because of the patronage of two major communist powers, and following the end of the Cold War and the collapse of this patronage this became a major factor in the country's decision to develop its own nuclear program to deter a U.S. nuclear attack (as covered in Chapter 19).

The West's Loss of Air Superiority and the Beginning of the End

Western military powers have relied overwhelmingly on air superiority in all major foreign military interventions since the Second World War. The unchallenged control of the air in early stages of the Korean War allowed the United States to destroy what was essentially the whole of North Korea – and most of the south along with it. Although North Korea initially did not receive support from the USSR, following American provocations along China's border and the PLA's entry into the war, the Soviet Union began to grant limited assistance to both China and the DPRK. While military aid to boost the two Asian powers' naval and ground warfare capabilities was extremely limited, the USSR did provide far more generously to strengthen their aerial warfare capabilities. This was in part due to the fact that combat aircraft were far less likely to get captured in the field than modern tanks or small arms, thus preserving Soviet technological secrets, but also because deploying its latest fighters was a relatively simple way of denying the Western Bloc its much needed air superiority advantage.

Demonstrating the capabilities of the latest Soviet made fighters in a limited deployment to protect the Manchurian border was also an effective means of deterring the United States and its allies from expanding the war beyond the Korean Peninsula – an outcome both Moscow and Beijing were keen to avoid. The MiG-15 jet fighter, arguably the most advanced fighter aircraft in the world at the time, was thus placed in Chinese and North Korean hands and was deployed to undermine Western air superiority. American bombers were increasingly targeted effectively, challenging their ability to attack targets in Korea[133] and undermining the previous principle known as 'the bomber will always get through,' a self-explanatory idea which had largely proven true at the close of the Pacific War and in the war against Nazi Germany in Europe, and which had been heavily relied on for nuclear delivery.

The deployment of the MiG-15 led to a substantial shift in the balance of power in Korea. As U.S. Air Force General Charles Cleveland stated, parity in the air was something the Western Bloc was not used to facing even in the Second World War: 'You have to remember that the little MiG-15 in Korea was successful doing what all the Focke-Wulfs and Messerschmitts of World War II were never able to do: Drive the United States bomber force right out the sky.'[134] The air became the only field where the Chinese and North Koreans had any semblance of technological parity with the Western Bloc. Britain's Chief of Air Staff noted of the MiG-15: 'not only is it faster than anything we are building today, but it is already being produced in very large numbers [...] The Russians, therefore, have achieved a four year lead over British development in respect of the vitally important interceptor fighter.'[135] The vast majority of fighters in the fleets of the United States and its allies were left effectively obsolete in the face of the new challenge, and only the U.S. was capable of engaging the MiG by rushing its newest and most advanced air superiority platform, the F-86 Sabre, into action. The discrepancy in capabilities favoring the MiG was somewhat compensated for both by the vast numerical superiority of U.S. aircraft deployed to Korea as well as by the superior caliber of U.S. pilots, who could draw on extensive experience from the Second World War in a way their novice Chinese and North Korean counterparts could not. In this way, the war in the air was very much an inversion of the war on the ground in terms of which party could rely on superior skill and which depended on a technological edge.

The Western powers' loss of air superiority over much of North Korea significantly changed the nature of the war. British Air Vice-Marshal W. M. Yool noted: 'There have been many puzzling aspects of the campaign in Korea, of which not the least has been the apparent failure of airpower to exercise any great influence upon the course of events.'[136] Yool further noted: 'We have had a situation in which the United Nations forces enjoyed practically complete air supremacy both before and after the intervention of the Chinese, and yet their [U.S. and allied] forces were almost thrown into the sea at the outset of the campaign, and subsequently, after their triumphant advance to the Yalu River, were driven back headlong south of the 38th Parallel.'[137] While the U.S. and their allies struggled even when they had uncontested control of the skies, the fact that the Chinese and North Koreans had begun to undermine this advantage boded ill for the future of their U.S. led campaign on the ground.

One pivotal event which turned the tide of the war was the Battle of Namsi, which came to be known among Western forces as Black Tuesday. Nine U.S. B-29 bombers and their fighter escort had flown from Okinawa to target an airfield under construction in North Korea and had been intercepted and destroyed by MiG-15 fighters. Only three bombers survived this encounter.[138] American Air Force Colonel Earl McGill, after extensively researching the battle and its implications, concluded that it 'would forever change the conduct of strategic aerial bombardment.'[139] The Western military powers' belief that their unparalleled air superiority capabilities would allow them to win any war quickly and with minimal loss of life, as it did in the late stages of the Pacific War against Japan, was seriously undermined and as a result a swift and absolute victory in Korea appeared all the more out of reach. When at the outset of the Korean War the United States Air Force had been granted permission to fight, the British *National Air Review* had predicted that it would end the war within 72 hours.[140] Given this faith in the potential of Western air power to work as an overwhelming decisive factor in their favor, the success of Soviet built planes flown by Asian pilots forced Western powers to seriously reconsider their military doctrine.

I. F. Stone noted at the time regarding this development: 'The Air Force suddenly faced the prospect of losing control of the air over Korea. It found that the long-distance strategic subsonic bomber, one which the Americans had relied for delivery of the atom bomb, was obsolete. It woke up to discover that the despised and technologically backward Soviet Union was producing better jet planes than the United States [...] To examine the situation carefully was to see that the Battle of Namsi and its aftermath represented a military, technological, and strategic setback of the first magnitude.'[141]

The shock the battle induced in American military leaders was clear from the sudden change of tone in their statements. U.S. Director of Central Intelligence and Second Air Force Chief of Staff General Hoyt Vandenberg had stated the day before the battle 'Our boys are knocking their socks off.' A month after the battle however he admitted that the U.S. 'suffered our heaviest loss of any single action of the Korean War.' He told the press at the Pentagon on November 21 'as regards the air situation in Korea, a significant and, by some standards, even sinister change has occurred [...] Almost overnight China has become one of the major air powers of the world [...] the air supremacy upon which we have relied in the past is now faced with a serious challenge.'[142]

General Vandenburg also revealed during the same press conference the extent to which the development of a powerful Chinese, Korean and possibly even Soviet Air Force presence in North Korea could affect the course of the war. He stated that American intelligence had discovered three 'particularly large airfields about ninety miles below the Manchurian border in northwestern Korea were being expanded and improved with amazing speed.' They had runways of at least 6,400 ft. and were obviously 'intended for jet use' due to the way they were constructed. Very strong anti-aircraft defenses were being established around the airfields. Vandenburg indicated the seriousness of this situation, stating: 'Their use by enemy aircraft would give Communist air power an effective operational range which could pose a menace to United Nations air and ground operations in the battle zone, operations which have been virtually unopposed by enemy air [assets] since the early days of the war.'[143] This would allow these air forces to operate effectively across all of northern Korea – where they had previously been restricted to operations near the Sino-Korean border far from the 38th Parallel frontlines.

The United States Air Force attempted to attack the new air bases in North Korea, though it was forced to admit that its ability to dominate the air had been seriously compromised and had to shift to night bombing. 'The Air Space between the Yalu and Pyongyang in which we had previously been able to operate unhindered, is now a "no man's air" and has become the area of decision in the Korea War [...] Unmistakably the enemy is intensifying the efforts in the air despite his forced acceptance of a stalemate on the ground. And we must expect that if he wins in the air the stalemate on the ground is not likely to continue.'[144]

With the loss of air supremacy a victory for the U.S. led forces appeared highly unlikely and the possibility emerged of losing the war and perhaps even losing all of Korea and being forced onto the defensive. Growing Soviet assistance to Chinese and Korean forces and the limited but increasing participation of the Soviet Air Force further worsened the situation for the already hard-pressed U.S. led coalition. The loss of uncontested air superiority was a crucial factor in forcing Western powers to end the Korean War. Having lost the ability to operate freely in the air, under which favorable circumstances they had been unable to secure victory, if air supremacy was lost entirely then prospects for the ground war looked dim. Indeed, had the Chinese and North Koreans gained air superiority themselves, as they may well have been on course to do, then the U.S. and their allies may have faced an absolute defeat – particularly if the Soviets provided greater assistance in supplies and logistics essential to facilitating a PLA and KPA drive south. An armistice was therefore the best option for the United States and its allies to both avoid defeat, end a growingly unpopular war and maintain several of their interests in southern Korea. The USSR, North Korea and China on the other hand were, as they had been before the war, more interested in a swift and peaceful end to the conflict. China had much to do to industrialize and rebuild after its own civil war and was forced to divert much of its resources to the war effort. The DPRK had suffered a great deal and by some estimates by Western experts 30 percent of its population were dead,[145,146] with many more severely wounded. It too sought a swift peace.

Outcome and Consequences of the Korean War

Peace talks concluded in 1953 and Korea has remained technically at war but under an armistice since then. The Western Bloc, having resorted to targeting civilians and rice fields, using biological and chemical weapons and very nearly using nuclear weapons, could not defeat the joint Korean-Chinese forces. The U.S. and their allies had initially been highly reluctant to resolve the war with any significant compromise, as demonstrated by the firebombing of Sinuiju on the Chinese border during peace talks among other events. This reluctance was in part due to the West's perception of their adversaries as beneath them and their inability to comprehend being bested by a 'peasant army' of Asiatics, so scantly armed and clad as they were. Indeed, this was the first time in over a century that an Asian army had forced an alliance of Western nations to negotiate rather than be allowed to dictate terms to end a major war – much to their chagrin. As U.S. and UN Supreme Commander General Ridgeway advised: 'To sit down with these man and deal with them as representatives of an enlightened and civilized people is to deride one's own dignity and to invite the disaster their treachery will bring upon us.'[147]

While Western military powers could not bring themselves to believe that Asian nations had proven so formidable or that Soviet-made aircraft had matched their own, it dawned on them for the first time since reclaiming Seoul that Korea would never be the easy victory they had hoped for. Since mid-1951 two years prior they had failed to permanently take ground and fighting had been localized to the 38th Parallel. U.S. President Truman's approval ratings had fallen to the lowest in American history – a record he would hold for over 50 years.[148] This was largely attributed to his failure in Korea, a war which cost thousands of American lives and had little public support. Facing an inevitable stalemate or worse, President Eisenhower did not wish to see the same fate himself.

As the North Korean government had not been removed from power and the peninsula reunified under Syngman Rhee's government, the United States had failed to achieve one of its primary objectives. They had however succeeded in preventing a peaceful reunification and the democratic victory of the northern government in the country, which had previously been considered inevitable with the election of a parliament just days before the war's outbreak strongly supporting such a unification process. Syngman Rhee too was able to remain in power in the south where his unpopularity prior to the war had meant his loss of power previously appeared imminent. The 'communist invasion' only gave further pretext to strengthen his position domestically. The U.S. meanwhile had successfully emerged from the postwar economic recession and has maintained a large and permanent military industrial complex and standing army ever since – ensuring that the crucial stimulant for its economy would remain indefinitely.

China's armed forces, though suffering considerable casualties, proved for the first time in over a century that it was advanced and competent enough to combat Western forces in Asia. The Korean People's Army also performed far more capably than the U.S. military leadership had ever imagined, particularly in the early stages of the war. They changed Western perceptions of Asian military performance, which until then had been that 'Chinamen can't fight' (as neatly summed up by MacArthur) and proved themselves a force to be reckoned with. General MacArthur had himself within a few weeks of engaging North Korean forces changed his assessment entirely, stating: 'The North Korean solider must not be underestimated. He is a tough opponent, well led.'[149,150] The United States has remained highly wary of North Korea's military capabilities ever since.

The Korean War would shape the rest of the Cold War and the future of Western interventionism in the Asia-Pacific. After several catastrophic defeats at the hands of the Japanese Empire less than ten years prior, to be matched by Chinese and Korean forces as well was a second blow to Western prestige and confidence in their outright superiority over and perceived right to dominate Asian nations and their peoples. This belief had previously prevailed to the extent that it was believed Caucasians must be flying the Chinese planes for them – how could the 'little yellow men' possibly match Westerners in air battles. Stories emerged that MiG-15s were being flown by captured, and presumably 'brainwashed,' Americans and Europeans, something entirely unfounded in reality but which nevertheless satisfied the prevalent racial prejudices. I. F. Stone reported that as the U.S. and their allies began to lose control of the air: 'The anti-aircraft gunnery on the ground and the flying skill in the air which the enemy began to show in the fall of 1951 was indeed a source of speculation as to the possible presence of "Caucasians" on the Red side. If complicated guns were so well manned and complicated planes so well flown, surely there must be white men at the controls. There was even speculation that maybe Americans were flying the planes for the Reds [...] No "Caucasians" had yet been reported found in downed planes. There was no doubt that most of the fliers were of Asian colored races – and doing a competent job.'[151] *Aviation Week* reported in December of that year that while it was unknown who flew the MiG fighters, there was speculation that they were flown by ex-American Second World War pilots.

The United States was forced to revise its military doctrine based on developments in the war. Having lost air superiority their bombers had become easy targets for Soviet fighters and they could no longer rely on the 'bomber will always get through' concept to win wars from the air and deliver nuclear strikes. This had implications well beyond Korea. Prospects for a nuclear offensive against the USSR and China dimmed as a result, and would never again become a feasible prospect due to both the rapid development of a Soviet and later a Chinese nuclear arsenal, the Soviet development of intercontinental ballistic missiles and the later emergence of the principle of mutually assured destruction.

The Western powers' failure to best China's People's Liberation Army on the battlefield despite their considerable advantages across the spectrum would lead to a serious reconsideration of policy towards the country. Prospects for rolling back Chinese communism through direct military intervention as General MacArthur and Chiang Kai-shek had hoped, likely backed by nuclear arms and a firebombing campaign, appeared wholly unfeasible, leading to a new approach to subduing the East Asian power. The United States would continue to maintain pressure on China following the Korean War's end, largely through the support of various Guomindang aligned armed groups and separatist factions alongside an economic blockade to hinder the country's prospects for modernization. This new policy was effectively summarized by Assistant Secretary of State for Far Eastern

Affairs Walter Robinson, who stated: 'our hope of solving the problem of the mainland of China was not through attack on the mainland but rather by actions which would promote disintegration from within.'[152] The Office of Policy Coordination, a covert operations wing of the CIA, would thus receive directives 'to initiate psychological warfare and paramilitary operations against the Chinese Communist regime,' which according to a national security memo the following year was intended to 'foster and support anticommunist elements both outside and within China with a view to developing an expanding resistance in China to the Peiping [Beijing] regime's control.'[153] These efforts were fully comprehensive, from airdrops of rocket propelled grenades to CIA trained saboteurs on Chinese soil to the forging and distribution of falsified communist party leaflets intended to intensify conflict and factionalism during the Cultural Revolution.[154]

For the Korean people the end of the war left their country in ruins. As General MacArthur had testified to the U.S. Congress: 'The war in Korea has already almost destroyed that nation of 20 million people. I have never seen such devastation. I have seen, I guess, as much blood and disaster as any living man, and it just curdled my stomach the last time I was there.' He referred to the war as 'a slaughter never heard of in the history of mankind.'[155] With their food production capacities having been devastated due to a combination of the firebombing campaign, scorched earth policies, targeting of irrigation dams and the loss of up to 30 percent of the workforce, North Korea was forced to rely almost entirely on food from abroad. American estimates of the numbers of Koreans killed range up to 5 million.[156,157] An estimated 20–30 percent of North Koreans had died in the war. Yet more were wounded, homeless, unable to work and otherwise adversely affected. The extent of the bombing and destruction remains unparalleled in history.[158] As former CIA Operations Officer and intelligence expert Robert R. Simmons observed of the results of U.S. intervention: 'a potentially swift and relatively bloodless reunification was converted into a carnage.'[159] As American reporter Hugh Deane concluded forty years later: 'Korea is the least remembered of the post-World War II American interventions. It ought to be remembered as the most genocidal of them.'[160]

South Korea had also suffered significantly in the war's initial months, and had lost approximately 1 million of its population, many of them from the military. The country remained under a U.S. sponsored dictatorship under Sygman Rhee and would see little improvement to its quality of life, among the very lowest in the world, until his overthrow. South Korean professor Seong Won Park noted that: 'The Korean War [...] destroyed Korean society. In the 1960s, South Korea was one of the poorest countries in the world.' The country relied on the United States heavily, with prostitution serving U.S. military personnel making up 25 percent of gross national product.[161] In 1965, 85 percent of its population were still in abject poverty.[162] It was not until two decades later that the economy finally began to improve under a new military government, with Prime Minister General Park Chung Hee providing far more competent and independent leadership than the American installed Rhee regime.

North Korea managed to quickly rebuild, and achieved economic growth rates of over 20 percent. Through mass mobilization of its population under an independent leadership they were able to recover and economically outpace the South despite having suffered the vast majority of wartime destruction. While there were no Korean or Chinese bombing raids on Seoul or other South Korean cities, American B-29 bombers were very thorough in destroying every building over two storeys high in the North. Unexploded munitions meanwhile continue to be dug up almost 70 years later, posing a danger to civilians ever since and continuing to cause injuries. The cleanup operation is expected to take at least 100 years.[163] North Koreans today consider the Korean War a victory, though it is one for which they paid a very high price. The city of Kaesong near the border became part of the North following the end of the war, as did the small Onjin peninsula, though overall the borders changed little. The country remains divided until today and tensions on the border remain high.

North Korea today remains heavily influenced by its experience in the Korean War – referred to as 'a confrontation between the rifle and the atomic bomb'[164] – which has played a formative role in shaping many aspects of the country's modern identity, from its education, art and theatre to its foreign policy, defense doctrine and more recently it pursuit of a nuclear deterrent. While Western sources are often quick to criticize Pyongyang's historically high defense expenditure, the context of the Korean War and the loss of approximately one quarter of the population – which could have potentially been averted had the state been better armed and better prepared to either wage or deter a war – is scarcely mentioned. The Korean People's Army's focus on air defense, underground fortifications, and more recently retaliatory strike capabilities, appear to be heavily shaped by the experiences of the Korean War and a strong desire to prevent its reoccurrence – namely the vast destruction wrought by the Western Bloc's bombing campaign, the vulnerability of population centers to air attack, and the threats to use nuclear force which the country was unable to retaliate against or deter even at the most basic level without Soviet support.

Shortly after the war's end Pyongyang became the only city in the world other than Moscow to receive the protection of the Soviet S-25 (NATO Reporting SA-1) long range surface to air missile network, a heavy platform with multichannel guidance capabilities unique for its time which was relied on heavily to defend the Soviet capital until the early 1980s. The DPRK's air defense network today remains among the densest and most heavily fortified in the world[165] – deploying sophisticated indigenous[166,167] and Russian made systems.[168] North Korea is also the most tunneled country in the world, with the dual purpose of allowing the military to shield its assets from air attack while protecting the population from suffering the same fate they did during the American firebombing campaign of the 1950s. Pyongyang's metro is a prime example, and was designed to double as a shelter against strikes from the hundreds of nuclear warheads the U.S. had deployed just across the 38th Parallel – which necessitated making it the very deepest in the world.

The Korean War is referred to in the West as a limited war, in that the Western Bloc did not use all means in their disposal against their enemies, nor did they fully expand the war to China. While it is true that there were limitations, these came not voluntarily but rather largely due to the fear of Soviet intervention which served as a potent deterrent against expansion of the campaign. The United States did not use nuclear weapons in Korea, and refrained from attacking civilian population centers near the Soviet border to avoid provoking the superpower into taking a more direct role in the conflict. The presence of the Soviet air force over China, and particularly of substantial numbers of Soviet bombers in China's Northeast near the Korean border and in range of American bases in Japan, deterred the United States from expanding the conflict too far beyond Korea.[169,170] These factors limited the means of the Western powers – not because they wanted to limit the scale of the campaign for humanitarian reasons, but rather because they feared the consequences of open war with the USSR. As chairman of the Joint Chiefs of Staff General Omar Bradley and Defence Secretary James Marshal themselves admitted, they would have been in favour of bombing China had they been sure the Soviets would not intervene.[171] In the eyes of the West the Russians were not 'little yellow men' and their military potential, so recently demonstrated in the Second World War against a broad coalition of European powers led by Germany, was feared and respected.

The U.S. and its partners, while refraining from launching nuclear strikes, employed other weapons of mass destruction better suited to the battlefield situation in Korea. These included incendiary bombs and biological warfare against Chinese and Korean civilians, the deployment of chemical weapons as well as the targeting of dams, burning of fields and destroying of food in an attempt to starve the population. This showed all the markings of an absolute war, one in which the entire population was a target and any means to defeat the enemy were considered acceptable. The Korean War was therefore a near absolute war against the independent North Korean state and its people, from children gunned down in fields by low flying aircraft to the cities and villages and infrastructure destroyed by incendiary bombings. While the actions of the US-led coalition in Korea are not internationally recognized as genocide, historians and investigators from across the world including several from the West and from South Korea have concluded that the crimes committed primarily by the United States constitute genocide against the North Korean people (as explored further in the following chapter).[172,173,174]

The DPRK would continue to be targeted for Western regime change and face decades of severe economic sanctions and continuous military threats aimed at bringing the 'defiant,' as it is so often called, Asian power to its knees and extending Western influence north of the 38th Parallel. Indeed, the stances of the United States towards the small Asian country in the twenty-first century closely mirrors that of the Korean War, with the U.S. military leadership as recently as November 2017 strongly advocating an approach to 'close that country down economically, starve them, cut their fuel, drive them into the ground, those are the kind of steps that need to be taken.'[175] These were the exact measures taken during the Korean War, short of the deployment of biological weapons, with measures such as starving the population and driving them into the ground resonating particularly strongly with North Korea's wartime experience. The United States' shipping of live anthrax samples to U.S. military facilities in South Korea for testing, which North Korea claimed was aimed and developing biological warfare agents, hardly helped the situation in this regard.[176] North Korea today is shaped by the war and the imminent threat of its recurrence, and with the Korean Peninsula remaining under armistice the war has never officially ended.

Notes

1 Fifield, Anna, 'Why does North Korea hate the United States? Let's go back to the Korean War,' *Washington Post*, May 17, 2017.
2 Connelly, Matthew, 'Notes on Cabinet Meeting,' 12 September 1952, Connelly Papers, HSTL.
3 Lockwood, Jeffrey A., *Six-Legged Soldiers: Using Insects as Weapons of War*, Oxford, Oxford University Press, 2009 (p. 189).
4 *We Accuse*, Report of the Committee of the Women's International Democratic Federation in Korea, May 16–27, 1951 (p. 4–5).
5 Chomsky, Noam, *Who Rules the World?*, London, Hamish Hamilton, 2017 (p. 215).
6 Hanley, Charles J. and Choe, Sang Hun and Mendoza, Martha, *The Bridge at No Gun Ri: A Hidden Nightmare from the Korean War*, New York, Henry Holt and Company, 2001 (p. 163).
7 Stone, I. F., *Hidden History of the Korean War*, Amazon Media, 2014 (p. 256).
8 *We Accuse*, Report of the Committee of the Women's International Democratic Federation in Korea, May 16–27, 1951 (p. 5–6).
9 Hanley, Charles J. and Choe, Sang Hun and Mendoza, Martha, *The Bridge at No Gun Ri: A Hidden Nightmare from the Korean War*, New York, Henry Holt and Company, 2001 (p. 121).
10 Deane, Hugh, *The Korean War, 1945–1953*, San Francisco, CA, China Books and Periodicals, 1999 (p. 143).
11 Hanley, Charles J. and Choe, Sang Hun and Mendoza, Martha, *The Bridge at No Gun Ri: A Hidden Nightmare from the Korean War*, New York, Henry Holt and Company, 2001 (p. 175, 234).
12 Ibid. (p. 177).
13 LeMay, Kurtis and Kantor, MacKinlay, *Mission with LeMay: My Story*, New York, Doubleday, 1965 (p. 382).
14 Neer, Robert M., *Napalm: An American Biography*, Cambridge, MA, Belknap Press, 2013 (p. 100).

15 *We Accuse*, Report of the Committee of the Women's International Democratic Federation in Korea, May 16–27, 1951 (p. 6).
16 Ibid. (p. 5–6).
17 Deane, Hugh, *The Korean War, 1945–1953*, San Francisco, CA, China Books and Periodicals, 1999 (p. 143).
18 Hanley, Charles J. and Choe, Sang Hun and Mendoza, Martha, *The Bridge at No Gun Ri: A Hidden Nightmare from the Korean War* (pp. 195–196).
19 Jackson, Robert, *Air War Over Korea*, London, Ian Allen, 1973 (p. 61).
20 Stone, I. F., *Hidden History of the Korean War*, Amazon Media, 2014, (Chapter 34, 'Lost and Found').
21 Ibid. (Chapter 43, 'Talks on Whether to Talk).
22 Ibid. (Chapter 34, 'Lost and Found').
23 Grosscup, Beau, *Strategic Terror: The Politics and Ethics of Aerial Bombardment*, London, Zed Books, 2003 (Chapter 5, Cold War Strategic Bombing: From Korea to Vietnam, Part 4, The Bombing of Korea).
24 Futrell, Robert F., *United States Air Force Operations in the Korean Conflict*, 1 July 1952–27 July 1953, USAF Historical Study no. 127, Maxwell Air Force Base, Ala, USAF Historical Division, Research Studies Institute, Air University, 1956 (p. 183–207).
25 Deane, Hugh, *The Korean War, 1945–1953*, San Francisco, CA, China Books and Periodicals, 1999 (p. 145).
26 Moon, Katherine H. S., *Sex Among Allies*, New York, Colombia University Press, 1997 (p. 51).
27 Hohn, Maria, and Moon, Seungsook, eds., *Over There: Living with the U.S. Military Empire from World War Two to the Present*, Chapel Hill, NC, Duke University Press 2010 (p. 51).
28 Choe, Sang-Hun, 'After Korean War, brothels and an alliance,' *New York Times*, January 8, 2009.
29 Deane, Hugh, *The Korean War, 1945–1953*, San Francisco, CA, China Books and Periodicals, 1999 (p. 191).
30 Chossudovsky, Michel, 'KNOW THE FACTS: North Korea Lost Close to 30% of its Population as a result of the U.S. Bombings in the 1950s,' *Centre for Research on Globalization*, November 27, 2010.
31 Lindqvist, Sven, *A History of Bombing*, New York, The New Press, 2001 (p. 131).
32 Harden, Blaine, 'The U.S. war crime North Korea won't forget,' *Washington Post*, March 24, 2015.
33 Cumings, Bruce, 'Nuclear Threats Against North Korea: Consequences of the "forgotten" war,' *The Asia-Pacific Journal*, Japan Focus, Volume 3, Issue 1, Number 0, January 13, 2005 (p. 2).
34 Harden, Blaine, 'The U.S. war crime North Korea won't forget,' *Washington Post*, March 24, 2015.
35 Garner, Dwight, 'Carpet-Bombing Falsehoods About a War That's Little Understood,' *New York Times*, July 21, 2010.

36 Young, Marilyn, 'Bombing Civilians from the Twentieth to the Twenty-First Centuries,' in 'Bombing Civilians: A Twentieth Century History, ed. Tanaka, Yuki and Young, Marilyn, New York, New Press, 2009, (p. 157).

37 Cumings, Bruce, *The Korean War: A History*, New York, Modern Library, 2010 (p. 152).

38 Kohn, Richard H., and Harahan, Joseph P., *Strategic air warfare: an interview with generals Curtis E. LeMay, Leon W. Johnson, David A. Burchinal, and Jack J. Catton*, Washington, DC, Office of Air Force History, 1988 (p. 88).

39 Williams, Christopher, *Leadership Accountability in a Globalizing World*, London, Palgrave Macmillan, 2006 (p. 185).

40 Townsend, J., 'They Don't Like Hell Bombs,' *Armed Forces Chemical Journal*, January 1951.

41 'Napalm Jelly Bombs Prove a Blazing Success in Korea,' *All Hands*, April 1951.

42 Bullene, E. F., 'Wonder Weapon: Napalm,' *Army Combat Forces Journal*, November 1952.

43 Cumings, Bruce, *The Korean War: A History*, New York, Modern Library, 2010 (p. 146).

44 Williams, Christopher, *Leadership Accountability in a Globalizing World*, London, Palgrave Macmillan, 2006 (p. 185).

45 Perry, Richard E., and Levin, Rebert J., 'Where the Innocent Die,' *Redbook*, January 1967 (p. 103).

46 Neer, Robert M., *Napalm: An American Biography*, Cambridge, MA, Belknap Press, 2013 (p. 129).

47 Milton, Giles, 'Winston Churchill's shocking use of chemical weapons,' *The Guardian*, September 1, 2013.

48 Lewis, Julian, *Changing Direction: British Military Planning for Post-war Strategic Defence, 1942–1947*, Abingdon, Routledge, 2008 (Appendix 8).

49 Deane, Hugh, *The Korean War, 1945–1953*, San Francisco, CA, China Books and Periodicals, 1999 (p. 144).

50 MacDonald, Callum A, 'Korea: The War Before Vietnam,' London, Macmillan, 1986, (p. 234–235).

51 McCormack, Gavan, 'Cold War Hot War: An Australian Perspective on the Korean War,' Sydney, Hale and Iremonger, 1983, (p. 132).

52 Omara-Otunnu, Elizabeth, 'Napalm Survivor Tells of Healing After Vietnam War,' *University of Connecticut Advance*, November 8, 2004.

53 Fifield, Anna, 'Why does North Korea hate the United States? Let's go back to the Korean War,' *Washington Post*, May 17, 2017.

54 *Report on U.S. Crimes in Korea*, Commission of International Association of Democratic Lawyers, March 31, 1952 (p. 12).

55 Russell, Edmund, *War and Nature: Fighting Humans and Insects with Chemicals from World War I to Silent Spring*, Cambridge, Cambridge University Press, 2001 (pp. 187–188).

56 'New war, old warlord,' *Time*, December 11, 1950.
57 Russell, Edmund, *War and Nature: Fighting Humans and Insects with Chemicals from World War I to Silent Spring*, Cambridge, Cambridge University Press, 2001 (pp. 187–188).
58 Ibid. (pp. 188–189).
59 *New York Times*, August 9, 1970, IV (p. 3).
60 Thames Television, transcript for the fifth seminar for *Korea: The Unknown War*, November 1986.
61 Dean, William F., *General Dean's Story, as told to William L. Worden*, New York, The Viking Press, 1954 (p. 274).
62 Hynes, Patricia, 'The Korean War: Forgotten, Unknown and Unfinished,' *Truthout*, July 12, 2013.
63 'The Three Year Plan,' *Kyŏngje kŏnsŏl* [Economic Construction], September 1956 (p. 5–6).
64 Kim, Monica, *The Interrogation Rooms of the Korean War: The Untold History*, Princeton, NJ, Princeton University Press, 2019 (p. 320).
65 Boggs, Carl, *Masters of War: Militarism and Blowback in the Era of American Empire*, Abingdon, Routledge, 2003 (p. 205).
66 Gwertzman, Bernard, 'U.S. Papers Tell of '53 Policy to Use A-Bomb in Korea,' *New York Times*, June 8, 1984.
67 Winnington, Alan, and Burchett, Wilfred, *Plain Perfidy, The Plot to Wreck the Korea Peace*, Britain-China Friendship Association, 1954 (p. 12).
68 Callum MacDonald, *Korea: The War Before Vietnam*, London, Macmillan, 1986 (p. 241–242).
69 Armstrong, Charles K., 'The Destruction and Reconstruction of North Korea, 1950–1960,' *The Asia-Pacific Journal*, Volume 7, Issue 0, March 16, 2009.
70 Balázs Szalontai, 'The Four Horsemen of the Apocalypse in North Korea: The Forgotten Side of a Not-So-Forgotten War' in Springer, Chris, and Szalontai, Balázs, *North Korea Caught in Time: Images of War and Reconstruction*, Reading, Garnet Publishing, 2010 (p.xiv-xv).
71 SSSR i Korea, Moscow: USSR Academy of Sciences, 1988 (p. 256).
72 Williams, Christopher, *Leadership Accountability in a Globalizing World*, London, Palgrave Macmillan, 2006 (p. 185).
73 Cumings, Bruce, *The Korean War: A History*, Modern Library Edition, 2010 (p. 147).
74 Kolko, Gabriel, 'Report on the Destruction of Dikes: Holland, 1944–1945 and Korea, 1953' in Duffett, John, *Against the Crimes of Silence: Proceedings of the Russell International War Crimes Tribunal, Stockholm and Copenhagen*, New York, O'Hare Books, 1968 (pp. 224–226).
75 Chomsky, Noam, *Who Rules the World?*, London, Hamish Hamilton, 2016 (pp. 132–133).

76 Williams, Christopher, *Leadership Accountability in a Globalizing World*, London, Palgrave Macmillan, 2006.

77 Armstrong, Charles K., 'The Destruction and Reconstruction of North Korea, 1950–1960,' *The Asia-Pacific Journal*, Volume 7, Issue 0, March 16, 2009.

78 McCurry, Justin, 'Unit 731: Japan discloses details of notorious chemical warfare division,' *The Guardian*, April 17, 2018.

79 Nie, Jing Bao, 'The West's Dismissal of the Khabarovsk trial as "Communist Propaganda": Ideology, evidence and international bioethics,' *Journal of Bioethical Inquiry*, Volume 1, Issue 1, April 2004 (pp. 32–42).

80 Taylor, Jeremy, 'Biology at War: A Plague in the Wind,' *BBC Horizon*, October 29, 1984.

81 Blum, William, *Killing Hope: U.S. Military and C.I.A. Interventions Since World War II*, London, Zed Books, 2003 (p. 26).

82 Chaddock, Dave, *This Must Be the Place: How the U.S. Waged Germ Warfare in the Korean War and Denied It Ever Since*, Seattle, Bennett & Hastings, 2013.

83 Marks, John, *The Search for the Manchurian Candidate: The CIA and Mind Control*, New York, Times Books, 1979, (p. 8). In September 1950, the *Miami News* published an article by Edward Hunter titled *'Brain-Washing' Tactics Force Chinese into Ranks of Communist Party*. It was the first ever printed use in any language of the term 'brainwashing.' Hunter, a CIA propaganda operative who worked undercover as a journalist, turned out a steady stream of books and articles on the subject for the purpose of delegitimising the claims of returned American veterans.

84 McCormack, Gavan, 'Korea: Wilfred Burchett's Thirty Year's War,' in Ben Kiernan (ed.), *Burchett: Reporting the Other Side of the World, 1939–1983*, Quartet Books, London, 1986 (p. 204).

85 Blum, William, *Killing Hope: U.S. Military and C.I.A. Interventions Since World War II*, London, Zed Books, 2003 (p. 26).

86 Hearings, United States Congress House Committee on Un-American Activities (p. 1652).

87 Knightley, Philipp, *The First Casualty: The War Correspondent as Hero and Myth-Maker from the Crimea to Kosovo* (revised edition), London, Prion, 2000 (p. 388).

88 Williams, Peter, and Wallace, David, *Unit 731; Japan's Secret Biological Warfare in World War II*, The Free Press (British edn.), 1989 (Chapter 17: 'Korean War').

89 Caute, David, *The Great Fear: The Anti-Communist Purge Under Truman and Eisenhower*, New York, Touchstone, 1979 (p. 415).

90 Deane, Hugh, *The Korean War, 1945–1953*, San Francisco, CA, China Books and Periodicals, 1999 (p. 155).

91 Cornwell, John, *Hitler's Pope: The Secret History of Pius XII*, New York, Viking, 1999 (p. 260).

92 Carroll, Rory, 'Church helped Nazis in Italy,' *The Guardian*, July 3, 2000.

93 Catechism, Paragraph 2425.

94 Giangreco, D. M., and Moore, Kathryn, *Dear Harry: Truman's Mailroom, 1945–1953*, Mechanicsburg, Stackpole Books, 1999 (p. 320).

95 Blum, William, *Killing Hope: U.S. Military and C.I.A. Interventions Since World War II*, London, Zed Books, 2003 (Chapter 30: 'Cuba 1959 to 1980s: The Unforgivable Revolution').
96 Hornberger, Jacob C., *'The Pentagon's B-52 Message to North Koreans,' Future of Freedom Foundation*, January 15, 2016,
97 Deane, Hugh, *The Korean War, 1945–1953*, San Francisco, CA, China Books and Periodicals, 1999 (p. 155).
98 Ibid. (p. 156).
99 *Report on U.S. Crimes in Korea*, Commission of International Association of Democratic Lawyers, March 31, 1952 (p. 7–8).
100 Harris, Sheldon H., *Factories of Death: Japanese Biological Warfare, 1932–1945, and the American Cover-up*, Abingdon, Taylor & Francis, 2002 (p. 220).
101 Zhang, Shu Guang, *Mao's Military Romanticism: China and the Korean War, 1950–1953*, Lawrence, University Press of Kansas, 1995 (p. 185).
102 Méray, Tibor, *On Burchett*, Kallista, Victoria, Australia, Callistemon Publications, 2008 (pp. 261–262).
103 Deane, Hugh, *The Korean War, 1945–1953*, San Francisco, CA, China Books and Periodicals, 1999 (p. 158).
104 Zhang, Shu Guang, *Mao's Military Romanticism: China and the Korean War, 1950–1953*, Lawrence, University Press of Kansas, 1995 (p. 185).
105 Wise, David, and Ross, Thomas, *The Invisible Government*, New York, Random House, 1965 (p. 114).
106 'The People of the CIA ... John Downey & Richard Fecteau,' Website of the Central Intelligence Agency, News & Information, November 14, 2007.
107 Lockwood, Jeffrey A., *Six-Legged Soldiers: Using Insects as Weapons of War*, Oxford, Oxford University Press, 2010 (p. 189).
108 Giangreco, D. M., and Moore, Kathryn, *Dear Harry: Truman's Mailroom, 1945–1953*, Mechanicsburg, PA, Stackpole Books, 1999 (p. 320).
109 Ham, Paul, *Hiroshima Nagasaki: The Real Story of the Atomic Bombings and their Aftermath*, New York, Doubleday, 2012 (p. 503).
110 Magdaleno, Johnny, 'Algerians suffering from French atomic legacy, 55 years after nuke tests,' *Aljazeera*, March 1, 2015.
111 'The Gallup Brain: Americans and the Korean War,' Gallup, <http://www.gallup.com/poll/7741/Gallup-Brain-Americans-Korean-War.aspx>.
112 Haynes, Richard F., *The Awesome Power: Harry S. Truman as Commander-in-Chief*, Baton Rouge, Louisiana State University Press, 1999 (p. 95).
113 'Majority Supports Use of Atomic Bomb on Japan in WWII,' Gallup, <http://www.gallup.com/poll/17677/Majority-Supports-Use-Atomic-Bomb-Japan-WWII.aspx>.
114 Tannenwald, Nina, *Nuclear Taboo: The United States and the Non-Use of Nuclear Weapons Since 1945*, Cambridge, Cambridge Studies in International Relations, 2008 (pp. 129–130).

115 Deane, Hugh, *The Korean War, 1945–1953*, San Francisco, CA, China Books and Periodicals, 1999 (p. 145).
116 U.S. National Archive, FR7: 1326.
117 Hastings, Max, *Korean War*, London, Michael Joseph, 1988 (p. 192).
118 'Thaw in the Koreas?,' *Bulletin of Atomic Scientists*, Vol. 48, No. 3, April 1992 (pp.18–19).
119 Cumings, Bruce, *Korea's Place in the Sun: A Modern History*, New York, W. W. Norton & Company, 1997 (p. 149).
120 Gwertzman, Bernard, 'U.S. Papers Tell of '53 Policy to Use A-Bomb in Korea,' *New York Times*, June 8, 1984.
121 J. Whitfield, Stephen, *The Culture of the Cold War*, Baltimore, MD, Johns Hopkins University Press (p. 6–7).
122 Winnington, Alan, and Burchett, Wilfred, *Plain Perfidy, The Plot to Wreck the Korea Peace*, Britain-China Friendship Association, 1954 (p. 12).
123 Gwertzman, Bernard, 'U.S. Papers Tell of '53 Policy to Use A-Bomb in Korea,' *New York Times*, June 8, 1984.
124 Elliot, David C., 'Project Vista and Nuclear Weapons in Europe,' International Security 2:1, Summer 1986, (p. 163–183).)
125 Cumings, Bruce, *Origins of the Korean War: The Roaring of the Cataract, 1947–1950*, Volume 2, Princeton, NJ, Princeton University Press, 2004 (p. 752).
126 Gwertzman, Bernard, 'U.S. Papers Tell of '53 Policy to Use A-Bomb in Korea,' *New York Times*, June 8, 1984.
127 Bennett, Bruce W., 'A surgical strike against North Korea? Not a viable option,' *Fox News*, July 14, 2017.
128 Cumings, Bruce, *Korea's Place in the Sun: A Modern History*, New York, W. W. Norton & Company, 1997 (p. 150).
129 Mizokami, Kyle, 'Everything You Need to Know: The History of U.S. Nuclear Weapons in South Korea,' *The National Interest*, September 10, 2017.
130 Kristensen, Hans M., *A History of U.S. Nuclear Weapons in South Korea*, September 28, 2005, Federation of American Scientists.
131 McGreal, Chris, 'Papers reveal Nixon plan for North Korea nuclear strike,' *The Guardian*, July 7, 2010.
132 Foster, Peter, 'Richard Nixon planned nuclear strike on North Korea,' *Telegraph*, July 8, 2010.
133 Krylov, Leonid, and Tepsurkaev, Yuriy, *Soviet MiG-15 Aces of the Korean War*, Oxford, Osprey, 2008 (Chapter 1: 'Korean War Resources').
134 Joiner, Stephen, 'The Jet that Shocked the West, How the MiG-15 grounded the U.S. bomber fleet in Korea,' *Air & Space Magazine*, December 2013.
135 Aldrich, Richard J., 'British Intelligence and the Anglo-American "Special Relationship" during the Cold War,' *Review of International Studies*, Vol. 24, No. 3, July 1998 (p. 331–351).
136 Stone, I. F., *Hidden History of the Korean War*, Amazon Media, 2014, (Chapter 47, 'Six Months of Futile Slaughter').

137 Ibid.
138 Joiner, Stephen, 'The Jet that Shocked the West, How the MiG-15 grounded the U.S. bomber fleet in Korea,' *Air & Space Magazine*, December 2013.
139 McGill, Earl, *Black Tuesday Over Namsi: B-29s vs MiGs – The Forgotten Air Battle of the Korean War, 23 October 1951*, Warwick, Helion & Company, 2013.
140 Stone, I. F., *Hidden History of the Korean War*, Amazon Media, 2014 (Chapter 47: 'Six Months of Futile Slaughter').
141 Ibid.
142 Cited in: Nash, Chris, *What is Journalism? The Art and Politics of a Rupture*, London, Palgrave Macmillan, 2016 (p. 91).
143 Stone, I. F., *Hidden History of the Korean War*, Amazon Media, 2014 (Chapter 47: 'Six Months of Futile Slaughter').
144 Ibid.
145 Chossudovsky, Michel, 'KNOW THE FACTS: North Korea Lost Close to 30% of its Population as a result of the U.S. Bombings in the 1950s,' *Centre for Research on Globalization*, November 27, 2010.
146 Lindqvist, Sven, *A History of Bombing*, New York, The New Press, 2001 (p. 131).
147 U.S. National Archive, Ridgway to JCS, June 21, 1951.
148 'Bush's Final Approval Rating: 22 Percent,' CBS News, January 16, 2009.
149 Cumings, Bruce, *Origins of the Korean War: The Roaring of the Cataract, 1947–1950*, Volume 2, Princeton, NJ, Princeton University Press, 2004 (p. 693).
150 Schnabel, James F., and Watson, Robert J., *The Korean War*, part I, History of the Joint Chiefs of Staff, (p. 178–181).
151 Stone, I. F., *Hidden History of the Korean War*, Amazon Media, 2014, (Chapter 47, 'Six Months of Futile Slaughter').
152 Grunfeld, A. Tom, *The Making of Modern Tibet*, Abingdon, Routledge, 1996 (p. 100).
153 Ibid. (pp. 99–100).
154 Deane, Hugh, *Good Deeds & Gunboats*, San Francisco, CA, China Books & Periodicals, 1990 (p. 184).
155 Neer, Robert M., *Napalm: An American Biography*, Cambridge, MA, Harvard University Press, 2013 (p. 100).
156 Lindqvist, Sven, *A History of Bombing*, New York, The New Press, 2001 (p. 131).
157 Grosscup, Beau, Strategic Terror: The Politics and Ethics of Aerial Bombardment, London, Zed Books, 2003 (Chapter 5, Cold War Strategic Bombing: From Korea to Vietnam, Part 4, The Bombing of Korea).
158 Deane, Hugh, *The Korean War, 1945–1953*, San Francisco, CA, China Books and Periodicals, 1999 (p. 191).
159 Ibid.
160 Ibid. (p. 192).
161 Moon, Katherine H. S., *Sex Among Allies*, New York, Colombia University Press, 1997 (p. 44).

162 Park, Seong Won, *The Present and Future of Americanization in South Korea*, Journal of Futures Studies, August 2009, 14(1), The Hawaii Research Center (p. 51–66).
163 Talmadge, Eric, '64 years after Korean War, North Korea still digging up bombs,' *Yahoo News*, July 24, 2017.
164 Kim, Jong Un, *War Veterans Are Our Precious Revolutionary Forerunners Who Created the Indomitable Spirit of Defending the Country*, Congratulatory Speech Delivered at the Fourth National Conference of War Veterans, July 25, 2015.
165 Kopp, Carlo, *Operation Odyssey Dawn – the collapse of Libya's relic air defense system*, in Defence Today, vol. 9, no. 1, 2011, Strike Publications (p. 14).
166 'KN-06 Surface to Air Missile System Enters Mass Production; The Importance of Air Defence Development for North Korean Security,' *Military Watch Magazine*, June 7, 2017.
167 Panda, Ankit, 'North Korea Declares KN-06 Surface-to-Air Missile System Operational After Successful Test,' *The Diplomat*, May 29, 2017.
168 'NATO Will "Drag Serbia Into Major Fight" Over Possible S-300 Deliveries,' *Sputnik*, August 26, 2017 (Russian State Media Confirms Presence of S-300 Missile Batteries in North Korea).
169 Wilson Lewis, John, and Goranchov, Sergei and Litai, Xue, *Uncertain Partners: Stalin, Mao and the Korean War*, Stanford, CA, Stanford University Press, 1993 (p. 200).
170 Hastings, Max, *Korean War*, London, Michael Joseph, 1988 (p. 177).
171 Levine, Alan J., *Stalin's Last War; Korea and the Approach to World War III*, Jefferson, McFarland & Company, 2005, (p. 207)
172 *Report on U.S. Crimes in Korea*, Commission of International Association of Democratic Lawyers, March 31, 1952 (p. 7–8).
173 Kim, Dong-Choon, 'Forgotten war, forgotten massacres – the Korean War (1950–1953) as licensed mass killings,' *Journal of Genocide Research*, vol. 6, issue 4, December 2004 (p. 523–544).
174 Cumings, Bruce, *The Korean War: A History*, New York, Modern Library, 2010 (p. 154).
175 'US, China can financially drive North Korea into the ground: Tom McInerney,' *Fox Business*, November 28, 2017.
(Lt. Gen. Thomas McInerney on North Korea: 'We can close that country down economically. We can starve them. We can cut their fuel. We can drive them into the ground. And I think those are the kind of steps that need to be taken.')
176 'U.S. military carried out anthrax & bubonic plague tests in S. Korea – probe,' *RT*, December 18, 2015.

CHAPTER 10

The Korean War: Conduct of Western Militaries on the Ground

> Sexual violence by invading forces against the local population is a means of articulating and demonstrating power over the victim, emphasizing their helplessness.[1]
>
> — SARA MERGER

> The fact that many Korean women in the villages were often raped in front of their husbands and parents has not been a secret among those who experienced the Korean War. It was known that several women were raped before being shot at No Gun Ri. Some eyewitnesses say that U.S. soldiers played with their lives like boys sadistically playing with flies.[2]
>
> — 1993 Report in the *Journal of Genocide Research* by Professor Kim Dong Choon of South Korea's Truth and Reconciliation Committee on the conduct of the U.S. military

American Massacres: Cover-ups and South Korean Complicity

The conduct of Western militaries during the Korean War, not only through their firebombing campaigns and employment of weapons of mass destruction against civilian targets, but also through their conduct towards Korean civilians on the ground, provides essential context to both the background of Korean relations with the West today as well as the nature of the Western Bloc's intentions towards the peoples of Korea and East Asia. As the only major conventional land war fought by the Western Bloc in Asia in the modern era, the Korean War provides valuable insight into the nature of Western forces and the potential consequences for Asian populations

– both Western aligned and otherwise – of their military involvement in the region in potential future conflicts.

During the Korean War an estimated 1 million South Korean and 4 million North Korean civilians lost their lives. As with many aspects of the war it remains widely unknown that up to 200,000 South Korean civilians, many of them refugees, were killed by U.S. forces and their allies – forces which were deployed to the country under the pretext of protecting the Korean people.[3] While many of these killings occurred at the hands of U.S. and allied air and naval assets, with population centers south of the 38th Parallel bombarded as thoroughly as those to the north when briefly under the control of North Korean forces, U.S. military personnel on the ground also received direct and specific orders to target fleeing civilians leading to a number of massacres. Due to the nature of South Korea's Syngman Rhee government, an American dependency and client state, no official investigation into these incidents was made for several decades. The only sources available are reports from the U.S. military itself and interviews with U.S. servicemen and South Korean survivors, which reveal the nature of the massacres that took place. Several Korean survivors and American soldiers have been interviewed and recalled the incidents when U.S. forces intentionally targeted South Korean civilians. These sources not only give a good account of the events that took place, they also show the human tragedy that many suffered as only firsthand sources can – with the lives of both the survivors and perpetrators having been irrevocably changed by the massacres. The targeting of Korean civilians on both sides of the 38th Parallel strongly supports the case that the Western Bloc's intervention from the outset targeted not only the government in Pyongyang, but the Korean people as a whole.

During the war, as a result of the scorched earth policies employed by retreating ROK and U.S. forces, South Korean civilians were displaced from their homes in their millions. These civilians were deliberately targeted by the U.S. Army, Air Force and Navy. There was a prevailing attitude among the U.S. military that Koreans as a people could not be trusted – in part due to the large numbers of South Korean soldiers who had either abandoned their positions or defected to join northern forces in the early stages of the war.[4,5] Military records further shed light on the orders given to target Korean civilians. On July 25, 1950, the U.S. 5th Air Force Advanced Headquarters reported: 'The army has requested that we strafe all civilian parties that are approaching our positions. To date we have complied with the army request.' The following day the 25th Infantry Division reported: 'General Keene directed that all civilians moving around in the combat zone will be considered as unfriendly and shot.' It later became increasingly clear that what was considered the combat zone was far from limited to the frontlines of conflict.[6]

British author Elizabeth Comber accompanied American forces in the early stages of the war and observed much of their conduct towards and massacres against the South Korean population. She wrote in her diary on July 14, 1950, regarding U.S. forces in Korea: 'they think every Korean is an enemy, firing at, and sometimes killing refugees.' Two weeks later she described a more serious situation, writing of the U.S. military: 'Day after day with their aircraft the Americans are laying waste towns and cities, killing fifty civilians for every one soldier.'[7]

One of the most notorious massacres of South Korean civilians was that at the village of No Gun Ri. Survivor, Suh Jong Gap, recalled in an interview: 'The Americans forced us out of our village. We didn't know anything, so we just followed them because they said they would take us to safety.' The civilians were forced onto a railway line overlooked by the 7th Cavalry's main positions. Suh Jong Gap recalled: 'I was at the head of a long line of people. I could see the American soldiers standing with rifles, trying to keep us on the tracks. They seemed to make sure that we couldn't move at all.' Troops then withdrew and left the refugees on the railway line. 'Just after 1 o'clock I could see a reconnaissance plane circling above us. Then the Americans seemed to talk to each other on the radio.' Planes from the U.S. Air Force appeared overhead, 'and then they dropped bombs on the contained group of people.' Survivor Cho Soo Jaoc recalled of the same event: 'I crawled out from under my mother and climbed on top of her. I shouted "mum, mum" but she was dead. When I stroked her head with my hand, I found my hand sliding inside. I didn't know what hit my mother, but the back of her head was blown off.'[8]

One South Korean survivor, Yang Hae Chan, recalled when interviewed: 'American soldiers broke into our house with rifles and bayonets.

They didn't even take off their boots. They searched inside the house with a torch, found us and ordered us out. I was young and scared. I hid behind my mother and father clinging to them. My father said the Americans had come to evacuate us, and we should pack up and leave our home.' He and his family too, along with those of Suh and Cho, were intentionally targeted by U.S. personnel and aircraft. Chan then recalled: 'After the strafing and bombing everything went quiet. Then I saw the American soldiers reappear. They started checking through the dead and the living, poking the bodies lying on the railway line with their bayonets. Those who were still alive were forced to get up at gunpoint. The Americans herded us further down the railroad tracks, so those of us who survived the bombing were made to move on again.' Many of the survivors of the bombing were badly wounded, but they were all herded on towards the village of No Gun Ri, directly beneath the guns of the 2nd Battalion of the 7th Cavalry. They were then exterminated by small arms fire from U.S. forces.[9]

Joe Jackman from the U.S. Army's 7th Cavalry 2nd Battalion recalled of the targeting of civilians near No Gun Ri that his unit were ordered in regards to the Korean civilians to: '"kill them all." Then of course there was a lieutenant who was screaming like a mad man "fire on everything, kill them all" [...] There was a hell of a lot of fire going. Hell of a lot of shooting. A *hell* of a lot of shooting. Because I know the infantrymen, the infantrymen, we used to carry 10–15 bandoliers of ammunition, and even help machine gunners carrying ammunition. There was a hell of a lot of expenditure of ammunition.' Regarding the nature of the targets he recalled: 'Kids, there was kids out there. It didn't matter what it was. 8 to 80, blind, crippled or crazy they [U.S. personnel] shot them. It just seemed like all Koreans were the enemy.'[10]

George Early of the 7th Cavalry's heavy mortar company recalled being given the order to massacre Korean refugees: 'A lot of refugees came down the road in a group. It was 50–60–70 people. So I ran up the road there by the railroad tracks to Captain Johnson and told him. He said go down, take the machine gun, shoot those people and we'll pull out. I said we can't kill all these people, and he pulled out his handgun, a 45, and pointed it at my head and he said, he said I said kill them, said you're disobeying a direct order in combat. He says I will kill you myself. He said go back there and kill those people. I said "yes sir."'[11]

Hundreds of survivors at No Gun Ri ran into railway tunnels seeking shelter. They remained there under fire for the next three days. Survivor Yang Hae Chan recalled: 'The floor inside the tunnel was a mix of gravel of sand. People clawed with their bare hands to make holes to hide in. Other people piled up the dead like a barricade, and hid behind the bodies as a shield against the bullets.' George Early of the 7th Cavalry's heavy mortar company recalled the situation as follows: 'Everybody just ceased moving. No one was moving over there. They either were dead, or so seriously wounded they couldn't move, or if there were alive they weren't moving. Because if they move they know they're gonna be fired at some more.'[12] Early later recalled: 'I remember seeing this woman on her hands and knees. She was crawling. You could just see the bullets bouncing… bouncing around her. She kept crawling, crawling. And finally I guess she was just hit. And that was it. And she just stopped, just, just like that. Just like she was hanging on the side of this hill with her fingers.' Buddy Wenzel, another serviceman from the 7th Cavalry, also testified to his role in the No Gun Ri massacre. Wenzel, recalling the orders he received, stated: 'Word came through the line, open fire on them. They were running toward us and we opened fire. … We understood that we were fighting for these people, but we had orders to fire on them and we did.'[13]

A Korean survivor at No Gun Ri recalled the desperation of the victims: 'A baby boy's mother was killed during the strafing on the rail track. The father managed to get the baby to the tunnels, but the boy was hungry and frightened. He cried and cried. And the American troops fired their guns into the tunnels whenever the boy cried. The bullets fired in the direction of the crying. People screamed that more would be shot if the baby kept crying. The father didn't know what to do. He might have thought the baby would die anyway, but he decided to silence it in order to save the others. He took to boy to the back of the tunnel and pushed him face down into a pool of water. I watched him doing that and thought, *what could be more tragic than this.*' Yang Hae Chan recalled the incident: 'I clung to my mother and, despite her pain and injuries, she hugged me tightly. I cried like mad. I was so scared of the dead bodies piled up inside the tunnels. I still have vivid memories of people crying and moaning because of the shooting. There were so many cries in the tunnel. I can still see bodies writhing in agony.'[14] Koreans who strayed outside the tunnel to collect food or drink stream water were shot. One survivor, Koo Hun, recalled: 'It looked like the Americans were shooting us out of boredom.'[15]

Many of the Korean survivors have presented their cases against the United States military. The Pentagon dismissed all such allegations as impossible, claiming the U.S. Army 7th Cavalry was not in the area where the massacre took place. It was only after a private investigation was launched into the allegations of the survivors that the claims which had been so flatly denied could be proven. The investigators mapped the movements of U.S. forces on combat maps based on evidence from the time, as well as analyzing documents from high ranking officers which attested to treating Korean refugees as hostile targets. The final report shocked Americans and many Koreans, whose preconceived ideas regarding the U.S. military made such conduct difficult to comprehend. The Pentagon amended its position in response to the evidence presented, reporting the deaths as unfortunate tragedies inherent to war, but did not take responsibility for the actions of U.S. forces. They claimed no orders were given to target Korean civilians, despite substantial evidence, including claims made by soldiers there at the time, to the contrary. The Pentagon declined to be interviewed on the matter when presented with evidence by investigators.[16]

According to the investigators there were orders for the Air Force to strafe refugees, but this evidence was omitted from Pentagon's report. The Pentagon report claimed that the strafing of civilians by the Air Force was not deliberate. Other evidence however, such as a memo written the day before the events at No Gun Ri by Air Force Colonel Turner Rogers, strongly indicates that the Air Force had orders to target civilians and supports the claims of investigators against those of the Pentagon. The memo states: 'The Army has requested we strafe all civilian refugee parties that are noted approaching our positions. To date, we have complied with the army request in this respect.'[17] The reports of South Korean civilians who survived the strafing strengthen the claim of the investigators that strafing took place.

Korean War Veteran, Former U.S. Congressman and Pentagon advisor Pete McCloskey confirmed that the U.S. pilots had orders to target

South Korean civilians. He stated that U.S. jets 'did have orders to strafe "people in white" [a term for Korean civilians, who traditionally wore white] approaching their position. At the Valley Forge [aircraft] carrier they unearthed a log that the Navy pilots were told to shoot any group of eight or ten civilians approaching the army position. I don't think there is any question that the strafing occurred – under orders. There was no question that that was the order the Air Force was obeying from the army – strafe the refugees.'[18]

Charles Hanley, an award-winning Special Correspondent for the *Associated Press* who was heavily involved in the No Gun Ri investigation, indicated that there was a cover-up by the U.S. military during the investigation to prevent the orders to target civilians from being publicized. During his investigation, the log for the 7th Cavalry which contained a record of the orders they were given, including any orders to target civilians, inexplicably disappeared from the Pentagon's archives. Hanley stated: 'What is extremely important to realize is that the single critical document that would have carried the orders to shoot the refugees at No Gun Ri, the 7th Cavalry regiment log, is missing inexplicably. And not only is it missing, but the Pentagon report does not disclose the fact that it is missing. And yet this report declared that there were no orders at No Gun Ri, declared that flatly although it does not have the document that would prove that one way or the other.'[19]

If the Pentagon admitted to having ordered its soldiers to target and kill hundreds of South Korean civilians, it would seriously tarnish the image of the military and undermine its primary pretext for retaining a sizeable presence on the Peninsula – the protection of the South Korean people. While orders from command were recorded in the communications logs of each division, and the log of the 8th Cavalry and others were all available, only the 7th Cavalry communications log, which based on the testimonies of witnesses from both sides would have been the most incriminating source of evidence, had disappeared. Based on these highly suspicious circumstances, it is likely that the information logged in the 7th Cavalry communications record held evidence the Pentagon preferred to keep away from the public and the investigators. George Preece, a career soldier who was present during the massacre, concluded regarding the disappearance of the log: 'it must have been covered up.'[20]

Charles Hanley commented on the potential threat to the image of the U.S. military should the orders given to soldiers at No Gun Ri have surfaced: 'This is a Pandora's Box for the U.S. government. It does seem that a decision was made that they had to close the door on No Gun Ri in order to close the door on God knows how many other cases.' Despite the orders tying directly to No Gun Ri being absent, at least 14 other documents from high ranking officers in the first months of the war point to a widespread policy of treating South Korean refugees as the enemy and targeting them accordingly. These include orders such as: 'shoot all refugees coming across the river,' 'refugees will be considered "enemy" and dispersed by all available fire including artillery' and 'all refugees are fair game' among many other such orders. While they do not directly indicate a massacre at No Gun Ri itself, they shed light on the prevailing U.S. military stances towards South Korean refugees and thus support the claims of both the survivors and the perpetrators. These documents were conveniently absent from the Pentagon's report.[21,22]

Despite many South Koreans having demanded justice and further investigations into other alleged massacres, the U.S. government has said that it will not investigate any more reported incidences of attacks on civilians. Pete McCloskey, former U.S. Congressman and advisor to the Pentagon, commented on the U.S. approach to allegations of war crimes: 'The American government, the Pentagon, don't want the truth to come out if it will embarrass the government. I think it is almost a rule of political science. It is a law. The government will always lie about embarrassing matters. I think the army just chose to try to downplay the terrible character of army leadership in 1950.'[23] Evidence of massacres by U.S. forces would have undermined the U.S. and ROK government's attempts to portray the U.S. military presence in South Korea as necessary protection from a hostile military force. It was essential for both the U.S. military and the South Korean government to maintain the positive image of the U.S. armed forces, and so to cover up any signs of American misconduct towards South Korean civilians.

Witnesses and survivors of both the U.S. forces and of South Korea's own pre-war atrocities against civilians, such as the Rhee government's massacres of those considered to hold leftist sympathies and killings of 2 percent of the ROK's population, were kept silent under the threat of being labeled communist sympathizers – an accusation which often led to a similar fate.[24] On the eve the first *Associated Press* report of the No Gun Ri massacre was published South Korean attempts to cover up evidence of the massacre came to light. The No Gun Ri Survivors' Committee discovered that South Korean authorities had plastered over the bullet holes inside the tunnel where they had hidden from the U.S. 7th Cavalry years before. One of the survivors and members of the committee said: 'When we saw the national railroad plaster this tunnel up, we couldn't help thinking there must be someone behind this cover-up. There must be hundreds of tunnels in Korea that are leaking. We are convinced that they plastered it in order to cover it up.' Yang Hae Chan said: 'All the eyes of the world are looking to America to speak the truth about the events at No Gun Ri. They should not ignore the voices of weaker countries. I believe this attitude of the Americans should be known throughout the world, so the U.S. changes its position and repents.'[25]

The consistency of the accounts of both the U.S. perpetrators with those of the Korean victims diminishes considerably the possibility of fabrication. The lack of any incentive to fabricate atrocities, and by contrast the pressure not to testify at all due to the risks that come with doing so particularly on the Korean side because of the dangers of criticizing the U.S. military in the country, make allegations that a massacre of civilians took place at No Gun Ri highly likely to have been true. The U.S. military was considered beyond reproach and any criticism, particularly allegations of war crimes, were strictly forbidden by the ROK's government, which gained much of its legitimacy from supposedly defending the Korean people from the 'evils of communism' alongside U.S. forces – a legitimacy which rested heavily on covering up the reality of the U.S. military's conduct in Korea. As one No Gun Ri survivor, Eun Yong, recalled: 'We couldn't say publicly that the Americans committed such things during the war. The United States was such a powerful country. Speaking against the Americans was tantamount to calling yourself a communist.'[26] This was at a time when suspected communists were disappeared, shot and buried in mass graves – a fate which awaited any suspected dissenters against the ROK government or its U.S. ally. With testifying against the U.S. military itself extremely dangerous, atrocity fabrication by the victims remains highly unlikely.

Further supporting the claims of both the survivors and the U.S. soldiers, journalists accompanying the North Korean military, which arrived at No Gun Ri in the wake of the American retreat, reported finding 'indescribably gruesome scenes' in the town. Journalist Chun Wook reported: 'Shrubs and weeds in the area and a creek running through the tunnels were drenched in blood and the area was covered with two or three layers of bodies. About 400 bodies of old and young people and children covered the scene so that it was difficult to walk around without stepping on corpses.'[27] With chances of co-ordination between the North Korean journalists, South Korean refugees and American soldiers in their testimonies negligible to non-existent it is highly likely that the stories of all three match one another because all were reporting the truth as they saw it.

The No Gun Ri massacre was hardly a unique case of American misconduct in Korea, but it was unique in that it had such a well-publicized investigation carried out to support the claims of survivors against the governments involved. Much like My Lai did in the Vietnam War, the single most well known massacre was remarkable only because it happened to be investigated and its details publicized – not because such occurrences were not commonplace. The targeting of civilians at No Gun Ri did not take place on the initiative of American soldiers themselves, but rather was ordered by the military's command with similar orders being given to Army and Air Force units across the country. The private investigators who covered No Gun Ri did not attempt to prove any other of the several allegations of the massacre of civilians made against the United States military by South Korean victims. Claims by survivors that U.S. forces carried out massacres remain common. The United States elected not to pay compensation to the victims of No Gun Ri, issue an apology or co-operate with any further investigations.[28] There remained a risk of setting a precedent allowing the victims of numerous massacres throughout the country to similarly make claims against the U.S. military – worse still that victims of hundreds of alleged massacres in North Korea, former South Vietnam and other countries could testify as well. David Straub, the political chief at the U.S. Embassy in Seoul during the No Gun Ri investigation, noted that meeting survivors' demands would have set an undesirable precedent for similar cases.[29]

The South Korean authorities have logged reports of 61 massacres of civilians carried out by U.S. forces at the time, including the naval shelling of refugees at the port of Pohang in September 1950 and killings of families sheltering in a shrine at Kokkan Ri.[30] South Korean survivors, in interviews with foreign investigators many decades later, recalled similarly grotesque scenes of carnage.[31] Oh Won Rok, president of a South Korean association of 80 groups of massacre survivors, indicated in 2010 that the investigations had so far revealed very little of the full extent of the massacres carried out against South Korean civilians by both U.S. and South Korean forces. Oh also noted the efforts made by the ROK government to prevent the emergence of the truth regarding the massacres. He stated: 'They have so far uncovered just a tip of the iceberg. So many victims did not come forward, out of fear. The current conservative government wants to keep it all buried.'[32]

A week after the No Gun Ri massacre the U.S. 1st Cavalry Division allegedly carried out a massacre at the Naktong River. The division had just retreated across the river via the bridge. Thousands of refugees massed on the other side, eager to cross the bridge. U.S. General Hobart Gay ordered the demolition of the bridge which, according to his own memoirs, went down with hundreds of refugees still on it. The advancing North Korean forces, which had forced the U.S. 1st Cavalry's retreat, would not arrive at the river for another four days. The decision to kill the refugees was in no way prompted by urgency. A second bridge elsewhere on the front was also blown up on the same day by the 14th Combat Engineers as refugees were running across it. The Engineers noted: 'results excellent,' failing to mention the substantial collateral damage from the deaths of Korean civilians.[33,34] Pfc. Leon L. Denis reported of the Korean civilians killed: 'They were average folks, ladies, children and old men, carrying their baggage on their heads.'[35] The extent to which the U.S. military did not consider South Korean people's lives to be of any value, to kill them in such numbers so easily and carelessly with so little remorse, is revealing of their perception of and resulting conduct towards the Korean people – consistent with wartime conduct towards East Asian peoples in general.

Cut off with the bridges blown, South Korean civilians waded across the river. A survivor, Kim Jin Suk, recalled: 'when we were half way across the river, what looked like American soldiers began shooting at us. First my father, who was in front, was shot. Then my brother was hit. I hid behind our cow, holding its tail. As the shooting became heavier, I saw piles of dead bodies floating down the river like straw.'[36] Kim later identified that they were American soldiers which had fired on him, and he recalled that his father and many other refugees died soon afterwards. Cho Koon Ja, another refugee, similarly reported U.S. troops firing on refugees crossing the river and the resulting carnage. Cho survived and fled to her hometown, No Gun Ri, where a more terrible sight awaited her.[37]

Melvin Durham, an American serviceman of F Company, recalled the orders to fire on civilians to prevent them from crossing the river: 'We was holding that railroad bridge to keep them from coming across that. But those people – there was women, children, old people – we had to eliminate them [...] Our orders was to start opening fire and when we did, there wasn't nothing standing but a couple of cows. We fired for about an hour, an hour and a half.'[38] The 8th Cavalry too were ordered by their commander, Col Raymond D. Palmer, on August 9 to 'shoot all refugees coming across the river.' These stranded Koreans carried with them a sign stating 'Americans, We Are Not Communists,' unaware that U.S. commanders knew this and knowingly gave the orders to target Korean refugees. Whether they were communist or not was irrelevant – all Korean people in the area were targets. U.S. Air Force P-51 fighters proceeded to strafe the Korean refugees on the far side of the river, even those who did not attempt to cross.[39]

It seemed that nowhere was safe for the refugees of the American scorched earth campaign. On August 11, 1950, refugees sheltering in a Confucian shrine were massacred by U.S. forces of the 25th Infantry Division. Survivors recall that 80 were killed in that incident alone.[40] A few days later thousands of South Korean civilians took refuge from a battle on a sheltered beach, where they remained for days in apparent safety. While they seemed to have escaped the U.S. Army, they were in full view of U.S. Navy warships stationed off the coast. In the morning hours of September 1, 1950, the warships suddenly opened fire on the civilians. This was done completely without warning, and there were no North Korean military personnel nearby. The U.S. Navy was found by an investigation conducted by the ROK's Truth and Reconciliation Commission decades later to have knowingly targeted refugees sheltering on the shoreline at Pohang.[41] Park Ke San, a survivor, recalled: 'Of all the terrible images I remember the most, it is the moment my sister's head was blown off and my mother lost one of her breasts. These two images have haunted me for my entire life. A little baby from our family was also killed. But how could I possibly forget seeing my sister's head being blown off in front of my own eyes.'[42]

Orders to target South Korean civilians were not exclusively given in the opening stages of the war. On January 3, 1951, the 8th Army Headquarters sent the secret command: 'You have complete authority in your zone to stop all civilian traffic. Responsibility to place fire on them to include bombing rests with you.'[43] This effectively authorized the U.S. military to target civilians. Strafing of South Korean civilians continued to be a widespread practice of the U.S. Air Force. Though strict censorship prevented him from reporting it, Associated Press correspondent Sean Swinton wrote in a letter to his parents on January 30, 1951: 'the most horrifying part of this last advance has been the hundreds of refugees killed by our strafing. The children weren't hit; they just tumbled off their mothers' back and froze to death on the roadside ... Do not the enemies we make among the civilian population counterbalance and more than counterbalance the damage we do to the Reds?' Other reports of the strafing of civilians were common. A four-plane mission flying near Taejon for example reported strafing fishing boats when military targets could not be found. Much like the North Koreans, South Korean civilians in areas occupied by northern soldiers adapted to hiding in the daytime and cultivating their rice fields only at night to avoid being targeted by American planes, who regularly gunned civilians down in their fields. South Korean civilians recalled after the war ended North Korean soldiers warning them not to go out in the daytime, advising them how best to avoid being targeted by U.S. aircraft.[44]

In January 1951 South Korean refugees were still being targeted by the U.S. Air Force, even those as far from the battlefront as several miles south of Seoul. Air Force planes were known to target refugees with incendiaries without provocation, killing hundreds at a time. Col. Turner C. Rogers, operations chief of the Fifth Air Force, had previously recommended that the army should shoot the refugees themselves rather than rely on the Air Force to do it for them. This recommendation was not heeded, and even years after the war when the U.S. Army War College conducted a study on the lessons learned in Korea on handling refugees they concluded: 'strafing fire from low-flying aircraft is very effective in clearing a road.' There was no remorse nor was the tactic, which was a severe war crime, considered at all undesirable – at least not when conducted against the supposedly 'racially inferior' Korean people.[45]

The International Association of Democratic Lawyers, an international NGO which researches legal issues affecting human, political and economic rights worldwide, working as a consultative organization with the UN, UNESCO, UNICEF and ECOSOC, with headquarters in Brussels and Tokyo, conducted an extensive study of American conduct towards civilians during the Korean War. They found that massacres of refugees by the American military occurred not only in South Korea, but very extensively in North Korea as well. They noted that these massacres occurred primarily in two periods as follows:

a) When the American troops were advancing Northwards in September and October 1950, large number of refugees fleeing northwards were cut off by the advancing troops particularly in the areas of Sinchon and Anak. These refugees were clearly distinguishable as refugees, whole families including women and children. The men wearing traditional Korean white clothes, and the women long skirts in color who were not at the time intermingled with troops of the Korean People's Army. It was these groups which were systematically exterminated.
b) When the American troops retreated in November-December 1950, it is established that large numbers of the inhabitants of the major cities were induced by leaflets and threats to believe that the atom bombs would be dropped and that they should move south with the American troops. These refugees were deliberately exterminated in their thousands by American forces.[46]

Other incidents were also reported by Western observers and press. Though the DPRK and Chinese forces witnessed several similar such massacres their accounts were inevitably not given any regard by Western press. Western and international reports did however portray very similar stories. *New York Times* correspondent Charles Grutzner, citing U.S. military sources, reported 'the slaughter of hundreds of South Korean civilians, women as well as men, by some U.S. troops and police of the Republic [of Korea].'[47] An article in the American Newark *Star-Ledger* in July 1950 stated: 'It's not the time to be a Korean, for the Yankees are shooting them all.' This corroborated with several other Western sources which indicated the indiscriminate killings of Koreans, northern and southern, by U.S. forces. Park Chan Hyun, a South Korean lawmaker, found during an investigation in the 1960s that an estimated 10,000 had been executed in Busan. American Air Force intelligence officer Donald Nichols attested in his 1981 memoir of witnessing an 'unforgettable massacre' of 'approximately 1,800' at Suwon during the war.

In several incidents South Korean lives were sacrificed en masse to achieve highly limited military objectives against North Korean forces. An example of this was the bombing of Yongsan on July 16, 1950, when U.S. bombers targeted Seoul's Yongsan district in order to slow down North Korean forces. This led to the deaths of 1,587 South Korean civilians, but was considered a military necessity.[48] However other killings, such as those which took place in No Gun Rhee, were far from any North Korean forces and had negligible military benefit for U.S. forces. These massacres of South Korean civilians reflected not military necessity, but a combination of disregard for the lives of the 'racially inferior' Korean people and a sense of enmity towards the Koreans as a race and people. The massacre of so many Korean civilians makes it, as the U.S. serviceman Joe Jackman said, 'seem as if all Koreans were the enemy.' While targeting civilians for strategic benefit, as the U.S. Air Force did at Yongsan, is a severe war crime, even the need for strategic gain could not be used to justify the widespread massacres of civilians under wholly different circumstances.

The conduct of the United States, far from being an inevitable part of the nature of war, bears a strong contrast to that of the Chinese and Koreans they were fighting – the 'most primitive of peoples' in the words of the *New York Times*' military editor. The attitude of the American military towards the South Korean people can be effectively summarized by a quote from appraised fighter pilot Ensign David Tatum: 'I figured if we had to kill 10 civilians to kill one soldier who might later shoot at us, we were justified.' His statement was published in *Time* magazine on January 1, 1951, the edition which awarded the American Fighting Man with the man of the year award for their conduct in Korea in which stories from such 'exemplary' U.S. personnel were published.

Chinese military personnel by contrast were not only strictly forbidden from any forms of vandalism or destruction against Korean property, they were also given the following instructions by Chairman Mao Zedong upon entering the war: 'The Chinese comrades must consider Korea's cause as their own and the commanders and fighters must be instructed to cherish every hill, every river, every tree and every blade of grass in Korea and take not a single needle or a single thread from the Korean people, just the way we feel about our own country and treat our own people. This is the political basis for winning victory. So long as we act this way, final victory will be assured.'[49] Just as the good conduct of the PLA towards China's rural population, a stark contrast to the U.S. backed Guomindang, had been instrumental in winning the Chinese Civil War and gaining mass public support, so too was this prioritized in the Korean theatre.

New York Times reporter George Barrett noted the stark contrast between the Korean people's perception of Chinese forces compared to those of the United States and other Western nations as a result of their vast discrepancy in their conduct. He wrote that widespread and regular rapes committed by U.S. and Canadian forces 'have created a deep animosity among large sections of the Korean populace.' The Koreans noted in particular that Western soldiers could commit crimes, including sexual crimes against civilians, without reprimand by their superiors. By contrast, Barrett noted, the Chinese military 'have impressed many Koreans with the discipline of their troops. Many residents of Seoul seem to go out of their way to tell about the good Chinese behavior, and especially about executions of two rapists the Chinese are said to have held.'[50]

One critical difference between Chinese and Western forces intervening in Korea was that there was no institutional racism against the Korean people, or as per the case of the United States and its Western allies against Asian peoples in general, in the Chinese military. Racial contempt towards Asian peoples, communist or otherwise, was prevalent at the highest levels of the United States military and UN command, and this allowed its soldiers to conduct themselves as conquerors and brutalize the 'mere gooks' who they were fighting. This was far from the case for the Chinese military, which not only lacked a resentment of the Korean race and people, but punished any transgressions against them severely. It is notable that Chinese forces left North Korea five years after the end of the war in 1958, after aiding the North with reconstruction, and have never returned to date.[51] The United States military by contrast has maintained tens of thousands of personnel in South Korea to this day and continues to maintain wartime operational command over the South Korean military. The distinction between a lesser client state and an ally and equal partner was clear both during and after the war.

North Koreans in their brief occupation of the south were, according to the accounts of South Korean villagers given years later, highly respectful. They treated South Koreans well, though this kindness did not extend to members of Rhee's government, many of whom were landowning former Japanese collaborators who had their land confiscated and distributed to those who worked on it. Villagers interviewed particularly noted North Korean's respect for local women, which bore a stark contrast to the American soldiers who had committed widespread rapes. CIA intelligence reports stated that even in Seoul, the stronghold of the Rhee government, most of the student population actively worked with the North Koreans and welcomed the arrival of the Korean People's Army.[52] According to eyewitness reports later declassified by the U.S. military, when American soldiers recaptured Seoul in the Autumn of 1950 they had gathered several hundred politically suspect Korean women and held them by force in a warehouse. There they had been used by force to satisfy the sexual needs of the American military personnel – sexual slavery.[53] When ROK forces regained control of their territories collaborators with the north were executed and it was strictly forbidden for many decades to speak well of the North Korean military.[54]

Pulitzer Prize winning investigative reporter Charles Hanley noted regarding the popularity of the North Korean forces: 'Many [South] Koreans were simply disgusted with the corrupt, autocratic Rhee years. That opposition deepened with the bloodbath of executions carried out by the retreating government through the summer, when military police and other agents shot thousands of leftist political prisoners and dumped their bodies in mass graves outside Taejon and Taegu and elsewhere in the South.' Hanley noted that the restoring of people's committees, which had briefly governed the country and enjoyed widespread support until their forcible abolishment under U.S. military rule, as well as the promotion of women's organizations and redistribution of land all served to make North Korean forces more popular among South Koreans.[55] The contrasting brutality of the U.S. and ROK forces only exacerbated this.

The Conduct of Western Military Forces in the Occupation of North Korea

American war crimes in Korea were not restricted to firebombing population centers, dive-bombing hospitals or machine-gunning civilians. Reports from multiple sources indicate that U.S. personnel on the ground also committed rape and sexual torture of Korean women on a large scale, particularly in northern Korea, alongside widespread destruction and deliberate targeting of Korean cultural and religious heritage. During the war the vast majority of sources on the events that took place in northern Korea were communist, mostly North Koreans themselves. There were however non-communist international commissions sent to observe and investigate claims of war crimes being carried out by U.S. forces, as well as some foreign journalists who reported from the north. It is these international sources which can be better relied on to more impartially give an account of the conduct of U.S. forces and their allies in North Korea.

The Women's International Democratic Federation (WIDF) an international women's rights organization founded in Paris in 1945, sent a commission to Korea during the war. The Federation was considered the most influential women's organization of the post-1945 era,[56] and was a consultant to the United Nations' Economic and Social Council. A monthly Federation magazine called *Women of the Whole World* was also published in English, French, Spanish, German and Russian. The Federation issued a report after visiting Korea and observing the severe misconduct of Western and ROK forces and the devastating impacts this had on the North Korean people. Detailing the ordeals faced by Koreans under this occupation, the report stated: 'In the district temporarily occupied by American and Syngman Rhee forces, in the period of occupation, hundreds of thousands of civilians, entire families, from old men to little children, have been tortured, beaten to death, burned and buried alive. Thousands of others have perished from hunger and cold in overcrowded prisons in which they were thrown without charges being leveled against them, without investigation, trial or sentence. These mass tortures and mass murders surpass the crimes committed by Hitler's Nazis in temporarily occupied Europe.'

As a result of their reports on the U.S. military actions in Korea, at a time when criticism of anti-communist policy was little tolerated in then strongly McCarthyist America, the WIDF was labeled a communist front organization. This label came from the strongly McCarthyist House Un-American Activities Committee, referred to by the BBC as 'McCarthy's House Un-American Activities Committee.'[57] Ties to communist powers or a communist agenda at the time were never proven, and indeed it was highly common at the time for any dissenters in the United States to be labeled 'communist agents' – or in the case of military personnel who gave accounts of U.S. war crimes 'brainwashed' by the communists.

The commission visited the Pyongyang Museum after American forces had withdrawn from the city. They testified to the fact that U.S. forces had robbed the museum of all its treasures including two famous statues of Buddha which were over 2,000 years old. Priceless frescoes discovered in thirty ancient tombs in North Korea were robbed, and six of these tombs had been used for torturing Korean women – the 'recreation' of American personnel. Cultural relics such as the shrine of Mo Ran Bon and the Yen Myen Sa temple of Buddha among others were destroyed. This ancient temple of Buddha, Yen Myen Sa, stood overlooking a hill surrounded by nothing but parkland, far from any military targets. It was deliberately targeted by American forces after they evacuated from Pyongyang. The Western Bloc notably claimed moral high ground over communists for adhering to religion, but in Korea they were shown to destroy places of worship and ancient relics which the DPRK's government took great efforts to restore after the war.

The WIDF commission reported that the occupation of areas of North Korea by Western forces entailed brutal conduct and grotesque sexual crimes. It stated in its report on Pyongyang: 'The Americans made the Opera and the remains of the adjoining house into an Army-brothel. To this brothel they took by force women and young girls caught in the streets. As she [a young girl interviewed] feared a similar fate, she didn't leave her dug-out for 40 days.' Most North Koreans at the time were forced to live in such small dugouts as almost all housing in the country was targeted and destroyed by U.S. military – 'every brick standing on top of another' in the words of Assistant Secretary of State Dean Rusk.[58] The commission's report continued: 'The husband of her friend, Ri San Sen, was beaten up by Americans because he hid his wife from them. An inhabitant of Pyongyang [...] confirmed this statement. Many other residents of Pyongyang recounted the atrocities by Americans. Kim Sun Ok, 37, the mother of four children killed by a bomb, stated that she was evacuated in the village by the Americans, among them the secretary of the local women's organization. The Americans led her naked through the streets and later killed her by pushing a red-hot iron bar into her vagina. Her small son was buried alive.' Similar punishments were frequently given to women who resisted rape by occupying soldiers. In Mih Yen Ri three women who defended themselves against rape by American soldiers had their breasts cut off. They were then killed by having red hot irons thrust into their vaginas. This was reported by the commission, though it was not an exceptional case.

Members of the commission from Austria, China, Cuba (not communist at the time), Canada, the USSR and England visited the province of Whang Hai. Their investigation found that along with the 120,000 civilians who had been killed by American, British and ROK forces, civilian prisoners including children as young as two years old were kept for 15 days without food in cells so crowded that there was no room to sit. They were beaten with iron bars by ROK forces under American instruction. Afterwards the prisoners, including the women and young children, were taken to the hills nearby and buried alive in trenches. A young mother who had been buried alive managed to dig herself out, but she was captured and buried again. There was a separate mass grave especially for children. These reports were based on the testimonies of North Korean survivors. One survivor, Kim San Yen, found his son and his son's wife's bodies dead and buried with no wounds – as they had been buried alive. He told the commission that he was a religious Christian man, and could not bring himself to believe that Western Christians would conduct themselves in such a way. North Korean government sources have since discovered the mass graves of civilians killed by live burial, of which they presented photographic evidence, affirming the findings of the WIDF commission and the testimonies of survivors.[59] Such reports are highly consistent with verified reports from South Korea which show almost the exact same conduct, confinement in cramped cells and burials of women and children including infants in mass graves – making reports of similar conduct towards civilians in the north far from implausible. Women and children have been found executed and buried in mass graves on both sides of the 38th Parallel by U.S. and ROK forces, so such reports from an international commission in the north are hardly remarkable or unusual.[60,61,62]

Reports from the Women's International Democratic Federation commission stated that victims of the U.S. military were peasants and workers, the vast majority of whom had no connections with the DPRK's government. A woman who survived said that American soldiers who had killed her family had tortured her by shoving red hot knitting needles under her fingernails. The commission observed the clear signs of disfigurement, as well as the blood on the walls of the prisons which were evidence of the beatings. An 11-year-old girl called Shin Soon Dza said that she and her mother and sister had been captured by American forces. Her mother and sister were shot and she was severely beaten and put in prison. Deep scars in her head as a result of the beatings were observed by members of the commission.

Kin Sen Ai, another 11-year-old girl from the same school as Kim Sen Ai, said that she was in the fourth class in school when American soldiers entered her village and put her in prison with her parents. Her father was tortured and thrown in a river. Her mother was a member of the Workers' Party, and so earned special treatment – her breasts were cut off. Kin's four-year-old sister was then buried alive. She asked to be able to speak to the commission and gave the mutilation of her family as evidence for her claims. In Wonsan, the capital of Northern Kang Won province, the majority of the population were said to have been killed under bombings and then occupation by U.S. led forces before 1952. Of the 123,127 inhabitants only 57,667 remained, the rest having fled or been massacred. Of the 27,345 houses only 9,257 remained – many of them severely damaged.

Ree Sam Sil, a leading member of Kaichen's women's organization, was jailed by American soldiers, tortured by electricity, stripped, raped by two soldiers and dragged naked through the streets. On the day of the withdrawal of U.S. military forces she managed to escape and survived the ordeal.[63] The Chairman of the Wonsan women's organization, aged 25 and nine months pregnant, was arrested and beaten by American soldiers for being a 'red.' She was exposed publicly in the town square, and she and her child were killed when a rod was thrust into her womb by two Americans and an ROK soldier. Eyewitnesses were forced to be present. Jo Ok Hi, a young girl who was Chairman of the Haiju women's organization was imprisoned and submitted to slow torture. Her eyes were pulled out, and after some time her nose was then cut off. Later on they cut off her breasts. Korean women associated with the government or any women's organizations consistently received such treatment. Tzen Man Suk, the Chairman of Ko Ri village's women's organization was arrested by Americans as a 'red,' and raped by soldiers repeatedly for two days. A large part of these rapes was to assert dominance over the society of the DPRK and over symbols of an independent and self-governed Asian nation. U.S. soldiers did so by particularly targeting Korean women in leadership positions with sexual violence.

Yan Yen Dek, a 28-year-old woman, said her five children and husband had all been killed. She was imprisoned by American soldiers with her two-year-old child who was trampled on by the Americans until its intestines fell out. She was taken by two American soldiers who raped her. She was then tortured by the soldiers, but survived the ordeal. Kim Chun Dze, a 20-year-old nursing student, had nails put in her ear by U.S. soldiers. She was stripped naked, had a drum strapped to her back, and was paraded through the street. She was then put in a prison where the soldiers tried to rape her. She resisted successfully, and so was bayonetted to death. Her mother found her body mutilated and cut in two.

In the Song San Ri locality in Anak in October 1950 American soldiers forced all adults and children into a school building. One woman, Kim Hwa Sil, defended herself against attempted rape and was put naked in the courtyard. The population was forced to watch her torture as a club one meter long was forced into her vagina. She immediately died and her body was hung on a telegraph pole, where it remained for the rest of the occupation. These scenes were photographed by American soldiers. Ten other women were then raped in succession by two or three soldiers, beaten by clubs, kicked, and had clubs forced between their legs. Children were taken from their mothers and beatings, rapes and murders went on for eight days. On October 26, the survivors were taken to the seashore and shot. One witness escaped the convoy when it was held up on the road, and was the only survivor. Atrocities by American soldiers occurred across the province. In nearby Sam Seng Ri a 12-year-old boy who tried to defend his father from a beating by American troops had his eyes gouged out.[64]

One 42-year-old woman was raped by American soldiers in succession (soldiers tended to be from 18 to 20 years old). Unlike many of the Korean women raped by U.S. personnel she survived, though at the time of the commission's investigation she was still very ill and bedridden. Older women were also raped by the young soldiers one third their age, such as in a report of American soldiers gang-raping a 56-year-old woman when they occupied Sariwon, or a 64-year-old woman in Soonchen.[65] These aforementioned cases represent only a small sample of the numerous and widespread cases of war atrocities under occupation that the WIDF commission recorded. The commission in turn collected only a very small sample of reports of what North Koreans suffered under the occupation of Western, predominantly American, military forces. This indicates the scale of the carnage, slaughter and brutal conduct of Western military forces against the Korean people.

The Women's Commission's findings were strongly supported by North Korean journalistic and military reports,[66] and North Korean accounts of their experience of the U.S. occupation point to extremely similar conduct. This is also highly consistent with South Korean reports of U.S. conduct in their own country. Reports from the northern side of the conflict by international journalists were relatively few. Two journalists who did gain access to North Korean victims however, Alan Winnington and Wilfred Burchett from Australia and Britain, gave accounts regarding the conduct of U.S. personnel which strongly supported the findings of the Women's Commission's investigation. The two journalists reported from both sides of the war, and their testimonies were considered invaluable by Western media who otherwise had very restricted access to information due to wartime censorship.[67,68,69] Burchett was renowned by many major U.S. media outlets as a reliable source,[70] praised even by hardline anti-communist papers such as the *U.S. News and World Report* which stated that Burchett 'never lied, so far as anyone could discover.'[71] In 1971 he would later be invited to the White House by Secretary of State Henry Kissinger who consulted him regarding prospects for peace in Vietnam, a war which Burchett also covered extensively.[72]

Burchett and Winnington interviewed North Korean women captured by the U.S. military. One woman, Kim Kyong Suk, gave the following account, as several other women who were captured with her sat at the interview and affirmed her story – correcting various dates and details. Kim had been put into a prison for juveniles at Kaesong under the U.S. military occupation, then sent to a large group of around 150 women at Inchon. She recalled: 'The Americans treated us like animals from the day we were captured. On the pretext of searching us, they forced us to strip nude. They hurled insults at us. They paraded us naked in the streets with their bayonets prodding us along and almost bursting through our skin. They brought along photographers and took pictures which they later posted on our prison compound notice board. Americans would come with ROK troops and select girls for raping.'

Kim recalled having been paraded naked through Seoul along with 50 other women in October 1950. She went on to state: 'No one was safe from their bestialities. They even violated one 14-year-old girl whom they had rounded up as a "prisoner of war." At the Inchon camp, two mothers with babies on their backs were repeatedly dragged off at bayonet-point. The children had their mouths gagged while the mothers were taken into the American guards' quarters and raped.' Kim reported that at least one young girl who had suffered from rape and torture lost her mind as a result of the psychological trauma.[73]

Winnington and Burchett observed evidence of the North Korean women's testimony. Where they alleged they had suffered from torture, including nails being put under their fingernails, severe beatings or electric torture they had the physical scars and burn marks to prove it. The two journalists noted that the 'sadistic crimes' committed against the Korean people by U.S. forces were due to a highly racialist mentality akin to that which had cause the Nazi German atrocities shortly beforehand. It was the frustration of victory over the 'inferior races' eluding them which led them to carry out such reprisals against the populations of these races.[74] For his coverage of the brutality of allied U.S. and ROK forces, the British cabinet considered charging Winnington with treason.[75]

What was notable about Winnington's reporting was its accuracy, in that while reports on war crimes committed by Western forces in North Korea could not be verified – reports on similar crimes committed in South Korea, which were at the time adamantly denied by the U.S. government as 'atrocity fabrication,' turned out to be entirely true when American intelligence reports, photographic evidence and other documents were decades later declassified. On example was his description of the massacres of South Korean civilians, who were then buried in mass graves – at the time dismissed but later verified entirely by U.S. military sources.[76] Based on the accuracy of Winnington's reporting on war crimes in the ROK, and of the United States' attempts to deny their involvement, there is little reason to believe that his claims regarding the conduct of the United States military in northern Korea would not be true as well.

The reports by the few non-communist sources which reported from North Korea during the war on the conduct of U.S. occupying forces all reached very similar conclusions and strongly support one another. While non-communist sources reporting from North Korea were few, the conduct of Western militaries in their occupation of the North was far from unbelievable based on the evidence of their conduct in South Korea. If anything, conduct towards North Korean civilians would be expected to be at least as brutal as that towards the supposedly allied South Koreans, if not more so. A member of the South Korean government's Truth and Reconciliation

Committee, a government body established in 1993 at the official end of the country's authoritarian rule to investigate incidents in Korean history, reported in 2004 on the conduct of American personnel towards South Korean civilians. The report stated that as a result of American soldiers' 'deep racial prejudices' atrocities against Korean civilians were carried out.

The report detailed the following: 'With total ignorance of Asia, young soldiers regarded Koreans and Chinese as "people without history." They usually called Koreans "gooks", a term used during World War II for Pacific Islanders. The fact that many Korean women in the villages were often raped in front of their husbands and parents has not been a secret among those who experienced the Korean War. It was known that several women were raped before being shot at No Gun Ri. Some eyewitnesses say that U.S. soldiers played with their lives like boys sadistically playing with flies.'[77]

The fact that the testimonies of North Korean survivors of massacres carried out by U.S. forces were so similar to those separately collected from South Korean survivors of similar massacres, all carried out by the very same perpetrators, primarily the U.S. military, strongly indicates the veracity of their claims. Indeed, considering the many corroborating sources, the conduct of U.S. forces in South Korea, the prior conduct of U.S. troops towards civilians in the Pacific War, and the conduct towards Vietnamese civilians soon afterwards, there is little reason to doubt the veracity of these reports on the conduct of U.S. personnel towards North Koreans – as it is entirely consistent with their conduct elsewhere as confirmed by numerous sources from all sides.

The Commission of International Association of Democratic Lawyers gave similar accounts regarding the conduct of Western militaries when occupying the DPRK. These investigators and reporters, all independent, reporting very similar conduct and reaching similar conclusions based on their results of independent studies, indicates their veracity. The two international commissions concluded, based on their own independent investigations, that the United States forces had committed genocide against the Korean people. The Lawyers' Commission noted that the research was carried out to ensure that conclusions reflected the reality of the situation. As an impartial international organization with no agenda concerning the Korean War their claims can be considered reliable. They also stated that they witnessed evidence merely weeks after the departure of U.S. forces, and based on this reached conclusions regarding the conduct of Western militaries and the suffering of the North Korean people, which applied to all of occupied North Korea – not just the areas mentioned. The commission investigated only a few sample cases to gain an understanding of a wider phenomenon.

One account by the Commission sent by the International Association of Democratic Lawyers details that conduct of American soldiers in Sinchon, which was highly similar to that described by the Women's International Democratic Federation. Describing one case it states: 'Wool Mal Che's daughter-in-law, seeing the American soldiers torturing her father-in-law tried to defend him. The Americans attached her by the hair to a tree, cut off her breasts, put a wooden club in her vagina, poured fuel-oil on it and set fire to it. They then poured oil over her and burned her alive. About 20 American soldiers took part in this murder.'[78]

The Lawyers' Association's report concludes regarding the conduct of American soldiers in occupied areas:

> The tortures and bestialities committed against individuals again reveal a common pattern of behavior throughout the area visited, and cannot be passed over as the sadistic excesses of individuals. The whole series of cases cited in this chapter of the report must not be taken as the whole evidence of cases committed but as typical of a vast number of similar cases brought to the attention of the Commission for examination [of which but a small fraction are listed]. [Accounts of] the torturing of people by beating, kicking, electric shocks, pouring water in the nose and throat to excess, cutting off various parts of the body, mutilation and the killing by shooting, bayoneting, suffocation, blowing up, burning alive and burying alive could be repeated again in sickening detail.[79]

The report further stated: 'the Commission has confined itself to a statement of those facts which were proved by direct evidence which in the opinion of the Commission was corroborated and established beyond doubt. A considerable volume of written statements was submitted to the Commission, which have been taken into account only by way of corroboration of facts proved by primary evidence. We were invited to investigate many similar cases to those stated above in various parts of the country, and it was time alone that prevented this from being done.'[80]

The Lawyers' commission's report concluded: 'Taking the view that the extensive murders are not the result of individual excesses, but indicate a pattern of behavior by the U.S. forces throughout the areas occupied by them [...] the Commission is of the opinion that the American forces are guilty of the crime of Genocide as defined by the Genocide Convention of 1948.' The United Nations Genocide Convention defines genocide as acts committed 'with the intent to destroy, in whole or in part, a national, ethical, racial or religious group.' This would include 'deliberately inflicting on the group conditions of life calculated to bring about its physical destruction in whole or in part.' This definition entered into force in 1951, as the United States carried out massacres of South Korean civilians in tandem with massacres, indiscriminate use of incendiaries and weapons of mass destruction against population centers and the destruction of dams and crops intended to cause starvation in the north. The war appeared to be waged against the Korean people themselves. This claim has a tangible basis in reality, and the U.S. bombing campaign was criticized as having racialist anti-Korean anti-Asian motives behind it by much of the media. It could very well be called a genocide against the Korean people by the United States.

Unlike other severe war crimes, the atrocities committed in northern Korea against its people continue to go unrecognized despite their severity – with the war continuously portrayed in the West as a noble if perhaps unnecessary war against a communist menace.[81] While U.S. war crimes in Korea are a scarcely covered subject outside of North Korea, allegations of genocide have been made by a number of respected sources on all sides. Kim Dong Choon, a South Korean professor at Song Kong Hoe University in Seoul and a member of the ROK's Truth and Reconciliation Commission published his findings in an article for the *Journal of Genocide Research* in 2004. Professor Kim himself found the United States military to have arguably been guilty of genocide during the Korean War. He cited massacres such as that at No Gun Ri and the intentional mass killings of Korean civilians to prove this point. Regarding the scarcity of investigations into the matter, Kim noted that it was due to the demonization of North Korea which 'served to justify any methods that the U.S. and South Korean army employed to oppose it. This is why existing books or articles dealing with massacres or genocides have never included the cases of the Korean War. Except for a few Western scholars who dared to mention the misconduct of American soldiers and the brutality of the ROK army, only a small number of scholars or reporters have ever raised the issue of 'criminal' actions of the U.S. and ROK army.' Anti-communism was in such fervor that even genocidal actions could be somewhat condoned in the war against a communist Asian power.[82]

Michel Chossudovsky, a Canadian Professor at Ottawa University, Director of the Center for Research on Globalization, similarly concluded that the United States had committed genocide during the Korean War. This was based on the death toll among North Korean civilians, which he stated was at least 25 percent, as well as the conduct of the United States' bombing campaign. Chossudovsky, citing several U.S. military sources, concluded that what was done to the North Korean people would be classified as genocide under international law.[83] American professor Patricia Hynes similarly concluded when analyzing the conduct of the U.S. air campaign, orders to 'wipe out all life in tactical sites' when targeting population centers, and the intentional targeting of irrigation dams at the onset of rice growing season to starve the North Korean population, that the actions of the United States amounted to genocide.[84]

Bruce Cumings, an American Professor of East Asian studies holding South Korea's honorable Kim Dae Jung Academic Award for Outstanding Achievements and Scholarly Contributions to Democracy, Human Rights and Peace, himself reached the same conclusion regarding the United States' conduct in Korea. Citing the United Nations Genocide Convention, signed in 1948 and implemented in 1951, as well as the Red Cross Convention on the Protection of Civilians in Wartime in 1948, Cumings concluded that though both of these were fully in effect during the Korean War, 'neither measure had the slightest impact.' Through their actions in Korea, particularly their air campaign, the United States violated both conventions and was guilty of crimes of genocide against the Korean people.[85]

U.S. and South Korean forces were far from the only ones to commit war crimes against the Korean people during the war. Other Western powers involved in the war were known to commit serious war crimes. British troops were heavily involved in fighting in North Korea and in occupying areas of the country. Kim Sun Sek, mother of Kim Chun Dze, stated in a testimony given to the WIDF commission that U.S. and British forces had upon taking control of her village rounded up the most beautiful girls to serve as comfort women for their own soldiers. The less beautiful girls were kept aside and given to ROK forces. 240 of these girls died due to the treatment they received at the hands of American and British troops, while only three survived.[86] Pak On In from Sa Ok Ri said her husband was arrested along with his three brothers. All were peasants and non-combatants, but all were killed in custody. She said she saw a teenage girl raped and killed by both American and British soldiers in front of her. She later found her husband's body, his head beaten open and burned. Song Chun Ok, a 42-year-old woman also interviewed by the WIDF commission, said all her family had been killed including her young children. American and British soldiers used axes and knives to do this. 'It was not only the American soldiers who did these things. It was the English soldiers too,' she recalled. 'I will go to the front and do anything until the whole of Korea is free from Americans,' was her defiant response to the slaughter of her family.[87]

Yu Tong Dze, a woman from Kwon Chou village, attested in 1951 to the killing of 35,000 innocent non-combatants in her district alone. Her husband and five-month-old child were killed. Massacres were carried out by both British and American soldiers. She said both equally behaved 'like beasts,' and she saw with her own eyes how American and English troops threw innocent people in the river. She said she could identify them only by their different uniforms, but their conduct had been the same. 'Do they have no pity in England? Do they believe in killing little children?' she asked.[88] Hwan Ik Su, a fourteen-year-old Korean girl from San Chen Ri village, said several of her family members were killed by American, British and Canadian soldiers. She was arrested and showed marks attesting to the beatings the soldiers gave her.

Canada notably carried out its own severe war crimes in Korea. Dr John Price, professor at the University of Victoria, gave a lecture titled 'Burying the Past, Canadian War Crimes in Korea' in which he outlined several crimes of the Canadian military during the war and how they were 'conveniently' forgotten. Dr Price claimed, based on his own research, that were these war crimes better publicized and made known today, Canada would likely not hold its current reputation as a moderate and peaceful nation. According to Price Canadians would very frequently kill and rape innocent Korean civilians during the war, and those convicted of such crimes most often went unpunished – with the Canadian government, specifically the ministry of defense, remaining reluctant to reopen these cases today. The motivation for this misconduct likely lay in the power military personnel felt they had over Korean peoples and in anti-Asian racial hatred. This is strongly indicated by Price's conclusion that the number of crimes committed against Koreans 'was substantial and exceeded anything seen during the fighting in Europe and WWII.' Fighting in Europe just five years before had been almost without incident by comparison. With little time for social changes between the two wars, the cause for the difference in conduct is likely due to racial factors.[89]

Through publicizing his findings Price wanted to expose the myth of the 'Kind Canadian' and the notion that Canadians held themselves to a higher moral standard that others. He argues that Canadians were as violent as the United States and British forces.[90] Ultimately all Western powers at war with Asian nations, even those perceived to be the most moderate, have historically had strong tendencies towards committing severe war crimes against those they perceived to be their racial inferiors. Price commented: 'it is time to expand and coordinate the research on war crimes.'[91] Indeed, only by doing so can the true nature of the conduct of Western military powers towards Asian peoples be exposed. This may grant victims, whether Koreans who saw their families killed and raped or those from Japan, Laos, Cambodia, Vietnam, China, the Philippines or elsewhere who suffered similarly, some degree of justice. Only through developing an awareness of the past and of the intentions of Western powers towards the region can a more secure future be built.

Proponents of Western dominance and advocates for continued Western military intervention in Asia or the 'liberation' of North Korea until today, of which there are many, would find it difficult to believe that the supposedly 'superior civilization' would conduct themselves in such a way. Others argue that any power would conduct themselves in such a way in war, and that brutalities and atrocities are part nature of war. This however is far from the case. The conduct of North Korean and

Chinese forces, which suffered greater casualties and far greater hardship with poorer equipment, fewer supplies and even a lack of winter clothing in battles at sub-freezing temperatures, colder than those of Stalingrad, were found by international reports to have committed no comparable acts. Atrocities in war are often considered by both military experts and psychologists to be at least in part results of the hardships and stresses faced by soldiers, and development of such conditions as post-traumatic stress disorder, which increase soldiers' likelihood to commit crimes and violent acts.[92,93] However in the Korean War Chinese and North Korean soldiers, facing far worse conditions, conducted themselves far better in their adherence to rules of war and conduct towards their enemies. The misconduct of Western forces was therefore hardly understandable or inevitable – much less excusable.

The two critical factors which allowed people to commit atrocities in war were, according to West Point psychologist Dave Grossman, 'an intense belief in moral superiority' and racial factors which allowed an enemy to be dehumanized. These factors both strongly applied to the U.S. military in Korea.[94] Indeed when it came to atrocities they were not endemic to the nature of war, but rather to how the forces involved perceived themselves, as conquerors or equals, and how they perceive the population, as racial inferiors or not. Western military powers in the Asia-Pacific have consistently shown themselves to be the latter – and the Korean War provides an exemplary case of this.

Medical Experiments and the Treatment of War Prisoners

Treatment of prisoners of war had long been considered one of the most critical indicators of the ethicality and general nature of warring parties, and reflects both their overall conduct towards and perceptions of their adversaries. As renowned Russian writer and philosopher Fyodor Dostoevsky famously observed: 'the degree of civilization in a society can be judged by entering its prisons,' and this applies equally if not more so to the treatment of prisoners of war. It is therefore vital to understanding the nature of the parties involved in the Korean War, as well as being a useful insight into the potential conduct of these parties in future wars in the region.

Treatment of Americans held prisoner by the Asian powers was significantly worse during early stages of the Korean War, as battle lines were constantly changing and North Korean forces were forced to quickly withdraw. Prisoners could only be kept with troops at the constantly moving front, to which supply lines were strained. Food for American captives, as well as for Korean soldiers, was therefore scarce. During long and cold marches accompanying Korean troops, some American soldiers died. As a result of the extensive firebombing campaigns North Korea had been brought to ruin, and Korean civilians were often eager to take revenge against the American military by attacking prisoners. North Korean soldiers often intervened to protect prisoners from civilians. An order of the DPRK's advanced headquarters strictly forbade 'the unnecessary killing of enemy personnel when they could be taken prisoners of war [...] Those who surrender will be taken as prisoners of war.'[95]

The opening months of the war were by far the most difficult for the Americans in North Korean custody, particularly after the Inchon landings and the withdrawal northwards, as no prisoner of war camps could be established and the KPA were hard pressed to feed and clothe even themselves. The vast majority of U.S. prisoners who died, an estimated 90 percent, died in the first year of the war.[96] American reporter Hugh Deane, former Coordinator of Information and naval intelligence officer on General MacArthur's staff, stated that 'during this early chaotic period the plight of the prisoners was often no worse than that of the northern soldiers and people. An unknown number of prisoners were killed along with North Korean civilians when U.S. planes bombed and strafed villages immediately south of the Yalu.'[97]

Evidence indicates that not all North Korean personnel followed orders when it came to sparing prisoners' lives, particularly after seeing the devastation wrought on their country by the scorched earth policies and bombing campaigns. An order given on August 26, 1950, in the 2nd Division stated: 'some of us are still slaughtering enemy troops that come to surrender. Therefore, the responsibility of teaching the soldiers to take prisoners of war and to treat them kindly rests on the Political Section of each unit.'[98] The 'Political Section' referred to the KPA's General Political Bureau which was responsible for exerting political authority over the military and ensuring that it complied with state policy.

As North Korean forces withdrew there was at times a risk that prisoners would either substantially slow the retreat or else fall back into enemy hands. In such cases prisoners were often executed out of strategic necessity, in the traditional military manner with a bullet in the back of the head. There were no reports of sadistic excesses, unprofessionalism or the causing of unnecessary suffering by KPA personnel, but executing prisoners still not only contravened high level orders, but was also a war crime committed at the lower levels of the military. The options of KPA personnel who did choose to disobey their orders in such a way were however highly limited – the only alternative was slowing down and risking death and the hands of the fast pursuing U.S. military or else freeing prisoners and risking their giving away valuable intelligence and seeing these same American soldiers continue the war against them and their people.

Within a year of the war's outbreak fighting was localized to the 38th Parallel and secure prison camps were quickly established behind Chinese and North Korean battle lines. Conditions for American prisoners quickly improved and these camps were opened to press including Western reporters. Though reports of 'communist atrocities' against prisoners were spread by the U.S. military and particularly by General MacArthur's Tokyo Command, they strongly contradicted the reports of the press and the pictures of decently fed smiling prisoners who were allowed exercise – prisoners who Tokyo Command alleged had been slaughtered. As Field Marshal Lord Richard Carver, Britain's former Chief of Defense Staff, observed: 'The UN prisoners in Chinese hands, though subject to "reeducation" processes [...] were better off in every way than any held by the Americans, whether the latter's compounds were dominated by the Communists or by the Korean or Chinese Nationalists (Guomindang).' Reeducation involved communist propaganda and lessons on the 'evils of capitalism' and the history of Western imperialism.[99] Evidence of Chinese or Korean forces slaughtering prisoners at this time was non-existent, and such reports were proven by U.S. reporters themselves to have been fabrications to rouse anti-communist feeling among military personnel who were increasingly coming to view the war as meaningless and among whom morale and the will to fight were quickly dropping.[100,101]

American prisoners reported Chinese prison guards would invite them to their quarters 'for drinking and talking' and liked to play music with them in joint 'jam sessions.'[102] One American prisoner of war, Shelton Foss, recalled regarding his treatment that he alongside his North Korean captors 'played chess, sang American songs ... and talked generally about the U.S. and Korea.'[103] Another U.S. prisoner recalled upon being freed regarding conditions in Chinese camps:

> Prisoners rose at 7 a.m. and either took a short walk or performed light calisthenics. They washed their faces and hands, and at 8 a.m. representatives from each squad drew the appropriate number of rations from the kitchen. Food was cooked by the Chinese and the diet was essentially the same as that provided the Communist soldiers consisting of singular items such as sorghum seed, bean curd, soya bean flour, or cracked corn and on certain special occasions such as Christmas or Lunar New Year, the prisoners received small portions of rice, boiled fatty pork, candy and peanuts.[104]

The *Associated Press* reported on April 12, 1953, as U.S. prisoners were first being released, that 'American soldiers returning from Communist prison camps told a story today of generally good treatment.' One former prisoner, Kenyon Wagner, had much praise for his medical treatment, saying he had been given 'the whole works.' Another former prisoner interviewed, Corporal Theodore Jackson, similarly praised the quality of medical treatment he and his fellow prisoners had received. 'To my idea' he said, 'they did fair, about the best they could do with the medicines they had.' Former British prisoner Arthur Hunt said that there was a daily sick call and prisoners' health was well taken care of, with inoculations given against various diseases. Albert Hawkins, another former British prisoner, said that he had reported his feet were feeling slightly numb, and was carefully attended to and fed vitamin pills as a result. Former prisoner Pfc. William R. Brock Jr. stated that conditions in prison camps were agreeable and he had never seen a prisoner ill-treated. He said that there was no barbed wire around the camps and that each man was issued with a quilt and blanket and their houses had floor heating.[105] Upon examination when returning home, the U.S. Military was surprised by the excellent physical health and low number of fatalities among the prisoners.[106] Statements from American prisoners indicated that interrogation rooms in Chinese and Korean camps were devoid of torture.[107] Thus the contrast between the treatment of the American prisoners by the North Koreans and Chinese, and the treatment of East Asian prisoners by the U.S. and their allies, could not have been starker.

Despite the severe war crimes committed by the American military and their partners in Korea, the North Korean and Chinese leadership made provisions for the humane treatment of prisoners and provided food and sanitation equal to what they provided for their own troops. By contrast to the conduct of Korean and Chinese forces, mistreatment of North Korean and Chinese prisoners by U.S. forces and their allies was widespread and often sadistic. This was however motivated far less by military necessity and more by genuine neglect and at times racial hatred towards prisoners. Renowned British military author and journalist specializing in military affairs Max Hastings found when interviewing American officers that many 'admitted knowledge of, or participation in, the shooting of communist prisoners when it was inconvenient to keep them alive. It is fair to suggest that many UN soldiers did not regard North Korean soldiers as fellow combatants, entitled to humane treatment, but as near animals, to be treated as such.'[108]

One case of such mistreatment was that of Park Sang Hyong, a KPA officer who was repeatedly interrogated, severely beaten, half-starved and kept in solitary confinement. What followed was perhaps more degrading. Park was kept in a six-by-three-foot cage with no walls – only strands of barbed wire. He was given one blanket and no shoes, and left outdoors for three winter months. He recalled after his release: 'I lived like an animal. I collected every scrap of refuse. Every bit of dried grass or grain stalk was a treasure to me. I used everything I could find for padding in my clothes. I burrowed into the dirt like a rabbit and wrapped my feet up with bits of grass, straw, paper and old rags.' Park said he did not believe he would be repatriated, until an ambulance door opened and he saw Korean People's Army uniforms, and a minute later a North Korean general was hugging him.[109]

Conditions for regular North Korean prisoners were similarly inhuman. A British officer noted that U.S. forces treated prisoners 'as cattle' and subjected them to racial abuse. Similarly, 'like animals,' Korean prisoners were often subjects of medical experimentation at the hands of U.S. forces – a severe war crime. They were often operated on to give young surgeons practice – in line with their status as subhumans in the eyes of their captors.[110,111] Hugh Deane noted when reporting this experimentation: 'The American doctors, if they had qualms, could always remind themselves that the purpose was to add to medical knowledge, making possible saving of more lives, and that the victims were inferior beings, gooks to many, near animals to others.'[112]

Experimentation took place in two large military hospitals, the U.S. 14th Field Hospital near the Busan prison camp and the U.S. 64th Field Hospital at Koje. Evidence of this experimentation was collected and analyzed by both China's Xinhua agency and by British and Australian journalists Alan Winnington and Wilfred Burchett. One of their sources was North Korean doctors released after the war, who were then interviewed. It was revealed that three North Korean doctors who had been captured as prisoners were transferred to different camps for complaining about the widespread 'unnecessary amputations' being carried out on Korean prisoners. A fourth doctor who had raised the issue was arrested and never heard from again.

One doctor, Kim Yong Suk, who had been a prisoner at the No. 4 Compound of the 14th field hospital noted that over a period of just 10 months from October 1950 to August 1951 over 4,000 prisoners had died, most of them due to dysentery. He stated:

> We were living in tents, two patients sharing an army stretcher and one blanket. It was bitterly cold. For the first twenty days after my arrival, there was no medical attention at all. Patients were merely ordered to remain on their stretchers [...] Later the dysentery patients began to get treatment that can only be described as experimental – patients in the same stages of disease receiving widely different treatments. One group would be ordered to take 8 sulfadiazine tablets, another group 16 or 24, 32 or up to 48 tablets daily. The maximum liquid they got with the pills was two cups of cold water daily and patients became seriously ill [...] Many patients were also suffering from hunger endema [...] There could be no doubt that it was experimentation to test the effects of very high sulfa intake and many patients died of sulfa poisoning.[113]

Dr Kim continued: 'Schistosomiasis [a disease caused by parasitic worms in the intestines] cases were not treated at all, but were examined under the direction of an American, Dr. Berry, who was interested only in determining the distributions and localization of this disease.' Another Korean doctor, Park Chu Bong, was barred from the surgical section at Pusan after protesting the severe misconduct of medical staff towards North Korean prisoners. He recalled that limbs stiff from lack of exercise or from having just been released from plaster casts were amputated.[114]

The former chief of the Korean People's Army 10th Division Hospital, Dr Rhee Tok Ki, was removed for surgery after his capture for protesting malpractices. He noted: 'This hospital had no floors in the tents. Twenty patients were packed onto stretchers into each tent as close as they could be fitted. Air circulation was very poor. There was no regular medical treatment [...] Patients went where they wanted for toilet needs. Later they built their own toilet. There was no purified water. If we POW medical assistants asked too often for drugs, or if the American doctor was in a bad mood, or didn't like the patient, we would be taken off and beaten up for "agitation." [...] Twice daily and nightly patients were forced to strip naked to prove they had no concealed weapons or "propaganda."'[115] Sanitary conditions in Korean camps were so poor that there were often outbreaks of disease, primarily forms of dysentery. Prisoners held on Koje Island by U.S. forces described the state of their captivity in a letter they signed in 1952: 'Koje Island is a living hell. The shores of this island are no longer washed by sea water, but by our tears and blood. There is no breath of fresh air here, the pungent stench of blood fills our nostrils in every corner of the island.'[116]

From January 1951 to August 1952 around 2,700 patients died in captivity, mostly from prolonged starvation and lack of medical treatment. The results of the mistreatment of prisoners became clear when prisoners were exchanged at Panmunjom near the end of the war. American journalist Hugh Deane reported on this:

> The American ambulances and trucks bringing wounded and ill prisoners to the exchange site at Panmunjom were an appalling sight – many were emaciated and so many lacked one or more limbs. The American correspondents heard their angry words and press conferences but knew better than to report them. Accompanying interviews confirmed and added details to the American shame. For some months what passed for hospitals were thin mats in tents. There was little or no organized sanitation, rarely latrines, no water purification. Teams of young surgeons arrived every few months, served several months and were replaced. They operated in surgeries from which other medical personnel were barred and performed many amputations, on occasion as many as five or six on a single prisoner. Repeated amputations were performed on a single limb. Of 170 chest operations on prisoners suffering from bronchitis or pleurisy, between April 1951 and July 1952 only 37 survived.[117]

Reports of the dire conditions faced by the Koreans and Chinese and their widespread mistreatment when in Western custody also emerged from the *American Medical Association*. In two articles from the 1953 March and April editions the treatment of 1,408 cases of acute amoebic dysentery at Koje was described. In lieu of treatment, an experiment was carried out. One group of patients was given no treatment, only bed rest, nutritional supplements, sedatives and fluid replacement. They were not expected to recover, only to act as a control group for the experiment. These 66 patients were essentially denied any real treatment. The other five groups were given five different drugs in various dosages, the effects of which were closely monitored. This methodology was clearly one of experimentation rather than treatment.

A report from *The American Journal of Tropical Medicine and Hygiene* similarly showed that the primary concern towards sick prisoners was experimentation rather that treatment. One epidemic at Koje resulted in 19,320 hospitalizations and a very high 9 percent fatality rate – 1,729 deaths. This was referred to as '150 epidemics in one.' It was inexplicably not reported to Washington for four months. Treatments varied greatly, and some 1,600 cases of the same disease followed 18 different treatment and dosage schedules. The article noted: 'the Korean outbreak demonstrated again that an epidemic situation provides the opportunity to accumulate valuable scientific data very rapidly.' This seemed to be the priority, rather than the wellbeing of the Korean and Chinese patients. The conduct of the United States towards prisoners was a war crime contrary to the Geneva Convention, which in Articles 13 and 19 stated that medical or scientific experimentation on prisoners against their will was forbidden, and that detaining powers were 'bound to take all sanitary measures necessary to ensure the cleanliness and healthfulness of camps and to prevent epidemics.'

Separate crimes were committed against Korean women, who often fought alongside men in the KPA and of whom there were many among the prisoners of war. Women were particularly singled out for abuse by their captors. Pulitzer Prize winning American historian John Tolland, the war's contemporary, described this in his own study. He stated in one case: 'One girl, Kim Kyung Suk, told how they had forced a group of women prisoners into a large room. Here they were stripped. Then nude male North Korean prisoners were shoved in. "We heard you Communists like to dance", an American shouted.

"Go on! Dance!" They pointed bayonets and revolvers at the prisoners, who began to dance, while drunken, cigar smoking, guffawing American officers stubbed out cigars on the girls' breasts and committed indecencies.'[118]

Alan Winnington and Wilfred Burchett, who were present in Korea during the prisoner exchange, witnessed the stark contrast in the health of prisoners from either side being exchanged and the quality of treatment they had received. They described the North Korean prisoners being returned to their country as: 'Haggard, with faces dank and moist like corpses, bearing the hideous mutilations of experimental surgery, some vacant eyed, girls driven mad by attempted rapes [...] Half of the prisoners in many ambulances were lacking legs, often both legs. Even men missing two legs and without artificial ones were not treated by the Americans as stretcher cases, so plentiful were amputees. In a single hour it was possible to see six people delivered who lacked all four limbs – hacked back to mere torsos.'[119] They noted the stark contrast this bore to the treatment of Americans in Chinese and Korean custody. For example they noted that the Koreans and Chinese had given even those U.S. prisoners with minor leg injuries a stretcher.[120] It is highly indicative that the treatment of Korean and Chinese prisoners in the custody of what was by far the world's richest nation was far poorer and conditions including accommodation, food and above all medication were far worse that those provided by war torn and impoverished East Asian communist nations to the Americans in their custody.

Despite their harrowing experiences in American camps, General MacArthur had said to President Truman in October 1950 regarding the treatment of prisoners of war: 'The prisoners are the happiest Koreans in Korea. They are clean and well-fed for the first time.'[121] While this proved to be wholly untrue, as the war neared its end prisoners increasingly became critical to the United States' strategic interests. Specifically, when it was clear that the war could not be won, the United States attempted to win a moral victory for the Western-led 'free world' by demonstrating the unpopularity of communism. To this end it became important to depict the prisoners as reluctant to return to their communist homelands in North Korea and China – and thus demonstrate the superiority of life in the 'free world.' Attempts to win a moral victory in this way led to major prisoner repatriation issues, as the United States claimed that as they believed prisoners did not want to return home, they would not be repatriated. CIA Director Allen Dulles declared that the issue of repatriation of prisoners of war was 'one of the greatest psychological victories so far achieved by the free world against communism.'[122]

Looking at the circumstances surrounding the prisoner repatriation issue, and the alleged unwillingness of prisoners to return home, there is significant evidence that there was substantial and often brutal coercion used to ensure that prisoners would agree to refuse repatriation in order to give the 'free world' the affirmation of their moral superiority which they so needed to compensate for military failure.

In early April 1952, during peace talks with the Chinese and North Koreans, American estimates projected that 116,000 prisoners would be repatriated and only a very small number would refuse to return home. The two Asian powers had accepted this figure and peace talks continued to go forwards. However the U.S. revised their approach drastically in only two weeks, altering this figure to only 70,000 prisoners, which stunned the Chinese and Korean negotiators and meant a loss of 46,000 men. The *New York Times* reported at the time that a quick solution to the issue of war prisoners was upset – something which would stall the end of the war substantially.

Hugh Deane reported on the American strategy to turn military failure into a moral victory as follows based on his own investigation:

> Reduced estimates reflected the results of savage coercion in the compounds. President Truman and an increasing number of others in the leadership had come to envisage a substitute for the victory the U.S. had failed to win on the battlefield – a propaganda triumph in line with the rollback doctrine that was prevailing over mere containment. An impressive number of prisoners were to refuse adamantly and publicly to go home to the communist evils awaiting them.
>
> To do the brunt of the dirty work in selected compounds (there were 32 of them on Koje, all overcrowded) the U.S. secured some 75 persuaders from Taiwan, mostly from Chiang Kaishek's equivalent of the Gestapo, and a larger number of members of terrorist youth groups sent in by the Syngman Rhee government. Some wore neat American uniforms, others were posing as prisoners ... Their continuing task was to locate prisoners who wished repatriation and to do whatever was necessary to dissuade them. Control of the food supplies was a powerful means, and that, threats, beatings, slashings and the killing of the most stubborn, led to a gratifying number who muttered 'Taiwan, Taiwan, Taiwan' when asked the key question ... Thus many

> Chinese who didn't want to go to Taiwan found themselves there. Of the Chinese prisoners 6,670 were repatriated to China, 14,235 were sent to Taiwan.[123]

Deane's report on the brutal coercion used to persuade prisoners to refuse repatriation was strongly supported by U.S. Admiral Charles Turner Joy, the chief negotiator in the peace talks. Joy wrote in his diary, citing army interpreters, that those communists who expressed a wish to return home at a preliminary screening were 'either beaten black and blue or killed [...] the majority of the PWs [same as POWs] were too terrified to frankly express their real choice. All they could say in answer to the question was "Taiwan" repeated over and over again.'[124]

Comparisons of prison camps where Chinese and North Korean personnel were held to Nazi concentration camps were common in internal U.S. reports.[125] John Muccio, U.S. Ambassador to the ROK, himself alleged that the Taiwanese representatives involved in repatriation were 'members of Chiang Kai-shek's Gestapo.' He passed on reports that Chinese prisoners were being forced to sign petitions in blood and undergo tattooing to prove they were anti-communists and wanted to go to Taiwan. One report from a prison stated, regarding the harsh enforcement of this policy: 'In early 1952, the brigade leader, Li Da'an, wanted to tattoo every prisoner in Compound 72 with an anti-Communist slogan [...] He ordered the prison guards to beat those who refused the tattoo in front of the five thousands prisoners. Some of those who couldn't stand the beatings gave up and agreed to the tattoo. One prisoner, however, Lin Xuepu, continued to refuse the tattoo. Li Da'an finally dragged Lin up to the stage, and in a loud voice asked Lin: "Do you want it or not?" Bleeding and barely able to stand up, Lin, a nineteen-year-old college freshman, replied with a loud "No!" Li Da'an responded by cutting off one of Lin's arms with his big dagger. Lin screamed but still shook his head when Li repeated the question. Humiliated and angry, Li followed by stabbing Lin with his dagger [...] Li yelled to all the prisoners in the field: "whoever dares to refuse the tattoo will be like him."'[126,127]

U.S. State Department officers A. Sabin Chase and Philip Mansard were sent to Korea to ascertain why such large numbers of prisoners refused repatriation. They concluded in their report that the main reason was 'violent tactics of the PW (POW) trustees before and during the screening process.' They reported a 'police state type of rule' over the Chinese prisoner compounds and that prisoners were not only subjected to an 'information blockade,' but also that physical terror including organized threats, beatings and murders before and during the polling process were all widespread. While the investigation found substantial evidence of coercion, they did not find any significant lack of support for the Chinese communist government or the People's Liberation Army among Chinese prisoners.[128]

North Korean doctor Rhee Tok Ki concurrently reported that ill patients were harassed to the detriment of their recovery to ensure that they would refuse repatriation. He stated: 'TB patients especially need rest, but they were hounded day and night as a sort of specially refined torture to get them to renounce repatriation.'[129]

The Red Cross similarly reported 'some very grave incidents' regarding the treatment of communist prisoners, particularly surrounding the issue of prisoner repatriation and coercion. Though reporters were not allowed near prison camps, one reporter for the *Toronto Star* managed to enter with a British delegation. His report affirmed that the prisoners were choosing not to be repatriated due to 'physical threats, often carried out.' In some cases prisoners were instead given the option either to remain imprisoned indefinitely or to go to Taiwan, and so voted to go to Taiwan based on false information.[130] The final report by the Neutral Nations Repatriation Commission gave the same conclusion, that 'any prisoner who desired repatriation had to do so clandestinely and in fear for his life.'[131]

A U.S. prisoner imprisoned in a Chinese camp, Howard Adams, reported not only the far better treatment of prisoners in Chinese and Korean camps compared to those of the United States and their partners, but also of the mishandling of peace talks and extensive coercion of prisoners by U.S. forces. He recalled in an interview: 'the [American] prisoners' hopes soared when the peace talks began. We thought we'd be free soon. The Chinese thought so too at one point and gave us a feast, but the talks dragged on and on as the U.S. side made ridiculous demands regarding prisoners and other issues.' Adams strongly opposed the treatment of Chinese prisoners, who he alleged were subjected to immense pressure to defect, and as a result many Chinese families never found out what happened to their sons.[132]

Ultimately not only was there rampant abuse, murder and scientific experimentation performed on prisoners, but also unnecessary and severe bodily mutilation, sexual abuse of female prisoners, a lack of sanitation or conditions fit for human beings, and extensive coercion to prevent prisoners from returning home. The moral victory of the Western 'free world' over communism in Korea, referred to in most Western histories of the Korean War as a key event, was truly a hollow one which reflected not the moral superiority of the United States and their partners, but rather their true depravity and the hollowness of their claims to represent any sort of 'free world.'

The Consistency of Reports on U.S. War Crimes and Implications for a Future Korean War

While the war crimes committed by the United States and their allies are a scarcely known phenomenon outside North Korea, they remain a critical factor in shaping the country's perception of the U.S. and their intentions until today. What many researchers from the United States and South Korea have termed a genocide is essential to understanding both the motives for North Korean foreign policy since 1950 and the potential impacts of American military intervention in the Asia-Pacific region in future – both on allied and enemy populations. Based on facts corroborated by numerous sources, American, British, Australian, South Korean and predominantly Western international commissions, which have been highly consistent, as well as similar conduct displayed both against Japan five years prior and in Vietnam throughout the following decade and beyond, the reports on the atrocities which were carried out against the North Korean people remain highly credible.

Indeed, considering the conduct of the U.S. military against those under its power even in more recent conflicts, the claims made by international observers and journalists seem entirely consistent. Examples include American soldiers found to have taken girls as young as 12 as sex slaves in

Yugoslavia in the 1990s,[133,134] or the sadistic horrors and sexual tortures reported to have been carried out at the hands of U.S. soldiers at Abu Ghraib prison in Iraq, including against young children, which according to photographic[135] and video[136] evidence and testimonies from both U.S. journalists[137] and members of the military[138,139] show conduct extremely similar to that carried out against the North Korean people – though on a far smaller scale as fitting with a lower key and less brutal war. As renowned U.S. journalist Seymour Hersh, who had been involved in uncovering the My Lai massacre in Vietnam, said when given full access to the recordings of abuses by U.S. personnel: 'You haven't begun to see evil [...] horrible things done to children of women prisoners, as the cameras run.'[140] There was substantial photographic evidence of soldiers sodomizing prisoners with broomsticks and chemical lights and raping young boys in front of their families[141,142] – though the vast majority of evidence has been withheld as, according to the then President Obama, they would 'inflame anti-American public opinion.'[143] Western militaries have shown themselves to be particularly brutal in their conduct towards those under their power relative to those of other nations – prominent examples being the gross misconduct, mass rapes and sexual sadism committed by French,[144] Belgian, Canadian[145] and Italian soldiers[146] under UN command in Africa, including mass child rapes, proliferation of illegal drugs, and even forced bestiality for children.[147] This was a stark contrast to soldiers from nations such as Bangladesh on the very same UN missions who, according to the *New York Times*, conducted themselves with distinction relative to the Western militaries and had even minor infringements harshly punished.[148]

While this has not been exclusive to Western nations, with the Chinese Guomindang's conduct towards the native Polynesian inhabitants of Taiwan[149,150,151] or the Suharto government's conduct to the East Timorese[152,153] having been results of a similar sense of superiority, the West has proven to be the most frequent and historically by far the most consistent perpetrator of such atrocities against subjugated peoples – and has done so with an arguably far greater severity. Having committed numerous genocides for centuries, including effectively wiping out the indigenous populations of three continents, and doing so employing means unheard of by other peoples or nations, their conduct remains outstanding until today in its depravity. Indeed, the conduct during the brief occupation of North Korea closely resembles that shown on numerous other occasions from the genocides against Native Americans and the indigenous people of Australia centuries before to the conduct towards the Japanese just five years before – and the conduct towards the Vietnamese both by the French Empire which coincided with the Korean War and by the United States which began shortly afterwards. There is a degree of consistency in wars with those the West deems 'savages' and 'racial inferiors' which makes the claims of misconduct in Korea difficult to dismiss.

As demonstrated by the Korean and Vietnam Wars and other smaller conflicts involving Western military powers such as America's war against insurgents in the Philippines where claims of genocide were also widespread, when the Western Bloc goes to war in Asia all people are seen as the enemy – and a Western military presence in the region is thus a danger to civilians on all sides, whether governed by a U.S. client or ally or a hostile enemy. Orders to massacre South Korean civilians, and the genocide simultaneously committed against North Korea's population, presents but one example of how the people of neither side are safe – and the threat to all Asia-Pacific peoples however their governments may be aligned remains one and the same. A future Korean War would almost certainly entail such conduct. Indeed, it is precisely because of the Western powers' record of conduct towards subjugated peoples abroad, consistent over several centuries, that their military presence in the Asia-Pacific is so dangerous for the region's peoples. Should war break out it is highly likely that such conduct will be repeated.

Notes

1 Meger, Sara, *Rape Loot Pillage: The Political Economy of Sexual Violence in Armed Conflict*, Oxford, Oxford University Press (p. 61).

2 Kim, Dong-Choon, 'Forgotten war, forgotten massacres – the Korean War (1950–1953) as licensed mass killings,' *Journal of Genocide Research*, vol. 6, issue 4, December 2004 (p. 523–544).

3 Tremblay, Regis, *Ghosts of Cheju* (Documentary), 2013.
4 Stokesbury, James L., *A Short History of the Korean War*, New York, William Morrow and Company, 1988 (p. 39, 42–43).
5 Gould, Dudley C., *Follow Me UP Fool's Mountain: Korea, 1951,'* Southfarm Press, Middletown, Conneticut, 2002 (p. 76).
6 Williams, Jeremy, "Kill 'Em All": The American Military in Korea,' *BBC.*
7 Han, Suyin (penname of Elizabeth Comber), *Love is a Many Splendored Thing*, London, Jonathan Cape, 1952 (p. 342 and 349).
8 '"Kill 'Em All": American War Crimes in Korea,' *Timewatch*, 2002.
9 Ibid.
10 Ibid.
11 Ibid.
12 Williams, Jeremy, "Kill 'Em All": The American Military in Korea,' *BBC.*
13 Hanley, Charles J., Choe, Sang Hun and Mendoza, Martha, *The Bridge at No Gun Ri: A Hidden Nightmare from the Korean War*, New York, Henry Holt and Company, 2001 (p. 126).
14 Williams, Jeremy, "Kill 'Em All": The American Military in Korea,' *BBC.*
15 Hanley, Charles J. and Choe, Sang Hun and Mendoza, Martha, *The Bridge at No Gun Ri: A Hidden Nightmare from the Korean War*, New York, Henry Holt and Company, 2001 (p. 129).
16 '"Kill 'Em All": American War Crimes in Korea,' *Timewatch*, 2002.
17 Ibid.
18 Ibid.
19 Ibid.
20 Hanley, Charles J., Choe, Sang Hun and Mendoza, Martha, *The Bridge at No Gun Ri: A Hidden Nightmare from the Korean War*, New York, Henry Holt and Company, 2001 (p. 142).
21 '"Kill 'Em All": American War Crimes in Korea,' *Timewatch*, 2002.
22 Hanley, Charles J. and Choe, Sang Hun and Mendoza, Martha, *The Bridge at No Gun Ri: A Hidden Nightmare from the Korean War*, New York, Henry Holt and Company, 2001 (pp. 140–141).
23 Williams, Jeremy, "Kill 'Em All": The American Military in Korea,' *BBC.*
24 Cumings, Bruce, *The Korean War: A History*, New York, Modern Library, 2010 (p. 189).
25 '"Kill 'Em All": American War Crimes in Korea,' *Timewatch*, (Documentary), February 1, 2002.
26 Hanley, Charles J. and Choe, Sang Hun and Mendoza, Martha, *The Bridge at No Gun Ri: A Hidden Nightmare from the Korean War*, New York, Henry Holt and Company, 2001 (p. 246).
27 *Chosun Minbo*, August 19, 1950.

28 Choe, Sang-Hun, 'Korean War Panel Finds U.S. Attacks on Civilians,' *New York Times*, July 9, 2010.
29 Straub, David, *Anti Americanism in Democratizing South Korea*, Stanford, CA, Shorenstein Asia-Pacific Research Center, 2015 (p. 65).
30 Williams, Jeremy, "Kill 'Em All": The American Military in Korea,' *BBC*.
31 Hanley, Charles J. and Choe, Sang Hun and Mendoza, Martha, *The Bridge at No Gun Ri: A Hidden Nightmare from the Korean War*, New York, Henry Holt and Company, 2001.
32 Choe, Sang-Hun, 'Korean War Panel Finds U.S. Attacks on Civilians,' *New York Times*, July 9, 2010.
33 Williams, Jeremy, "Kill 'Em All": The American Military in Korea,' *BBC*.
34 *Washington Post*, September 30, 1999 (p. 1), October 14 (p. 14), December 29 (p. 19).
35 Hanley, Charles J. and Choe, Sang Hun and Mendoza, Martha, *The Bridge at No Gun Ri: A Hidden Nightmare from the Korean War*, New York, Henry Holt and Company, 2001 (p. 151).
36 '"Kill 'Em All": American War Crimes in Korea,' *Timewatch*, February 1, 2002.
37 Hanley, Charles J. and Choe, Sang Hun and Mendoza, Martha, *The Bridge at No Gun Ri: A Hidden Nightmare from the Korean War*, New York, Henry Holt and Company, 2001 (p. 188, 189).
38 Ibid. (p. 133).
39 Ibid. (p. 163, 187).
40 Ibid. (p. 164).
41 Comprehensive Report, Volume 1, Part I, Truth and Reconciliation Commission of the Republic of Korea, December 2010 (p. 121).
42 '"Kill 'Em All": American War Crimes in Korea,' *Timewatch*, February 1, 2002.
43 Williams, Jeremy, "Kill 'Em All": The American Military in Korea,' *BBC*, February 17, 2011.
44 Hanley, Charles J. and Choe, Sang Hun and Mendoza, Martha, *The Bridge at No Gun Ri: A Hidden Nightmare from the Korean War*, New York, Henry Holt and Company, 2001 (p. 177, 163, 195, 183).
45 Ibid. (p. 176, 181).
46 *Report on U.S. Crimes in Korea*, Commission of International Association of Democratic Lawyers, March 31, 1952 (p. 21).
47 Blakely, Ruth, *State Terrorism and Neoliberalism: The North in the South*, Abingdon, Routledge, 2009 (p. 87).
48 Gil, Yoon-hyeong, 'U.S.'s Yongsan bombing of 1950 caused 1,587 civilian deaths U.S. air raids accounted for 25 percent of civilian deaths in the first 3 months of the war,' *Hankyoreh*, July 16, 2010.
49 Mao, Zedong, *Directive to the Chinese People's Volunteers: The Chinese People's Volunteers Should Cherish Every Hill, Every River, Every Tree and Every Blade*

of Grass in Korea, January 19, 1951 in *Selected Words of Mao Tsetung, Volume V*, Oxford, Pergamon Press, 1977 (p. 44).
50 'Koreans Watch U. N. Murder Trial as Test of Curb on Unruly Behavior,' *New York Times*, August 21, 1951.
51 Zhang, Shu Guang, *Mao's Military Romanticism: China and the Korean War, 1950–1953*, Lawrence, University Press of Kansas, 1995 (p. 529).
52 Hanley, Charles J. and Choe, Sang Hun and Mendoza, Martha, *The Bridge at No Gun Ri: A Hidden Nightmare from the Korean War*, New York, Henry Holt and Company, 2001 (pp. 195–196).
53 Pollock, Sandra, *Let the Good Times Roll: Prostitution and the U.S. Military in Asia*, New York, New Press, 1992 (pp. 172–173).
54 Hanley, Charles J. and Choe, Sang Hun and Mendoza, Martha, *The Bridge at No Gun Ri: A Hidden Nightmare from the Korean War*, New York, Henry Holt and Company, 2001 (pp. 195–196).
55 Ibid. (pp. 195–196).
56 De Haan, Francisca, *The Women's International Democratic Federation (WIDF): History, Main Agenda, and Contributions, 1945–1991*, Women and Social Movements, International-1840 to Present, Central European University, 2012.
57 Brown, Sarah, 'Pleading the Fifth,' *BBC News*, February 5, 2002.
58 Harden, Blaine, 'The U.S. war crime North Korea won't forget,' *Washington Post*, March 24, 2015.
59 'Sinchon Accuses the U.S. Barbarians,' 2002, Pyongyang Cultural Preservation Center. Also see records at Sinchon's Museum of American War Atrocities.
60 Hanley, Charles J. and Choe, Sang Hun and Mendoza, Martha, *The Bridge at No Gun Ri: A Hidden Nightmare from the Korean War*, New York, Henry Holt and Company, 2001 (pp. 195–196).
61 Cumings, Bruce, *The Korean War: A History*, New York, Modern Library, 2010 (p. 168, 181).
62 *The Times* (UK), December 18, 21 and 22, 1950.
63 *Report on U.S. Crimes in Korea*, Commission of International Association of Democratic Lawyers, March 31, 1952 (p. 20).
64 Ibid. (p. 18).
65 Ibid. (p. 19, 20).
66 'Sinchon Accuses the U.S. Barbarians,' 2002, Pyongyang Cultural Preservation Center. Also see records at Sinchon's Museum of American War Atrocities.
67 Winnington, Alan, *Breakfast With Mao: Memoirs of a Foreign Correspondent*, London, Lawrence and Wishart, 1986 (p. 128).
68 Cumings, Bruce, *The Korean War: A History*, New York, Modern Library, 2010 (p. 84).
69 Parrott, Lindesay, 'Peiking Radio is Busy,' *New York Times*, October 12, 1951.
70 Fromson, Murray, 'Parallels in Crisis,' *Saturday Review*, June 1, 1968 (p. 29).

71 'Mouthpiece for the Reds: The Strange Role of Wilfred Burchett,' *U.S. News and World Report*, February 27, 1967 (pp. 19–20).
72 Burchett, Wilfred, *At the Barricades*, London, Quartet Books, 1971 (pp. 274–79). (In the introduction to the book, Harrison Salisbury described Burchett as a 'well-informed, useful source and a warm and decent friend.')
73 Winnington, Alan, and Burchett, Wilfred, *Plain Perfidy, The Plot to Wreck the Korea Peace*, Britain-China Friendship Association, 1954 (p. 69, 71).
74 Ibid. (pp. 71–72).
75 Jenks, John, 'The Enemy Within: Journalism, the State and the Limits of Dissent in Cold War Britain, 1950–1951,' *American Journalism* 18, no. 1, winter, 2001.
76 Carter, Dave, and Clifton, Robin, *War and Cold War in American Foreign Policy, 1942–1962*, London, Palgrave Macmillan, 2002 (pp. 159–160).
77 Kim, Dong-Choon, 'Forgotten war, forgotten massacres – the Korean War (1950–1953) as licensed mass killings,' *Journal of Genocide Research*, vol. 6, issue 4, December 2004 (p. 523–544).
78 *Report on U.S. Crimes in Korea*, Commission of International Association of Democratic Lawyers, March 31, 1952 (p. 18).
79 Ibid. (p. 21).
80 Ibid. (p. 21).
81 Remarks of President Bill Clinton, Dedication of Korean War Memorial, Washington D.C., July 27, 1995.
82 Kim, Dong-Choon, 'Forgotten war, forgotten massacres – the Korean War (1950–1953) as licensed mass killings,' *Journal of Genocide Research*, vol. 6, issue 4, December 2004 (p. 523–544).
83 Chossudovsky, Michael, Presentation to the Japanese Foreign Correspondents Club on U.S. Aggression against the People of Korea, Tokyo, August 1, 2013 (<https://off-guardian.org/2017/05/08/video-u-s-crimes-of-genocide-against-korea/>).
84 Hynes, Patricia, 'The Korean War: Forgotten, Unknown and Unfinished,' *Truthout*, July 12, 2013.
85 Cumings, Bruce, *The Korean War: A History*, New York, Modern Library, 2010 (p. 154).
86 *We Accuse*, Report of the Committee of the Women's International Democratic Federation in Korea, May 16–27, 1951.
87 Ibid.
88 Ibid.
89 Denney, Steven, 'Speaking the Truth to Power: Canadian War Crimes in Korea,' *The Diplomat*, November 3, 2014.
90 Ibid.
91 Ibid.
92 Morris, David J., 'War Is Hell, and the Hell Rubs Off,' *Slate*, April 17, 2014.

93 Green, Bonnie L., *Trauma Interventions in War and Peace: Prevention, Practice, and Policy*, New York, Springer, 2003 (pp. 274–275).
94 Alvarez, Alex, *Governments, Citizens, and Genocide: A Comparative and Interdisciplinary Approach*, Bloomington, Indiana University Press, 2001 (p. 15).
95 Hastings, Max, *The Korean War*, New York, Simon and Schuster, 1987 (p. 298)
96 Ibid.
97 Ibid.
98 Cumings, Bruce, *Origins of the Korean War: Liberation and the Emergence of Separate Regimes, 1945–1947, Vol. 1*, Yeogsabipyeongsa Publishing Co, 2004 (pp. 702–703).
99 Deane, Hugh, *The Korean War, 1945–1953*, San Francisco, CA, China Books and Periodicals, 1999 (p. 164).
100 Stone, I. F., Hidden History of the Korean War, Amazon Media, 2014, (Chapter 45: 'Atrocities to the Rescue').
101 Stone, I. F., Hidden History of the Korean War, Amazon Media, 2014, (Chapter 46: 'Weird Statistics').
102 Paschall, Rod, *Witness to War: Korea*, New York, Perigee Trade, 1995 (p. 173).
103 Sayre, George, 950774-RECAP-K, Intelligence Document File, Assistant Chief of Staff, G-2, Intelligence, Box 1025, RG 0319 Army Staff, NARA, College Park, Maryland.
104 Kim, Monica, *The Interrogation Rooms of the Korean War; The Untold History*, Princeton, NJ, Princeton University Press, 2019. (p. 330).
105 Winnington, Alan, and Burchett, Wilfred, *Plain Perfidy, The Plot to Wreck the Korea Peace*, Britain-China Friendship Association, 1954 (p. 19).
106 Mayer, William E., Beyond the Call: Memoirs of a Medical Visionary, vol. 1, Albuquerque, Mayer Publishing Group International, 2009, (p. 350).)
107 Kim, Monica, The Interrogation Rooms of the Korean War; The Untold History, Princeton, NJ, Princeton University Press, 2019. (p. 338).)
108 Deane, Hugh, *The Korean War, 1945–1953*, San Francisco, CA, China Books and Periodicals, 1999 (p. 166).
109 Ibid.
110 Winnington, Alan, and Burchett, Wilfred, *Plain Perfidy, The Plot to Wreck the Korea Peace*, Britain-China Friendship Association, 1954 (several severe medical malpractices detailed, particularly in Chapter X).
111 Williams, Peter, and Wallace, David, *Unit 731; Japan's Secret Biological Warfare in World War II*, The Free Press (British edn.), 1989 (pp. 385–387) (citing Associated Press).
112 Deane, Hugh, *The Korean War, 1945–1953*, San Francisco, CA, China Books and Periodicals, 1999 (p. 176).

113 Ibid. (p. 177).
114 Ibid.
115 Ibid. (p. 178).
116 Ibid. (p. 166).
117 Ibid. (p. 178).
118 Toland, John, *In Mortal Combat: Korea, 1950–1953*, New York, William Morrow & Co., 1991.
119 Winnington, Alan, and Burchett, Wilfred, *Plain Perfidy, The Plot to Wreck the Korea Peace*, Britain-China Friendship Association, 1954 (p. 9).
120 Ibid. (p. 19).
121 Substance of Statements Made at Wake Island Conference on 15 October 1950, compiled by General of the Army Omar N. Bradley, Chairman of the Joint Chiefs of Staff.
122 Memorandum of discussion at the 181st meeting of the NSC, January 21, 1954; Eisenhower Library, Eisenhower papers, Whitman file.
123 Deane, Hugh, *The Korean War, 1945–1953*, San Francisco, CA, China Books and Periodicals, 1999 (p. 167).
124 Joy, C. Turner, and Goodman, Allan E., *Negotiating While Fighting: Diary of Admiral C. Turner Joy at the Korean Armistice Conference*, Stanford, CA, Hoover Institution Press, 1978 (p. 116).
125 Carruthers, Susan Lisa, C*old War Captives: Imprisonment, Escape and Brainwashing*, Oakland, University of California Press, 2009 (p. 125).
126 Westad, Odd Arne, *The Cold War; A World History*, London, Allen Lane 2017 (p. 180).
127 Peters, Richard, and Li, Xiaobing, *Voices from the Korean War: Personal Stories of American, Korean and Chinese soldiers*, Lexington, University Press of Kentucky, 2005 (pp. 244–245).
128 Foot, Rosemary, *A Substitute for Victory: Politics of Peacemaking at the Korean Armistice talks*, Ithaca, NY, Cornell University Press, 1990 (pp. 120–121).
129 Deane, Hugh, *The Korean War, 1945–1953*, San Francisco, CA, China Books and Periodicals, 1999 (p. 178).
130 Ibid. (p. 178, 169).
131 Young, Charles S., *Name, Rank, and Serial Number: Exploiting Korean War POWs at Home and Abroad*, Oxford, Oxford University Press, 2014 (p. 89).
132 Deane, Hugh, *Good Deeds & Gunboats*, San Francisco, CA, China Books & Periodicals, 1990 (Chapter 22).
133 Vine, David, *Base Nation, How U.S. Military Bases Abroad Harm America and the World*, New York, Henry Holt and Company, 2015 (Chapter 9, 'Sex for Sale,' Section 5, 'Sold Hourly, Nightly or Permanently').

134 O'Meara, Kelly Patricia, 'US: DynCorp Disgrace,' *Insight Magazine*, January 14, 2002.
135 Gardham, Duncan, and Cruickshank, Paul, 'Abu Ghraib abuse photos "show rape",' *The Daily Telegraph*, May 28, 2009.
136 Higham, Scott, and Stephens, Joe, 'New Details of Prison Abuse Emerge,' *Washington Post*, May 21, 2004, (p. A01).
137 Sealey, Geraldine, 'Hersh: Children sodomized at Abu Ghraib, on tape,' *Salon* July 15, 2004.
138 Harding, Luke, 'After Abu Ghraib,' *The Guardian*, September 20, 2004.
139 Taguba, Antonio, '"The Taguba Report" On Treatment Of Abu Ghraib Prisoners In Iraq,' *Findlaw.com*, May 2004.
140 Sealey, Geraldine, 'Hersh: Children sodomized at Abu Ghraib, on tape,' *Salon*, July 15, 2004.
141 Taguba, Antonio, '"The Taguba Report" On Treatment Of Abu Ghraib Prisoners In Iraq,' *Findlaw.com*, May 2004.
142 Higham, Scott, and Stephens, Joe, 'New Details of Prison Abuse Emerge,' *Washington Post*, May 21, 2004 (p. A01).
143 Gardham, Duncan, and Cruickshank, Paul, 'Abu Ghraib abuse photos "show rape",' *The Daily Telegraph*, May 28, 2009.
144 '"Horribly possible": More child-rape cases by peacekeepers could emerge – UN,' *RT*, May 2, 2015.
145 'Photos reveal Belgian paratroopers' abuse in Somalia,' *CNN*, April 17, 1997.
146 'Italy Says Its Soldiers Tortured Somalis,' *New York Times*, August 9, 1997.
147 '"Forced sex with dog": 98 Central African Rep. girls report shocking abuse by UN peacekeepers,' *RT*, April 1, 2016.
148 Crossette, Barbara, 'The World: When Peacekeepers Turn Into Troublemakers,' *New York Times*, January 7, 1996.
149 *Los Angeles Times*, February 24, 1992.
150 Anderson, Scott, and Anderson, Jon Lee, *Inside the League: The Shocking Expose of How Terrorists, Nazis, and Latin American Death Squads Have Infiltrated the World Anti-Communist League*, New York, Dodd Mead, 1986 (pp. 47–49).
151 Hutchings, Graham, *Modern China, A Guide to a Century of Change*, Cambridge, MA, Harvard University Press, 2001 (p. 259).
152 Harris Rimmer, Susan, *Gender and Transitional Justice: The Women of East Timor*, Abingdon, Routledge, 2012 (p. 16).
153 *Los Angeles Times*, October 13, 1989 (p. A6).

CHAPTER 11

The U.S. Military in South Korea: Comfort Women and Destitution

> If someone called attention to the ceaseless orgy, all the usual bromine pour forth to drown out the faint cries of peasant girls yanked off a train in Seoul and thrown into a brothel, a thousand little justifications for the abasement of a thousand little girls at American hands ... the social construction of every Korea female as a potential object of pleasure for Americans. It is the most important aspect of the whole relationship and the primary memory of Korea for generations of young American men who have served there.[1]
>
> — BRUCE CUMINGS

The Western Role in Determining the Future of Governance in South Korea and Korean Independence

In 1882 the United States and the ruling Choson dynasty of Korea signed the Shufeldt Treaty, the first article of which stipulated that should either nation be subjected to 'unjust or oppressive' treatment by a third party the other would intervene on its behalf. The British Empire signed a similar treaty the following year, the United Kingdom-Korea Treaty. By the late 1890s Japan made no secret of its plans to incorporate Korea into its growing empire, part of its effort to become a 'civilized nation' and imperial power with overseas colonies following the European example. King Kojong, the last Korean king, sent emissaries to Washington in 1896 and 1905 requesting American assistance to ensure Korea's independence, which under the US-Korea treaty they were obliged to provide. The United States however reneged on their obligations under Article 1, instead coming to an imperial agreement with Japan that the two powers would recognize one another's claims to their respective colonies of the Philippines and Korea. Japan agreed to this, confirming that it recognized the Philippines as a colony of the United States and had no aggressive designs against the territory. The United States in turn agreed to recognize Korea as a part of the Japanese Empire. Britain too reneged on their treaty obligations and agreed with the Japanese Empire that Korea would be recognized as a part of the empire if Japan reciprocated by recognizing India as part of the British Empire. Article Three of the treaties signed by Hayashi Tadasu, the Japanese ambassador to Britain, and the British foreign minister stated that since 'Japan reserves special interests, political, military and economic, in Korea the United Kingdom acquiesces in the right of Japan to take measures in Korea for guidance, administration and protection and promotion of these interests.'[2,3]

The United States and Britain both unilaterally abandoned their respective treaty obligations with Korea and concluded separate treaties with Japan to further their own interests. The two leading Western powers thereby effectively handed Korea over to Japanese rule – offering no explanation to the ruling Choson dynasty. Betrayed and now vulnerable, Korea was forcibly made a protectorate of the Japanese Empire in 1905 following the Japanese-Russian war. Adding insult to injury, when viewed from a Korean perspective, the settlement of the war and division of the spoils was mediated by U.S. President Theodore Roosevelt, who was awarded the Nobel Peace Prize for his contribution. In 1910 Korea went on to become a Japanese colony in full and the Choson dynasty was abolished.

During the Second World War the Japanese Empire inflicted a series of defeats on Western imperial powers throughout Asia and went on to occupy several Western colonies. The British, Dutch, French and Americans all lost valued colonial possessions, and the United States and Britain at this point revised their policy on Korea. As Japan had challenged the Western powers' administration of their own colonial possessions, it was in the best interests of the Western powers to no longer recognize Korea as a part of Japan. As the Japanese promised self-rule and self-determination to several Asian nations under Western colonial rule such as India, Malaysia and the Philippines, so too did the United States reciprocate and promise Korea self-determination and independence. As Japan had the advantage of being seen as a liberator from Western imperialism, which won it considerable popular support across the region, the Western powers made similar promises to negate this advantage and win support among the Korean population.

At the Cairo Conference in 1943 the American, British and Guomindang Chinese leaders Roosevelt, Churchill and Chiang drafted the Cairo Declaration, in which they stated they would 'apply merciless pressure on the barbarous enemy state [Japan]' and laid out objectives of the anti-Japanese war. The draft also touched on the postwar fate of Korea. The first version read that Korea should become a free and independent state 'at the earliest moment' after Japan's defeat. Checking this on November 25, President Roosevelt replaced the word 'earliest' with 'proper.' This slight and subtle change had significant implications for Korea's fate, as it altered the substance of the draft. Debating the draft, British Prime Minister Churchill suggested changing the phrase 'at the proper moment' to 'in due course.' This British proposed version was fixed as the final version on the Korean issue, which read: 'Our three great powers, mindful of the enslavement of the people of Korea, are determined that in due course Korea shall become free and independent.' Its implications were very different from the original draft, and these changes were indicative of the Western powers' agenda towards Korea – namely that they were in no hurry to grant it autonomy.[4]

The Korean Peninsula had long been considered a key strategic position in Asia, connecting Japan to the Asian mainland, and it was highly valued by both Imperial Japan and subsequently by the United States and its allies who saw control of the peninsula as vital to their strategic interests once Japan was defeated. 'In due course' was open to interpretation and highly ambiguous, leaving the Western powers with a great deal of room to maneuver in their policy making but avoiding binding them to any particular commitments to the Korean people – while still presenting themselves as liberators of Korea against Japanese 'barbarism' before the world.

During the period of Japanese occupation several Koreans in exile had set up a 'Provisional Government of Korea' in China. On December 4, 1943, three days after the issuing of the declaration, members of the Korean provisional government visited the U.S. embassy in China. They asked for clarification as to the meaning of the term 'in due course.' The U.S. embassy avoided giving an answer, and reported their inquiry to the U.S. government. The United States, Britain and Guomindang China all declined to comment on this in any official capacity. The December 3,

1943 issue of the *New York Times* commented that the decisions made in Cairo may not be in the best interests of the Korean people, and that this was no more than a plan to paralyze Japan by taking back all it had taken before. Former U.S. Secretary of State Cordell Hull wrote that the Cairo agreement on Korea was a thoughtless act, and the Korean people hoped to win independence as soon as the Japanese were defeated, rather than 'in due course.'[5] How long this 'due course' would be would of course not be decided by the Korean people, but by the Western powers themselves as best suited their own interests.

Referring to the Korean issue in a press interview President Roosevelt stated that Korea's independence would take the same course as that of the Philippines, implying perhaps 20 or 30 years of American 'trusteeship.'[6] It would also most likely mean significant U.S. influence over political, economic and military matters long afterwards – in much the same way as the Philippines (as previously covered in Chapter 5).[7] This was far from a genuine promise to grant independence, and revealed the Western Bloc's true intention regarding Korea. The Philippines too was governed by the United States for decades, supposedly as a period of 'preparation for independence,' and the granting of self-rule to U.S. selected elites was under the condition that the United States be granted continued access to military facilities in the country and extensive economic concessions. Was this to be the fate of Korea as well? Roosevelt's pledges at the Cairo declaration were far better publicized and well known than the implications of his interview, and so the misleading declaration served its purpose.

The U.S. Military in South Korea: New Comfort Women for a New Occupier

The Japanese Empire surrendered on August 15, 1945, and 24 days later the first U.S. troops landed on the Korea Peninsula to establish a military government below the 38th Parallel. Korea had been governed by people's committees in the interim under the newly formed People's Republic of

Korea (PRK), a democratic state which had quickly been set up by Korean nationalists following Japan's defeat. The PRK sought redistribution of land held by Japanese collaborators and the nationalization of major Japanese industries such as mining and transportation. The new republic governed the country through various people's committees. While these people's committees were recognized in the northern half of the country under the Soviet military occupation, in the south these Korean initiatives were abolished by military decree and a U.S. military government was imposed in its stead. Based on the conduct of the U.S. military in numerous aspects of its subsequent occupation, the office of commanding General John R. Hodge observed at the time: 'Americans act as though Koreans were a conquered nation rather than a liberated people.'[8,9] Common American perceptions of the Pacific War with Imperial Japan as a race war against an Asian power threatening 'combine most of the Asiatic peoples against the whites'[10] likely had a key influence over perceptions of Asian populations placed under their power in the war's aftermath towards greater animosity. Their conquerors' attitude would manifest itself strongly in the treatment of Korean women.

The use of comfort women by U.S. forces in South Korea began as soon as U.S. troops first entered the country in September 1945. The Japanese Empire had previously taken Korean comfort women by force to serve their soldiers in wartime. Upon taking control of the Japanese stations which employed these Korean women, they were raped by U.S. forces.[11] Japan's system of comfort stations was later vastly expanded by the Americans and women were provided with modest salaries. Many of the first generation of prostitutes working for the U.S. were in fact former comfort women for the Japanese army, working under a remarkably similar system on a larger scale.[12] This was despite prostitution being illegal under both Korean and American law.

David Vine, associate professor at American University in Washington, DC concluded in his research: 'With the assistance of Korean officials, U.S. authorities continued the system absent formal slavery, but under conditions of exceedingly limited choice for the women involved.'[13] In the center of downtown Seoul the U.S. Army occupied the 640-Acre Yongsan garrison that had been built and used by the Japanese. It switched hands, much as control of the country did. The neighborhood filled with brothels servicing U.S. troops, and GIs called the area 'Hooker Hill.' Boston College Professor Arissa Oh wrote in her research on the subject: 'During the period of U.S. occupation (1945–1948) camptowns, or *kijichi'on* quickly sprang up around American military bases throughout South Korea. The system of US-oriented prostitution was built on the foundation established by the Japanese colonial government (1910–1945).'[14]

Korean President Syngman Rhee's wife of Austrian origin, Franziska Donner, had claimed that the ROK government had had little choice but to establish the camptowns where Korean women would serve American soldiers. She said this was a necessary measure, as foreign military men had previously kept 'taking' any woman they wanted.[15] From a woman who strongly supported the occupation, whose husband had been hand-picked by the U.S. military to assume power, this admission was a powerful indicator as to the extent of the sexual crimes being perpetrated by the U.S. forces in Korea. Mass rapes committed by U.S. forces, later by their Western allies under UN command, were widely reported by the victims and their families, and this further prompted complaints by South Korean officials to U.S. commanders.[16] Comfort stations were seen as a way to prevent this by giving Western armies controlled access to Korean women. An army taking any women they want and raping them does not paint the picture of a benevolent savior, rather of a brutal and rapacious occupier.

Investigators Maria Hohn and Seungsook Moon noted regarding the fate of Korean women under U.S. occupation:

> The demise of [Japanese] colonial rule did not end the use of women's sexual labour for foreign soldiers in Korea. Projecting its image as a 'benevolent liberator' to teach democracy to Koreans, the U.S. military was deeply implicated in various forms of prostitution from the dawn of its occupation of Korea [...] The so-called decolonizing process led by the U.S. military continued to provide fertile soil for the rapid growth of private and unregulated prostitution (sach'ang) in Seoul, Ascom, Taejon, Kwangju, and Pusan [...] Well-paid American soldiers aggressively sought out local women for sexual services. American GIs chased after Korean women in the context of racialized cultural difference, coupled with racism against the Koreans by GIs [...] Military authorities had to deal with the pervasive problems of the deterioration of military courtesy, discipline, appearance, and training. Under the category of courtesy, the authorities addressed widespread racism against the Koreans, ranging from the

> use of the racial slur 'gooks,' physical assaults, reckless driving, and undue arrests of Koreans to making aggressive passes at Korean women [...] GIs viewed sexual access to Korean women outside the respectability of marriage as their entitlement, as agents of European colonialism did towards colonized women of color.[17]

There are scant records of the individual cases of rape, as it was in the interest of neither the South Korean government under Syngman Rhee nor the occupation forces' interests to keep such records. There is however substantial evidence from both Korean and American sources that widespread rapes did take place, including testimonies from South Korean victims. One source which emerged was an interview with a South Korean soldier who recalled the conduct of U.S. forces, stating: 'I was conscripted into the ROK army and had to do sentry duty at the house of a big-shot American. Each night they took our Korean girls in there to be defiled. I don't want your sort of "Free World."'[18] Professor Arissa Oh noted regarding these incidents: 'Rape of local women was largely undocumented but widespread enough to prompt complaints from South Korean officials.' It was highly in keeping with their conduct elsewhere for U.S. troops deployed across the Asia-Pacific to commit rapes en masse against women. While it was an essential part of their occupation to try to be seen as benevolent democratizing saviors, rather than as rapacious conquerors, the latter appeared to be closer to the truth based on accounts from the time. According to the U.S. National Archives and Records Administration the Korean population, though they somewhat tolerated the GIs' relations with prostitutes, complained of the widespread rapes of women who were unwilling.[19] Professors Seungsook Moon and Maria Hohn found in their own study that many South Korean women under U.S. occupation were 'trafficked through force and deception.'[20]

The prime function of the U.S. military government in South Korea was descried by U.S. Colonel Donald Portway as being little more than a pimping for the Americans. He stated: 'The American Military government had as its basic purpose the provision of banquets, gifts and feminine company.'[21] After the outbreak of the Korean War in 1950, arrangements granting Western military personnel better access to Korean women were expanded and further formalized with the close cooperation of the American installed ROK government. The *Pusan Daily* wrote on August 11, 1950: 'The municipal authorities have already issued the approval for establishing UN comfort stations in return for the Allied Forces' toil. In a few days five stations will be set up in the downtown areas of new and old Masan. The authorities are asking citizens to give much cooperation in the coming days.'[22,23]

As the Syngman Rhee government argued that the provision of comfort women was a necessity to satisfy American forces in Korea, so too was it forced to better justify the need for a U.S. military presence for which such a high price needed to be paid. To this end constant portrayal of an imminent North Korea threat became essential, and speaking well of the North Korean government was punishable by death. Only in this way could the suffering and humiliation endured appear at least somewhat justifiable. In her study of military prostitution in Korea, *Sex Among Allies*, Katherine H. S. Moon wrote: 'The sexual domination of tens of thousands of Korean women by "Yangk'I foreigners" [she later puts the total figure at around 1 million] is a social disgrace and a "necessary evil" that South Koreans believe they have had to endure to keep U.S. soldiers on Korean soil, a compromise in national pride, all for the goal of national security. Such humiliation is a price paid by the "little brother" in the alliance for protection by the "big brother."'[24]

The extent to which chastity was valued in Korean society, and extramarital sex or prostitution was abhorred, had few equals in the world. In her comprehensive study of the evolving Korean perceptions of chastity, Professor Katrina Maynes repeatedly emphasized how for a woman to be respected and considered of value, she had to be chaste. She wrote: 'Respectable women [...] were expected to uphold their chastity at all times. Their virginity was their greatest asset and their key to an honourable marriage. They were instructed to guard their chastity with their life, and in the case of rape, women were taught that suicide was preferable. Respectable women could prove their honour through demonstrating chastity and upholding their husbands in life and death.'[25]

Considering Korea's highly conservative culture, the widespread rapes by American and allied soldiers were particularly devastating for the Korean people. Bearing in mind the beliefs of Korean traditional culture experiencing rape in their society was especially terrible for the Korean communities made victims of sexual attacks by Western forces. The culture's emphasis on chastity shows that Korean women must truly have been desperate and had few alternatives if they were to turn to sex work. They had to 'guard their chastity with their lives,' and so to become a sex worker for foreign soldiers was more humiliating and undesirable than it would be in most cultures. The U.S. military and South Korean government referred to these women as 'hostesses,' 'comfort women,' 'special entertainers' and 'businesswomen.' Both governments viewed prostitution as a way to advance 'friendly relations' between the two countries. This was highly symbolic of the unequal partnership between the dominant Western superpower and the subjugated Asian client state. The prostitutes were meant to keep the U.S. soldiers 'who fight so hard for the freedom of the South Korean people' happy. The irony of the idea that the U.S. soldiers were there to free Korea, while extorting their women as conquerors, was great indeed.

Recruitment of Comfort Women for the U.S. Military: Coercion 'for the Sake of Freedom'

Renowned American professor and historian of East Asia Bruce Cumings, a specialist in Korea, holder of South Korea's honorable Kim Dae Jung Academic Award for Outstanding Achievements and Scholarly Contributions to Democracy, Human Rights and Peaceand former member of the U.S. Peace Corps stationed in Korea, concluded in his study of US-ROK relations:

> One element in the Korean-American relationship has been constant: the continuous subordination of one female generation after another to the sexual servicing of American males, to the requirements of a trade in female flesh that simply cannot be exaggerated. It's the most common form of Korean-American interaction, whether you're a private in the Army, a visiting Congressman (for who special stables are maintained), or a Peace Corps teacher [...] It's also the most silent exchange, as if the trade were chaperoned by the deaf, dumb and blind [...] It is the aspect that most

> struck me when I first lived in Korea, creating indelible impressions of a relationship that, because of the use made of Korean women, *could not be* what it was said to be: a free compact between two independent nations dedicated to democracy and anticommunism.[26]

In October 1959 a member of the South Korean national assembly stated in regards to the issue of comfort women: 'It is inevitable that there are prostitutes who cater to foreign soldiers [...] We should [...] train those catering to foreigners on American customs, (entertainment) facilities, or language and etiquette.'[27] A legislator made the claim: 'As long as the U.S. continues to stay in the ROK, we must acknowledge that the majority of the troops are single and by human nature want entertainment [sexually] ... we could provide luxurious accommodations/facilities around Seoul for these men so that they don't have to go to Japan [where comfort stations were already established on a large scale].'[28] This was recorded in parliamentary transcripts. The legislator's claim indicates that it was desirable for the ROK government to sell their women. These claims are strongly contradictory, first alluding to prostitution and sexual entertainment of American soldiers as undesirable inevitability, a necessary evil, but then advocating that the Korean government should prevent it from being outsourced. If it truly was seen as an unfortunate inevitability, why not allow the soldiers to 'go to Japan'? Attempts to prevent prostitution from being outsourced strongly indicate that the South Korean government in the Rhee years actively encouraged the practice not as an unfortunate inevitability, but quite the opposite – as a beneficial opportunity they did not want to lose to the Japanese. 'The idea was to create an environment where the guests were treated well in the camp towns to discourage them from leaving.'[29]

During 12 years in office the Syngman Rhee government never instituted a national economic policy and the ROK made almost no economic or social progress as a result. Though U.S. aid made up for one third of the country's budget, little was done to monitor its use and much of these funds were diverted by officials for their personal use as a result. As Professors Uk Heo and Terrence Roehrig noted in their study of South Korean political history, alongside rampant corruption, 'Rhee also had little expertise or interest in economic development, and his economic ministers were similarly inexperienced and untrained in economic policy making.'[30,31]

Any semblance of a beginning of an economic rise in South Korea came long after the Rhee government was ousted.[32] Professors Seungsook Moon and Maria Hohn concluded in their own study that the Rhee government relied heavily on prostitution to provide currency because it was otherwise incapable of managing its economy and providing for its people. They wrote: 'In the face of dire wartime poverty, the way the Korean government viewed prostitution was an inevitable means to feed its people.'[33] Ms. Kim, a former prostitute, recalled: 'They urged us to sell as much as possible to the G. I.s, praising us as "dollar earning patriots."'[34] By the 1960s the South Korean government had allowed itself to rely on camptown prostitution selling sex to U.S. forces to an extent that it provided nearly 25 percent of the country's Gross National Product (GNP).[35] It was clear that, unable to otherwise provide for their people, the ROK government relied on selling its young women and girls to foreign soldiers. As Kim Ae Ran, a 58-year-old former prostitute interviewed in 2009, said: 'Our government was one big pimp for the U.S. military.'[36]

Government involvement in camptown prostitution was little investigated for years, largely due to the highly repressive nature of former ROK governments. Only decades later was the *New York Times* able to conduct an investigation, interviewing former prostitutes who claimed the government was heavily involved in human trafficking in relation to the sex trade and provision for the U.S. military for many decades. The paper reviewed South Korean and American documents, which they concluded: 'do provide some support for many of the women's claims.' Though the government remained silent on the issue, in 2006 Kim Kee Joe, a government official and former high level liaison to the United States military, admitted in a television interview: 'Although we did not actively urge them to engage in prostitution, we, especially those from the county offices, did often tell them that it was not something bad for the country either.'[37] This somewhat broke the general silence of the South Korean government on the matter.

The promotion and encouragement of prostitution by the Rhee government was confirmed in a ruling by the Seoul High Court on February 8, 2018, which for the first time acknowledged that the ROK government had actively encouraged prostitution with the operation of U.S. military camptowns for the sake of both strengthening the military alliance and earning foreign currency. The court concluded: 'In regarding the right to sexual self-determination of the women in the camp town and the very character of the plaintiffs as represented through their sexuality as means of achieving state goals, the state violated its obligation to respect human rights.' The court reported: 'according to official Ministry of Health and Welfare documents, [the state] actively encouraged women in the military camp towns to engage in prostitution to allow foreign troops to "relax" and "enjoy sexual services" with them.'[38]

The incentives for Korean women to go into sex work went beyond a nod of encouragement from the government. Rather than rape women outright, U.S. occupation forces found it was effective to rely on hunger and financial incentives to force women into prostitution. The United States military's thorough scorched earth campaign and incendiary bombings had destroyed the livelihoods of millions of South Koreans during the Korean War. The U.S. forces' military intervention caused mass poverty and desperation among South Koreans, and they went on to fully take advantage of this desperation they had themselves caused to gain sexual access to the women of Korea. As Professor Arissa Oh concluded: 'Many women had few options other than questionable employment in tearooms, restaurants, and bars, where a thin line separated the hostess and the sex worker. Other women were seduced through false promises, or raped. Widows often resorted to sex work to support their children.'[39] It was often the reality that women had to either sell their bodies to Western soldiers or see their children starve. It would be difficult for mothers to allow the latter, and so they had little choice but sex with occupation forces. In 1952, the final year of the Korean War, the U.S. State Department reported that of the 'UN Aunties,' a term for the prostitutes servicing the Western soldiers, half were widows. This statistic alone is highly indicative as to the true nature of prostitution in wartime and postwar South Korea and the desperation of those who entered the trade.

In their research publication on the effects of what they referred to as the 'U.S. Military Empire' Seungsook Moon and Maria Hohn publicized their findings of the methods of coercion used to obtain comfort women for American forces after the Korean War: 'It appears that, while some women would have been trafficked through force and deception, the masses of impoverished Korean women, single and married, were mainly recruited by private businesses that secured approval from authorities. The majority of women working in UN comfort stations were married, which suggests that sexual labor was a desperate attempt to feed children and families. The force of abject poverty and the death, disability, and displacement of men during the Korean War further multiplied the number of women who had to prostitute themselves for survival.' Based on an analysis of the circumstances, it is clear that what was called consensual was actually very far from consensual work. The conditions which forced women into prostitution were caused by the very occupiers who benefited from having access to large numbers of desperate Korean women.

As Korean professor Jin-Kyung Lee noted, the 'consent' of South Korean women to serve American soldiers was hardly worthy of the term. It was in fact very similar to the system of 'comfort women' Japan operated, but on a far greater scale. She concluded: 'Prostitution is an occupation "choice" that is largely forced on them as a matter of bare subsistence and survival [...] prostitution is an institutionalization of sexual violence via commercialization, for the ways in which the "consent" is forcibly manufactured out of unequal social and economic relations among sex workers, their employers and their clients. In other words, considering this inherent coerciveness and structural violence built into prostitution, I would like to conceptualize prostitution as another kind of necropolitical labor.' This is a term she coined for forced labor, in which there are significant risks of violence and death, evidenced by the number of prostitutes killed or otherwise seriously harmed in their work by soldiers, but the alternative to which is death – such as slavery or concentration camp labor.[40]

In her 'Research for the Reform of Law and the Prevention of Prostitution' Elaine Kim wrote that the Korean War and the US-Republic of Korea Mutual Defense Treaty provided all the raw materials to ensure the 'Rest and Recreation' prostitution system would take off. The war and its destruction brought poverty and chaos. Families were separated and millions were orphaned or widowed, all of which 'mass produced' women who had no choice but to work as prostitutes. The war left many women and young girls without homes or livelihoods.[41] Korea was bombed down to the smallest hamlet, and U.S. forces and their allies conducted a scorched earth policy which impoverished millions (see Chapter 8). Rural people lost their villages, their farmland, their homes and their families. The women would seek food and shelter where U.S. forces were deployed, and so go on to serve them as subsistence work. This was essentially an indirect way of forcing women into sexual slavery. By destroying a people's lives and their ability to provide for themselves, they could be made helpless as slaves. Then a reliance on one's own resources could be fostered, at a price, such as a supply of women to sexually exploit. This is essentially how the United States sexually enslaved hundreds of thousands of Korean women.

American sociologist Kathleen Barry noted the similarities between the 'industrialization of sex' and the scale of sexual exploitation under a new form of Western colonialism in occupied South Korea with the sexual exploitation of conquered women by traditional conquerors.[42] Professor Jin Kyung Lee at the University of California also noted that the approach of the United States to guaranteeing access to Korean women was merely a 'shift from the Japanese Imperial System of Comfort Women.'[43] The exploitation of South Korean women in desperate circumstances on such a scale had much in common with sexual slavery.

Bruce Cumings, himself a former member of the U.S. Peace Corps, described the debauchery he witnessed and the prevalent attitudes among Americans towards Korean society – particularly their sense of entitlement to exploitation of the country's women, as follows: 'If someone called attention to the ceaseless orgy, all the usual bromine pour forth to drown out the faint cries of peasant girls yanked off a train in Seoul and thrown into a brothel, a thousand little justifications for the abasement of a thousand little girls at American hands [...] the social construction of every Korea female as a potential object of pleasure for Americans. It is the most important aspect of the whole relationship and the primary memory of Korea for generations of young American men who have served there [...] When I told an older "Korea hand" that I was going to Seoul with spouse, he remarked, "why take a sandwich to a banquet?"' It seems that is exactly what Korea was to the Americans.[44]

In his description of the 'whoring district' near an American military base Cumings described what he saw: 'ridiculous-looking painted Korean girls – often very young – peer from the doors [...] a middle aged woman with two kids hanging on to her who, in the middle of the street, asked me to come and "hop on" in the chimdeh [bed].' Cumings described: 'Goofy-looking, stupid soldiers walk arm-in-arm with whores who are often only young girls – *very, very* young girls. How do these men justify this to themselves [...] [Koreans] simply hate them [the Americans] and exist by pandering to their ever-base desires [...] the adults avert their eyes when you look at them, and if they don't, they glare at you with a hatred that can be measured – an American who speaks Korean is the only things that shocks them.'[45]

According to Cumings, Korean prostitutes of all ages, including children, were sold. While child sex tourism exists in many poorer Asia-Pacific nations today and caters heavily for Westerners,[46,47,48,49] it seemed it was common for Americans to take very young girls in Cold War era Korea as well. Cumings wrote: 'In Seoul women were available on almost every block – in a bathhouse, massage room, restaurant, or in the ubiquitous tea houses all over the city. You could get them very young, probably around twelve; kids were shanghaied into a kind of slavery as they got off the train from the countryside, looking for work to support their peasant families. Kidnapped, gang-raped and beaten by pimps while learning their few necessary words of English, they were ready for the street in a week.'[50]

Regarding the means by which South Korean women entered prostitution, other than the desperation of the Korean War and postwar years, coercion and fraud were also extremely common. Flesh-traffickers and pimps would often wait by train and bus stations to greet young girls coming from the countryside, promising them employment and a place to stay. These girls, who often left the countryside to seek work, would then be taken in and 'initiated' through rape. They would then be employed in sex work or sold to brothels in the camptowns. Many advertisements offering jobs as waitresses, shopkeepers and singers were used to lure women to their 'initiation ceremonies,' after which they would have been psychologically broken by the shock and social shame of rape, and be sold into prostitution. Once a girl or woman was in the power of such a system, it was extremely difficult to get out. Cultural and psychological reasons were a significant factor as these women were now considered fallen and would face significant social stigma and isolation from society. However, pimps and brothel owners who coerced women into prostitution also made extensive use of a debt-bond system, confiscating women's incomes, getting them into debts and punishing any transgressions with violence.[51,52] It was not unusual for Korean women to have to hand over 80 percent of their earnings to brothel owners, making it near impossible for them to pay debts.[53]

The South Korean police, then notoriously corrupt, were themselves allegedly involved not only in trading drugs, but also in trafficking women. According to a study by International and Political Studies Professor Lukasz Kamienski, 'the police were [...] actively involved in trafficking in women and smuggling them to brothels, thus providing cover and protection for the entire underground sex and drug trade economy.' With police themselves heavily involved in trafficking women, it is difficult to claim that they went into such work willingly.[54]

Katherine H. S. Moon's research revealed the reluctance of women to work as prostitutes. It was strongly against their culture whether they were desperately poor or not. She shows how women were broken down by force to be able to provide sexual services to the American soldiers, stating: 'Most women do not come into the clubs equipped with the "hostessing skills" and the willingness to share flesh with the GIs [American soldiers]. For women who are new to the club scene, an initiation process often takes place. Some women attest to having been raped by their pimp/manager; others have been ordered by the club owner to sleep with a particular soldier; yet others stumble into bed with GIs. On their own; some receive advice on the type of man to avoid (e.g. violent types) from more experienced prostitutes.'[55]

Jeon, a former sex worker aged 71 at the time, gave an interview to the *New York Times* in 2009, which portrayed the desperation that forced South Korean women to seek out sex work. Jeon had been orphaned by the war. She had gone to the Dongducheon camptown near the North Korean border and began to work selling sex for American soldiers' 'rest and recreation' when she was 18 years old. She had a son in the 1960s, but gave him up for adoption when he was 13. When interviewed, Jeon was subsisting by selling items she picked up from trash for a living. Her outlook revealed something of the reality of many women's lives in South Korea as a result of the U.S. military presence there. She said: 'The more I think about my life, the more I think women like me were the biggest sacrifice for my country's alliance with the Americans. Looking back I think my body was not mine, but the government's and the U.S. military's.'[56] The U.S. military's conduct destroyed the lives of many Koreans, leading to deplorable living situations and abuse of Korean women – the effects of which are still profound.

'Johnston's Mom' was the pseudonym used by one of these women. She lived in Songsan, Uijongbu, north of Seoul. Her interviewer described where she lived as 'a run-down cement building-front off an alley [...] a small dark room with gray cement walls and a few pots and pans-the kitchen.' 'Johnston's Mom' was in her late twenties, and had been living in the tiny unheated cold cement hut for months with her two sons. Her sons were both the children of different American servicemen. An American soldier, the father of neither of the boys, had previously been living with them. He had provided food for her and her sons, and in return she had provided her body – given him sexual services whenever he wanted. This 'contract cohabitation' was common in camptowns. She could not bear to sell her sons (Caucasian-looking children sold for $50–200) and was forced to resume working as a prostitute to feed them. The interviewer discovered that as per their 'contract,' 'Johnston's Mom' would have regular sex with the U.S. soldier in the same room as the young boys, as there was nowhere else to go. This case was not particularly outstanding among the millions of relations that a million prostitutes had with U.S. soldiers.[57,58] Such poverty, depravity and exploitation were commonplace, and such circumstances were the experience of so many Korean women.

In the 1950s the South Korean population was just 19 million. Of these just over half were females (96.1 males to 100 females as of 1956)[59] and around half again were young women. When the fighting in Korea ended in 1953 it was not under a peace agreement but rather an armistice. South Korea was officially termed a battle zone as a result, so American soldiers deployed to the country had short deployments of around one year. Soldiers with wives were discouraged from bringing them. The short rotations and significant number of soldiers deployed meant that between

1950 and 1971 around 6 million American soldiers served in Korea. In this time it is estimated that around 1 million Korean women worked in camptowns as prostitutes for the soldiers' 'recreation.'[60] This was at least five times the number that worked for the Japanese army, the highest estimate for which was 'up to 200,000 women, mostly from Korea, but also from other parts of Asia' (meaning well under 200,000 from Korea itself).[61] For 1 million comfort women to have worked servicing the U.S. military out of a total female population of approximately 8.7 million meant that a very significant proportion of young women served as American comfort women. This figure also discounts the significant number of women who were raped by the U.S. military and the armies of other Western powers from 1945 onwards, as the rapes committed were not recorded by the government or police. There is only evidence from testimonies that they did take place and on a very wide scale, but there are no exact figures.

When observing Korean-American and Korean-Japanese relations in the twenty-first century the question often arises: why is Japan's use of under 200,000 Korean comfort women (the majority of its 200,000 comfort women from all Asia, as a highest estimate) frequently made an issue by politicians and activists, and is a well publicized crime, while more recent American use of 1,000,000 South Korean comfort women under terrible conditions and with often questionable consent, as well as the rapes of many more, is not something that is mentioned or addressed. South Korea demands apologies from the Japanese government, builds statues in the honor of the comfort women, and is paid reparations. On the other hand however the South Korean government never mentions the many similar crimes the U.S. committed on a larger scale. Meanwhile the trafficking of comfort women to serve the U.S. forces in the ROK continues on a considerable scale in the twenty-first century, though many are now trafficked from abroad from countries such as the Philippines and sold at auction.[62,63] This was confirmed by a 2002 report by the U.S. State Department.[64,65] Trafficked Filipina women working in the ROK in the 2000s were found to have been so desperate and hungry as to beg U.S. soldiers to bring them bread.[66] A study carried out in 2007 by three professional researchers similarly concluded that U.S. bases in the ROK were 'a hub for the transnational trafficking of women from the Asia-Pacific and Eurasia to South Korea and the United States.'[67] Is the ROK today therefore consistent in its condemnations?

Comparing the coercion of Korean women into military sex work by the Japanese Empire with the far larger scale on which this took place under the U.S. military does not exempt the former or lessen the rapaciousness or degradingness of its crime against the Korean people, but rather brings to light the inherent double standards present in South Korea's claims against Japan when put in perspective with the more recent crimes committed by the United States. One explanation for these double standards is that the U.S. and South Korea are allies – with the latter heavily dependent on the former in the military and economic spheres. Just as the Japanese collaborators in Korea did not raise the issue of the empire's use of comfort women, publicize the suffering of Korean comfort women, or demand compensation for their countrymen, so too would it be unlikely for closely U.S. aligned South Korean governments to make a case against the United States. A second reason is that the comfort women in Korea were in most cases unpaid by the Japanese, and were essentially slaves.‡ The women serving the United States on the other hand are more often depicted as having chosen sex work consensually for financial benefits. While the first is a plausible explanation, the common notion that Korean women consented to sell themselves to the American soldiers, and that the means the U.S. military used to obtain comfort women were therefore significantly different from those used by the Japanese Empire, proves to be largely untrue.

‡ The United States Office of War Information reported based on interviews with 20 Korean comfort women servicing Japanese forces in Myanmar that they were induced by the offer of plenty of money, an opportunity to help provide their families and pay off family debts, easy work, and for some a new life in Singapore. Many Korean women enlisted for overseas duty based on these promises, and were even rewarded with an advance payment of a few hundred yen. The women were forced to remain abroad until they paid their debts, after which many returned to Korea. While this was not how all Korean women who served the Japanese forces were recruited, it draws a revealing comparison with how the United States recruited women to serve their own forces (<http://www.exordio.com/1939-1945/codex/Documentos/report-49-USA-orig.html>).

While recruitment was allegedly consensual, the methods used to recruit comfort women to serve American soldiers involved rape and violence to disorient and break women in who would afterwards have little choice but to 'consent' to sex work for the U.S. military. This mirrored the methods of the Japanese in Korea, who had similarly used middlemen to recruit women to serve their soldiers rather than recruit them directly. Pimps recruiting women for the U.S. forces would often advertise jobs as nurses or factory workers and would then take the respondents and press them into sexual slavery. One major difference was that the Japanese saw comfort women as a temporary wartime measure to satisfy soldiers, and began recruiting them in large numbers only in wartime when they believed men risking their lives for the Empire required special rest and recreation. The recruitment of comfort women was not however ever meant to be a permanent state of affairs which would continue into peacetime. By contrast, though there was no open war in Korea for several decades, the U.S. military recruited hundreds of thousands of comfort women. In fact the prostitution industry in South Korea expanded significantly after the war had ended, after the signing of the Korea-U.S. Mutual Defense Treaty in 1953.[68] While access to comfort women has been considered by a number of militaries throughout history to be a way for men risking their lives and enduring the stresses and exhaustion of combat to cope, even this somewhat feeble defense used by Imperial Japan could not be put forward as an excuse by the United States military for their conduct in South Korea.[69] For the American military access to comfort women could not be considered a necessary evil of wartime. It was in fact a permanent and indefinite state of affairs even in peacetime.

Due to the poor state of the ROK's economy under the Rhee government South Korean women had hunger, even in peacetime, as an incentive to sell themselves. The Japanese Empire, for all its flaws in governing conquered territories, had not left the Asian peoples they conquered starving in peacetime, and to the contrary had made efforts to increase agricultural[70] and industrial[71] outputs of their overseas territories which were highly successful. One example was the construction of the Sui-ho dam in northern Korea, the second largest irrigation dam in the world, to increase to agricultural output of Korean farming and generation electricity. By the end of the Japanese occupation 75 percent of northern Korea's rice production relied on this efficient dam-based irrigation system.[72] Had the Japanese instead left Koreans starving as the American imposed Rhee government had, perhaps they would have not needed to forcibly recruit comfort women – and could instead have left them desperate and paid them a bare subsistence wage as Americans would later do. Would this really have been 'consensual' and 'voluntary,' as many claim prostitution was under the U.S. occupation? Equally had Japan firebombed Korea and enacted scorched earth policies to destroy the people's means of providing for themselves perhaps more Korean women would have been drawn to 'consensual' sex work out of desperation as they were as a result of the actions of the United States military. How genuine was the 'consent' of Korean women serving the U.S. military, who outnumbered those serving the Japanese many times over, and was America's conduct really more moral than that of the Japanese Empire, or could it be considered even more immoral and depraved?

The Myths and Reality of a 'Prostitution Culture': How American Servicemen Were Conditioned to Perceive Korea

It was commonplace for the U.S. military to offer sexual access to women in Korea and other Asia-Pacific countries as an incentive for young men to enlist. Perceptions of Asian peoples, and of their women's 'role' in servicing the brave Western men sailing overseas to protect their freedom, strongly influenced conduct of U.S. personnel towards peoples across the region. American Army Chaplains often attested to the prevalence of such attitudes towards Asian peoples, with one interviewed in 1991 stating: 'What the soldiers have read and heard before ever arriving in a foreign country influence prostitution a lot. For example, stories about Korean or Thai women being beautiful, subservient – they're tall tales, glamorized ... U.S. men would fall in lust with Korean women. They were property, things, slaves ... Racism, sexism – it's all there. The men don't see the women as human beings – they're disgusting, things to be thrown away … They speak of the women in the diminutive.'[73] This attitude is strongly reflected in their conduct in Asia. American Professor Laurie Weinstein came to the same conclusion in her research, stating: 'Racist norms and myths prevalent in American society have also helped induce and even justify sexual abuse of women through military men's participation in prostitution.'[74]

The way Koreans were perceived by Americans, particularly in the military, was shown clearly in the American military newspaper *Stars and Stripes*. Asian, in this case Korean, women appeared to exist solely for the pleasure of Western men – with little regard given to them as a people or as a culture in themselves. The paper highlighted the advantages for U.S. military personnel of being posted to Korea by very strongly objectifying Korean women and giving the image of sexually available and docile Korean women – thus encouraging Americans to view Koreans in this way. It wrote: 'Picture having three or four of the loveliest creatures God ever created hovering around you, singing, dancing, feeding you, washing what they feed you down with rice wine and beer, all saying at once: "you are the greatest." This is the Orient you heard about and came to find.' The use of the word 'creatures' is particularly revealing. The paper encouraged American soldiers to take part in Korea's 'night-time action,' calling it 'the ultimate experience.'[75] Access to women and the prevalence of prostitution were depicted as inalienable parts of Korean and Asian culture – 'this is the Orient' – and such a depiction not only made such deployments more attractive, but also critically shaped the perceptions of American personnel towards Asian cultures and peoples.

The lure of 'the loveliest creatures God ever created,' referring to perfectly sexually available Asian women, was relied on to entice American soldiers into enlistment – notably similar to the strategy used by terrorist organizations today offering women of conquered countries as a 'just reward' to jihadists in warzones.[76] The mentality is similar; as both promote the idea that their own soldiers 'deserve' access to the women in conquered and 'liberated' lands. Approximately 84 percent of Americans deployed in the Korea surveyed admitted to having been with a prostitute. A U.S. captain deployed in Korea said there was an 'overwhelming cultural pressure among enlisted men' to seek out prostitutes, and even those initially against the idea would end up participating. When U.S. Navy ships were set to dock in the Philippines or Korea, officers 'threw the men condoms as if they were Hallmark cards.' Officers were known to tell their men that prostitution was a way of life for Asians, and that Asians like prostitution, which they 'enthusiastically promoted.'[77] There were similar attitudes to other Asian sites of military bases, such as the Philippines which was widely known as 'Uncle Sam's main squeeze sight in this part of the world' (a euphemism for 'America's whorehouse').[78] This is far from true in Asian culture, as previously mentioned. However in areas surrounding Western military bases in Asia prostitution became a 'way of life' not because it is how Asian culture or people are, but because it is what the Western powers shaped peoples under their influence to be.

As previously mentioned, by imposing a government which encouraged such practices, destroying people's means of subsisting and condoning the partaking prostitution by literally millions of American soldiers, among other factors, the United States military effectively served to create a prostitution culture in South Korea – with the prevalence of the trade having no relation to or sanction in Korean culture. The idea that prostitution was part of Korean culture, as well serving to shift the blame for its rampancy to the Korean people themselves, was also used to justify the exploitation of the country's women. A notable flaw in the argument is that both North and South Korea have the same traditional culture, and considering that the North Korea government strictly enforced the outlawing of prostitution entirely and established formal legal equality for women in 1946, where the trade was actively encouraged by the American imposed South Korean Rhee government, it makes it extremely difficult to attribute prostitution to a Korean 'way of life.' North Korea, which also had a brief Soviet and later Chinese military presence, never sold its women for sex to foreign personnel – nor did the Soviet or Chinese militaries request such services. The country remains highly sexually conservative until today, where adultery is a serious crime by law and even divorce is strongly discouraged.[79] American personnel for their part were wholly unaware that South Korea's prostitution culture was of their country's own making, and assumed that the north must in the same way be something of a bordello. Bruce Cumings noted on returning from North Korea, when he confirmed the extremely stark contrast between attitudes to the sex trade in the two countries, 'Upon returning from my first visit to North Korea, I lectured at a military graduate school about my experience. The students asked about this and that but waited until we sat down for a beer to put the most important, albeit alternative, question for the accomplished Korean hand: "what is the price of pussy [sex] in Pyongyang."' Associating Korea with easy sexual access to local women, they were wholly ignorant of the far darker reality of the situation.

Numerous South Korean officials interviewed in the post-Korean War years, including those at the Blue House, all expressed concern that the perceptions of U.S. servicemen of Korea were based heavily on their experiences in camptowns and the prostitution industry, as this was essentially all Korea was to them – a bordello.[80] As Bruce Cumings noted, access to Korean women was 'the primary memory of Korea for generations of young American men who have served there.' These Korean officials feared that American servicemen would take poor perceptions of the country back home, and such perceptions would spread and ultimately affect U.S. policy towards Korea. The *Korea Herald* similarly noted this phenomenon in an editorial in June 1971.

American Conduct Towards Korean Women and the Lasting Legacy of 'Rest and Recreation' Services

Widespread perceptions of Korea as a 'prostitution culture' were but a part of a greater disdain held by Americans for the country and its people, which manifested itself strongly both in the conduct of individuals and to some extent in the policies of the military. As the office of commanding General John R. Hodge had observed: 'Americans are ignorant of Korean customs, show no appreciation of Korean art or culture, and openly ridicule the idea that there can be any good in anything Korean.'[81] A U.S. survey carried out in the 1960s in South Korea and West Germany showed the way the attitudes of American personnel towards peoples in countries where their military was deployed had a strong influence on how they were perceived by the local populations. Of South Koreans questioned, only 13 percent thought Americans 'liked them' while 70 percent of West Germans assumed Americans not only liked them but viewed them 'as friends.'[82] The reason for the discrepancy was the nature of relations between countries. Germany was viewed as a close partner of the United States, its culture was regarded with respect as a European and Western culture and its population were viewed more as human beings and less as 'creatures.' By contrast Korean culture was regarded with contempt and Koreans were severely exploited and mistreated by Americans as 'racial inferiors.'

Indeed, the U.S. military itself appeared to officialise the discrepancy in attitudes to South Korea and Germany through its publications. While Stars and Stripes advertised deployments to Korea for the easy access men would have to local women, in Germany exploring cultural sites such as castles and learning about a new country were used to promote deployments. Though Americans had fought against and defeated the Germans and had greater reason to view them as a conquered or inferior people, as a Western nation they and their culture were guaranteed respect in a way Koreans and their country never were. U.S. personnel were not provided adequate leisure facilities in Korea and hardly any forms of entertainment compared to deployments in Europe precisely because Korean women in camptowns were relied on for their 'entertainment' – or in other words the military had a 'prostitution culture' to fall back on. Though prostitution existed in Europe, it was never encouraged, officialised or promoted as it was in Asia.

It was not only in Europe where U.S. personnel were expected to hold their conduct to a higher standard than in Korea, but also in the Middle East. As two U.S. Army chaplains noted: 'command spells out what's o. k. and not o. k. in terms of interactions with the locals, including women. In Saudi Arabia, it was definitely "Thou salt not."' A second chaplain further stated that '[in] Saudi Arabia, even before the soldier could go near a local woman and get caught by Arabs, we'd get him before the Arabs could; that's how strict we were.'[83] Military personnel were given special 'Arab Cultural Awareness' brochures teaching them the local etiquette such as not to shake with the left hand, so as to avoid causing even the slightest offense to the locals. The brochure stated that men were expected to stand when women entered a room. The brochure's 'what not to do section' read in red bold print:[84]

> Do not shake hands with an Arab woman unless she offers her hand first, or if you are a woman. Do not flirt, hit-on, touch, hug or talk in private with women. IT COULD ENDANGER THEIR SAFETY!
>
> Do not talk in public to professional Arab women unless it is business related.
>
> Do not try and engage a woman in conversation unless you have been formally introduced.
>
> Do not stare at women or maintain eye contact.
>
> Do not ask an Arab questions about his wife or other female members of his family.

This presents an incredibly stark contrast to their conduct in the Asia-Pacific region, which was not in fact down to a cultural difference – as both cultures had similar views on women and chastity which if anything were stricter in traditional Korean culture (there are no suicides for loss of chastity in the Middle East). This shows that the behaviour of the U.S. forces in Korea and throughout the region was largely based on racial prejudices rather than on an inescapable and unavoidable part of their military deployments.

Ill feeling of South Koreans towards Americans came not only from exploitation of its women but also from the soldiers' abusive treatment of Korean civilians. Historian Lloyd Lewis noted on U.S. personnel's perception of Asian peoples in the 1970s: 'soldiers in all branches of the armed services recount receiving the same indoctrination,' that the 'enemy is Oriental and inferior.'[85] This racism, encouraged by the United States military, led to mistreatment of the local populations. Based on these racial perceptions several hate crimes were carried out. The U.S. Eighth Army reported in 1951 regarding the apparently sadistic pleasure personnel took in tormenting the Korean people – those they had been taught to view as subhuman. The report stated that the soldiers: 'take a perverse delight in frightening civilians' and using force to 'drive the Koreans off roads and into ditches.'[86,87]

British Military historian Max Hastings, in reference to the same phenomenon, reports the comments of a U.S. Marine which effectively summarized the attitude of Americans in Korea: 'They're just a bunch of gooks. Who cares about the feelings of people like that?'[88]

While U.S. personnel regularly committed violent, humiliating and abusing acts against regular South Korean civilians who had worked for them,[89] their conduct in dealing with women and sex workers was at times far worse. The reflections of Asian women servicing American personnel strongly reflected the American's perceptions of them as inferiors, existing solely for their sexual and often sadistic pleasure. As one prostitute commented: 'that's what they think of us, the Americans, they we really are pigs.' Another stated: 'what I felt about the Americans when I did floor shows is that they seemed brutal.' She reported the 'sadism' of some customers, particularly those on drugs who were a danger to women and who often purposely tried to harm them sexually for their own pleasure.[90] Reports that men were sadists or would pass on diseases made many women reluctant, but due to financial pressure and high debts to clubs and pimps they often had little choice. As another claimed: 'The customers, the Americans, don't treat the women well. The Americans are dogs. Sometimes they beat the women.'[91]

Korean comfort women were very often afraid of and highly reluctant to enter into sexual relations with American soldiers. Most women had to take drugs or alcohol to be able to get through their sex work. The 'sexual favors' the soldiers required were often extreme. One comfort woman, 'Ms. Pak,' expresses her feelings towards working at the GI club serving American soldiers. Though she had already sold sex to Korean men, she was afraid of sex with American men and did not know if she could physically handle their large bodies. She was particularly afraid of sex with black American soldiers, and wondered how dark their genitals would be. 'If I do it with him, will my skin turn black?' she wondered. Though she was reluctant, her club owner ordered her to have sex and she had to follow his order. He 'warned that I had to do it,' she recalled.[92]

Korean women were expected to cater for the soldiers' variety of sexual fantasies. These included strip teases, peeve shows, the 'vaginal coin suck,' but there was a common desire for unusual and extreme sexual actions, such as the demand for 'three holers' among the women who served them.[93] In many cases due to the context of a dominant military power subjugating a small dependent nation, which had a significant impact on the perceptions of Koreans and their position in regards to the United States, sex was largely about degrading and humiliating the women for the soldiers' pleasure – a means for one to assert dominance over the other. One military chaplain quoted by *Time* magazine noted that U.S. personnel tended to view Korean women as property, much as Westerners serving at imperial postings across the world once 'owned' sex slaves of conquered nations in Africa, the Americas and elsewhere, stating: 'Some of them *own* their girls ... before leaving Korea, they sell the package to a man who is just coming in.'[94]

An independent survey of 243 South Korean prostitutes servicing U.S. personnel found that well over two thirds experienced 'beating, sexual violence, theft and robbery, in declining order of frequency' at the hands of American soldiers. Based on these findings, sexual violence and aggression against South Korean women by American personnel can be considered extremely common.[95] As one prostitute said anonymously when interviewed, 'some GIs are mean and nasty, especially when they are drunk ... at worst a woman encounters a GI who beats her and murders her.' American conduct towards Korean women, as in many other Asia-Pacific nations, was strongly influenced by perceptions that they were dealing with an inferior people.

Koreans were perceived as a culture and people with whom Americans were entitled to do as they pleased, including inflicting abuse and demanding sexual favors. According to a Korean sex worker interviewed, GIs would tell Korean women that they would never beat women in America – but as they were in Korea they were free to so to Korean women – supposedly to justify their behavior. It was common for Korean women to be harshly beaten by drunk soldiers.[96] One comfort woman, Uijeongbu, recalled: 'I met an American but he was suspicious of me. He had been divorced twice. He was always beating me up ... I lived with him for about three months. Then he said he was leaving. I asked why. I don't know what he said. At that time, I didn't know any English.' She then went on to meet another, a soldier two years younger who she later discovered had a Korean wife: 'He was all right, but he would drink too much and pee in the bed. He was always drinking. I thought: "just don't mistreat me, and it's fine."'[97] 'Yun Kumi,' a Korean sex worker, encountered a more extreme case of a violent GI. She was killed by Private Kenneth Markle. Her body was found 'naked, bloody, and covered with bruises and contusions – with laundry detergent sprinkled over the crime site. In addition, a coke bottle was embedded in Yun's uterus and the trunk of an umbrella driven 27 cm into her rectum.' Several other cases of brutal treatment of Korean women, and at times children,[98] by U.S. forces in crimes referred to by Korean courts as 'sadistic,' have continued into the twenty-first century.[99]

Considered fallen women with little hope to return to a normal life in their own country, many Korean prostitutes hoped to marry GIs to find a new life in the United States. These hopes tended to be short-lived, however. For the few women who did get soldiers to marry them around 80 percent of marriages ended in divorce. Many American soldiers who married Korean women worked with criminal gangs, using marriage as a means to bring a woman to the United States and then sell her to traffickers in the America. Korean women deceived in such a way would then be abandoned by their husbands and forced into sex work in a new country, reliant wholly on the traffickers in a relationship closely resembling formal slavery.[100]

Police Chief William Dwyer, who worked on cases involving the trafficking of Korean women to the United States in the mid-1980s, said regarding the issue: 'We learned servicemen had married some of the defendants in the case and brought them over here for a certain amount of money – $5,000 to $10,000 … It was a slavery thing.' Police sources indicate that this continued throughout the 1990s. A U.S. Midwestern police officer involved in raids on 'massage parlors' and brothels employing trafficked Koreans revealed that some of the women trafficked there through marriage were as young as 18. He stated in an interview in 2002 that the American men marrying and trafficking the women 'are paid $1500 to marry the Korean woman. In San Francisco, the divorce is already arranged as soon as he gets her into the country. Then he gets another $1500.' A police Sergeant, Jim Lalone, stated in 2002 regarding the primary means by which Korean women were trafficked into the United States: 'The military is the key! I've never seen it any other way.' According to the U.S. Army Criminal

Investigation Division, 'soldiers are seldom punished even when sham marriages are suspected.'[101]

Many Korean women would enter relationships or marriage to Americans hoping for a better life and education. The vast majority of prostitutes until the end of the 1970s had little to no formal education, but given the Confucian culture of Korea, education was very highly prized. One woman admitted she married an American serviceman so she could 'go to study in America.'[102] It was not education for its own sake, but to equip them to provide for themselves without having to sell their bodies, allowing them to make real contributions to their country. One comfort woman interviewed stated that if she had power in government she would 'take the women away from the pimps and owners and put them into vocational schools and really put the women to work for the nation's good.'[103] While women's labor was largely responsible for the economic growth in South Korea, for several decades it was stifled due to a lack of educational opportunities.[104] Women who could have and were eager to help their country were instead forced, with the government 's encouragement, to sell sex to young Americans stationed there.

With the use of Korean comfort women so widely prevalent among U.S. personnel, a number of sexually transmitted diseases, foremost of which was Venereal Disease (VD), began to spread among the armed forces. Measures taken to protect the American personnel from contracting these diseases effectively demonstrated the military's disdain for Korean women. Prostitutes were required to wear tags so the soldiers could more easily identify them, with U.S. personnel in East Asia often complaining of a genuine inability to tell people apart from one another. This had been a particular problem in the past when training the Guomindang Chinese soldiers in the 1940s.[105] Women suspected of being ill were held by force in guarded facilities with barred windows known as 'monkey houses,' where conditions were found to be 'poorly lighted and quite filthy.'[106] These women were required to take large doses of medication for VD[107] with often detrimental effects on their general health, including high doses of penicillin to which approximately 5 percent were allergic.[108] Many Korean physicians, even years into the program, remained 'reluctant to give such large doses ... because such doses in subjects allergic to penicillin could result in the death of the patient.'[109] It appeared however that the health of U.S. personnel was a priority, and unnecessarily large doses were administered to get the comfort women back into service as quickly as possible despite considerable risks to the health of the Korean women.

Once they reached an older age prostitutes most often lacked families to support them. Clubs would not accept them and due to their old age they were paid very little by American soldiers for sex. Nevertheless these women had to find ways to subsist, often by providing cheap 'tricks' for Americans' sexual gratification. There were women in their sixties and older streetwalking, offering American soldiers a sex trick for a few dollars. Ultimately, they had little choice: perform sexually for men a third their age or face starvation. For a Confucian society this was deeply abhorrent on many levels.

Many of the profound social issues South Korea continues to face, namely a high prevalence of prostitution – often referred to as a culture of prostitution – has largely been a result of the decades long U.S. military presence. By 1989 Korea's 'entertainment' of nightclubs, bars and entertainment made up 5 percent of the Gross National Product. By this time 400,000 establishments offered sexual services and between 1.2 and 1.5 million South Korean women sold sex (this was one fifth of the total number of women aged 15 to 29). A variety of services were offered at a variety of locations, from seedy inns to luxury hotels, to cater for the very large numbers of clients.[110,111] The sex trade in South Korea now makes up 4 percent of GDP, as much as fishing and agriculture combined.[112] Up to one fifth of South Korean women between 15 and 29 today have at some point worked in the sex industry, over 1 million women.[113,114] A report by the U.S. State Department released in 2008 indicated that young girls and women from South Korea are very often made victims of human trafficking to Western nations in significant numbers. These include Western Europe, Canada, Australia, New Zealand and the United States as well as to Japan.[115]

The culture of prostitution in the ROK continues to flourish as it has for decades since being established by the United States' military. Just as Thailand's previously negligible sex industry grew exponentially during and after the Vietnam War, so too has prostitution and the sex industry been made a part of South Korea today, from the services to locals and other Asian nations, the elderly women who continue to offer sex on the streets of Seoul[116] and the ever present camptowns servicing the American military. As Katherine H. S. Moon noted regarding the social changes which occurred in South Korea as a result of the U.S. military presence: 'Increasingly Koreans view the history of prostitution and the contemporary forms of sex tourism in Korea as manifestations of foreign domination over the country.'[117] Whether these manifestations of Western dominance can be remedied in the coming years remains to be seen.

Notes

1 Pollock, Sandra, *Let the Good Times Roll: Prostitution and the U.S. Military in Asia*, New York, New Press, 1992 (p. 170).

2 Sung Chol, Ryo, *Korea: The 38th Parallel North*, University Press of the Pacific, 2004 (p. 10).

3 Paine, S.C.M., *The Japanese Empire: Grand Strategy from the Meiji Restoration to the Pacific War*, Cambridge, Cambridge University Press, 2017, (p. 79–80).

4 Foreign Relations of the United States, Diplomatic Papers, Cairo and Tehran Conferences, 1943, Washington, 1961 (pp. 402–404).

5 Hull, Cordell, *Memoirs*, Volume II, New York, Macmillan, 1948 (p. 1580).

6 Pak Chi, Young, *Korea and the United Nations*, Cambridge, Kluwer Law International, 2000 (p. 3–4).

7 For election rigging, drafting of stringent military appropriation terms and terms of trade designed to overwhelmingly advantage American companies, assassination of rival politicians and other means employed by the United States to heavily influence politics and economy in the Philippines long after granting it nominal independence, see Chapter 5 of this work.

8 'Report on Standards of Living Conditions, Military Courtesy Discipline, and Training,' April 29, 1946; 'Deterioration of Standards,' May 3, 1946; 'Courtesy Drive,' November 6, 1946; 'Message from the Commanding General, USAFIK,' January 17, 1947; 'Instructions to Courtesy Patrol Officers,' July 21, 1948; 'Personal Conduct,' August 27, 1948, all in NARA, RG 554, box 50.

9 Hohn, Maria, and Moon, Seungsook, eds., *Over There: Living with the U.S. Military Empire from World War Two to the Present*, Chapel Hill, NC, Duke University Press, 2010 (p. 43).
10 Diary of Admiral William Leahy, October 20, 1942 (quoted in Thorne, Christopher, *Allies of a Kind: The United States, Britain and the War Against Japan, 1941–1945*, Oxford, Oxford University Press, 1978, p. 157).
11 Schrijvers, Peter, *The GI War Against Japan: American Soldiers in Asia and the Pacific During World War II*, New York, New York University Press, 2005 (p. 212).
12 Moon, Katherine H. S., *Sex Among Allies*, New York, Colombia University Press, 1997 (p. 46).
13 Vine, David, *Base Nation, How U.S. Military Bases Abroad Harm America and the World*, New York, Henry Holt and Company, 2015 (p. 164).
14 Oh, Arissa, *To Save the Children of Korea: The Cold War Origins of International Adoption*, Stanford, CA, Stanford University Press, 2015.
15 Oh, Arissa H., *To Save the Children of Korea: The Cold War Origins of International Adoption*, Stanford, CA, Sanford University Press, 2015 (p. 49).
16 Hanley, Charles J. and Choe, Sang Hun and Mendoza, Martha, *The Bridge at No Gun Ri: A Hidden Nightmare from the Korean War*, New York, Henry Holt and Company, 2001 (p. 189).
17 Hohn, Maria, and Moon, Seungsook, eds., *Over There: Living with the U.S. Military Empire from World War Two to the Present*, Chapel Hill, N, Duke University Press, 2010 (p. 43).
18 Winnington, Alan, and Burchett, Wilfred, *Plain Perfidy, The Plot to Wreck the Korea Peace*, Britain-China Friendship Association, 1954 (p. 129).
19 Association with Korean Women, January 25, 1947, National Archives and Records Administration, RG 554, box 50.
20 Hohn, Maria, and Moon, Seungsook, eds. *Over There: Living with the U.S. Military Empire from World War Two to the Present*, Chapel Hill, NC, Duke University Press 2010 (p. 52).
21 Portway, Donald, *Korea: Land of the Moring Calm*, London, George G. Harrap, 1953 (p. 291).
22 Moon, Katherine H. S., *Sex Among Allies*, New York, Colombia University Press, 1997 (p51).
23 Maria Hohn and Seungsook Moon, eds., *Over There: Living with the U.S. Military Empire from World War Two to the Present*, Chapel Hill, NC, Duke University Press, 2010 (p. 51).
24 Moon, Katherine H. S., *Sex Among Allies*, New York, Colombia University Press, 1997.

25 Maynes, Katrin, 'Korean Perceptions of Chastity, Gender Roles, and Libido; From Kisaengs to the Twenty First Century,' *Grand Valley Journal of History*, Volume 1, Issue 1, Article 2, February 2012.
26 Hanley, Charles J. and Choe, Sang Hun and Mendoza, Martha, *The Bridge at No Gun Ri: A Hidden Nightmare from the Korean War*, New York, Henry Holt and Company, 2001.
27 Cho, Hyoung, and Chang, P'ilhwa, 'Perspectives on Prostitution in the Korean Legislature: 1948–1989,' Women's Studies Review (p. 95).
28 Moon, Katherine H. S., *Sex Among Allies*, New York, Colombia University Press, 1997 (pp. 44–45).
29 Ibid.
30 Heo, Uk, and Roehrig, Terence, *South Korea Since 1980*, Cambridge, Cambridge University Press, 2010 (p. 18).
31 Henderson, G., *The Politics of the Vortex*, Cambridge, MA, Harvard University Press, 1968 (pp. 348–349).
32 Heo, Uk, and Roehrig, Terence, *South Korea Since 1980*, Cambridge, Cambridge University Press, 2010 (p. 26).
33 Lee, Na Young, 'The Construction of U.S. Camptown Prostitution in South Korea: Trans/Formation and Resistance,' University of Maryland, Department of Women's Studies, 2006.
34 Choe, Sang-Hun, 'After Korean War, brothels and an alliance,' *New York Times*, January 8, 2009.
35 Moon, Katherine H. S., *Sex Among Allies*, New York, Colombia University Press, 1997 (p. 44).
36 Choe, Sang-Hun, 'After Korean War, brothels and an alliance,' *New York Times*, January 8, 2009.
37 Ibid.
38 Kim, Min-Kyung, 'Court Finds that South Korean Government Encouraged Prostitution Near U.S. Military Bases,' *Hankyoreh*, February 9, 2018.
39 Oh, Arissa, *To Save the Children of Korea: The Cold War Origins of International Adoption*, Stanford, CA, Stanford University Press (p. 49).
40 Lee, Jin-Kyung, *Service Economies: Militarism, Sex Work, and Migrant Labor in South Korea*, Minneapolis, University of Minnesota Press, 2010 (p. 82).
41 Kim, Elaine, 'Research for the Reform of Law and the Prevention of Prostitution,' *The Women's Studies Quarterly*, 8:1 Seoul, Korea Women's Development Institute, Spring 1990 (p. 89).
42 Barry, Kathleen, *The Prostitution of Sexuality*, New York, New York University Press, 1996.

43 Lee, Jin-Kyung, *Service Economies: Militarism, Sex Work, and Migrant Labor in South Korea*, Minneapolis, University of Minnesota Press, 2010 (p. 79).
44 Pollock, Sandra, *Let the Good Times Roll: Prostitution and the U.S. Military in Asia*, New York, New Press, 1992 (p. 170).
45 Ibid. (p. 171).
46 'UN warns Britain over child voodoo rituals, pedophile sex tourists,' *RT*, June 20, 2014.
47 'Unwanted Visitors,' *The Economist*, August 21, 2008.
48 Klein, Naomi, *The Shock Doctrine: The Rise of Disaster Capitalism*, London, Penguin, 2008 (p. 273).
49 'Asia's child sex tourism rising,' *BBC*, August 22, 2000.
50 Pollock, Sandra, *Let the Good Times Roll: Prostitution and the U.S. Military in Asia*, New York, New Press, 1992 (p. 173).
51 Hye Seung Chung, *Kim Ki-duk*, Champaign, University of Illinois Press, 2012 (p. 34).
52 Moon, Katherine H. S., *Sex Among Allies*, New York, Colombia University Press, 1997 (pp. 19–20, 23, 24, 132).
53 Ibid. (p. 131).
54 Kamienski, Lukasz, *Shooting Up; A History of Drugs in Warfare*, London, C. Hurst & Co. Publishers Ltd, 2016 (p. 148).
55 Moon, Katherine H. S., *Sex Among Allies*, New York, Colombia University Press, 1997 (p. 20).
56 Choe Sang Hun, 'After Korean War, brothels and an alliance,' *New York Times*, January 8, 2009.
57 Moon, Katherine H. S., *Sex Among Allies*, New York, Colombia University Press, 1997 (pp. 4–5).
58 Hye Seung Chung, *Kim Ki-duk*, Champaign, University of Illinois Press, 2012 (p. 34).
59 Hohn, Maria, and Moon, Seungsook, eds. *Over There: Living with the U.S. Military Empire from World War Two to the Present*, Chapel Hill, NC, Duke University Press 2010 (p.351).
60 Oh, Arissa H., *To Save the Children of Korea: The Cold War Origins of International Adoption*, Stanford, CA, Sanford University Press, 2015 (p. 50).
61 'Japan PM urges S. Korea to remove "comfort woman" statue,' *The Korea Herald*, January 8, 2017.
62 Vine, David, *Base Nation, How U.S. Military Bases Abroad Harm America and the World*, New York, Henry Holt and Company, 2015 (pp. 167–169).
63 Irvine, Reed, and Kincaid, Cliff, 'The Pentagon's Dirty Secret,' *Media Monitor*, August 7, 2002.

64 Moon, Katherine H. S., *Sex Among Allies*, New York, Colombia University Press, 1997 (p. 346).
65 Gillem, Mark L., *America Town: Building the Outposts of Empire*, Minneapolis, University of Minnesota Press, 2007 (p. 67).
66 Demick, Barbara, 'Off-Base Behavior in Korea,' *Los Angeles Times*, September 26, 2002.
67 Hughes, Donna M., and Chon, Katherine Y., and Ellerman, Derek P., 'Modern-Day Comfort Women: The U.S. Military, Transnational Crime, and the Trafficking of Women,' *Violence Against Women* vol. 13, no. 9, 2007, (p. 918).
68 Seungsook Moon, *Regulating Desire, Managing the Empire: U.S. Military Prostitution in South Korea, 1945–1970*, Durham, Duke University Press, 2010.
69 Mikaberidze, Alexander, *Atrocities, Massacres, and War Crimes: An Encyclopedia*, Santa Barbara, CA, ABC-CLIO, 2013 (p. 7).
70 Hsiao, Mei-Chu W., and Hsiao, Frank S. T., *Taiwan in the Global Economy – Past, Present and Future, Section V., Taiwan in the Global Economy During the Japanese Period*, University of Colorado at Boulder, University of Colorado at Denver.
71 '朝鮮総督府統計年報 昭和１７年 [Governor-General of Korea Statistical Yearbook 1942].' Governor-General of Korea. March 1944.
72 Williams, Christopher, *Leadership Accountability in a Globalizing World*, London, Palgrave Macmillan, 2006 (p. 185).
73 D'Amico, Francine J., and Weinstein, Laurie L., *Gender Camouflage: Women and the U.S. Military*, New York, New York University Press, 1999 (p. 212).
74 Ibid.
75 Moon, Katherine H. S., *Sex Among Allies*, New York, Colombia University Press, 1997 (p. 33).
76 Volokh, Eugene, 'ISIS Enshrines a Theology of Rape,' *New York Times*, August 13, 2015.
77 Nyen Chan, Emily, 'Engagement Abroad: Enlisted Man, U.S. Military Policy and the Sex Industry,' *Notre Dame Journal of Law, Ethics and Public Policy*, Volume 15, Issue 2, Symposium on International Security, Article 7, 2012 (pp. 631–632).
78 Ibid. (p. 632).
79 Pollock, Sandra, *Let the Good Times Roll: Prostitution and the U.S. Military in Asia*, New York, New Press, 1992.
80 Moon, Katherine H. S., *Sex Among Allies*, New York, Colombia University Press, 1997 (p. 118).
81 Hohn, Maria, and Moon, Seungsook, eds. *Over There: Living with the U.S. Military Empire from World War Two to the Present*, Chapel Hill, NC, Duke University Press 2010 (p. 43).

82 Moon, Katherine H. S., *Sex Among Allies*, New York, Colombia University Press, 1997 (p. 119).
83 Ibid. (p. 37).
84 *Arab Cultural Awareness: 58 Factsheets*, TRADOC DCSINT Handbook No. 2, Office of the Deputy Chief of Staff for Intelligence, U.S. Army Training and Doctrine Command, Ft. Leavenworth, Kansas, January 2006.
85 Lewis, Lloyd B., *The Tainted War: Culture and Identity in Vietnam Narratives*, Santa Barbara, CA, Praeger, 1985 (p. 55).
86 Voorhees, Melvin B., *Korean Tales*, Franklin Classics, 2011 (p. 150).
87 Steinberg, David I., *Korean Attitudes Toward the United States: Changing Dynamics*, Abingdon, Routledge, 2015 (p. 234).
88 Hastings, Max, *Korean War*, London, Pan Books, 2012 (Chapter 12: 'The Stony Road,' Part 3: 'The Cause').
89 Hanley, Charles J. and Choe, Sang Hun and Mendoza, Martha, *The Bridge at No Gun Ri: A Hidden Nightmare from the Korean War*, New York, Henry Holt and Company, 2001 (pp. 201–202).
90 Pollock, Sandra, *Let the Good Times Roll: Prostitution and the U.S. Military in Asia*, New York, New Press, 1992 (124, 126).
91 Ibid. (p. 155).
92 Moon, Katherine H. S., *Sex Among Allies*, New York, Colombia University Press, 1997 (p. 20).
93 Pollock, Sandra, *Let the Good Times Roll: Prostitution and the U.S. Military in Asia*, New York, New Press, 1992.
94 'South Korea: A Hooch is Not a Home,' *Time*, October 9, 1964 (p. 48).
95 Hohn, Maria, and Moon, Seungsook, eds., *Over There: Living with the U.S. Military Empire from World War Two to the Present*, Chapel Hill, NC, Duke University Press 2010 (p. 351).
96 Hanley, Charles J. and Choe, Sang Hun and Mendoza, Martha, *The Bridge at No Gun Ri: A Hidden Nightmare from the Korean War*, New York, Henry Holt and Company, 2001 (p. 214).
97 Ibid.
98 Lee, Jiyeon, 'U.S. soldier gets 10 years in prison for rape in South Korea,' *CNN*, November 1, 2011.
99 Yea, Sallie, *Trafficking Women in Korea: Filipina Migrant Entertainers*, Abingdon, Routledge, 2018 (pp. 31–32).
100 Terito, Leonard, and Kirkham, George, *International Sex Trafficking of Women & Children: Understanding the Global Epidemic*, New York, Looseleaf Law Publications, 2009 (pp. 209–210).
101 Ibid. (pp. 210–211).

102 Moon, Katherine H. S., Telephone interview with Mrs. Chong via Mr. An, March 10, 1993.
103 Moon, Katherine H. S., Telephone interview with Mrs. Pak Mrs. Smith, April 2, 1993.
104 Draudt, Darcie, 'The Struggles of South Korea's Working Women,' *The Diplomat*, August 26, 2016.
105 Mitter, Rana, *China's War with Japan, 1937–1945: The Struggle for Survival*, London, Allan Lane, 2013.
106 Subcommittee Minutes, #25, February 22, 1974, Enclosure entitled 'Report on Situation in Tongduchon' (by Ministry of Transportation).
107 Choe, Sang-Hun, 'After Korean War, brothels and an alliance,' *New York Times* January 8, 2009.
108 Sherwood, Col. Robert W., *Trip Report to EUSA, Korea, July 7, 1972*, Washington, DC, U.S. Dept. of the Army, Office of the Surgeon General.
109 Subcommittee Minutes, #16, January 12, 1973.
110 Shin, Hei Soo, 'Women's Sexual Services and Economic Development: The Political Economy of the Entertainment Industry and South Korean Dependent Development,' Ph.D. dissertation, Rutgers University, New Brunswick, NJ, 1991 (p. 58).
111 Moon, Katherine H. S., *Sex Among Allies*, New York, Colombia University Press, 1997 (p. 45).
112 Ghosh, Palash, 'South Korea: A Thriving Sex Industry In A Powerful, Wealthy Super-State,' *International Business Times*, April 29, 2013.
113 Moon, Katherine H. S., *Sex Among Allies*, New York, Colombia University Press, 1997 (p. 45).
114 Ghosh, Palash, 'South Korea: A Thriving Sex Industry In A Powerful, Wealthy Super-State,' *International Business Times*, April 29, 2013.
115 U.S. Department of State, Under Secretary for Civilian Security, Democracy and Human Rights, Trafficking Persons Report 2008.
116 Williamson, Lucy, 'The Korean grandmothers who sell sex,' BBC, June 10, 2014.
117 Moon, Katherine H. S., *Sex Among Allies*, New York, Colombia University Press, 1997 (pp. 46–47).

CHAPTER 12

Targeting North Korea: Cognitive Dissonance and Information War

> It is not a matter of what is true that counts, but a matter of what is perceived to be true.[1]
>
> — HENRY KISSINGER

North Korea's emphasis on military readiness and the development of a heavily self-reliant economy – more recently named as the policy of *Songun* and ideology of *Juche* – have since the Korean War meant that the country has been well prepared to endure both a military attack and economic pressure by its adversaries. Military options against the country by the United States are widely considered unfeasible – with Pentagon and U.S. experts estimating that a conventional invasion would lead to the loss of approximately 200,000 American military personnel.[2,3] Other reports indicate that the Pentagon predicts a loss of up to 500,000 troops under its command within 90 days of the outbreak of war, though this figure includes South Korean military losses as well.[4] These did not account for North Korean weapons of mass destruction or its ability to deliver them to U.S. territories such as Guam or Hawaii – let alone the U.S. mainland itself. Economic warfare, though waged for several decades,[5] has had limited success – with the DPRK sustaining economic growth and keeping both exchange rates[6] and prices for most basic goods stable despite harsh economic sanctions.[7,8,9] As *USA Today* reported at the end of 2017, a year of unprecedented Western sanctions against the country: 'North Korea's economy has proven resilient and seems to have fended off the suffering President Trump has sought to force to halt the country's nuclear program.' This was in reference to the DPRK's stable living standards and continued economic growth – something other nations targeted by U.S. and Western sanctions such as Iran,[10,11] Iraq[12] and Russia[13] were unable to achieve despite significantly less economic pressure being applied and far greater endowments of natural resources.[14]

One field in which North Korea has proven particularly vulnerable has been in promoting its image abroad and developing its soft power, which have been restricted by the country's small economy, language barriers with the outside world and international isolation since the end of Many of its longtime allies were absorbed into the Western Bloc's sphere of influence. The result has been that the United States and its partners have had a freer hand to undertake an extensive campaign of demonization against their longstanding adversary, which has successfully influenced public opinion across much of the world against the country. While all states conducting foreign policies in ways opposed by the Western Bloc are demonized to some degree, what is unique about North Korea is that the country's small size and extreme post-Cold War isolation has given its Western adversaries a free hand to depict it almost however they wish. There is an unwritten but often enforced rule, particularly in the United States, that North Korea cannot be mentioned in media or scholarship without harsh criticism following – even from supposedly apolitical sources. Whether it be a travel guide, a book on flag designs or a collection of mountain scenery there will almost always be additional commentary on the 'most vicious, paranoid, murderous dictatorship' (from a 2016 British book on flag designs) or some similar description.[15]

The highly negative depiction of North Korea by the United States and its partners is facilitated by their tremendous control of information and soft power. In determining public opinion, 'media might makes right.' U.S. Republican Congressman Ron Paul, himself a staunch anti-communist, said of the position taken by the United States towards the DPRK and its use of its media to target the small Asian nation: 'I would say they [the United States government] make no effort to come across as being consistent. Or at least their inconsistencies are totally ignored because of our media and the propaganda … They [North Korea] get targeted … I think it's our hegemony, our fortress and our empire that we have to protect that they [the US] will do and say anything necessary to protect that power.

But they couldn't do it if they didn't have almost absolute control of the major media outlets in this country.'[16]

Dr Anthony Di Maggio, Professor of Political Science at the University of Illinois, though a staunch critic of the North Korean government, noted regarding the nature of the coverage of major Western media outlets when reporting tensions on the Korean Peninsula: 'Efforts to escalate the conflict between the U.S. and North Korea are a major cause of concern for those who are intent on defusing this nuclear crisis. Media pundits are typically more likely to blame the North Korean regime for fueling tensions with the U.S. than they are to level substantive criticisms against American political leaders for their share in provoking a nuclear crisis ... Attention is focused less, if at all, on the United States' well-documented efforts to aggravate an already volatile situation by labeling North Korea as part of an "Axis of Evil" – as well as other American actions that have provoked a standoff.' Di Maggio notes as examples U.S. reconnaissance flights into North Korean airspace, positioning nuclear bombers near the country, and publishing documents such as Operation Plan 5030 which outlined a plan for nuclear strikes against the country and the violent overthrow of its government[17,18] – none of which were covered by any major Western media outlets as provocations. He goes on to state: 'What are considered acceptable or warranted responses to the North Korean predicament proposed throughout the media range from intimidation and isolation to a full out military strike.'[19]

Not only are U.S. threats towards North Korea rarely covered, but positive imagery of the country is almost always dismissed or otherwise interpreted negatively ('they are being forced to applaud for their leader or to cry for his death,'[20] etc.). David Shim and Dirk Nabers wrote in their article for the German Institute of Global Area Studies that the West tightly and effectively censored positive images of North Korea. Images of the DPRK were made to both alienate its people and at the same time present them as a 'threat' to the rest of the world. They wrote: 'Images of North Korea showing its military "strength" and internal "weakness" are highlighted as idiosyncratic aspects to emphasize its Otherness. The use of images marks North Korea in particular ways, which separate "them" from "us" ... A good example of what is made almost invisible in Western representations of North Korea is smiling or joyful ordinary North Korean people.'[21]

One minor example of suppression of positive imagery of the DPRK was the footage taken by British video blogger Louis Cole. Cole had a substantial Internet following and when visiting North Korea he depicted it positively, focusing on the quality of the food, the waterparks and the kind local people. Due to the popularity of his blog, Cole's account and footage risked undermining the Western narrative on the DPRK. He was heavily criticized by organizations such as the Western NGO Human Rights Watch for failing to mention the 'true' North Korea – the invisible one that is never seen on camera but which Western sources insist represent the true nature of the country:[22] one where seemingly happy and well fed people are, if Western reports are to be believed, secretly starving and behind closed doors. Cole was even widely accused of being a paid agent of the DPRK's government.[23] Though his visit was apolitical and he was not a journalist, he was still strongly expected to take a political stance against the government despite seeing nothing in the country which would prompt this.

Several Western journalists have attested to the unreliability of major news outlets' reporting on the DPRK. *The Telegraph* and *Business Insider* both published articles claiming that Western reporting on the DPRK as a whole was largely based on hearsay and political biases, and that reporting on the country was therefore highly unreliable. *The Telegraph* wrote: 'when it comes to covering news about the "Hermit Kingdom" it seems that sometimes the rule book is thrown out the window.'[24,25] Max Fisher from the *Washington Post* wrote that regarding North Korea: 'almost any story is treated as broadly credible, no matter how outlandish or thinly sourced.'[26] Isaac Stone-Fish wrote in *Foreign Policy* that: 'as an American journalist you can write almost anything you want about North Korea and people will just accept it.' He admitted to having done the same himself, detailing a severe 'North Korean Drug Epidemic' without substantial evidence, which later proved to be entirely false.[27] As the story depicted the country negatively however, it was widely accepted regardless. The fact that false stories consistently portray the country as worse than the reality strongly indicate an agenda of demonization rather than merely poor journalism.

Charles K. Armstrong, Professor of Korean Studies at Colombia University, noted that due to North Korea's isolation it was far easier for Western powers to depict the country in any way they chose. He wrote that isolation 'has served in the West as a blank screen on which many – often mutually contradictory – fears and fantasies have been projected.'[28] Any story which would tarnish the image of the country is picked up and reported as fact. There is often no need to check sources; if it is demonizing or demeaning then it will be accepted.

One example was the rumor that all men in the DPRK were required to get a haircut identical to that of the country's leader Kim Jong Un. This was initially reported by Radio Free Asia (RFA),[29] an American based and U.S. government funded nonprofit broadcasting corporation with the stated purpose of 'advancing the goals of U.S. foreign policy.'[30,31,32] The absurdity of this new 'law' reinforced the image of an absurd and repressive leadership in Pyongyang, and it was re-reported by major news outlets such the BBC as fact without evidence or fact-checking.[33] Typically of such stories, it turned out to be entirely false. Gareth Johnson, General manager of the Young Pioneers tour company who was in Pyongyang at the time the story was released, stated: 'we were in the country last week, and saw no-one with said haircut.'[34] Adray Abrahamian, director of the Singapore based NGO Choson Exchange who was also in North Korea at the time said the story was 'just stupid.'[35] Radio Free Asia has been found to have fabricated many of the most absurd stories about North Korea, consistently citing 'anonymous sources,' which in turn are repeated by major Western news outlets as fact.[36] Another such case was in 2017 when RFA reported that the Chinese Foreign Ministry had advised all Chinese citizens in the DPRK to immediately evacuate the country for their safety, at a time when military tensions with the United States had spiked.[37] While some Chinese citizens who heard the broadcast did evacuate, there was no record of the Chinese embassy or ministry ever giving such a warning,[38] and the Chinese Foreign Ministry had to release a statement to deny the report, calling it Fake News.[39] By using false information to demonize the DPRK, Radio Free Asia fulfills the purpose for which it receives its government funding: to 'advance the goals of U.S. foreign policy' by depicting North Korea as a pariah state and exacerbating tensions around the country.

One such story which was publicized by major Western media was that the country's recently appointed leader Kim Jong Un 'fed his uncle to dogs,' supposedly demonstrating the brutality and depravity of the DPRK's leadership.[40] This claim proved to be entirely false.[41] The story originated from a satirical Chinese social media post that was re-reported by Western media.[42] Among the most fantastical example of Western reporting however was the story in 2012 that the North Korean government claimed to have discovered a 'unicorn lair.'[43,44] This was repeated primarily by American media outlets, 'Crazy Kim Regime Claims to have Discovered Unicorns' etc. as well as in several books on the country such as the *New York Times* endorsed bestselling guide to the country: *North Korea, Unmasking Three Generations of Madmen*. When the original Korean statement was analyzed, it in fact announced the discovery of an archeological site associated with the ancient capital of King Dongmyeong of Goguryeo – a poetic term for which is 'kiringul,' a unicorn lair. A combination of cultural ignorance and a willingness to depict the country negatively led to this false reporting.

Those who have worked with North Koreans have very consistently given feedback which strongly contrasts with the country's depiction in the Western media and undermines its narratives. Serbian volleyball coach Branislav Moro, who trained North Korea's national team, noted that reporting on the country was largely detached from reality. As an example, he noted that major Western media outlets had reported on the executions of North Korean athletes as punishment for their poor performance at international competitions. Moro stated: 'for example, I sit right next to one of those "killed" athletes and I'm too ashamed to tell him that he's supposed to be dead. I even used my cellphone to check on the internet to confirm his identity. Basically there is very little truthful information out there.' Moro noted that this represented a wider phenomenon regarding demonizing misreporting on the country.[45] Indeed, Western reports of 'executions' of high profile North Korean figures, from leading pop singers[46,47] to Generals,[48] have more often than not turned out to be entirely false with these same supposedly dead figures reappearing on camera. A short disappearance from high profile meetings or television is so often treated as an opportunity by Western journalists to write a sensationalist piece about a brutal purge by an erratic leadership.

Many of those who write or comment on North Korea have little knowledge or experience of the country itself, but still go on to give it extensive negative coverage. In the introduction to his book *Only Beautiful*

Please John Everard, former British Ambassador to the DPRK, wrote of those who seek to portray the country negatively: 'I have realized whilst writing this book that there is an industry of DPRK watchers, many of whom have never set foot in the country, who make a living travelling from conference to conference to exchange the same ideas with the same people. It sometimes seems to me that the passion with which some of them defend their positions is in inverse relation to their knowledge of the DPRK. In this book I have made no secret either of my affection for the people of North Korea – which will anger those DPRK watchers determined to portray them all as brainwashed automatons.' It is from such individuals that the majority of Western reporting on the country seems to originate.[49]

Widespread ignorance of Korean culture was used to depict the death and mourning of Korean Leader Kim Jong Il in 2011 to slander the country. Videos of Koreans weeping hysterically, pounding their fists and shaking fists at the sky was taken to mean not sadness for their leader's passing, as this would contradict the image built of the 'oppressive and tyrannical' DPRK leadership, but was instead spun to exemplify the 'Madness of the Kims' grim dominion over North Korea.'[50] Koreans were reportedly crying so hysterically out of fear that if they did not do so they would be executed by the government. This story too was widely accepted, those who did not 'cry hard enough' would be shot. Koreans were, according to Western media, irrefutably mourning 'on command.'[51] In fact it was clear to anyone versed in Korea's Confucian culture – South Koreans included – mourning the death of a father figure traditionally is done by exactly such hysteric wailing, fist pounding and shaking fists. Indeed, one would see the same thing at traditional Korean funerals for many centuries before the division of the peninsula. Again, cultural ignorance and a strong Western bias towards negative interpretations facilitated false reporting to tarnish the country's image.

North Korea operates a tight security system and strict control of information due to perceived security threats from the United States and its allies. This has proven effective in making it the most difficult country for hostile Western powers to collect intelligence on. Because of the DPRK's extensive security precautions Western sources are often unable to gain access to the country to gather information. Donald Gregg, former

U.S. ambassador to South Korea, national security advisor and CIA officer, described his country's understanding of North Korea as 'the longest running intelligence failure in the history of U.S. espionage.' Isaac Stone Fish of the American *Foreign Policy* publication described the country as an 'information black hole,' as U.S. intelligence is uniquely almost completely denied intelligence and information. CIA director Robert Gates similarly described the country as a 'black hole' and 'without parallel the toughest intelligence target in the world.'[52]

Western policymakers themselves are very often unable to analyze North Korea objectively, as the information available from Western media sources is very often heavily biased against the country, if not entirely fabricated, which leads to strong prejudices in all levels of government. CIA analyst John Nixon, who worked on cases for both North Korea and Iraq, noted that the United States' leadership would consistently put their own prejudices and preconceptions above what intelligence and evidence on the countries actually indicated even if it was in complete contradiction. Nixon noted regarding the way this restricted policymakers' ability to objectively analyze states which they had been conditioned to see as 'evil,' stating after several meetings in the White House and with military and intelligence officials: 'I can conclude that U.S. policymakers were prisoners of what they thought they knew ... countervailing intelligence be damned.'

Members of the administration Nixon served under were, in relation to their own prejudices towards these 'rogue states,' 'convinced it was right, no matter what the intelligence showed.' When Nixon reported intelligence on either Iraq or North Korea which did not fit in with their images as maniacal and essentially evil regimes under which their people suffered, this intelligence was consistently dismissed. In North Korea's case, when working for the CIA he noted that 'The Agency seemed completely locked into its interpretations of Kim [Jong Il],' and evidence which contradicted their preconceived ideas was never accepted.[53] This phenomenon which appears widespread in the West in regards to North Korea is known as cognitive dissonance – under which information which undermines certain preconceptions is ignored, or in the case of North Korea labeled 'staged' or 'fake,' so as to prevent this information from challenging one's worldview. Renowned French philosopher Frantz Fanon stated regarding this condition: 'Sometimes people hold a core belief that is very strong. When they are presented with evidence that works against that belief, the new evidence cannot be accepted. It would create a feeling that is extremely uncomfortable, called cognitive dissonance. And because it is so important to protect the core belief, they will rationalize, ignore and even deny anything that doesn't fit in with the core belief.'[54] Accordingly the demonization of the DPRK and the widespread preconceived ideas on the country foster prejudices which impact U.S. policy at all levels. According to Nixon, what key decision makers from the White House to the CIA think they know is far more important than what intelligence reports the reality may be.[55]

The impact of the phenomenon referred to by Nixon on Western intelligence at the highest levels was exemplified by the testimony of former U.S. Secretary of State Madeleine Albright, who when visiting the country in the 2000s was seriously misinformed by anti-Korean propaganda and prejudices. She said: 'I went having been briefed on what kind of a weirdo he [Kim Jong Il] was from our own people. He was portrayed as reclusive-like with many girlfriends and watching porno movies – basically a very weird kind of person.' After meeting him she expressed her surprise that the way he had been portrayed to her had been completely wrong. 'He was actually quite charming ... He was very, very well prepared, responded without notes, was not only respectful but also interested in what I had to say.' To her complete surprise the talks were a success.[56,57] If the reality of the country, its rationality and willingness to negotiate were better known there may well be more calls for negotiation and diplomacy rather than military confrontation.

Dr Konstantin Asmolov, leading fellow at the RAS Institute for Far Eastern Studies' Korean Studies Center, noted based on his extensive research of the DPRK both extensive demonization by its adversaries and cognitive dissonance in the West when analyzing developments in the country – under which all positive aspects and achievements of the state are denied based entirely on speculation. Asmolov stated:

> the author sees one more aspect associated with the fundamental demonization of the DPRK as the Land of Darkness. After all, from the standpoint of the demonizing propagandists, such a state is fundamentally unable to create something positive, especially something aimed at improving the living standards of the population [...] If

> something is noticed there which is along the lines of improving the living standards of the population, it is propaganda, and the actual situation does not work that way. If they invent something useful, that is not actually their own invention, they just stole it. If something is built there, then the building has been erected on the bones of countless prisoners, or it has something to do with the Potemkin village [a term for façade or 'show city' unrepresentative of the 'true reality'].[58]

More impartial non-Western sources which do not have agendas against the country have repeatedly reported highly positively on North Korea – as doing so does not so starkly contradict their preconceived world views. Japanese citizens of Korean origin of all ages can be seen in their hundreds in Pyongyang during the holiday seasons – and though they are fully exposed to the world and to the ROK they still maintain their close cultural and educational ties to and prefer to visit the north. As one 22-year-old Japanese student of Korean origin studying a summer course in Pyongyang in 2017 told the writer on the flight out of the country: 'life is much better here, food is better. There is more of the traditional Korean culture. There are less social issues and people are far more open and welcoming than in the south.' When asked, she said she had visited the south before. Some 75,000 Koreans living in Japan have since North Korea's formation repatriated there.[59] This is not to say that the north is necessarily better – only that unlike it is so often portrayed by highly politicized Western reporting the north is not categorically worse and its people aren't forced to 'pretend' to enjoy their lives for the cameras. The Japanese Koreans, coming from a country with among the highest living standards in the world, live among the North Korean people as Koreans for extended periods and choose to return for study, work and tourism regularly in large numbers. Were the country's virtues truly a complete illusion as consistently claimed by Western media, this could not explain the actions of the Japanese Koreans who actively choose to return to the country and live among its people.

The UN workers, telecommunications executives and embassy staff from non-Western backgrounds the writer spoke to, who had all spent an extended time in North Korea, were all full of praise for a country many of them had previously known little about. Ambassadors and visiting government officials of non-aligned countries have consistently come to similar conclusions, with Egypt's renowned U.S. trained General Saad El-Shazly referring to it in his memoirs as 'that extraordinary republic, an inspiring example of what a small nation of the so-called Third World can achieve with its own resources.'[60] Syrian ambassador to the country, Tammam Sulaiman, three-year resident of Pyongyang, took this further in 2017 stating, regarding the DPRK's achievements relative to those of other nations including his own, 'I visited many other countries, [but when] I look at this country I see that out of severe poverty ... they do miracles here, really. And it's not like I'm saying what the state media says. In our country we don't have this: we thought that we were living in prosperity before the war. This country, after the sanctions and with the skills that they have, they are making miracles ... What if they were not under sanctions? They would do even more.'[61]

The sources cited by Western reporters, other than their extensive use of 'anonymous sources,' have often proven to be highly dubious. Several North Korean defectors who have become celebrities in the West as a result of their denouncing of their former homeland have given inconsistent or otherwise unreliable testimonies – from which they have derived substantial financial benefits. Shin Dong Hyuk was one such defector, whose allegations of severe human rights abuses were accepted without evidence as fact in the West. Shin's life story, *Escape from Camp 14: One Man's Remarkable Journey from North Korea to Freedom in the West*, whose title is notably indicative of the agenda it represents, the story of 'Western good' against 'Asian communist evil,' became a bestseller promoted in Western countries as a key reference for understanding the DPRK. The book was translated into 27 languages and sold worldwide – while Western human rights organizations based several of their reports on the DPRK heavily on Shin's testimony.

Following Shin's testimony and its worldwide promotion and wide endorsement, his editor and renowned former *Washington Post* journalist Blaine Harden stated that Shin had fabricated much of his story.[62] Shin later revealed that he had 'altered details' of his testimony. Harden stated that Shin was an 'unreliable narrator' and re-emphasized that 'Shin was the only source of information about his early life,' giving him substantial room to alter his testimonies as they were accepted without any need for evidence – also noting that he would not be surprised if Shin made further alternations to his testimony in future.[63] While Shin's testimony had been the basis for Western economic sanctions against the DPRK and its leadership, and was said to have 'shifted the global discourse about North Korea,'[64] these sanctions were never reconsidered in light of Shin's admission as to his falsification of information – nor did they lead the West to question their depictions of the country.[65]

The only other defector with prominence equal to or eclipsing that of Shin was Yeonmi Park, who rose to fame shortly after the flaws in Shin's testimony were revealed, and was endorsed and promoted in the West in much the same way. It has been widely reported by other North Korean defectors, and even by some prominent Western reporters with a basic knowledge of the DPRK, that Park's stories were highly inconsistent with reality and at times nonsensical. Award-winning documentary producer Mary Ann Jolley, having interviewed Park several times, noted very telling inconsistencies in her stories. In an article for the *Diplomat* Jolley details how interviews Park gave changed completely depending on when she told the story. She also noted that several facts Park gave did not stand up to reason, for example she wrote: 'In telling of her escape from North Korea, Park often says she crossed three or even four mountains during the night to get to the border and describes the pain she endured because her shoes had holes in them. However, Hyesan where Park was living is right on the river that divides the two countries and there are no mountains to cross.'[66] This was but one of many impossible claims that Park made, added to a list of severe contradictions between her different interviews. Several other observers including journalist Michael Basset concluded that Park's statements regarding the DPRK were not synonymous with the reality in the country, using outright lies to harm the country's image. Park has meanwhile reaped a small fortune from her 'sensationalized' speeches, from which she earns over $12,500 per speech according to her speaking agent.[67]

Je Son Lee, a North Korean defector, noted that several facts about Park's story were clearly fabricated. Regarding some of Park's claims she commented 'no one would believe this unless they were an idiot.'[68] South Korea professors Shi Eun Yu and Kim Hyun Ah who worked at the ROK's processing sector for North Korean refugees strongly refuted several of

Park's statements. 'It's not possible' they commented outright regarding one of her claims.[69] Another notable critic was Swiss businessman Felix Abt who had worked and traveled extensively in North Korea for seven years. He strongly refuted Park's claims about life in the DPRK based on his own experience there. Though he admitted that the stories of some defectors *may* be true even though they crucially 'cannot be verified,' Abt said he would 'only challenge claims that are obviously exaggerated or plain false.'[70]

Stories such as those of Shin and Park have been endorsed and promoted because they suit the Western agendas towards North Korea. They are able to gain such traction because of the general ignorance of the country around the world and North Korea's lack of global media with which to counter this misrepresentation. Among those with even a basic understanding of the country however, there is generally a consensus that the stories pushed by the West and on which Western Human Rights organizations and reports have based their testimonies are unreliable – often bordering on absurd. North Korea is however an ideal target for such demonization and false reporting precisely because of its isolation.

One prominent case regarding a propaganda coup against the DPRK due to a defection was that of 12 North Korean waitresses employed in China, who reportedly sought asylum in the ROK in 2016. This was hailed by Western media as yet another sign of the disillusionment of the country's population with their leadership.[71] While Pyongyang continued to insist that its waitresses had been kidnapped, publicizing interviews with their bereaved families, the ROK government of President Park Geun Hye prevented the women from accessing the press or lawyers for several months. North Korean claims were inevitably dismissed as propaganda. With the coming of a new administration in Seoul, it emerged in 2018 that North Korean claims were in fact true and the waitresses had been kidnapped by South Korean intelligence, reportedly on orders of President Park, and wished to return home. Only after being reported by South Korean media was it was later re-reported by a number of Western outlets and extensively covered by the *New York Times*. The supposed defections represented an abduction of North Korean citizens for political gain by the country's adversaries.[72] Many other supposed defectors claim to have been coerced or tricked into moving to South Korea from China.[73]

The number of defectors who have either returned to North Korea or sought to do so but been prohibited from leaving the south significantly undermines the Western narrative of the country.[74,75,76,77] Numbers of North Koreans seeking to return to their country after experiencing life in the south continue to rise, and life in the ROK has often failed to meet the expectations of defectors. As one North Korean living in Seoul, Kwon Chol Nam, said when interviewed in 2017: 'even though North Korea is poorer, I felt more free there. Neighbors and people help each other and depend on each other. Life is simpler there and here they are just slaves to money.' Kwon was arrested by South Korean police for attempting to return to the DPRK. His case was far from exceptional, with many North Korean defectors similarly seeking but unable to return home due to South Korean laws.[78,79] Indeed, on the very day that Kwon's interview was published a UN human rights hearing on North Korea held in Seoul was interrupted by a tearful defector, Kim Ryon Hui, who begged to be allowed to return home. She had over several years repeatedly attempted to return to the north.[80] Stories which challenge the narrative of an ROK indisputably superior to the DPRK are inevitably little mentioned in Western reporting, while reports from those who are most critical of North Korea are publicized and strongly endorsed, often leading such defectors to gain celebrity status.

While the fact that several North Koreans have defected to the south is used by The West to support their claims regarding the poor quality of life under a depraved and ineffectual government, it is also little mentioned that the ROK has offered up to $860,000 dollars per person for defections – and that the vast majority of defectors go to the ROK from third countries such as China or Mongolia or from various diplomatic postings across the world where they have access to information regarding these financial rewards.[81,82] Indeed, if such sums were offered to defectors from even the richest of countries, they would see significant numbers leaving to South Korea. South Koreans by contrast seem to need no financial incentives to seek a better life abroad, with 88 percent of the population under the age of 35 preferring to leave the country and live abroad. It is not uncommon for South Koreans to leave high-end professions as doctors and lawyers to work in low wage manual labor overseas – as was covered extensively in the Al Jazeera news network's 2016 report aptly titled 'Fleeing South Korea.'[83]

Several other statistics about the country, suicide rates,[84,85] widespread and growing alcoholism[86] and widespread underage prostitution[87] being but a few examples, indicate that the ROK is hardly the indisputably superior civilization relative to the DPRK that the West claim. By both glossing over the drawbacks of the Western aligned ROK while magnifying or even fabricating information to demonize the DPRK, the West paint a picture of angels and demons which, while strongly in line with its agenda, is far from balanced. Each state has its advantages and its flaws, and both can be considered highly successful though imperfect societies based on their handling of their respective circumstances. With the Western Bloc for years exerting what U.S. policymakers have referred to as 'maximum pressure' through both military exercises and extensive measures to cut North Korean trade and undermine the country's economy, it is only natural that it would also attempt to weaponize its extensive control of information to turn international opinion against the East Asian state. Due largely to the overwhelming discrepancy in their control of information and ability to promote their narratives internationally, this campaign has been highly successful.

Notes

1 Smith, Joanne R., and Haslam, S. Alexander, *Social Psychology: Revisiting the Classic Studies*, London, Sage, 2017 (p. 58).

2 Paul, Ronald, and McAdams, Daniel, *B-52s Over Korea ... Protecting Our Homeland?* (7:20), Ron Paul Institute for Peace and Prosperity, Ron Paul Liberty Report, January 11, 2016.

3 Bechton, Bruce E., *Military Proliferation to the Middle East in the Kim Jong-un Era: A National Security and Terrorist Threat*, (Presentation), Shurat HaDin Israeli Law Center (1:08:00) (<https://www.youtube.com/watch?v=Z8UJ-1bwOAM>).

4 'North Korea: The War Game,' *The Atlantic*, July/August 2005.

5 Harrison, Selig S., 'Promoting a Soft Landing in Korea,' Foreign Policy, No. 106, Spring 1997, (p. 60).

6 'North Korea's Stable Exchange Rates Confound Economists,' *Associated Press*, November 16, 2018.

7 Kim, Christine, and Chung, Jane, 'North Korea 2016 economic growth at 17-year high despite sanctions: South Korea,' *Reuters*, July 21, 2017.

8 Lankov, Andrei, 'Sanctions working? Not yet …,' *Korea Times*, May 29, 2016.
9 Pearson, James, and Park, Ju-Min, 'Despite sanctions, North Korea prices steady as Kim leaves markets alone,' *Reuters*, August 8, 2016.
10 Peterson, Sabrina M., 'Iran's Deteriorating Economy: An Analysis of the Economic Impact of Western Sanctions,' *International Affairs Review*, Elliott School of International Affairs at George Washington University, July 1, 2012.
11 'How Sanctions Affect Iran's Economy,' *Council on Foreign Relations*, May 22, 2012.
12 'Iraq Sanctions Kill Children, U.N. Reports,' *New York Times*, December 1, 1995.
13 'Russian economy shrinks 2% as sanctions bite – Medvedev,' *BBC*, April 21, 2015.
14 Dorell, Oren, 'North Korean Economy Keeps Humming Despite Ever-Tighter Sanctions,' *USA Today*, November 24, 2017.
15 Marshall, Tim, *Worth Dying For: The Power and Politics of Flags*, London, Elliott & Thompson, 2016 (p. 165).
16 Paul, Ronald, and McAdams, Daniel, *B-52s Over Korea … Protecting Our Homeland?*, Ron Paul Institute for Peace and Prosperity, Ron Paul Liberty Report, January 11, 2016.
17 Kim, Suk Hi, *The Survival of North Korea: Essays on Strategy, Economics and International Relations*, Jefferson, NC, McFarland, 2011 (pp. 49–50).
18 Park, Kyung Ae, *New Challenges of North Korean Foreign Policy*, London, Palgrave MacMillan, 2010 (p. 218).
19 Di Maggio, Anthony, *Mass Media, Mass Propaganda: Understanding the News in the 'War on Terror,'* Lanham, MD, Lexington Books, 2009 (pp. 295–296).
20 Sifton, John, 'North Korean mourners, crying to survive?,' *CNN*, December 22, 2011.
21 Shim, David, and Nabers, Dirk, *North Korea and the Politics of Visual Representation*, German Institute of Global and Area Studies, GIGA Research Programme: Power, Norms and Governance in International Relations, April 2011.
22 Robertson, Phil, 'Louis Cole's Merry North Korea Adventure,' *Human Rights Watch*, September 20, 2016.
23 Butterly, Amelia, 'Vlogger Louis Cole Denies North Korea Paid for Videos of his Trip,' *BBC*, August 18, 2016.
24 O'Carroll, Chad, 'North Korea's invisible phone, killer dogs and other such stories – why the world is transfixed,' *The Telegraph*, January 6, 2014.
25 Taylor, Adam, 'Why You Shouldn't Necessarily Trust Those Reports Of Kim Jong-un Executing His Ex-Girlfriend,' *Business Insider*, August 29, 2013.
26 Fisher, Max, 'No, Kim Jong Un probably didn't feed his uncle to 120 hungry dogs,' *Washington Post*, January 3, 2014.

27 Stone Fish, Isaac, 'The Black Hole of North Korea,' *New York Times*, August 8, 2011.
28 Armstrong, Charles K., 'Korea and its Futures: Unification and the Unfinished War, Review,' *The Journal Of Asian Studies*, Vol. 60, No. 1, February 2001.
29 (In Korean) 'North Korean University Students Copy Kim Jong Un's Hairstyle,' *Radio Free Asia*, March 25, 2014.
30 Welch, David, *Propaganda, power and persuasion from World War I to Wikileaks*. New York, I. B. Tauris, 2014.
31 Sosin, Gene, *Sparks of Liberty: an insider's memoir of Radio Liberty*, University Park, Pennsylvania State University Press, 1999 (p. 257).
32 Radio Free Asia, 'About.' Broadcasting Board of Governors. n.d. Retrieved June 5, 2016.
33 'North Korea: Students required to get Kim Jong-un haircut,' *BBC*, March 26, 2014.
34 Quigley, J. T., 'That Viral Kim Jong-Un Haircut Story is Another Hoax,' *The Diplomat*, March 27, 2014.
35 Macdonald, Hamish, 'Why men's Kim Jong Un hairstyle requirement is unlikely true,' *NK News*, March 26, 2014.
36 Asmolov, Konstantin, 'How the Radio Free Asia released the whole set of baloney,' *New Eastern Outlook*, November 26, 2016.
37 'China Warns its Citizens in North Korea to Leave as Conflict with U.S. Looms,' *Sputnik*, May 2, 2017.
38 Ibid.
39 Ministry of Foreign Affairs of the People's Republic of China, Foreign Ministry Spokesperson Geng Shuang's Regular Press Conference, May 2, 2017.
40 Dier, Arden, 'Report: Kim Jong Un fed uncle alive to 120 starved dogs,' *USA Today*, January 3, 2014.
41 Kaiman, Jonathan, 'Story about Kim Jong-un's uncle being fed to dogs originated with satirist,' *The Guardian*, January 6, 2014.
42 'A lot of money rides on constant promotion of North Korean threat,' *RT*, May 14, 2015.
43 'North Korea Says It's Found a "Unicorn Layer",' *U.S. News*, November 30, 2012.
44 'Unicorns' Existence Proven, Says North Korea,' *Time*, November 30, 2012.
45 'Serbian Coach Reveals How Mainstream Media "Kills" North Korean Athletes,' *Sputnik*, September 16, 2017.
46 'Kim Jong Un's Ex-Lover Hyon Song-Wol "Executed By North Korean Firing Squad After Making Sex Tape",' *Huffington Post*, August 23, 2018.

47 'Kim Jong Un's "executed" ex-girlfriend comes back from the dead with appearance on state TV,' *Mirror*, May 17, 2014.
48 'Former North Korean general believed executed turns up alive,' *Fox News*, May 10, 2016.
49 Everard, John, *Only Beautiful, Pease, A British Diplomat in North Korea*, Washington, DC, Brookings Institution Press, 2012 (Preface).
50 Gourevitch, Philipp, 'Unreality Check: From Kim to Kim in North Korea,' *The New Yorker*, December 19, 2011.
51 Ibid.
52 Litwak, Roberto, *Rogue States and U.S. Foreign Policy: Containment After the Cold War*, Washington, DC, Woodrow Wilson Center Press, 2000 (p. 223).
53 Nixon, John, *Debriefing the President; The Interrogation of Saddam Hussein*, London, Bantam Press, 2016 (pp. 204–205, 220).
54 Fannon, Franz, *Black Skin, White Masks*, London, Pluto Press, 2008.
55 Nixon, John, *Debriefing the President; The Interrogation of Saddam Hussein*, London, Bantam Press, 2016 (pp. 204–205, 220).
56 'Nuclear Nightmare: Understanding North Korea,' *Discovery Times*, (Documentary), 2003 (00:35:50–00:37:42).
57 *Gender in Mediation: An Exercise for Trainers*, CSS Mediation Resources, ETH Zurich Centre for Security Studies and Swisspeace 2015 (p. 59).
58 Asmolov, Konstantin, 'Korea: Large Construction Baloney,' *New Eastern Outlook* August 21, 2016.
59 Hart-Landsberg, Martin, 'Korea: Division, Reunification and U.S. Foreign Policy,' New York, Monthly Review Press, 1998.
60 El-Shazly, Lt. General Saad, 'The Crossing of the Suez,' *American Mideast Research*, 2003 (p. 83).
61 O'Carroll, Chad, 'A long way from Damascus: Life as Syria's ambassador to North Korea,' *NK News*, January 31, 2017.
62 Fifield, Anna, 'Prominent N. Korean defector Shin Dong-hyuk admits part of story are inaccurate,' *Washington Post*, January 17, 2015.
63 Power, John, 'Author of book on North Korea's founding addresses Shin controversy,' *NK News*, March 18, 2015.
64 Donghyuk, Shin, Dalhousie University, Academics, Convocation, Ceremonies, Honorary Degree Recipients, Honorary Degree 2014.
65 Dorell, Oren, 'U.S. puts N. K. leader Kim Jong Un on sanctions list for human rights abuses,' *USA Today* July 6, 2016.
66 Jolley, Mary Ann, 'The Strange Tale of Yeonmi Park,' *The Diplomat*, December 10, 2014.

67 O'Carroll, Chad, 'Claims N. Korean defector earns $41k per speech "completely incorrect",' *NK News*, June 30, 2015.
68 Je Son Lee, 'Why defectors change their stories,' *NK News*, January 21, 2015.
69 Jolley, Mary Ann, 'The Strange Tale of Yeonmi Park,' *The Diplomat*, December 10, 2014.
70 Power, John, 'North Korea: Defectors and Their Sceptics,' *The Diplomat*, October 29, 2014.
71 Ripley, Will, 'Tearful North Korean waitresses: Our "defector" colleagues were tricked,' *CNN*, April 20, 2016.
72 'Tale of North Korean Waitresses Who Fled to South Takes Dark Turn,' *New York Times*, May 11, 2018.
73 Yun, David, 'Loyal Citizens of Pyongyang in Seoul,' (Documentary), October 16, 2018.
74 Choe, Sang-Hun, 'A North Korean Defector's Regret,' *New York Times*, August 15, 2015.
75 Taylor, Adam, 'Why North Korean Defectors Keep Returning Home,' *Business Insider*, December 26, 2013.
76 Yoon, Soo, 'North Korean defectors see American dream deferred as reality sets in the US,' *The Guardian*, June 13, 2016.
77 'South Korea to deport Korean-American accused of praising North,' *The Guardian*, January 9, 2015.
78 'After Fleeing North Korea, some defectors want to go back to life under Kim Jong Un,' *ABC News*, December 14, 2017.
79 Yun, David, 'Loyal Citizens of Pyongyang in Seoul,' (Documentary), October 16, 2018.
80 'North Korean defector interrupts UN human rights event to plead tearfully to be allowed to return to Pyongyang,' *The Telegraph* December 14, 2017.
81 Hancocks, Paula, and Masters, James, 'South Korea to quadruple reward fee for North Korean defectors,' *CNN*, March 5, 2017.
82 'South Korea boosts reward for defectors from North to $860,000,' *BBC*, March 5, 2017.
83 'Fleeing South Korea' (Documentary), *Aljazeera*, December 29, 2016.
84 'South Korea still has top OECD suicide rate,' *Korea Herald*, August 30, 2015.
85 Novak, Kathy, '"Forgotten": South Korea's elderly struggle to get by,' *CNN*, October 23, 2015.
86 Chao, Steve, and Gooch, Liz, 'The country with the world's worst drink problem,' *Aljazeera*, February 7, 2016.
87 Chang, Jennifer, 'South Korea's runaway teen prostitution,' *Aljazeera*, November 12, 2012.

PART III

A Shifting Balance of Power and the West's Role in Asia Today

CHAPTER 13

Modern Japan and Western Policy in Asia

> Why must the State Department insist that only the lives of American boys be used? Why cannot other peoples of the earth be used also to help create the necessary seawall of blood and flesh and steel to hold back the communist hordes?[1]
>
> — SENATOR JOSEPH McCARTHY

> It was still difficult to imagine a sovereign Japan as anything other than dependent on and subordinate to the United States – a client state in all but name.[2]
>
> — JOHN DOWER

Japan and the United States: Assimilating the Empire of the Sun into the Western-led Pacific Order

Following the defeat of the Japanese Empire and the occupation of most of its former territories by Western military forces, the United States took over and continued to employ much the empire's apparatus for its own ends. The U.S. continued to operate Japanese imperial assets to serve its foreign policy designs in the Asia-Pacific, examples of which are numerous. Japanese military forces stationed in China were, following the empire's surrender, kept armed and co-opted into the United States' war effort there. Japanese imperial soldiers were placed under U.S. command to fight alongside 50,000 U.S. Marines and allied Chinese Guomindang forces against the Chinese communist movement. This was described by U.S. President Truman as 'using the Japanese to hold off the communists.'[3] Japanese military scientists who had worked on developing weapons of mass destruction by experimenting on Chinese civilians, including several leading figures from Japan's infamous Unit 731 biological warfare unit, were also absorbed into the United States' own biological weapons program. The scientists, war criminals of the first degree, were given full amnesty by the United States and went on to contribute to the development of American biological weapons and provide invaluable information relating to the results of their human testing. These Japanese scientists were reportedly heavily involved in the U.S. biological weapons attacks during the Korean War.[4,5]

While in North Korea Japanese collaborators were purged from government; in South Korea the United States took over much of the apparatus of the Japanese Imperial government and kept the vast majority of its elites, from administrators to military officers, in power.[6,7] A study conducted by the South Korean government in the early 2000s found that over 90 percent of pre-1990 South Korean elites had ties to collaborationist families or individuals.[8] South Korea emerged from decades of military and authoritarian rule only in the 1990s, and until then the same regime of the Japanese imperial period had largely prevailed and been used as an asset by the United States. Japanese collaborators made up much of the American installed government from 1945, including several former high-ranking Korean members of the Japanese military. Examples included the country's first Chief of Staff General Yi Ung Jun, who had previously pledged fealty to the Emperor of Japan in blood, and Kim Chong Won, former Japanese officer in the Philippines and New Guinea, who was prized as a military commander by the new government for his brutal tactics. American Ambassador Muccio called him 'ruthless and effective.'[9]

Pak Hung Sik, a Japanese collaborator and adviser to the United States' Korean Economic Mission, had testified that the ROK military was mainly led by former Japanese commanders serving the new government, saying: 'the central figures in charge of national defense are mostly graduates of the former Military College of Japan.'[10] They enforced the will of the U.S. military government highly effectively, responding to any suspected communist or anti-government sentiments among the population with force and committing numerous atrocities against the South Korean population – according to both South Korean and American reports.[11]

Japanese counterinsurgency forces were also reportedly deployed by the United States to South Korea to combat the Cheju insurgency, a conflict which some South Korean reports indicate killed up to 60,000 of the island's population within a single year.[12,13] Japanese naval units operated by former personnel of the Imperial Navy were also used to support U.S. naval operations during the Korean War, including minesweepers paving the way for the landing of the U.S. Marines at Inchon in September 1950. With Japan under direct U.S. military rule until 1952, thousands of Japanese technicians could be sent by the U.S. to aid their war effort in Korea.[14,15] Another prominent example was at the Battle of Inchon, where 79% of tank landing ships carrying the U.S. Marines into their most pivotal battle against the North Koreans were Japanese manned.[16] According to accounts from American prisoners of war, there were Japanese nationals held in the Chinese and North Korean camps. There is little doubt that Japan played a covert but not insignificant role in the Western war effort against China and the DPRK.[17] Even the comfort stations used by Japanese soldiers in Korea, which took Korean women as sex slaves, were taken over and expanded by the United States to allow military personnel access to Korean women by force in much the same way, only on a far greater scale.[18,19] The apparatus of Japan's government of South Korea was largely maintained to govern the country, only now under Washington rather than Tokyo. In this sense at least, the occupation of South Korea never truly ended with the 'liberation' by U.S. troops. It was more the case that the occupation 'changed hands' while its enforcers remained the same.

Much like its assets overseas, the Japanese imperial order was largely kept intact but placed under new American directives following the end of the war, with the economy built to be heavily reliant on the United States and the U.S. also frequently interfering in Japanese political processes to further its own goals in the country (as covered in Chapter 2). As renowned U.S. historian, Asia specialist, MIT professor and award winning author John Dower noted: 'it was still difficult to imagine a sovereign Japan as anything other than dependent on and subordinate to the United States – a client state in all but name.'[20] Bruce Cumings similarly referred to Japan as a key part of 'a historically unprecedented system of semi sovereign states,'[21] which began during the Korean War and continued into the twenty-first century, under which the East Asian power was dominated by the United States.

The close but highly unequal partnership between the former Japanese Empire and the current U.S. led Pacific regional order, or 'American Empire' as it is often unofficially termed, has continued to greatly benefit U.S. designs in the Asia-Pacific region. With the escalation of the Cold War soon after Japan's defeat the United States made significant and persistent efforts to coerce Japan to quickly remilitarize. This was strongly encouraged across several Western client states to create subservient military forces, which were expected to contribute to future US-led wars as an invaluable asset against the Soviet Bloc. Considering the unequal relationship between the two governments and Japan's subservience to U.S. interests particularly in matters of foreign policy, a modern Japanese military would serve to help the U.S. led Western Bloc in furthering its designs and combating adversaries such as North Korea, China, North Vietnam and years later Iraq – against all of which Japan contributed significantly to American war efforts. A stronger Japanese military was therefore a great asset to the interests of the Western Bloc, much as Japan's formidable imperial apparatus had been an invaluable asset to the United States.

Early U.S. Attempts to Engineer Japanese Remilitarization

With Japan under a U.S. military government, the United States had written a strictly pacifist constitution in the immediate aftermath of the Second World War which prohibited Japan from re-establishing its armed forces. Under Article 9 of the constitution, Japan was to 'forever renounce war as a sovereign right of the nation and the threat or use of force as means of settling international disputes.' This put serious constraints on the country's ability to rearm itself, and was seen as a guarantee that the country would not restore itself as a military power. The article further stated: 'land, sea, and air forces, as well as other war potential, will never be maintained. The right of belligerency of the state will not be recognized.'[22]

At the time the constitution was drafted the American public sought assurances that Japanese militarism would never rise again, and the grueling experience of the Pacific War would never be allowed to re-occur. More importantly however, the United States expected a highly favorable balance of power in the Asia-Pacific region, with China's Guomindang having been expected by both Cold War superpowers to emerge victorious from the civil war. Chiang Kai-shek's highly militaristic and closely Western aligned government would have been more than sufficient as a military partner for the United States in the Pacific and it was only after the wholly unexpected communist victory in China, despite Washington's very best efforts, that rearming Japan emerged as an imperative for the American position in the region.

With Japan directly governed by the U.S. military until 1952, the United States moved early on to capitalize on the power they had over what was formerly one of the world's leading great military and economic powers. Japan could potentially be shaped into a potent asset against the newly formed People's Republic of China (PRC) as well as the USSR, North Korea and other states which threatened the new U.S. dominated Pacific order. A draft of U.S. policy document NSC 48, written just weeks after the declaration of the PRC, described the island chain formed by Japan and Guomindang held Taiwan as 'our first line of offense from which we can seek to reduce the area of communist control, using whatever means we can develop, without, however, using sizeable U.S. armed forces.' Calls to support Japan's 'renaissance' as a great military power under the U.S. alliance, to be used as a formidable asset against China and the Soviet Union, escalated the following year after the string of defeats suffered by U.S. forces against Asian armies on the Korean Peninsula.[23] Having witnessed the potency of the Japanese military during the Second World War, the resurrection of Japan's Imperial era might as a junior partner in an American led alliance was seen as an invaluable asset in the escalating Cold War. As a result, particularly after the failure of the U.S. military intervention to keep Chiang Kai-shek's Guomindang government in power in China in 1949 and the subsequent and wholly unexpected U.S. military failures in the opening months of the Korean War, efforts were made to slowly but surely bend Japan's constitutional constraints on militarization.

The Japanese public remained both war weary and highly supportive of pacifism, despite the constitution's restrictions on military force having been externally imposed, and the U.S. military government was forced to make extensive efforts to disguise the establishment of a Japanese armed force because of this. With the outbreak of the Korean War on June 25, 1950, the U.S. military government rapidly arranged the inauguration of

Japan's first postwar ground force within a month. Though these forces were called the 'National Police Reserve,' they were equipped by the United States with weapons for modern warfare rather than domestic police action. The American Sherman and Chaffee tanks supplied were called 'special vehicles' to avoid the impression of remilitarization – so officially Japan had no heavy armored units. By 1956 Japan would be testing its first postwar domestically manufactured battle tanks, supposedly also for its 'Police Reserve,' which were fielded alongside artillery and combat aircraft. The legality of this rearmament program was seriously questioned even by U.S. officers responsible for training the Police Reserve.[24]

Chief of Staff of the U.S. Military Advisory Assistance Group in Tokyo, Colonel Frank Kowalski, played a leading role in overseeing the training the first American armed Japanese forces – describing them as 'a little American army.'[25] This had been a consistent trend across the United States' Asian client states – the formation of close military ties with the United States, adoption of military systems closely based on the U.S. military and reliance on American weaponry. Similar patterns were observed in South Korea, South Vietnam, and the Philippines among others. What distinguished Japan from other U.S. clients however, aside from its size and its history as a major imperial power which was seen to give it a greater military potential, were both its strong public desire to avoid remilitarization and its pacifist constitution – a unique means with which to resist demands for comprehensive and immediate remilitarization. Though the constitution was bent and reinterpreted numerous times, it was almost impossible without an absolute revision to allow Japan to send military forces to fight alongside the United States abroad due to Article 9. This was however not the case for South Korea, the Philippines and Thailand whose own 'little American armies' committed tens of thousands of personnel to US-led foreign wars against North Korea, North Vietnam, China and years later Iraq.

Initial American attempts to remilitarize Japan in the first decade after the Second World War were opposed by both the country's conservative Yoshida government and by prominent business circles. There was little to no Japanese popular support in any sectors of society, but with the country largely subservient to U.S. interests this went ahead regardless. Prime Minister Yoshida maintained that the constitution would need to be revised before Japan could acquire 'fighting potentiality.' What exactly this meant was unclear, but his opposition was largely ignored as the United States bent and reinterpreted the rules to create a heavily armed 'National Police Reserve.' With the U.S. rapidly expanding the Police Reserve, Prime Minister Yoshida publicly denied the country was rearming. A poll conducted in February 1952 showed that 48 percent of the Japanese population believed their Prime Minister was outright lying when he denied the country's remilitarization, while only 12 percent believed he was telling the truth.[26] As John Dower noted: 'Yoshida's posture enshrined sophistry concerning remilitarization as official policy.'[27]

Had the Yoshida government, the country's business elites and the Japanese people not collectively taken a strong stance against remilitarization in the 1950s with support from the U.S. drafted constitution, Japan in all likelihood would have fully remilitarized at an early stage under American pressure and gone on to aid the U.S. more extensively and overtly in its military interventions abroad. With the disaster the Americans faced in the Korean War the U.S. continued to secretly urge Japanese leaders to create a far larger standing army of between 300,000 to 350,000 men. This was widely seen to be a highly reckless demand made of the Japanese people and economy – one made out of fear and panic induced by the fast deteriorating situation on the ground in Korea. Prime Minister Yoshida argued that this would not only overwhelm and distort Japan's economy, but also provoke violent protest throughout the country which may well have destabilized the new state. He also argued that it would seriously agitate other Asian nations whose populations, unlike the Americans, had lived under Imperial Japanese occupation themselves and viewed prospects of a remilitarized Japan with much apprehension. Yoshida also believed, quite accurately based on the precedents set by the United States' other clients, that if Japan had a sizeable military it would come under immense pressure to provide more direct military assistance in the Korean War and later regional conflicts.

By maintaining their pacifist constitution and lack of a sizeable military, Japan's 'little American army' was able to avoid being brought in to fight overseas alongside the 'big brother American army.' Prime Minister Yoshida was eager to keep Japan from militarizing and being used by Washington to fight America's wars. When U.S. Secretary of State John Foster Dulles visited Tokyo to push for remilitarization Yoshida sent clandestine emissaries to two Japanese Socialist Party leaders urging them to hold protest demonstrations outside his office to persuade the Americans of the extent of popular opposition to militarization and the implications were it to take place.[28] Due to the unequal nature of the countries' relations, the Prime Minister could not easily withstand pressure from the United States alone. He therefore sought to persuade the United States of his position and of the dangers of remilitarization for domestic stability by demonstrating the unpopularity of the move and thus threatening instability in a vital U.S. client state. Were Japan to be destabilized the United States would risk losing a key ally in Asia, something highly undesirable especially at the time of the Cold War. Indeed, with lingering anti-American sentiments from the Imperial era and from the families of the millions of civilians killed or maimed by the U.S. firebombing campaign against Japanese population centers, there was a risk instability in Japan could end in a sharp pivot away from the Western Bloc and into an alliance with the Soviet Union and China. In this way the Yoshida government used Washington's fear of considerable backlash from the Japanese public to keep the 'National Police Reserve' at 75,000 men – thus avoiding diverting Japan's resources to support American military interventions abroad and instead focusing on economic development and retaining a pacifist non-interventionist foreign policy.[29]

75,000 men and the gradual introduction of tanks, warships and fighters was a compromise between the United States' interest in seeing a full and rapid remilitarization and its fear of the potential dangers should it force this process too quickly. Nevertheless Washington's goal to eventually see a fully militarized Japan ready to fight by its side was never abandoned – only the circumstances necessitated a gradual process rather than sudden change. Chief of Staff Kowalski referred to: 'a calculated, creeping rearmament well tuned to the will of the Japanese public and the Allied reaction,' further noting that this was not a process initiated due to the will of the Japanese public or leadership itself – but rather due to the strategic interests of the United States. Observing the stimulus which had brought about the rearmament process, the Colonel noted: 'The Japanese did not initiate the rearmament of their nation [...] Japan has an Army, Navy and Air Force now only because General MacArthur, assuming international authority, expanded the police forces of the nation.'[30] Japanese forces were expanded to 110,000 personnel in 1952, when the United States faced a stalemate and a serious and wholly unanticipated near-peer challenge to its military might on the Korean Peninsula.[31] By 1972 Japan's forces numbered 150,000, and they would grow considerably more in the years to come.[32] The constitution would be bent and reinterpreted slowly but surely, and it would be a matter of decades before the Japanese military would be deployed abroad to fight alongside the US, as had always been the intention of the Western superpower towards its East Asian client state. Japan's refusal since 1950 to accept and acknowledge the constrained but nevertheless significant remilitarization on which it had embarked would continue for decades – leaving the country in a decades-long twilight zone of rearmament.

Terms of Independence: Keeping Japan Subservient to U.S. Foreign Policy Objectives and Maintaining a Rift Between Asia's Two Great Powers

While direct Western military rule over Japan ended in the 1950s, a time when American and European rule over Asia-Pacific nations under formal colonialism began to come to an end, the Western Bloc went to great lengths to maintain its influence in the strategically important region. This was particularly critical in a time of the Cold War, when it was essential to guarantee that former colonies, upon gaining their independence, would not seek to form ties with the Soviet Bloc or with China and thus undermine the West's dominant position by breaking the ranks of U.S. led alliance. Western imperial powers thus largely adopted an approach bearing significant similarities to that of the Soviet Union in Mongolia and the Warsaw Pact nations of Eastern Europe. Direct military occupation gave way to indirect rule to ensure the countries' continued subservience to the interests of the dominating power – leaving former colonies as nominally independent client states. The policies of the West's client states were largely influenced by their former rulers and occupiers – particularly when pertaining to foreign policy and one's economic and diplomatic relations with states outside the 'free world.' Client states would also, when required, allow for a continued military presence of their former occupiers. The stances states took to various foreign policy issues, from the U.S. firebombing of Vietnam to the Soviet military intervention in Czechoslovakia, were also largely dictated by the dominating powers. Independence in foreign policymaking for such countries was largely illusory rather than genuine.

While Soviet client states that were granted token independence were restricted to some of the territories the USSR had formerly occupied, namely Mongolia and parts of Eastern Europe where communist rule would collapse with the fall of the USSR,* the Western bloc's effective neocolonies extended worldwide as its empires had, encompassing much of Latin America, Africa, the Middle East, and the Pacific – Japan included. These states, much like those in the Warsaw Pact, were given little room to determine their own foreign policies, and were required to support the positions of their masters. Their right to self-determination was thus highly constrained. As renowned U.S. strategist Zbigniew Brzezinski would later observe in regard to the emergence of token sovereignty in a growing number of former colonies as direct foreign rule receded: 'Sovereignty is a word that is used often but it has really no specific meaning. Sovereignty today is nominal. Any number of countries that are sovereign are sovereign only nominally and relatively.' Brzezinski made this statement to support the declaration of a nominally sovereign and independent U.S. client state – a means by which to 'gain political legitimacy' which direct American rule lacked while also continuing to ensure U.S. interests were fulfilled.[33]

Following the end of U.S. military rule, Japan proved a key example of a Western client state which was 'sovereign only nominally and relatively,' and the U.S. went to great lengths to ensure a continued position of power

* While Soviet aligned states such as Yugoslavia, North Korea, Cuba, Laos and Vietnam prevailed following the Bloc's collapse precisely because they were very much independent, the USSR's semi-sovereign client states all but collapsed with the Cold War's end.

over the country. In 1952 the United States' formal occupation of Japan ended with the implementation of the San Francisco Treaty. In practice however Japan was obliged to abide by several conditions imposed by the United States, which overwhelmingly dictated the terms of Japanese independence and of the peace treaty. John Dower analyzed the terms of Japan's peace treaty, which were very revealing as to the new status Japan was to have as an unequal partner to the United States:

> Although in the end the peace treaty would involve scores of nations, the Americans controlled the peacemaking process; and the exact price Japan would be called on to pay for incorporation into a Pax Americana became apparent only bit by bit. Rearmament under the American 'nuclear umbrella' was but one part of that price. The continued maintenance of U.S. military bases and facilities throughout the country was another. Okinawa was excluded from the restoration of sovereignty (just as it had been excluded from the occupation reforms) and consigned as a major U.S. nuclear base to indefinite neocolonial control [...] The communist countries would refuse to participate in a settlement that locked Japan so tightly into U.S. containment policy. In the parlance of the day, Japan had been given the choice of a 'separate peace' or no peace treaty at all; although Japanese progressives and leftists called with great passion for an 'overall peace' coupled with Japan's disarmed neutrality, this was not a realistic option.[34]

The Yoshida government learned how high the costs of independence would be, with the United States largely dictating the nature of Japan's future foreign relations in accordance with American interests. As the United States lamented the 'loss of China' through the successful overthrow of its American aligned Guomindang government in 1949, a prospective Sino-Japanese partnership appeared in the 1950s as perhaps the most serious threat to U.S. dominance in the region. Great efforts were therefore undertaken, using the United States' dominance of postwar Japanese policy as leverage, to undermine the formation of positive bilateral relations between the two countries. Japanese businessmen were keen to trade with China and gain access to its vast market – while Japanese Prime Minister Yoshida strongly supported forming diplomatic relations both for financial reasons and because he believed that Japan had the potential to influence Chinese politics in future. He believed that Japanese investment in the country would facilitate a 'fifth column for democracy.' Though the United States sought the complete isolation of the communist People's Republic of

China, Yoshida long remained adamant that Japan would pursue political and economic ties to the new state 'whether it was red or green.'[35]

Prime Minister Yoshida's apparent defiance sparked fierce opposition in Washington, and the United States was resolute that it would bring Japanese foreign policy into line with its own interests in East Asia. John Foster Dulles, soon to be Secretary of State but then still President Eisenhower's special emissary for East Asian affairs, paid the Prime Minister a visit in Tokyo to straighten out his policy. Yoshida was presented with an ultimatum to commit his country to severing any diplomatic ties to the Chinese People's Republic and instead to recognize Chiang Kai-shek's Republic of China – which by then governed only Taiwan and a few minor surrounding islets and was of negligible importance to Japan either strategically or economically. Should Yoshida fail to comply, Dulles threatened, the United States Senate would refuse to ratify the San Francisco Treaty under which Japan's sovereignty would be restored and U.S. military rule would continue indefinitely – a threat Washington was in a strong position to carry out. The threat was clear – if Japan did form ties to China then there would be no Japanese state, and the U.S. military government certainly would not permit any ties to communist China under its rule and would likely choose a successor to Yoshida who would be more accommodating of their wishes. Japan acquiesced and, as a price for its statehood, it recognized the Taiwan based Republic of China in a peace treaty in 1952 and did not form diplomatic or economic ties with the Chinese mainland – much to the chagrin of its economic elite and to the detriment of Japanese national interests.

It was not only Japan which had sought constructive relations with the People's Republic, but China's own leadership which had warmly welcomed a postwar Sino-Japanese partnership. Premier Zhou Enlai told a visiting Japanese parliamentary delegation that the war between the two countries was 'already in the past and we should let go the history and ensure that history is never repeated.' Chairman Mao Zedong believed that not only would close ties to Japan benefit both countries economically, but they could also potentially help to draw Japan out of the United States' sphere of influence through economic interdependence with China – leading to the undermining of the Western Bloc's embargo against the country. He told a visiting Japanese parliamentary delegation regarding the prospective positive ties the country and future relations' departure from their wartime animosity: 'you cannot be asked to apologize every day, can you?'[36] Despite both war-torn Asian states being keen on establishing diplomatic and business ties however, the United States successfully came between them – cementing both its near absolute influence over Japan and the near complete isolation of the People's Republic of China.

Japan was forced to accept surrender terms that seriously hindered its relations with many of its closest neighbors when such relations were in conflict with U.S. interests and Washington's containment strategy against the communist world. This served to alienate the two major Asian powers of the time from one another and thus weaken both. By doing so any true hopes of an Asian power axis based on its two emerging economic superpowers would be quashed for decades. Until today Sino-Japanese cooperation remains limited, and relations between the two have never reached their full potential. Had Japan stepped out of line in regard to its relations with the Western Bloc's adversaries they would have been punished harshly by the United States, much as they were in later years for a relatively minor infringement – violating the U.S. drafted export control limits when Japanese corporations sold dual use technologies to the Soviet Union in the 1980s.[37]

The United States' ability to hold the Japanese sovereignty as leverage to shape the country's foreign policy and ensure that the America itself would remain closer to both Asian powers, China and Japan, than they were to one another was critical to continued American primacy in the region. The policy proved largely successful. It was somewhat ironic therefore that the United States would be the one to first normalize relations with the People's Republic of China after 22 years, which it did in 1971 without notifying Japan beforehand. The Japanese, largely beholden to the United States in their foreign policymaking as they were, could only begin to normalize relations with their neighbor once Washington had set the precedent and given them the green light, which they proceeded to do September 1972.

Japan's eventual recognition of the People's Republic of China was still considered a potential threat to the United States' position in the region even after Washington had extended that same recognition. A strategy of divide and rule to prevent strong relations from forming between the two had to be implemented – largely playing on both states' historical fears of one another. For the United States to maintain its dominant position in East Asia, President Richard Nixon and his advisers planned for the United States to be portrayed to each state as its protector which could be relied on to reign in the other. As the president told his national security advisor Henry Kissinger in 1971 regarding his strategy to divide the two powers and guarantee the U.S. a dominant position: 'I believe that we have got to frankly scare the bejeezus out of (China) on Japan ... They have got to become convinced that a Japan ... without the United States is potentially more dangerous than with the United States.'[38]

Richard McGregor, award winning Australian journalist and expert on Sino-Japanese relations and the policy of the United States in East Asia, wrote regarding President Nixon's plan: 'He had a clear strategy – to stoke China's memories of the (Second World) war and with it fears of a Japanese military resurgence – to underline the benefits of keeping the United States in East Asia ... Nixon's argument was in fact a familiar one at that time, portraying the presence of U.S. forces in the region as the cork in the bottle of Japan's congenital militarism. Never mind that it was at odds with the constitution that the United States had written for Japan and the peaceful path the country had set itself on in the war's aftermath ... If China had been willing for practical reasons to sideline its wartime history with Japan, Nixon and Kissinger had decided they would now deliberately play it up.' According to McGregor, Nixon had traveled to Asia and Japan as few politicians of his era had and he understood better than anyone that Japan's politicians and people were highly unwilling to play a more assertive military role in the region. 'In this sense, Nixon's warnings about a remilitarized Japan seemed confected and cynical. His real criticism of Japan was not that it was militaristic but that it wasn't militaristic enough.'[39]

For the U.S. State Department, the historical animosity between China and Japan was the key reassurance they needed that the establishment of diplomatic relations between the countries would not lead to an undermining of the United States' dominant position or a change in the regional status quo guaranteed by the terms under which America had granted Japan self-rule. Secretary of State Henry Kissinger too believed that both China and Japan posed threats to the United States' position in East Asia but understood that should the two states remain primarily concerned with the threat each posed the other then the U.S. would be the ultimate beneficiary. He noted that Japan 'could become a big problem' and threaten U.S. interests just as China did should the balance of power shift – but so long as the two states continued to co-operate with the United States largely out of fear of one another, the balance of power would remain in America's favor.[40] This strategy has continued to be a central part of the United States' strategy in East Asia into the twenty-first century, with the Donald Trump administration in particular on the one hand deepening Japan's reliance on U.S. military protection and increasing arms sales to the country as a result of the 'threat' of China – and to some extent North Korea as well. On the other hand the U.S. President warned China that should it fail to co-operate with the United States in regard to the Korean peninsula, it would face a 'big problem' with the 'warrior nation' Japan – a reference to Japan's resurgent remilitarization.[41] Just as had been the case under Nixon, the U.S. sought to portray itself to China as the only country able to hold this 'warrior nation' in check. The United States can therefore emerge again as the prime beneficiary from each party's fear of the other – potentially guaranteeing an American dominated regional order in perpetuity.

Free, Yet Not Free: Security Treaties and U.S. Attempts to Secure an Indefinite Military Presence in Japan

As with many Western client states throughout Asia and beyond, true independence remained a distant illusion for Japan. The US-Japan Security Treaty and a related administrative agreement that accompanied the San Francisco Treaty and granting of self-rule turned out to be perhaps more inequitable than any other bilateral arrangement the United States entered into in the postwar period. The U.S. retained exceptional extraterritorial rights, and the number of military installations they demanded was far in excess of what anyone had anticipated. Hanson Baldwin, the oracular military commentator for the *New York Times*, accurately pronounced this the inauguration of 'a period when Japan is free, yet not free.'[42]

The end of the formal occupation period did not mean the end of the vast American military presence – considered by many Japanese a continuing occupation with tens of thousands of U.S. personnel deployed to this day to both Okinawa and the main islands. There were almost no changes to the deployments of American military personnel in Japan. Washington needed its forces to stay in Japan, and stay they would, particularly so long as challengers to the American-led regional order remained. To many of the Japanese population who opposed the continuation of the U.S. military presence in their country the move from U.S. military rule to a subordinate independence and continued military occupation was not seen as a significant change – restoration of nominal sovereignty was hardly worth celebrating. In a poll conducted at the time Japanese people were asked whether their country had become an independent nation. Only 41 percent answered affirmatively,[43] to the majority it was clear that Japan was still an occupied and externally controlled nation. Following their military defeat and domination by the United States however, there was little they could do.

Regarding Japan's status as a U.S. vassal state following the Second World War Michael Cox, Professor of International Relations at the University of London, LSE, noted:

> a series of unspoken but well-understood bargains between the United States and Japan's dominant ruling coalition for over half a century, Japan's Liberal Democratic Party.† The first was an acceptance by Japan that Japan would accept its subordinate position within an American-led Pacific order in exchange for an American guarantee of its security. This in turn assumed low military spending by Japan and a declaration that it would never possess, or even seek to acquire, weapons of mass destruction. The second part of the bargain was more specifically economic. This not only allowed Japan easy access to U.S. markets, it also placed Japan at the very heart of the East Asian economic region for the next forty years. Finally, underpinning

† The LDP faced no serious political challenges from their first office in 1955 until 1993, and it was only in 2009 when the first non-Liberal Democratic Party government emerged, though this lasted only until 2012.

> the relationship was a recognition that while Japan might pursue certain external policies of its own, these would never be at the expense of the United States. Japan in effect would be a semi-sovereign state with only a limited capacity to determine its own foreign policy choices.[44]

While Japan would benefit economically from its privileged position relative to other Western client states in East Asia, the 'well understood bargains' referred to were far from consensual – with the Japanese leadership's role in setting the terms negligible and Tokyo being left with little room to move towards a more independent position.

Three days after the 1952 peace treaty came into effect over 1,000,000 Japanese citizens took to the streets in 330 May Day rallies across the nation. It came to be known as bloody May Day. The major May Day rally in Tokyo was largely organized by the Sohyo labor federation on the grounds of a Meiji Shrine. Around 400,000 people gathered to protest the state of affairs. They endorsed slogans such as 'Oppose rearmament – fight for the independence of the race,' and supported opposition to war, U.S. military bases, Okinawa's status as an American colony and the demands of Japanese workers. There was notably a communist undertone to the protests, with hand-drawn placards portraying Stalin, Mao Zedong and purged leaders of the Japanese Communist Party. They referred to April 28, the day of the peace treaties, as 'the Day of National Disgrace.'[45]

Near the end of the rally the protestors began to march to the plaza in front of the Imperial Palace. The Japanese government however had forbidden the use of the Imperial Plaza for such protests and defied a Japanese court order that revoked this ban. The protestors ran to the palace chanting anti-government and anti-American slogans. Several placards read 'go home Yankee' written in English. Violence between the protestors and the police then erupted without warning when the police attacked with tear gas and firearms. As the protestors fled violence continued and many on each side were injured. Over 8,000 policemen and almost double the number of protestors were injured. Many were wounded in the back as they attempted to flee police retaliation. Bloody May Day strengthened the image of a divided Japan – with the country's position in the Cold War and the acceptance of its new subservience relationship with the United

States being a key cause of conflict. Prime Minister Yoshida appropriated an image of Korea, saying a 'thirty eighth parallel' ran through the heart of the Japanese people.[46]

In Okinawa occupation and the status of subservience of the Japanese people was even more profound. The reforms instituted elsewhere in Japan never affected Okinawa and sovereignty was not restored there for decades after it was granted to the main islands. Okinawa remained under what was essentially a U.S. military dictatorship for 26 years. The territory continues to bear the majority of the U.S. military presence in Japan to this day and its people have suffered as a result. The U.S. military presence continues to expose Okinawans to frequent sexual assaults by U.S. servicemen[47] including gang rapes of children 'just for fun' – in the words of the American perpetrators,[48] as well as drink driving, murder, disfiguring of the dead,[49] crashes and noise from military aircraft, and extreme pollution of the environment endangering local wildlife.[50] As one Okinawan victim of assault by American personnel, Yumi Tomita, recalled regarding the state of fear and widespread crimes under the 26-year American military rule: 'So many were being raped … U.S. soldiers often barged into people's homes looking for women. Locals used to ring a warning bell whenever a soldier was nearby. People protected women by hiding them in closets whenever they heard the bell.' As a schoolgirl she remembered: 'sometimes I'd be walking down the street, and I'd be chased by a U.S. soldier. I had heard of women being raped in our area, but those incidents were not reported.'[51]

Okinawa was returned to Japan in 1971 under the Okinawa Reversion Agreement, which imposed steep terms on Tokyo in return for the return of its territory. Much like the San Francisco treaty before it, it was drafted as an extremely one-sided accord strongly favoring U.S. interests at Japan's expense. The treaty protected American military administrators of the occupation period from being held accountable for any crimes they had committed in the 26 years of military rule, forced Japan to pay $320 million over the next five years for the reversion of its territory, and stated that Japan had to agree to a continued U.S. military presence on the island as a precondition for restoration of the territory.[52] The terms of the treaty, in particular the continuation of the U.S. military presence without giving Tokyo any freedom to reject it, were highly unpopular throughout the country and sparked violent protests in which a police officer was killed.[53] Okinawa too experienced rioting and attacks on American soldiers.[54]

Though Okinawa has since 1972 been under Japanese rule U.S. personnel are effectively immune to being tried for the crimes they have frequently committed against the population under a system of extraterritoriality much like citizens of Western imperial powers in China and Japan were under the Unequal Treaties.[55] U.S. forces carry out surveillance of the island's residents and particularly of anti-base organizations, activists, protest groups and journalists – a continuing but highly illegal practice under Japanese law.[56] Okinawa remains by far the poorest of all of Japan's provinces, while the transfer of governance from Washington to Tokyo had little impact on the United States' military's ability to operate from the key strategic position. It did however transfer the costs of the sizeable military bases to the Japanese government, allowing the United States to continue to operate from the strategically located territory with an effective subsidy from Japanese tax revenues.

Keeping Japanese Foreign Policy in Line: Washington's Continuing Leverage Over Tokyo

A number of different methods have long been used by major powers to keep their client states' foreign policies in line with their own, from control of food and water supplies and threats to apply force to influence over and education of a country's future political and military elites. A combination of such means became very common among imperial powers, and in many cases remain so to this day. Indeed such means were employed by the Imperial Japan itself over Manchuria, Vietnam, Indonesia, the Philippines and other overseas territories which were granted varying degrees of self-rule and independence so long as they did not step out of line with the Empire's interests. The United States has long sought to similarly maintain influence over post-imperial Japan – which it has done highly successfully since 1945 with Tokyo rarely stepping out of line with Washington in matters of foreign policy.

With the end of U.S. military rule the Japanese Liberal Democratic Party relied heavily on support from the United States both to determine the fates of its leaders and to ensure it remained in power. The Liberal Democratic Party was itself heavily reliant on the United States to remain in power, and was provided extensive funding and other support for its election campaigns through the CIA. One CIA official involved in making payments to the LDP interviewed by the *New York Times*, under what the paper indicated was a major case of corruption and foreign influence over the elections, stated: 'that is the heart of darkness and I'm not comfortable talking about it, because it worked.' Alfred C. Ulmer Jr., who had formerly directed all the CIA's Far East operations, similarly confirmed reports that the agency had been financing the LDP. Roger Hilsman, head of the State Department's intelligence bureau, referred to these payments made to the Japanese ruling party by American intelligence as 'established and so routine.' Former U.S. ambassador to Japan U. Alexis Johnson also confirmed these allegations. CIA officials further attested to the importance of obstructing the progress of the Japanese opposition and directly recruiting and funding LDP party members. 'We had penetrations of all the cabinet agencies,' one CIA official recalled regarding the extent to which the Japanese government had been infiltrated by U.S. intelligence.[57]

The U.S. pardoned a number of key war crimes suspects from the Imperial era who would later go on to assume leading positions in the LDP, Class A war crimes suspect Prime Minister Nobusuke Kishi (grandfather of later Prime Minister Shinzo Abe) among the most prominent of them, and these leaders owed their freedom and often their exemptions from execution or lengthy prison sentences to the good graces of the United States. This was part of a broader policy of offering former Imperial era officials implicated in war crimes pardons in exchange for service to further the interests of the United States. The pardoning of scientists from the military's infamous Unit 731, which had conducted crimes against humanity including medical experimentation on live Chinese prisoners – claims at the time denied by the United States but later admitted to – remains the most prominent example.[58,59] With the LDP in power for almost the entirety of Japan's post war history, influence over the party and many of its early leading members was one of many effective means to ensure that extensive American influence over Japanese policymaking would prevail.

The need to keep the LDP in power has been particularly critical for the United States given the foreign policy stances of major opposition parties – from the prominent and vehemently anti-American communist party in the 1950s to the Democratic Party of Japan (DPJ) in the 2000s. Coming to power briefly from 2009, the DPJ openly pursued the formation of far closer comprehensive ties to China and other East Asian states, prioritized new regional exclusivist trade agreements with neighbors over trade with the US,[60] and sought changes to the Japanese-American partnership unprecedented ever since the LDP had first come to power in 1955. While the LDP has often been closely associated with the legacy of the Japanese Empire, from visits paid by its leaders to the Yasukuni shrine to alleged glorification and rewriting of imperial history – glossing over major war crimes committed against Japan's Asian neighbors – the DPJ appears to have picked up on a different aspect of the country's imperial past, namely the pan-Asian ideology under which Japan had prioritized close co-operation with its neighbors and opposed Western domination of the regional order. The effect of this policy has borne a strong contrast to the LDP's approach, which has alienated Japan's potential regional partners – South Korea and China in particular.[61] While the LDP's form of Japanese nationalism has very often played in to the hands of the Western Bloc, diminishing prospects for the formation of a Sino-Japanese power bloc while leading to calls for remilitarization targeting American adversaries at the exact time that the United States and its Western partners most require support to sustain their regional dominance, the DPJ's foreign policy, closely resembling pan-Asianism and regional nationalism, by contrast threatens to strengthen co-operation between Asia-Pacific as a whole to the detriment of the Western position.[62]

As a result of the moves taken by the DPJ to strengthen trade ties with China in particular, reports were widespread in the United States that a major shift in Japanese foreign policy was imminent – with the *New York Times* reporting with much apprehension on Washington rapidly 'losing diplomatic ground to China' in what was at the time the world's second largest economy.[63] The party's less controversial stances regarding Japanese imperial history, with a leftist support base which contrasted strongly with the rightist populism of the LDP, did much to ease anti-Japanese sentiment in neighboring China and South Korea – a significant first step towards a major shift in its foreign policy orientation towards these nations.[64] The DPJ has hardly been alone in calling for such a foreign policy shift, which appeared imminent had the Hatoyama administration's time in office not been cut short. A shift towards prioritizing relations with other Asian states has become increasingly popular given the economic rise of China and South Korea the potential for closer trade ties to revive the long stagnant Japanese economy while granting greater autonomy from Washington.[65] The importance of a dominant LDP government to U.S. and Western interests in the Asia-Pacific, and the potential implications for the regional balance of power should it lose power and Japanese foreign policy be revised on similar lines to those proposed by the DPJ, thus cannot be overstated.

Former Japanese Prime Minister Yukio Hatoyama strongly indicated that the U.S. retained extensive influence over Japanese policymaking and that the Japanese leadership remained unable to deviate away from the American position – particularly in matters of foreign policy. He elaborated on this prevailing state of affairs in his country, commenting in 2016 on the United States' prevailing and potent influence over Japan's relations with its neighbors and its means of coercing the Japanese government. When asked why Japan reported regularly to America regarding development of its peace negotiations with Russia for example, and looked to U.S. for guidance on this matter, he said:

> We have a special relationship with America. We are close allies, and America is respected by the Japanese more than other partners ... I think it represents a big problem that when making foreign policy decisions, Tokyo is always guided by the United States' approach. Japan depends on America. When Russia and Japan discussed the Kuril Islands sixty years ago, Prime Minister Ichiro Hakoyama was determined to resolve the territorial dispute and was ready to accept the two [of four disputed] islands, but America strongly disagreed with this position. Washington threatened to take Okinawa [then under U.S. military rule] if Tokyo agreed to the two islands compromise. As a result, Japan failed to return the two Kuril Islands [from Russia]. Things stayed the same, and have not been resolved since. Essentially, the Kuril issue should be settled between the two countries, Japan and Russia, but

> it is very possible that the outcome of the [future] negotiations will also depend on the United States' position.

Yukio Hatoyama was hardly the only Prime Minister to openly attest to Japan's lack of independence in its foreign policymaking, with former Prime Minister Yoshiro Mori stating to much the same effect that in regard to the conduct of its foreign policy: 'Japan is bound by certain obligations to follow the US.'[66]

Regarding the resulting stances of the Japanese media and government to political issues and how these would always primarily reflect the interests of the United States, Prime Minister Hatoyama stated: 'The Japanese media and government cannot navigate away from the Cold War attitudes … They always take America's side. Tokyo is dependent on the US' views … Japan will continue to side with America and the G7 countries [Western powers].' Such profound influence over the foreign policies of regional 'allies,' as in Japan's case, has been crucial to the policy of divide and rule and to ensuring Western dominance of the Asia-Pacific region.[67] The importance of U.S. influence over Tokyo to maintaining American economic dominance of the Pacific, namely by ensuring Japan, as the world's third largest economy, does not lend clout to regional economic initiatives that are not approved by the US, is discussed in Chapter 15.

The Kuril Islands were former territories of the Japanese Empire which became part of the Soviet Union and later the Russian Federation after the Second World War. Prime Minister Ichiro Hatoyama was determined to resolve the territorial dispute over the islands with Russia which would have facilitated the signing of a peace treaty and significantly improved relations between the two neighbors – and only the opposition of a third party which sought to disrupt the accord between the two neighbors, the United States, prevented this. The USSR and Russia have both never concluded peace treaties with Japan largely due to U.S. interventions opposing such moves and using its influence in Japan to prevent their realization.

Preventing a resolution of the Kuril Islands dispute and formation of closer ties between Japan and Russia, much like Washington has long sought to prevent close ties from forming between Japan and China since 1949, remain but two major examples of times Tokyo's foreign policy has been strongly shaped by American influence – against Japan's own interests and the interests of co-operation and friendly relations among East Asian states. This has long served to isolate the country regionally, particularly during the early stages of the Cold War before the Sino-U.S. rapprochement. Former CIA operative and contractor for the American National Security Agency (NSA) Edward Snowden, having been stationed in Japan, revealed some of the means the U.S. used to maintain influence over Tokyo. This provided an invaluable insight into the relationship between the East Asian state and its former occupier. Not only did the United States collect intelligence through surveying the entire country, against Japanese law, but they also placed malware throughout Japan's crucial civilian and military infrastructure, including hospitals and dams, which could be activated 'in case Japan was no longer an ally' destabilize the country.

As the endorsed narrative of Snowden's operations in Japan stated: 'We bugged the country anyway, of course [despite it being against Japanese law]. And we did not stop there. Once we had their communications we continued with the physical infrastructure. We sneaked into small programs in their power grids, dams, hospitals. The idea was that if Japan one day was not our allies we could turn off the lights.'[68] In such a vulnerable position and facing such devastating consequences for potentially stepping out of line, it would be extremely difficult for Japan and other similarly affected U.S. clients to do anything other than continue to comply with Washington's demands – or else. Japan's independence and willingness to comply with American initiatives in the region are likely not done as freely as it would appear.

Japan's Place in the Post-Cold War World: The United States Again Pushes for Remilitarization

Since the Korean War successive administrations in the United States have consistently sought to obtain greater Japanese commitments to participate in American war efforts across the world – much as Washington's other client states such as the Philippines, Thailand and South Korea did. The potential of a fully or even partially militarized Japan, considering its history as a leading imperial power and the size of its economy, has long been and today remains great indeed. Assistance from such a power against American adversaries, from the Soviet Union and North Vietnam during the Cold War to China and North Korea today, has thus been a much sought after asset for the United States to help the country retain a favorable balance of power in the Far East. Spending just 1 percent of GDP on its armed forces, at times less, the Japanese armed forces nevertheless remain among the most capable in the world – consistently ranked within the top 10 military powers worldwide, worldwide and since the mid-2010s surpassing the military prowess of any of America's European allies.[69] Japanese naval power projection capabilities are considered particularly formidable, with the third largest destroyer fleet and third most numerous carrier fleet in the world, and the potential of an even moderately militarized Japan, perhaps spending 2.6 percent of GDP on its military as South Korea does, would be great indeed and would dramatically shift the Asia-Pacific balance of power in favor of the U.S. led regional order.[70]

The process of remilitarizing Japan has faced numerous obstacles over many decades, and has been carried out gradually and highly cautiously. During the 1991 Persian Gulf War the United States formed a coalition to fight by its side against the Ba'athist Republic of Iraq. Though Iraq and Kuwait where the fighting took place were nowhere near East Asia, Iraq being over 5,000 miles from Japan, and Baghdad had never threatened Tokyo or its interests, there was still an expectation the Western Bloc's allies and client states, collectively known to themselves as the 'free world,' would partake in the American led offensive to overthrow the 'illegitimate' Republic of Kuwait, an Iraqi client, restore the Kuwaiti monarchy, a Western client, and punish Iraq for its transgression against the new Western dominated world order.

Due to Japan's constitution it was possible to refuse American requests to dispatch troops to the Middle East, though the United States government and particularly its military were nevertheless openly displeased. There was much ill feeling towards Japan in the Western world at this time due to their unwillingness to provide direct military assistance to Western led operations. While the U.S. military hardly lacked the capabilities needed to defeat the disorganized and poorly led Iraqi forces, the image of a coalition from across the world reigning in a 'rogue state' was far better than that of a superpower relentlessly bombing a small third world country – and to this end the endorsement of Japan through the dispatch of its soldiers was given much importance.

With the United States having strongly expressed its disapproval, Tokyo moved quickly to announce that it would contribute $10 million to fund the coalition on August 29, 1990 – months before open hostiles begun. The U.S. responded coldly and again disapprovingly, following which the Japanese Ministry of Finance came out with the amended figure of $1 billion (a 10,000 percent increase). Japan's reluctance however furthered its reputation, which was propagated by much of the Western media, that it was a self-centered country and not an altruistic alliance member of the 'free world' – as the Western powers in contrast portrayed themselves. The Japanese government supplemented the already significant sum with a further $13 billion dollars in order to save face, following persistent pressure from Western powers (alone a 130,000 percent increase on the sum originally offered). This was a significant sum, greater than the annual defense budgets of all but the world's very largest militaries at the time. The country the war was allegedly fought to liberate, Kuwait, had one of the highest GDPs per capita in the world, and the war was fought under the pretext of defending them and other highly oil rich Arab nations such as Saudi Arabia. Despite this Japan was pressed into paying for a war to defend these wealthy Western clients which little served Tokyo's own strategic or economic interests. The United States, however, continued to press for more from Japan.

Following the outbreak of open hostilities Tokyo announced a further $9 billion of military support. Whether this was denoted in dollars or yen however was unclear. Japan announced the contribution would be denominated in yen, only for the United States to demand the payment in dollars – costing the Japanese treasury considerably more. Due to the highly unequal nature of their relationship however the Japanese had little choice other than to again yield to American demands.

Despite Japan's colossal financial contribution to a war effort waged in far-off deserts that had little to do with its own interests, and in spite of its well-known pacifist constitution and the limitations it placed on military action, the country was still shamed for its lack of a personnel contribution.* At a time when Japan's economy was rising and there was a genuine fear in the West that for the first time in centuries the technological and economic prowess of a non-Western nation would eclipse their own. Negative views of the country as a self-interested nation seeking economic dominance over others gained currency both among the American public and in Congress itself. Theories as to the true nature of Japan's economic success, with harsh negative undertones, were propagated throughout Western media. With the Cold War ending there was no longer a common threat emanating from the USSR, and many in the West now felt threatened by Japan as a rival to their dominance and primacy. Themes of 'yellow peril,' consistently applied by the West to all rising Asian powers in the past, were again applied to Japan.[71]

Japan's public shaming in 1991 was not something easily forgotten. As hostilities broke out Japanese ground forces major Nozomu Yoshitomi was attending joint war games in Tokyo with U.S. officers. Watching the conflict unfold live on CNN, Yoshitomi recalled the great shame he felt when asked 'how Japan could be a true U.S. ally if it hadn't sent troops.' It was made clear more that in the post-Cold War world order, under the New World Order of American primacy as referred to by President George H. W. Bush, American allies were expected to stand beside them in full no matter what. The U.S. ambassador to Japan at the time, Michael Armacost, thus gained the nickname 'Mistua Gaiatsu' – Mr. External Pressure.[72]

Financial contributions no matter how great, for great they were, were insufficient to prove oneself a 'true ally.' For this a nation had to commit itself to fighting America's wars across the world and risk the lives of its

* As a prominent British expert and Senior Fellow of the Foreign Policy Research Institute think tank told the writer regarding the American led operation: "the war was waged relatively cheaply. Not if you are Japanese, because the Japanese paid for it, and obviously not if you are Iraqi." The Western powers and their Arab allies which benefitted most from Iraq's defeat thus to a large extent did so at the expense of the East Asian country as a result of the considerable political pressure applied to Tokyo.

soldiers. The West's wars were everybody's wars. Though Tokyo contributed not only colossal financial aid, but also aided in minesweeping operations after the fighting had ended, the United States and its other allies made it clear that Japan's contribution was insufficient. In Kuwait's official thanks, following the return of the American aligned Arab monarchy to power, Japan did not receive mention. Though dozens of other countries were listed in the full-page advert the Kuwaiti monarchy published in the *New York Times*, the Japanese who had contributed so significantly were not. Was this deliberate? Pacifist constitution or not, manpower contributions were expected and this was a key factor influencing a gradual series of policy changes which continue to affect Japan until today.

Japan's response came in October of the same year when a United Nations Peace Cooperation Bill was submitted to the Diet (Japanese Parliament). This bill would provide a legal framework for Japan to contribute to military operations overseas. The bill aimed to organize domestic institutions for appropriate and quick co-operation with United Nations peacekeeping and other operations – a first and more publicly acceptable step towards the sanctioning of Japanese military deployments abroad. Opinion was divided within both the Diet and the Ministry of Foreign Affairs however, and ultimately legislation failed to pass. With the opposition holding a majority in the upper house of the Diet it was unlikely that the closely Western aligned Liberal Democratic Party, which was by far the most supportive of militarization, could pass. The vast majority of the Japanese population opposed the motion, with only around 20 percent supporting it, and the bill was shelved on November 8. This far from ended the debate regarding remilitarization.

Prime Minister Kaifu had continuously stressed that 'checkbook diplomacy' was no longer adequate, stating in the aftermath of the 1991 Gulf War: 'I think it is widely understood we have to make personnel contribution as well as financial ones.'[73] The U.S. led 'New World Order' had spoken, and it was now Japan's turn to act. Either compliantly militarize and abandon pacifism, however gradually, or defy the world's one superpower, that which had such tremendous influence over Japan. There was little real choice – only a question as to how militarization could take place in a means acceptable to the firmly pacifist Japanese population.

Despite strong opposition Japan's Peace Cooperation Law was passed in 1992, allowing the country's Self Defense Force – the official name of the Japanese armed forces – to participate in United Nations peacekeeping operations abroad. This is widely considered a response to the country's international shaming a year beforehand, and though to many the Peace Cooperation Law seemed benign to others it appeared but a step towards full remilitarization. As senior General Tetsuya Nishimoto of the Ground Self Defence Force said of the first UN mandated Japanese military deployment abroad, 'that was the starting line.'[74] The shaming of Japan in the Gulf War had led to debate as to the nature of Japan's alliances, with a new stress being put on the importance of the Japanese-American military and security alliance in the post-Cold War world. The incident thus served to drive Japan into a closer military alliance with the United States.

In 1997, Tokyo and Washington formulated the 'Guidelines for Japan-U.S. Defense Cooperation.' As General Nishimoto observed: 'We learnt from the Gulf War that just sending money and not people would not earn us international respect.' The two powers began work on a possible emergency contingency to fight a war in Korea should it break out.[75] The United States had long sought to topple the government in Pyongyang, and now that the USSR had fallen and the United States reigned almost unchallenged it seemed an opportune time to do so. The U.S. had very real plans for an attack on North Korea in the 1990s, a state whose military forces and deterrence capabilities were at the time a shadow of the formidable strength they would reach 20 years later. Japan was set to be a part of and contribute to any such war efforts, and would work with the U.S. soon afterwards on a joint missile defense system under the pretext of a North Korean threat.[76]

The legacy of the Gulf War and its impact on the perceptions of both the Japanese military and the Liberal Democratic Party, regarding the need to bring about change to the country's non-interventionist policy, would remain a prominent influence for over two decades. The country's shaming was a key influence on its movement away from the pacifism that had defined it since the Second World War, several Japanese officials involved told Reuters – with this shame being described as a burden on the country's shoulders. Tomohiko Taniguchi, adviser to Prime Minister Shinzo Abe on foreign policy, said following Japan's commitment to support the American military in 2015: 'For the first time, we are just about to be able to exercise collective defense with the U.S. and others, so the feeling is we have finally been able to get the [Gulf War] burden off our shoulders.'[77] That year the Japanese military began its first joint offensive drills with the United States to train for amphibious assaults and capturing of strategic islands – an offensive role and far cry from the renouncement of military force. The country would three years later inaugurate its own Marine Corps specialized in carrying out offensive amphibious warfare operations.[78] The extent to which United States has been able to influence Japan's policy and coerce it to act as suits their interests, namely to remilitarize to support American war efforts, was great indeed. As one Japanese anti-militarization protestor observed: 'they [the United States] can't bear all the military costs on their own, so they want Japan to share the costs. My impression is that Japan is legislating the security bills in response to the US' request.'[79]

Following the passage of the Peace Cooperation Law in 1992, the Japanese Diet would build on it with a very considerable further step towards militarization in 2003. On July 25 of that year the Diet made its most significant deviation from their post war pacifism yet, approving the dispatch of Japanese forces to support the United States in Iraq. This was not a UN peacekeeping mission, and America's 2003 Iraq war had been strongly opposed by the United Nations – one of the few motions which ever faced a significant majority opposition on the Security Council. Then Japanese Prime Minister Junichiro Koizumi overrode significant opposition, a no confidence vote, and a late-night filibuster to pass the highly unpopular legislation – which gave the American war effort, widely labeled an illegal act of aggression, valuable endorsement from an internationally respected Asian power. Despite having sent small numbers of troops as UN mandated peacekeepers abroad in the past decade, involvement in the Iraq War was hardly comparable and entirely unprecedented. No Japanese soldier had fired a gun or been killed in action since the Second World War, the actions of peacekeepers mainly being regulated to reconstruction and other activities with little to no risk.

To legalize the deployment of Japanese troops in Iraq, Prime Minister Koizumi pushed the Iraq Assistance Special Measures Law through parliament – which built on the 1992 Peace Cooperation Law and moved Japan considerably further down the path of militarization. To allow its passage the law forbade participation in active fighting, requiring Japanese troops to be deployed in 'areas where no combat is taking place.' This however could never be practically guaranteed in Iraq at the time, where the operations of several insurgent groups meant that there were no well-defined battle lines. American officials for their part made it clear that Japanese forces needed to be fully armed when deployed. The law also differed from the Peace Cooperation Law in that Japan would send personnel to an open warzone – and they would do this not as neutral UN peacekeeping forces, but actively taking a side in an ongoing war.

With United States military taking casualties in the tens of thousands against Iraqi insurgents, they were finally ready to call upon the assistance of their Asian partner to fight and die by their side in a war half a world away. Japan's path to reach a state where it was ready and able to do so had been slowly paved over time – in line with the United States' need for active support from its ally. Without the international shaming during and after the Gulf War the Japanese most likely would not have moved to allow their defense forces to participate in UN peacekeeping actions abroad. Without the prior deployments of Japanese troops abroad as peacekeepers, deployment to Iraq would have been too sudden a departure from pacifism. Involvement in Iraq was hailed by some as the 'end of an era' in the history of Japan.[80] Over time, little by little, the restrictions on the use of Japanese military force abroad were lifted.

Award-winning British journalist Jonathan Watts observed at the time regarding the Japanese government's actions and their divergence from the original meaning of the constitution and Article Nine: 'Mr Koizumi and his predecessors have steadily eroded the significance of this document to allow the SDF [Self Defense Force] to serve as a more active ally to the US.'[81] The greatest beneficiary of this was clear – and the same party will continue to be the primary beneficiary of an increasingly militarized Japan. Prime Minister Koizumi himself pledged Japanese backing in the Iraq war to President Bush, knowing full well not only that this would be very unpopular at home, but that it would likely considerably tarnish his image domestically as well. After voicing his strong support for the U.S. led invasion his domestic disapproval rating soared to 49 percent – exceeding his approval rating of only 40 percent.[82]

Participation on the ground not only seriously undermined Japan's image as a neutral nation, but also endangered Japanese civilians around the world, who were now made legitimate targets by international terrorist organizations and insurgent groups operating in Iraq just as the country's soldiers were. As a Japanese anti-war protestor and history student noted when interviewed in 2015, Japan being dragged into wars alongside Western powers in dangerous regions such as the Middle East would endanger the country's citizens. She stated to this effect: 'If Japan shares the same policy beliefs with the [United] States, Japan could be targeted by terrorists just like Britain and other U.S. allies.'[83] This proved to be true, and Japanese civilians have since become the targets of Islamic terrorist organizations on multiple occasions as a direct result of the country's active support for Western interventionist wars.[84] Japanese citizens were put at a far greater risk from terrorist attacks because of the country's participation in the Iraq War, and were targeted on several occasions. Two Japanese diplomats in Iraq were shot and killed in November 2003 while working to finalize preparations for the deployment, and in 2004 Iraqi insurgents took hostage three Japanese citizens – threatening to burn them alive unless Japan withdrew its forces from Iraq. They were subjected to psychological torture, though many of the scenes were notably not shown by Japanese media. The hostages were to be spared only if Japan withdrew from the war.[85] Though the three citizens were eventually released under unclear circumstances,[86] other kidnappings and killings occurred including the capture and beheading of backpacker Shosei Koda in 2004.[87] The new danger Japanese citizens very quickly found themselves under now that the country had abandoned pacifism and neutrality remained considerable.

Japan's considerable deviation from its post war pacifist principles led to a dilemma regarding maintaining its image as a neutral supporter of international consensus and peaceful resolution while participating in the United States' military interventions which were very much unilateral. This became particularly apparent at the time of the 2003 Iraq War, when the United States again showed it was prepared to make war without UN or even NATO support to ensure foreign policy objectives abroad using its status at the time as an unchallenged military power. A high-ranking Japanese diplomat observed: 'As is obvious from the case of the Iraq War, the United States is prepared to act in its capacity as sole world superpower.' He went on to write:

> Unlike the days when coordination among Western powers aligned behind the United States was absolutely essential ... today broad international coordination is not always compatible with the Japan-U.S. alliance, no matter how fundamental both of them may be in shaping Japan's foreign policy. This incompatibility was inherent in the question of whether or not Japan should support the US- and UK-led military action against Iraq, because that action did not enjoy the full consent of the international community ... It the context of their [US-Japan] bilateral alliance, it is difficult to imagine Japan and the United States taking divergent approaches in their basic security policies in a situation such as the conflict in Iraq.[88]

By aligning itself so closely with the United States, so much so as to support them even when acting directly against a UN consensus, Japan was largely sacrificing its own valuable and carefully cultivated image and neutrality. The diplomat's comments also show that Japan was very much beholden to the United States in its foreign policy. Theirs was far from an equal alliance – rather an Asian nation forced to follow in the steps of the Western superpower. This was wholly out of step not only with pacifism, but perhaps even more so with their Imperial era foreign policy under which committing troops to fight in the West's wars and serve as a vassal state for Western imperialism was unthinkable. Indeed, as hawks in the Japanese leadership called for it to become a 'normal country' and remilitarize– this new Japan would lack both the valuable freedom not to fight of the pacifist postwar era and the freedom to choose when and against whom to fight and how to conduct its foreign policy as in the Imperial era.[89] A remilitarized Japan serving as a U.S. vassal state is very much the worst of both worlds when it comes to Japanese interests – lacking both the dignified independence and self-determination of the Empire and the peace, security and low defense spending of the postwar years.

Japanese public opinion has consistently, though to varying degrees, been opposed to militarization, with the greatest benefit of the United States' occupation in the 1940s and 1950s widely considered in Japan today to be that it brought a democratic system and facilitated low defense spending. It seems however that to a great extent the government has not been beholden to the will of its people, willing to sharply defy public opinion and put Japanese citizens in harm's way for little apparent benefit other than appeasing the United States, undermining the country's much valued pacifism. In his book *The US-Japan Alliance: Balancing Soft and Hard Power in East Asia* Professor Tsuneo Akaha wrote of Japan's involvement in the 2003 Iraq War:

> It should be noted that the Japanese government's decision to support the U.S. military action in the absence of international consensus was met with strong disapproval among the Japanese public, who remained unconvinced that all peaceful means had been exhausted before the military action was taken. Japan's popular pacifism, the geographical distance between Iraq and Japan, and Japanese unfamiliarity with the Iraqi situation were behind the public's reluctance to endorse the US-led military attack on Iraq. The Japanese government's alliance realism vis-à-vis the United States had trumped the wisdom of the Japanese people.[90]

The deployment of the SDF to Iraq was but one stage in Japan's gradual remilitarization, a process which the United States has sought to further hasten since the implementation of the Obama Doctrine and Pivot to Asia in the early 2010s due to the increasingly unfavorable military balance it faces the Pacific. With U.S. forces deployed to the Asia-Pacific region set to be outmatched by those of the Chinese People's Liberation Army, a seeming inevitability based on an analysis of a number of decisive factors (as covered in Chapter 17), the U.S. needs Japan more than ever to commit personnel and funding to preserving the Western dominated Pacific regional order – which rests heavily on military supremacy.

Japan's acquisition of aircraft carriers, a key power projection asset, has come gradually hand in hand with its emergence as a major partner for American initiatives overseas – and has been highly symbolic of the erosion of Japanese pacifism through slow but incremental steps. The Japanese Navy first developed two 19,000 ton helicopter carriers, the Hyuga Class warships, which it commissioned from 2009. These were followed by the larger 27,000 ton Izumo Class which entered service in 2015 and 2017. While the commissioning of the Izumo Class was seen as a step towards developing a carrier fleet, the Navy maintained that the carriers were 'helicopter destroyers' – a loophole Russia has similarly used for its own aircraft carrier in terming it a 'heavy aircraft carrying missile cruiser.' With Japan's 'helicopter destroyers' able to operate STOVL (short takeoff vertical landing) capable fighters such as the American F-35B stealth jet, Japan in 2017 expressed interest in acquiring the aircraft – allegedly not for carrier use but rather for operations from short runways. It later emerged that the Izumo Class warships were in fact purpose built to deploy fixed wing fighter jets from the outset.[91] The military would later express its intention to operate the F-35B from the Izumo Class ships – giving the country its first aircraft carriers since 1945.[92] Between them carrying approximately 40 fighters, this would make Japan a formidable carrier power. With Japan's leadership having called for the commissioning of a 'mothership,' potentially the first of many much larger carrier warships, this could well be the first step of many to developing a sizeable carrier fleet.[93]

While commissioning a dedicated aircraft carrier directly would have been too direct a deviation from the constitution and faced widespread opposition, doing so in gradual stages has allowed Japan's ruling party to overcome this challenge. The approach to requiring a carrier capability is very much symbolic of the wider approach to remilitarize Japan – laying groundwork through small, incremental, and often seemingly benign steps. The end of Japanese pacifism has thus come to resemble the death of a frog in boiling water – a slow and unrealized descent into a new era.

Japan has escalated its military presence in the East China Sea significantly since the announcement of the United States' 'Pivot to Asia,' and commissioned several new advanced weapons systems since then. More recently Japan has supported the United States by deploying its navy to the South China Sea, an area where it has no territorial claims but nevertheless has played a key role in supporting the Western Bloc's initiatives against Chinese interests there.[94] In 2018 Japan deployed a 27,000 ton Izumo Class carrier to carry out several months of patrols in the South China Sea – likely the first of many such deployments which in future could include fixed with stealth fighters.[95] Submarines and destroyers were also deployed.[96] Japan has also increased participation in military drills alongside U.S. and South Korean forces simulating a war against North Korea,[97] while its Navy has conducted extensive reconnaissance near North Korean coasts and reported findings directly to the United States.[98] Tokyo has also used the perceived threat from North Korea, which has threatened retaliatory strikes against U.S. military bases throughout the Pacific including those in Japan if attacked, to push for the development of pre-emptive strike capabilities.[99] These have included plans to induct long-range U.S. built cruise missiles, the JASSM-ER, which when mounted on its fighter aircraft would allow the country to strike enemy targets with precision over 2000 km from its shores – giving Japanese fighters coverage of Beijing, Shanghai, Taiwan, Russia's Far East and the entire Korean Peninsula. Though North Korea's induction of missiles with similar ranges was deemed an unacceptable threat to regional peace by the Western Bloc, as a Western partner Japan could quietly acquire such missiles without any issues being raised. While acquisition of such military capabilities is hardly unusual for a major power, Japan's enhanced military capabilities are set to be used not to benefit Tokyo's own foreign policy goals – but rather to support those of the United States against regional powers which oppose the Western led regional order as Japan once did. It was for this reason that the beginning of the LDP's renewed remilitarization drive coincided with the U.S. 'Pivot to Asia' in the early 2010s. Unlikely to enhance Japan's security, adopting a closely U.S. aligned interventionist policy when geographically situated so closely, well within strike range, of the Western Bloc's three foremost potential military adversaries puts the country and its citizens at considerable risk.

In July 2014, as the U.S. military's Pivot to Asia began to gain considerable momentum, Japan's Liberal Democratic Party led by Prime Minister Shinzo Abe forwarded and strongly supported legislation calling for a reinterpretation of country's pacifist constitution, specifically Article 9, to allow the Japan to intervene militarily abroad to defend 'allied states.' There was little doubt that this the 'allied state' in mind was the United States, which was seeing fast rising tensions with China, Russia and North Korea – all countries closely bordering Japan by sea. Involvement of the Japanese military would be an invaluable asset to the U.S. should war with any of these countries break out – and such legislation made Japanese participation in such wars far more likely. The legislation was passed, though by means which were widely viewed as having been illegitimate as Prime Minister Abe circumvented the constitutional amendment procedure and unilaterally dictated a radical change to the meaning of one of the

Constitution's most fundamental principles without Diet debate, public approval or a vote – all of which would have likely halted the passage of the legislation.[100]

Opposition to the legislation was predominantly based on the argument that it would lead to Japan being involved in external conflicts to support the Western Bloc's military adventurism across the world. As Taro Yamamoto, head of the opposition party, claimed: 'If this legislation passes, we will absolutely be caught up in illegal American wars.' Mizuho Fukushima of the Social Democratic opposition party noted that such legislation could lead Japan to become 'accomplices to murder' by aiding the United States in its foreign wars. The belief that Japan's government was unable to refuse requests by the United States to deploy its military however it is required by American interests was widespread in the country, and fueled opposition to the legislation. As Tsuneo Watanabe, senior fellow at the Tokyo Foundation policy research group concluded: 'It's partly about public distrust of Japan's own government. People think Japanese leaders are too weak to say no to the U.S.'[101]

In May 2017 Prime Minister Abe sought to build on the legislation passed in 2014 by setting a 2020 deadline for passing further revisions to Article 9 to recognize the country's military.[102] Passing constitutional recognition for the military would be one of the most significant constitutional amendments yet, and would have consequences for Japan's future involvement to support the United States militarily. The *New York Times*[103] and Japanese papers such as *Asahi Shimbun*[104] noted that the vast majority of Japan's population supported the pacifist constitution. Future amendments may well have to be enacted in much the same way as the collective defense legislation of 2014, the only way for the Abe government to make changes to the constitution without the support of parliament or the public.

Prime Minister Abe stated in 2017 regarding his intentions to amend the constitution and make Japan a 'normal country' in regards to its right to retain military capabilities: 'Now is precisely the time to unchain ourselves from the post-World War II regime, and that includes rewriting the Constitution.'[105] Japan is a sovereign state with every right to alter its constitution and pursue militarization, particularly considering that this constitution was written by the United States for Japan under an occupying military government. The move may be seen as a means for Japan to reclaim a part of its sovereignty lost to it since 1945, and ending of the U.S. imposed 'post-World War II regime.' Constitutional amendments facilitating remilitarization however are in fact if anything representative of a loss of sovereignty and self-determination for the Japanese people due to two critical factors. The first is that they are strongly opposed by the Japanese public, who support and have benefited immensely from the country's pacifism in light of both the low defense spending required and the security the country has long enjoyed due to its non-interventionism. The second is that remilitarization, far from being carried out to free Japan from the diktats of the United States, are being carried out primarily for the benefit U.S. and Western interests in the Asia-Pacific region at Washington's urging. The 'perfect time to unchain ourselves' Prime Minister Abe referred to coincided with the time the U.S. more than ever needed a remilitarized Japan to support it.

Japan's latest drive towards militarization began as the U.S. led Western Bloc sought to further integrate the country into its own military alliances. As Victor Cha, former director for Asian affairs at the White House's National Security Council and senior advisor at the Center for Strategic and International Studies think tank, noted in 2007: 'As Japan extends its security profile to become more of a global player, it is doing so wholly within the context of a US-Japanese alliance.'[106] Japan's remilitarization is very closely tied to the needs of the United States to dominate the Asia-Pacific. In 2016 European powers attempted to expand the U.S. led Western military organization NATO to Asia by encouraging Japan to join the organization. Prime Minister Abe responded that it may be possible in the future, but at the time not only did he fear a deterioration of relations with Russia, but also a harsh public condemnation of such a move.[107]

Despite the much touted threats to Japan allegedly posed by China and North Korea, which have served as valuable pretexts for remilitarization, the Japanese people continue to oppose an interventionist foreign policy. Nevertheless the United States wishes that Japan be militarized, and though military rule of the mainland officially ended over half a century ago, Washington's influence remains unchallenged and can be rarely be opposed by Japan's government – regardless of public opinion. The nation remains 'free but not free,' as so many Western client states do in Asia and beyond. Japan never gained full autonomy, and the U.S. forces deployed there are set to stay indefinitely as the country remains a subservient but increasingly active partner, increasingly relied on to shoulder the burden of maintaining the Western dominated order in the Pacific – the very same order the Japanese Empire had seven decades prior expended such great efforts to end.

The United States Military in Japan: Controversy and Beneficiaries

The United States has maintained a significant military presence of tens of thousands of personnel in Japan for over 70 years since the country's surrender in 1945. These have been a crucial asset to the United States in its interventions in the Asia-Pacific, from the CIA's war in Indonesia where Okinawa was used as a staging ground for operations, to the Chinese Civil War, the Korean War, the Vietnam War and the recent tensions following the 'Pivot to Asia.' In all of these cases the use of extensive military facilities in Japan were instrumental in allowing the United States to project its power across the region. The United States' Council of Foreign Relations for this reason named the extensive American military facilities in Japan as the 'anchor of the U.S. security role in Asia.'[108]

The American military presence has been indefinitely maintained under the pretext of providing security against potential aggression by the USSR during the Cold War, though afterwards the military presence remained. Following Japan's independence there was a significant movement calling for the removal of U.S. personnel, and only the outbreak of the Korean War allowed the United States to retain their military facilities.[109] New pretexts for the continued American military presence in Japan were continually found, and even the very existence of the slightest opposition to the U.S. led regional order in the Asia-Pacific can be used as a pretext for Japan to require American protection. For example in the 1990s James R. Lilley, former CIA agent stationed in Asia then U.S. Ambassador to South Korea, then to China, made interesting remarks regarding U.S. policy's need to give the image of a 'threat' in Asia to maintain their military presence – reportedly stating: 'If North Korea did not exist, we would have to create it to give us the excuse to keep our Seventh Fleet in Japan after the end of the Cold War.'[110] Given his credentials he was one of the most well-informed people on the strategy of the United States in the region. The very existence of North Korea, the only state other than China which rejected the regional Pax-Americana, which at the time had negligible military capabilities and was suffering from severe food shortages, was used as a pretext to maintain the vast U.S. military presence in Japan.

While pretexts for a continued military presence in Japan have varied over several decades, the real reason for the United States' military deployments to the country are little spoken of and remain largely elusive. There may not in fact be any 'real' military threat to Japan, until recently a pacifist and non-interventionist nation with few resources and a highly capable and modern Self Defense Force giving little incentive to any of its neighbors to attack it. Maintaining a strong military presence in the Japan, while it may not be needed to defend the country, is vital to both granting the United States influence over the affairs of the country and to allowing it to project power throughout the region.

The Asia-Pacific continues to increase its economic prowess and move to become a potential center of the global economy. As countries in the region become increasingly interdependent for trade, with China replacing the United States as the leading trading partner for most Asian states, the U.S. must focus more on asserting its military supremacy and relying on force to maintain any claim to regional leadership in the face of a declining economic supremacy relative to those of regional powers. This was attested to by Political Science Professor Joseph Cheng who stated: 'The U.S. still wants to maintain its influence in the region, which it considers to be one of the most important strategic regions in the world for the U.S. … In the view of the rising economic strength of countries like China, Japan and even South Korea, the U.S. will have to rely much more on this military presence to maintain that kind of influence. Certainly, nowadays it seems that many Southeast Asian countries including Japan are adopting various types of what they call "hedging strategies", which means strengthening military capabilities on their part as well as strengthening military cooperation with the US.'[111]

Despite Japan's welcoming of the United States' military presence and its adherence to the diktats of U.S. policy, the United States has made clear that its own affinities will continue to lie with Western nations over Japan. The United States does not account for Japanese interests, and very often significantly endangers them, while the Japanese accommodate for American and Western regional interests to their own detriment. This was shown in the case of the United States spying on the government of Japan and major Japanese companies, which was revealed in 2015. A list released a list of 35 'top secret' Japanese targets which were spied on by the American NSA, which also included Cabinet officials, major banks and leading companies that competed with Western economic interests. They also spied on the 'content of a confidential prime ministerial briefing that took place at Shinzo Abe's official residence.'[112]

The United States proceeded to share this intelligence information with Canada, Britain, New Zealand and Australia. When this spying activity was leaked by Wikileaks its founder Julian Assange commented: 'The lesson for Japan is this: do not expect a global surveillance superpower [the United States and its Western allies] to act with honor or respect. [In their relations with other states, even allies] there is only one rule: there are no rules.'[113,114]

Former U.S. Marine and Vietnam War veteran Douglas Lummis, today an anti-war activist resident in Okinawa, similarly advised against Japan's continuing faith in the military partnership with the United States stating: 'Many young people don't even know there was a war in Vietnam and those that do remember haven't grasped that the U.S. lost that war – and almost every war since ... The Japanese government insists that Japan should stick with the U.S. for its defense, but we need to rethink what power really is.'[115] American operations and their military presence in Japan have not gone unopposed by the Japanese people, who despite their central government's general subservience to the Western Bloc's interests in military and foreign policy issues, have organized significant protests and campaigns to limit or end the American military presence in the country.

Despite the unequal nature of their partnership the Japanese leadership seems on the whole to be committed to adhering to the will of the Western Bloc, particularly in the conduct of its foreign policy. Since the 'Pivot to Asia' and the resulting escalation in regional tensions it has become clear what role Japan's military is set to play in the West's designs for the region. Japan has recently expanded its military activities not only in the East China Sea but also in support of Western powers in the South China Sea where it has no territorial claims. The Japanese Defense Minister stated in September 2016: 'Japan, for its part, will increase its engagement in the South China Sea, for example, Maritime Self-Defense Force joint training cruises with the U.S. Navy and bilateral and multilateral exercises with regional navies.'[116] This development strongly indicates that Japan's remilitarization has far more severe implications than as a token force against terrorist insurgents in the Middle East, but that it has the potential to provide significant backing to Western militaries both in the Asia-Pacific and further afield. The stronger Japan's military becomes and the fewer restraints put on its actions, the greater an asset the United States will have in the region.

Notes

1 Hanley, Charles J. and Choe, Sang Hun and Mendoza, Martha, *The Bridge at No Gun Ri: A Hidden Nightmare from the Korean War* (p. 144).
2 Dower, John, *Embracing Defeat, Japan in the Wake of World War II*, New York, W. W. Norton & Company, 2000 (p. 408).
3 Truman, Harry S., *Memoirs, Volume Two: Years of Trial and Hope, 1946–1953*, New York, Doubleday, 1956 (p. 66).
4 Harris, Sheldon H., *Factories of Death: Japanese Biological Warfare, 1932–1945, and the American Cover-up*, Abingdon, Taylor & Francis, May 3, 2002 (Chapter 17).
5 Deane, Hugh, *The Korean War, 1945–1953*, San Francisco, CA, China Books and Periodicals, 1999 (p. 156).
6 Kim, Monica, The Interrogation Rooms of the Korean War; The Untold History, Princeton, NJ, Princeton University Press, 2019. (p. 48, 55, 219).
7 Millett, Alan R., 'Captain James H. Hausman and the Formation of the Korean War, 1945–1950' *Armed Forces and Society 23*, no. 4, 1997 (p. 515).
8 Cumings, Bruce, *The Korean War: A History*, New York, Modern Library, 2010, (p. 58).

9 Ibid. (Chapter 7: Part 5, 'Mr. Massacre').
10 Rozman, Gilbert, and Armstrong, Charles K., *Korea at the Center: Dynamics of Regionalism in Northeast Asia*, New York, M. E. Sharpe, 2006 (p. 85).
11 Shaines, Robert A., *Command Influence: A Story of Korea and the Politics of Injustice*, Parker, Outskirts Press, 2010 (p. 395).
12 Cumings, Bruce, *Korea's Place in the Sun: A Modern History*, New York, W. W. Norton & Company, 1997 (p. 221).
13 'The Background of the Present War in Korea,' *Far Eastern Economic Review*, 31 August 1950 (pp. 233–237).
14 Cumings, Bruce, *Origins of the Korean War: The Roaring of the Cataract, 1947–1950*, Volume 2, Princeton, NJ, Princeton University Press, 2004 (p. 726).
15 Chen, Jian, *China's Road to the Korean War: The Making of the Sino-American Confrontation*, New York, Colombia University Press, 1996 (p. 147).
16 Levine, Alan J., Stalin's Last War; Korea and the Approach to World War III, Jefferson, McFarland & Company, 2005, (p. 83–84).
17 Kim, Monica, The Interrogation Rooms of the Korean War; The Untold History, Princeton, NJ, Princeton University Press, 2019. (p. 321).
18 Schrijvers, Peter, *The GI War Against Japan: American Soldiers in Asia and the Pacific During World War II*, New York, New York University Press, 2005 (p. 212).
19 Oh, Arissa, *To Save the Children of Korea: The Cold War Origins of International Adoption*, Stanford, CA, Stanford University Press, 2015.
20 Dower, John, *Embracing Defeat, Japan in the Wake of World War II*, New York, W. W. Norton & Company 2000 (p. 408).
21 Stone, I. F., *Hidden History of the Korean War*, Amazon Media, 2014 (Foreword by Bruce Cumings).
22 The Prime Minister of Japan and His Cabinet, *The Constitution of Japan*, November 3, 1946.
23 *New York Times*, December 22, 1950.
24 Kowalski, Frank, *An Inoffensive Rearmament: The Making of the Postwar Japanese Army*, Annapolis, MD, Naval Institute Press, 2014 (Chapter 3: 'Basic Plan').
25 Ibid. (p. 72).
26 Dower, John, *Embracing Defeat, Japan in the Wake of World War II*, New York, W. W. Norton & Company 2000 (p. 547).
27 Ibid. (p. 548).
28 Dower, John, *Embracing Defeat, Japan in the Wake of World War II*, New York, W. W. Norton & Company, 2000 (p. 548).
29 Ibid.

30 Kowalski, Frank, *An Inoffensive Rearmament: The Making of the Postwar Japanese Army*, Annapolis, MD, Naval Institute Press, 2014, Chapter 3: 'Basic Plan.'
31 Kowalski, Frank, *An Inoffensive Rearmament: The Making of the Postwar Japanese Army*, Annapolis, MD, Naval Institute Press, 2014 (p. 72).
32 *The Military Balance*, Volume 108, International Institute for Strategic Studies, 2008 (pp. 408–411).
33 Congressional Record: Volume 149 Part 23, November 25, 2003 (p. 31866).
34 Dower, John, *Embracing Defeat, Japan in the Wake of World War II*, New York, W. W. Norton & Company, 2000 (p. 552).
35 McGregor, Richard, *Asia's Reckoning; The Struggle For Global Dominance*, London, Allen Lane, 2017 (p. 26).
36 Ibid. (p. 28).
37 Rosenblatt, Robert A., 'Toshiba: Soviets Already Had Technology: French Submarine Equipment Found in USSR, Company Claims,' *Los Angeles Times*, September 10, 1987.
38 *Foreign Relations of the United States, 1969–1976, Volume XVII, China, 1969–1972, 165*, 'Memorandum From the President's Assistant for National Security Affairs (Kissinger) to President Nixon,' undated, Office of the Historian, United States of America Department of State.
39 McGregor, Richard, *Asia's Reckoning; The Struggle For Global Dominance*, London, Allen Lane, 2017 (p. 42).
40 Ibid. (p. 51, 52).
41 Johnson, Jesse, 'Trump warns China it could face "big problem" with "warrior nation" Japan over North Korea,' *Japan Times*, 4 November, 2017.
42 *New York Times*, April 19, 1952.
43 Dower, John, *Embracing Defeat, Japan in the Wake of World War II*, New York, W. W. Norton & Company 2000 (p. 553).
44 Cox, Michael, and Stokes, Doug, *U.S. Foreign Policy*, Second Edition, Oxford, Oxford University Press, 2012 (p. 262).
45 Dower, John, *Embracing Defeat, Japan in the Wake of World War II*, New York, W. W. Norton & Company, 2000 (pp. 554–555).
46 Ibid.
47 'Okinawa Suspect allegedly admits to rape of woman before killer her,' *Japan Times*, May 21, 2016.
48 Watanabe, Teresa, 'Okinawa Rape Suspect's Lawyer Gives Dark Account: Japan: Attorney of accused Marine says co-defendant admitted assaulting 12-year-old girl "just for fun,"' *Los Angeles Times*, October 28, 1995.
49 'Brutal Rape and Murder of Okinawa Woman Gets U.S. Marine Life in Prison,' *Sputnik*, March 12, 2017.

50 'Endangered Okinawa dugong's habitat to be bulldozed for the sake of U.S. military base,' *RT*, April 29, 2015.
51 Vine, David, *Base Nation, How U.S. Military Bases Abroad Harm America and the World*, New York, Henry Holt and Company, 2015 (Chapter 10: 'Militarized Masculinity').
52 Albertson, Eileen, *The reversion of Okinawa: its effect on the international law of sovereignty over territory*, Judge Advocate General's School, U.S. Army, March 30, 1973 (p. 114).
53 Eldridge, Robert D., 'Post-Reversion Okinawa and U.S.-Japan Relations,' *U.S.-Japan Alliance Affairs* Series No. 1, May 2004.
54 Masamachi, Inoue, *Okinawa And the U.S. Military: Identity Making in the Age of Globalization*, New York, Columbia University Press, April 17, 2007 (p. 312).
55 McNeill, David, 'Rape victim marks 10 years on lonely crusade for justice,' *Japan Times*, April 10, 2017.
56 Mitchell, Jon, 'How the U.S. military spies on Okinawans and me,' *Japan Times*, October 19, 2016.
57 Weiner, Time, 'C. I. A. Spent Millions to Support Japanese Right in 50's and 60's,' *New York Times*, October 9, 1994.
58 Harris, Sheldon H., *Factories of Death: Japanese Biological Warfare, 1932–1945, and the American Cover-up*, Abingdon, Taylor & Francis, 2002 (p. 220).
59 Taylor, Jeremy, 'Biology at War: A Plague in the Wind,' *BBC Horizon*, (Documentary), October 29, 1984.
60 Tabushi, Hiroko, 'Japan Unveils Plan For Growth, Emphasizing Free Trade in Asia,' *New York Times*, December 30, 2010.
61 Rachman, Gideon, *Easternisation, War and Peace in the Asian Century*, New York, Vintage, 2017 (pp. 88–89).
62 Tabuchi, Hiroko, 'Japan's New Prime Minister Takes Office, Ending an Era,' *Japan Times*, September 16, 2009.
63 Valencia, Mark J., 'In Japan, U.S. Losing Diplomatic Ground to China,' *New York Times*, January 24, 2010.
64 Saeki, Satoshi, 'China Proposes Hatoyama Visit Nanjing Incident Site,' *Daily Yomiuri*, January 22, 2010.
65 'As security pact with U.S. turns 50, Japan looks to redefine relations,' *The Japan Times*, January 19, 2010.
66 'Ex-Japan FM: I Told Putin We Follow U.S. Policy as We're Surrounded by Nuke States,' *Sputnik*, May 22, 2018.
67 'Stationing American troops in Japan will lead to bloody tragedy – ex-PM of Japan,' *RT*, (televised interview), November 6, 2016.
68 Stone, Oliver, and Fitzgerald, Kieran, *Snowden* (2016) (details of biographical film confirmed by Edward Snowden). (Rebello, Lara, 'Snowden "uncomfortable"

with the accuracy of Joseph Gordon-Levitt's portrayal of him in new Oliver Stone film,' *IB Times*, September 12, 2016.)

69 'National Rankings by Military Strength,' Military Watch Force Comparison (2018), *Military Watch Magazine* (<https://militarywatchmagazine.com/forceapp/countries/>).

70 'Military expenditure (% of GDP),' *The World Bank* (<http://data.worldbank.org/indicator/MS.MIL.XPND.GD.ZS>).

71 Dower, John, *War Without Mercy: Race and Power in the Pacific War*, New York, Pantheon, 1986 (p. 10).

72 Kelly, Tim, and Kubo, Nobuhiro, 'Gulf war trauma began Japan's retreat from pacifism,' Reuters, December 20, 2015.

73 Statement by Prime Minister Toshiki Kaifu regarding the Dispatch of Minesweepers to the Persian Gulf, April 24, 1991.

74 Kelly, Tim, and Kubo, Nobuhiro, 'Gulf war trauma began Japan's retreat from pacifism,' *Reuters*, December 20, 2015.

75 Ibid.

76 Kelly, Tim, and Kubo, Nobuhiro, '1991 Gulf war trauma began Japan's retreat from pacifism,' *Japan Today*, December 21, 2015.

77 Kelly, Tim, and Kubo, Nobuhiro, 'Gulf war trauma began Japan's retreat from pacifism,' *Reuters*, December 20, 2015.

78 Panda, Ankit, 'Japan Actives Amphibious Rapid Deployment Brigade,' *The Diplomat*, April 9, 2018.

79 Soble, Jonathan, 'Japan Parliament Approves Overseas Combat Role for Military,' *New York Times*, September 19, 2015.

80 Watts, Jonathan, 'End of an era as Japan enters Iraq,' *The Guardian*, July 26, 2003.

81 Watts Jonathan, 'Koizumi has time on his side,' *The Guardian*, September 22, 2003.

82 Shinoda, Tomohito, 'Japan's Top-Down Policy Process to Dispatch the SDF to Iraq,' *Japanese Journal of Political Science*, Volume 7, Issue 1, April 2006 (pp. 71–91).

83 Soble, Jonathan, 'Japan Parliament Approves Overseas Combat Role for Military,' *New York Times*, September 19, 2015.

84 Mullen, Jethro, and Botelho, Greg, 'ISIS threatens to kill 2 Japanese hostages unless Tokyo pays $200 million,' *CNN*, January 21, 2015.

85 'Get out of Iraq or we burn hostages alive, Japan told,' *The Guardian*, April 9, 2004.

86 'Three Japanese Hostages Released,' *CNN*, April 14, 2004.

87 'SDF logs cast doubt over legality of Japan's Iraq mission,' *Nikkei Asian Review*, April 17, 2018.

88 Akaha, Tsuneo, *Japan Alliance: Balancing Hard Power in East Asia*, Abingdon, Routledge, 2011 (pp. 66–67).
89 'After his election success, Japan's leader takes aim at pacifism,' *The Economist*, October 26, 2017.
90 Akaha, Tsuneo, *Japan Alliance: Balancing Hard Power in East Asia*, Abingdon, Routledge, 2011 (p. 67).
91 'Japan's Izumo Class Warships Designed as Aircraft Carriers from the Outset, Met with Much Apprehension Abroad,' *Military Watch Magazine*, February 28, 2018.
92 Gady, Franz-Stefan, 'Japan Approves Plans to Convert Izumo-Class Into F-35-Carrying Aircraft Carriers,' *The Diplomat*, December 19, 2018.
93 'Japanese Supercarrier Coming Soon? Leadership Call for Commissioning of 'Mothership' for Power Projection Operations,' *Military Watch Magazine*, June 16, 2018.
94 'China warns Japan against militarism, says Tokyo must learn lessons of history,' *Press TV*, March 23, 2017.
95 'Japan Deploys Newest Carrier to the South China Sea; Extensive Implications of Tokyo's Growing Military Involvement in Western Led Regional Initiatives,' *Military Watch Magazine*, July 7, 2018.
96 'With a Submarine, Japan Sends a Message in the South China Sea,' *New York Times* September 18, 2018.
97 Lendon, Brad, 'US, South Korea, Japan start drills off North Korea,' *CNN*, March 14, 2017.
98 'Japan Tightens Patrols Around N Korea at U.S. Request – Reports,' *Sputnik*, January 13, 2018.
99 Gady, Franz-Stefan, 'Deterring North Korea: Japan Lawmakers Push for Preemptive Strike Capability,' *The Diplomat*, March 9, 2017.
100 'Reinterpreting Article 9 endangers Japan's rule of law,' *Japan Times*, June 27, 2014.
101 Soble, Jonathan, 'Japan Parliament Approves Overseas Combat Role for Military,' *New York Times* September 19, 2015.
102 Tatsumi, Yuki, 'Abe's New Vision for Japan's Constitution,' *The Diplomat*, May 5, 2017.
103 Rich, Motoko, 'Shinzo Abe Announces Plan to Revise Japan's Pacifist Constitution,' *New York Times*, May 3, 2017.
104 'EDITORIAL: Japan should extol, not negate, 70-year history of Constitution,' *Asahi Shimbun*, May 3, 2017.
105 Ibid.

106 Cox, Michael, and Stokes, Doug, *U.S. Foreign Policy*, Second Edition, Oxford, Oxford University Press, 2012 (p. 263).
107 'Merkel Offered Shinzo Abe NATO Membership, Reports Japanese Press,' *Sputnik*, May 2, 2016.
108 Xu, Beina, 'The U.S. –Japan Security Alliance,' *Council on Foreign Relations*, July 1, 2014.
109 Stone, I. F., *Hidden History of the Korean War*, Amazon Media, 2014 (Chapter 6: 'Time Was Short').
110 Engdahl, F. William, 'Behind the Putin Invite to Kim Jong-un,' *New Eastern Outlook*, February 18, 2015.
111 'U.S. relies on military presence to maintain its influence in Asia,' *RT*, May 27, 2016.
112 'Target Tokyo,' *WikiLeaks*, July 31, 2015.
113 Ibid.
114 Becker, Jo, and Erlanger, Steven, and Schmitt, Eric, 'How Russia Often Benefits When Julian Assange Reveals the West's Secrets,' *New York Times*, August 31, 2016.
115 Mitchell, Jon, 'Battle Scars: Okinawa and the Vietnam War,' *Japan Times*, March 7, 2015.
116 'Japan to boost South China Sea role with training patrols with U.S.: minister' *Reuters*, September 15, 2016.

CHAPTER 14

Economic War on Asia: South Korea and the Asian Tigers

> A market is not politically neutral; its existence creates economic power which one actor can use against another.[1]
>
> — ROBERT GILPIN

A leading cause of leading Western powers' newfound focus on the Asia-Pacific region has been its increasing economic prosperity since the end of European and American colonial rule.[‡] While the West once held a monopoly on the modern industrialized economy, the undermining of this monopoly by the Japanese Empire, and more so later by the USSR, posed a serious threat to the West's nations' global primacy in the mid-twentieth century. Asia's economic rise has particularly since the 1990s, with the Soviet challenge to Western dominance settled, thus been perceived as a key threat to the West's position as a global center of power.

Though the importance of a retention of Western military primacy has been repeatedly emphasized by analysts and policymakers, it is at least as important if not more so for the Western Bloc to maintain economic primacy – the latter being a key facilitator of the former. Western policy towards the Asia-Pacific has long sought to ensure that the region cannot rival the West in its economic prowess. This was referred to by renowned American scholar George Kennan, chair of the State Department's Policy Planning staff, who stated that the policy goal of the United States in the

‡ For those that dispute that the United States was ever a colonial power, in the Pacific alone one need only look to the annexation of the Philippines, Guam and Hawaii and the former status of Okinawa.

region should be to maintain its 'position of disparity' separating the wealth of the U.S. and Western Europe from the poverty of Asian nations.[2] As a key report by the U.S. State Department's Policy Planning Staff, marked top secret but since declassified, stated: 'Disparity [in wealth] is particularly great as between ourselves and the peoples of Asia. In this situation, we cannot fail to be the object of envy and resentment. Our real task in the coming period is to devise a pattern of relationships which will permit us to maintain this position of disparity without positive detriment to our national security.'[3] Maintaining this disparity remains crucial to the West's continuing status as world's dominant force – giving the Western Bloc considerable freedom to shape world affairs in line with its own interests. Development and modernization in Asian nations has thus been perceived as a potential major threat to Western power.

Asia-Pacific nations starting with Japan and followed by the 'Asian Tiger' economies of Hong Kong, Singapore, South Korea and Taiwan – have since the 1970s emerged as fast modernizing economic powers with the potential to eclipse the stagnating economies of the West and become a new center of the global economy. This trend has only increased with time, and by the mid-1990s the 'Asian Tiger Economies' were well on their way to joining Japan in becoming global economic powers, with rising living standards and technological development which threatened to potentially eclipse those of leading Western nations. The Tiger Economies were themselves closely followed by the success stories of less developed but fast-rising and more populous Asian economies of Indonesia, Malaysia and Thailand. Behind these was the far more populous nation with perhaps the greatest economic potential of all. China's economy was by the 1990s fast rising with annual growth rates well into the double digits, and having eradicated the widespread illiteracy and drug addiction which had hindered it for so long the country was rapidly modernizing and growing. With the downfall of the USSR in 1991, these rising Asian economies emerged as by far the greatest threat to the Western Bloc's position of primacy – leading to a major shift in Western policy towards these countries.[4] Renowned U.S. foreign policy specialist, award winning journalist and chief foreign affairs columnist for the *Financial Times* Gideon Rachman was one of many who observed that the root cause of the West's growing inability to shape international affairs as it once did was 'the extraordinary economic development in Asia' – namely the Asia-Pacific region – which led to a 'long run shift in global economic power.'[5] By allowing Asian economies to rise peacefully, the West had effectively failed to maintain its 'position of disparity' – with serious results for the balance of power in the world which threatened to undermine hundreds of years of undisputedly Western dominated world order.

Michael Cox, professor of international relations at the University of London, LSE, noted the Asia-Pacific's unique potential to eclipse the West as a center of economic power. He stated: 'The region overall appears to be economically "blessed," not so much in terms of raw materials but with other, more intangible, but important assets, including a culture of hard work, a system of entrepreneurial values, a plentiful supply of labor, a huge reservoir of capital, and a set of political and economic structures that allow the state to play a critical role in engineering successful economic outcomes.'[6] Cox was far from alone in observing this phenomenon – one as true today as it was in the 1990s.

As a result of the growing threat posed by the phenomenal economic rise and modernization taking place in Asia in the 1990s, steps had to be taken to undermine the region's progress. One major asset the Western Bloc had to destabilize Asian economies was its position as the center of the global financial system – from its near monopoly on the global reserve currencies used for international trade to its control of the world's leading financial markets. Acting as a center of what is often termed the 'wiring' of the global financial system was compounded by massive dominance of what have come to be known as the 'Bretton Woods institutions' – the International Monetary Fund (IMF) and the World Bank – both of which were conceived in a conference in Bretton Woods, New Hampshire, in the United States. These would play a key role in tackling the challenge posed to the West by a rising Asia. Both of these institutions, exerting considerable influence over the global economy, are based in Washington D.C. – with the former consistently headed by a European and the latter by an American. These institutions, overwhelmingly run by the West, have, despite names which indicate an internationalist orientation, consistently served the interests of the Western Bloc. With no alternative non-Western institutions having been formed at the time, and with the Soviet Union no longer available as a source of economic assistance, the West's effective monopoly of such global institutions proved an extremely potent tool to handle the threat of an emerging Asia. With emerging Asian economies integrated into the Western centered global financial system, and relying on Western dominated institutions for consultations and loans, they proved highly vulnerable. In 1997 the West's assets were put to use with great effect to destabilize the rising economies of Asia – causing devastation from which the region's economies would not recover for well over a decade.

Just weeks before crisis hit, the 'Asian Tigers' were heralded as the success stories of 1990s and the great 'emerging market' for the future. Indonesia, Thailand and Malaysia too were seen as among the most promising with good prospects to become middle-to-high-income countries in the near future. Stockbrokers were advising their clients that there was no better investment than this new Asian market. The hard work, endurance and investments of these Asian peoples in themselves, producing a dedicated, educated and healthy workforce, were propelling them to economic success. They had all made many sacrifices to strengthen their economies, which were facilitated largely by export-led growth. However this positive future which these peoples were set to achieve was not to be permitted by those developed high income nations whose position was threatened. The free market principles the West claimed to support had allowed many Asian nations to achieve economic miracles – showing the success of a fair market based economic system and how it rewarded an educated, hard-working and efficient people. The Western Bloc revealed however that it was willing to sacrifice the free market principles it had long advocated to further its own strategic interests. It would be a hard lesson that for all the talk of free trade and a fair global financial system, under which the best and most efficient economies would be rewarded, under which East and Southeast Asia's economies had thus thrived, the system could be rigged by the nations that founded it against those which threatened their interests.

To take South Korea, one of the region's most prominent success stories, as an example – the following events instigated by Western financial institutions led to its economic catastrophe. In the mid-1990s, shortly before the financial crisis, South Korean and other Asian governments came under pressure from the International Monetary Fund and World Trade Organization (WTO) to restructure their economies. South Korea was under considerable pressure from the United States government to implement a financial liberalization program and deregulate its financial markets. This came as part of a broader effort by the Western Bloc, and the United States in particular, to promote neoliberal ideology abroad. The Organization for Economic Cooperation and Development (OECD), an intergovernmental organization founded entirely by and overwhelmingly comprised of Western states, itself made further demands of the South Korean economy to dispense with its system of capital account control and open its market.[7] The protection of domestic interests had to go, as did the regulation of financial centers which allowed Seoul some control over capital flows in and out of the country. The ROK government was also pressured to privatize key state-owned companies. The response to these demands and the pressure to reform was to meet them half way. Barriers to financial sectors were lifted, allowing for open currency trading and little to no control over the flow of money in and out of the country. National firms however remained off limits to foreign ownership and key state-owned companies would not be privatized. The Western Bloc had shown itself to be if anything uncompromising in the pursuit of its interests in Asia however, and with open currency trading Asian markets, including those of the ROK, were now open and highly vulnerable to speculation – a vulnerability which the Western financial institutions would exploit to achieve the ends the Western Bloc sought.[8] With no capital controls, South Korea's most potent means of protecting itself from speculative attacks from Western financial institutions was lost.

Ha Joon Chang, Director of Development Studies at Cambridge University, and National University of Singapore Professor Shin Jang Sup stated in their study of the ROK's economy: 'The post-1993 financial liberalization in Korea was critical in generating the current crisis as, for the first time in the country's history, it instituted a very substantial, if not a complete, capital account liberalization.' It incentivized borrowers to contract short-term loans from abroad and left the market vulnerable to speculation while failing to strengthen the supervision system.[9] The primary reason why this took place was political pressure from Western nations and Western based international organizations such as the IMF and WTO. With capital controls lifted colossal sums of money flowed into Korean markets unregulated by the Korean government. Free capital flows had begun to occur in several other rising Asian nations such as Malaysia and Thailand at around the same time – also overwhelmingly due to external pressure.

Colombia University Professor, Nobel Prize Winner and renowned economist Joseph Stiglitz concluded that the cause of Asia's economic crisis was rapid market liberalization, primarily the sudden deregulation of capital flows – the lifting of capital controls. He noted that these were exactly the policies that the U.S. Treasury and IMF had strongly advocated and pressured nations such as South Korea to adopt. This in turn laid the ground for the country's vulnerability to speculative attacks from the West. Following the economic advice of Western governments and institutions was thus by far the greatest cause of the Asian financial crisis which came soon afterwards.[10] American International Relations Professor and former Oxford University Foreign Service Program director Rodney Bruce Hall similarly argued that the primary cause of the crisis was an IMF attempt at 'demolition' of the Asian development model – using the lifting of capital controls to set the stage for harsh speculative attacks.[11]

South Korea's compromise and its lifting of its capital controls facilitated lethal speculative attacks by Western financial institutions which devastated its now vulnerable markets. In 1996 Western brokers had invested approximately $100 billion in the South Korean economy. Within just weeks, based on pure speculation and without any changes to the South Korean economy taking place, this all changed. In 1997 investment into South Korea turned to negative $20 billion, and though the economic and political situation of the country was improving there was an unexplained discrepancy of $120 billion. Western financial sectors sharply pulled out with devastating effect. Speculative attacks did not punish Korea for economic failures, ideology, opposing Western foreign policy or anything else. The other Asian countries targeted all differed significantly in all of these aspects – but what all had in common was that they were rising Asian economic powers whose growing prosperity threatened the position of the West. As HSBC's global chief economist Stephen D.

King argued in his aptly titled work, *Losing Control; The Emerging Threats to Western Prosperity*, the rise of Asian economies, regardless of their political orientation, posed a fundamental threat to the West's position and its global economic primacy.[12] King was but one of many prominent figures in the West who had made this case – drawing attention to the need for drastic measures, such as those implemented in the 1990s, to forestall Asia's rise. Rising Asian powers, whether triumphing militarily or economically, invoked the West's feared 'yellow peril' of old – that the Asia-Pacific would rise to supplant the West as the world's center of power.

On the face of it the financial crisis had no apparent rational cause. What suddenly happened to Asian markets was referred to as 'Asian Flu,' later 'the Asia Contagion,' for lack of a better explanation. The previously booming Asian economies were devastated, with the Thai Baht, Malaysian Ringgit, Indonesian Rupiah and South Korean won all suffering. *The Economist* called the resulting losses 'a destruction of savings on a scale more usually associated with a full-scale war.'[13] These nations had adopted Western economic models, which while not necessarily flawed in themselves, when opened to global financial markets left them at the mercy of the Western centered financial system. Whatever they built could be taken from them, for the center of the economic system was in the West. The economies of their Asian nations could do little to protect themselves as they were attacked. It became clearer with time that the crisis was due to Western actions rather than Asia's own shortcomings. A *Financial Times* editorial wrote: 'The Asian crisis showed the world how even the most successful countries could be brought to their knees by a sudden outflow of capital. People were outraged at how the whims of secretive hedge funds could apparently cause mass poverty on the other side of the world.'[14] Those developed Western nations at the center of the global financial system retained a significant advantage in their ability to use economic measures – in this case speculative attacks – to destabilize the economies of developing countries which had no potential to rival them in the future.

As brokers sold all their Asian investments and advised their clients to do the same Asian currencies sunk rapidly. Asian governments were forced to drain their foreign currency reserves to prop up their own currencies. Western markets and brokers responded with increased selling which quickly depleted these reserves. As growing economies they could not compete with the economic might of the established Western financial institutions. The lifting of capital controls a year prior under immense Western pressure meanwhile meant that Asian governments had no means of regulating markets and were extremely vulnerable to speculation. In one year $600 billion had disappeared from the stock markets of these Asian nations, wealth that had been built with great effort by the peoples of these countries over several decades.[15]

In South Korea people responded in solidarity, encouraged by advertising campaigns calling on citizens to donate their belongings, particularly gold and jewelry, to save their country's economy. Within a few weeks over 3 million donated jewelry, medals, trophies, wedding rings and more. The BBC reported at the time regarding the gold donation initiative, a public attempt to save the country's hard-earned economic achievements: 'Housewives gave up their wedding rings; athletes donated medals and trophies; many gave away gold "luck" keys, a traditional present on the opening of a new business or a 60th birthday. The campaign has exceeded the organizers' expectations, with people from all walks of life rallying around in a spirit of self-sacrifice. According to the organizers ten tons of gold were collected in the first two days of the campaign. But perhaps the most extraordinary aspect of the campaign is not the sums involved, but the willingness of the Korean people to make personal sacrifices to help save their economy.'[16,17] Over 200 tons of gold were collected,[18] a huge amount from a small developing nation, and enough to drive down the world gold price.[19,20] Even this was not enough – it could never be enough. The predominantly Western based financial markets were unrelenting, and speculation would not stop driving the Korean Won down until Western goals had been achieved.

The power to determine whether Asian economies would be spared or not lay in the West's hands. Three years prior to the Asian crash a similar crisis had occurred in Mexico, the Tequila Crisis, which had been ended by Western financial institutions themselves which did not wish to see Mexico fall. Swift action was taken to stop the crisis and the U.S. treasury loaned Mexico enough money to restore faith in its markets and end the destructive speculative cycle. They would not let Mexico fail and it was well within their power to save it. No moves were made to help the Asian markets whatsoever. Indeed, several Asian economists had predicted during the Tequila Crisis that should a similar crisis occur in their own region, they were unlikely to receive the financial support that Mexico did as it was not in line with Western interests to support Asian economies as it was to prop up that of Mexico. These included Toyoo Gyohten and Hajime Shinohara of the Japanese Institute for Monetary Affairs – who realized the resulting need for an Asian monetary fund independent of the United States to support a bailout where the U.S. wouldn't.[21] Their prediction proved entirely correct. When the Asian crisis occurred it was in line with U.S. and Western interests not only to see the crisis go through, but to exacerbate the effect it had on its economic rivals. Several of the most renowned names in Western finance came out to present a unified message, not to help or lend to Asia – a stark contrast to the message for the Mexican crisis. Milton Friedman, the world famous and influential American Economics professor, made a very rare appearance in his mid-80s on CNN to say he opposed any form of bailout, and that (unlike Mexico) the Asian market should be left to 'correct itself.' That essentially meant that it should be left to crash, and Asia's should return to its 'correct' place.[22]

The view that Asian markets should be allowed to crash was also echoed by Morgan Stanley. Jay Pelosky, one of their primary emerging market strategists, made it clear to a conference in Los Angeles hosted by the Milken Institute that the U.S. Treasury and IMF should do nothing to lessen the pain of the crisis Asia was suffering. It was imperative that these two organizations held back from saving Asian markets. As Pelosky said: 'what we need now in Asia is more bad news. Bad news is needed to keep stimulating the adjustment process.'[23]

In November 1997 the Asia Pacific Economic Cooperation Summit was held in Vancouver four months after the market crash had begun. When the issue of the Asian financial crisis was raised U.S. President Bill Clinton enraged his Asian counterparts by referring what they saw as an economic catastrophe as 'A few little glitches in the road.'[24] The United States was not willing to help its supposed Asian allies and friends, though as they had demonstrated with Mexico it was entirely within their power to do so.

Alongside the perceived threat to its primacy posed by a rising Asia, the West had much to gain economically which further incentivized it to exacerbate an economic crisis in the Asia-Pacific. South Korea's economy, along with those of Malaysia and Thailand, had rapidly developed under strong protectionist policies, under which foreigners were banned from owning land or buying out national firms. These countries had kept several sectors such as transportation and energy publicly owned, while many imports from Japan and Western countries were strongly discouraged to strengthen domestic production. They were success stories, but entirely Asian success stories the benefits of which were enjoyed by their own people. Western investment banks wanted more benefits from Asia's success for themselves while Western multinationals did not want strong Asian firms providing for their own markets, and potentially competing for exports. They also wanted open access to Asian markets themselves and an end to any protectionist policies. In South Korea, as companies such as Samsung, Hyundai, Daewoo rose to prominence and success, Western investors wanted the rights to buy up the best of them. This was forbidden by the South Korean government. Asia's success was to be enjoyed by the Asian peoples, something which sounded reasonable but for the West was unacceptable. These considerable financial incentives, along with the aforementioned impact of Asia's rise in undermining the West's longstanding primacy and the political consequences this had, made exacerbation of the crisis strongly in line with Western interests.

Morgan Stanley strategist Jay Pelosky told things as they were in his analysis. If the crisis was left to worsen all foreign currency would be drained from the target Asian nations, leaving Asian companies unable to operate. They would be forced either to sell themselves or to close down – both of which suited Western interests very well. The aim was to leave Asian corporations desperate. Pelosky said in relation to the 1997 crisis: 'I'd like to see closure of companies and asset sales ... Asset sales are very difficult; typically owners don't want to sell unless they're forced to. Therefore, we need more bad news to continue to put the pressure on these corporates to sell their companies.' Pelosky thus strongly advocated withholding support for Asian markets – something from which Western corporations would go on to benefit greatly.[25]

Eisuke Sakakibara, Japan's top international finance bureaucrat at the time, noted regarding the performance of the IMF in the region: 'Absurdly, they forced fiscal consolidation on countries at a time of crisis. They shut down financial institutions – a measure that will squeeze the economy. They also introduced capital liberalization, forcing countries to move from a pegged exchange system to a flexible one. If you do that at a time of crisis, the outcome is obvious – it will cause the currency to collapse. All these measures exacerbated the Asian financial crisis.' Could provoking a currency collapse and exacerbating the currency crisis not have been the intention of the Western run IMF considering both the predictability of the results of their adjustments and, critically, the very substantial benefits the West derived directly from the destruction of Asian currencies?[26]

Canadian journalist, award-winning author and political analyst Naomi Klein stated in her analysis of the Asian financial crisis and its beneficiaries: 'What few were willing to accept to admit at the time is that, while the IMF certainly failed the people of Asia, it did not fail Wall Street – far from it. The hot money may have been spooked by the IMF's drastic measures, but the large investment houses and multinational firms were emboldened ... [The firms] now understood that as a result of the IMF's "adjustments," pretty much everything in Asia was now up for sale – and the more the market panicked, the more desperate Asian companies would be to sell, pushing their prices through the floor.' Klein speculated that the IMF could have likely intended to deepen the crisis intentionally to benefit Western firms at Asia's expense, but in the best case was 'recklessly indifferent' when intervening in Asia's economies. She stated that whatever the IMFs intentions, it was clear who had benefited from their harmful policies.[27]

British Professor of Anthropology David Harvey noted in his own study of the Asian crisis, regarding Western Bloc's ability to use its position as the center of the global financial system as a means to 'liquidize' its potential rivals: 'Liquidation can come by a variety of means ... IMF austerity programs implemented at the behest of the U.S. Treasury can be used with equally destructive effect as physical force. The distinctive role of U.S. financial institutions and the U.S. Treasury backed by the IMF in visiting a violent devaluation of assets throughout East and South-East Asia, creating mass unemployment and effectively rolling back years of social and economic progress on the part of huge populations in that region, is a case in point.'[28] Regarding incentives for the United States in particular to use its power over the global financial system to bring ruin to the Asian economies, Harvey noted that the purpose was to eliminate a threat to its place as the center of the world economy and the world's leading power, stating: 'It is hard to imagine that the U.S. would peacefully accept and adapt to the phenomenal growth of East Asia and recognize ... that we are in the midst of a major transition towards Asia as the hegemonic center of global power. It is unlikely that the U.S. will go quietly and peacefully into that goodnight.'[29]

The United States took up its opportunity to reshape Asian nations' economies in line with its own interests. As Jose Pinera, senior fellow at the highly influential Cato Institute think tank in Washington D.C., said 'the day of reckoning has arrived' – referring to the fall of the Asian Tigers as 'the fall of a second Berlin Wall.'[30,31] The Western world had won a victory in taking their primary rival, the Soviet Bloc, under their economic influence following its disintegration. Now they would neutralize emerging economic rivals in Asia as well. The devastating effect of this form of economic sabotage was clearly seen by the fall not only of Asian nations' currencies, but also the extreme and sudden economic contraction of these states. Gross National Product (GNP) of many nations fell so quickly and so greatly that it exceeded the economic devastation resulting from many of the century's major wars.[32]

Table 1

Currency	Exchange rate (per US$1)		Currency Depreciation
	June 1997	July 1998	
Thai baht	24.5	41	▼ 40.2%
Indonesian rupiah	2,380	14,150	▼ 83.2%
Philippine peso	26.3	42	▼ 7.4%
Malaysian ringgit	2.48	4.88	▼ 45.0%
South Korean won	850	1,290	▼ 34.1%

Country	GNP (US$1 billion)		GNP Contraction
	June 1997	July 1998	
Thailand	170	102	▼ 40.0%
Indonesia	205	34	▼ 83.4%
Philippines	75	47	▼ 37.3%
Malaysia	90	55	▼ 38.9%
South Korea	430	283	▼ 34.2%

The IMF, whose responsibility it was to prevent such crises, responded to the Asian crisis only after the worst was over. When they did so it was with a long list of demands for economic restructuring. The crisis was not something to be averted, but rather an opportunity to further push forward the United States' neoliberal agenda onto Asian nations. Alan Greenspan, Chairman of the U.S. Federal Reserve, perhaps the world's most influential economic policymaker, described the fall of Asia's markets as 'a very dramatic event towards a consensus of the type of market system we have in this country (United States).'[33] It was the birth of a new Asia, born into the United States' economic dominance. As Greenspan observed at the time: 'the current crisis is likely to accelerate the dismantling in many Asian countries of the remnant of a system with large elements of government-directed investment.'[34,35]

Malaysia was notably an exceptional case, and by refusing to comply with the 'advice' of Western financial institutions to restructure and adopt neoliberal policies it was spared the worst of the crisis. The country had relatively little debt even after the crisis and chose to resist the demands and pressure of the West and the IMF. As Prime Minister Mahathir Mohamad said, he should not have to 'destroy the economy in order that it should become better.'[36] That was essentially what other nations were forced to do, at great cost to their own peoples. Mahathir used any opportunity at domestic and international forums to raise awareness of and speak against the West's 'movement to turn all Asian economies [into] Anglo-Saxon laissez faire market economies.' He accused the World Bank and IMF of being instruments of the West's 'neocolonialism' and the Western financial system and currency traders of artificially devaluing Asian currencies 'so the so-called East Asian economic tigers suddenly turn into meowing cats.'[37]

As it became evident to increasing numbers of observers that the crisis was caused largely as a result of the lifting of capital controls and the resulting ease with which money could flow in and out of Asian economies unregulated, many lawmakers in other afflicted Asian states suggested simply reinstating capital controls. Malaysia did so, and their economy recovered soon afterwards. Though Prime Minister Mahathir's defiance produced results, or perhaps because of it, he was portrayed as a dangerous economic extremist in the West – all the better to prevent Malaysia's common sense approach from being adopted by neighboring states which suffered from similar economic issues. Other Asian governments relied heavily on advice from the IMF, having largely outsourced their decision-making to the fund in return for loans. As Thailand's deputy premier Supachai Panitchpakdi said at the time, while its IMF drafted economic reforms were passed by four emergency degrees to avoid parliamentary debate: 'We have lost our autonomy, our ability to determine our macroeconomic policy. This is unfortunate.'[38] The IMF meanwhile dismissed such ideas as Mahathir's as absurd without explanation.[39] The Washington based institution acted in accordance with the strategic interests of the Western Bloc – seeking not to amend the crisis or look to its causes but rather to leverage the crisis to further weaken the Asian nations and undermine their independence and their formerly successful economic models.

The IMF's own internal audit by the IMF Independent Evaluation Office during the Asian crisis was itself highly critical of the Fund's leveraging of the economic crisis to impose reforms on Asian nations. It stated that, contrary to IMF policy at the time, 'crisis should not be used as an opportunity to seek a long agenda of reforms just because leverage is high, irrespective of how justifiable they may be on merits.' It referred to the stringent structural adjustment demands as 'ill advised,' 'broader than seemed necessary' and 'not critical to resolving the crisis.' Regarding the IMF's efforts to prevent Asian nations from reinstating capital controls as Malaysia previously did, the audit stated: 'If it was heresy to suggest that financial markets were not distributing world capital in a rational and stable way, then it was a mortal sin to contemplate' capital controls. Capital controls were not, the audit stated, dismissed on the basis of their merits or lack of them, but the IMF was determined to prevent their imposition regardless.[40,41] The highly critical report by the Independent Evaluation Office did not emerge until 2003, by which time it was far too late for Asian nations affected to reconsider their near unconditional acceptance of IMF structural adjustments and economic reforms.

The IMF offered negotiations only after the crisis had run its full course, when Asian governments were deeply in need of foreign currency and unable to negotiate effectively. As Stanley Fischer, Former Governor of the Bank of Israel and Vice Chairman of the Federal Reserve System's Board of Governors, then in charge of talks for the IMF, said: 'You can't force a country to ask you for help. It had to ask. But when it's out of money, it hasn't got many places to turn.'[42] The great irony remained that the IMF's own pressure, along with the WTO, had forced the Asian nations to remove the capital controls and initiate reforms which first caused the crisis. Now these same nations were forced to turn to the very same IMF and follow its own programs to further reform their economies. One could compare the situation to asking a man who is responsible for torching your house to help put out the fire.

The first stage of the IMF reform process was to strip countries of active state participation in their own economies. What was removed was nothing less than the 'trade and investment protectionism and activist state intervention that were the key ingredients of the "Asian miracle,"' according to political scientist Professor Walden Bello.[43] With their own states unable to intervene in their interests, Asian peoples and economies were left entirely at the mercy of Western institutions. Fischer admitted that the IMF's own investigation had in fact concluded that the crisis in Korea and Indonesia was unrelated to government overspending, yet he went ahead to enforce severe and sudden austerity measured regardless. Whatever one's opinions of state interventionism in an economy, the key point was that it was pulled back not as a response to economic necessity or stimuli, or at the request of the people, but rather as an external imposition to further foreign interests. It was nothing to do with helping Asia recover. One *New York Times* reporter wrote that the IMF's actions while working to reform Asia's economies were 'like a heart surgeon who, in the middle of an operation, decided to do some work on the lungs and kidneys, too.'[44]

Singaporean political and economic analyst Cheong Yip Seng noted in 2010 that the policies advocated by the IMF and Western institutions for Asia were utterly hypocritical considering their response to the West's own financial crisis in 2008. He wrote:

> The West – including the International Monetary Fund and World Bank – prescribed bitter medicine. They extolled traditional free market principles: Asia should raise interest rates to support sagging currencies, while state spending, debt, subsidies should be cut drastically. Banks and companies in trouble should be left to fail, there should be no bail-outs. South Korea, Thailand, Indonesia were pressured into swallowing the bitter medicine … Western credibility was torn to shreds when the financial tsunami struck Wall Street [2008]. Shamelessly abandoning the policy prescriptions they imposed on Asia, they decided their banks and companies like General Motors were too big to fail. How many Asian countries could have been spared severe pain if they had ignored the IMF?[45]

The supposedly internationalist Western led institutions prescribed austerity and a selling off of corporations in the rival economies of Asia, with devastating effect, but advised generous bailouts to save their Western counterparts. Market principles were not applied consistently, but rather in a way that best suited Western economic interests.

The IMF, an organization founded in the United States in 1946 with its headquarters in Washington D.C., whose managing directors have all been Westerners, was inevitably working to further Western interests throughout the Asian crisis. During the negotiations between the IMF and the South Korean government David Lipton, U.S. Treasury Undersecretary for International Affairs, flew to South Korea and checked into the Seoul Hilton – the hotel where negotiations were taking place. He attended to ensure that the interests of U.S. firms were represented and reflected in the final agreements. Korea's economy was being rewritten to reflect Western interests. As *Washington Post* and *Wall Street Journal* economic reporter Paul Blustein wrote, Lipton's presence at the negotiations was 'a visible manifestation of the influence the United States wields over IMF policy.'[46]To reflect Western economic interests the IMF went on to privatize basic services, all of which were open to be bought by foreigners – something formerly illegal in several Asian countries including South Korea. Central banks were made independent and workforces were made more 'flexible' as Western firms – then best positioned to buy out their Asian rivals – wanted assurances that they could radically downsize them. Korea was forced to lift its laws protecting its workers against mass layoffs,[47] and the IMF set them strict layoff targets. Korea's banking sector was forced to shed 50 percent of its workers, though this figure was later reduced to 30 percent.[48] A year beforehand South Korea's unionized workforce held immense influence, but now following the crisis the government was forced to crack down on them in accordance with Western demands made through the IMF. Social spending was also reduced significantly.

South Korea was devastated and when the next presidential elections took place two of the four leading presidential candidates ran on anti-IMF platforms. This was a threat to IMF policy and Western interests in South Korea – whose reform process was just beginning. The IMF responded by refusing to release the money it would loan to South Korea, that for which Seoul had already made extensive concessions, unless an extra condition was met. All four main presidential candidates had to pledge in writing that they would stick to the deal with the IMF if they won. There would be no return to government control and protection of the country's economy against foreign interests. With the country held to ransom all candidates had little choice but to sign.[49] South Koreans could vote of course, but they could not have any say in the future running of their country's economy. It was not to be run in their interests anymore.[50] The day of the signing was fittingly known as the country's 'National Humiliation Day.'[51,52]

Within a year the economies of Thailand, Indonesia, the Philippines and South Korea had been hugely restructured and remade under the regime of the IMF, in accordance with Western interests. *Financial Times* commentator Martin Wolf referred to this imposed restructuring as 'the humiliating dictation by IMF officials operating under the thumb of the U.S. Treasury.'[53] The idea behind the IMF's restructuring was that the now remade and efficient Asian economies would supposedly attract all the currency that flowed out back in. However after a year of IMF reforms, many of them wholly unnecessary, the markets were not emboldened to invest in a new Asia – but rather panicking. The reasoning was, if Asia needed such a severe makeover as the extent of IMF reforms was widely interpreted to indicate, it must truly be a dire situation indeed and not a good place to put one's investment. While, as the IMF Independent Evaluation Office would later confirm, the institution's restructuring of Asian economies was highly excessive and was wholly unrelated to inefficiencies in these economies, this was not how speculators perceived the massive restructuring program. As the IMF had insisted on removing capital controls, the only form of defense against the destructive effects of such speculation, money again flowed out. Traders and brokers took more and more money out of Asia, further weakening the Asian currencies. South Korea was losing $1 billion every day and its debt was downgraded to junk. As Jeffery Sachs, American Economist, Colombia University Professor and director of the Earth Institute put it: 'Instead of dousing the fire, the IMF in effect screamed "fire" in the theatre.' They had turned a severe crisis into an outright catastrophe, for which target Asian nations would pay the price.[54]

The human cost of economic disaster in Asia was very high. 24 million people in the affected countries lost their jobs. In Indonesia the unemployment rate tripled. In South Korea 300,000 workers lost their jobs every month, largely due to the IMF's demands to lay off workers – which proved to be totally unnecessary and if anything counterproductive. South Korea's unemployment rate nearly tripled while its 'middle class' all but collapsed. In 1996, 63.7 percent of South Koreans had 'middle-class' living standards and incomes. By 1999, after just two years of IMF restructuring, the middle class was down to 38.4 percent. 20 million people fell into poverty during this period as a direct result of this crisis brought on by a combination of Western pressure to remove capital controls, its financial institutions' speculative attacks, and finally the Washington based IMF's painful restructuring of their economies.[55,56]

The extent of the human suffering was greater than statics could show. Through destroying economies people's lives were devastated which had horrific consequences – many of which would commonly be associated with famine or total war. Economic war targeted Asia specifically for exploitation. As the middle classes across Asia fell, the poor fell further. Many rural families in the Philippines and South Korea were left with little choice but to sell their daughters to human traffickers. These young girls would go on to work in the sex trade in Australia, Europe and the United States.[57] Without firing a shot, the West had looted not only Asia's riches and economy, but their young women as well. In Thailand public health officials reported that child prostitution had increased by 20 percent in just one year, the year following the IMF reforms.[58] The Philippines noted the same trend.[59] Again it would be primarily Westerners who would benefit from a more desperate population and resulting child sex industry in Asia, with the prime destinations for trafficking being synonymous with the Western world.[60,61] The BBC similarly reported a rise in sex tourism and child sex tourism, largely catering to Western clients, occurring as a direct result of the Asian financial crisis.[62]

Khun Bunjan, a Thai community leader, said when interviewed on the impacts of the crisis: 'we the poor pay the price ... even our limited access to schools and health is now beginning to disappear.' Khun's husband had lost his factory job, and she had been forced to send her children to work as scavengers. Young women increasingly turned to prostitution, catering especially to Western foreigners, while drug dealing became increasingly attractive to the now destitute young men.[63] Given this it was painfully ironic when U.S. Secretary of State Madeleine Albright visited Thailand in March 1999 and scolded the Thai people for turning to prostitution and 'dead end drugs.' She emphasized how it was 'essential that girls not be exploited and abused and exposed to AIDS. It's very important to fight back.' Despite this she expressed her 'strong support' for the severe austerity policies dictated by the IMF which were forcing them into such vice. On the same trip she lobbied hard to sell U.S. fighter jets worth hundreds of millions of dollars to the impoverished nation – and combined with the harsh austerity measures it appeared that the United States was encouraging Thailand to spend money on anything but its increasingly desperate population.[64,65]

While the IMF's operations had devastated the lives of the Asian peoples, they had benefited Western interests tremendously. As a result of the IMF's adjustments everything was now for sale dirt-cheap (from their daughters to Hyundai and Daewoo). The more the markets panicked, the further prices fell and the more Asian firms would be forced to close or sell. As Jay Pelosky had said, Asia needed 'more bad news to continue to put pressure on these corporates to sell their companies.'[66] It was now time to scavenge the broken Asian economy and take what could be taken at bargain prices unthinkable before 1997.

Jeffrey Garten, former U.S. Undersecretary of Commerce, had predicted that when the IMF was finished with Asia, 'there is going to be a significantly different Asia, and it will be an Asia in which American firms have achieved much deeper penetration and much greater access.'[67] Asia's crash was dubbed 'the World's biggest going-out-of-business sale' by the *New York Times.*[68] *Business Week* called it a 'business-buying bazaar.'[69] The apparatus of the Asian economy, the workforce, consumer base, and brand value built up by Korean firms particularly were coveted, and fell under Western control. Western firms entered not to build their own businesses, but rather to buy up businesses. These would then often be broken up and downsized or shut down completely to eliminate competition to Western brands.

Observing Asia's colossal losses and the West's equally colossal gains as a result of the crisis, British economists Robert Wade and Frank Veneroso predicted that 'the Combination of massive devaluations, IMF-pushed financial liberizations, and IMF-facilitated recovery may even precipitate the biggest peacetime transfer of assets from domestic to foreign owners in the past fifty years anywhere in the world.'[70] Indeed, why invade Asia to acquire its wealth and forestall its growth through military means as in imperial times when economic warfare seemed to work just as well but far more subtly.

The Korean giant Samsung was broken up and sold for parts. S. C. Johnson & Son took its pharmaceuticals arm. Volvo took its heavy industry division. General Electric took its lighting division. Daewoo's car division previously valued at $6 billion was sold to General Motors for a mere $400 million.[71] Nissan bought one of Indonesia's biggest car companies. General Electric bought the controlling share in Korea's previously successful refrigerator manufacturer LG. The large Korean electricity and gas company LG Energy was bought up by the British Powergen. Other large Western companies which benefited directly from Asia's crisis included: Coca Cola, Seagram's, Hewlett-Packard, Nestle, Interbrew and Novartis, Carrefour, Tesco and Ericsson.[72,73]

Western financial institutions also gained a great deal. Two months after the IMF reached its final deal with South Korea *The Wall Street Journal* published an article titled: 'Wall Street Scavenging in Asia-Pacific,' which detailed how Morgan Stanley among others had 'dispatched armies of bankers to the Asia-Pacific region to scout for brokerage firms, asset management firms and even banks that they can snap up at bargain prices. The hunt for Asian acquisitions is urgent because many U.S. securities firms, led by Merrill Lynch & Co. and Morgan Stanley, have made overseas expansion their priority.' These banks managed incredible deals and acquired valuable assets.[74]

AIG bought Bangkok Investment for a small fraction of its prior worth. JP Morgan bought a significant stake in the Korean car giant KIA Motors. Merrill Lynch bought both Japan's Yamaichi Securities[75] and Thailand's largest securities firm Phatra Thanakit.[76] Travelers Ground and Salomon Smith Barney bought several companies including Korea's largest textile company.[77] The Carlyle group became a major shareholder in one of Korea's largest banks, as well as buying Daewoo's telecom division and SsangYong Information and communication, one of Korea's largest high-tech firms.[78]

Asian governments were also forced to sell off publicly owned services to Western interests. This had been predicted by the United States which sought to benefit from buying up what had been property of the Asian peoples at very low prices. To make a case for the U.S. Congress authorizing billions to the IMF to help remake Asian economies, the U.S. trade representative Charlene Barshefsky said that the agreements with the IMF would force Asian nations to 'accelerate privatization of certain key sectors – including energy, transportation, utilities and communications.' This was put forward as a positive step not because it would help Asia to recover, but because it would 'create new business opportunities for U.S. firms.'[79]

A wave of privatizations took place all across Asia, the main benefactors of which were Western interests. Bechtel bought the water and sewage systems in Eastern Manilla,[80] as well as beneficial contracts to build an oil refinery in Indonesia's Sulawesi.[81] Motorola took full control over South Korea's appeal telecom.[82] Sithe, an American energy giant, took a large stake in the Cogeneration, Thailand's public gas company. Indonesia's state-owned water systems were split between Britain's Thames waters and France's Lyonnaise des Eaux. A massive Indonesian government power plant project was taken by Canada's Westcoast Energy. British Telecom purchased large stakes in Malaysian and South Korean postal service. Bell Canada took a piece of Hansol, Korea's telecom.[83,84,85] These were but a few of the many Western acquisitions of Asian publicly owned companies.

Professor of Anthropology David Harvey noted regarding how the United States, having played a key role in orchestrating the Asian crisis, was now the key beneficiary:

> Various bouts of devaluation and destruction of capital were visited, usually through the good graces of IMF structural adjustment programs … The hedge funds' attack upon the Thai and Indonesian currencies in 1997, backed up by the savage deflationary policies demanded by the IMF, drove even viable concerns into bankruptcy throughout East and South-East Asia. Unemployment and impoverishment were the result for millions of people. That crisis also conveniently sparked a flight to the dollar, confirming Wall Street's dominance and generating an amazing boom in asset values for the affluent in the United States.[86]

The West had vested interests in seeing other nations adopt neoliberal economic systems under which emerging industries could not be protected from external acquisitions. While such economic models, as well as the reforms and 'adjustments' which lead to them, have been promoted by Western states, academic institutions and media as being in the best interests of the peoples and countries in which they were implemented – the prime benefactors of their implementation were always the parties which advocated them rather than the countries in which they were implemented. As the *American Interest* noted, implementation of neoliberalism in independent states was seen highly favorably by Western nations because it brought about 'co-option and an evolutionary change in values.'[87] These political, economic, and resulting social changes and the weakening of the role of foreign states in protecting their own emerging industries have benefited Western designs to maintain their own economic primacy.

In the case of many nations affected by the crisis, perhaps most prominently South Korea, it was the elite of American educated economists who supported Western governments and institutions in advocating the neoliberal policy that proved so disastrous. As Ha Joon Chang, Director of Development Studies at Cambridge University, and National University of Singapore Professor Jang Sup Shin stated in their study of the ROK's economy noted of the liberalization process in South Korea: 'What was decisive in this process was the increasing conversion of the intellectual elite, especially the bureaucratic elite, to Neo-Liberalism. The increasing number of elite bureaucrats and academics who got advanced degrees from the U.S. at the height of its Neo-Liberal revolution meant that there were more and more people inside the government who were convinced of the virtues of the free market and saw developmentalism as a "backward" "mistaken" ideology. It needs to be added that in this ideological battle, the Neo-Liberals were critically helped by the ideological dominance of the Anglo-American academia and media at the world level.' This pressure from American educated Koreans was an invaluable asset to external actors which were pressing the country to change course and adopt economic reforms in line with their own interests – and these in turn led the economy to disaster.[88]

Despite the great costs to the peoples in affected countries the Asian crisis is largely considered in the West to have been a positive development. It is not spoken of as something that hugely benefited the West at Asia's expense, but rather as a chance for Asia to 'correct' itself by conforming to Western economic ideals – a remaking of the region in the West's image and in line with Western interests. The Asia-Pacific was no longer a strong and rising economic region, but rather an impoverished crisis, yet this was lauded as a great new step for Asian nations. *The Economist* wrote: 'it took a national crisis for South Korea to turn from an inward looking nation to one than embraced foreign capital, change and competition.'[89] The reality in Korea, however Western sources chose to word their analyses, was in fact one of suffering, economic loss, suicides and destitution. In 1998 the suicide rate spiked, with the greatest increase occurring among those over 60 who had sought to lessen the economic burden on their children. Korean authorities pointed out that there was a tremendous increase in family suicide pacts, in which fathers would lead their household in group suicide pacts. According the South Korean media these family suicide pacts meant that the official suicide rate was in fact far below the nation's actual rate. Under a family suicide pact one member of the family would hold the responsibility of killing the others – then finally themselves. As a result: 'only the [family] leader's death is classified as suicide while the rest are listed as murders, the actual number of suicides is far higher that the statistics released.'[90,91] The crisis was hailed as a positive development only because it benefited Western interests at the expense of the Asian populations.

Three times Pulitzer Prize winner Thomas Friedman wrote in his book *The Lexus* that the destruction of Asian economies in the crisis had a positive effect. He wrote: 'Globalization did us all a favor by melting down the economies of Thailand, Korea, Malaysia, Indonesia ... in the 1990s, because it laid bare a lot of rotten practices and institutions.'[92,93] What he failed to explain was how these countries, if they really were so 'rotten' were so successful before they had been pressured by the West to lower capital controls and expose themselves to speculation. What had led them to crash was not their 'rotten institutions and practices' but rather external pressures followed by external destruction of their currencies, then adoption of IMF policies which sabotaged their economies. Whether he viewed them as 'rotten' or not, they had produced far better results for their populations when then had been in place than afterwards.

Analyzing the crisis and its long-term implications on Asian populations affected ten years afterwards in 2007, Naomi Klein noted the extent of the devastation. She stated:

> The truth is that Asia's crisis is still not over, a decade later. When 24 million people lose their jobs in a span of two years, a new desperation takes root that no culture can easily absorb. It expresses itself in different forms across the region, from a significant rise in religious extremism in Indonesia and Thailand to the explosive growth in the child sex trade. Employment rates have still not reached pre-1997 levels in Indonesia, Malaysia and South Korea. And it's not just that the workers who lost their jobs during the crisis never got them back. The layoffs have continued, with new foreign owners demanding ever-higher profits for their investments. The suicides have also continued. In South Korea, suicide became the fourth most common cause of death, more than double the pre-crisis rate, with thirty-eight people taking their own life every day [the world's highest suicide rate].

Klein attributed the fast growth of brothels, slums, human trafficking, child prostitution, and suicide in the Asian countries affected to the Western financial centers' attacks on their economies and to the policies of the IMF which exacerbated the situation.[94]

Could this catastrophe on a massive scale be another lesson in the results of trying to compromise with Western interests when they seek to dictate policy to a country? To try to compromise with the uncompromising can hardly yield positive results. Notably the countries that avoided towing the Western line fared much better. As economic professors Damien Cahill and Martijn Konings noted regarding neoliberalism's discredited track record and the reason why the West was so eager to see China's emerging economy adopt such a system after attempts to promote destabilization and topple the ruling Communist Party in 1989 failed: 'the Asian crisis of 1997 ... did much to undermine the idea that following neoliberal strategies offered a viable development model. This was in part due to the sheer severity of the crisis and the way the currency speculation plunged an entire region of the world into a prolonged economic recession, but also due to the simple fact that those countries following the IMF rulebook had been affected most severely, whereas those that were quick to impose capital currency controls in fact remained somewhat shielded from the worst effects of the crisis.' They noted that Russia, which had also implemented the IMF's reforms and adopted neoliberal policies, had seen crises of their own within years of the Asian crisis, and that these collectively largely discredited the neoliberal ideology the Western Bloc was so avidly promoting, often imposing, on rest of the world through its economic institutions.[95]

Mainland China and North Korea were not hit by crisis at all. Though China had long been advised by several prominent Western economists and pressured to lower its capital controls, it had refused to do so. Western powers have since 1997 made extensive efforts to press China to transition to adopt a neoliberal economic system.[96] As British economist Stephen D. King indicated, it was precisely because China, unlike Thailand, South Korea, Indonesia and Malaysia, did not adopt the economic policy advocated by the West, that it withstood the crisis where others were devastated.[97]

British Professor, Lecturer and China specialist Jude Woodward noted regarding the agenda behind the United States' efforts to persuade China to adopt a neoliberal policy, namely to leave its markets vulnerable as those of other Asian nations had been:

> The U.S. tried to persuade China to pursue a range of neoliberal policies – privatization, deregulation, ending or reducing state and state-aided investment and so on – which would open the Chinese economy up to both U.S. commodities and capital while slowing its growth. Such tactics had succeeded with Yeltsin's Russia [also in the 1990s] where 'shock therapy' led to catastrophic destruction of the Russian economy

> [a 45 percent GDP contraction in five years][98] and thus its potential to act as a global counterweight to the US. But China had no equivalent of Yeltsin – a leader willing to comply with the West's demands – and so U.S. economic policy interventions against China have been confined to an assault from think tanks, the economic and financial media, Western business schools and economics departments arguing China should urgently depend market 'reform' through privatizations and deregulation.[99]

Nobel laureate in economics and chief economist of the Roosevelt Institute Joseph E. Stiglitz noted in a similar vein regarding the Asian financial crisis that Beijing had only been spared the effects of the crisis because it had refused to adopt many of the market liberalizations strongly advocated by the West. He further stated that the West continued to press China to adopt such economic reforms, similar to those undertaken by Russia, long after the Asian crisis and the catastrophic impacts of these reforms had become clear.[100] What this indicates is that the West's economic 'advice,' in both the Asia-Pacific and in Russia, was a means by which rival economic and political entities could be weakened – with the Western Bloc taking advantage of the authority of the prestige of its academic and financial institutions to push for the adoption of economic policies which would leave rival states vulnerable to economic destabilization.

It became increasingly clear, particularly in the early 2010s, that it was unlikely for China to adopt a neoliberal economy or to leave itself vulnerable by fully adopting the West's economic philosophy and exposing its markets to speculators. The *American Interest* noted in 2015 China's 'unequivocal rejection of Western political philosophy and values, raising serious doubts about the neoliberal presumption that China's current regime would ever embrace a U.S.-led liberal political-economic world order.'[101] Western press such as the *New York Times* reported in 2013 that Chinese ruling party had themselves openly rejected ideas such as neoliberalism and radical economic reforms along the lines of Western interests as those imposed across much of Asia in the years preceding the 1997 crash.[102] At a meeting in December 1997 Vice Premier Zhu Rongji told the Chinese central bankers and financial executives that the country was 'lucky' to have not been involved in the Asian financial crisis – which he attributed to state controls on the country's financial system. The extent to which China's combination of a far more independent political system and awareness of the intentions of

Western financial institutions towards its economy saved it economic and social hardship therefore cannot be overstated.[103] While Western sources, from the media to financial analysts to leadership continue to call for China to open its market and harshly criticize its protectionist actions, and have clear motives for making such calls, the Chinese leadership remains largely aware of the benefits of a more closed system.[104]

China's policy independence and refusal to reform its economic and political systems are key factors in making it the only Asian power capable of ending Western primacy and seriously challenging the Western Bloc's regional dominance. This is something states which continue to see Western influence over their internal affairs are unable to achieve. Indeed, it is worthy of note that the Republic of China's Guomindang government was never able to diverge significantly in its policy from the influence of the West, in particular the United States, and it is precisely for this reason that Western media and scholarship today continue to lament the 'loss of China' in 1949.[105,106,107] A Chinese government heavily beholden to the West in its policymaking could never challenge the Western Bloc's economic primacy as the Chinese People's Republic, by virtue of its fully independent policymaking, does today. Like South Korea, Thailand, and the Philippines, the 'other China' would always have been vulnerable to pressures from the West to 'reform,' allowing the Western Bloc to cripple its economy at will should it pose a threat to their primacy – much like what happened to emerging Asian powers in 1997. A Guomindang ruled China was favorable to the West not only because it would have been a Cold War ally – but perhaps more importantly because it could never have been a challenge to Western primacy. China's economic success under the People's Republic today therefore, and its ability to challenge the West, have largely been facilitated by the victory over the GMD in the Civil War – which gained the country an invaluable and genuine sovereignty and policy independence from the Western Bloc. Because China continues to plot an independent course it has now become arguably the greatest threat to continued Western primacy – while the Western Bloc is powerless to enact economic measures to derail its success (as covered in the following chapter).

Behind the demands for denuclearization and disarmament, a key demand of Western powers from North Korea remains the granting of 'enhanced opportunities for economic cooperation.'[108] Based on Western policy towards other developing nations, this would very likely involve instigating neoliberal reform that would leave the East Asian state vulnerable to economic warfare in the future in much the same way. In the case of Malaysia its shrewd leadership quickly realized the true nature of the threat and responded accordingly – reinstating capital controls against all the advice of Western experts. The Malaysian economy recovered soon afterwards and continued to be run in the interests of its own people – without the painful austerity measures, IMF restructuring and asset sell offs that neighboring states would suffer from.[109] Only those states which lacked genuine independence in policymaking and remained blind to the nature of Western financial institutions and the hostile designs of several Western nations could thus be brought down, while states which continued to conduct policy independently could not. This has crucial implications regarding the potential for nations to grow to challenge the West economically in future.

Notes

1 Gilpin, Robert, *The Political Economy of International Relations*, Princeton, NJ, Princeton University Press, 1987 (p. 23).
2 Chomsky, Noam, *Who Rules the World?*, London, Hamish Hamilton, 2016 (p. 73).
3 'Report by the Policy Planning Staff, Review of Current Trends, U.S. Foreign Policy, February 24, 1948,' Office of the Historian, Foreign Relations of the United States, 1948, General; the United Nations, Volume 1, Part 2, United States of America Department of State.
4 Pempel, T. J., *The Politics of the Asian Economic Crisis*, Ithaca, NY, Cornell University Press, 1999 (p. 41).
5 Rachman, Gideon, *Easternisation, War and Peace in the Asian Century*, New York, Vintage, 2017 (p. ix, 3, 4).
6 Cox, Michael, and Stokes, Doug, *U.S. Foreign Policy*, Second Edition, Oxford, Oxford University Press, 2012 (p. 271).
7 Shin, Jang Sup, and Chang, Ha Joon, *Restructuring 'Korea Inc.': Financial Crisis, Corporate Reform, and Institutional Transition*, Abingdon, Routledge, 2003

(3.4.1, 'The Decline of the Development State' and 3.4.2, 'Mismanagement of Financial Liberalisation').

8 Klein, Naomi, *The Shock Doctrine: The Rise of Disaster Capitalism*, London, Penguin, 2008 (p. 267).

9 Shin, Jang Sup, and Chang, Ha Joon, *Restructuring 'Korea Inc.': Financial Crisis, Corporate Reform, and Institutional Transition*, Abingdon, Routledge, 2003 (3.4.1, 'The Decline of the Development State' and 3.4.2, 'Mismanagement of Financial Liberalisation').

10 Stiglitz, Joseph E., *Globalization and Its Discontents*, New York, W. W. Norton & Company, 2002 (p. 89).

11 Bruce Hall, Rodney, *International Studies Quarterly*, Volume 4 (pp. 87–88).

12 King, Stephen D., *Losing Control: The Emerging Threats to Western Prosperity*, New Haven, CT, Yale University Press, 2010.

13 'The Weakest Link,' *The Economist*, February 6, 2003.

14 Isimbabi, Michael J., *Globalization and the WTO Agreement on Financial Services in African Countries* (p. 11).

15 McNally, David, 'Globalization on Trial,' *Monthly Review*, September 1998.

16 'Selling Pressure Mounts on Korean Won – Report,' *Korea Herald* (Seoul), October 27, 1998.

17 'Koreans give up their gold to help their country,' *BBC*, January 14, 1998.

18 Hur Nam Il, 'Gold Rush ... Korean Style.' *Business Korea*, March 1998.

19 'South Koreans sell jewellery to help economy,' *BBC*, January 10, 1998.

20 'South Korea's gold collection campaign draws public support,' *Minnesota Daily*, January 7, 1998.

21 Lipsey, Phillip Y., 'Japan's Asian Monetary Fund Proposal,' *Stanford Journal of East Asian Affairs*, Volume 3, Number 1, Spring 2003 (p. 94).

22 'Milton Friedman Discusses the IMF,' *CNN Moneyline with Lou Dobbs*, January 22, 1998.

23 Milken Institute, Global Conference 1998, Global Overview, March 22, 1998.

24 'Why did Asia crash?,' *The Economist*, January 8, 1998.

25 Milken Institute, Global Conference 1998, Global Overview, March 22, 1998.

26 'Looking back at the "Asian IMF" concept,' *Nikkei Asian Review*, June 22, 2017.

27 Klein, Naomi, *The Shock Doctrine: The Rise of Disaster Capitalism*, London, Penguin, 2008 (p. 274).

28 Harvey, David, *The New Imperialism*, Oxford, Oxford University Press, 2005 (pp. 38–39).

29 Ibid. (p. 77).

30 Pinera, Jose, *The 'Third Way' Keeps Countries in the Third World*, Prepared for the Cato Institute's 16th Annual Monetary Conference cosponsored with *The Economist*, Washington, DC, October 22, 1998.

31 Pinera, Jose, *The Fall of a Second Berlin Wall*, October 22, 1998.

32 Cheetham, R., 1998. Asia Crisis. Paper presented at conference, U.S.-ASEAN-Japan policy Dialogue. School of Advanced International Studies of Johns Hopkins University, June 7–9, Washington, DC.

33 Bell, Daniel A., *Beyond Liberal Democracy: Political Thinking for an East Asian Context*, Princeton, NJ, Princeton University Press, 2006 (p. 256).

34 'Text – Greenspan's Speech to New York Economic Club,' *Reuters*, December 3, 1997.

35 'U.S. Senate Committee on Foreign Relations Holds Hearing on the Role of the IMF in the Asian Financial Crisis,' February 12, 1998.

36 Interview with Mahathir Mohamad, July 2, 2001, for *Commanding Heights: The Battle for the World Economy* (https://www.pbs.org/wgbh/commandingheights/shared/minitext/int_mahathirbinmohamad.html).

37 Verma, Vidhu, *Malaysia, State and Civil Society in Transition*, Boulder, CO, Lynne Rienner Publishers, 2002 (p. 38).

38 Bello, Walden, 'A Siamese Tragedy: The Collapse of Democracy in Thailand,' *Transnational Institute*, September 29, 2006.

39 Grenville, Stephen, *The IMF and the Indonesian Crisis*, Background Paper, Independent Evaluation Office of the IMF, May 2004 (p. 8).

40 *The IMF and Recent Capital Account Crimes: Indonesia, Korea, Brazil*, Washington, DC: , Independent Evaluation Office of the International Monetary Fund, September 12, 2003 (p. 42–43).

41 Grenville, Stephen, *The IMF and the Indonesian Crisis*, background paper, Independent Evaluation Office of the IMF, May 2004, page 8.

42 Interview with Stanley Fischer, May 9, 2001, for *Commanding Heights*.

43 'The Influence of Trade Liberalization on Deindustrialization,' *IOSR Journal of Business and Management*, Volume 17, Issue 10, October 2015.

44 Kahn, Joseph, 'I. M. F.'s Hand Often Heavy, A Study Says,' *New York Times*, October 21, 2000.

45 Cheong, Yip Seng, *Oh Marker: My Straits Times Story*, Kuala Lumpur, Straits Times Press, 2012.

46 Blustein, Paul, *The Chastening: Inside The Crisis That Rocked The Global Financial System And Humbled The IMF*, New York, PublicAffairs, 2003 (p. 7).

47 Hart-Landsberg, Martin, and Burkett, Paul, 'Economic Crisis and Restructuring in South Korea: Beyond the Free Market-Statist Debate,' *Critical Asian Studies* 33, no. 3, 2001.

48 Ambrose, Soren, 'South Korean Union Sues the IMF,' *Economic Justice News* 2, no. 4, January 2000.

49 Sachs, Jeffrey, 'Power Unto Itself,' *Financial Times*, December 11, 1997.

50 Klein, Naomi, *The Shock Doctrine: The Rise of Disaster Capitalism*, London, Penguin, 2008 (p. 270).
51 Sheng, Andrew, *From Asian to Global Financial Crisis: An Asian Regulator's View of Unfettered Finance in the 1990s and 2000s*, Cambridge, Cambridge University Press, 2011 (p. 40).
52 'Maldives,' *The World Factbook*, Central Intelligence Agency, 2007.
53 Tett, Gillian, 'What Asians learnt from their financial crisis,' *Financial Times*, May 22, 2007.
54 Sachs, Jeffrey, 'The IMF and the Asian Flu,' *The American Prospect* no. 37, March–April 1998.
55 International Labour Organization, 'ILO Governing Body to Examine Response to Asia Crisis,' press release, March 16, 1999.
56 Jordan, Mary, 'Middle Class Plunging Back to Poverty,' *Washington Post*, September 6, 1998.
57 Klein, Naomi, *The Shock Doctrine: The Rise of Disaster Capitalism*, London, Penguin, 2008 (p. 273).
58 Sawatsawang, Nussara, 'Prostitution – Alarm Bells Ringing Sound Amid Child Sex Rise,' *Bangkok Post*, December 24, 1999.
59 Baguioro, Luz, 'Child Labour Rampant in the Philippines,' *Straits Times* (Singapore), February 12, 2000.
60 Klein, Naomi, *The Shock Doctrine: The Rise of Disaster Capitalism*, London, Penguin, 2008 (p. 273).
61 'Asian Financial Crisis Rapidly Creating Human Crisis: World Bank,' *Agence France-Presse*, September 29, 1998.
62 'Asia's child sex tourism rising,' *BBC*, August 22, 2000.
63 Robb, Caroline M., *Can The Poor Influence Policy: Participatory Poverty Assessments in the Developing World*, World Bank Publications, 2002 (p. 186).
64 Myers, Laura, 'Albright Offers Thais Used F-16s, Presses Banking Reforms,' *Associated Press*, March 4, 1999.
65 Klein, Naomi, *The Shock Doctrine: The Rise of Disaster Capitalism*, London, Penguin, 2008 (p. 273).
66 Milken Institute, Global Conference 1998, Global Overview, March 22, 1998.
67 Hahnel, Robin, *Panic Rules!: Everything You Need to Know about the Global Economy*, Boston, MA, South End Pres, 1999 (p. 74).
68 Lewis, Michael, 'The Real Asian Miracle; The World's Biggest Going-Out-of-Business Sale,' *New York Times*, May 31, 1998.
69 'Invasion of the Bargain Snatchers,' *Business Week*, March 2, 1998.
70 Wade, Robert, and Veneroso, Frank, 'The Asian Crisis: The High Debt Model Versus the Wall Street-Treasury-IMF Complex,' *New Left Review*, 228, March–April 1998.

71 'Chronology-GM Takeover Talks with Daewoo Motor Creditors,' *Reuters*, April 30, 2002.
72 Klein, Naomi, *The Shock Doctrine: The Rise of Disaster Capitalism*, London, Penguin, 2008 (pp. 274–275).
73 Ozawa, Tertutomo, and Zhan, James, *Business Restructuring in Asia: Cross-Border M&As in the Crisis Period*, Copenhagen, Copenhagen Business School Press, 2001 (pp. 96–102).
74 Raghavan, Anita, 'Wall Street Is Scavenging In the Asian-Pacific Region,' *The Wall Street Journal*, February 10, 1998.
75 McCarthy, Roy, 'Merrill Lynch Buys Yamaichi Branches, Now Japan's Biggest Foreign Broker,' *Agence France-Presse*, February 12, 1998.
76 'Phatra Thanakit Announces Partnership with Merrill Lynch,' *Merrill Lynch Press Release*, June 4, 1998.
77 'Advisory Board for Salomon,' *Financial Times*, May 18, 1999.
78 'JP Morgan – Carlyle Consortium to Become Largest Shareholder of KorAm,' *Korea Times*, September 9, 2000.
79 Bello, Walden, *Dilemmas of Domination: The Unmaking of the American Empire*, New York, Holt Paperbacks, 2006 (p. 122).
80 'International Water – Ayala Consortium Wins Manila Water Privatization Contract,' *Business Wire*, January 23, 1997.
81 'Bechtel Wins Contract to Build Oil Refinery in Indonesia,' *Asia Pulse News Agency*, September 22, 1999.
82 'Mergers of S. Korea Handset Makers with Foreign Cos on the Rise,' *Asia Pulse News Agency*, November 1, 2004.
83 United Nations Conference on Trade and Development, World Investment Report 1998, (p. 337).
84 Klein, Naomi, *The Shock Doctrine: The Rise of Disaster Capitalism*, London, Penguin, 2008 (pp. 274–275).
85 Ozawa, Tertutomo, and Zhan, James, *Business Restructuring in Asia: Cross-Border M&As in the Crisis Period*, Copenhagen, Copenhagen Business School Press, 2001 (pp. 96–102).
86 Harvey, David, *The New Imperialism*, Oxford, Oxford University Press, 2005 (p. 66).
87 Eikenberry, Karl W., 'China's Place in U.S. Foreign Policy,' *The American Interest*, June 9, 2015.
88 Shin, Jang Sup, and Chang, Ha Joon, *Restructuring 'Korea Inc.': Financial Crisis, Corporate Reform, and Institutional Transition*, Abingdon, Routledge, 2003 (3.4.1, 'The Decline of the Development State').
89 'The Weakest Link,' *The Economist*, February 6, 2003.
90 'Economic Woes Driving More to Suicide,' *Korea Times*, April 23, 1998.

91 'Elderly Suicide Rate on the Increase,' *Korea Times*, October 27, 1999.
92 Friedman, Thomas L., *The Lexus and the Olive Tree, Understanding Globalisation*, New York, Farrar, Straus and Giroux, 1999 (pp. 452–53).
93 Veseth, Michael, *The Rise of the Global Economy*, Chicago, Fitzroy Dearborn Publishers, 2002 (p. 43).
94 Klein, Naomi, *The Shock Doctrine: The Rise of Disaster Capitalism*, London, Penguin, 2008 (p. 277).
95 Cahill, Damien, and Konings, Martijn, *Neoliberlism*, Cambridge, Polity Press, 2017 (pp. 64–65).
96 Shoup, Lawrence H., *Wall Street's Think Tank: The Council on Foreign Relations and the Empire of Neoliberal Geopolitics, 1976–2014*, New York, Monthly Review Press, 2015 (pp. 244–246).
97 King, Stephen D., *Grave New World; The End of Globalization, The Return of History*, New Haven, CT, Yale University Press, 2017 (p. 63).
98 Menshikov, S., 'Russian Capitalism Today,' *Monthly Review*, 51:3, 1999 (pp. 82–86).
99 Woodward, Jude, *The U.S. vs China: Asia's New Cold War?* Manchester, Manchester University Press, 2017 (p. 9).
100 Stiglitz, Joseph, 'The Asian crisis 10 years later,' *The Guardian*, July 2, 2007.
101 Eikenberry, Karl W., 'China's Place in U.S. Foreign Policy,' *The American Interest*, June 9, 2015.
102 'China Takes Aim at Western Ideas,' *New York Times*, August 19, 2013.
103 Xin, Zhou, 'How Beijing and Hong Kong sent billionaire George Soros packing the last time he attacked Asian markets,' *South China Morning Post*, January 27, 2016.
104 E. Looney, Robert, *Handbook of Emerging Economies*, Abingdon, Routledge, 2015 (p. 518).
105 'Post-War China, Alternatively Chiang's China. What if Mao Zedong's Communist Party had lost the Chinese civil war to Chiang Kai-Shek's Nationalist Party?,' *The Economist*, July 1, 2015.
106 David Baker, Benjamin, 'What if the Kuomintang Had Won the Chinese Civil War?,' *The Diplomat*, December 24, 2015.
107 Kaplan, Robert D., 'Mao Won the Battle, Chiang Kai-shek Won the War,' *Foreign Policy*, March 24, 2014.
108 Welch, David A., 'Bringing North Korea Into Line,' *The Diplomat*, January 17, 2016.
109 Harvey, David, *The New Imperialism*, Oxford, Oxford University Press, 2005 (p. 73).

CHAPTER 15

Asia Divided: Unifying Economic Initiatives in the Asia-Pacific as a Threat to Western Primacy

A kingdom divided in itself cannot stand.[1]
—THOMAS HOBBES

Divide and Rule: The Western Imperative of Preventing an Asian Power Bloc from Forming

The Asia-Pacific has all the prerequisites to form a power bloc to challenge Western primacy in its economic, technological, military and soft power on the world stage. These include the region's unique endowment of what Michael Cox, professor of international relations at the University of London, LSE, listed as: 'intangible, but important assets, including a culture of hard work, a system of entrepreneurial values, a plentiful supply of labour, a huge reservoir of capital, and a set of political and economic structures that allow the state to play a critical role in engineering successful economic outcomes.'[2] The rise of the Asia-Pacific to eclipse the West has since the era of European colonialism been seen as the greatest threat to the Western centric world order. Fears of the potential of the 'little yellow man' led to what came to be known as the 'yellow peril,' leading to further repression by European imperial powers against Asian populations under their control.

For the Western Bloc to maintain its global primacy today it is essential that no independent Asian powers be permitted to modernize economically, technologically and culturally independently of the West – something which Imperial Japan had set out to achieve with much success. It remains imperative for Western powers to ensure that two factors remain unchanged in Asian international relations. First, Asia-Pacific nations must remain divided, with economic, military and in some cases cultural ties to Western powers, namely the United States, eclipsing ties to their neighbors. Second, Asian countries must remain economically and militarily dependent on Western powers, unable to compete in critical high end industries and granting the West substantial influence over their military and economic development – thereby preventing any independent developments which could challenge the Western Bloc. Should these be established Asia will continue to be a secondary center of global power, culture and influence under the West's global hegemony.

One key advantage European powers had in the colonial era was that centuries of war in Europe had led to new definitions of statehood and identity. Countries were largely divided into large states rather than small tribes or principalities, while the idea of a greater common European identity also began to emerge. When encountering peoples who lacked this unifying state identity, it was far easier for European powers to play different factions off against one another for their own gain. An example of this was in India, which was at the time of British conquest was ruled by several dozen rival kingdoms. Had the kingdoms united, the relatively tiny and poorly armed British military could have been defeated quickly, as although the Indian kingdoms lacked the military experience of European powers which had been waging war for some time they more than made up for this in the quantities of their manpower and the quality of their advanced military technologies and the gargantuan scale of their economy relative to that of Britain. Indeed in the eighteenth and nineteenth centuries Indian kingdoms very often deployed superior firepower to the British, such as in the Battle of Plassey in 1757 when the Mughal Empire deployed 53 artillery pieces to the British eight – and those of the Mughals were of a superior caliber. From 1845 in the Anglo-Sikh war against the Sikh Empire meanwhile the British faced modern artillery which caused massive casualties among their forces.[3]

The British Empire nevertheless managed to conquer all of India, except for the small enclaves held by other competing Western empires, largely due to their successful application of the strategy of 'divide and rule.' By encouraging conflict between Indian factions Britain was able to conquer the subcontinent one piece at a time, and so gained total dominance over a region many times greater in power and military capability than themselves. An example was the subjugation of the Tipu Sultanate which was a potent military adversary that vehemently resisted the British Empire. The British therefore sought out the assistance of the Marathas, a rival Indian kingdom to which they promised substantial rewards. With the assistance of the Marathas the British subjugated the Tipu, then went on to conquer the Marathas in turn and claim dominion over the two. By turning them against one another and posing as a friend to one, both could be defeated far more easily than if the intentions of the conqueror had been made clear from the beginning – which would have likely united the two kingdoms. This was the concept of divide and rule, critical to which was an ability to mask one's intentions. Such scenarios repeatedly played out across the Indian subcontinent and Africa as the European imperial powers sought to subjugate their peoples.

The West had the advantage of defining themselves as a greater whole where their adversaries did not, and this was a key facilitator of the successful implementation of divide and rule. Had there been a greater African or Indian state, or even a concept of pan-Africanism or pan-Indianism to cement the idea of a common identity and affiliation among their peoples, these regions most likely would not have come to be dominated by Western imperial powers. Dr Stephen Howe, British professor of History and Cultures of Colonialism and author, noted on the matter: 'European invaders were very often able to exploit division and disunity among their opponents. In most cases, they could recruit the bulk of their fighting men from among the colonized populations themselves. If Africans or Indians had united against the colonialists, then colonization would have been impossible except at staggering, unacceptable human and financial cost. But to do that, they would have had to think of themselves as "Africans" or "Indians," a single people with shared interests, in the first place. Before the twentieth century very few could even potentially do so.'[4]

Today the West enjoys an advantage in the Asia-Pacific which is conceptually similar to that it enjoyed in Africa and India in the colonial era. Having created a broader 'Western Bloc' which since 1945 has consistently acted politically and military in unison through organizations such as NATO, this grants the West a significant advantage in its attempts to dominate the Asia-Pacific region. The Asia-Pacific today is deeply divided, and lacks a prominent concept of pan-Asianism or a unifying political, military or even economic bloc. Asian states can therefore be divided against one another by the Western Bloc much as they divided African and Asian states against one another in the colonial era – and thus cement their dominance over the region. As a result the prospective formation of all such blocs, from the Japanese Co-prosperity Sphere to the Beijing-Pyongyang-Hanoi-Phnom Penh-Jakarta Axis, have inevitably been vehemently opposed by the Western Bloc which has gone to great lengths to dismantle them.

The Western Bloc has since 1945 consistently presented a joint front against Asian nations deemed to be a threat, from joint sanctions against the People's Republic of China[5] to European NATO members' increasing military involvement in U.S. led deployments in Asia from Afghanistan and the Persian Gulf to the South China Sea and Korean Peninsula. This was evident particularly in the Korean War, when the United States, Canada, Turkey, Britain, France, Australia, New Zealand, Greece, Belgium, the Netherlands, Luxembourg and even South Africa, then under the apartheid rule of a small European elite and very much a member of the Western Bloc, all jointly committed forces under U.S. command to a war against China and North Korea. They received support from Spain, Sweden, Denmark, Italy, Norway, and West Germany. In more recent years actions taken by the Western Bloc in the Asia-Pacific in support of the of the 'Obama doctrine' targeting Chinese interests, as covered in Chapter 18, demonstrate the continuation of this united front against independent Asia-Pacific states.

As in the colonial era, the Western Bloc has in the modern era continued to exploit division and disunity and recruit vast fighting forces from compliant Asian states to use against the non-compliant. Examples of this include the British use of Nepalese and Indian forces in an attempt to suppress Indonesian nationalists – with these forces taking the majority of casualties among the British intervention force, the rebuilding of the Japanese military and encouragement of remilitarization into what Americans termed 'a little American army,'[6] or the training of a Filipino army in the 1940s for deployment under U.S. command in Korea and Vietnam – later Iraq and Afghanistan. Perhaps the best example however has been the military of South Korea, which including reservists accounts for almost 4 million personnel all placed directly under U.S. military command should any war on the peninsula break out.[7] The United States could on their own authority issue orders after the outbreak of war for ROK forces to deploy beyond the Korean Peninsula to engage Chinese or Russian forces in the event of a wider regional conflict.[8] These are critical assets for the Western Bloc, which seeks to dominate those parties which challenge the Western dominated order by using its client states against them – much as the British used the Marathas against the Tipu before asserting their dominance over both parties.

The emergence of some form of unifying Pacific Asian Bloc is the most effective means to counter the Western Bloc's attempts to maintain its primacy and dominate the region – or as the popular Imperial Japanese slogan stated, much to the chagrin of the European colonial powers, to create an 'Asia for the Asiatics.'[9] While the emergence today of a closely co-operating Sino-Russian bloc, and organizations such as the Shanghai Cooperation Operation (as covered in Chapter 16), have increasingly served to unify China and Russia with Central and South Asia militarily and economically, ultimately these remain primarily strategic and lack the common cultural, historical and ethnic background to form close bonds to the same extent that the Western Bloc has. An Asia-Pacific Bloc encompassing Southeast Asia, China, Japan and the Koreas potentially could do this, and should these states establish the concept of a pan-Asian identity and solidarity as the Western Bloc did long ago – this would effectively negate the Western advantage and could well be key to leading the region into becoming the new global center of power.

The Asian Monetary Fund: How the United States Sabotaged Prospects for a Regional Alternative to the Western Controlled IMF

At the height of the Asian financial crisis in 1997, the Western-dominated International Monetary Fund and World Bank were the only financial institutions able to handle such a crisis and provide bailouts – and as a result they were able to impose harsh terms on the struggling Asian economies in accordance with Western economic interests – as covered in the previous chapter. Observing this effective monopoly, Japan proposed the creation of an Asian Monetary Fund (AMF). With the terms set by the IMF being highly unpopular among both Asian populations and their governments, which nonetheless had little choice but to comply, the proposed creation of a regional alternative was met with much enthusiasm across Southeast Asia and in South Korea. In the West however, particularly in the United States, the AMF was perceived as an intolerable threat to the monopolistic position of the IMF and the Western powers' resulting ability to effectively dictate economic policy in the Asia-Pacific region through the fund.

ASEAN countries had already been discussing the potential for a proposal similar to the AMF in response to the financial crisis, which would reduce their dependence on Western institutions. Indeed, such an initiative had been under consideration since the Mexican crisis of 1996, the year before the Asian crisis, as many economists were aware that the West would not have an interest in supporting their economies as it did that of Mexico if crisis hit.[10] An Asian institution capable of organizing such a bailout as a safety net for regional economies was considered essential. Such proposals had widespread support, particularly from the Thai government – and for good reason given the impact the crisis would eventually have on the country's economy. Japan, then by far the region's largest economy, portrayed itself as responding to the ASEAN nations' proposal rather than pushing for it too openly and directly. Officials from Japan's Ministry of Finance nevertheless observed that an 'Asian consensus' had been created which to some extent legitimized Japan's role, then the world's second largest economy, as a regional leader at the expense of the dominant Western powers.[11]

According to Eisuke Sakakibara, a senior official from Japan's Ministry of Finance who served as Vice Minister of Finance for International Affairs and who was heavily involved in planning and promoting the AMF, the International Monetary Fund had done 'great damage' to the Asian economies and taken measures with 'obvious outcomes' – exacerbating the financial crisis and causing a currency collapse.[12] He also noted that 'the IMF proposed many structural reform plans, but they didn't work. Asia has its unique economic structure, characterized for example by large family-owned conglomerates. The IMF and the U.S. called it cronyism and tried to change it. All they had in mind was to 'reform' the economy. But a country's economy is rooted in its culture and has a long historical background. It cannot be changed overnight.'[13]

By contrast to the IMF, Sakakibara noted an 'Asian sense of solidarity' pervaded while the AMF was being planned with other Asian nations and was a key factor in his decision to promote the initiative.[14] Pooling Asian reserves under a regional fund such as the AMF could prove a highly effective strategy to deal with the financial crisis while minimizing reliance on the West. The AMF would also obviate time-consuming consensus building among regional nations by automating their commitments. While Asia-Pacific countries were in great need of an Asian Monetary Fund, and Japan was more than willing to fund and organize such an institution, such a development was considered intolerable for the Western Bloc's regional interests and those of the United States in particular. Sakakibara stated in regard to this: 'At the time, the IMF didn't properly address the crisis. We were angry about that. That is why we planned to establish Asia's own version of the IMF. The ASEAN countries and South Korea supported the idea, but the U.S. didn't. The former U.S. Treasury Secretary Lawrence Summers strongly opposed it, because he foresaw it weakening America's financial influence in Asia.'[15]

Upon obtaining information regarding the AMF, of which it had purposely not been informed by Japan and the other members, the United States moved quickly to preempt its formation. Deputy Treasury Secretary Larry Summers called Sakakibara directly at his residence at midnight and angrily berated him: 'I thought you were my friend.'[16] Summers had a heated two-hour discussion with the Japanese official and criticized the plan on the sole basis that it both excluded the United States and undermined the IMF by allowing Asian nations to act autonomously of it. America's fierce opposition to the AMF was due to the fear that Japan was posing a threat to its regional hegemony.[17]

The AMF was set to be a $100 billion fund with ten members including Japan, South Korea, China, Hong Kong, Indonesia, the Philippines, Malaysia, Singapore, Thailand and Australia. Upon learning of the initiative the United States applied significant pressure to many of these nations to abandon it. It was particularly critical to undermine Chinese support for the proposal, as it was the region's second largest economy at the time and its support for the AMF alongside Japan could well have cemented the fund's formation. The United States lobbied China not to lend the initiative support by emphasizing that it posed a threat of 'Japanese hegemony.'[18] Using a longstanding strategy first devised under President Nixon in the 1970s when the United States first permitted Japan to form diplomatic relations with the People's Republic of China,[19] the U.S. used the two leading Asian powers' fears of one another to divide them and thus to further American regional interests.[20] As a result the AMF faced both strong opposition from the US, the most dominant and influential regional actor, while China showed neither an approving solidarity nor direct opposition. While Chinese support for the Japanese initiative could well have given the proposal the clout it needed to withstand American protests, without strong Chinese support the Asian Monetary Fund lacked the backing it needed. The proposal eventually floundered and Asian nations suffering from the crisis were forced to accept the harsh terms and restructuring imposed by the IMF. U.S. interests were served well and the dominance of Western financial institutions in the region remained unchallenged.

Malaysia's East Asian Economic Group and the Imperative of Regional Exclusivist Agreements

Malaysian Prime Minister Mahathir Bin Mohamed, in power from 1981 to 2003 and later re-elected to office from 2018, was a prominent nationalist figure who oversaw the rapid economic transformation of his country from a third world postcolonial state to a highly industrialized upper middle income country with the highest living standards in Southeast Asia – with the exception of the small trading states of Brunei and Singapore.[21] During his first tenure as Prime Minister Mahathir proposed the formation of a regional bloc of East and Southeast Asian countries called the East Asia

Economic Group (EAEG). This group was considered to represent exclusivist Pacific Asian regionalism and promoted close trade relations and co-operation among Asian states above those with external and Western powers. The group was considered to be a counterweight to the North American Free Trade Agreement (NAFTA) agreement and the European Union, both of which represented exclusivist American and European regionalist ideas themselves. The idea of an Asian exclusivist organization was perceived as a major threat to Western interests in, and continued dominance of, the Asia-Pacific region however, and so was strongly opposed by Western powers.[22]

In Malaysia Mahathir was an outspoken critic of the Western Bloc, particularly what he perceived to be its gross double standards in conducting foreign policy.[23] He notably led a boycott of all British goods in Malaysia himself in his first three years in office, in what came to be known as the 'Buy British Last' campaign from 1981 to 1983. He was also particularly critical of the foreign policy of the United States.[24] Mahathir believed that Asian nations should co-operate more closely together and reduce dependence on Western powers. Although he prioritized relations with other Asian nations and was highly critical of the West, relations with Europe and the United States never became openly hostile.

Seeking closer ties with Asian powers, and intending to use Asian led development initiatives to facilitate regional integration and enhanced co-operation, Mahathir's administration enacted Malaysia's Look East Policy during its first year in power. At the time Japan had by far the largest and the most developed economy in the Asia-Pacific region and the administration believed that by learning from Japan's development process and emulating it Southeast Asia could undergo economic transformation independently of the West. Although Japan had been a close Western strategic partner since the end of the Pacific War, Mahathir hoped that Tokyo would play a leading role in the united and co-operating Asian economic group he sought to build. To this end it was proposed by Malaysia that EAEG was to be led by Japan. It is possible that granting Japan such a significant role in the EAEG was an incentive encouraging it to form closer ties with Asian nations even if it came at the expense of its ties with the West. Although it was hardly the leading member of the US-Japan alliance or of the G6 political forum, the latter being termed a 'steering group for the West' by senior figures the U.S. Council on Foreign Relations,[25] Japan was offered a leadership position should it join the new Asian group.

Considering Japan's decades of economic, military, strategic and information co-operation with the United States as a junior partner since 1945 and the United States' substantial influence over Japanese foreign policy decisions, it was near impossible for Tokyo to participate in Mahathir's EAEG without Washington's approval.[26] As Former Japanese Prime Minister Yukio Hatoyama noted: 'I think it represents a big problem that when making foreign policy decisions, Tokyo is always guided by the United States' approach. Japan depends on America.'[27] At a time when Japan was widely seen in both the West and the Asia-Pacific as a power with the potential to become the world's leading economy, the establishment of a regional sphere of influence through a body such as the EAEG would have been ideal for forming regional ties and gaining an advantage in Southeast Asian export markets over extra-regional competitors such as the United States and Europe – similar to what the United States enjoyed through NAFTA and Germany did through the fast expanding European Union. Despite this potential, Japan remained beholden to the United States and as such was unable to establish itself as a leading regional power – instead largely keeping to itself as it had since 1945.

Ultimately the EAEG initiative failed primarily because the United States strongly opposed its realization. The EAEG did exactly what the Western Bloc needed to ensure no Asian power could achieve – to unite much of the Asia-Pacific economically and to some extent politically by facilitating trade among countries in the region in an exclusivist organization – one which by definition did not include Western powers. As Europe and in particular the United States were leading trade partners of most potential members of the EAEG, these Asian nations could be pressurized by Western powers not to join the Asian organization or else risk worsening economic relations with their Western trading partners who held much leverage over them. The *Encyclopedia Britannica* strongly indicated that failure of the EAEG was due to the fact that it opposed Western interests, stating: 'The EAEG encountered strong opposition from the United States and Australia. Under President George H. W. Bush the United States successfully pressured key Asian allies, especially South Korea and Japan, not to support the EAEG. Fear of U.S. protectionism or a U.S. backlash was enough to persuade most East Asian states, whose economic and political survival depended on access to the U.S. market, to withhold their support for the EAEG. East Asian states subsequently rejected the EAEG proposal.'[28]

The role of the United States in terminating the EAEG was also attested to by Diane K. Mauzy, Professor of Political Science at the University of British Colombia and Professor R. S. Milne, founder of the University of Singapore's political science department and Professor of Political Science at the University of British Colombia. In their analysis of the EAEG they wrote: 'Indonesia and some of the other ASEAN states were not receptive to the EAEG, since they believed that they would be cutting themselves off from important regions and trade partners. The United States was hostile, and apparently urged Japan ... and South Korea to reject the proposal.'[29] Evi Fitriani, Head of International Relations at the University of Indonesia wrote of Western measures to prevent Asian unification and co-operation: 'History teaches us that the reasons behind the absence of solid Asian regionalism and identity derive not only from domestic problems and inter-state distrust among Asian countries, but also from the presence of external powers like the U.S. in the region.'[30]

The reason consistently given for the Asian nations' lack of receptiveness to the EAEG by a number of separate analyses is that it was opposed by the West. Asian nations could not integrate their own region for their own benefits because it displeased Western powers, and the majority of countries in the region were highly cautious of the potential consequences of stepping out of line with Western interests in the conduct of their foreign policies. As a paper by Stanford University stated: 'Although some Japanese officials viewed the EAEG proposal favorably, the Japanese government nevertheless had to oppose it publicly in the face of strong opposition of the United States. Without the support of Japan, Malaysia had to recast the EAEG proposal as an East Asian Economic Caucus (EAEC), which called for periodic consultations among East Asian countries on economic issues of common concern. This reformulation of the initiative implied that the EAEC would only serve as a platform for accelerating economic integration in East Asia by promoting the coordination of economic policies.' Even this however could never occur, as it too was strongly opposed by the Western Bloc which Asian leaders were highly unwilling to displease. Western displeasure with the EAEC was reflected in the popular jibe at the time that what the group's initials actually stood for was East Asia Excluding Caucasians – in that it did not include Western or even ethnically European Oceanic countries. 'Nevertheless, the continued suspicions and strong objections of the United States meant that the EAEC was for all intents and purposes a stillborn proposal.'[31]

The failure of the EAEC demonstrated the degree to which so many Asia-Pacific nations, including Japan, were beholden to act in accordance with the strategic interests of the Western Bloc. Because of this, regional integration projects which would effectively allow the region to assert its own interests and offer it a significant degree of independence from the West can never receive sponsorship from or be initiated by such countries. The subservience of Asian leaders to Western interests in the majority of states and the lack of genuine independence in policymaking guarantees that these states can never lead the region out of such subservience and into a position from which it can eclipse the West as a global center of power. This status quo remains perfectly in line with the Western Bloc's interests.

The United States reportedly predicted the emergence of an East Asian Economic bloc, with NAFTA and the EU starting at around the same time, and thus took measures to prevent an exclusively Asian group from forming. The United States thus supported the Asia Pacific Economic Cooperation (APEC) which notably included itself, Australia and other external members. It could therefore function as an alternative to any initiative such as the EAEC with the crucial difference that was not an exclusivist regional bloc. *Encyclopedia Britannica* describes how the United States chose to fight a potential EAEC or equivalent by preempting them: 'Under President Bill Clinton the United States continued to oppose the EAEG but did so mainly by giving new support to APEC. U.S. support for APEC is widely seen as a successful preemptive move against the EAEG and any other East Asia-type arrangements. The EAEG and APEC are often perceived as rivals.'[32]

Prime Minister Mahathir himself proved to be ahead of his time in realizing the need for a joint Asian economic bloc. He understood the ill intentions of the Western Bloc towards Asian development – as evidenced by declassified reports from the U.S. State Department's own policy planning staff underlining the importance of maintain 'a position of disparity' between Western wealth and Asian poverty,[33] which would soon after be demonstrated in the 1997 financial crisis. Response to this threat necessitated the formation an exclusively East Asian economic bloc to safeguard the region's interests against Western intervention. Neighboring countries which rejected prospects for such an organization for their part largely failed to understand this, and to see the importance of excluding Western powers from an Asian regional agreement, because they did not fully comprehend the intentions of the Western Bloc towards the Asia-Pacific and its economic development.

Prime Minister Mahathir was proven to be entirely correct – with the devastating East Asian Economic crisis of 1997 in which Asian nations were deliberately targeted by the West for economic sabotage proving his point. This was then followed by an austerity regime strictly imposed by the IMF, the terms of which were largely dictated by the United States, as covered in the previous chapter, which devastated Asian populations across the region – lowered living standards significantly while failing to yield economic benefits. By engineering the Asian economic crisis, and further exploiting it afterwards, the West revealed its hand in the region and its intentions became far clearer. The crisis was purposely exacerbated by the West which then benefited greatly from one-sided business with its crippled emerging economic competitors which were now effectively neutralized as a threat to its economic primacy. The human costs imposed on East and Southeast Asian populations was truly phenomenal, with severe poverty, suicides and sex trafficking of women and children to Western countries increasing rapidly in its aftermath.[34,35,36] Malaysia's government, always wary of the West's designs as it was, had notably prevented the crisis from worsening by refusing the West's advice to implement neoliberal reforms – instead instating capital controls which hindered the ability of speculators to attack the Malaysian Ringgit. Malaysia was thus spared the worst of the crisis.

Chief Executive of the think tank Global Institute For Tomorrow, Chandran Nair, regarding the lasting impact of the West's handling of the Asian Financial Crisis on Asians' impressions of the West, stated: 'the way the region was both misadvised and humiliated by western institutions and political leaders. Asian leaders who spoke up against the prescriptions of the west, such as Mahathir Mohamed, were severely criticized but later proved right. Lessons were learned and not forgotten.'[37] It was only after the West's hand was revealed by the Asian economic crisis that the necessity of an exclusivist Asian Bloc became clear to the leaderships of more Southeast Asian states. The Western Bloc's claims to be acting altruistically in the greater good of the Asia-Pacific nations were proven false. As International Business Professor Young Chan Kim wrote in his paper 'RCEP vs. TPP: The Pursuit of Eastern Dominance':

> The financial crisis in East Asia signalled for the emerging economies to embark on various feats to further the notion of economic regionalism in the areas of international trade and global finance. The crisis further stimulated the region's economies, which were in prior years progressively interdependent towards the U.S. market, to acknowledge the value of the regional economic cooperation among themselves and to proceed to institutionalize such interdependence. Since November 2001, the notion of regional economic integration was initiated via the free trade agreement between the Chinese and the ASEAN nations, and from then on, more than 30 agreements were penned between subsequent members. Throughout the course of this period, the majority of the East Asian economies acknowledged the fact that unless they were to develop their own method of regional trade, they will undoubtedly be disadvantaged in the field of international trade and multilateral agreements.[38]

In the immediate aftermath of the crisis in December 1997 a summit between ASEAN states and East Asian States China, Japan and South Korea was the first exclusive East Asian regional grouping that had been created. This was known as the ASEAN+3. The summit formed the APT (ASEAN Plus Three) framework in that same meeting, which focused primarily on improving regional financial governance. New schemes such as the Chiang Mai Initiative (CMI) and the Asian Bond Market Initiative (ABMI) all co-operated to organize financial policy co-operation among East Asian nations.

The APT's framework has expanded to include not only finance but several areas of regional co-operation including infrastructure logistics, food and health security issues, human resources development, e-commerce, energy resource management, small business development, pollution, maritime piracy, international migration, ICT, customs information exchange, agricultural technology and management training programs. Co-operation is between almost all Asian nations, and crucially is between Asian nations exclusively. The framework also comprises of 49 consultative bodies which work in 17 specified fields. The APT framework has also formed the East Asia Vision Group and East Asian Study Group to provide ideas on how to advance future regional co-operation. APT members have also held regular meetings as they founded the East Asia Summit (EAS). The APT and EAS are considered a revival of the EAEC initiative, with many of the same features of the previously proposed group.[39] Proposing the EAEC however proved to be ahead of its time, as it took a Western induced financial and social catastrophe for other Asian nations to realize the necessity of an exclusivist economic and political bloc and the nature of the threats arrayed against regional development by extra-regional actors. The future of the bloc, particularly as the Asian financial crisis fades from recent memory with the passage of time, remains to be seen.

China as Number One

While the rapid economic growth of the People's Republic of China has long been considered a threat to the Western Bloc's interests, this threat appeared all the more serious after 2008 when North America and Europe bore the brunt of a devastating financial crisis which pushed much of the Western-centered global economic system into recession. Though global GDP registered a negative growth of –2.01 percent in 2009, the Chinese economy by contrast continued almost unaffected – weathering the crisis as it had others before it. The result was a loss of confidence in the Western economies' ability to maintain primacy in the medium to long term and increased confidence in China's ability to continue its dynamic growth. The question was no longer whether China would overtake the United States to become the world's largest economy – but how long this would take.

From 2007 to 2014 China's incremental GDP growth set it apart from the rest of the world, with growth greater than that of the next seven countries (USA, Brazil, India, Russia, Australia, Germany, Indonesia) combined – gaining $6.85 trillion. The U.S. economy by contrast grew only $2.939 trillion.[40] China surpassed the United States as the world's largest trading nation in 2013, while the country's GDP accounting for Purchasing Power Parity (PPP) overtook that of the United States as the world's largest in 2014. With the U.S. having held the position as the world's largest economy for almost 150 years since 1871, the IMF's announcement that the Chinese economy had eclipsed it in size came as a major blow to America's international standing – where just a decade prior the country's leadership and several influential think tanks and strategists had been planning for a 'New American Century' in which its dominance of global affairs for the coming 100 years was being mapped out – all based on the assumption that the primacy of its economic might, and the unparalleled military prowess this would facilitate, would continue to go unchallenged.

Purchasing Power Parity is considered a better measure of the size of an economy by the majority of economists, and is based directly on a country's productivity while avoiding often absurd incidences which allow the size of an economy on paper to change by double digits within weeks based on fluctuations in currency markets while productivity remains essentially the same. While it was notable that this system of measurement was widely disparaged by Western economists in the aftermath of China's emergence as the world's largest economy, Chinese GDP measured in terms of Real GDP, the second major means of measuring the size of an economy which gives high income countries producing expensive goods with stronger currencies a considerable advantage, is also set to eclipse that of the United States in the early 2020s.

A prominent result of China's economic rise and America's apparent decline in 2008, a year when China's balance of trade surplus hit an unprecedented $268 billion, has been increased calls in the United States for drastic measures, possibly a trade war, to undermine the Chinese economic advantage over the US. Barack Obama in his 2008 presidential election campaign pledged that he would take measures to label China a currency manipulator – a promise that won him much popularity among the American public as it was seen as an effective means to prevent or at least forestall the apparently inevitable rise of China to become the world's largest economy – which supposedly was taking place at the expense of America's workforce.[41] Such policy was extensively lobbied for by numerous interest groups which represented American workers – including the Alliance of American Manufacturers, and several workers' unions. This popular platform of 'coming down hard on China' resonated well with the American population, and was adopted by numerous presidential hopefuls including Obama's Republican challenger in the 2012 presidential election Mitt Romney[42] and the 2016 election winner Donald Trump.

While economic measures to 'get tough on China' and curb its economic advantage were popular among the American public, under both Presidents Obama and Trump there remains little the United States can do to reverse this overwhelming trend. Such measures were by the 2010s never feasible in practice – though they did make good platforms for election campaigning. With their economies so interdependent, a trade war with China would hurt the American economy and affect its living standards at least as much as, if not more than, it would those of China. The result of such measures would be not only a decline in American exports, but also a rise in prices as competitive Chinese imports were substituted by less cost effective alternatives. While such policies may well hurt China more than the United States, any president who enacted such measures, which would have a noticeable effect on American living standards, would quickly lose domestic support. Though President Donald Trump's so called trade war initiated in the summer of 2018 was seen as a departure from this trend, within weeks U.S. lawmakers were working to remove tariffs so recently placed on Chinese goods,[43] and a number of leading analysts have speculated that it was likely that new restrictions on Chinese imports will be lifted altogether in exchange for a pledge from Beijing to import more American goods such as soybeans and fossil fuels.[44] Chinese exports, meanwhile, continued to grow steadily regardless[45] – while much of President Trump's support base remained particularly vulnerable to a decline in Chinese imports of American commodities.

Though the use of some limited tariffs as a temporary leverage to potentially extract limited concessions from China could well be feasible, the drastic measures needed to effect genuine change in China's set path to become the world's prime economic power are highly unlikely to ever be implemented. American consumers are set to pay a considerably higher price for these measures than their Chinese counterparts,[46,47,48] while according to the prominent U.S. investment bank Morgan Stanley, President Trump's tariffs will not have any major effect on the Chinese economy.[49] As well as the unacceptable damage it would incur on the U.S. economy, waging a large scale trade war remains highly questionable in its effectiveness or its ability to reverse the trend towards China's rise to surpass the U.S. as the world's largest economy.[50]

While China continues to foster initiatives to promote regional growth and offset the United States' longstanding economic dominance of the Asia-Pacific, there remains little the U.S. can do in terms of economic measures to forestall its economic rise. 'Getting tough' on China by means such as sanctions, while they may fulfil American long-term strategic interests in hindering Chinese growth, would be a disaster for the country's short term economic interests and lead to significant economic contraction because of the U.S. economy's dependence on trade with its strategic rival. America's leaders cannot afford to sacrifice the prosperity of today to maintain the economic dominance of tomorrow, even if such measures could prove effective, and this plays well into Beijing's hands.

Chinese Economic Initiatives

The Western Bloc has long been wary of China's potential, particularly since the founding of the People's Republic of China in 1949 when over a century of Western influence and extensive Chinese concessions came to an end, to emerge as a major power capable of challenging the West's global dominance. The perceived threat posed by China comes not only from the country's potential to develop itself into a challenger to Western dominance – but more so because it threatens to create a sphere of influence in the Asia-Pacific region which will both pull Asian states out of their dependence on the West while facilitating greater economic growth among Asian nations to eliminate Western nations' position of economic disparity. While the Japanese Empire threatened to form such a sphere of influence through coercion, China may well be able to do so through economic ties and mutually beneficial trade relations – or 'win-win' as the Chinese themselves regularly refer to it.[51]

Despite the devastating economic crisis of 1997 which affected much of Southeast Asia, the region's economic prowess has grown rapidly since the end of the Cold War. Most regional economies grew more than fivefold in the period from 1991 to 2010,[52] and growth rates continue to be among the highest in the world. In this same period of phenomenal growth, Southeast Asia also saw a significant rise in trade with China and the beginnings of economic interdependence – with bilateral economic co-operation growing from under $8 billion to $300 billion.[53] While China replaced the United States as the world's largest trading nation in around 2013 (depending on the source, this varies from 2012 to 2014) it had begun to emerge as the primary trading partner of Southeast Asian nations long before this – reducing the economic influence of the Western Bloc as a whole in the strategically critical region. China's share of trade with the ASEAN market almost tripled within a decade from 5 percent in 2001 to 13 percent in 2011 while trade between Western powers (U.S. and EU) has nearly halved from 30 percent to 18 percent.[54] Through the establishment of institutions such as the Asia Infrastructure Development Bank meanwhile, China has attempted to support the economic development of Southeast Asian nations – improving the markets of its neighbors to further enhance trade.

Asian Infrastructure Investment Bank

In 2014 the Asian Infrastructure Investment Bank (AIIB), a Chinese proposed and predominantly Chinese funded initiative, was launched alongside 21 other countries. The purpose of the bank was to boost growth in East and Southeast Asian economies by raising $100 billion for regional infrastructure investment. The formation of the AIIB was widely perceived to be a challenge to the American-led World Bank and the IMF's Asian Development Bank.[§] The United States therefore strongly opposed the AIIB, which it saw as threatening to undermine the US-led international financial architecture based around the American and European dominated IMF and World Bank. This was but the latest in a long series of Asian regional initiatives which threatened make the region more independent of the US, and which were thus opposed by America – other key examples including the aforementioned Japanese proposed Asian Monetary Fund in 1997 and the Malaysian proposed East Asian Economic Group in 1990.

The U.S. put significant pressure on its allies to prevent them from joining the AIIB, just as it had to undermine the AMF and EAEG, but in this case such efforts proved unsuccessful. Close U.S. partners Thailand, the Philippines, Singapore, South Korea and Taiwan all signed up – the first three as founding members. The failure to undermine this initiative, where previous such attempts against others had succeeded, underlined Washington's waning economic dominance relative to China and the resulting undermining its diplomatic strength and its influence over regional powers. As Asian nations in the 1990s were far more reliant on economic ties to America than to Japan, let alone Malaysia, they could be pressured by the U.S. to undermine initiatives led by these two states. This was not the case with China in the 2010s however, which was the main trading partner of most countries in the region – meaning that the United States could not put itself in an 'us or them' position to undermine the AIIB. The result was something of a coup against U.S. interests – referred to by *Foreign Policy* as 'Washington's big China screw-up.'[55]

The World Bank has consistently imposed neoliberal economic reforms as a precondition for loans, something which has drawn stringent criticism for the hardship it has caused – South Korea and Southeast Asia in 1997 being but one example. The World Bank's Special Adjustment

§ For indications of American leadership: all World Bank presidents without exception have been American citizens, as have the majority of its Chief Economists. The United States maintains more voting power than any three leading states combined. This is strongly reflected in the bank's policy.

Programs (SAPs), which largely involved destruction of welfare and subsidies, were an example of such neoliberal reforms which most often, as in the case of the Asian economies in the 1990s, had little to no positive impact on their economies but substantially lowered the living standards of much of their populations.[56] The AIIB by contrast does not have the Western Bloc's neoliberal agenda behind it, and will therefore likely have an advantage over the World Bank in its appeal to developing countries and effectively challenge the Western institution's monopoly. Indeed, had such an institution existed in 1997, the outcome of the Asian financial crisis very likely would have been very different – with Western institutions having been free to dictate terms to Asian states due to the lack of alternative sources of economic assistance. Given the importance of this monopoly to Western interests, as demonstrated by the vast benefits derived from the Asian financial crisis, the detriment to Western interests and the Western position as a result of the formation of a viable alternative is great indeed.

The purpose of the AIIB has been to address Asia's infrastructure needs, and it was expected to lend $10–15 billion a year to finance these projects – the majority of which would be provided by China. The sums are set to increase substantially over time. After decades of relations with the IMF, World Bank and Western dominated initiatives, infrastructure in much of Southeast Asia nations has largely been neglected. Infrastructure needs at the time of the bank's formation were considered 'absolutely enormous.' Chinese Premier Li Keqiang stressed that infrastructure and connectivity were crucial for Asia to be the most dynamic region for economic growth.[57] Chinese Premier Xi Jinping stated regarding the goal of the AIIB to help China's Pacific neighbors modernize their economies by providing critical infrastructure: 'If you want to get rich, you have to build roads first. The AIIB should accelerate the pace of boosting infrastructure connections in the region, promote regional cooperation and inject new dynamics for Asian economic development.'[58]

A poor state of infrastructure in many Southeast Asian nations has long hindered regional economic growth, and as the establishment of the AIIB is set to support growth through infrastructure development independently of the Western Bloc it has been perceived as a challenge to the

Western 'position of disparity' and thus inevitably been met with strong opposition. While the Western Bloc's interests ultimately lie in maintaining a disparity between their own advanced economies and those of Asia, China benefits from the economic growth of its neighbors to boost regional growth and thus improve regional trade – while the establishment of institutions such as the AIIB allow it to form a sphere of influence in the region by supporting this growth.

As a result of the threat posed by the AIIB, the United States undertook extensive lobbying efforts to prevent Asian nations from joining the Chinese initiative upon its establishment – much as the U.S. had done for the Malaysia sponsored EAEG beforehand. The *New York Times*, citing senior U.S. officials, reported: 'In quiet conversations with China's potential partners, American officials have lobbied against the development bank with unexpected determination and engaged in a vigorous campaign to persuade important allies to shun the project.'[59] *The Diplomat* reported that such initiatives were opposed because they challenged the status quo of a Western dominated Asia, stating: 'The key point is that the U.S. foreign policy community was always opposed to China or any other nation trying to upend the regional order in Asia, and there was never any reason to think the U.S. wouldn't be opposed to initiatives that do just that, such as the AIIB.'[60] This status quo involves leaving much of Southeast Asia underdeveloped and lacking in infrastructure, while remaining economically heavily reliant on the United States and its allies and firmly in the Western sphere of influence both politically and economically.

The need for more integrated Asian markets in response to the threat of Western designs in the region was observed by International Business Professor Young Chan Kim. Kim wrote in his paper 'RCEP vs. TPP: The Pursuit of Eastern Dominance' that the Asian financial crisis in 1997 had

> exposed the need for an abridged regional paradigm and a new wave of regional integration in Asia, which allows it to stand without the aid of external Western partners. Furthermore, prior to the financial crisis, the USA dominated the trading market and was a lead importer in terms of internal trade with the members of the ASEAN. The national wealth of the member nations depleted due to the influence of Western financial institutions similar to hedge funds, and as a result, the members of the ASEAN started to search for a subsequent nation to enable the level of

> trade to sustain. The answer they found was China. This was greatly aided by the considerable number of Sino-businesses within the ASEAN region that enabled the integration process to proceed with greater ease.[61]

With the region's infrastructure estimated to require $8 trillion of investment, and Southeast Asian states already having experienced the consequences of implementing the stringent neoliberal reforms pushed for by the World Bank and IMF in exchange for loans, the AIIB emerged as an invaluable means for Asian economies to build the infrastructure necessary to facilitate their own economic growth. The modernization and growth of regional economies is strongly in line with Chinese long-term interests, and China thus has much to benefit from making the infrastructure investments in Southeast Asia. The AIIB grants it an ideal means of doing so. As an international institution, the AIIB is governed independently meaning that political issues which could arise from direct Chinese investment in and ownership of the majority of developing Asian nations' major infrastructure projects are largely mitigated. Thus both developing Asian countries and China itself will benefit substantially from the AIIB, with the former strengthening the regional economy as a whole and finding a good investment for some of its multi trillion dollar foreign exchange reserves, while the latter will gain key infrastructure necessary for their rising economies to flourish. Only Western Bloc's interests in the Asia-Pacific will be undermined.

Regional Comprehensive Economic Partnership

Of all China's economic initiatives, it is perhaps the Regional Comprehensive Economic Partnership (RCEP) free trade agreement which could have the greatest strategic impact. Should the RCEP come into effect its 16 members would account for around 40 percent of world trade between them. The free trade agreement will facilitate lower tariffs and enhanced technical and economic co-operation between members, while promoting investment among them. It will also cover settlement disputes and other such issues, and under such a framework members states are set to see enhanced co-operation in several fields. The combined GDP of the member states in 2016 was $21.3 trillion. Considering member countries' projected economic growth the joint GDP of member states is predicted to grow to over $100 trillion by 2050.[62] The RCEP is set to dominate global trade and become a global center of economic power. It is however not a regional exclusivist economic agreement, including India, Australia and New Zealand alongside the major Asia-Pacific economies, including China, South Korea, Japan and all the 10 ASEAN members. The Asia-Pacific centered economic agreement has the potential to serve in a highly complementary role to an Asia-Pacific regional exclusivist economic bloc.

The RCEP was opposed by much of the Western Bloc for undermining its regional interests – with the United States in particular seeing it as a manifestation of China's growth to eclipse the U.S. as the center of trade in the region. This aspect of American policy towards Asian economies, the opposition of any initiatives which challenged what Henry Kissinger referred to as the 'Asian regional order' – that under which external powers were a dominant and integral force in the region – was attested to by Dr Young Chan Kim. Dr Kim, an expert on China's trade relations with ASEAN, wrote: 'The main yardstick with which Washington measures Asian initiatives is how they affect its ability to be the dominant power in the region. The thrust of U.S. foreign policy, in the words of the former U.S. Secretary of State, James Baker, is always to avoid any institutional device that "would draw a line down the middle of the Pacific and threaten to divide East Asia and North America".'[63] It is for this reason that initiatives such as the RCEP, AIIB and Malaysia's East Asian Economic Group (EAEG) have all been met with strong opposition in Washington. With the latter two the U.S. undertook extensive lobbying efforts to prevent regional powers from joining,[64,65] while with the first the Obama administration attempted to create its own rival alternative to secure American interests in Asian markets, the Trans-Pacific Partnership – while dismissing the RCEP as failing to prioritize U.S. interests in the region in the way an American drafted agreement would.[66]

Where Malaysia's EAEG failed in the 1990s, China's RCEP is likely to succeed for a number of reasons. China offers prospective members far more than Malaysia was ever able to, in that while the United States may well threaten regional powers with reduced economic relations should they join an Asian regional bloc, China is more vital to trade and economic prosperity than the United States throughout the region. Malaysia's small economy and the importance of trade with the country could never, even to neighbors such as Brunei and Indonesia, contend with the importance of trade relations with the United States. Indonesia for example would not consider sacrificing its substantial economic relationship with the U.S. for its ties with Malaysia – the harsh terms it was given by Washington when the EAEG was proposed in the 1990s. In a similar vein in the 2010s Indonesia's ties to China eclipse those to the U.S. in importance, as they do for most ASEAN member states. While the U.S. could effectively lobby ASEAN members to reject the EAEG in the 1990s, when it was at a position of unparalleled economic dominance, China's eclipsing of the U.S. in its trade relations with the vast majority of regional powers means that the U.S. does not have the undisputed leverage it once did over Asian economies to prevent them from joining a regional grouping. The RCEP is therefore likely to succeed where the EAEG failed.

The Trans-Pacific Partnership: The Obama Administration's Attempt to Maintain Regional Leadership in the Asia-Pacific

The United States responded to the Asia-Pacific's fast growing economic interdependence, and the growing importance of regional powers' economic ties to China in particular, with an American dominated trade agreement – the Trans-Pacific-Partnership (TPP). It is widely considered to be an attempt to undermine the Chinese-led RCEP with an American-led alternative to prevent the emergence of an Asian-led economic partnership. This trade agreement was specifically written to ensure the continuing dominance of the United States in Asia, as attested to by U.S. President Obama, who strongly supported instating the TPP trade agreement as quickly as possible to secure the U.S. position in the region. Getting Asian nations to sign the treaty would, according to Obama, ensured that the United States would continue to play a leading role in the Asia-Pacific, strongly indicating that this was America's role rather than China's. He wrote: 'The Asia-Pacific region will continue its economic integration, with or without the United States. We can lead that process, or we can sit on the sidelines and watch prosperity pass us by. As we speak China is negotiating a trade deal [RCEP] which would carve up some of the fastest growing markets in the world at our expense.'[67]

President Obama said that the TPP trade agreement would 'make sure we [the US] write the rules for the 21st century.' He rejected the Chinese proposed RCEP on the grounds that it did not prioritize U.S. interests in the same way as the TPP. His article directly stated that the U.S. did not seek to establish equal partnerships with Asian nations, but rather sought to dominate relations for the coming century at the expense of countries in the region – notably at China's expense. In his own words, all states 'should play by the rules set by America.'[68] Obama's National Security Advisor Thomas E. Donilon called the agreement a potential game changer and the 'economic lynchpin of U.S. rebalancing strategy in Asia.'[69]

Dr Young Chan Kim observed the connection between the United States' implementation of the TPP and the coinciding military 'Pivot to Asia' (the latter covered in detail in Chapter 17). He wrote:

> From Washington's perspective, her [America's] economic policy has always been in tandem with the regional strategic policy. Thus, it is apparent that the TPP served as a viable route to bridge her economic relations with the ASEAN regions via the implementation of a newly reenergized strategic approach to East Asia ... the notion of the TPP synthesizes with the idea of combatting heightening Chinese influence in the East Asian region. In a world of propagating FTAs [free trade agreements], the U.S. government is powerless to hinder East Asian governments from establishing agreements among themselves, and thus, the creation of a subsequent trade group that includes the USA serves as a beacon of U.S. influence in contesting increasing Chinese prestige in these regions.[70]

While increasing its military presence in Asia significantly, the United States sought to maintain its strategic advantage of being 'closer to each of them than they are to one another' in the region. A binding American-centric trade agreement seemed an ideal way to do so.

Dr Kim's conclusions were strongly supported by a later statement by President Obama in September 2016: 'TPP is a core pillar of America's rebalance towards the Asia-Pacific. And the trade and the growth it supports will reinforce America's security alliances and regional partnerships ... Failure to move ahead with TPP will not just have economic consequences, but call into question America's leadership in this vital region.'[71] Essentially President Obama believed that should the TPP fail, the economic influence of the United States in Asia would be seriously threatened and prospects for regional co-operation independent of the U.S. would more likely be realized. As the president stated, revealing a particularly hegemonic take on international relations: 'We have to make sure America writes the rules of the global economy. And we should do it today, while our economy is on the position of global strength. Because if we don't write the rules for trade around the world – guess what – China will.'[72] The president further reiterated this when signing for the trade agreement, stating: 'TPP allows America – and not countries like China – to write the rules of the road in the 21st century.'[73] The importance of undercutting China's economic expansion in the Asia-Pacific was clearly a critical selling point of the trade agreement, which notably excluded China, and it was thus reiterated by the president and several of the TPP's other advocates on several occasions. The urgency was spurred by China's rapid economic growth and expanding economic ties throughout Southeast Asia at a rate far eclipsing the United Sates – forcing a rapid response from Washington to cement its position before all was lost.

China itself has proven to be fully aware of the TPP's nature as a trade agreement set to divide Asia and undermine Beijing's position. The state run paper *People's Daily* stated in an article in 2011: 'the U.S. does not want to be squeezed out of the Asia-Pacific region by China ... [the] TPP is superficially an economic agreement but contains an obvious political purpose to constrain China's rise.'[74] Professor Song Guoyou, deputy director at Fudan University's Centre for American Studies, observed that the TPP member countries were almost all close U.S. allies – which he felt demonstrated the fact that the U.S. had followed its traditional pattern of choosing economic partners based on its military alliances. U.S. collaboration with its military allies would thereby be strengthened through a closer trade relationship, while the risk of improved trade relations with China drawing these allies closer to China would be reduced. This strategic element led several analysts to refer to the TPP as 'economic NATO.'[75]

The TPP reflected China's growing regional influence not only by revealing the desperation of the United States in the face of its declining regional influence, but also of the newfound influence China held as a result of its booming economic ties to Asian nations. As a result of this three long-standing U.S. regional allies, Thailand, Indonesia and South Korea, all opted out of the TPP largely due to its confrontational position towards China.[76]

While the TPP was a cornerstone of the 'Obama Doctrine' and key to the U.S. strategy for continued regional dominance, the deal was undermined significantly by numerous leaks and ultimately grew unpopular among the U.S. public. Though the details of the trade deal were originally kept secret from the public in all nations where it was set to be implemented, when details were leaked the deal turned out not only to be cementing the position of the United States in the Pacific – but also cementing the rights of American corporations over workers. Julian Assange, the founder of Wikileaks wanted by the United States for exposing state secrets and responsible for publicizing the leaked TPP documents, commented on the impact of the TPP on the lives of populations of signatory countries that the agreement 'would trample over individual rights and free expression, as well as ride roughshod over the intellectual and creative commons. If you read, write, publish, think, listen, dance, sing or invent; if you farm or consume food; if you're ill now or might one day be ill, the TPP has you in its crosshairs.'[77] The predominantly American multinational corporations, which were largely involved in drafting the TPP themselves, gained rights to veto government regulations which could threaten their profits – whether they were environmental regulations, increases to minimum wages or related to state healthcare under a set of supranational laws which all signatories were bound to. This applied not only to the Asia-Pacific signatories, but to the United States itself.[78] This and the common perception in the U.S. that the TPP would make it easier for U.S. corporations to outsource work to developing countries, thus threatening American jobs, made the TPP highly unpopular.

The TPP did in fact significantly harm American workers' interests, reducing tariffs on goods from member nations and making outsourcing of labor to developing countries far more feasible. While China's economy was competitive and it could afford a regional trade agreement without its workforce suffering, the United States had been able to attract partners in the Pacific such as Japan and Vietnam only by pledging to lower its protectionist measures and tariffs for its far less competitive economy.[79] By signing the TPP, the Obama administration was largely sacrificing the interests of its workforce in a desperate attempt to further strategic interests in Asia.

The unpopularity of the TPP domestically made its cancellation a popular policy during the U.S. presidential election campaigns of 2016, with Donald Trump among other Republican candidates pledging to cancel the deal and thus protect American workers if they were elected.[80,81] As Trump pledged on campaign: 'I will stop Hillary [Clinton]'s ObamaTrade [TPP] in its tracks, bringing million of new voters into the Republican Party. We will move manufacturing jobs back to the United States and we will make America great again.'[82] While Hillary Clinton had as Obama's Secretary of State been largely responsible for the initial implementation of the Obama Doctrine and the planning of the TPP, her defeat in the presidential elections and Trump's inauguration brought the end of the agreement. As he had pledged to, Trump cancelled the TPP almost immediately after being sworn into office.

President Trump's decision was criticized by many in the U.S. government for ridding the United States of a crucial asset in the Asia-Pacific and thus benefiting China.[83] The Japanese government similarly concluded that a trade agreement which did not include the United States would be 'meaningless,' tacitly acknowledging the American-centric nature of the initiative which had included 11 other nations.[84] The Achilles heel of the TPP was not that it hadn't strengthened U.S. interests in the Asia-Pacific, but that it had done so while compromising the position of American workers – thus leaving it vulnerable to a form of economic populism which saw its immediate cancellation with the coming of the new administration. Whether the United States will attempt to revive some form of Asia-Pacific trade deal, possibly following the Trump administration's departure, remains to be seen, but by that stage the RCEP will likely have gained too much traction to be undermined by a new American led alternative.

Ultimately excessive Western influence over key financial institutions and dominance of key trade agreements, used to the detriment of the interests of Asia-Pacific nations, has led regional powers to seek alternatives which will better serve their own interests. As demonstrated by 1997, the potential impacts of failing to do so are devastating – and with that crisis also showing the potency of Western influence over both the global financial system and institutions such as the IMF and World Bank, the undermining of these key assets is a major blow to prospects for continued Western primacy and regional dominance. As an Australian government white paper concluded based on an exhaustive study of predominant trends in the global economy: 'Asia is set to overtake the combined economic output of Europe and North America within the decade to 2020.'[85] A study by the United States' National Intelligence Council, which brings together intelligence from several American agencies including the CIA, similarly reported: 'By 2030 Asia will have surpassed North America and Europe combined in terms of global power, based upon GDP, population size, military spending and technological spending.'[86] The vast majority of this Asian economic and military strength would be focused in the Asia-Pacific, the driver of growth on the continent, and it remains likely that the Asia-Pacific will surpass the combined West in the size of its economy (GDP accounting for PPP) in the near future – and may well do so in terms of real GDP by the late 2030s if not sooner.

Without the ability to engineer future crises to forestall the rise of Asia's economies, the prospects for the West of being surpassed by the Asia-Pacific as a new center of global power appear far more likely. If, to take the example used in the previous chapter, South Korea were to find itself in a similar economic situation to that of the mid 1990s, not only would it be less susceptible to pressure from Western institutions, from the U.S. treasury to the IMF, to enact measures which endanger its economy, such as the lifting of capital controls and later submitting to an extremely damaging IMF restructuring program – thus making a crisis considerably more difficult to engineer from the outset – but should a crisis occur, Seoul would be able to look to institutions such as the AIIB – possibly even the Chinese dominated New Development Bank (BRICS Bank) – thus robbing Western powers and their institutions of the effective monopoly position which was so valuable in 1997.

As Vice Chairman of the Federal Reserve System's Board of Governors Stanley Fischer, in charge of talks for the IMF during the 1990s Asian bailout, had said at the time, countries were highly receptive to the Fund's program largely due to the lack of alternatives for loans.[87] Should the IMF press a hard neoliberal line for loans today, while Western economists hail the benefits of 'more bad news' from the Asian economies as they did in the 1990s, any Asia-Pacific country would have an alternative pole to turn to which lacks the hostile agenda of the West – namely regional institutions which would have interests in protecting rather than undermining Asian economic achievements. The importance of breaking this Western monopoly to supporting regional growth therefore cannot be overstated given the scale of the devastation which took place under this monopoly from 1997.

Regarding the differing intentions of these new institutions towards Asian growth relative to their Western dominated counterparts, Singaporean Prime Minister Lee Hsien Loong observed the way that Chinese initiatives designed to stimulate growth in Southeast Asia had proven highly beneficial for the region, stating: 'The Chinese are very engaged ... They come, they have a pitch, they have specific proposals and they back it up with resources. So they'll cooperate with you on maritime research or they'll help with education. They'll have a list of seven or eight items and they'll make sure they've covered the ground and they want that relationship to be a good one.'[88] By contrast while the West's policy has long been based on retaining a critical 'position of disparity' between their own wealth and the relative poverty of others, for China the cultivation of an economically developed Asia – and by extension a larger global economy – will in turn provide more local trading partners and better stimulate growth domestically. Japan and Malaysia for their part appear to have similarly sought to strengthen the regional economy as a whole through their own aborted initiatives, but only China appears to have had the political strength and regional influence necessary to resist Western pressure against such initiatives. The stark differences in Chinese and Western policy towards the Asia-Pacific are strongly reflected by the impacts of their initiatives, and the support of Chinese institutions and assistance is likely to be instrumental in raising living standards and modernizing much of Southeast Asia in a relatively short span of time – where by contrast under the IMF and World Bank infrastructure development across the region had been stagnant – and in many cases in decay.

As well as providing an alternative to Western institutions, regional exclusivist economic blocs can go a long way towards bringing about greater unity among Asia-Pacific nations. Regarding the imperative of a continually divided Asia as a prerequisite for Western primacy to prevail, several Western analysts have long taken comfort in the considerable existing divisions – noting that they are likely to serve to prolong the dominance of a more unified Western Bloc even if between them Asian powers should surpass Western economic, military and technological prowess.[89] As renowned U.S. foreign policy specialist and chief foreign affairs columnist for the *Financial Times* Gideon Rachman noted 'divisions and rivalries within Asia itself' served as the primary obstacle 'to the smooth Easternisation of global political power.'[90] By both ending the monopoly of Western financial institutions, as well as acting as a unifying force for Asia-Pacific nations – much like NAFTA and to some extent the European Economic Community have done in the West, the prospects for divisions within Asia are reduced considerably by new institutions and power blocs. The importance of these institutions, organizations and trade agreements therefore, from the Japanese AMF and Malaysian EAEG which were terminated under Western pressure to the Chinese AIIB and RCEP today – and even to some extent the Shanghai Cooperation Organization (covered in the next chapter) as a broader Asian power bloc – cannot be understated. Whether they succeed will be a key determinant of the future of world order and the Asia-Pacific's ability to rise to succeed the West as a center of power and protect its hard won economic gains from external intervention.

Notes

1 Hobbes, Thomas, *Leviathan*, 1651 (Chapter 18, 'On the Rights of Sovereigns by Institution').

2 Cox, Michael, and Stokes, Doug, *U.S. Foreign Policy*, Second Edition, Oxford, Oxford University Press, 2012 (p. 271).

3 Gady, Franz-Stefan, 'This Is How Europe Conquered Asia,' *The Diplomat*, August 3, 2017.
4 Howe, Stephen, *Empire; A Very Short Introduction*, Oxford, Oxford University Press, 2002 (pp. 94–95).
5 Weitz, Richard, 'EU Should Keep China Arms Embargo,' *The Diplomat*, April 18, 2012.
6 Barnet, Richard J., *The Alliance: America-Europe-Japan Makers of the postwar world*, New York, Touchstone 1985 (p. 91).
7 'Goodbye to America's 4 Million Man Army? Inter-Korean Summit Risks Compromising U.S.' Most Formidable Pacific Asset,' *Military Watch Magazine*, April 28, 2018.
8 'Time for South Korea to regain wartime operational control of its military,' *The Hankyoreh*, September 29, 2017.
9 Hotta, Eri., *Pan Asianism and Japan's War 1931–1945*, New York, Palgrave Macmillan, 2007 (p. 217).
10 Lipsey, Phillip Y., 'Japan's Asian Monetary Fund Proposal,' *Stanford Journal of East Asian Affairs*, Volume 3, Number 1, Spring 2003 (p. 94).
11 Ibid. (p. 95).
12 'Looking back at the "Asian IMF" concept,' *Nikkei Asian Review*, June 22, 2017.
13 Ibid.
14 Sakakibara, *Nihon to Sekai ga Furueta Hi* [The Days Japan and the World Were Shaken], Tokyo, Chuokoronshinsha, 2000 (pp. 180–182).
15 'Looking back at the 'Asian IMF' concept,' *Nikkei Asian Review*, June 22, 2017.
16 Sakakibara, *Nihon to Sekai ga Furueta Hi* [The Days Japan and the World Were Shaken], Tokyo, Chuokoronshinsha, 2000 (p. 185).
17 Ibid.
18 Lipsey, Philip Y., 'Japan's Asian Monetary Fund Proposal,' *Stanford Journal of East Asian Affairs*, Volume 3, Number 1, Spring 2003 (p. 96).
19 'Memorandum From the President's Assistant for National Security Affairs (Kissinger) to President Nixon,' Office of the Historian, Foreign Relations of the United States, 1969–1976, Volume XVII, China, 1969–1972, United States of America Department of State.
20 Ibid.
21 United Nations Development Program Human Development Report.
22 Ba, Alice D., 'East Asian Economic Group (EAEG); Proposed Regional Economic Bloc,' *Encyclopedia Britannica.*
23 Richter, Frank-Jürgen, *Asia's New Crisis*, Singapore, John Wiley & Sons, 2004 (Preface by Mahathir Mohamad).
24 'Commanding Heights: Dr. Mahathir bin Mohamad,' *PBS*, July 2, 2001.

25 Laub, Zachary, *The Group of Eight (G8) Industrialized Nations*, Council on Foreign Relations, March 3, 2014.
26 'Stationing American troops in Japan will lead to bloody tragedy – ex-PM of Japan,' *RT*, (televised interview), November 6, 2016.
27 Ibid.
28 Ba, Alice D., 'East Asian Economic Group (EAEG); Proposed Regional Economic Bloc,' *Encyclopedia Britannica*.
29 Milne, R. S., and Mauzy, Diane K., *Malaysian Politics under Mahathir*, Abingdon, Taylor & Francis, 2002 (p. 130).
30 Fitriani, Evi, 'ASEAN and contemporary U.S. diplomacy in East Asia,' *Jakarta Post*, August 13, 2010.
31 Kiat Yip, Wei, 'Greater East Asia, Prospects for Closer Economic Integration in East Asia,' *Stanford Journal of East Asian Affairs* (p. 107).
32 Ba, Alice D., 'East Asian Economic Group (EAEG); Proposed Regional Economic Bloc,' *Encyclopedia Britannica*.
33 'Report by the Policy Planning Staff, Review of Current Trends, U.S. Foreign Policy, February 24, 1948,' Office of the Historian, Foreign Relations of the United States, 1948, General; the United Nations, Volume 1, Part 2, United States of America Department of State.
34 Sawatsawang, Nussara, 'Prostitution – Alarm Bells Ringing Sound Amid Child Sex Rise,' *Bangkok Post*, December 24, 1999.
35 Baguioro, Luz, 'Child Labour Rampant in the Philippines,' *Straits Times*, February 12, 2000.
36 Klein, Naomi, *The Shock Doctrine: The Rise of Disaster Capitalism*, London, Penguin, 2008 (p. 273).
37 Nair, Chandran, 'Why is the West seen as the greatest threat? From Asia, the answer is clear,' *The Guardian*, March 6, 2014.
38 Kim, Young Chan, 'RCEP vs. TPP: The Pursuit of Eastern Dominance,' Springer Institute Publishing, January 2016.
39 Dent, Christopher M., *China, Japan and Regional Leadership in East Asia*, Cheltenham, Edward Elgar, 2008 (p. 19).
40 Figures from the October 2014 update of the International Monetary Fund's World Economic Outlook Database.
41 Whitesides, J., Bohan, C., 'Obama and Clinton vow to get tough with China,' *Reuters*, April 14, 2008.
42 Branigan, Tania, 'Mitt Romney renews promise to label China a currency manipulator,' *The Guardian*, October 23, 2012.
43 Sullivan, Andy, 'U.S. Senate quietly votes to cut tariffs on hundreds of Chinese goods,' *Reuters*, July 27, 2018.

44 Robert D. Atkinson, 'Who Lost China?,' *The National Review*, July 26, 2018.
45 'Trump's Tariffs Have Fully Kicked In – Yet China's Exports Grow,' *Wall Street Journal*, November 8, 2018.
46 'Trade War's Next Salvo to Hit U.S. Shoppers Harder Than Chinese,' *Bloomberg*, September 6, 2018.
47 'American shoppers set to pay higher price than Chinese for trade war,' *South China Morning Post*, September 6, 2018.
48 Heeb, Gina, 'Trump's trade war is probably hitting the US economy a lot harder than China's, HSBC says,' *Business Insider*, January 4, 2019.
49 'The trade war won't cause any "major" hit to China's economy,' *CNBC*, August 29, 2018.
50 Trigkas, Vasilis, and Feng, Qian, 'Why the U.S. Trade War on China Is Doomed to Fail,' *The Diplomat*, August 28, 2018.
51 Zheng, B. J., *China's peaceful rise, speeches of Zheng Bijian*, Washington, DC, Brookings Institution Press, 2005 (p. 5).
52 Fu, Y., and Wu, S. C., 'South China Sea: how we got to this stage,' *The National Interest*, May 9, 2016.
53 Ibid.
54 Kim, Young Chan, 'RCEP vs. TPP: The Pursuit of Eastern Dominance,' Springer Institute Publishing, January 2016.
55 Roach, Stephen S. and Zha, Daojiong and Kennedy, Scott, and Chovanec, Patrick, 'Washington's big China screw-up,' *Foreign Policy*, March 2015, p. 26.
56 Fujita, Sanae, *The World Bank, Asian Development Bank and Human Rights: Developing Standards of Transparency, Participation and Accountability*, Cheltenham, Edward Elgar Publishing, 2013 (p. 31).
57 Wong, Sue-Lin, 'China launches new AIIB development bank as power balance shifts,' *Reuters*, January 16, 2016.
58 'China leads countries in signing up for US$50b Asian infrastructure bank,' *South China Morning Post*, October 25, 2014.
59 Perlez, Jane, 'U.S. Opposing China's Answer to the World Bank,' *New York Times*, October 9, 2014.
60 Keck, Zachary, 'Why the U.S. Is Trying to Squash China's New Development Bank,' *The Diplomat*, October 10, 2014.
61 Kim, Young Chan, 'RCEP vs. TPP: The Pursuit of Eastern Dominance,' January 2016.
62 'Understanding and applying long-term GDP projections,' *East Asian Bureau of Economic Research*, June 17, 2016.
63 Kim, Young Chan, 'RCEP vs. TPP: The Pursuit of Eastern Dominance,' Springer Institute Publishing, January 2016.

64 Ba, Alice D., 'East Asian Economic Group (EAEG); Proposed Regional Economic Bloc,' *Encyclopedia Britannica.*

65 Bird, Mike, 'China's new development bank is becoming a massive embarrassment for Obama,' *Business Insider*, March 31, 2015.

66 Obama, Barack, 'President Obama: The TPP would let America, not China, lead the way on global trade,' *Washington Post*, May 2, 2016.

67 Ibid.

68 Ibid.

69 Shoup, Lawrence H., *Wall Street's Think Tank: The Council on Foreign Relations and the Empire of Neoliberal Geopolitics, 1976–2014*, New York, Monthly Review Press, 2015 (p. 242).

70 Kim, Young Chan, *Chinese Global Production Networks in ASEAN*, Amazon Digital Service, 2016 (p. 25).

71 The White House, Office of the Press Secretary, 'Remarks of President Obama to the People of Laos,' September 6, 2016.

72 The White House, Office of the Press Secretary, 'Remarks by the President on Trade,' May 8, 2015.

73 The White House, Office of the Press Secretary, Statement by the President on the Signing of the Trans-Pacific Partnership, February 3, 2016.

74 Ding Gang (丁刚) and Ji Peijuan (暨佩娟)，美力促“泛太平洋伙伴关系”学者称有明显主导亚洲经贸格局意图，*People's Daily* (人民日报), July 27, 2011.

75 Wu, S., 'Why the TPP is an "economic NATO,"' *Huffington Post*, October 19, 2015.

76 Kirk, D., 'China, Russia, U.S.: Looming Face-Off in Asia Over TPP with Korea at the Vortex,' *Forbes Asia*, September 29, 2015.

77 'Secret Trans-Pacific Partnership Agreement (TPP) – IP Chapter,' *Wikileaks*, November 13, 2013.

78 'Robert Reich: A Trans-Pacific Partnership is a corporate hijacking,' *Salon*, May 5, 2015.

79 Mourdoukoutas, Panos, 'How Lower Tariffs Under TPP Could Send More Nike Jobs to Vietnam – And Harm the Company,' *Forbes*, May 9, 2015.

80 'Donald Trump will withdraw U.S. from TPP "on day one" as he gives major policy address on what he will do in first 100 days as president,' *The Telegraph*, November 22, 2016.

81 Boyle, Matthew, 'Rand Paul comes out swinging against Obama's secret trade deal amid collapse,' *Breitbart*, May 12, 2015.

82 Smith, Allan, 'Donald Trump is staring down decades of Republican party orthodoxy on an signature issue,' *Business Insider*, July 3, 2016.

83 Carney, Jordain, 'McCain disappointed with Trump withdrawal from TPP,' *The Hill*, November 22, 2016.
84 Takenaka, Kiyoshi, 'Japan PM says TPP trade pact meaningless without U.S.,' *Reuters*, November 21, 2016.
85 'Australia in the Asian Century,' Australian Government White Paper, October 2012 (p. 53).
86 'Global Trends 2030 – Alternative Worlds,' U.S. National Intelligence Council (p. 4).
87 Interview with Stanley Fischer, May 9, 2001, for *Commanding Heights*.
88 Rachman, Gideon, 'Lunch with the FT, Lee Hsien Loong,' *Financial Times*, April 11, 2014.
89 Rachman, Gideon, *Easternisation, War and Peace in the Asian Century*, New York, Vintage, 2017 (p. 16).
90 Ibid. (p. 15).

CHAPTER 16

The Russian Factor in the Asia-Pacific

> I cannot forecast to you the action of Russia. It is a riddle wrapped in a mystery inside an enigma; but perhaps there is a key. That key is Russian national interest.[1]
>
> —WINSTON CHURCHILL

The Sino-Soviet Alliance and the Threat to the Western Bloc's Global Primacy

The end of the Chinese Civil War and establishment of the People's Republic of China (PRC) in 1949 saw the end of over two decades of war and over a century of hostile foreign military deployments on the country's territory and extensive interference in its domestic affairs – referred to by the Chinese people as the 'century of humiliation.' The Western powers had in the eyes of the new PRC government revealed themselves to be unremittingly hostile, not only historically since the British Empire had pillaged large swathes of Chinese territory and propagated opium addiction to improve its own balance of trade,[2] but also the actions of the U.S. military during the Chinese Civil War and in the early 1950s. This included the United States' extensive support for Chiang Kai-shek and deployment of the U.S. Marines against the Chinese communists, the blockade and trade embargo placed on the country, and the threats to invade and 'roll back' Chinese communism which had led U.S. troops to approach the Chinese borders and threaten an attack on the country during the Korean War. Support for insurgent groups in and regular CIA incursions into Chinese territory further worsened the situation. They came alongside the United

States' threat to use nuclear weapons against the new state on numerous occasions in the 1950s, and U.S. President Eisenhower's statement that the U.S. military should use nuclear weapons 'as you would use bullets' across the Chinese mainland should China threaten U.S. interests in the Taiwan.[3] The extensive use of biological weapons including anthrax, bubonic plague and cholera among others during the Korean War, combined with these other factors, only increased China's perception of the U.S. led Western Bloc as unremittingly hostile and an existential threat to its security (as previously covered in Chapters 3, 8 and 9).

Devastated by over 20 years of war and facing an imminent threat to its statehood, the newly formed People's Republic increasingly turned towards the Soviet Union for support. While the USSR had not supported the Chinese communists during the country's Civil War, they did provide the new PRC with loans, technological assistance and military aid. During the Korean War the Soviets provided China with limited material support, including medical equipment to prevent the spread of plague following U.S. biological warfare efforts and state of the art MiG-15 fighter jets which were critical to negating the advantage of American air power. With the two states having signed the Sino-Soviet Treaty of Friendship, Alliance and Mutual Assistance in February 1950, just four months before the war begun, each party was under Article One obligated to come to the aid of the other should it come under direct attack. The threat of direct Soviet intervention was thus key to deterring the United States from using its nuclear weapons against Chinese population centers and military installations during the war – something for which the military had prepared and which Presidents Truman and Eisenhower had both seriously considered. Firebombing campaigns against Chinese cities, similar to those which had caused millions of civilian casualties in North Korea, and in Japan just five years prior, never took place against Chinese population centers, largely as a result of the Soviet protection China enjoyed.

After the Korean war China was able to assert its independence against growing U.S. threats largely due to both the protection of the Soviet nuclear umbrella and later its own nuclear weapons, which were developed with considerable Soviet assistance in the face of regular threats by the United States to strike Chinese population centers. Assistance for a Chinese nuclear program began immediately after the United States began to station nuclear missiles on Taiwan – and were seen by Moscow as key to providing its ally with a form of nuclear parity against growing American nuclear threats just over 130 km from its territory.[4] The USSR provided advisers to aid in the production of fissile materials,[5] as well as providing prototype missiles for the delivery of nuclear warheads – such as the SS-2 Sibling missile based on which the Chinese developed the Dongfeng 1. A prototype bomb and other related technologies were also transferred to China. Following its first successful nuclear test in 1964 the Chinese government acknowledged that such an achievement would have been impossible without the substantial assistance it received from the Soviet Union.[6]

The USSR too faced significant threats from the Western Bloc on its own borders, and by posing a threat to the very existence of both countries the Western Bloc did much to push China and the Soviet Union together. The USSR under General Secretary Joseph Stalin had long been seen as the greatest threat to the West's dominant position – to the extent that many Western leaders were initially willing to support Nazi Germany and its fascist European allies to fight against it.[7,8] Before the Second World War had ended the United States had already begun exploring means to undermine and ultimately defeat the USSR in the postwar world and thereby cement its position as the sole hegemonic center of power. Even before its nuclear strikes on Hiroshima and Nagasaki the U.S. military had begun to look into potential uses of nuclear arms to launch a preventative war on the USSR to ensure that it could not develop weapons of its own to gain nuclear parity or emerge as a major power capable of challenging the U.S. led Western Bloc. Within a month of Japan's surrender the Pentagon had planned for nuclear strikes against 66 Soviet cities, requiring an 'optimum' of 204 atomic bombs. The purpose of these strikes was to obliterate most of the Soviet Union's population and industry – chiefly its capacity to refine oil and produce aircraft and battle tanks.

Major General Lauris Norstad, Deputy Chief of Air Staff at Army Air Forces HS met Leslie R. Groves, the United States Army Corps of Engineers officer who directed the Manhattan Project on the September 15, 1945. He told Groves that America and Russia 'will be the outstanding military powers' for the next ten years. The destruction of the USSR's capability to wage war must serve as the 'basis upon which to predicate the U.S. atomic bomb requirements.' The Army Air Forces Study conceded it might not be necessary to remove all 66 Soviet population centers, and that wiping out the first 15 'first priority cities' may have the same impact. 'The primary for the application of the atomic bomb is ... the simultaneous destruction of these 15 first priority targets.' Cities such Moscow, Leningrad, Tashkent, Novosibirsk and Nizhny would each be hit by six nuclear bombs, with the remaining cities being hit by five or less nuclear bombs. Bombs planned for these strikes would have a far greater payload that those used on Hiroshima and Nagasaki. Groves was responsible for the manufacture of bombs for the future, and more bombs were built as a result. In this scenario 10,151,000 would be killed, wounded or displaced. Around 600 square kilometers of urban areas would be devastated.[9] This would hardly be the last time the United States seriously considered preventative nuclear strikes against a country to prevent it from gaining nuclear parity – as was the case with China in the 1960s[10,11] and North Korea in the 2010s.[12,13,14,15]

Despite the intentions of the Pentagon and its destructive war plans the U.S. State Department still claimed: 'It is generally recognized throughout the world that the United States has no aggressive designs on any other nation and is, therefore, the safest possessor of the [nuclear] secret.'[16] A secret memo released from FBI archives revealed that this was not exclusively an American strategy. British Prime Minister Winston Churchill persistently lobbied U.S. President Truman to launch a preventative nuclear attack on the USSR insisting: 'the only salvation for the civilization of the world would be if the President of the United States would declare Russia to be imperiling world peace and attack Russia.' If the Kremlin could be hit by nuclear weapons, 'wiping it out,' it would then be 'a very easy problem to handle the balance of Russia, which would be without direction.'[17] Churchill feared that should the United States fail to launch a nuclear attack, the USSR would create their own bomb and gain limited and eventually full nuclear parity – thus undermining the Western Bloc's advantage. According to Churchill, who had referred to the Russian peoples as 'not human beings at all. They are lower in the scale of nature than the Orangutan,'[18] initiating nuclear strikes on the USSR was necessary because if the West lost its primacy 'civilization will be wiped out or set back many years.'[19] It was considered imperative to destroy any potential competitor to ensure the West's own position – something which applied very much to the USSR and would later in the 1950s apply to China as well.

Plans to initiate a preventative nuclear attack on the USSR never materialized due to a number of factors. The United States had difficulty producing the hundreds of atomic bombs required due to both financial and technological constraints. The surprise Soviet development its own nuclear weapons in 1949, half a decade before the U.S. had anticipated, closed the window for a safe preventative nuclear strike prematurely. Soviet leader Joseph Stalin had long prioritized the development of nuclear weapons, and after the attacks on Japan allocated more scientists and resources to the project. The third setback to the United States' plans for a preventative strike was the new reality the U.S. Air Force had to contend with during the Korean War – when the ability of its bombers to deliver nuclear strikes was put to serious question by the heavy losses they were sustaining against small numbers of Soviet made MiG-15 fighters deployed to Korea – which were fielded in their thousands by the USSR itself. The United States had previously relied on long-range subsonic bombers to deliver its nuclear weapons, but this suddenly ceased to be a viable strategy. As American Journalist I. F. Stone noted regarding the setback to the United States of an advanced Soviet Air Force: 'the subsonic bomber proved obsolete over Korea and with it the foreign policy based upon the subsonic bomber. The atom bomb was still a "deterrent to aggression" – from either side. It was no longer a threat with which either side could hope to dictate terms. The Truman-Acheson dream of "building up strength," to the point where Moscow – and half the world with it – would be forced into unconditional surrender, had disintegrated in the skies over Korea.'[20] Half the world referred to the USSR and its allies at the time – including the Warsaw Pact nations, Mongolia, China and North Korea.

When the Sino-Soviet Alliance formed it became the utmost priority of the Western Bloc to hinder its development. Many Western analysts predicted that this alliance would result in the two countries surpassing the West's longstanding primacy and lead to their 'Complete World Victory' and 'Universal Empire.'[21,22,23] Indeed, considering the substantial economic achievements made by the USSR under General Secretary Stalin, widely termed an 'economic miracle' at the time, which had unprecedentedly turned a backward country suffering from multiple epidemics and regular famine into a global superpower in little over ten years[24] – should the far larger People's Republic of China undergo a similar process undisrupted it would have been a disaster for the Western Bloc's position. The collective effort of China, the USSR and the latter's satellite states not only during the Korean War, but also afterwards in their joint reconstruction program in North Korea, was a unique event which symbolized the height of the Sino-Soviet alliance.

The Sino-Soviet Split and the Western Imperative of Dividing Two Superpowers

In response to the Sino-Soviet alliance the United States masterfully applied the strategy of divide and rule to break the communist bloc into two. Following the death of Joseph Stalin in 1953, who had been widely revered by the Chinese communist leadership, the USSR's new leader Nikita Khrushchev took a new stance to relations with both China and the West. This materialized in the late 1950s when Khrushchev began to seek rapprochement with the Western Bloc, and in doing so increasingly abandoned his commitments to China which gained him significant approval from Western leaders. As British Professor, Lecturer and China specialist Jude Woodward noted regarding Khrushchev's pivot to the West undermining relations with China:

> On 20 June 1959 Khrushchev abruptly withdrew from China's nuclear program, and in July 1960 all Soviet technical support and personnel were pulled out of China without any prior consultation. Behind this move lay Khrushchev's determined orientation towards a rapprochement with Eisenhower's U.S., including his 1958 proposal for an international ban on nuclear testing to be initially agreed between the USSR, the U.S. and Britain. Withdrawing China's access to Soviet nuclear technology strengthened Khrushchev's hand before meeting Eisenhower at Camp David later in 1959. These events precipitated the Sino-Soviet split, which was to adversely

> affect their relations for the next 25 years and allowed the U.S. to manipulate each country against the other, weakening both.

U.S. President Richard Nixon would years later in 1982 refer to Khruschev's premiership as primarily responsible for the Sino-Soviet split, which he stated represented the greatest setback of the Western Bloc's adversaries and 'the most significant geopolitical event since World War II.'[25] Khrushchev's rapprochement with the Western Bloc would ultimately fail and he would later be deposed from the Soviet Premiership. His policies nevertheless did lasting damage both to his own country, which began to stagnate economically and saw its defense sector fall behind that of the United States, and to relations with China which would give the Western Bloc a significant and lasting advantage.[26]

Henry Kissinger, U.S. National Security Advisor and Secretary of State under the Nixon administration, one of the most influential figures in the U.S. foreign policy, advocated 'triangular diplomacy' with the USSR and China. This strategy is revealing not only of the United States' approach to bilateral relations between China and Russia today – but also to relations throughout the Asia-Pacific where similar strategies continue to be implemented. Secretary Kissinger crucially noted the advantages the United States sought to gain if they were to encourage a rift between the two and at the same time 'to be closer to either Moscow or Peking than either was to the other.' He further reiterated this point in his book *Diplomacy* when he stated that the position of the United States 'would be strongest when America was closer to *both* Communist giants than either was to the other.' This was again reiterated in his book *World Order* in which he stated that the design of his 'triangular diplomacy' was to balance 'China against the Soviet Union from a position in which America was closer to each Communist giant than they were to each other.' Kissinger repeats this point four times throughout his writings precisely because it is so crucial to American foreign policy – very likely the greatest U.S. victory of the Cold War and arguably the cornerstone of the Western Bloc's eventual prevalence over the Soviet Union.

The Western Bloc gained an advantage over the Sino-Soviet Bloc by exploiting divisions between and offering each party benefits if it co-operated with the West against the other. The United States courted Khrushchev in the late 1950s which led to his abandonment of support for China for what he believed would be stronger ties to the West. The Soviet Union ultimately gained little from pursuing this détente – while the United States had successfully offered the prospect of rapprochement to manipulate the new Soviet leader, who went on to somewhat naively sacrifice his most important ally in exchange, leading to the breakup of what was fast becoming the most powerful alliance in the world. The strategy was repeated in the 1970s – a time when the USSR had fallen under somewhat more capable leadership and the United States, with its international prestige having dropped as a result of its failure and brutal misconduct in Vietnam, its first ever trade deficit in 1971, and the devaluation of its currency, was in a weakened position and sought to use China to counter its major adversary. In exchange for international recognition, a seat at the United Nations and a scaling back of economic sanctions China began to co-operate more closely with the Western Bloc in its efforts to undermine the USSR.

Francis P. Sempa, American author, Political Science Professor and contributing editor to *American Diplomacy*, elaborated on the exploitation of the strained relations by the United States for its own gains. He wrote: 'The geopolitical threat [to Western power] posed by the Sino-Soviet Bloc gradually receded when the Sino-Soviet split emerged and was successfully exploited by the Nixon administration with its famous "opening" to China.'[27] In President Nixon's own words, his strategy was 'to play Russia and China off against each other.'[28] Indeed, China did perceive an imminent threat to its sovereignty from the growing Soviet-Indian-Vietnamese axis on their northern, southern and western borders – particularly since the Soviet intervention in Czechoslovakia which showed that the country was willing to use force to bring divergent communist nations into line, and China could well be next. A group of four Chinese Marshals who were tasked with assessing China's defensive options at the time of the rapprochement warned that while the hostile Soviet Union posed a threat to China, the United States would attempt to leverage a Sino-Soviet conflict to position itself 'sitting on top of the mountain watching a fight between two tigers.'[29]

The United States' moves to exacerbate the divisions among their enemies was indeed critical to ensuring the Western Bloc's continued position as the dominant power bloc.[30] The resulting Sino-Soviet split not only divided the West's two greatest adversaries, but also undermined the efforts of smaller powers to oppose Western interests worldwide. In Vietnam the war effort against the United States was seriously compromised by division between the country's two major sponsors, China and the Soviet Union. The result was a lack of the formidable united front which had proven so effective in Korea. This gave the United States and its allies a significant advantage – as war against a Vietnamese resistance force supported by two major superpowers acting in unison rather than contending with one another would have been a far more difficult prospect.

Examples of how the Sino-Soviet split undermined the Vietnam War effort, in stark contrast to their co-operation in Korea, are many. While the U.S. Air Force conducted bombing raids and dropped napalm on Vietnamese population centers causing massive destruction, Soviet attempts to provide the North Vietnamese military with means to counter American air power were seriously undermined by their rivalry with China. The most advanced surface to air missile system in use in the North Vietnamese military was the S-75 (NATO reporting SA-2). While this took a toll on U.S. aircraft, the USSR had access to a number of newer systems including the complementary S-125 (NATO reporting SA-3) and 2K12 Kub (NATO reporting SA-6) missile systems. These missiles proved to be lethal against U.S. made aircraft in the 1973 Arab-Israeli war, and were able to deny even the most advanced American fighters such as the F-4E Phantom access to airspace covered by their range. As the U.S. Air Force relied on the same aircraft as Israel had to gain control of the skies – the deployment of a wider variety of more modern air defense systems to Vietnam could have seriously undermined the U.S. war effort and potentially turned the tide of the air campaign much like it did when deployed in the Middle East. The USSR did not transfer these missiles, and many other state of the art weapons systems, because arms transiting to North Vietnam almost all passed through Chinese territory. There was much concern among the Soviet military leadership that the Chinese People's Liberation Army would obtain the some of the USSR's most sophisticated weapons in transit and acquire their technological secrets – allowing them to develop similar systems for use against the Soviet Union itself. The only beneficiaries of this conflict were the United States and its allies, whose combat aircraft had far better access to Vietnamese airspace as a result while China, the USSR and most of all the Viet Minh themselves all lost out.

The Chinese took steps to further undermine Soviet influence in Vietnam, in so doing undermining the war effort against the United States. A CIA report from 1968, marked Top Secret and declassified in 2007, details several incidences of China preventing Soviet aid from reaching Vietnamese forces as a result of the tensions between the two superpowers, something from which the United States again benefited directly. Anti-aircraft guns, various MiG fighters, military technical workshops and other valuable supplies, all of which transited through China, were prevented by the Chinese from reaching North Vietnam on numerous occasions between 1965 and 1968 according to the report.[31] As the Vietnamese war effort suffered and the United States benefited, Ho Chi Minh and the Viet Minh leadership implored the two communist powers in vein to act as a united front as they had in Korea – to no avail.

When the Soviet Union offered to send their own military to North Vietnam to deter the U.S. from escalating the conflict, something which would almost certainly have changed the course of the war, they were unable to do so because the Chinese refused to tolerate the presence of Soviet troops on their Southern border. The United States genuinely feared and took extensive measures to avoid any direct confrontation with Soviet military, a caution which the Americans did not extend to the armed forces of Vietnam or China – then seen as a 'third world peasant armies.' The Soviets had similarly given the Viet Minh a bleak choice – 'either us or the Chinese' – which for a small nation fighting the United States and a broad coalition of its allies was hardly constructive considering that it would need all the aid it could get from both communist powers.[32]

Vietnam was far from a unique case of a crucial independence movement being undermined as a result of the rift between China and the USSR. Conflict between the two communist powers severely undermined the positions of emerging nations which were relying on the support of the superpowers to oppose the Western Bloc, leading several leaders to raise their concerns. President Nasser of the United Arab Republic, a leading anti-imperialist figure who had with Soviet support waged wars against Britain, France and a number of the Western Bloc's Middle Eastern clients, had tried to maintain strong relations with both the USSR and China. He implored the Soviet leadership in 1965: 'We've tried with you, and we've tried with the Chinese, but it's no use. Both of you are asking us to take sides and that puts the whole Afro-Asian [anti-imperialist] movement in a terrible dilemma.'[33] Several states suffered similarly and neutrality was discouraged, dividing former allies across the world. North Korea too, for insisting on a neutral stance and refusing to condemn China, saw its military relations with the USSR deteriorate.[34] Pyongyang's refusal to downgrade its ties with the Soviet Union on the other hand lead to a deterioration of its relations with Beijing, which began to view its neighbor with much suspicion. As the united front against the Western Bloc was lost, the positions of all Soviet and Chinese allies were weakened as a result. The prime beneficiary inevitably was the Western Bloc itself. Animosity between the USSR and China would continue for the rest of the Cold War, and Sino-Soviet relations would never return to what they had been in the 1950s.

The Russian Factor: The Nature of Post-Soviet Russia's Relations with the West and its Implications for the Asia-Pacific Region

During the 1990s, following the collapse of the USSR, the Russian Federation which emerged long acquiesced to the interests of the Western Bloc in its former sphere of influence. Under President Boris Yeltsin Russia did not object to the expansion of the West's NATO military alliance eastwards towards its borders in the 1990s – nor did it take any measures whatsoever to counteract the unilateral NATO military intervention against Yugoslavia, a close Russian ally, where civilian infrastructure was extensively targeted and the formerly prosperous economy was devastated.[35] Following the disintegration of the country and its division into several smaller republics, many of these were integrated into the NATO alliance. Although the expansion of NATO further east than Germany was forbidden under the terms that ended the Cold War, the NATO alliance violated this agreement through its rapid expansion – and thus increasingly threatened Russian national security.[36] According to a statement given at the alliance's 2009 international summit, NATO had 'concluded that the end of the Cold War provided a unique opportunity to build improved security in the entire Euro-Atlantic area and that NATO enlargement would contribute to enhanced stability and security for all.'[37] This notably failed to take into account Russian security concerns however.

Russia's Yeltsin era government, credited with opening the country to Western influence and introducing a Western neoliberal economic system, quickly became very unpopular both for its failure to protect national security interests and for its gross mishandling of the economy – leading to a public approval rating of just 6 percent.[38] Yeltsin's government had fully applied the neoliberal economic policies strongly advocated by the West and by Western institutions such as the International Monetary Fund and World Bank during the 1990s, with disastrous effects for the Russian economy. From 1991 to 1999 the Russian economy's GDP contracted by a staggering 45 percent in size, while economic mismanagement and rampant corruption led to huge sections of the population losing their incomes, savings and pensions.[39] Russian life expectancies fell dramatically in under five years, with the male life expectancy falling by six and a half years according to the Russian Federation Federal State Statistics Service. The World Bank estimated that the poverty rate had increased from 1.5 percent to between 39 percent and 40 percent of the Russian population in under eight years.[40] As a result of these policies over 80 percent of Russian farms were bankrupt between 1991 and 1998 and around 70,000 state factories closed. 74 million Russians, around half the population estimated at 147 million in 1995, had suddenly fallen below the poverty line in their living standards. 25 percent of the population lived in desperate poverty.[41]

Young Russian women were sold for sex in Western countries and human trafficking, which had previously been negligible to non-existent, suddenly became highly prevalent. *Human Rights Review* noted that this was caused directly by the Western imposed economic policies. The paper 'Human Trafficking in Russia and Other Post-Soviet States Since the collapse of the Soviet regime' states: 'post-communist states have rapidly learned the modern face of slavery. Slavic women have been trafficked to the sex markets of Western Europe, Asia, and North America. The surge in human trafficking is the result of numerous factors, including the dramatic fall of the economic system and complete deterioration of the social safety net.' The paper went on to state: 'no less than 500,000 have been trafficked from the country since the collapse of the Soviet Union. Russia has become one of the largest exporters of women for the sex industry.'[42] Drug addiction also increased by 900 percent, the suicide rate doubled and HIV became a nationwide epidemic.[43] Policies enacted under President Yeltsin's government, which served to critically weaken the nation which had so recently been a superpower, were however met with strong approval from the Western Bloc and particularly from the United States – which strongly advocated for and supported his policies[44] and even aided his election campaigns – reportedly with a decisive impact.[45,46]

Alongside the destruction of the Russian economy under neoliberal policies, which were not only endorsed by the United States, but were to a large extent imposed on the country by the IMF and World Bank as conditions for aid, Russia also faced potent Western-backed security threats. In particular radical Islamist forces which had been organized, funded, armed and directed by the Western Bloc and their Arab partners to destabilize the Soviet aligned government of Afghanistan, and were later supported to further Western interests in Yugoslavia,[47] would continue to be an invaluable asset to press the offensive against the now weakened Russian Federation in the 1990s. This was noted by the CIA National Council on Intelligence's Deputy Director Graham E. Fuller, a key architect in the creation of the Mujahedeen army – a predecessor of Al Qaeda. Fuller stated regarding the CIA's strategy in the Caucasus in the 1990s: 'The policy of guiding the evolution of Islam and of helping them against our adversaries worked marvelously well in Afghanistan against the Red Army. The same doctrines can still be used to destabilize what remains of Russian power.'[48]

The U.S. Congressional Task Force on Terrorism and Unconventional Warfare's director, Yossef Bodansky, detailed the extent of the CIA's strategy to destabilize Central Asia by using Islamist proxies and thereby threaten Russia: 'A formal meeting in Azerbaijan in December 1999 in which specific programs for the training and equipping of Mujahedeen from the Caucasus, Central/South Asia and the Arab world were discussed and agreed upon, culminating in Washington's tacit encouragement of both Muslim allies [Arab states and Turkey] and U.S. "private security companies" ... to assist the Chechens and their Islamist allies to surge in the spring of 2000 and sustain the ensuing Jihad for a long time ... Islamist Jihad in the Caucasus as a way to deprive Russia of a viable pipeline route through spiraling violence and terrorism.'[49] Russia's government claimed to have evidence of contacts between Islamist fighters and Western intelligence groups.[50] These proxies of Western and Arab interests working to destabilize Russia and Central Asia were known as the 'Arab Mujahedeen in Chechnya.' Though the largest ethnic group were Arabs, they came from a variety of nationalities united only by their Arab Wahabist ideology.

With the situation in Russia looking extremely bleak, President Yeltsin's successor Vladimir Putin who assumed the presidency in 2000 recalled that the country was set to undergo the same scenario as Yugoslavia – chaos, destabilization and eventual fragmentation – likely followed by a Western military presence on its soil. He would go on to recall years later in 2015: 'At the end of the 1990s Russia was pretty close to following the Yugoslav scenario.'[51] The president believed that the Western Bloc, through its support for various separatist factions including Islamist terror groups, was meant to instigate such a Yugoslav style collapse, stating in 2014: 'The support of separatism in Russia from abroad, including the informational, political and financial, through intelligence services, was absolutely obvious. There is no doubt that they would have loved to see the Yugoslavia scenario of collapse and dismemberment for us with all the tragic consequences it would have for the peoples of Russia.'[52] President Putin believed that the Western Bloc still sought to undermine and eventually dismantle Russia in this way – and took it as his administration's responsibility to prevent this.[53] As U.S. political journal *Politico* noted of the new Russian government: 'They rejected the liberal, democratic Russia that President Boris Yeltsin was trying to build.'[54] What this meant was a rejection not only of Western neoliberal economic policy, but also Western political influence and the adoption of a more independent foreign policy. The result was an economic, military and foreign policy resurgence by which the country dramatically changed course – and from the brink of total collapse Russia would in little over a decade return to become a major world power.

Russia's new administration quickly struck hard against the U.S. backed Islamist insurgents in the Caucuses, working extensively to boost the military's then severely battered morale and making good use of special forces, aerial bombardments and mines to destroy the bulk of the enemy forces. A change in economic policy and the rejection of the Western advocated neoliberalism meanwhile foreshadowed a significant economic resurgence, and from 2000 to 2008 real incomes more than doubled while poverty halved. 30 percent of the population lived below the poverty line in 2000, while this was at 14 percent in 2008 and has continued to decrease since then. The average wage was $90 in 2000 but reached $500 in 2008, while pensions increased from $33 to $140. Wages and benefits have consistently grown faster than inflation. GDP increased by 70 percent in eight years and industrial growth increased by 75 percent.[55] Reinvestment in research and development for the country's historically advanced military, largely facilitated by the country's economic resurgence, gave it much needed modern capabilities and made Russia a world leading, and in many fields *the* world leading, military power.

Russia's economic and military resurgence was inevitably met with disdain in the West, seen as both a contradiction and threat to the post-Cold War 'end of history' – under which a Western-centric hegemonic world order had been predicted to prevail indefinitely. Interestingly, the downfall of the Western client regime in Russia was met with a similar response to that with which the West had met the defeat of Chiang Kai-shek's Guomindang in the Chinese civil war – and Western Russophobia in the early twenty-first century became comparable to the Sinophobia of the 1950s. Indeed, just as the United States had lamented the 'loss of China' in 1949, so too did the West begin to refer to having 'lost Russia' – the return of a term which had not been used in such a context ever since the Chinese case.[56] There was no civil war or revolution in Russia, but President Putin and his supporters had effectively carried out a coup against the Western-backed oligarchy.

The expansion of NATO towards Russia's borders had effectively overturned the balance of power laid out in the terms by which the Cold War had ended, and in the early 2000s further military activities undertaken by the Western Bloc in Europe were perceived in Moscow as a further threat to Russia's security interests. The proposed integration of the Baltic States and Georgia into NATO, the former which began to take place in the early 2000s, only further exacerbated tensions with Russia. In 2002 the United States withdrew from the longstanding Anti-Ballistic Missile Treaty which had restricted the deployments of anti-missile systems for both parties. The purpose of the treaty had been to maintain continued parity of the countries' nuclear missile forces – thus preserving the Cold War era concept of mutually assured destruction and preventing either side from gaining an advantage to facilitate the initiation of nuclear war against the other. Upon its withdrawal NATO began the deployment of long-range interceptor missiles and radar tracking systems in the Czech Republic and Poland, soon followed by a number of other states in the former Soviet sphere of influence very near to Russia's borders. This inevitably drew stringent criticism from Russia, which perceived the deployment as an attempt by the Western Bloc to neutralize Russia's nuclear deterrent with anti-missile technologies – something which constituted an imminent threat to its national security.[57] The withdrawal was referred to by President Putin as having 'delivered a colossal blow to the entire system of international security' by restarting an arms race and attempting to undermine the mutual vulnerability which he referred to as having 'guaranteed the safety of humanity from major conflict over the past seventy years. It was a blessing rooted in "mutual threat" but this mutual threat is what guaranteed mutual peace on a global scale.'[58,59] Russia would respond by developing advanced missile defenses of its own[60,61] as well as advanced hypersonic missiles, entering service from March 2018, which were effectively immune to interception.[62,63,64]

Alongside the militarization of Eastern Europe, Russia has perceived several of the Western Bloc's actions to seriously threaten its national security – leading to a significant deterioration of relations. The United States' arming and training of radical Islamist forces since 2011, many of them with ties to Al Qaeda,[65,66,67] and its attempts to use these forces to overthrow Russia's longstanding ally, the Syrian Arab Republic, led to a number of major confrontations. These worsened further when the Russian military began to find evidence of what it believed to be American co-operation with the Islamic State terror group.[68,69,70] The United States' support for an involvement in the overthrow of the Ukrainian government in 2014, another close Russian partner, and Russia's retaliatory reconquest of Crimea – a strategic peninsula which should it fall under NATO control would have seriously compromised Russian security – further soured relations and led to both the Western Bloc and Russia imposing harsh economic sanctions on one another. These were among the most significant events which led to a deterioration of Russian-Western relations in the early twenty-first century. Having suffered tremendously as a Western client in the 1990s and since faced growing national security threats from the Western Bloc, including support for Islamic terrorist forces to undermine its interests, Russia has increasingly turned towards the Asia-Pacific region to establish new partnerships independently of the hostile Western world. The deterioration of Russian-Western relations was thus key to facilitating a strategic partnership in the economic and military fields which has come to dominate the twenty-first century – Russia's own 'Pivot to Asia' – and in particular the re-establishment of a close Sino-Russian alliance.

As prospects for cordial relations with the Western Bloc, much less the healthy partnership which Secretary Gorbachev staked the country's future on, increasingly appear an impossibility for Russia, and the Asia-Pacific region by contrast grows as a new center of global economic power far more attractive not only in political terms, but also economically relative to the stagnant West, Moscow appears to have set in motion its own pivot to Asia. In many ways this has been more decisive than that of the United States which, mired by commitments in the Middle East and lacking historical roots in Asia, has found the transition difficult. Russia by contrast, with its origins as a country extensively influenced by its Mongol heritage and the source of its wealth historically having been its vast Asian territories, appears in many ways more at home in Asia – with its landmass extending to the Korean Peninsula and just 40 km away from the Japanese coast. As Vyacheslav Nikonov, chairman of Russia's parliamentary education committee and highly influential supporter of an Asian pivot – culturally, strategically and economically – noted regarding his country's origins and its place in the world as a separate entity to the West: 'We have different roots from the West ... We don't have the Greek-Roman heritage, we have the Mongol heritage, which came from China ... They established the Chinese tax system and the system of communication that went all the way to the Pacific.'[71] Russia's future as an Asian nation and a pivot eastwards thus closely reflect and are harmonious with its past and its origins.

The strong perception of a social and economic decline in the West combined with the perceived hostility of the Western Bloc has led a number of influential figures to lend their support to a Russian pivot to Asia. Editor of the highly influential journal *Russia in Global Affairs*, Fyodor Lukyanov, noted: 'The Atlantic is no longer the sole center of world events and engine of global progress. The Pacific [is] … taking over the main stage of world development.'[72] Dmitri Trenin, one of Russia's leading strategic analysts, was one of several key figures who proposed that Russia would do better to shift the seat of its government, and gradually the bulk of its economy, to its far east – where it would border the Koreas, China and Japan – very likely to be the most economically prosperous region of the twenty-first century. The contrast between Northeast Asia and Eastern Europe, where Russia's capital is currently located, is stark in economic terms – with the former holding two of the world's three largest economies, China and Japan – and with both Koreas very likely to become two of the leading economies in terms of expansion rates, technology, and living standards in the coming century. As Vladislav Inozemtsev, a prominent professor at Moscow State University, noted: 'Russian policymakers … have fallen in love with the idea of a push to the East' – apparently with good reason.[73]

While Russia is no longer the major power it once was, with its economy, science, technology and living standards a shadow of what they were in the Soviet era, and while its previously booming population faces a sharp decline, it nevertheless remains a formidable force in world affairs which has, by lending support to Asia-Pacific nations against the ambitions of the Western Bloc, aided considerably the region's rise to become a new global center of power. While prospects for a world order centered around Moscow died in 1991, an Asian led world order based on countries which have historically been far more friendly towards Russia remains far preferable to one dominated by the hostile Western Bloc. It was not for no reason that Russia was widely seen to hail the rise of the Asia-Pacific over the West as a highly positive development, with British journalists describing leading Russian politicians as 'exultant' over the news that China's economy had surpassed that of the United States in size in 2014 being just one example[74] – a development which boded well from Russia's own position.

China and Russia: A Partnership to Shape the Twenty-first Century

With the end of the Cold War both China and Russia perceived themselves to be under threat under a U.S. led unipolar world order. While the United States was by a considerable margin the world leader in the number of military interventions it carried out overseas during the Cold War, the fall of the USSR removed the most important check and balance on American power and led to a significant further escalation in such interventions. The U.S. engaged in 46 military interventions abroad during the Cold War period from 1948 to 1991. From 1992 to 2017, however, this increased to 188 military interventions – an increase of over 600 percent in the number of interventions per year. Independent states across the world came under attack under a number of pretexts – consistent only in that they either acted independently of or directly opposed the Western Bloc's interests.[75]

The threat posed by increasingly frequent Western military interventions worldwide led to a growth in co-operation between states which were potential targets – one such case being vastly improved Sino-Russian co-operation, particularly in the field of defense. In the 1990s Russia transferred critical Soviet defense technologies to China which were instrumental in the country's military modernization during that period. Perhaps the most prolific example has been the J-11 air superiority fighter, the backbone of the Chinese Air Force in service from 1997, which was in fact a license built variant of the Soviet Union's prime fighter jet the Su-27. Its entry into Chinese service changed the balance of power in the skies over East Asia irrevocably.[76]

While the end of the Cold War saw an abating of tensions and some military co-operation, mainly in the form of an impoverished Russia selling modern arms and technological secrets to an economically booming China in the 1990s, it was only in the 2000s with the end of the Yeltsin administration that genuine bilateral co-operation began to take place. The first stage of this was the signing of the Treaty of Good Neighborliness and Friendly Cooperation in 2001 between the two countries. This treaty served as a basis for extensive economic, diplomatic and geopolitical co-operation. Perhaps most significantly however its ninth article is also implicitly a defense pact between the two countries which binds both parties to respond jointly to any threats to the security interests of either state. The future sharing of military intelligence and technologies was also laid out and would prove critical for both countries to counterbalance the power of the then dominant Western Bloc.[77]

China and Russia further cemented their military alliance through the creation of the Shanghai Cooperation Organization (SCO), a political, economic and security bloc which entered into force in September 2003. The founding signatories were China, Russia, and several former Soviet republics in Central Asia including Kazakhstan, Kyrgyzstan and Tajikistan. These republics were all members of the Collective Security Organization (CSO), a Russian led military alliance established in 1992 through which a number of former Soviet states co-operated closely on sensitive military affairs. China's military alliance with the CSO states through the SCO has facilitated close security co-operation – leading a number of Western analysts to conclude that the SCO was a Sino-Russian led military alliance formed as a counterbalance to the U.S. led NATO alliance.[78,79,80]

The vast and expanding NATO military presence on Russia's Western borders and the United States' redeployment of the bulk of its military forces to East Asia, where they have repeatedly trespassed into what China perceives to be its territorial waters, have led both countries to perceive significant threats to their sovereignty from the Western Bloc. China and Russia have thus taken considerable steps to strengthen their military co-operation and jointly respond to the threat. Sino-Russian military co-operation has developed to encompass even the most sensitive fields – part of what Russian President Putin referred to as an 'all embracing and strategic partnership.'[81] The depth of the partnership is unprecedented for either of the two countries.

An indicator of the extent of this military co-operation was the joint military exercise held in 2016 simulating a joint response to a hostile ballistic missile attack which was, according to many analysts, indicative of a 'a new level of trust' between the two powers.[82] The exercises involved sharing very highly classified information on missile systems and early warning systems – one of the most sensitive defense secrets of any nuclear power. Vasily Kashin, a Russian military expert specializing in the Chinese People's Liberation Army, noted the significance of the decision between the two states to share such sensitive information. 'The ability to share information in such a sensitive area as missile launch warning systems and ballistic missile defense indicates something beyond simple co-operation,' he stated.[83] Indeed, the Soviet Union did not share such information even with its Warsaw pact allies – nor do the United States or France with their NATO allies or one another. It indicates a level of co-operation and intelligence sharing beyond a usual alliance, allowing the two militaries to effectively integrate and fight efficiently almost as a single force would.

China and Russia have also engaged in joint war games on numerous occasions, the scale of which have increased since Russian Defense Minister Sergei Shoigu's announcement in 2016 that both countries intended to continuously expand joint military exercises.[84] Crucially, exercises have been held to present a joint front against threats faced by both nations. Upon the announcement that the United States, Britain and France would increase their naval deployments to the South and East China Seas, where they would carry out joint military exercises, Russia began to strengthen its own forces in the region and held joint Pacific war games with China. This was a sign that China did not stand alone in the region and had the support of the Russian Navy in the face of growing threats.[85] The Russian military's development of a number of game changing new weapons technologies key to dominating the Pacific theatre, unmatched by those of either China or the Western Bloc, including long range ship hunting hypersonic missiles which entered service in 2018 and can seriously threaten Western warships across the South and East China Seas, means its increased military involvement in the region could well play a decisive role.[86]

With Russia's growing military involvement in the Syrian conflict, and in the aftermath of the United States' threat to use military force to overthrow the Russian aligned Syrian government, the Chinese Navy sailed to the Mediterranean to conduct joint naval drills with the Russian fleet. As Russia's naval facilities in Syria were at the time key to deterring U.S. attacks on the country, support from the Chinese Navy, which had also supported Russia in vetoing Western backed UN resolutions against Syria, sent a strong signal of a united front against the Western Bloc's designs in the region.[87] With the war in Syria turning in Russia's favor by late 2016, the United States conducted direct but limited airstrikes on Syrian forces then engaged against the Islamic State terror group in September 2016, causing over 150 casualties using its A-10 attack jets.[88] This was followed by further strikes in April[89] and May 2017[90] and the shooting down of a Syrian strike fighter deep within the country's own airspace in June.[91] With Russia offering stern warnings that it would not tolerate such attacks on its ally, and deploying advanced military hardware to the region, the Chinese Navy was seen in the Mediterranean in July 2017 for joint naval drills with Russian forces – again presenting a joint front.[92]

In April 2018, as tensions between Russia and the Western Bloc again escalated amid new rounds of Western economic sanctions against Moscow and Western threats both to take military action against the Syrian government and to retaliate for an alleged but unproven Russian chemical weapons attack on British soil, China more directly stated its support for its strategic partner. Chinese Defense Minister and State Councilor Wei Fenghe traveled to Russia from April 1 to April 5 on his first foreign visit since assuming the post. The minister referred to the two countries' defense partnership as 'as stable as Mount Tai' and was explicit regarding their defense co-operation being aimed at countering threats from Western Bloc specifically. At the Moscow Conference on International Security, which Minister Wei attended alongside Foreign Minister and State Councilor Wang Yi, the Defense Minister stated: 'the Chinese side has come to show Americans the close ties between the Armed Forces of China and Russia, especially in this situation. We have come to support you.'[93] A week later on April 12, China announced large-scale live fire naval drills in the Taiwan Strait, which were according to a number of military analysts scheduled to coincide with Western threats against Russia and a buildup of Western military forces near Syria as a sign of solidarity with Moscow – thus pressing the Western Bloc on multiple fronts.[94]Chinese military expert Teng Jianqun, senior research fellow from the China Institute of International Studies, observed that the military partnership between Russia and China had quickly become closer and more trusting, particularly regarding the sharing of sensitive information. He said: 'They are not afraid to share intelligence and technical capabilities with each other and it is a good basis for strong military relations … It shows a solid level of trust between the two countries. If you look at the evolution of the development of maritime drills, the first one was initiated in 2012. At that time, the two sides were very cautious of each other because that was the first contact in maritime engagement. After at least four runs of the drill, the two sides have become very familiar with each other and they are good at communication.' He said these increasingly positive military relations were 'laying the foundation for good relations overall between Russia and China,' stressing their many common strategic interests.[95]

Alongside their close military co-operation, China and Russia have significantly improved their economic ties since the year 2000. Annual trade in 2014 was almost 1,200 percent of what it had been in 2000, rising from just $8 billion to $95.4 billion. In this period Russian annual exports to China grew from $5.8 billion to $41.6 billion, while annual imports from China increased from $2.2 billion to $53.8 billion. This made China Russia's largest trading partner other than the European Union.[96] While Russian trade has long overwhelmingly been dominated by the EU, with the reliance on trade with Europe growing rapidly following the USSR's collapse, as relations with the West soured and those with China improved the country has undergone a massive economic shift under which China has in a very short period gone from a negligible trading partner to the most important for Russia's economy. In 2018 the two countries saw an increase in trade of over 25 percent compared with the previous year, and should these trends continue Chinese importance as an economic partner for Russia will far surpass the EU and the United States combined by the mid-2020s.[97]

While Russia is only China's ninth largest trading partner, bilateral trade is continuing to rapidly increase while the critical strategic importance of Russian imports makes them far more significant than their ranking would indicate. As China's rapidly growing economy finds itself increasingly in need of fossil fuels, Russia provides by far the most reliable and secure foreign source of these resources. With the United States military deployed both throughout the Persian Gulf, allowing it to potentially cut off fossil fuel supplies from Arab states and Iran, and perhaps more critically with growing U.S. military deployments surrounding the critical Malacca and Lombok straits through which most of China's oil imports transit, China remains vulnerable to having its energy sources cut off by the United States military (see Chapter 17). This is particularly vital considering that U.S. war plans with China such as Air Sea Battle project the blockading of the Malacca Strait and the disruption of energy supplies as a key means to cripple the Chinese economy in times of war. As a result China's ability to obtain fossil fuels over land from Russia is an invaluable and irreplaceable asset to the country's economic security.

In January 2011 Russia's East Siberia-Pacific Ocean pipeline, the country's first ever pipeline to carry oil eastwards, was opened to more efficiently deliver fossil fuels to China. The pipeline was operational at full capacity by 2013, and several expansions have since been planned. In March 2013 Russia's state owned oil company Rosneft announced an agreement to more than triple its oil exports to China to 45–50 million tonnes annually, making China by far the largest importer of Russian oil. The deal reportedly included joint development of Russian oil deposits in eastern Siberia and offshore deposits near the Barents Sea.[98] Eight months later in November Rosneft signed a deal to use the Kazakhstan-China oil pipeline, which was extended to export Russian oil to China. In May 2014 Russia's Gazprom proceeded to sign the largest deal for natural gas supplies in its history, a deal worth over $400 billion to supply gas to China over 30 years.[99] China's Board of Energy Affairs has since sought to further increase fossil fuel imports from Russia.[100] Alongside fossil fuels, from 2012 the Chinese state power grid also began to import electricity from Russia. This co-operation has served to reduce both China's reliance on energy imports by sea, vulnerable to blockade by the United States and its allies, and Russia's own reliance on European energy markets, also vulnerable to Western sanctions.

Referring to progress in the relations between China and Russia in the ten years since the signing of the critical 2001 Treaty of Good Neighborliness and Friendly Cooperation, Russian President Putin stated: 'we have brought Russia-Chinese relations to a very high level. I would even say it is the highest peak in the history of our relations. First and foremost, we have achieved an unprecedented level of trust in international affairs. We cooperate very closely on the international arena. Of course, both Russia and China are large countries. They are both major players on the international arena. Russian-Chinese cooperation on the international arena has become a major influence on global politics. We have learned to coordinate our efforts in order to protect our legitimate interests.' He referred to enhanced economic co-operation, joint manufacturing, joint research and development programs, a rapid increase in bilateral trade, close co-operation in disaster relief efforts and highly successful cultural exchanges as signs of the emerging partnership between the two countries.[101]

Referring to the potential of a new Sino-Russian partnership to mirror that of the formidable Sino-Soviet alliance, British China expert Professor Jude Woodward noted that during the Cold War the division of the two powers had been key to the Western Bloc retaining its dominant position. The professor noted that during the Cold War the United States had attempted to '"triangulate" their relations to their own advantage, first courting Russia to isolate and threaten China and then drawing China into its Cold War strategies against the USSR. If, rather than exploiting Sino-Soviet divisions, the U.S. had faced them united, the outcome of the Cold War might have been quite different. Today a newly arisen China and a resource-rich and militarily powerful Russia acting in concert could offer each other critical mutual economic and military support, and exercise a formidable geopolitical influence. Hence it is well understood throughout the U.S. foreign policy community that success in containing China requires preventing Russia and China from coming together, and instead redeploying the old Cold War triangular strategies for today's circumstances.'[102] Whether the strategy of dividing the two powers would succeed will again be key to determining the future of the twenty-first century – as the Western Bloc's prospects for maintaining its global dominance against a joint Sino-Russian axis are far slimmer than they would be against the two states should they act separately, or better yet should Sino-Russian relations deteriorate to an openly hostile state as they did from the late 1950s.

Preventing the emergence of a world order centered around a Sino-Russian partnership remains a high priority for the Western Bloc as evidenced by its policies. The emergence of the Sino-Russian alliance was referred to by Henry Kissinger in 2017 as 'one of the key problems of our period.'[103] While U.S. and European foreign policy analysts had long advocated that the Western Bloc co-opt Russia to 'balance' the growing power of China,[104] their hostility towards the country and its experience of the eventual impacts of the West's 'divide and rule' strategy – the unipolar order of the 1990s under which Russia suffered profoundly – had led Moscow to instead pursue closer ties with Beijing.

With a strong alliance forming between China and Russia, and diplomatic, economic and military ties closer than ever before in their history, it is imperative now more than ever before for the Western Bloc to engineer a rift between the two powers. As Zbigniew Brzezinski, U.S. political scientist, strategist and presidential advisor and one of the most influential figures in American foreign policy, stated in a speech in December 2016: 'The U.S. must be wary of the great danger that China and Russia could form a strategic alliance … Nothing is more dangerous to the U.S. than such a close connection.'[105] Brzezinski himself strongly advocated the essentiality of dividing the two powers against each other to yield results akin to the Sino-Soviet split – thus weakening the positions of both powers. Only by doing so could the U.S. led Western Bloc gain some chance of securing its position as the world's dominant power. Brzezinski stated: 'it behooves the United States to fashion a policy in which at least one of the two potentially threatening states becomes a partner … in containing the least predictable but potentially the most likely rival'[106] (i.e. partnering with one to divide it against the other to end the threat of an alliance). This was the exact same strategy the United States had used in the Cold War. As U.S. President George W. Bush stated in 2006, quoting a saying from the state of Tennessee: 'Fool me once, shame on you. Fool me twice, shame on me.'[107] Re-implementing the same strategy successfully a second time remains unlikely, particularly under today's Russian and Chinese governments which not only are arguably far more competent in their foreign policies than their counterparts in the 1960s – but are now extremely familiar with the results of the strategy's successful implementation – namely a Western dominated world order under which the sovereignty and prosperity of both countries would be seriously threatened.

Notes

1 Churchill, Winston S., *The Gathering Storm: The Second World War*, New York, Rosetta Books, 2002 (p. 403).
2 Kort, June M. Grasso, and Jay Corrin, Michael, *Modernization and revolution in China: from the opium wars to the Olympics*, Abingdon, Routledge, 2009.
3 Eisenhower, Dwight D., presidential news conference, March 16, 1955.
4 Lewis, John, and Xue, Litai, *China Builds the Bomb*, Stanford, CA, Stanford University Press, 1988 (Chapter 3, The Strategic Decision and Its Consequences).
5 Burr, William, and Richelson, Jeffery T., 'Whether to "Strangle the Baby in the Cradle": The United States and the Chinese Nuclear Program, 1960–1964,' *International Security*, vol. 25, no. 3, Winter 2000–2001 (pp. 54–99).
6 Jersild, Austin, *Sharing the Bomb among Friends: The Dilemmas of Sino-Soviet Strategic Cooperation*, Cold War International History Project, Wilson Center, October 8, 2013.
7 McCullough, David, *Truman*, New York, Simon & Schuster, 1992 (p. 262).
8 Aris, Ben, and Campbell, Duncan, 'How Bush's grandfather helped Hitler's rise to power,' *The Guardian*, September 25, 2004.
9 Ham, Paul, *Hiroshima Nagasaki: The Real Story of the Atomic Bombings and their Aftermath*, New York, Doubleday, 2012 (pp. 488–490).
10 Gady, Franz-Stefan, 'How a State Department Study Prevented Nuclear War With China,' *The Diplomat*, October 25, 2017.

11 Burr, William, and Richelson, Jeffery T., 'Whether to "Strangle the Baby in the Cradle": The United States and the Chinese Nuclear Program, 1960–1964,' *International Security*, vol. 25, no. 3, Winter 2000–2001 (pp. 54–55, 58).

12 Friedman, Uri, 'Lindsey Graham Reveals the Dark Calculus of Striking North Korea,' *The Atlantic*, August 1, 2017.

13 Sevastaopulo, Demetri, 'Trump and North Korea: the perils of a pre-emptive strike,' *Financial Times*, January 9, 2018.

14 Brown, Daniel, 'Republican congressman says the U.S. should preemptively strike North Korea,' *Business Insider*, September 22, 2017.

15 Peters, Ralph, 'The moral answer to North Korea's threats, Take them out!' *New York Post*, September 4, 2017.

16 Ham, Paul, *Hiroshima Nagasaki: The Real Story of the Atomic Bombings and their Aftermath*, New York, Doubleday, 2012 (p. 494).

17 'Winston Churchill wanted to nuke Kremlin "to win Cold War," FBI memo reveals,' *RT*, November 9, 2014.

18 Reynolds, David, 'World War Two: 1941 and the Man of Steel,' ClearStory, BBC Four, (Documentary), June 13, 2011.

19 'Winston Churchill wanted to nuke Kremlin "to win Cold War," FBI memo reveals,' *RT*, November 9, 2014.

20 Stone, I. F., *Hidden History of the Korean War*, Amazon Media, 2014 (Chapter 47, 'Six Months of Futile Slaughter').

21 Burnham, James, *Containment or Liberation*, New York, The John Day Company, 1954.

22 Sempa, Francis P., 'Is Kissinger's Triangular Diplomacy the Answer to Sino-Russian Rapprochement?,' *The Diplomat*, August 2, 2016.

23 Aron, Raymond, *The Century of Total War*, New York, Doubleday, 1954.

24 Evans, David, and Jenkins, Jane, *Years of Russia, the USSR and the Collapse of Soviet Communism*, London, Hodder, 2008 (Chapter 8: 'Stalin's Economic Policies 1928–1939').

25 Nixon, Richard, *Leaders*, New York, Simon & Schuster, 2013 (Chapter 6: Nikita Khrushchev The Brutal Will To Power).

26 Woodward, Jude, *The U.S. vs China: Asia's New Cold War?* Manchester, Manchester University Press, 2017 (p. 86).

27 Sempa, Francis P., 'Is Kissinger's Triangular Diplomacy the Answer to Sino Russian Rapprochement?,' *The Diplomat*, August 2, 2016.

28 Farrell, John A., *Richard Nixon, The Life*, New York, Random House, 2017 (p. 438).

29 Ibid. (p. 439).

30 Athwal, Amardeep, 'The United States and the Sino-Soviet Split: The Key Role of Nuclear Superiority,' *The Journal of Slavic Military Studies*, Vol. 17.

31 *The Sino-Soviet Dispute on Aid to North Vietnam (1965–1968)*, Central Intelligence Agency, United States of America, Directorate of Intelligence, Intelligence Report, Reference Title ESAU XXXIX.
32 Ibid. (p. 151).
33 Heikal, Mohamed, *Sphinx and Commissar, The Rise and Fall of Soviet Influence in the Arab World*, New York, HarperCollins, 1979 (pp. 150–151).
34 Chin, O. Chung, *P'yongyang Between Peking and Moscow: North Korea's Involvement in the Sino-Soviet Dispute, 1958–1975*, Tuscaloosa, University of Alabama Press, 1978 (p. 118).
35 Dobbs, Michael, 'NATO's Latest Target: Yugoslavia's Economy,' *Washington Post*, April 25, 1999.
36 Cox, Michael, and Stokes, Doug, *U.S. Foreign Policy*, Second Edition, Oxford, Oxford University Press, 2012 (pp. 244–245).
37 North Atlantic Treaty Organization, *NATO Enlargement* (<http://www.nato.int/summit2009/topics_en/05-enlargement.html>).
38 Bump, Philip, 'The Lesson of Vladimir Putin's Popularity Isn't the One Donald Trump Seems to be Taking,' *The Washington Post*, September 8, 2016.
39 Menshikov, S., 'Russian Capitalism Today,' *Monthly Review*, 51:3, 1999 (pp. 82–86).
40 Milanovic, Branko, *Income, Inequality, and Poverty During the Transformation from Planned to Market Economy*, Washington, DC, The World Bank, 1998 (pp. 186–90).
41 Klein, Naomi, *The Shock Doctrine: The Rise of Disaster Capitalism*, London, Penguin, 2008 (Chapter 11: 'Russia Choses the Pinochet Option: Bonfire of a Young Democracy').
42 Yulia V. Tverdova, 'Human Trafficking in Russia and Other Post-Soviet States,' *Human Rights Review*, December 11, 2016.
43 Klein, Naomi, *The Shock Doctrine: The Rise of Disaster Capitalism*, London, Penguin, 2008 (Chapter 11: 'Russia Choses the Pinochet Option: Bonfire of a Young Democracy').
44 'Bill Clinton, Boris Yeltsin, and U.S.-Russian Relations,' Office of the Historian, Milestones 1993–2000, United States of America Department of State.
45 Randolph, Eleanor, 'Americans Claim Role in Yeltsin Win,' *Los Angeles Times*, July 9, 1996.
46 'Yanks to the Rescue, the Secret Story of How American Advisers Helped Yeltsin Win,' *Time Magazine*, Vol. 148, No. 4, July 15, 1996.
47 O'Neil, Brandon, 'How We Trained Al Qaeda,' *Spectator*, September 13 2003.
48 *Congressional Record*, V. 151, PT. 17, U.S. Congress, October 7 to 26, 2005.
49 'American political scientist: Western Intelligence used Azerbaijan to export terrorism into Russia,' *Panorama*, May 30, 2015.

50 'Putin accuses U.S. of directly supporting Chechen militants,' *Press TV*, April 26, 2015.
51 Bechev, Dimitar, *Rival Power: Russia's Influence in Southeast Europe*, New Haven, CT, Yale University Press, 2017 (Chapter 1).
52 Presidential Address to the Federal Assembly, President of Russia, Kremlin, December 4, 2014.
53 'Putin says Russia will not be dismantled like Yugoslavia,' *Reuters*, December 4, 2014.
54 McKew, Molly K., 'Putin's real long game,' *Politico*, January 1, 2017.
55 'Russia's economy under Vladimir Putin: achievements and failures,' *Sputnik*, March 1, 2008.
56 Conradi, Peter, *Who Lost Russia? How the World Entered a New Cold War*, London, Oneworld Publications, 2017.
57 'Putin: U.S. missile defence aimed at neutralizing Russia nukes, N. Korea & Iran just a cover,' *RT*, November 10, 2015.
58 Russian President Addresses Representatives of International Media Organizations at St Petersburg International Economic Forum, June 17, 2016.
59 Kremlin, President of Russia, *Plenary session of St Petersburg International Economic Forum*, June 17, 2016.
60 Bryen, Stephen, 'Russia's S-400 Is Way More Dangerous Than You Think,' *The National Interest*, January 18, 2018.
61 'President Putin Orders Preparation of Russia's New S-500 Missile System for Mass Production,' *Military Watch Magazine,* May 22, 2018.
62 'U.S. Plans to Surround Russia with 400 Anti Ballistic Missiles; Why Moscow Prioritises Strengthening it Deterrent with Hypersonic Missiles,' *Military Watch Magazine,* March 7, 2018.
63 'Russia and China are "aggressively developing" hypersonic weapons – here's what they are and why the U.S. can't defend against them,' *CNBC*, March 21, 2018.
64 Speier, Richard H., and Nacouzi, Georgem and Lee, Carrie, and Moore, Richard M., 'Hypersonic Missile Nonproliferation, Hindering the Spread of a New Class of Weapons,' *RAND Corporation*, 2017.
65 Hughes, Michael, 'U.S. Support for Al Qaeda-Linked Rebels Undermines Syrian Ceasefire,' *The Huffington Post,* May 22, 2017.
66 Fisk, Robert, 'America siding with "terrorists" like al-Nusra? It's not a conspiracy theory,' *The Independent*, June 14, 2015.
67 '"Americans are on our side": Al-Nusra commander says U.S. arming jihadists via 3rd countries,' *RT*, September 26, 2016.

68 'U.S. special ops forces& hardware spotted at ISIS positions north Deir ez-Zor – Russian MoD,' *RT*, September 24, 2017.
69 'U.S. Support for Terrorists in Syria Main Obstacle of Defeating Them – Russian MoD,' *Sputnik*, October 4, 2017.
70 'Drones used by Syrian terrorists "require advanced training" – Russian MoD in response to US,' *Sputnik*, January 9, 2018.
71 Vyacheslav Nikonov interview with Gideon Rachman, Moscow, October 3, 2014.
72 Kadri, Liik, 'Russia's Pivot to Asia,' *European Council of Foreign Relations*, May 29, 2014 (p. 18).
73 Ibid. (p. 62).
74 Rachman, Gideon, *Easternisation, War and Peace in the Asian Century*, New York, Vintage, 2017 (p. 189).
75 Duffy Toft, Monica, 'Why is America Addicted to Foreign Interventions?,' *The National Interest*, December 10, 2017.
76 Ait, Abraham, 'How Did Japan Lose Its Air Superiority Advantage?,' *The Diplomat*, February 17, 2018.
77 *Treaty of Good- Neighborliness and Friendly Cooperation Between the People's Republic of China and the Russian Federation*, Ministry of Foreign Affairs of the People's Republic of China, July 24, 2001.
78 Tannock, Charles, 'Backing Kazakhstan's "great game,"' *The Guardian*, February 18, 2008.
79 Fels, Enrico, *Assessing Eurasia's Powerhouse. An Inquiry into the Nature of the Shanghai Cooperation Organisation*, Winkler Verlag, Bochum, 2009 (pp. 23–27).
80 Roney, Tyler, 'The Shanghai Cooperation Organization: China's NATO?' *The Diplomat*, September 11, 2013.
81 'Putin praises "all-embracing" partnership of Russia, China,' *Daily Mail*, June 25, 2016.
82 Clover, Charles, 'Russian and China learn from each other as military ties deepen,' *Financial Times*, June 23, 2016.
83 Ibid.
84 'Bear and Dragon: Russia, China to Intensify Joint Military Drills in 2016,' *Sputnik*, April 27, 2016.
85 'China, Russia to Begin Massive Eight Day Naval War Games in South China Sea,' *Sputnik*, September 11, 2016.
86 Ait, Abraham, 'Russia Inducts Its Own "Carrier Killer" Missile, and It's More Dangerous than China's,' *The Diplomat*, May 12, 2018.
87 Gady, Franz-Stefan, 'China and Russia Conclude Naval Drill in Mediterranean,' *The Diplomat*, May 22, 2015.

88 'US-Led Coalition Used 4 Planes, 1 Drone in Deir ez-Zor Strike – Russian MoD,' *Sputnik*, September 16, 2016.
89 *Statement from Pentagon Spokesman Capt. Jeff Davis on U.S. strike in Syria*, U.S. Department of Defense, April 6, 2017.
90 Risk, Robert, 'U.S. air strikes in Syria: Why America really attacked pro-Assad militia convoy,' *The Independent*, May 19, 2017.
91 Browne, Ryan, 'New details on U.S. shoot down of Syrian jet,' *CNN*, June 22, 2017.
92 Gady, Franz-Stefan, 'Chinese Navy Conducts Live-Fire Drill in Mediterranean,' *The Diplomat*, July 13, 2017.
93 Tiezzi, Shannon, 'China, Russia, "Show Americans" Their Close Relationship,' *The Diplomat*, April 10, 2018.
94 'China to mount navy drills in Taiwan Strait "to support Russia,"' *South China Morning Post*, April 12, 2018.
95 'Russia-China Drills in South China Sea Show "Solid Level of Trust,"' *Sputnik*, September 12, 2016.
96 United National Commodity Trade Statistics Database, published figures, July 2015.
97 'China quickly catching up to EU in trade with Russia – Kremlin,' *RT*, September 3, 2018.
98 Soldatkin, Vladimir, 'Rosneft to triple oil supplies to China,' *Reuters*, March 22, 2013.
99 'Russia signs 30-year gas deal with China,' *BBC*, May 21, 2014.
100 'China wants to buy more natural gas from Russia and diversify supplies,' *RT*, September 6. 2018.
101 'Russia and China: from cooperation to synergy,' *RT*, October 12, 2011.
102 Woodward, Jude, *The U.S. vs China: Asia's New Cold War?* Manchester, Manchester University Press, 2017 (p. 83).
103 '"Triangular Diplomacy": What's Really Behind Kissinger's Turn Toward Russia,' *Sputnik*, January 22, 2017.
104 De Haas, Masja, *Russia's foreign security policy in the 21st century: Putin, Medvedev and beyond*, Abingdon, Routledge, 2010 (p. 72).
105 Brzezinski, Zbigniew, 'How To Address Strategic Insecurity In A Turbulent Age,' *Huffington Post*, January 3, 2017.
106 Zbigniew Brzezinski, 'Toward a Global Realignment,' *The American Interest*, April 17, 2016.
107 'Remarks by the President on Teaching American History and Civic Education,' *The White House*, September 17, 2002.

CHAPTER 17

Western Militaries in the Asia-Pacific Today: Part I – China's Rise and the End of the 'Anglo Saxon Lake'

> The Pacific is now an Anglo Saxon Lake.
>
> — General DOUGLAS MACARTHUR on the new Asia-Pacific regional order following the defeat of the Japanese Empire

> America should write the rules. America should call the shots. Other countries should play by the rules that America and our partners set, and not the other way around.
>
> — U.S. President BARACK OBAMA on his vision for the future of the Asia-Pacific region in the twenty-first century

China's Rise as a Threat to the Established Order of a Western-Dominated Pacific

The Western Bloc has sought to contain the influence of China since 1949, when the fall of the client Guomindang government and declaration of the new People's Republic threatened their hegemonic interests in Asia. Isolating China became a priority which involved numerous military, diplomatic and covert efforts. Western influence throughout the region was used to forestall prospects for an Asian power bloc forming around the new Chinese republic, much as they had been used to isolate Imperial Japan beforehand. Indeed, the nature of the threat posed by Imperial Japan was in many ways similar to that posed by China from 1949. U.S. Admiral William Leahy noted of the Japanese Empire that it posed an imminent danger to the West because it had the potential to 'succeed in combining most of the Asiatic peoples against the whites.'[1] President Roosevelt too feared this unification of Asia under Japan, particularly after Asian leaders met in Tokyo in 1943 to declare their solidarity in the pan-Asian cause, noting: '1,100,000,000 potential enemies are dangerous.'[2] The Pentagon papers would later state regarding their new Asian adversary: 'China … looms as a major power threatening to undercut our importance and effectiveness in the world and, more remotely but more menacingly, to organize all of Asia against us.'[3]

The West feared a 'Yellow Menace' threatening to unite Asia whenever a major independent Asian power threatened to overturn the status quo in the Pacific and undermine the Western dominated regional order. As MIT professor and award winning author John Dower noted: 'the visceral hatred of the Japanese tapped Yellow Peril sentiments that, before the turn of the century, had been directed mainly against the Chinese.'[4] With the re-emergence of China as a major independent power from 1949 the image of a 'Yellow Menace' in the West was again applied to China after its successful application against Imperial Japan.[5] Indeed, the fear of a rising 'Asiatic' power had such resonance in the Western world that the United States also undertook extensive efforts to depict the Soviet peoples themselves as 'essentially oriental in their thinking' and 'the descendants of Genghis Khan' – stressing their ethnic Mongol and non-Western descent to stoke strong anti-Soviet feeling among Western populations.[6] These themes were more subtly returned to in the 2010s as relations between Russia and the Western Bloc again worsened.[7]

During the Pacific War the Japanese, for being both modern and Asian, were widely described in the United States as a 'racial menace' as well as a cultural and religious one. There were calls to arms against Japan as part of the 'perpetual wars between Oriental ideas and Occidental.' Fighting Japan was depicted a crusade for both Western civilization and Christianity against a heathen, subhuman and barbaric enemy. It was described by popular American writers as 'a holy war, a racial war of greater significance than any the world has heretofore seen.'[8] Attitudes to China following the establishment of the PRC in 1949, and particularly following Chinese military successes against the United States and its European allies in Korea, were little different. Not only were themes of race war, a clash of civilizations, and a threat to Western dominance of the Pacific applied to both countries – but the theme of a Christian Holy War also applied to both Imperial Japan and communist China. The former had for centuries banned Christian missionaries which it viewed as agents of Western influence seeking to destabilize the Empire.[9] The latter suppressed Christianity, particularly after evidence emerged of the Catholic Church's involvement in espionage against the PRC on behalf of the Western Bloc.[10,11] China had before the establishment of the PRC been widely perceived in the West as a Christian nation in the making, with the religion spreading both with generous Western and particularly American support and funding and with the blessing of Guomindang leader Chiang Kai-shek – himself a devout Christian convert and close Western ally.

The Western Bloc, led by the United States, would take extensive measures to counter the threat of an emerging independent Chinese state to their regional dominance. These measures, which commenced in the early 1950s, included a complete trade embargo, deployment of nuclear weapons to Taiwan, South Korea and Japan, and the rapid expansion of air and naval bases in the two countries to further encircle China. A number of military treaties and alliances with various allies and client states, all with the primary goal of countering China's regional standing, were quickly signed. These included Australia, New Zealand, Japan and the Philippines in 1951, which for the latter two was a condition for the U.S. granting them sovereignty and statehood, and treaties with South Korea in 1953 following the end of the Korean War. The Southeast Asia Treaty Organization (SEATO), a U.S. led alliance similar to NATO in Europe which had been designed to counter Soviet power in the Western hemisphere, was established in 1955. Alongside the U.S. it included Pakistan on China's Western border, as well as the Philippines, Thailand – the only Southeast Asian members of the treaty – Australia and New Zealand. Britain and France, which still maintained imperial colonial possessions in the region also joined the alliance – the primary target of which was China. U.S. bases from Hawaii and Midway to Guam and the Philippines were rapidly expanded alongside the growth of the U.S. military presence in the region. Support for Chiang Kai-shek's government in Taiwan was also critical to deny China access to the Taiwan Strait, where the U.S. Navy's Seventh fleet also maintained a strong presence. The United States signed a mutual defense treaty with

Taiwan in 1954 and proceeded to deploy nuclear weapons to the territory to complete China's encirclement.

During the Cold War the United States had, as reported by the Japanese magazine *The Diplomat*, considered as means to undermine China 'infiltration, sabotage, invasion by Chinese Nationalists, maritime blockades, South Korean invasion of North Korea, conventional air attacks on nuclear facilities, and the use of tactical nuclear weapons on selected targets.'[12] While plans for nuclear strikes never fully materialized, many others including extensive sabotage, an invasion of North Korea and extensive provocations on the Chinese border during the Korean War, did. The constant presence of U.S. nuclear weapons and vast forces encircling China meant that there was an ever-present threat of attacks of any nature – against which the country had few means to defend itself. With the end of the Cold War the United States did little to reduce its military presence in the Asia-Pacific region. Though SEATO was largely considered a failure and eventually dissolved and U.S. nuclear weapons were eventually withdrawn from South Korea and Taiwan, with advances in nuclear tipped ballistic and cruise missiles technologies and the deployment of more survivable nuclear armed ballistic missiles, and attack submarines making such deployments essentially obsolete, the military containment of China still remained key to guaranteeing the United States' continued dominance of the Asia-Pacific region.

Though attitudes towards China had softened after the initial 'red scare' of the 1950s, particularly following the Sino-Soviet split and Chinese co-operation with the United States against the communist superpower, the Western Bloc remained wary of China's potential to 'organize Asia against them' – using their Pacific military deployments to keep it tightly contained. With China's rapid modernization its ability to challenge the Western Bloc has grown. Perhaps more than any time since the 1950s the 2010s have led to a renewed 'red scare' and 'Yellow Peril' in Europe and the United States in which China again threatens the primacy of the West. As a result the 'Pivot to Asia,' a redirection of the United States' foreign policy and military attentions towards the Asia-Pacific region including deploying over 60 percent of America's armed forces to the region to contain China, has been carried out under the pretext of countering what is commonly referred to in the West as the 'rise of China.' This 'rise' refers to the country's military and economic development and its increasing soft influence and economic ties throughout Asia and the wider world.

As a modern Asian economy, many of China's cutting-edge high-tech industries which have been developed apace for over a decade threaten to seriously undermine Western monopolies and near monopolies key to the Western Bloc's current prosperity. Just as the existence of an independent Japan in the Imperial era following its rapid nineteenth-century economic development, as the only modern and industrialized state in Asia, was perceived as a considerable threat to continued Western primacy, so too does China's modernization today and its potential to compete in several high end technologies make it a threat to the Western Bloc.[13] As reported by *The Diplomat*, a considerable threat is perceived from:

> China's high-tech industries, to be more specific, industries identified by China's 'Made in China 2025 initiative.' This national strategy aims to build up 10 strategically and technologically important sectors such as 5G networks and cyber security, high end precision tools and robotics, and aerospace. Most of these areas are now exclusive domains of Western companies. But China, by launching a national strategy to advance its domestic high-tech sectors, can be seen as posing a threat to U.S. dominance in these fields. Lorand Laskai, a research assistant at the Council on Foreign Relations, made this clear by writing that the 'Made in China 2025' policy is 'shaping up to be the central villain, the real existential threat to U.S. technological leadership.'[14]

China today also poses a considerable threat to the Western Bloc because its independent development has offered an alternative to Asian peoples from their longstanding dependence on the West. This dependency comes in many forms – examples being a lack of alternatives to Western proposed development models, a reliance on the U.S. dollar as a reserve currency or dependence on loans from Western led institutions such as the Asia Development Bank and World Bank. The Western Bloc's effective monopolies in these fields have granted it considerable advantages and served as a critical guarantor of continued Western primacy in the region, as demonstrated by the financial crisis of 1997 when these assets were all put to good use undermining emerging Asian economies to suit Western interests – as covered in Chapter 13. The loss of these considerable assets as a result of China's growing financial clout and internationalism thus represents the stripping of one of the key facilitators of primacy from the Western powers. China is increasingly giving Asia-Pacific nations alternatives to the West in a number of fields, setting an example through its own highly successful development model, strengthening of the Yuan as a reserve currency and establishing institutions such as the Asian Infrastructure Investment Bank and the New Development Bank to rival their long-established Western equivalents to give but a few examples. It is China's very independence as a major Asian power, and the significant potential this has to end Western hegemony in the region, which the American led Western Bloc perceives to be a very significant threat.

In an interview Paul Craig Roberts, former Assistant Secretary to the U.S. treasury, alluded to this and gave more details as to the motives of the United States regarding its policy in Asia. Roberts stated:

> The United States has an ideology of world hegemony and does not accept any prospect of any country being sovereign or acting on its own. You have to be an American vassal state. Just as the United States has turned all of Europe, Canada, Australia and Japan into vassal states that is the only terms on which the United States can accept Russia and China. It will not accept them as sovereign, independent countries following their own interests. The demonization of Russia's leader and the country will continue [and occurs in the case of China's own leadership today]. The situation will become more and more hostile. It's not going to go away, because the United States is guided by … ideology of American world hegemony which means hegemony over Russia and China …
>
> Facts don't matter to propaganda. Washington is using propaganda. The Russians [and all independent nations] need to wake up, they have an enemy. The enemy intends to destroy you. That's what the fact is. There's no sense in playing that this is somehow a mistake, or we can get the facts out or people will come to their senses. The United States has a policy of world hegemony and you're seeing that.[15]

While this interview primarily concerned Russia what was said applies to China as well, as the West's posturing towards both states has been highly similar in many ways.

Under the Western powers' model for relations among Asian nations the region is to remain comprised of clients largely subservient to Western interests while nations' culture, ideology, policies and economics are heavily influenced by the West. High end industries meanwhile will continue to be dominated by Western producers, while Western products will retain a dominant position in Asian markets. The 'Asian Regional Order,' unlike those of Europe or North America, must maintain external powers, namely the United States, as key players in regional affairs. As renowned U.S. foreign policy strategist and former secretary of state Henry Kissinger noted regarding the nature of this 'Asian Order': 'The historic European order had been self-contained … Occasionally, European powers enlisted outside countries to strengthen their positions temporarily – for example, France courting the Ottoman Empire in the sixteenth century or Britain's early-twentieth-century alliance with Japan – but non-Western powers … had few interests in Europe and were not called on to intervene in European conflicts. By contrast, the contemporary Asian order includes outside powers as an integral feature.'[16]

The dominance of Western imperial interests backed up by overwhelming military force increasingly became a part of the 'regional order' since the Portuguese first expanded their empire to the Asia-Pacific and began to take control of strategic ports in the sixteenth century. They were quickly followed by other Western imperial powers – the last of which was the United States which waged wars to subjugate the peoples of Hawaii, Guam, the Philippines and several other Pacific territories in the late nineteenth century – the last which they acquired after 300 years of Spanish rule. While the Japanese Empire sought to end this regional order and temporarily succeeded during the 1940s, their defeat heralded a new era in which the dominance of the United States, and Britain to a lesser extent, between them had complete and unchallenged dominance of the Asia-Pacific region. As General MacArthur proclaimed following the defeat of Japan: 'the Pacific is now an Anglo Saxon lake,' and this would leave the now U.S. led Western Bloc as the undisputed dominant power in the region for three quarters of a century.

China's economic and military rise threaten the West's longstanding dominance in the Asia-Pacific, potentially facilitating regional integration and increased interdependence and independence from external powers and establishing an Asian regional order based on the interests of regional players above those of extra-regional actors. China also poses a threat by successfully pursuing its own domestic policy, allowing the country to develop its own economic, political and social models which can rival those of the West and thus present an example to Asia and much of the developing world of an alternative path to prosperity to that under Western leadership. China's immunity to the effects of the 1997 financial crisis, under which Western aligned Asian governments following economic models advocated by the IMF and World Bank suffered, is but one significant example of this.

Should its economic successes continue China could well become an example to much of the region, just as the West's own economic success led developing nations to emulate its institutional, political and economic structures. While the West has continually preached that only a Western style liberal democracy can lead to a modern, prosperous and stable society, China's successes have seriously undermined this drive to promote a Western governance model across the Pacific through its economic and technological progress and continued social stability under a party state. The country's potential to do so has hardly gone unnoticed in the West, with the *New York Times* observing with much apprehension that China had built 'an alternative value system that competes with Western liberal democracy,'[17] while the Wall Street Journal noted just a few weeks earlier that the success of China's alternative model had done much to threaten the global 'triumph of liberal democracy.'[18] Indeed, since the 19th Congress of the Chinese Communist Party in October 2017, the country has pledged to more actively export its development model – a central aspect of the CCP's first true grand strategy spanning over 33 years to become a 'leading world power.'

Should China demonstrate the success of its independent path its economic policies could well seriously undermine the global standing of the West, much as the USSR was emulated by much of the developing world in the 1950s in the wake of its successful industrialization and modernization of its formerly backward and war torn economy in little over ten years.[19] The fact that this Soviet industrialization took place when the West was stagnating under the Great Depression only increased the prestige of this alternative political and economic model. Since the notable decline of Soviet soft power from the late 1950s, China's development model could well become the first to pose a feasible challenge to that of the West in its international prestige in half a century – and by extension the first major threat to Western influence in the developing world in over 50 years. The fact that this occurs at a time of Western stagnation and both political and economic instability unrivalled since the great depression makes the threat China's relative success poses to Western dominance only more acute.

The United States Military and the Post-Cold War Re-emergence of Near-Peer Threats

As a result of the threat China's rise poses to Western primacy, the United States and a number of its partners have increasingly been forced to rely heavily on and when possible apply their military might to protect their dominant position. Much as advanced military capabilities were key to gaining primacy in the Asia-Pacific region and to overcoming previous threats to the Western dominated order, namely Imperial Japan, so too are they set to be heavily relied on whenever possible to contain China. Perhaps the most essential facilitator of the West's longstanding dominance of the Asia-Pacific region has been its military supremacy. While the Japanese Empire's technological parity in the military field with the armies of the Western imperial powers allowed it to temporarily expel the combined forces of France, Britain, the Netherlands and the United States from the region, since the Empire's fall in 1945 the United States has committed itself to maintaining military dominance of the Pacific. U.S. Defense Secretary Carter was one of many who attested to America's intention to retain military dominance of the Pacific, stating in 2016: 'the United States will remain the most powerful military and main underwriter of security in the region [Asia] for decades to come – and there should be no doubt about that.'[20] Whether the gradual shift in the military balance of power in the Pacific will in the near future lead to the West's loss of its military primacy in the region, as has been widely predicted, is set to be decisive in determining Asia's future and the continued viability of Western leadership. This in turn could well determine whether the region, likely under Chinese leadership, will in the near future surpass the Western Bloc as a global center of power – or whether the United States and its partners may have a chance of containing the emerging Asian power and thus retaining their vital dominant position.

The United States pursues a form of military supremacy referred to by defense planners as 'full spectrum dominance' (FSD). It entails dominance of all air, land, sea, space, and cyberspace globally – allowing the U.S. military to project power freely across the world. The military today however faces challenges to its ability to project power far eclipsing those of the Cold War era, which bring doubt to its ability to remain the dominant power in the Asia-Pacific region. While in the Cold War era the U.S. and its allies faced a single modern military power bloc led by the Soviet Union challenging FSD, today American capabilities are tested by near-peer adversaries on multiple fronts. U.S. military planners refer to four potent military competitors, each with the ability to challenge American military supremacy in their respective regions. These are Iran, North Korea, Russia and the People's Republic of China, all of which have been repeatedly listed by the Defense Department as the primary adversaries of the United States military. A prospective conflict with any one of these powers is termed a 'great power war' by the U.S. Department of Defense, and the respective capabilities of these 'great powers' form the basis of United States' military planning.[24,25,26] China and Russia in particular were referred to as the United States military's most 'stressing competitors' by the country's Defense Secretary in 2016.[27] A war with any one or more of these four highly competent militaries would differ profoundly from any the United States has involved itself in since 1945 – and America's military leadership have themselves repeatedly expressed doubts as to whether they are capable of fighting a war against such adversaries.[28,29]

To contain the four adversarial 'great powers' the United States military is stretched between three major fronts – Eastern Europe facing Russia, the Middle East and Central Asia facing both Iran and China's Western border, and the Asia Pacific region facing North Korea, Russia's Far East and China. With each of these powers capable of challenging the American military presence in its respective region, and the capabilities of all four powers rapidly advancing, U.S. forces face a real risk of becoming overstretched and losing their military primacy across multiple fronts. The fact that the U.S. military planners did not foresee the re-emergence of near peer adversaries, underestimating Russia's ability to recover from economic disaster and re-establish a modern military,[30] North Korea's missile program[31] and conventional modernization,[32] China's military modernization[33] and the potency of Iran's ability to project power in the Middle East through well-armed proxies,[34] significantly worsened the current predicament. Complacency in the aftermath of the Cold War led to a cutting back on several cutting edge but costly defense programs made to fight near-peer adversaries such as the Soviet Union and a reconfiguring of the military to combat small rogue powers and wage the war on terror against various militant groups. The war on terror in particular, according to a report by the RAND Corporation military think thank: 'led the U.S. military to reorganize and re-equip may of its forces in way that maximizes counterinsurgency rather than conventional capabilities.'[35] The result was a military which is far less prepared to engage in a 'great power war' against near-peer adversaries, exacerbating the pressure on the already overstretched force.

An example was the premature termination of the F-22 fifth generation air superiority fighter program, with only 25 percent of the fighters planned for the Air Force having entered service. Export bans to key allies on the frontlines against U.S. adversaries such as Japan and Israel and the termination of the carrier variant entirely meant that the U.S. Navy and U.S. allies lack any fifth generation air superiority capabilities whatsoever.[36] U.S. allies were forced to instead rely on sturdy but dated platforms such as the F-15, a design over 40 years old, for such a role. The Navy's fourth generation air superiority fighter, the F-14, was also retired from service without replacement, leaving its air wings gravely underpowered[37] should they need to face a near-peer adversary – reducing U.S. carrier strike groups' area of influence by 77 percent and forcing it to rely on lighter jets with a considerably reduced payload/range capacity.[38,39] High end air superiority fighters are an asset of immense importance against near-peer adversaries, but of little use against insurgent groups or small states the U.S. were engaging in the 1990s and 2000s. Having cancelled the fifth generation program however, and with Russia and China both commissioning their own fifth generation air superiority fighters well before the U.S. predicted, and with analysts predicting that China's latest stealth fighters will be able to considerably outmatch the United States' own due to far greater investments in modernization,[40] the United States will be hard pressed to maintain any sort of advantage in the air as it did in the Cold War. This was affirmed by several military reports and papers published by renowned American think thanks and research institutes such as CSBA.[41] The same applies more so to the United States' high-level regional defense partners such as Japan.[42,43] The case of air superiority fighters represents but one example of a wider trend throughout the military.

Only in October 2017 did the Pentagon update its fighting manual to revert the military to its Cold War primary function of fighting near-peer adversaries. For over two decades prior the U.S. military advantage over such adversaries had meanwhile been 'steadily eroded,' according to Army Chief-of-Staff Gen. Mark Miley.[44] The Heritage Foundation military think tank, citing evidence such as the fact that only 11 percent of the U.S. Air Force's vast fleet were 'full spectrum mission capable,' reached much the same conclusion.' The result was an 'increasingly dangerous world threatening a significantly weaker America.'[45] The U.S. Congress's National Defense Commission came to similar conclusions thirteen months later, finding that the military was no longer in a strong position to win a war against near peer adversaries. The chairman of the Senate Armed Services Committee was among the many others who reached the same conclusion.[46,47,48]

Having been assured of its continued post-Cold War global dominance, the United States was caught entirely off guard by the sudden re-emergence of near-peer military adversaries, and the result has been complacency and the loss of much of the critical capability advantage the country once had.

China's Post-Cold War Military Modernization

The Chinese military had never been able to present a credible challenge to the United States following the deterioration of its relations with the Soviet Union in the late 1950s, as it was no longer able to acquire modern Soviet technologies for its air force, navy or missile forces to project power away from its shores. China's domestic military industries were negligible relative to those of the two superpowers, and other third parties able to provide modern defense technologies were few and far between. This was exemplified by the Chinese Air Force, which in 1990 still relied heavily on second generation J-7 combat jets, based on the Soviet MiG-21 in service since 1959, as its prime fighter. The Western and Soviet blocs were two generations ahead, both by this time having operated large fleets of fourth generation platforms for over a decade – and even the Koreas, Taiwan and Japan fielded air fleets qualitatively far surpassing those of their larger neighbor. Though China's ground forces were well trained and numerous and the country possessed a somewhat primitive nuclear missile program – assets which between them were able to deter direct attacks by the superpowers – the People's Liberation Army's ability to project power even onto Taiwan 130 km from its coast was in serious doubt. Chinese air defenses were also negligible to non-existent, which combined with its dated air force meant that the USA or USSR would have de-facto control of the skies in case of war.[49]

Since 1991 the PLA has embarked on a vast military modernization program, the results of which have changed the balance of power in the Asia-Pacific region dramatically. This modernization program was largely spurred by the performance of the U.S. military in the Gulf War, which demonstrated its ability to overwhelmingly dominate a large conscript army that lacked modern air defenses or air superiority aircraft to deny its adversary control of the skies – though severe deficiencies in training, planning, morale and leadership on the Iraqi side also played a significant role. The United States' ability to control the skies over Yugoslavia and devastate the country's civilian infrastructure from the air alongside its NATO allies shortly after its victory in Iraq would further reinforce the perceived need for modernization – as would the Clinton administration's decision to sail aircraft carrier battle groups through the Taiwan Strait in 1996 in a show of force to Beijing. With relations with the United States fast deteriorating in the post-Cold War period, and the lack of any third superpower to counterbalance the power of the West, China's military in its current state appeared poorly suited to defend the country.[50]

The end of the Cold War saw an end to Sino-Soviet tensions, and the economic desperation of several Soviet successor states allowed China to purchase some of the most advanced Soviet technologies available to modernize its own forces. From 1990 to 2007 Russian weapons accounted for 90 percent of Chinese arms imports, with much of the remaining 10 percent being accounted for largely by other former Soviet states such as Ukraine.[51] Combined with substantial investment in improving its domestic military industrial base this facilitated China's rise to become a modern military power within a decade. In 1991 China received the first of its 78 Russian Sukhoi Su-27 and 100 Su-30MK fourth generation fighters, at the time the most advanced air superiority aircraft in the world, which made it the first nation outside the Soviet Union to deploy the platforms. Considering the age and limited capabilities of the fighters which previously comprised the Chinese air fleet, this represented a sudden and revolutionary change. No single fighter acquisition had so dramatically shifted the regional balance of power in the air in China's favor since the first acquisition of the MiG-15 during the Korean War at the time of the Sino-Soviet alliance. China would go on to purchase more advanced variants of these potent long-range fighters, most recently the Su-35 in 2015,[52] and would manufacture its own derivatives domestically – the Chengdu J-11, J-15, and J-16. The result was the acquisition of Russia's most advanced aerial warfare systems in large enough numbers to make China a world leading aerial power, eventually fielding approximately 500 of the elite fighters.

As U.S. Director of Central Intelligence and Second Air Force Chief of Staff General Vandenburg had stated during the Korean War following deliveries of the MiG-15, which had also been the most advanced fighter of its time, to Chinese forces in the 1950s: 'a significant and, by some standards, even sinister change has occurred ... Almost overnight China has become one of the major air powers of the world ... the air supremacy upon which we have relied in the past is now faced with a serious challenge.'[53] These very same words are equally applicable to the situation which began to occur from 1991. Given the critical importance of air superiority to Western military doctrine, as demonstrated during the Korean War where the challenging of the U.S. fleet over North Korean skies played a key role in determining the war's outcome, it remains an example worthy of mention despite being only one of several fields where the capabilities of China's armed forces were revolutionized in an extremely short period. While the technology to produce a fully indigenous fourth generation air superiority platform was well beyond Chinese capabilities at the time, by the 2010s the country's domestic research and development had reached such an advanced state that China could in 2017 declare itself the second nation in the world after the U.S. to have developed a fifth generation air superiority fighter. Development of a sixth generation fighter already appears ahead of Russian and American programs,[54] and the People's Liberation Army's rapid transformation from a negligible third world force in 1990 to leading the arms race and successfully competing with both the United States and Russia just 25 years later represents an unprecedented leap forward without parallel among other major world military powers.

Acquiring the most cutting edge Soviet technologies also helped China to modernize its formerly negligible air defenses. In the 1990s China acquired 160 S-300 (NATO reporting SA-20) long range surface to air missile launchers, the most advanced systems of their kind in the Russian arsenal or anywhere in the world at the time, with all attendant radars, munitions and support equipment. With capabilities far more advanced than anything ever faced by a Western air force the S-300 turned the almost entirely unprotected Chinese airspace, which had until then relied on the early Vietnam War era S-75 systems, into one of the best defended in the world. Reverse engineering both Russian and Western technologies also allowed China to develop several indigenous air defense systems such as the HQ-9, HQ-10 and HQ-16 which further improved China's long range air defense coverage.[55] When China went on to become the first foreign customer for the Russian S-400 (NATO reporting SA-21) in 2017, the world's most advanced and versatile air defense system according to a number of experts, its airspace became arguably the best defended in the world against enemy aircraft after only Russia itself.[56] With a 400 km engagement range giving it full coverage over Taiwanese airspace as well as the Senkaku Islands disputed with Japan,[57] and with the ability to detect and target the United States' most advanced stealth aircraft,[58] the system shifted the balance of power significantly further in China's favor. Just as China's aerial warfare capabilities rapidly advanced, so too did parallel advances take place in the sophistication of its ground forces and its navy across the board.

In 2017 the International Institute for Strategic Studies, a leading military think tank based in the London, attested to the Western Bloc's sudden loss of its longstanding military advantage over China. John Chipman, the IISS director, presented the findings of a study titled *Military Balance 2017* in which the most prominent theme was the threat to Western global military supremacy and the rapid advance of Chinese military capabilities. Considering that Western militaries have overwhelmingly relied on air power in all conventional wars fought since the 1940s, it was critical that, Chipman noted: 'particularly in the air domain, China appears to be reaching near-parity with the West.' Chinese development of military technologies would in a potential conflict 'complicate the operations of any Western Air Force,' while undermining the global military supremacy and freedom of action the Western powers took for granted since the 1990s.[59] Chipman concluded: 'Western military technological superiority, once taken for granted, is increasingly challenged.'[60]

This conclusion was echoed by a number of analysts and experts for several years. In 2006 the threat of China's rapid military technological progress was noted in the *Quadrennial Defense Review* which stated that 'China has the greatest potential to compete militarily with the United States and field disruptive military technologies that could over time offset traditional U.S. military advantages.'[61] In 2014 Congress Deputy Undersecretary of Defense and Acquisition Frank Kendall similarly noted in regard to China specifically: 'the U.S. military's technological superiority is being challenged in ways I have not seen for decades, particularly in the Asia-Pacific region ... Technological superiority is not assured. This is not a future problem. This is a here-now problem.'[62] Chairman of the Senate Armed Services Committee John McCain in 2016 stated in the same vein, noting the technological progress of America's leading potential adversaries: 'From China and Russia, to Iran and North Korea, we see militaries that are developing, fielding, and employing long-range precision guided weapons, advanced fighter aircraft, anti-access and area-denial systems [air defense being a key example], growing space and cyber capabilities, and other advanced weapons. The result is that we are at real and increasing risk of losing the military technological dominance that we have taken for granted for thirty years.'[63]

China's military has rapidly modernized its capabilities across the spectrum so that in the 2010s the state of its ground, naval and air forces are all unrecognizable from what they were in 1990. The country's rapid military modernization has largely been facilitated by its economic growth, and its military budget has consistently increased by approximately 8.5 percent annually – roughly in line with growth rates. With two fifth-generation fighter programs, the fastest growing navy in the world and indigenous weapons systems leading the world technologically in several fields from destroyers to strategic bombers and hypersonic missiles, U.S. military planners have warned of China's rapid 'closing in on our capability advantage.'[64] The British think tank Royal United Services Institute for Defense and Security Studies noted in its own study the rapid quantitative and qualitative growth of the Chinese armed forces, stating in a 2017 report: 'it is hard to recall growth at a similar pace in any navy across history.'[65]

The emergence of China's People's Liberation Army as one of the world's foremost military organizations, currently ranked one of just three 'tier one military powers'[66] alongside the United States and Russia with a rate of spending and capability growth far surpassing the other two combined, has seriously upset the longstanding regional status quo of Western primacy in the Asia-Pacific. American chairman of the House Armed Services Subcommittee on Seapower Randy Forbes said that Chinese weapons tests, specifically the testing of hypersonic missiles which American military planners project would leave U.S. surface warships highly vulnerable across the Pacific, had worried him. He accused China of developing technologies which would seriously alter the balance of power in the region against the favor of the United States and its allies – stating on this basis: 'Beijing is committed to upending both the conventional military and nuclear balance, with grave implications for the stability of Asia.'[67] Indeed, the balance of power has shifted markedly against the Western Bloc in the Asia-Pacific and now threatens the American dominated regional order by undermining its key determinant – the unchallenged military supremacy of the United States and its allies.

America's Military Buildup in the Pacific

A key element of the United States' Pivot to Asia has been its commitment to vastly expand its military presence in the Asia-Pacific region. In late 2011 U.S. President Barack Obama announced his administration's new policy towards the Asia-Pacific, since termed the Obama Doctrine, on a visit to Australia. He stated:

> With most of the world's nuclear power and some half of humanity, Asia will largely define whether the century ahead will be marked by conflict or cooperation ... As President, I have therefore, made a deliberate and strategic decision – as a Pacific nation, the United States will play a larger and long-term role in shaping this region and its future ... I have directed my national security team to make our presence and mission in the Asia Pacific a top priority ... As we plan and budget for the future, we will allocate the resources necessary to maintain our strong military presence in this region. We will preserve our unique ability to project power and deter threats to peace ... Our enduring interests in the region demand our enduring presence in the region.
>
> The United States is a Pacific power, and we are here to stay. Indeed, we are already modernizing America's defense posture across the Asia Pacific. It will be more broadly distributed – maintaining our strong presence in Japan and the Korean Peninsula, while enhancing our presence in Southeast Asia. Our posture will be more flexible – with new capabilities to ensure that our forces can operate freely. And our posture will be more sustainable, by helping allies and partners build their capacity, with more training and exercises. We see our new posture here in Australia ... I believe we can address shared challenges, such as proliferation and maritime security, including cooperation in the South China Sea.[68]

President Obama's speech emphasized in particular the military aspects of the United States' new strategy – indicating that the military build-up was taking place with North Korea and China in mind due to the respective references to 'proliferation' and the South China Sea. With the high strategic importance of the Asia-Pacific region set only to grow in future, already very likely the most strategically critical region in the world, the importance of retaining dominance over Asia for both the United States and the wider Western Bloc is set only to increase. While outlining the new doctrine the U.S. president christened it appropriately with the announcement of the deployment of over 2,500 U.S. Marines to Darwin in Northern Australia – within striking distance of the South China Sea. This was followed by an extremely rapid redeployment of U.S. military assets to the region. By July 2016 United States Secretary of the Army Eric Fanning revealed that the number of U.S. troops deployed to the Asia-Pacific had increased by 30,000 since the announcement of the Obama Doctrine. 'The number of soldiers and civilian army workers in the Pacific region has shot up to more than 100,000, from 70,000 four years ago,' he stated.[69] These numbers are set to further increase. By 2020 the United States has pledged to have

60 percent of its military deployed in the region according to U.S. Defense Secretary Panetta – and this may well further increase beyond this date.[70]

In 2011 the United States military began to set up equipment depots in several Southeast Asian countries including Cambodia and Vietnam, which would mean a de-facto permanent deployment of U.S. personnel to these countries. U.S. forces also began joint military exercises with Vietnam that year, which were widely considered by Western analysts to be aimed at China.[71] The United States Navy has also since gained permission to make regular port calls in Thailand and Malaysia, while obtaining the rights to territory in the latter as a base for its surveillance drones. These developments and others which took place in 2011 marked only the beginning of what was to come, and the U.S. military has continued to rapidly expand its military presence in the Asia-Pacific region ever since with support from a number of its Western allies.

Examples of further expansion include the re-establishment of military facilities in the Philippines for which the U.S. gained permission in 2016,[72] described by Reuters as 'a 10-year military pact with the Philippines that opens the way for U.S. troops, planes and warships to have greater access to bases in the Philippines.'[73] That year the U.S. negotiated plans both to expand its marine base in Australia to host U.S. warships as well as to rotate long-range B-1B bombers in northern Australia – within strike range of but a relatively safe distance from China. B-1B heavy bombers were transferred from the Middle East, the United States' its previous area of prime military focus, to its Air Force base in Guam that same year.[74] Equipped for a ship hunting role with advanced cruise missiles, the bombers remain a critical asset against both the fast growing Chinese surface navy as well as land based targets.[75]

The United States has also escalated its participation in military drills alongside regional partners, several which practiced the application of offensive strategies against China. In September 2014 U.S. forces staged the Valiant Shield exercises in the Western pacific involving 18,000 soldiers. The aim was to test the Pentagon's Air-Sea battle concept against China in a potential war. First China's 'communications in space and cyberspace' would be blinded, before destroying land and sea weapons systems and eliminating all of China's deployed weapons. The blinding campaign would be a crucial stage at the beginning of the fight, to ensure the conflict would remain one-sided. The network of command centers, radar installations and satellites controlling Chinese missiles and other weapons would be destroyed.

In July 2015 the United States, Australia, Japan and New Zealand staged the two-week Talisman Sabre air-sea military exercise, the biggest in recent history, to train in 'high end warfare.' The aim was to rehearse blocking the Strait of Malacca, the Lombok Straits and other vital sea-lanes to cut off China's access to oil, gas and raw materials from Africa and the Middle East. China relies on these routes to transport 80 percent of its raw materials. Elaborating on the purpose of the drills, Australian Senator Scott Ludlam said that the 30,000 troops simulating for mass landing operations and task-force protection were not preparing for a defensive war. 'That's not what they're training for – it's about landing on beaches and invading other people's countries ... preparing for a war with China.' There was a wide consensus that the drills were rehearsing 'expeditionary wars and invasions' aimed at the People's Republic of China.[76] Australia, the Philippines and the United States navies the following year launched large scale military drills involving amphibious beach landings and the capture of oil and gas extraction facilities, with U.S. Marine Pacific Commander Lieutenant-General John Toolan commented that they 'absolutely' were training and preparation for a security crisis with China in the South China Sea.[77] These were but a few of the offensive drills which took place in the early days of the Obama Doctrine's implementation, and such exercises have since continued.

While the United States military has made an unprecedentedly rapid transfer of its assets to the Asia-Pacific region, its ability to remain the region's prime military power remains in serious doubt. It is notable that the growth of the American military presence in Asia has come as a result of transfers away from other regions – rather than a growth in the military itself which would require massive American economic growth to facilitate. With the U.S. unlikely to completely abandon critical defense commitments elsewhere in the world, there is a limit on the extent to which it can continue to transfer forces to Asia – and a continuous expansion of the U.S. military presence in the region at such a pace is therefore far from sustainable. The reallocation of forces under the Obama Doctrine represents a surge rather than a steady growth in American fighting power. China's People's Liberation Army by contrast, with a growth in its budget of approximately 8.5 percent per year facilitated by the country's rapid economic rise, is seeing not only an extremely fast growth in the size and capabilities of its navy and air force, but has experienced such growth as part of a steady process rather than a sudden surge as in the case of the United States which relies on drawing forces from elsewhere in the world. The strength of China's military in the Pacific therefore is not only growing faster than that of the United States, which even in the first years of the Obama Doctrine did not see its military capabilities expand by anything approaching 8 percent annually, but is also growing far more sustainably. So long as China's economic growth continues at a stable rate, the Obama Doctrine could never be considered a feasible plan to retain American military primacy in the Pacific in the medium to long term – at best only slightly prolonging it at the expense of other U.S. defense commitments.

U.S. Power Projection and a Global Reach vs. China's Territorial Defensive Strategy

While China's military capabilities deployed to the Pacific theatre can match if not exceed those of the United States, American power projection capabilities – the ability to deploy military force and conduct operations far from one's own homeland – remain far in advance of any regional or global challenger. This power projection is facilitated both by the global reach of the U.S. Navy and Air Force and by American military bases hosting forces across the world. A global network of military satellites and special forces operations in all but a select few countries further give the United States an ability to project power abroad unparalleled by its military rivals. While the Chinese Navy may well be able to match and very soon, if not already, overcome that of the U.S. in a confrontation near China's own territorial waters, the ability of the United States Navy to wage wars and project power in blue waters far from its own territories are unmatched. The U.S. Navy is currently the only one in the world capable of deploying sizeable aerial forces to wage an offensive war across an ocean, which is facilitated by its unparalleled fleet of tankers and high endurance blue water capable nuclear-powered supercarriers. Carriers and tankers are critical to projecting power away from one's borders and offensive warfare, and are assets the Navy is investing heavily in modernizing today.[78,79]

The U.S. carrier fleet outnumbers the rest of the world combined, with 20 carriers purpose built for projecting power abroad in service as of 2019. The Nimitz and Gerald Ford class nuclear powered supercarriers in particular, of which the United States fields 11, have no equivalent in any other navy and are essential tools of the United States' power projection. Britain, Australia, Japan and France also maintain carrier fleets which have all been deployed, or in Britain's case are pledged to be deployed, to support American patrols near Chinese waters – and very often into waters claimed by China as its own. These European and Oceanic carriers are far smaller, less sophisticated and less well suited to blue water offensive operations however – and relative to the capabilities of the United States Navy appear to represent little more than a token addition representing solidarity among the major powers of the Western Bloc. The United States also maintains a colossal aerial tanker fleet far outmatching that of any other nation in the world, fielding 59 McDonnell Douglas KC-10A Extenders and 397 Boeing KC-135 Stratotankers. These tankers are critical for projection of power and offensive actions, particularly over the vast waters of the Pacific separating potential target states China and North Korea from the majority of U.S. military facilities – extending the range of U.S. combat aircraft by allowing them to refuel aerially.

China's People's Liberation Army Navy and Air Force, in strong contrast to the capabilities of the United States, have negligible long range power projection capabilities. Indeed, the People's Liberation Army has paid so little attention to developing these capabilities that according to a number of Western sources they would struggle to deploy in such aggressive operations even against targets as near as Taiwan.[80,81] These claims can be made despite a strait of only 130 km separating Taiwan from the mainland, the relative softness of Taiwan as a military target[82,83,84] and the vastness of China's investment in its armed forces. This is because China's military buildup has always been overwhelmingly defensive, and this is strongly reflected in the composition of the PLA today. While developing power projection capabilities, a large fleet of amphibious assault vessels needed to conquer Taiwan or land troops abroad for example, are well within Chinese capabilities and far simpler and less costly tasks than several of the high-end defense projects currently being undertaken, the military has wholly neglected them – a strong sign of its defensive objectives.[85]

Chinese acquisitions under its modernization program have overwhelmingly been of defensive platforms such as land based missile launchers to target enemy ships near the Chinese coasts and defensive warships designed to operate near the country's own coasts.[86] While China maintains two aircraft carriers and has two more under construction, none are nuclear powered or suited to long-term operations far from the country's territorial waters – a stark contrast to the U.S. supercarriers which are built specifically for such high endurance operations. Indeed, three of China's four carrier classes are closely based on the Soviet Kuznetsov Class carrier designed for coastal defense, while the fourth, known as Type 003, is a larger more sophisticated platform with a similar role. China has the opportunity to acquire advanced nuclear supercarriers from Russia, with the country offering such platforms for export for relatively modest prices and having laid their keels down in the final days of the Soviet Union before the state's collapse brought about the programs' cancellation in early 1992. While supercarriers would allow China to project power offensively in the same way as the United States, these do not fit in with the country's overwhelmingly defensive doctrine.[87]

While U.S. carriers can between them theoretically deploy over 900 aircraft when operating at full capacity, over 70 each for supercarriers and 20 for the smaller Wasp and America class assault ships, China's two carriers deploy approximately 54 fighters between them – around 6 percent of the U.S. Navy's air wing. The Chinese carrier fleet is, by contrast to that of the United States, tailored heavily towards coastal defense. The Liaoning and future carriers are notably the only ones in the world which deploy heavy air superiority fighters exclusively, with China's only carrier based fighter the J-15 being tailored heavily to an anti-aircraft and anti-ship role and being poorly suited to strikes on ground targets. This combined with the design of the warships themselves as short range platforms indicates a carrier program overwhelmingly tailored to naval and air superiority in nearby waters – not far off power projection across the world or attacks on enemy territories. It is also notable that unlike other carrier powers, particularly the United States, China has grossly neglected investment in developing Carrier Onboard Delivery aircraft such as the American Grumman C-2 Greyhound necessary to support lengthy carrier operations far from shore. While developing such platforms would be well within China's capabilities given the size of its defense budget and the sophistication of its military aviation, this lack of investment again strongly indicates that the country's military development is not tailored to power projection operations far from China's own territory.

It is also worthy of note when assessing the nature of China's military modernization that the country's aerial tanker fleet has remained negligible with only three purpose built tankers currently in service, less than 1 percent the size of the U.S. tanker fleet, which reflects its air force's overwhelmingly defensive role. For a major power to field a tanker fleet smaller than that of nations such as Chile, Pakistan and Malaysia indicates a disproportionately small investment in power projection capabilities. The same trend is shown when comparing the Chinese and American bomber fleets, with the former lacking any intercontinental range bombers while the latter fields over 150 of these platforms. The composition of China's inventory indicates that the PLA would be unable to effectively project power beyond its territorial waters, and while its navy and air force have made formidable advances they have not seen fit to invest in obtaining such capabilities. Indeed, China's military modernization efforts and the expansion of its armed forces can hardly be considered balanced in this regard, and are overwhelmingly defensively oriented.

Dr Andrew S. Erickson, Professor of Strategy at and founding member of the U.S. Naval War College's China Maritime Studies Institute, noted regarding China's unwillingness to invest in power projection capabilities and a blue water navy capable of long distance offensive operations similar to that of the United States: 'China's Navy is not poised to speed across the Pacific to threaten America ... Such statements lack basis in fact and present an ideal strategic teaching moment to remind analysts and policymakers that Beijing's evolving naval structure and operations yet again show that China is not working off a traditional European, Soviet or American naval development playbook [all powers which invested heavily in projecting power away from their shores]. Even its most ambitious strategists and decision-makers do not seek what they would term a "global Far Oceans blue-water type" navy any time soon.'[88]

As British Professor, Lecturer and China specialist Jude Woodward similarly noted regarding the extent China's growing military could project power offensively as the U.S. Navy has been built to do: 'China will not challenge the U.S. in the far seas for many decades to come, even if it were pursuing that goal ... China has shown no interest in extending its naval operations out towards the Eastern Pacific and America's seaboards.' She went on to call the idea of China challenging the United States Navy anywhere beyond China's close territorial waters 'a figment of fevered imaginations.'[89] While the PLA will likely eclipse the combat capabilities of U.S. forces when operating near Chinese waters, due to its overwhelmingly defensive doctrine and lack of investment in power projection capabilities the U.S. is set to maintain a significant advantage in its ability to launch offensive operations.

An analysis of the power projection capabilities of the military powers active in the Asia-Pacific gives strong indications as to which parties do pose a risk of aggression. While the armed forces Asia-Pacific nations are all heavily defensively oriented relative to their Western counterparts, the ratio of combat assets to logistical support assets in the armed forces of the United States and many of its European allies strongly indicates that their orientation is primarily and overwhelmingly offensive. Furthermore, unlike in Asian nations, reservists in Western nations are primarily geared towards providing additional logistical support – rather than serving as extra combat personnel. This is due to the far greater strain placed on logistics by offensive operations, particularly those over long distances, hence why an analysis of investment in logistical assets can serve as an invaluable means of evaluating whether a military is primarily offensive or defensive in its orientation – with Western militaries largely corresponding to the former while Asian militaries correspond to the latter.

The United States is currently the only military power in the Pacific with the assets required for major power projection operations against faraway targets – and though several European militaries are heavily oriented towards performing similar roles their assets are considerably fewer and less capable than their American counterparts. Without the United States' unique offensive capabilities any prospects for a major war in the region are unlikely – as no Asian power comes close to its level of preparedness to operate offensively. China by contrast, with its three purpose built tankers, negligible amphibious fleet, low endurance short ranged carriers, and low ratio of logistics to combat assets, would struggle to mount a token offensive against neighboring Japan – let alone pose a threat of aggression to the entire Asia-Pacific region. U.S. forces have several hundred tankers to facilitate the movement of vast fighter fleets to Chinese or North Korean territory, and supercarriers capable of deploying hundreds more from forward positions. China by contrast does not have a military at all capable of any significant offensive power projection.

The other critical facilitator of a nation's power projection capabilities similarly indicates an overwhelming U.S. advantage – that of strategically located military facilities. The American *Nation* reported on the United States' 'empire' of military bases worldwide: 'While there are no freestanding foreign bases permanently located in the United States, there are now around 800 U.S. bases in foreign countries. Seventy years after World War II and 62 years after the Korean War, there are still 174 U.S. 'base sites' in Germany, 113 in Japan, and 83 in South Korea, according to the Pentagon. Hundreds more dot the planet in around 80 countries … Although few Americans realize it, the United States likely has more bases in foreign lands than any other people, nation, or empire in history.'[90]

95 percent of foreign military installations globally are American. The majority of the remaining 5 percent belong to allied Western military powers such as the United Kingdom and France. These costly military facilities and sustained military presences abroad serve to cement continued military supremacy globally – allowing the United States to intervene militarily across the world. Beyond the military bases U.S. Special Forces are deployed even more widely – able to operate to all but a few countries. In 2016 alone they were deployed to 138 nations, the only notable

exceptions being China, Russia, North Korea, Iran and South Africa.[91,92] This military prowess, with a truly global reach unparalleled in history, is a key asset directed largely against those states which have sought to in some way undermine the Western dominated world order.

In the Asia-Pacific the United States has built a supply chain to project its naval and air power across the region – stretching from the U.S. mainland to Honolulu in Hawaii and onto Guam, its small Pacific colony. The chain then stretches to Subic Bay in the Philippines, on to Singapore where extensive port and air force facilities are maintained, onto Diego Garcia – a remnant colony of the British Empire where U.S. bombers are stationed.** With military facilities across all of China's major trade routes, with the exception of overland routes through neighboring Russia and Pakistan, the United States' bases are a major asset which its up and coming military rival cannot hope to match. Alongside military deployments encircling the Chinese mainland, the United States' secondary priority in the Asia-Pacific region has been to gain control of China's seaborne energy supply chain. The only direct route from the Persian Gulf to China runs through the Malacca Strait, a strategically critical Southeast Asian sea route through which 80 percent China's energy imports pass.[93] Malacca is by far the busiest and most strategically important strait in the world, carrying 25 percent of all traded goods and 25 percent of all oil carried by sea. East and Southeast Asian nations' trade with Eurasia, and for the vast majority their energy supplies as well, are heavily reliant on the Malacca Strait for their economic wellbeing. Western imperial powers have sought control of the Malacca Strait since the early sixteenth century as a means to gain influence and dominate trade routes in the Asia-Pacific region, with Portugal first gaining control over the Strait in 1511 before being displaced by the Dutch in

** For those who would dispute the status of Guam and Diego Garcia as 'colonies,' the former is classified as a 'federal territory' whose population, the Chamorro people, lack the voting rights of U.S. citizens while having no say in the construction of military facilities on the island. The islanders of Diego Garcia meanwhile were forcibly evicted from their ancestral homes by the British military for resettlement in 1971 with little compensation and no right to object to make space for expanded military facilities at this strategic location.

1641, who would control it until 1825 when they relinquished control of the Strait to the British Empire. The Strait was then under British control until the mid-twentieth century.

Control of the Malacca Strait is perhaps more strategically important now than at any time since it first fell under Western control over 500 years ago – with traffic through the waterway today accounting for one third of all traded goods and the majority of China's imported oil. The third phase of the United States military's Air Sea Battle strategy for a war in the Pacific clearly states the potential for a blockade of the Malacca Strait, which would both devastate Chinese trade and cut off its access to the bulk of its fossil fuels. Referred to as 'distant blockade operations,' which allow the United States to cut China's economic lifeline without having to intervene militarily near Chinese waters – a far riskier prospect. Distant blockade operations capitalize on the United States' overwhelming advantage in power projection capabilities, as it can use facilities and naval forces across the world to blockade China while remaining well out of reach of China's coastal defenses and defensively oriented air force and navy. Taking advantage of the People's Liberation Army's lagging power projection capabilities, such a strategy can effectively attack China without directly engaging the country's advanced defenses. Signs that China may be considering an investment in some longer-ranged power projection capabilities for its Navy and Air Force with the express purpose of amending this potential weakness of a purely defensive force – namely to challenge the Western Bloc's ability to dominate strategically placed waterways key to the country's economic wellbeing, have begun to emerge since the details of Air Sea Battle were first publicized.

Leading American strategists, such as T. X. Hammes, a renowned research fellow at the U.S. Institute for National Security Studies, have strongly advocated a distant blockade, referred to by Hammes as 'offshore control,' as perhaps the most effective and risk free offensive strategy the United States can take against China.[94] As a result of the success of the People's Liberation Army's modernization program, strategies such as 'offshore control' offer perhaps the only feasible strategic prospect for the United States to leverage its military power to turn the tide in its escalating conflict with the Asian power. As one U.S. defense commentator for the

American *National Interest* magazine stated, the Obama administration did not shift over half of the United States' Naval assets to the Asia-Pacific to contain pirates.[95] As a result the U.S. military has taken measures to increase its military presence in Singapore, constructing facilities for the deployment of American aircraft carriers which have begun to deploy there more regularly[96] and the permanent stationing of Littoral Combat stealth warships from 2016.[97] Britain too maintains naval facilities in its former colonies of Singapore and Malaysia, and more extensive facilities in nearby Brunei. With the U.S. and British militaries deployed around the Strait, and U.S. military deployments growing fast since the 2010s, the two Western powers will with possible assistance from their allies gain the strategically invaluable capability to choke the energy supplies and seriously restrict the Eurasian trade of any Asia-Pacific power – including China. U.S. military planners have referred to Malacca as 'where we'd get them' – in reference to Western control over China's maritime trade routes being a key and outstanding weakness.[98] The lesser straits of Sunda, Lombok and Makassar are also highly vulnerable to blockade, with the Western powers leveraging their two key unrivalled assets, vast supremacy in power projection and a global network of strategically located military bases, to control these key waterways as needed.

China perceives the United States and its allies' undisputed military dominance over the Malacca Strait and other key trade routes as an imminent threat to its future economic wellbeing, particular as America's leading strategists have advocated for the Strait's closure under strategies such as Air-Sea battle. As professors of strategy at the U.S. Naval War College in Newport, Toshi Yoshihara and James R. Holmes, noted: 'Chinese leaders fret that the United States will deploy naval might to deny China access to the commons, retaliating against some Chinese transgression or even conceivably on the whim of an American president.'[99]

China has already responded to the threat posed by an offshore control strategy by attempting to rapidly diversify its energy supplies and establish alternative trade routes, with the signing oil and gas deals with Russia and Kazakhstan worth hundreds of billions of dollars and funding the construction of pipelines to facilitate them among other measures taken. China's substantial investments in improving infrastructure and transport networks on the Asian continent, from the One Belt One Road Initiative to revive trade along the ancient Silk Road trading networks to the China-Pakistan Economic Corridor, in which China helped Pakistan improve its transportation infrastructure to allow it to act as a conduit for Chinese trade. The development of Gwadar Port in Balochistan province in particular, and possible development of defensive military facilities nearby as well as considerable assistance provided to the Pakistan Navy to defend the key site,[100] will combined with the fast road and rail networks built linking it to Chinese territory allow the country to considerably reduce its reliance on Western controlled Malacca. Close to the Arabian Sea and Strait of Hormuz, Gwadar Port can provide a key conduit for Middle Eastern fossil fuels in particular – an effective means of reducing the impact of Malacca's potential closure. Construction of a pipeline infrastructure in Myanmar will similarly allow China to import Middle Eastern oil through the Southeast Asian nation's ports – also circumventing Malacca and a potential Western naval blockade.[101] Vast investments in renewable energies are, alongside concerns for a cleaner environment and more sustainable growth, also largely spurred by a sense of vulnerability given the situation in Malacca.

Ultimately the aforementioned measures taken by Beijing can only mitigate China's reliance on vulnerable sea trading routes such as the Malacca Strait, but they cannot eliminate this reliance entirely for the foreseeable future. The United States and its European allies' vast military presence in strategically critical Afghanistan, bordering China, Pakistan and Iran, further complicates prospects for relying too heavily on land based trade.

The United States Military's Disadvantage in the Pacific: Overstretched Forces and Inefficient Acquisitions

While the expansion of the U.S. military presence in the Asia-Pacific has come in response to China's own military modernization, an attempt to maintain the longstanding Western military primacy in the region, the United States faces several limitations which seriously undermine its ability to contend with China's People's Liberation Army and other near peer adversaries in the long term. The United States' defense spending, according to the London-based International Institute for Strategic Studies, is around $1 trillion annually. This is more that the total GDP of all but the world's 15 largest economies, exceeding the total defense spending of the next 42 nations combined. In the early 2010s U.S. military spending accounted for over 45 percent of all global military spending – around ten times that of China. Upon taking office in 2017, U.S. President Donald Trump's move to further boost U.S. military spending by approximately 10 percent further increased the discrepancy in their military budgets. This military spending surge notably required considerable cuts to be made to other critical sectors of the U.S. economy, and unlike the annual growth in Chinese defense spending of approximately 8 percent annually the surge in American defense spending was hardly sustainable. No similar spending increases could be expected for some years to come.

Despite the considerably larger budget of the United States military, China's military capabilities are considered a major challenge in the Asia-Pacific. A number of factors in China's favor allow it to potentially surpass the United States as the Asia-Pacific's dominant military power despite its far smaller expenditure. The People's Liberation Army's capabilities do not necessarily need to eclipse those of the United States for it to become the dominant military power in the Asia-Pacific. The United States military remains stretched across the world on three major fronts against near-peer adversaries, and otherwise deployed across the world across approximately 80 countries on six continents – as well as substantial deployments on the U.S. mainland itself.[102] While these widespread deployments are an asset for power projection, spreading forces so widely leaves U.S. military contingents in theatres where they face near-peer adversaries such as the Pacific at a greater risk of being outmatched – a disadvantage relative to other powers which can concentrate their assets. A common error made by a number of analysts has been to compare the entirety of the United States military with that of China in assessing whether the latter could challenge the regional primacy of the former. This approach would perhaps be viable for tensions between two states bordering one another and focusing the majority of their military prowess on countering their neighbor, a rare case in the modern world of which Ethiopia and Eritrea or Armenia and Azerbaijan serve as two of only a few examples – but for assessing the military balance in the Asia-Pacific is wholly unsuitable. With U.S. forces in the Asia-Pacific representing just a fraction of their military power, China need only develop its military to match this American contingent for it to pose a challenge to the United States' position as the region's dominant military power.[103] As Timothy A. Walton, a consultant and Asia-Pacific security specialist at the Alios Consulting Group defense and strategy firm, noted, such errors were frequently made by low-level analysts. Though the sum of U.S. forces were greater than those of China, 'Unfortunately, the United States does not fight on a chessboard. What really matters is the localized correlation of forces, and that may be a stronger factor toward deterrence in the region.'[104]

The American defense think thank RAND Corporation similarly noted regarding the United States' significant disadvantage in being stretched on too many fronts relative to China's concentration on the Asia-Pacific: 'A number of factors complicate the U.S. military position vis-à-vis China. The U.S. military is pulled in several directions by a range of world-wide demands, while the PLA enjoys the ability to focus more narrowly.' It noted both a refocusing of U.S. military efforts towards counterinsurgency due to commitments in the Middle East and Central Asia, which also diverted significant resources away from major fronts such as the Asia-Pacific. China meanwhile faced no such handicap.[105] Not only are U.S. forces spread widely, but the fact that they are deployed for power projection overseas rather than for territorial defense as Chinese forces are means that they must contend with far longer supply lines.

The United States military's struggle to maintain an advantage or even parity is further exacerbated by poor performance and high cost of many of its most prolific cutting edge defense programs. One example is the troubled $1.5 trillion[106] F-35 fifth generation multirole fighter program. The platform's underperformance was attested to by a number of sources from military think tanks such as NSN[107] and RAND Corporation,[108] organizations such as the Project on Government Oversight (POGO)[109] and individuals such as the Pentagon's chief weapons tester Michael Gilmore,[110] Marine Captain Dan Grazier,[111] and leading U.S. military aviation experts such as

Pierre Spray.[112] A combination of its poor maneuverability, low climb rate, minimal payload, short range, high maintenance, overreliance on complex electronics and stealth capabilities – a technology which has been compromised by relatively primitive U.S. adversaries in the past[113] – all serve to make the program unfit for operations against near-peer adversaries in the Pacific. The F-35 is set to serve as the backbone of the United States' Air Sea Battle strategy for war in the Pacific. It was referred to by General Lori R. Robinson, United States Air Force commander and former commander of the Pacific Air Force, as 'the keystone to future U.S. airpower,' with particular importance for the Pacific theatre. Considering that this aircraft is set to comprise the bulk of the fighter fleets of the U.S. Air Force, the Navy and the Marines, with over 2,500 jets planned, the fact that the F-35's extremely limited ability to combat near-peer forces significantly undermines the future operational capabilities of the U.S. military in the region.[114] This is particularly true considering that by diverting such colossal funds to the program, there have been less funds available for other potentially more cost effective defense programs.[115]

Senate Armed Services Committee Chairman John McCain referred to the F-35 as 'a textbook example' of the country's 'broken defense acquisition system.'[116] He further stated in a briefing to the Senate: 'the F-35 program's record of performance has been both a scandal and a tragedy with respect to cost, schedule and performance.'[117] Indeed, other next generation weapons programs have similarly suffered cost overruns and severe underperformance issues – an example being the B-2 Spirit bomber, a subsonic platform originally budgeted at under $500 million[118] which due to cost overruns had a final price of $2.13 billion dollars[119] with $3.4 million monthly maintenance costs per bomber.[120] The platform was so delicate that it required storage in special and highly costly air conditioned hangers,[121] while its stealth capabilities proved to be highly unreliable,[122] and maintenance requirements were so as high as to restrict it to at best conducting a sortie every two months.[123,124] Another was the Zumwalt Class destroyer, costing $7.5 billion each,[125] the flaws of which are too numerous to list but have led to regular breakdowns at sea and a near complete ineffectiveness in combat against rival destroyers commissioned at a fraction of the cost. The U.S. Conservative magazine *National Review* referred to it as 'an unmitigated disaster' and 'emblematic of a defense procurement system that is rapidly losing its ability to meet our national security needs.'[126] These are but a few of the multi-billion dollar weapons programs which have not only reached tremendously inefficient costs, but have also grossly underperformed – undermining their viability and the fighting capabilities of the military as a whole.

Rampant inefficiencies and, according President Donald Trump, severe corruption are prevalent throughout the U.S. defense acquisition system,[127] and have significantly undermined the quality of the weapons which have entered service while leading to huge cost overruns. These issues are considered a grave threat to American national security, as former Secretary of State Rumsfeld said in 2001: 'In fact, it could be said it's a matter of life and death.' He noted: 'The adversary has come closer to home. It's the Pentagon bureaucracy.' Secretary Rumsfeld went on to admit that significant sums of money went unaccounted for, stating: 'According to some estimates we cannot track $2.3 trillion in transactions.' The *New York Times* reported regarding these corruption scandals, citing military officials who had attested to the poor state of affairs in the Pentagon and the way this seriously undermined national defense: 'The Pentagon's spending of the public's money is a dirty business, one that too often has nothing to do with national defense, one in which secrecy and deception are valuable currencies.'[128] U.S. Army General Edward Hirsch, who had undertaken extensive efforts to make amendments to the military's acquisition system, referred to it as 'a system designed for failure – it isn't going to work.'[129] Danielle Brian, director of the Project on Governmental Oversight similarly observed: 'waste has become ingrained in the defense budget because opposition to defense spending is portrayed as unpatriotic, and legislators are often more concerned about winning Pentagon pork than controlling defense waste … You have a black hole at the Pentagon for money and a blind congress.'[130,131]

Gross cost overruns, a 'broken' defense acquisition system and serious performance failures with its latest weapons systems, significantly undermine any U.S. efforts to maintain regional primacy against a fast rising rival military power. The Pentagon's Defense Advanced Research Projects Agency (DARPA) noted in regards to this severe constraint on the U.S. military's ability to compete with near peer rivals in a report in mid 2018: 'our acquisition system is finding it difficult to respond on relevant timescales to adversary progress, which has made the search for next generation capabilities at once more urgent and more futile.'[132] The United States' four 'great power' adversaries on the other hand have demonstrated no remotely comparable inefficiencies in their acquisitions processes or weapons programs. With reported cases of corruption and inefficiency growing substantially following the end of the Cold War, this may well be a result of post-victory complacency – or Victory Disease as referred to by the U.S. military. Despite the phenomenally high U.S. defense budget, these gross inefficiencies in acquisitions combined with commitment to sizeable deployments across the world on six continents and three major fronts means that it will be extremely difficult for the United States to maintain its position as the dominant military power in the Asia-Pacific region.

Referring to China's closing of the technological gap between its own defense sector and that of the United States, achieved extremely quickly following the Cold War's end given the nature of the discrepancy that existed between the two in 1990, senior fellow at the prominent Washington based think tank Center for a New American Security Elsa B. Kania stated: 'The U.S. no longer possesses clear military-technical dominance, and China is rapidly emerging as a would-be superpower in science and technology.'[133] Reports by the U.S. Defence Intelligence Agency have similarly indicated a fast waning American military advantage - noting that China's People's Liberation Army has surpassed the United States military the sophistication of a number of its weapons systems. This trend is set to continue to grow as more and more PLA weapons programs lead to the deployment of systems which far surpass their American counterparts.[134] The fact that China can produce weapons systems of similar and often superior quality at far lower costs, examples being the Type 055 destroyer – coming at under one seventh the cost of the considerably less capable U.S. Zumwalt Class, the Type 054A Class frigate's advanced capabilities relative to the severely flawed but costly American Littoral Class,[135] the HQ-9B's low cost and high performance relative to the Patriot air defense system and the DF-41's vast superiority relative to the far less sophisticated U.S. Minuteman III ballistic missiles.

The Chengdu J-20 next generation air superiority fighter, while coming at well under a third of the cost of its U.S. analogue the F-22 Raptor,[136] is predicted to field considerably superior capabilities.[137] The result is likely to be a quantitative disadvantage combined with, at best, technological parity for the United States military in the Pacific – while the prospects for a considerable technological disadvantage relative to the PLA to compound this remains a likely prospect within a decade.

U.S. Army Chief of Staff General Mark Milley noted at a hearing at the Senate's defense appropriations subcommittee that countries such as China with more cost effective militaries, and with government owned research and development in particular, could effectively compete with the United States despite having just a fraction of its defense budget. The efficiency of China's defense industry and its military, also largely owing to the country's far greater purchasing power, by some estimates makes the Chinese People's Liberation Army a better funded organization than the U.S. military itself. A study published by Bloomberg in May 2018 came to this conclusion.[138] Considerably greater efficiency combined with China's ability to concentrate its forces in East Asia in a way the United States cannot, heavy investment in asymmetric defensive anti-access area denial weaponry and a fast growing and far more sustainable defense budget and an economy set to eclipse the United States in nominal GDP in the near future all strongly indicate that the United States is set to lose its position as the Asia-Pacific's prime military power – if this has not occurred already.

Taking into account defense spending alone without considerable additional 'defense-related' expenditures, the United States defense budget averaged nearly 4 percent of GDP from 2000 to 2017, while China's expenditure was just under 2 percent. With the U.S. military today having relied on spending and troop surges under Presidents Trump and Obama respectively to retain parity in the Pacific, there is little room for further expansion. China on the other hand can not only continue to expand its military at a rate the United States cannot compete with, but also retains the latent potential as a far smaller defense spender, in proportion to the size of its economy, to enact spending surges of its own if necessary – potentially increasing the defense budget to 3 percent or 4 percent if facing a major threat. The United States defense budget on the other hand has far less room to give further, and lacks this key latent potential.

With its forces thinly stretched, the U.S. military is unlikely to maintain an advantage over or even parity with a regional military superpower which can sustain a 7 to 8 percent defense budget growth annually, develop cutting edge indigenous weapons technologies, and rapidly expand the size of its modern air and naval fleets, and do so at a fraction of the cost that the United States can. China's annual military budget growth has been roughly in proportion to the country's economic growth whereas surges in American defense spending increases have been disproportionately high – and such spending boosts are less sustainable as a result. According to the International Institute for Strategic Studies (IISS), China's military spending is set to surpass that of the United States by 2023 as its economy and defense budget continue to grow far faster[139] – though the late 2020s may be more likely. China's already large and fast growing defense budget, combined with far more efficient expenditure and the ability to field equal and often superior weapons systems at a far lower cost makes prospects for continued U.S. primacy highly unlikely. The idea that the United States can with a fraction of its assets, retain primacy far from its own shores the Asia-Pacific region where the vast majority of Chinese assets are focused is in the long run essentially impossible.

Notes

1 Diary of Admiral William Leahy, October 20, 1942 (quoted in Thorne, Christopher, *Allies of a Kind: The United States, Britain and the War Against Japan, 1941–1945*, Oxford, Oxford University Press, 1978, p. 157).

2 Dower, John, *War Without Mercy: Race and Power in the Pacific War*, New York, Pantheon, 1986 (p. 7).

3 Draft Memorandum From Secretary of Defense McNamara to President Johnson, Washington, November 3, 1965.

4 Dower, John, *War Without Mercy: Race and Power in the Pacific War*, New York, Pantheon, 1986 (p. 10).

5 Ibid. (p. 14).

6 Barnet, Richard J., *The Alliance: America-Europe-Japan Makers of the postwar world*, New York, Touchstone, 1985 (pp. 107–108).

7 Trofimov, Yaroslav, 'Russia's Turn to Its Asian Past,' *The Wall Street Journal*, July 6, 2018.

8 Dower, John, *War Without Mercy: Race and Power in the Pacific War*, New York, Pantheon, 1986 (p. 7).

9 Dower, John, *Visualizing Japan (1850s-1930s): Westernization, Protest, Modernity, Black Ships and Samurai 1: Historical Background*, Harvard University Online Course, (Lecture 2.7, 'Japanese Seclusion').

10 'Religion: Prayer for China,' *Time Magazine*, September 17, 1951.

11 Bertuccioli, Giuliano, 'Informatori, avventurieri, spioni, agenti più o meno autentici in duemila anni di storia delle relazioni italo-cinesi,' in *Mondo Cinese*, 101, 1999.

12 Gady, Franz-Stefan, 'How a State Department Study Prevented Nuclear War With China,' *The Diplomat*, October 25, 2017.

13 'Is "Made in China 2025" a Threat to Global Trade?,' *Council on Foreign Relations*, August 2, 2018.

14 Liu, Wei, 'Trump's Trade War on China Is About More than Trade,' *The Diplomat*, July 20, 2018.

15 'The U.S. govt bent on world hegemony, Russia stands in its way – Reagan economic ex-advisor,' *RT*, December 4, 2014.

16 Kissinger, Henry, *World Order: Reflections on the Character of Nations and the Course of History*, London, Penguin, 2015 (pp. 208–209).

17 Li, Yuan, 'A Generation Grows Up in China Without Google, Facebook or Twitter,' *New York Times*, August 6, 2018.

18 Runciman, David, 'China's Challenge to Democracy,' *Wall Street Journal*, April 26, 2018.

19 Evans, David, and Jenkins, Jane, *Years of Russia, the USSR and the Collapse of Soviet Communism*, London, Hodder, 2008 (Chapter 8: 'Stalin's Economic Policies 1928–1939').

20 Brunnstrom, David, and Torode, Greg, 'U.S. flexes muscles as Asia worries about South China Sea row,' *Reuters*, June 4, 2016.

21 'Obama's FY 2017 Budget Addresses Russia, China, Iran, North Korea, Terrorism,' *U.S. Department of Defense*, February 9, 2016.

22 'Carter Outlines Security Challenges, Warns Against Sequestration,' *U.S. Department of Defense*, March 17, 2016.

23 The National Military Strategy of the United States of America 2015, The United States Military's Contribution to National Security, June 2015.

24 'Obama's FY 2017 Budget Addresses Russia, China, Iran, North Korea, Terrorism,' *U.S. Department of Defense*, February 9, 2016.

25 'Carter Outlines Security Challenges, Warns Against Sequestration,' *U.S. Department of Defense*, March 17, 2016.

26 The National Military Strategy of the United States of America 2015, The United States Military's Contribution to National Security, June 2015.
27 'Carter Outlines Security Challenges, Warns Against Sequestration,' *U.S. Department of Defense*, March 17, 2016.
28 'U.S. general says we could be screwed in a war against China or Russia,' *New York Post*, March 16, 2016.
29 Sharman, John, 'America could lose a war against North Korea, former U.S. commander says in leaked letter,' *The Independent*, November 10, 2017.
30 Sengupta, Kim, 'War in Syria: Russia's "rustbucket" military delivers hi-tech shock to West and Israel,' *The Independent*, January 29, 2016.
31 'U.S. general: North Korea ICBM threat advancing faster than expected,' *Reuters*, July 27, 2017.
32 'The Transformation and Rapid Modernization of North Korea's Defences in 2017; How U.S. Intelligence Underestimated Pyongyang's Military Industrial Capabilities,' *Military Watch Magazine*, January 23, 2018.
33 Walton, Timothy A., 'Are We Underestimating China's Military?' *The National Interest*, May 19, 2014.
34 Farquhar, Lieutenant Colonel Scott C., *Back to Basics, A Study of the Second Lebanon War and Operation CAST LEAD*, Combat Studies Institute Press, U.S. Army Combined Arms Centre, Fore Leavenworth, Kansas (pp. 14–20).
35 Heginbotham, Eric, *The U.S.-China Military Scorecard, Forces, Geography, and the Evolving Balance of Power 1996–2017*, Santa Monica, CA, RAND Corporation, 2015 (p. 43).
36 Ait, Abraham, 'How Did Japan Lose Its Air Superiority Advantage?,' *The Diplomat*, February 17, 2018.
37 Kopp, Carlo, *Operation Odyssey Dawn – the collapse of Libya's relic air defense system*, in Defence Today, vol. 9, no. 1, 2011, Strike Publications (p. 14).
38 Thompson, Roger, *Lessons Not Learned; The U.S. Navy's Status Quo Culture*, Annapolis, MD, Naval Institute Press, 2007 (Chapter 10).
39 'Leading Experts Warn F-18E's Gross Underperformance Threatens to Cut Carrier Strike Groups' Area of Influence by 77%; Why the U.S. Navy Urgently Needs a Replacement for the Super Hornet,' *Military Watch Magazine*, August 11, 2018.
40 'How China's New Stealth Fighter Could Soon Surpass the U.S. F-22 Raptor,' *The Diplomat*, March 30, 2018.
41 Watts, Barry, *The F-22 Program in Retrospect*, Center for Strategic Budgetary Assessments, August 2009.
42 Ait, Abraham, 'Why the F-35 Isn't Good Enough for Japan,' *The Diplomat*, April 28, 2018.

43 Ait, Abraham, 'How Did Japan Lose Its Air Superiority Advantage?,' *The Diplomat*, February 17, 2018.

44 'U.S. Army Shifts Focus to Fighting Technologically Advanced Near-Peer Foes,' *Sputnik*, 12 October 2017.

45 '"Significantly Weaker America" Fails to Project Military Might – DC Think Tank,' *Sputnik*, 5 October 2017.

46 Inhofe, Jim, 'Sen. Jim Inhofe: The U.S. military is outgunned, and we must to something about it,' *Tulsa World*, February 3, 2019.

47 Sonne, Paul, and Harris, Shane, 'U.S. military edge has eroded to "a dangerous degree," study for Congress finds,' *The Washington Post*, November 14, 2018.

48 National Defence Strategy Commission, *Providing For the Common Defence, The Assessment and Recommendations of the National Defence Strategy Commission*, Washington, DC, United States Institute of Peace, 2018.

49 Heginbotham, Eric, *The U.S.-China Military Scorecard, Forces, Geography, and the Evolving Balance of Power 1996–2017*, Santa Monica, CA, RAND Corporation, 2015 (Chapter 7, 'Scorecard 5: Chinese Anti-Surface Warfare').

50 McReynolds, Joe, *China's Evolving Military Strategy*, Washington, DC, Brookings Institution Press, 2016 (Preface, p. vii).

51 Harold, Scott Warren, and Schwartz, Lowell H., 'A Russia-China Alliance Brewing?' *RAND Corporation*, April 12, 2013.

52 Gady, Franz-Stefan, 'China Takes Delivery of 10 Russian Su-35 Fighter Jets,' *The Diplomat*, January 4, 2018.

53 Nash, Chris, *What is Journalism? The Art and Politics of a Rupture*, London, Palgrave Macmillan, 2016 (p. 91).

54 'Chinese Dark Sword is the First Sixth-Generation Warplane – Military Experts,' *Sputnik*, June 11, 2018.

55 McCarthy, Christopher J., *Chinese Anti-Access/Area Denial: The Evolution of Warfare in the Western Pacific*, Newport, U.S. Naval War College, 2010.

56 'China, Aircraft and Anti-Aircraft,' Military Watch Force Comparison (2018), *Military Watch Magazine* (<https://militarywatchmagazine.com/forceapp/aerial/capabilitiesbycountry/ china>).

57 Bryen, Stephen, 'Russia's S-400 Is Way More Dangerous Than You Think,' *The National Interest*, January 18, 2018.

58 Kazianis, Harry, 'Forget the S-300, Here Comes the S-400,' *The Diplomat*, May 14, 2013.

59 'Chinese military approaches technological "near-parity" with NATO in air domain – think tank,' *RT*, February 15, 2017.

60 Szoldra, Paul, 'China's military is approaching "near parity" with the West,' *Business Insider*, February 17, 2017.

61 *Quadrennial Defense Review Report*, Washington, DC, U.S. Department of Defense, February 6, 2006 (p. 29).

62 Walton, Timothy A., 'Are We Underestimating China's Military?' *The National Interest*, May 19, 2014.

63 John McCain, U.S. Senator, Arizona, 'Remarks by SASC chairman John McCain on the National Defense Authorization Act for FY17,' May 19, 2016.

64 Department of the Air Force, Presentation to the Senate Armed Services Committee Subcommittee on Airland Forces, United States, Senate, March 8, 2016, 2:30pm, *Subject: Fiscal Year 2017 Air Force, Force Structure and Modernization Programs*, Statement of: Ms Darlene J. Costello, Lt. Gen. James M. 'Mike' Holmes, Lt. Gen. John W. 'Jay' Raymond, Lt. Gen. Arnold W. Bunch, Jr.

65 'Beijing Outmaneuvering U.S. Navy in South China Sea,' *Sputnik*, March 1, 2017.

66 'National Rankings by Military Strength,' Military Watch Force Comparison (2018), *Military Watch Magazine* (<https://militarywatchmagazine.com/forceapp/countries/>).

67 'China successfully tests nuclear-capable hypersonic missile – Pentagon sources,' *RT*, April 27, 2016.

68 *Remarks by President Obama to the Australian Parliament*, The White House, Office of the Press Secretary, November 17, 2011.

69 'US-South Korea military drills to proceed despite North Korea's warning,' *The Guardian*, July 30, 2016.

70 'Leon Panetta: U.S. to deploy 60% of navy fleet to Pacific,' *BBC*, June 2, 2012.

71 Gady, Franz-Stefan, 'Deterring China: U.S. Army to Stockpile Equipment in Cambodia and Vietnam,' *The Diplomat*, March 18, 2016.

72 Robinson, S., 'U.S. Buildup in Philippines raises stakes in the region,' *Stars and Stripes*, February 3, 2016.

73 Felsenthal, Mark, and Spetalnick, Matt, 'Obama reassures allies, but doubts over "pivot" to Asia persist,' *Reuters*, April 29, 2014.

74 'U.S. flies all 3 types of bombers in "strategic power projection" stunt over Guam,' *RT*, August 18, 2018.

75 'Ship Hunting Lancers; U.S. B-1B Heavy Bombers Test Long Range Anti Ship Missiles Following Similar Developments for China's H-6 Fleet,' *Military Watch Magazine*, May 31, 2018.

76 Gady, Franz-Stefan, 'Australia and U.S. Conclude Major Military Exercise in Pacific Region,' *The Diplomat*, July 28, 2015.

77 'U.S., Philippines begin military exercises as maritime tension simmers,' *Reuters*, April 4, 2016.

78 'Troubles Facing the U.S. Military in the Pacific Today and Why the New MQ-25 Carrier Based Tanker Drone Represents and Effective Solution,' *Military Watch Magazine*, July 19, 2018.
79 'USS Gerald Ford; The First of a New Generation of U.S. Supercarriers Enters Service,' *Military Watch Magazine*, June 7, 2017.
80 Erickson, Andrew, 'Chinese Naval Shipbuilding : An Ambitious and Uncertain Course,' Annapolis, MD, Naval Institute Press, 2017.
81 Blasko, Dennis, *The Chinese Army Today: Tradition and Transformation for the 21st Century*, Abingdon, Routledge, January 15, 2006.
82 'Taiwanese Military Expert: "Not Even the Gods Can Save Taiwan" Unless Air Defences Upgraded,' *Military Watch Magazine*, December 31, 2017.
83 DeAeth, Duncan, 'Not even the Gods can save Taiwan unless air defenses upgraded, says expert,' *Taiwan News*, December 26, 2017.
84 Ait, Abraham, 'What China's Newly Inducted S-400 Means for the Balance of Power in the Taiwan Strait,' *The Diplomat*, August 14, 2018.
85 Roggeveen, Sam, 'Why China isn't planning to storm Taiwan's beaches,' The Lowy Institute, May 23, 2018.
86 Nathan, A. J., and Scobell, A., *China's Search for Security*, New York, Colombia University Press, 2012.
87 'Russia offers Indian Navy nuclear-powered carrier,' IHS *Jane's Defence Weekly*, July 15, 2016.
88 Erickson, A., and Collins, G., 'China's Real Blue Water Navy,' *The Diplomat* August 20, 2012.
89 Woodward, Jude, *The U.S. vs China: Asia's New Cold War?* Manchester, Manchester University Press, 2017 (p. 71).
90 Vine, David, 'The United States Probably Has More Foreign Military Bases Than Any Other People, Nation or Empire in History,' *The Nation*, September 14, 2015.
91 Durden, Tyler, 'U.S. Special Forces Deployed To 70 Percent of The World In 2016,' *Ron Paul Institute for Peace and Prosperity*, February 11, 2017.
92 Turse, Nick, 'Special Ops, Shadow Wars, and the Golden Age of the Grey Zone,' *Tom Dispatch*, January 5, 2017.
93 McCarthy, Christopher J., *Chinese Anti-Access/Area Denial: The Evolution of Warfare in the Western Pacific*, Newport, U.S. Naval War College, 2010.
94 Hammes, T. X., *Offshore Control is the Answer*, Proceedings, 138:12, 2012, (p. 1318).
95 P. Porter, 'Thucydides trap 2.0: Superpower Suicide?,' *The National Interest*, May 2, 2014.
96 LaGrone, Sam, 'Two Littoral Combat Ships to Deploy to Singapore Next Year, Four by 2017,' *USNI News*, April 24, 2015.

97 'USS America visits Singapore during 7th Fleet operations,' *Naval Today*, August 7, 2017.
98 Rachman, Gideon, *Easternisation, War and Peace in the Asian Century*, New York, Vintage, 2017 (p. 98).
99 Yoshihara, Toshi, and Holmes, James R., *Red Star Over the Pacific: China's Rise and the Challenge of U.S. Maritime Strategy*, Annapolis, MD, Naval Institute Press, 2013 (p. 10).
100 'China Gives Two Vessels to Pakistan's Navy to Protect New Trade Route,' *Sputnik*, January 15, 2017.
101 'Myanmar pipeline gives China faster supply of oil from Middle East,' *South China Morning Post*, April 12, 2017.
102 Vine, David, 'The United States Probably Has More Foreign Military Bases Than Any Other People, Nation or Empire in History,' *The Nation*, September 14, 2015.
103 Ait, Abraham, 'Will China Have 7 Aircraft Carriers by 2025?' *The Diplomat*, June 30, 2018.
104 Walton, Timothy A., 'Are We Underestimating China's Military?' *The National Interest*, May 19, 2014.
105 Heginbotham, Eric, *The U.S.-China Military Scorecard, Forces, Geography, and the Evolving Balance of Power 1996–2017*, Santa Monica, CA, RAND Corporation, 2015 (p. 43).
106 Wolff-Mann, Ethan, '7 Amazing Things America Could Have Bought Instead of a $1.45 Trillion Jet,' *Time*, May 2, 2016.
107 'Thunder Without Lightning, The High Costs and Limited Benefits of the F-35 Program,' *National Security Network*, August 2015.
108 Axe, David, 'Pentagon's big budget F-35 fighter 'can't turn, can't climb, can't run,'' *Reuters*, July 14, 2014.
109 Grazier, Dan, 'F-35 Continues to Stumble,' *Project on Government Oversight*, March 30, 2017.
110 'F-35 "scarcely" fit to fly: Pentagon's chief tester,' *Press TV*, April 3, 2017.
111 Grazier, Dan, 'FY16 DOD Programs, F-35 Joint Strike Fighter,' Project on Government Oversight.
112 'Extended Interview with Pierre Spray,' *The Fifth Estate*, CBC, September 28, 2012.
113 'Serb discusses 1999 downing of stealth,' *USA Today*, October 26, 2005.
114 Harrigian, Jeff, and Marosko, Max, 'Fifth Generation Air Combat: Maintaining the Joint Force Advantage,' *The Mitchell Forum*, July 2016.
115 Fredenburg, Mike, 'The F-35: Throwing Good Money after Bad,' *The National Review*, July 22, 2015.

116 McCain, John, 'U.S. Senator, Arizona, Opening statement by SASC Chairman John McCain on the F-35 Joint Strike Fighter Program,' April 26, 2016.
117 Ibid.
118 'U.S. to add one B-2 Plane to 20 Plane Fleet,' *Washington Post*, March 22, 1996.
119 'B-2 Bomber: Cost and Operational Issues Letter Report,' *United States General Accounting Office (GAO)*, August 14, 1997, GDO/NSIAD-97-181.
120 'The Gold Plated Hangar Queen Survives,' *Strategy World*, June 14, 2010.
121 U.S. General Accounting Office, September 1996 (pp. 53, 56).
122 'Key Senate Backer of Stealth Bomber Sees it in Jeopardy,' *New York Times*, July 23, 2009.
123 U.S. General Accounting Office, September 1996 (pp. 53, 56).
124 Capaccio, Tony, 'The B-2's Stealthy Skins Need Tender, Lengthy Care,' *Defense Week*, May 27, 1997 (p. 1).
125 *Defence Acquisitions: Assessments of Selected Weapon Programs*, March 2015 Report to Congressional Committees, United States Government Accountability Office.
126 Fredenburg, Mike, 'How the Navy's Zumwalt-Class Destroyers Ran Aground,' *National Review*, December 19, 2016.
127 'F-35 program "cost is out of control," Trump says,' *Fox News*, December 12, 2016.
128 Weiner, Tim, 'Corrupt From Top To Bottom,' *New York Times*, October 3, 1993.
129 Charette, Robert N., 'What's Wrong with Weapons Acquisitions?,' *IEEE Spectrum*, November 1, 2008.
130 Hossein-zadeh, Ismael, *The Political Economy of U.S. Militarism*, London, Palgrave MacMillan, 2006 (pp. 183–184).
131 Abate, Tom, 'Military waste under fire / $1 trillion missing – Bush plan targets Pentagon accounting,' *SFGate*, May 18, 2003.
132 Peck, Michael, 'Did the Pentagon Just Admit Stealth Technology May Not Work Anymore?' *The National Interest*, July 18, 2018.
133 Baculinao, Eric, 'These Chinese military innovations threaten U.S. superiority, experts, say,' *NBC News*, February 17, 2018.
134 'Some Chinese military tech surpasses US, Pentagon admits, citing hypersonic weapons,' *South China Morning Post*, January 16, 2019.
135 'U.S. Navy Does Not Have High Hopes for its Littoral Combat Ship; Reports Reflect Poorly on Next Generation Warship,' *Military Watch Magazine*, June 10, 2018.
136 'Powerful Dragon v Raptor: how China's J-20 stealth fighters compare with America's F-22s,' *South China Morning Post*, July 28, 2018.
137 'How China's New Stealth Fighter Could Soon Surpass the U.S. F-22 Raptor,' *The Diplomat*, March 30, 2018.
138 Harshaw, Tobin, 'China Outspends the US. On Defense? The Math,' *Bloomberg*, May 25, 2018.
139 'Daily Chart, the Military Balance,' *The Economist*, March 18, 2013.

CHAPTER 18

Western Militaries in the Asia Pacific Today: Part II – China's Twenty-first-century Confrontation with the West

> It was Europe's entrenched relationship with violence and militarism that allowed it to place itself at the center of the world. ... Europe's distinctive character as more aggressive, more unstable and less peace-minded that other parts of the world now paid off.[1]
>
> — PETER FRANKOPAN on the rise of the Western-dominated world order

Containment of China and the Importance of the South China Sea

The implementation of the Obama Doctrine and subsequent 'Pivot to Asia' represented not only an attempt by the United States to remain the Pacific's dominant military power, but also a critical part of a wider policy of 'containment' of China similar to the Western Bloc's Cold War efforts to 'contain' the Soviet Union before it. While containment has been implemented ever since the Western aligned Guomindang government lost power in 1949, the rapid growth of Chinese economic, military and soft power in the twenty-first century has led to a redoubling of efforts to limit the effects of its rise and thereby ensure continued Western dominance of Asia. This was certainly how China interpreted the move to station more U.S. forces in the Asia-Pacific and strengthen defense ties with Chinese neighbors – reinforcing the already formidable remnants of Cold War era deployments made to encircle the People's Republic at a time when it was considerably less powerful both economically and militarily. As Chinese Premier Hu Jintao remarked in 2012 regarding his country's growing sense of encirclement, the United States had 'strengthened its military deployments in the Asia-Pacific region, strengthened the US-Japan military alliance, strengthened strategic cooperation with India, improved relations with Vietnam, inveigled Pakistan, established a pro-American government in Afghanistan, increased arms sales to Taiwan, and so on. They have extended outposts and placed pressure points on us from the east, south, and west.'[2]

In trying to contain China there are five major fronts over which the Western Bloc would seek to assert its dominance and restrict Beijing's influence. On the northern front lies Russia, which in the Soviet era was successfully turned into a major Chinese adversary through the aforementioned engineering of the Sino-Soviet split. The Russian Federation's formation of close ties with the People's Republic of China in the fields of culture, economy, science and defense has since the Cold War's end been a considerable thorn in the side of Western efforts to isolate both countries. Relations continue to strengthen by the year, and the Western Bloc appears unable to engineer a second rift between Moscow and Beijing despite the urging of numerous leading analysts to prioritize dividing the two countries – as covered in Chapter 16.

To China's east last lie Japan and Korea, which the United States has secured effectively at gunpoint with around 80,000 military personnel deployed there. While Beijing's influence has steadily grown and relations with its East Asian neighbors have continued to improve as China replaced the United States as by far the leading trading partner of both countries, the U.S. for its part has made every effort to keep these strategically vital nations in its sphere of influence. Signs of a gradual shift in South Korean foreign policy under the Moon Jae In administration from 2017, which has prioritized close ties with Beijing and seen a sharp reduction in the formerly high tensions between the two states over the issue of U.S. missile deployments to the ROK threatening Chinese security,[3] indicate that Seoul's position today is increasingly far from that of an effective protectorate of the Western Bloc which it was during the Cold War. The joint hard line[4] taken by both Beijing and Seoul against the potential U.S.

preventative strikes on North Korea in 2017 further demonstrated the considerable common interests between the two East Asian powers in maintaining peace and preventing external powers from starting a potentially devastating regional war. The Moon administration has attempted to prevent further deployments of U.S. missile systems perceived by Beijing as a threat to Chinese security[5] – though the government in Seoul still remains under considerable pressure from large segments of its population to press the United States to remove American missile systems entirely which are already on Korean soil. South Korea's simultaneously growing economic[6,7] and defense[8,9] ties with Moscow at a time of unprecedented and growing tensions between Russia and the Western Bloc also indicate a considerable deviation from its Cold War policy which will see it play a more balanced role in the region.

To China's south lies India, with which the Western Bloc has made significant attempts to strengthen military co-operation – particularly through the Washington backed Quad security forum uniting Japan, the United States, Australia and India in an attempt to contain Chinese influence. While the success of Western attempts to win Delhi's support remain questionable, particularly following Washington's provocative threats to impose economic sanctions on India over its acquisitions of Russian arms in 2018,[10] the South Asian giant nevertheless remains highly resistant to Chinese influence. India's neighbor Pakistan, though a staunch Cold War era U.S. ally, has been far more receptive to Chinese overtures and established high level military and economic co-operation – including the joint manufacture and export of Sino-Pakistani fighter aircraft.[11] The Sino-Pakistani economic corridor project, with an estimated worth of over $60 billion, is further set to cement ties between the two countries while breaking China's encirclement westwards – connecting the country to Iran, Central Asia and the Middle East by road and rail. Pakistan's growing co-operation with China is a considerable factor in the United States' decision to revoke the Islamabad's status as a non-NATO ally and strip it of U.S. military aid. To the west of China lie Kyrgyzstan, Tajikistan and Afghanistan, where China has sought to expand its partnerships through the One Belt One Road initiative.[12] China is an increasingly important trading partner of these former communist states, and has emerged as a leading source of investment. The strong NATO military presence in Afghanistan however puts this too at a potential risk.

China's fifth frontier, that with very likely the greatest economic potential, is Southeast Asia – where the country has worked to enhance its economic, cultural and defense ties and expand its sphere of influence. Limiting Chinese influence in Southeast Asia remains the greatest imperative for the Western Bloc's containment strategy – if not second in importance only to preventing Sino-Russian economic and strategic ties. It was inevitable therefore that the South China Sea, which has for centuries linked China to Southeast Asia, would become a focal point of military tensions following the initiation of the Obama Doctrine. The strategic importance of controlling the South China Sea, a region where the United States Navy has long been the dominant military power, provides the Western Bloc with an invaluable opportunity to leverage its military might to isolate the People's Republic of China and contain its influence.

Alongside the alleged threat posed by North Korea's development of a nuclear missile deterrent against the United States, the primary pretext for increased Western involvement in the Asia-Pacific region from the 2010s has been to resolve longstanding territorial disputes between China – both the Taipei based ROC and Beijing based PRC – and several Southeast Asian nations in the South China Sea. A series of minor atolls, many of which are often below sea level, are at the center of this dispute. The three main island groups in the sea, the Spratlys, Paracels and Scarborough Shoal, are disputed by China and Taiwan, Vietnam, the Philippines, Malaysia and Brunei. These islands, of negligible size in themselves, grant whichever state controls them access to both ludicrous fishing grounds and a seabed containing fossil fuels under the Law of the Sea. Sovereignty over them is as a result a hotly contested issue, as while they are of negligible benefit to the large Chinese economy these resources are much coveted by its smaller and poorer neighbors. For China the value of these territories has come down to their strategic defensive value, namely that they lie adjacent to some of the world's busiest sea lanes vital to the country's trade with the rest of the world. The need to secure merchant shipping routes, through which around $5 trillion of international trade passes annually – much of it between China and Southeast Asia, was made a priority in U.S. military plans published by the Pentagon in 2013. Under these plans the United States Navy threatened to deploy its warships to blockade these routes – an effective means of strangling the Chinese economy and cutting it off from its emerging partners in ASEAN and beyond if necessary.[13] The nature of the threat has since grown, with U.S. planners reportedly setting up plans to directly blockade Chinese access to the sea – thereby crippling the economy of the world's largest trading nation.[14] China's perceived need to fortify these trade routes against a potential Western intervention has thus emerged in response to this threat – for which control of the contested strategically located islands remains imperative.

China's military activities in the South China Sea have not only been based on a defensive strategic necessity, but also on longstanding claims to a number of territories backed up by extensive historical documentation. While much of China's evidence supporting its claims goes back to the Han dynasty over 1,800 years ago, more recently these claims were recognized by the Second World War Allied Powers in 1945 regarding the restoration of Chinese territories seized by Japan. Had China's Western aligned Guomindang government remained in power, the restoration of these territories to Beijing's sovereignty by the Western powers would have gone ahead. As it was however the communist victory led to China's exclusion from the 1951 San Francisco peace conference which finalized the details of the peace treaty with Japan – while the then allied USSR was also not present to make China's case. As a result none of China's territorial claims, which had been promised to the country when it had been a Western ally under Chiang Kai-shek in 1945, were included in the final treaty. Japan's treaty, signed the following year with the Western aligned Taiwan based Republic of China, noted that Tokyo renounced all claims to the strategic islands in the region – former possessions of the Japanese Empire. The fact that a government in China disapproved of by the Western Bloc had come to power meant that China was not internationally recognized, and could not have its territories restored to it by Japan. There is little doubt therefore that if China was still the ROC, a close Western ally, all of its claims to the South China Sea – those currently derided by the West as threats to regional stability – would have been recognized.

While sovereignty over the disputed islands remained ambiguous, so long as the Western powers recognized the Republic of China based in Taipei, as the legitimate Chinese government and refused the PRC a seat at the United Nations, the islands were widely considered to be 'Chinese' territory and possessions of the Republic of China. From 1950 until 1979 when the United States still recognized the ROC government, American ships continued to apply for permission from Taipei to carry out mapping and nautical surveys off the islands as if it were the country's own territory, showing their recognition of a 'Chinese' claim.[15] These islands are now claimed as disputed by the Western Bloc as a result of both the altered status of Taiwan and the West's animosity towards Beijing.

It was only in the late 1970s when 'China' became synonymous with the Beijing based PRC government, which was not a Western client state as the ROC was, that the Western Bloc ceased to recognize 'Chinese' sovereignty over the islands and began to challenge its claims. This scenario is similar to that regarding the ROC and PRC's claims to Tibet, with those of the Western client state 'China' being irrefutably recognized and those of the independent PRC 'China' being made into a serious international dispute – in accordance with the strategic interests of the Western Bloc (see Chapter 3). Taiwan's continuing claims in the South China Sea are based on the very same evidence of China itself, and with China perceiving Taiwan to be a part of the same nation, Beijing has not opposed Taipei's claims.

With the re-emergence of territorial disputes with neighboring countries in the 1980s, Beijing took extensive measures to prevent these from harming relations with regional partners and avoided asserting its claims too strongly. Chinese Premier Deng Xiaoping proposed that such disputes be shelved and settled by 'wisdom of future generations.' As he told Filipino President Corazon Aquino in 1988: 'we can set aside this issue for the time being and take the approach of pursuing joint development.' Premier Deng underlined the importance of not letting 'this issue stand in the way of China's friendship with the Philippines and other countries.'[16] It was imperative for China not to let these disputes impair its relations with its neighbors – and at the time the lack of imminent security threats from the United States in the region meant that control of the islands was not critical to Chinese national security interests as it is today.

The Association of South East Asian Nations (ASEAN) has also taken measures to prevent tensions arising from territorial disputes through the establishment of the mutual Declaration on the Conduct of Parties in the South China Sea (DCPSCS) signed by ASEAN members and China in 2002. It laid out a consensual framework agreed to by all parties on how to proceed with seabed exploration and infrastructure development in disputed areas. Between the mediating role of ASEAN and China's restraint and prioritization of bilateral relations over asserting territorial claims, disputes were long considered a minor issue in a region which was growing increasingly economically interdependent, with relations between China and its neighbors rapidly improving as trade boomed. The violation of DCPSCS by a number of parties did increase tensions, but such issues tended to be resolved regionally through ASEAN.

Seeking greater involvement in the Asia-Pacific region as Asian economies became increasingly interdependent and less dependent on the West, the United States found that re-stoking the near dormant territorial disputes an ideal pretext for intervention. While the U.S. claimed the role of a mediator, its policy soon turned to a hardline stance against China's claims[17] – claims which Washington had de-facto recognized years before when made by the Republic of China. The U.S. attempted to create a rift between ASEAN and China by trying to create an American led consortium of Southeast Asian nations – if possible all of ASEAN – to formally and unilaterally declare Chinese activities to protect its claims in the South China Sea a threat to regional stability.[18] The regional initiatives towards an independent ASEAN-Chinese brokered agreement thus stalled or broke down altogether.[19]

To be able to create such a rift in the South China Sea the United States made effective use of one invaluable asset, its significant influence over several developing Southeast Asian nations. In particular the effective neo-colony of the Philippines was invaluable to sparking tensions at the very moment when the United States needed them to justify its 'Asia Pivot.' In key speech in July 2010 in Hanoi by U.S. Secretary of State Hillary Clinton, a key architect of the Obama Doctrine, she declared for the first time that the South China Sea was a sphere of U.S. 'national interest' and pledged greater American involvement in resolving the disputes. These disputes had until then been of negligible importance even within the region – let alone internationally. Immediately afterwards the government in Manila, as if on cue, took to the offensive and unilaterally invited foreign companies to drill for oil in disputed waters – breaking the ASEAN agreements which stipulated that such actions in disputed waters could only be undertaken jointly with other claimants.[20] The country's actions seriously undermined ASEAN brokered agreements which had for so long kept tensions to a minimum, and by doing so the Philippines was giving the United States exactly the pretext it required to follow through with the pledges made by Secretary Clinton in Hanoi – to involve itself in the regional disputes.

In response to Filipino attempts to unilaterally assert its claims in the disputed waters, to which it also laid claim, China began to station a permanent garrison on the Scarborough Shoal to protect its interests. China's actions were in violation of the ASEAN agreements and the spirit of Premier Deng's agreements to avoid tensions, but by then these had already been violated by the Philippines' moves to unilaterally explore for oil and were deemed by Beijing to be a necessary response. Similarly, though the construction of airstrips on disputed islands and the militarization of the region was against the spirit of the regional agreement, China began to construct airstrips on islands under its control as well as building numerous artificial islands on reefs in the territory it claimed. The construction of airstrips in disputed territories had however first been carried out by Taiwan, Vietnam, Malaysia and the Philippines on Taiping, Swallow Reef, Spratly island and Thitu respectively. It was only afterwards that China began to construct its own airstrips on the islands. As Beijing officially claimed in 2015: 'We have simply repeated what everyone else is doing.'[21]

China's construction of artificial islands on which it subsequently built extensive military facilities were in fact not in response to the construction of such facilities by regional powers, which had been occurring long before China initiated its own island construction program and preceded the Obama Doctrine by several years. Rather, they were initiated in response to the United States' growing military presence in the region and threats this posed to Chinese trade routes – though the fact that other claimants had previously carried out similar efforts did much to legitimize China's actions. U.S. war plans in the early 2010s began to increasingly refer to the importance of 'offshore control,' the ability to blockade China's trade in both the South China Sea and the Malacca Strait to cripple its economy.[22,23] U.S. Secretary of State Rex Tillerson would further threaten in 2017 to deploy the U.S. Navy to waters claimed by China to unilaterally blockade its access to islands it claimed as its own.[24]

Under the pretext of protecting freedom of navigation in the region, the United States military engaged in increasingly provocative maneuvers near Chinese controlled islands on numerous occasions. The Chinese Foreign Ministry has referred to such maneuvers by the U.S. Navy as having 'threatened China's sovereignty and security interests, jeopardized the safety of personnel and facilities on the reefs, and damaged regional peace and stability.'[25] Maneuvers were carried out by American nuclear capable strategic bombers as well as warships, with the Pentagon itself underlining the fact that bombers on these missions were under orders to ignore warnings from Chinese ground controllers.[26] The Commander of U.S. Pacific Air Forces General Lori Robinson was one of many who called on other nations to follow the example of the United States in conducting such maneuvers in waters claimed by China. She said regarding these maneuvers: 'We would encourage all nations in the region to do just that, just as the United States is doing.'[27] Such calls received at best a lukewarm reception from ASEAN, and despite their various territorial disputes with China these states have been highly reluctant to actively deploy force as part of the American initiative targeting Beijing while failing to directly sanction the actions of the United States military.[28,29,30] Other Western powers have been far more receptive however – deploying military assets to the region in support of the American initiative. As the perceived threats to its security have grown, China has moved to strengthen its defenses in the South China Sea and deploy effective anti-access area denial weapons systems to protect its interests amid escalating military involvement by the United States and a number of its European allies.[31,32]

The Asia-Pacific region as a whole had only to lose from the exacerbation of tensions over minor territorial disputes, hence both Premier Deng's calls to leave them to future generations and prioritize maintaining good relations with neighboring countries and the ASEAN agreements to manage territorial disputes agreed to by all nations staking a territorial claim. The United States, through its attempts to push tensions over the brink and make them a major international issue which it has allocated itself a leading role in resolving – has taken actions which are to the detriment of the interests of all regional powers. This in turn has served as a pretext to increase its military presence in the strategically critical waterways. The exacerbation in regional tensions meanwhile threatens to derail peace and stability, and as a result economic growth and prosperity in a region which is today the greatest emerging economic rival to the United States and the wider Western world. It is not without reason therefore that the United States and its allies can seek to benefit from promoting discord and conflict in the Asia-Pacific region – an effective means of intervening to undermine the stability of many of the world's fastest rising economic powers.

Chinese Premier Xi observed regarding the growing regional tensions and the Western powers' 'military first' approach to the situation: 'What the Asia-Pacific countries care about most is to maintain economic prosperity and build on the momentum of economic growth and regional cooperation. At a time when people long for peace, stability and development, to deliberately give prominence to the military security agenda, scale up military deployment and strengthen military alliances is not really what most countries in the region hope to see.'[33] Fears that intervention by Western powers would promote conflict in the prosperous Asia-Pacific region were voiced by Chinese state news agency Xinhua, which commented regarding the 'Pivot to Asia': 'There's no need for countries outside the region to forcibly dictate how affairs should be managed in the South China Sea. That should be left to the countries of East and Southeast Asia.' The agency warned that the West threatened to bring chaos to the Pacific as it had to the Middle East, and turn a prosperous Asia into a war zone.[34]

Noam Chomsky, a prominent MIT professor, political analyst and a hardline critic of American adversaries in the Asia-Pacific, China and North Korea foremost among them, nevertheless noted regarding the double standards of the American position in the region under the Obama Doctrine: 'The security dilemma arises over control of the seas off China's coasts. The United States regards its policy of controlling these waters as "defensive," while China regards it as threatening; correspondingly, China regards its actions in nearby areas as "defensive," while the United States regards them as threatening. No such debate is even imaginable concerning U.S. coastal waters. This "classic security dilemma" makes sense, again, on the assumption that the United States has a right to control most of the world, and that U.S. security requires something approaching absolute global control.'[35] The Chinese Foreign Ministry stated in much the same vein that 'freedom of navigation' was only a pretext for the assertion of regional hegemony and as 'violent means by which the U.S. promotes its unilateral claims.' It was a testament to 'the hegemonic logic of the U.S. towards international maritime order.'[36]

Ultimately due to a number of factors discussed in the previous chapter, namely the fast shifting military balance between China and the U.S. led Western Bloc and the unsustainability of a Western favoring balance of power in the Asia-Pacific region, the ability of the U.S. and its Western allies to pose a threat to Chinese shipping or realistically challenge the fast growth capabilities of the People's Liberation Army is increasingly limited. With even China's outlying fortified islets in the South China Sea today proving extremely challenging targets for Western navies due to the state of the art anti-access area denial weapons systems and combat jets deployed,[37] it is likely that the Western Bloc's 'freedom of navigation' patrols will not materialize into anything more than a nuisance, albeit a potentially dangerous one if improperly handled, for Beijing and Southeast Asian states. A return to dialogue and a form of joint sovereignty between China and ASEAN over disputed territories and their resources remain a distinct possibility and likely outcome in the long term.

Support From the Wider Western Bloc for the Pivot to Asia

While the United States, increasingly emphasizing its identity as a Pacific power, saw a surge in its military presence in the Asia-Pacific region during the eight-year presidency of Barack Obama, other Western powers have increasingly begun to deploy their own forces to support American efforts in the region. The reason for this is beyond an inclination to help a superpower ally in the Pacific. Leading European military powers, the armed forces of which have been increasingly overstretched in recent years, have made efforts to involve themselves in the Pacific due to the imperative of maintaining the centuries-long Western-dominated balance of power in what is arguably the world's most strategically critical region. Doing so is not just essential to U.S. interests, but to the interests of the Western Bloc as a whole since long before the United States involved itself. It is the primacy of the entire bloc that is at stake should the 'Asian order' become, for the first time in centuries, dominated by regional rather than external powers and the West's aforementioned 'position of disparity' with Asia be lost.

British Defence Secretary Michael Fallon attested to the Western Bloc's common interests in the United States' Pivot to Asia to respond to 'the emergence of China as a global power.' He stated in 2012, shortly after the implementation of the Obama Doctrine, that: 'the European NATO powers should welcome the fact that the U.S. is willing to engage in this new strategic challenge *on behalf of the alliance*.'[38] European imperial powers maintain a long history of operating in Asia – including in numerous wars against China. France, Germany, Italy, Britain, Sweden, Norway, Portugal, Austria, Hungary, the Netherlands and Spain all signed Unequal Treaties which they imposed on China using military force, granting their citizens extreme privileges in the country and immunity from the rule of law.[39] Since then the continued primacy and living standards of Europe have largely relied on no region rivalling its technology, education, economy and military, or as George Kennan, chair of the State Department's Policy Planning staff referred to it, the 'position of disparity'[40] between one's own wealth and advanced economies relative to those of the rest of the world – and Asia in particular.

Britain has led Europe in pledging further involvement in East Asia, and in 2015 the country announced plans to double the number of personnel involved in war games in Malaysia.[41] British Marines were in 2016 deployed to Japan for the first time in decades,[42] and in October of that year Royal Air Force (RAF) made an unprecedented deployment of its Eurofighter Typhoon fighters to Misawa airbase in Japan – referred to by an RAF officer as 'probably the most ambitious deployment that the Air Force has done to the Far East.' Tensions with China and preparation to participate in possible preventative strikes on North Korean targets were the stated reasons for this deployment.[43] In December the British envoy to the United States pledged that his country would increase its military presence in the South China Sea – which included sending the country's two aircraft carriers to the region.[44] This pledge was later reiterated by Foreign Minister Boris Johnson,[45] and the first carrier was dispatched to the region in early 2019. Britain has also increasingly taken a leading role in military drills alongside its American ally in the region, including jointly carrying out simulated strikes against North Korea's leadership using its Air Force.[46] Sources from the leadership of the British Royal Navy the following year indicated the country was willing to provide whatever support it could to a potential American attack on North Korean targets should Washington initiate a preventative war.[47] Several British warships have since taken a leading role in patrolling near the Korean Peninsula to closely monitor North Korean shipping and clamp down on potential violations of economic sanctions – alongside military assets from Australia, New Zealand and Japan.[48]

It is notable that amid moves to escalate its involvement in the Asia-Pacific region, Britain's armed forces have faced deep budget cuts[49] as a result of the country's severe economic difficulties which have forced the termination of several key military programs.[50,51] As the navies of several prominent Asia-Pacific nations have rapidly expanded and modernized alongside their economic ascendance, the British Royal Navy has been one of several formerly formidable Western military services which has fallen into a sharp quantitative and qualitative decline.[52,53] Qualitatively British assets have, alongside much of the rest of Europe, fared little better despite their phenomenal costs by Asian or American standards. While British warships were at the cutting edge during the Cold War with those of France and other European states close behind, they are today well below the standards of the United States, China, South Korea, and other Asian powers. Compounding quantitative and qualitative shortcomings, maintenance has also been a key issue in a number of European states, Britain included, which have left its real operational capabilities at a fraction of what they may appear on paper.

The Royal Navy in 2017 saw the vast majority of its vessels, 75 percent, fall into disrepair due to lack of funds for maintenance.[54] British warships have broken down at sea on several occasions as a result,[55,56] and the Navy is forced to keep its destroyer fleet in port most of the time despite its meagre size of just six ships. (To put this in perspective Japan has almost 40 and South Korea has 12. China adds approximately six to its fleet every year – and these are considerably more sophisticated and heavily armed than their British counterparts.). The Navy has struggled to operate even basic disaster relief exercises in British overseas territories, with First Sea Lord West referring to a 'hollowing out of defense' due to austerity which seriously compromised the capabilities of the armed forces.[57] First Sea Lord Admiral Sir George Zambellas similarly warned in 2017 that Britain was set to 'disappear into a Third World nation, security-wise' as a result of steep cuts to its already inadequate defense budget. He referred to the Royal Navy as the 'bottom of the efficiency barrel' – noting the service's struggle to accomplish simple tasks such as humanitarian missions to victims of Hurricane Irma in the British Caribbean Islands.[58] Global power projection aspirations aside, the Royal Navy's ability to perform the most essential task – patrolling Britain's own territorial waters – has itself been called to serious question.[59]

A 2016 report by the British parliamentary Defence Committee stated that the Royal Navy was 'way below the critical mass required for the many tasks which could confront it' with a critically overstretched fleet, the size of which was 'already pathetically low.'[60] This came amid reports by the country's National Audit Office of crumbling military infrastructure due to lack of investment, which seriously undermined the country's capabilities.[61] The Air Force fared little better, with only 137 serviceable combat aircraft as of 2017, many of them almost four decades old. The situation is unlikely to improve.[62] Economic difficulties, particularly the steep fall of the British pound, have also made the cancellation of up to half of the Navy and Air Force's initial orders for new fighters a distinct possibility – an issue which is set to stifle a number of the country's future weapons programs.[63,64] As the second most indebted nation in the world,[65] the fact that Britain has prioritized deployments to East Asia so highly despite the extremely poor and declining state of its military and economy indicate the importance of maintaining a favorable Western dominated balance of power in the Asia-Pacific. As a key facilitator of Western primacy, its importance to British interests and those of the wider Western Bloc cannot be overstated.

Alongside Britain and the United States, France has also moved to escalate its military involvement in the Asia-Pacific region. Much as in Britain's case, this has come despite deep cuts to its naval and air fleets since the Cold War, low levels of serviceability for its major assets – fighter jets in particular – and a considerably qualitative disadvantage particularly in its navy relative to either the United States or the major powers of the Asia-Pacific. Defense Minister Jean-Yves Le Drian nevertheless emphasized that it was in the interests of all European nations to support the 'Obama Doctrine' and strongly encouraged the deployment of armed forces to patrol waters claimed by China – with France assuming a leading role in this initiative. European naval patrols had to be 'regular and visible,' according to Le Drain.[66] France has since reinstated its dubious claim to be a 'Pacific Power,' contributing its strategically located Pacific colonial territories of New Caledonia and French Polynesia to the Western Bloc's joint efforts in the region.[67] France sent carrier warships to conduct joint military drills with Japan, the United States and the United Kingdom in East Asia, which were led by the French themselves and practiced offensive operations including amphibious landings to capture enemy territory. There was little doubt among British, Chinese or Russian media that these drills were conducted with China and North Korea in mind.[68,69]

France perceives China's rise to be a threat not only to the Western led Pacific order, but also to its economic interests in 'Francophone Africa,' France's imperial-era sphere of influence on which its modern economic prosperity is heavily reliant. China's growing diplomatic and economic ties with a number of former French colonies, Paris' effective neo-colonies, are perceived as a threat to France's hegemonic leadership and dominance in the region.[70] France's extreme reliance on benefits from its African former colonies and the potentially catastrophic impacts for the European state's fragile economy should its privileges in the region be undermined was attested to by former French President Jacques Chirac, who said in reference to 'Francophone Africa': 'Without Africa, France will slide down into the rank of a third world power.'[71] His predecessor, Francois Mitterrand, similarly stated in regards to the same issue: 'Without Africa, France will have no history in the 21st century.'[72] France has shown itself willing to use military force to protect this critical and resource rich sphere of influence,[73] and its increasing involvement in East Asian military drills aimed at undermining China's own interests may well be partly in response to this.

A wider coalition of Western powers has increasingly involved itself in the Pacific, and military personnel from Britain, France, Italy, Denmark, Australia, Canada and New Zealand have since 2016 all taken part in massive U.S. led military drills in South Korea. These drills practiced preventative strikes, an invasion of North Korea and decapitation of its leadership. Launching strikes on civilian targets including major cities were part of the drills.[74] The involvement of several European states strongly indicates that many Western military powers would contribute militarily to a U.S. led war effort in Asia should it break out. At a time when the United States was actively rehearsing for the initiation of preventative war on North Korea, NATO Secretary General Jens Stoltenberg himself attested to the importance of the Western alliance's involvement in America's conflict with the East Asian state[75] with high expectations that European military involvement on the peninsula was expected to grow.[76] During military exercises, forces involved also practiced for operations on the Russian and Chinese borders, with a senior South Korean defense official stating: 'This year's operations will involve recovering key facilities that are located deep within North Korea, all the way near its northern borders. The scenario will include the special operations forces being deployed to border areas adjacent to China and Russia.'[77] Several leading European military powers have increasingly involved themselves in military exercises targeting not only North Korea, but also Russia and increasingly China. Preparations for incursions deep into North Korean territory and operations on the country's Chinese and Russian borders are part of a growing trend in this regard.

A full scale war in Korea would almost certainly involve China and Russia, with the former having committed to intervene on the side of the DPRK should the United States initiate a war against it and being under treaty obligation to do so[78,79] and the latter strongly warning that it would not accept a U.S. attack on its Korean neighbor[80,81] and indicating that any U.S. attack on North Korea would be seen as an 'openly hostile' act towards Russia.[82] When tensions on the peninsula spiked in 2017 and the

U.S. threatened air and missile strikes against the DPRK, both China and Russia deployed advanced air defense systems and other high end assets near their the Korean borders – providing coverage over much of the peninsula and allowing them to intervene to prevent any unilateral military action which could lead to a wider conflict.[83,84] Such a war could very possibly pit a U.S. led alliance of Western powers directly against North Korea, China and Russia.

For China in particular, with a sizeable and growing alliance of Western powers pledging to deploy force to waters Beijing views as part of its own territory, Western actions appear highly reminiscent of the Eight Nation Alliance of imperialist military powers at the time of the Opium Wars – a conflict which brought about a century of humiliation and national decline. A cause for reservation among European powers in deploying their militaries to Asia has been their lack of power projection capabilities – with none of their navies amounting to even a fraction of the potency of that of the United States and the capabilities of their few aircraft carriers and destroyers dubious at best relative to those of more capable naval powers such as Japan, the U.S. and South Korea. European NATO members have repeatedly demonstrated staggering inefficiencies in defense, with few parallels elsewhere in the world, and resultingly extremely limited military capabilities – despite colossal military spending of approximately $200 billion annually between them. This was brought to light particularly by their underwhelming performance in the campaign against Libya in 2011, an incident which forced the United States to intervene heavily on their behalf to an extent it had not previously anticipated.[85] Performance in the Libyan campaign was but one of several incidents which strongly indicated that European militaries will very likely be out of their league in anything more than a very basic supporting role in the Asia-Pacific. Europe's lack of several critical high end military capabilities is also a factor, as is its preoccupation with contributing to both U.S. military coalitions in the Middle East and to the U.S. led military buildup near Russia's borders in Eastern Europe. As Europe faces a severe economic crisis, negligible growth and mounting debt, to allocate such funds to military operations so far from its borders, while strategically critical, remains extremely difficult both to fund and to justify publicly.

Moral Crusades: Western Pretexts for Intervention in the Asia-Pacific Region

While the West's centuries long need to assert military dominance over the Asia-Pacific has been motivated by the region's economic and strategic importance, Western empires have long depicted themselves as interventionist due to altruistic rather than imperialist motives. Pretexts for military action have included civilizing missions, spreading the word of God, protecting freedom of trade, democratization and the overthrow of 'tyrannical' Asian leaders, protection from communism, and most perhaps prominently in the 2010s freedom of navigation – among others. As renowned American philosopher Professor Edward Said noted in regard to pretexts for imperial domination and military intervention: 'Every single empire in its official discourse has said that it is not like all the others, that its circumstances are special, that it has a mission to enlighten, civilize, bring order and democracy, and that it uses force only as a last resort.'[86] The history of Western intervention in the Asia-Pacific is a case in point.

Caroline Elkins, professor of history at Harvard University, similarly noted in her study of severe British war crimes in East Africa during the Cold War: 'Whether it's Britain's "civilizing mission" or America's "freedom and democracy," the dark side of Western imperialism and the official wisdom behind it has not changed much in the last 50 years.'[87] Regarding the United States' first large scale military intervention in the Asia-Pacific region, and the pretexts under which not only aggression but also what he claimed were severe war crimes being carried out, renowned American writer and journalist Mark Twain noted his country was 'subjugating the remaining tens of millions by Benevolent Assimilation, which is the pious new name of the musket.'[88] The use of altruistic pretexts have all served as effective covers for the prevailing purpose of the Western nations' military involvement in the Asia-Pacific region – which have included gaining privileged access to natural resources in Southeast Asia, improving the balance of trade with China by fostering a reliance on opium imports, the elimination of rival empires as per the Pacific War with Japan and more recently maintaining the West's dominance over and position of economic disparity with Asian states.

The Western imperial powers initially came to dominate the Asia-Pacific region through gunboat diplomacy, which was essentially state-level piracy that allowed each European empire to impose taxation and reorganize regional trade to enrich itself through force. This left most of the region subservient to Western interests, whose claim to the region came from their military might. The United States has since 1945 taken the place of Britain, France, the Netherlands and Portugal as the leading Western imperial power in the region – with influential U.S. policymakers having openly advocated a role for their country modelled on that of the British Empire. Richard N. Haass, senior fellow at the highly influential Council on Foreign Relations and Director of Foreign Policy Studies at the Brookings Institution, published in Foreign Affairs in 1999 regarding the United States' role as an imperial power of the twenty-first century: 'American foreign policy must project an imperial dimension ... [and] organize the world along certain principles affecting both relations between states and conditions within them. The U.S. role should resemble that of nineteenth-century Great Britain.'[89] Considering the conduct of American foreign policy in the Asia-Pacific region, this has largely been heeded and a new 'gunboat diplomat' has emerged.

The role of 'gunboat diplomat' has involved Western navies dominating Pacific sea routes for centuries, with one dominant Western military power taking on the role since the Portuguese Navy first established colonies in the region in the early sixteenth century – over 500 years ago. The importance of control of the Pacific has long been clear to Western imperial powers. As renowned New Zealand professor of Security Studies Dr Robert Ayson noted: 'The mainstay of America's military presence in the [Asia-Pacific] region had long been at sea rather than on the land, continuing the pattern of Western maritime supremacy in Asia. That pattern had been largely unbroken since the Portuguese explorer Vasco da Gama sailed into Asian waters at the end of the fifteenth century, beginning what [Australian professor] Coral Bell described as "500 years of ascendancy of the West over Asia." The U.S. Seventh Fleet was always the supreme part of America's presence in the region, because it represented a unique post-war capacity to project armed force, including via America's aircraft carrier battle groups.'[90]

Coercion and military interventionism have long been the crux and key facilitator of the West's supremacy and a central part of their foreign relations – as ever disguised as altruism. As Dr Peter Frankopan, Oxford University research fellow and professor of history, noted regarding the initial rise of the West: 'European warfare had an even more important role, it prompted the rise of the west. Discussions about Europe in this period attempt to emphasize that the Enlightenment and the Age of Reason saw a coming of age where ideas of absolutism were replaced by notions of freedom, rights and liberty. But it was Europe's entrenched relationship with violence and militarism [following centuries of brutal wars with one another] that allowed it to place itself at the center of the world ... Europe's distinctive character as more aggressive, more unstable and less peace-minded that other parts of the world now paid off [as opposed to a commitment to freedoms and positive virtues].'[91] Professor of History and author Tonio Andrade similarly noted that it was not 'enlightenment' or even science which led the West to first achieve primacy, but rather that Europeans were far better at waging war because they experienced it far more frequently than states such as China. It was this primarily which led to Western dominance.[92]

Senior Fellow with the EastWest Institute think tank, military analyst and Associate Editor with *The Diplomat*, Franz-Stefan Gady reached a similar conclusion, noting that Europe did not have a military technological advantage over leading Asian powers but rather was far more experienced in warfare due to the less peaceful nature of the continent, resulting in more effective applications of often inferior technology which provided a significant advantage. The European powers did not have a monopoly of advanced weaponry, or even necessarily an advantage in firepower when they conquered Asia. Gady noted as an example that the British Empire in India often found itself outgunned by the artillery forces of the Mughal Empire, which were not only more numerous but also far superior in their capabilities.[93] Against the Tipu Sultanate the British faced the world's first iron-cased rockets, a predecessor to modern missiles and rocked artillery which far eclipsed anything any Western power had ever developed, and these were used to devastating effect against British forces.[94,95] What the Western powers did have however was experience from the near constant wars waged on their own continent, a result of Europe's 'less peaceful nature,' allowing them to develop modern military drills and techniques – perfection of the 'volley fire' being but one example – which gave them a lethal edge in war. This 'entrenched relationship with violence' was the key – though effective application of the divide and rule strategy would often prove a very significant asset. Based on his own extensive research on the subject Philip T. Hoffman, author of *Why Did Europe Conquer the World* and Harvard Professor of History, similarly noted that it was not 'enlightenment' or technology which gave Western powers an advantage – but rather a longstanding relationship with violence beyond what any of the scientifically advanced but peaceful Asian powers had experienced.[96]

Regarding pretexts the West has used for its continued military presence and right to forcefully intervene in the Asia-Pacific region, little has changed over centuries. When the European powers, namely Britain and France, waged a war against China in the 1850s they pillaged and destroyed the country with the same sense of moral superiority that other Western imperial powers currently claim over China. Indeed the current rhetoric towards China as well as North Korea is somewhat reminiscent of that during the Opium War. The British press reported at the time: 'Thus it has been the destiny of England to break down a government fabric ... to uncover to its own subjects its hollowness and its evils.'[97,98] The very same theme and idea persist, with remarkably similar pretexts still in use – that the West is intervening with its military and wreaking untold destruction to 'free' Asian people from 'authoritarianism' or 'communism' to bring them Western 'democratic values.' The theme of an American war against North Korea today for example being strongly in the interests of the Korean people remains highly prevalent in Western reporting today – though if one were to ask Koreans on either side of the 38th Parallel such logic would seem absurd.[99] Had the relatively prosperous Chinese in the first half of the nineteenth century read Western news, they would have been similarly confounded as the Koreans are today – particularly following the war's end when the effective collapse of the state and brutalities of the invading powers led to possibly the very darkest period in thousands of years of Chinese history.

Other reports from British press further stated that the Chinese government's 'mysterious and exclusive barbarism' could only be dismantled, for the good of its own people, by 'the force of active and intrusive Western Civilization.'[100,101] The language of a moral crusade was ultimately used to justify a war fought to ensure that the British Empire would maintain the rights to sell drugs to China, addiction to which was rampant and devastating the country until Mao Zedong's anti-drug campaign in the 1950s. The crippling of China in the aftermath of the Opium Wars allowed Western imperial powers to extract substantial economic, territorial and legal concessions – all under the guise of promoting free trade, enlightenment and civilization. Today Western powers again seek to stifle Asia's growth, and cement their own leadership and supremacy in the region based on justifications similar to those of the first Western 'gunboat diplomats' – and should this succeed the consequences for China and for the region will likely be similarly dire.

A Pivot From the Middle East: What Could Accompany the U.S. Military in its Move to Asia?

Before the United States' initiation of the Obama Doctrine and beginning of the 'Pivot to Asia,' the country's primary region of strategic focus had for decades been the Middle East and North Africa (MENA). This was a region which by the early 2010s had seen its few secular and progressive governments, most of them Russian aligned, undermined by US-led efforts to be replaced by sectarian or radical Islamist forces – as in the cases of Afghanistan, Egypt, Libya and much of Iraq and Syria. MENA saw the deaths of tens of thousands annually in war, suffering from an escalating cycle of bloodshed and sectarianism – and all wars in the region without exception had significant U.S. and Western involvement. MENA was left largely under the control of various state and non-state radical Islamist forces, from the Islamist governments imposing strict Sharia law in most of the Persian Gulf to prominent ISIS and Al Qaeda linked groups in Iraq, Libya, Syria, Afghanistan, Yemen, Sinai and Lebanon. The most prominent of these non-state Islamist forces had established themselves with arms and funding from Western powers to undermine secular governments such as Syria, Libya, Egypt and Afghanistan and which had at various stages opposed the Western Bloc's regional designs.

Congresswoman Cynthia McKinney, member of the U.S. House of Representatives, stated regarding the 'Pivot to Asia' and prospects for the region: 'Given what has happened to the Arab World with U.S. attention, the rest of Asia must shudder at the prospect of what could happen to it with President Obama's new doctrine: Pivot to Asia.'[102] Indeed, observing the United States and its allies' history of intervention and the parties it has supported politically, militarily and financially to further its strategic interests in MENA, one can hardly be optimistic about the impacts of increased Western intervention in Asia. This has not been lost on Asian analysts themselves, nor on the government of the People's Republic of China. Chinese state run news agency Xinhua noted in response to increased Western involvement in the Pacific: 'Western countries have a long history of failing to establish orderly rule over parts of the world. The Middle East is a classic example. Their intervention has led to chaos in Syria, Iraq and Libya. The Asia-Pacific has become a rising global economic power because of decades of regional peace and stability. Should Western countries intervene in the South China Sea and its surroundings, that stability would quickly come to an end. The Asia-Pacific would likely become another Middle East.'[103]

An understanding of the role of the Western Bloc in supporting a number of radical Islamist groups over several decades, which have been key to destabilizing a number of 'non-compliant' Soviet and Russian aligned states in the Cold War and its aftermath, has key implications for the Asia-Pacific – particularly considering the Western Bloc's growing animosity towards China. Just as the Soviet Union's sphere of influence in the Muslim world was undermined by Western-backed Islamist organizations, so too could these same agents of terror be employed to undermine the growing Chinese spheres of influence in Southeast and Central Asia as the Western powers increasingly turn their attentions eastwards. An understanding of the preceding history of Western support for Islamist forces therefore remains critical.

Examples of Western support for jihadist groups in MENA include U.S. intelligence's close ties with the Muslim Brotherhood in the 1950s and 1960s in the United Arab Republic to undermine its secular Soviet aligned government, the arming of the Islamic Mujahedeen[104] and Al Qaeda in the 1980s[105,106,107] to undermine the Soviet aligned Democratic Republic of Afghanistan and target the Soviet military, support for Al Qaeda linked militants to overthrow the Russian aligned government of Libya in 2011, as detailed in the emails of Secretary of State Hillary Clinton,[108] and more recently extensive support for Al Qaeda-linked jihadist groups in the 2010s to wage war on the government of Syria – Russia's leading regional partner.[109,110] Russia's General Staff alleged in December 2017 that the U.S. was hosting training camps for Islamist militants in Syria, including former members Islamic State terror group, citing data from satellite and other surveillance assets.[111] According to the Russian Defense Ministry and numerous other Russian military sources involved in counterterror operations in Syria, the United States has also given extensive support to the Islamic State (IS) terror group in the country on numerous occasions to further its foreign policy goals – namely the removal of the Syrian government.[112,113] The Defense Ministry noted on several occasions that U.S. military-controlled 'safe zones' in Syria became staging grounds for terror groups to launch attacks on Russian and Syrian forces.[114] The U.S. was also tacitly accused of providing IS and other jihadist groups with key intelligence using its advanced surveillance assets, which were key facilitators of jihadist drone and precision strikes launched against Russian forces on several occasions.[115,116]

Russia's repeated allegations of U.S. support for terror groups in Syria were supported unanimously by almost all non-Western parties with military forces on the ground in Syria, including the Iranian military which has been extensively involved in counterterrorism operations. Iran's deputy chief of staff General Mostafa Izadi in June 2017 alleged that the United States was using terrorist groups to wage 'proxy warfare' and were directly supporting Islamic State to fight its enemies – namely the Syrian and Iranian governments.[117] Syria's own government has also repeatedly claimed that the Western Bloc has been extensively supporting radical Islamist terror groups in the country since the outbreak of the war.[118] Turkish President Recep Tayyip Erdoğan, leader of a NATO member state whose relations with Syria and Russia have often been extremely hostile, also claimed in October 2017 that he had 'confirmed evidence' of U.S. and other Western nations' support for the Islamic State terror group among others. He stated: 'Islamic State, Al Qaeda, PKK – behind all these organizations you will see the shadow of the West ... They receive very serious financial support.'[119] The United States notably suspended its visa services to Turkey hours after these allegations were made in October 2017.[120] With thousands of Turkish military personnel deployed to both Iraq and Syria for counter-terrorism operations, the Turkish president's claims strongly supported those of both non-Western nations operating in the country, and were highly consistent with United States' history of supporting terror groups against its adversaries.[121]

Allegations that the United States was providing support to Islamist insurgents in Syria were tacitly supported by allegations from within the U.S. Congress, with Rep. Tulsi Gabbard accusing the U.S. president in September 2018 of 'standing up to protect the 20,000 to 40,000 Al Qaeda and other jihadist forces in Syria, and threatening Russia, Syria and Iran with military force if they dare attack these terrorists.' The Congresswoman referred to the U.S. Commander in Chief as acting 'as the protective big brother of Al Qaeda and other jihadists,'[122] and previously put forward the Stop Arming Terrorists Act (H.R. 608) alongside fourteen co-sponsors to prevent the Obama administration from using federal agency funds to provide covert assistance to Al Qaeda, Jabhat Fateh al-Sham, Islamic State, or any of their affiliates.[123,124] The Congresswoman's more recent allegations indicate that the policy of supporting jihadist groups has been carried forward by the Trump administration – and are supported by a number of claims that the United States has provided effective 'safe zones' to Islamic terrorists in Syria.[125] Jihadist strongholds granted Western protection in Syria,[126] the province of Idlib – the world's foremost Al Qaeda safe heaven according to leading experts at the U.S. state department[127] – being a prime example, have been used as effective staging grounds for terror attacks into Syrian territory and beyond. Writing for *Forbes* magazine, former Special Assistant to President Ronald Reagan, Senior Fellow at the renowned Cato Institute think tank Doug Bandow was thus one of many prominent analysts who referred to the policy of both the Obama and Trump administrations as 'turning Syria over to a mix of radicals, jihadists, and terrorists.'[128]

The United States has directly supported Islamist groups elsewhere in the world, including in Indonesia where they conducted acts of terrorism to undermine the Sukarno government[129] and in Bosnia as a means of combating Serb forces in the 1990s – where thousands of veterans from the Afghan 'Jihad' against the USSR the previous decade were aided by the Pentagon in redeploying to Eastern Europe to fight the Western Bloc's new enemy. Richard Holbrooke, America's chief Balkans peace negotiator, recalled that deployment of the Mujahedeen from Afghanistan was key to the survival of Western aligned Bosnian forces against the Russian aligned Serbs in that conflict.[130] In Chechnya the Mujahedeen terror group were trained and armed by the CIA – as detailed by the U.S. Congressional Task Force on Terrorism and Unconventional Warfare's director Yossef Bodansky[131] and CIA National Council on Intelligence's Deputy Director Graham E. Fuller.[132] Fuller notably wrote of the CIA's 'policy of guiding the evolution of Islam and of helping them against our adversaries.'[133] Russian and Turkish allegations regarding the more recent incident of U.S. support for Islamic State were given tacit support by the leaked emails of former U.S. Secretary of State Hillary Clinton, which revealed that the United States had largely turned a blind eye to its close Islamist Middle Eastern partners Saudi Arabia and Qatar's 'providing clandestine financial and logistic support to ISIS and other radical groups in the region.'[134] Allegations of support for such groups in the Syrian conflict are therefore hardly unfounded, neither is it impossible that such support could be given in future to similar such groups in other parts of the world, Western China and Southeast Asia being prominent examples, to further U.S. strategic goals in the Asia-Pacific region.

Tacitly supporting Deputy Director Fuller's claims, Saudi Arabian Crown Prince Mohammed Bin Salman stated in an interview with the *Washington Post* in April 2018 that the Western Bloc had during the Cold War requested that Riyadh take an active role in promoting the spread of Wahabist ideology, a radical branch of Sunni Islam adhered to by the

Mujahedeen in Afghanistan, Al Qaeda, the Taliban, and the Islamic State among other jihadist groups. This was done to help undermine the Soviet Union's sphere of influence in the Islamic World, a strategy which yielded favorable results for the Western powers in a number of Soviet and later Russian aligned Muslim countries including Afghanistan, Syria, Libya, Yugoslavia and even parts of Russia itself among several others.[135] This is likely what Deputy Director Fuller referred to regarding the CIA's 'policy of guiding the evolution of Islam and of helping them against our adversaries.'[136]

Alongside allegations of U.S. support for Islamic State and other military groups in Syria by a number of informed parties on the ground there, details of U.S. support for the terror group in Afghanistan have also emerged. Most notably former Afghan President Hamid Karzai, having served 13 years in his post and worked closely with the United States, noted regarding the U.S. nurturing of the terror group in his country: 'since the arrival Daesh [Islamic State] on the Afghan scene,' no action had been taken against them by the American military despite stationing tens of thousands of troops in the country. Karzai further stated: 'from the two years onwards to today, every day the local people, the local elders, government officials, media and others began to report that unmarked foreign helicopters, would go in and support extremists in all parts of the country ... there's a lot of evidence, unfortunately, that shows that these extremist forces are supplied from the foreign bases within Afghanistan.'[137] The only countries with sizeable 'foreign bases' in Afghanistan are the United States and its Western allies. It is notable that the same phenomenon, 'unmarked helicopters' allegedly U.S. linked supporting IS forces, was reported on numerous occasions in Syria, where the Western Bloc also retains a considerable military presence.[138]

Karzai continued: 'The support to Daesh [IS] in Afghanistan is not definitely meant for the purposes in Afghanistan. The U.S. has already established itself in Afghanistan. It doesn't need to have a reason to establish itself there. It must be for objectives beyond Afghanistan, to cause trouble in the region.'[139] Indeed, Karzai's allegations would hardly be unthinkable considering both the numerous precedents set for the United States supporting Islamist forces in Afghanistan and other regions, as well as the formidable asset the group's emergence in the country could provide the United States. An Islamic State presence bordering Iran, China and the Russian sphere of influence in Central Asia would have a severe destabilizing effect on all these U.S. adversaries, potentially spreading the insurgency to China's Sunni Muslim majority Xinjiang Autonomous Region as well as derailing the Chinese One Belt Road initiative to integrate Central Asian economies and develop trade routes through the region which would substantially benefit China's economy and enhance its regional influence. The U.S. Congressional Task Force on Terrorism and Unconventional Warfare's director, Yossef Bodansky, noted regarding plans to promote Islamic terrorism in Central Asia to undermine Russian interests: 'Islamist Jihad in the Caucasus as a way to deprive Russia of a viable pipeline route through spiraling violence and terrorism.'[140] As the region becomes increasingly critical to China's own interests, with Sino-Russian oil pipelines through Central Asia key to Beijing's plans to reduce reliance on vulnerable maritime oil imports, attempts to repeat such a strategy to undermine the West's new major adversary remain a considerably possibility.

The implications of the Western Bloc having persistently made use of a formidable terrorist apparatus to destabilize rival powers or undermine their interests abroad are manifold for the now fast rising Asia-Pacific region – today perceived to be the greatest threat to Western primacy. It is notable that as Islamic State forces saw unprecedented successes in Afghanistan in 2017, so too did Chinese security forces intercept an unprecedented number of 'trained jihadist fighters' attempting to enter China. This threat was particularly focused around Xinjiang Autonomous Region which borders Afghanistan. The number of jihadists captured showed a ten-fold increase on the previous year, and presented an imminent threat to the country's security.[141] With China already having faced Islamist terror attacks on civilian targets, notably widely blamed on Chinese authorities by Western media as a response to its alleged repression of Muslims,[142] should Islamic State's power continue to grow in Afghanistan it will present an imminent threat to Chinese security. The terror group has notably threatened to 'shed blood like rivers' and bring war to the PRC – an endeavor in which, based on the West's history for support of Islamist groups against its adversaries, it would very likely enjoy extensive Western backing.[143] China has responded to this threat by granting military aid including generous funding to Afghan security forces, as well as by mediating disputes and attempting to strengthen anti-terror co-operation between Afghanistan and Pakistan.[144] Both Pakistan and Myanmar, close Chinese partners lying on critical trade and energy routes respectively which are of great economic significance to China, are also highly vulnerable to the threat of Islamic terrorism – though the former has historically handled this threat far more effectively than the latter.

China for its part appears to perceive a considerable threat from the potential of a jihadist insurgency in its far west, and shortly following the rise of Islamic State in Afghanistan, the discovery of several thousand jihadists of Chinese origin in Syria operating under the Islamic State and a number of Al Qaeda affiliates, and direct attacks on Chinese interests – including the Chinese embassy in Kyrgyzstan in 2016[145] – by these groups, the country implemented a far reaching security campaign to curb the spread of Islamic extremism in the Xinjiang province. The rapid growth of Wahhabism in western China,[146] the aforementioned distinctly Middle Eastern brand of Islam supported by the West which has historically had no presence in the region and which is adhered to by Al Qaeda, the Islamic State and other jihadist groups – alongside open Western and Turkish support for the Munich-based World Uyghur Congress, which advocates a struggle to separate Xinjiang from the Chinese mainland, were other major factors which led Beijing to conclude that the treat was both serious and imminent. Numerous reports that jihadist groups in Syria have sought to target China's far west,[147] and active Western support for these groups, has exacerbated Chinese fears of a potential catastrophe in Xinjiang.[148] Premier Xi Jinping said regarding the state of affairs in the province: 'Xinjiang is in an active period of terrorist activities, intense struggle against separatism and painful intervention to treat this.'[149] Chinese state media outlet Global Times reported on the rapidly initiated security measures and re-education campaign, under which the population of Xinjiang was provided with compulsory month long education programs on the aforementioned radical Wahabist influences, that this was necessary to save the province from 'the verge of massive turmoil' – further noting: 'It has avoided the fate of becoming "China's Syria" or "China's Libya".'[150]

The rise of Islamic State in Afghanistan, Syria and elsewhere, reportedly with Western support, and potential for other jihadist groups like it to spread to western China could if improperly handled end up forcing Beijing to divert extensive resources to national security and domestic counterterrorism. A quagmire for the People's Liberation Army on Chinese territory could have serious implications for morale, undermine confidence in the country's leadership and potentially be a considerable drain on the East Asian state's resources. With the United States estimated to have spent $589 billion on homeland security related costs, lost $55 billion in physical damage, and suffered an economic impact of $123 billion dollars in response to the 9/11 attacks alone, a potentially far more menacing terror threat right on China's border could well have devastating impacts on the country's development.[151] Unlike in the case of Al Qaeda in its limited conflict with the United States, a jihadist movement in Xinjiang is likely to enjoy considerable support from a number of state sponsors – namely Beijing's Western adversaries, as well as Muslim states such as Turkey, which already support radical groups for strategic reasons in Syria[152] and Xinjiang independence organizations. These are many of the same state actors which were responsible for arming and supporting jihadist forces in Chechnya in a similar campaign to destabilize Russia in the 1990s. Disrupting Chinese trade with Central Asia and the Middle East, the One Belt One Road initiative in particular, and the emergence of a security state within China itself to protect potential terrorist targets across the country – already seen to some extent with growing and often disruptive counterterrorism measures implemented in Beijing in response to Islamist terror attacks carried out there, and the diversion of military resources away from the Pacific, could if not properly handled in its early stages lead to disaster. For the United States and the wider Western Bloc, for which China's economic rise is the primary global threat to their continued primacy, such an outcome would be strongly in line with their interests.

Zbigniew Brzezinski, national security advisor to U.S. President Jimmy Carter and one of the most influential figures on U.S. Cold War foreign policy, was a key architect of Operation Cyclone to arm Islamic extremists in Afghanistan against the Soviet Union and its allies. When asked following the USSR's collapse whether the policy of arming future terrorists was regrettable, he repeatedly emphasized the soundness of the strategy and that strengthening of Islamic terrorists was a price worth paying to bring about the fall of the Soviet Union and the 'liberation' of central Europe.[153] Considering the highly successful application of support for radical Islamist insurgent groups throughout both Muslim countries and countries with sizeable Muslim minorities, there is significant room to apply similar strategies in Southeast Asia and to China's Central Asian far West and neighboring states. Indeed, a precedent is also set by the CIA's extensive support and training provided to Tibetan insurgent groups from the 1950s to the 1970s which engaged in acts of terrorism to sabotage Chinese civilian infrastructure – as previously covered in Chapter 3. With the Western Bloc having benefited significantly from applying this strategy in the past to undermine the Soviet sphere of influence, there is little reason to think it would not be reapplied in the face of a new threat to Western primacy in the form of rising East Asian powers and a rising China in particular. As Central and Southeast Asia fall further into Beijing's sphere of influence, destabilization through support for Islamist groups remains a key asset which the Western Bloc is highly likely to employ – much as it has in the past.

The support of the United States and its allies for Islamic militant groups does not necessarily imply direct control over these groups and micromanaging of their operations. Rather, allegations made against the U.S. unanimously indicate a provision of logistical support, funding, intelligence, armaments, training, and even 'safe zones' from which to launch attacks against U.S. adversaries – as was alleged in Syria. Such assistance to these groups in Syria, Central Asia, China and potentially Southeast Asia in future empowers jihadist forces to go on to destabilize their respective regions and weaken Western adversaries or undermine Chinese allies in accordance with the Western Bloc's interests.

According to a statement from the UN Security Council Committee on Counterterrorism in October 2017, Islamic State and other Islamist militant groups have attempted to transfer fighters and resources away from Iraq and Syria where they face imminent defeat. The committee noted that the groups were in particular focused on Southeast Asia, where they were diverting significant resources to recruitment and propaganda efforts.[154] Similar observations regarding redeployment of assets by Islamist terror groups to Southeast Asia were made by a number of prominent think tanks such as the International Institute for Strategic Studies.[155] Singapore's leadership have issued similar warnings, noting as early as 2015 that the region was emerging as a 'key recruitment center' for Islamic State. As Singaporean Prime Minister Lee Hsien Loong said in regard to this emerging threat: 'the threat is no longer over there [Middle East]; it is over here ... It is not so far fetched that ISIS could establish a base somewhere in the region, in a geographical area under its physical control like in Syria or Iraq ... That would pose a serious threat to the whole of Southeast Asia.'[156] The Malaysian government has similarly warned that IS was attempting to create a destabilizing presence in the country by infiltrating universities, the military and political parties to further their regional goals – as well as plotting terror attacks.[157] Indonesia's Defense Minister and government, following a series of terror attacks with close links to Middle Eastern terror groups, expressed similar concerns.[158] Russia's Defense Ministry has raised the same issue regarding the growing security threat from the spread of Middle Eastern terror groups to Central and Southeast Asia based on intelligence collected while combating these jihadist forces in Syria and Iraq.[159]

Indonesia, Malaysia, the Philippines and Thailand, four major emerging economies and close Chinese economic partners, have already proven fertile ground for Islamic State and other terror group recruitment, with the former two having sent several hundred fighters to Syria to wage 'jihad' against the Russian, Chinese[160] and North Korean[161] backed Syrian government. These states have all suffered serious terror attacks linked to IS in the 2010s, while the terror groups Mujahidin Indonesia Timor in Indonesia and Isnilon Totini Hapilon in the Philippines have already pledged allegiance to IS. The Philippines and Indonesia have experienced IS affiliated terror attacks – which in the former manifested in a month's long battle with the Filipino army in Marawi in 2017, the capture of a city by IS forces and thousands of casualties. In Thailand, alongside bombings by other Islamist terror groups, Syrian IS members were also found in 2015 to have entered the country to plan attacks. Malaysia has also faced terror attacks, set to increase should the Malaysian nationals fighting in Syria return. Myanmar too has also faced growing incidents of Islamic terrorism linked to the Middle East, though not to IS specifically, with soldiers killed and non-Muslims massacred by the Arakan Rohingya Salvation Army – the leadership of which are largely based in Saudi Arabia.[162] This group has no known ties to Al Qaeda or Islamic State, this is likely to change in future.

If the Russian, Afghan, Turkish, Iranian and other allegations are true regarding U.S. support for and co-operation with Islamist militants, including IS, to destabilize those states which oppose U.S. interests – something strongly supported by the claims of Graham E. Fuller and other high ranking American officials regarding the CIA's policy of supporting Islamist militant groups to further U.S. policy goals[163] as well as the precedents set by Western support for similar groups during the Cold War, the move of IS and other terror groups to Southeast Asia and to China's western borders coinciding with the 'Pivot to Asia' could well prove an invaluable asset to the Western Bloc in the Asia-Pacific region. With China's rise posing arguably the greatest threat to Western primacy in modern history, surpassing that posed by the Soviet Union, and considering the success of support for Islamist groups in the past and the frequency with which the strategy has been employed, it remains highly likely that this will again be implemented.

Notes

1 Frankopan, Peter, *The Silk Roads: A New History of the World*, London, Bloomsbury, 2015 (p. 258).
2 Robert, *The World America Made*, New York, Alfred A. Knopf, 2012 (p. 65).
3 'China, South Korea agree to mend ties after THAAD standoff,' *Reuters*, October 31, 2017.
4 'Seoul warns Trump: U.S. must not strike North Korea without our consent,' *The Guardian*, November 15, 2017.
5 Maresca, Thomas, 'South Korean President Moon Jae-in suspends further THAAD deployment,' *USA Today*, June 7, 2017.
6 Stanley, Timothy, 'The Growing Russia-South Korea Partnership,' *The Diplomat*, May 24, 2018.
7 'Russia's 2nd Important Trade Partner in Asia-Pacific,' *Sputnik*, June 22, 2018.

8 'S-400 Coming to Seoul? How South Korean Indirectly Acquires Cutting Edge Russian Air Defences,' *Military Watch Magazine*, April 6, 2018.

9 'Does the South Korean Navy's New Dokdo Class Carrier Use Cutting Edge Russian Technology for Air Defence?,' *Military Watch Magazine*, June 29, 2018.

10 Pubby, Manu, 'Will not bow to U.S. pressure on Russian sanctions: MoD,' *The Economic Times*, July 14, 2018.

11 Wong, Katherine, 'China-Pakistan military ties set to get even closer as "iron brothers" eye new alliance,' *South China Morning Post*, January 7, 2018.

12 Micallef, Joseph V., 'Beijing's "One Belt-One Road" Strategy: Why Geography Still Matters,' *Military.com*, January 16, 2017.

13 Etzioni, Amitai, 'Who authorized perpetrations for war with China,' *Yale Journal of International Affairs*, 8:2, Summer 2013, (p. 37–51).

14 Brunnstrom, D., and Spetalnick, M., 'Trump team struggles for cohesion on tougher China policy,' *Reuters*, January 14, 2017.

15 Fu, Y., and Wu, S. C., 'South China Sea: how we got to this stage,' *The National Interest*, May 9, 2016.

16 'Set aside dispute and pursue joint development,' *Ministry of Foreign Affairs of PRC*, April 1988.

17 Taylor Fravel, M., *U.S. policy towards the disputes in the South China Sea since 1995*, Singapore, Nayang Technological University, S. Rajartnam School of International Studies, 2014.

18 Dyer, G., 'U.S. blames China for rising tensions in South China Sea,' *Financial Times*, February 9, 2014.

19 Woodward, Jude, *The U.S. vs China: Asia's New Cold War?* Manchester, Manchester University Press, 2017 (p. 177).

20 'Philippines to seek more oil in South China Sea,' *ABS-CBN News*, June 29, 2011.

21 Mitchell, T., and Dyer, G., 'U.S. military flight over South China Sea escalates tensions,' *Financial Times*, May 21, 2015.

22 Hammes, T. X., 'Offshore Control is the Answer,' *Proceedings*, 138:12, 2012, (p. 1318).

23 Hammes, T. X., *Offshore Control: A Proposed Strategy for an Unlikely Conflict*, Strategic Forum, National Defence University, Institute for National Strategic Studies, June 2012.

24 Brunnstrom, D., and Spetalnick, M., 'Trump team struggles for cohesion on tougher China policy,' *Reuters*, January 14, 2017.

25 'China angered over warships patrol near artificial islands, warns U.S. not to "create trouble,"' *Los Angeles Times*, October 27, 2015.

26 'U.S. strategic bombers fly close to Chinese islands, ignore "get away" orders,' *RT*, November 12, 2015.
27 'U.S. sends 3 B-2 bombers to Asia-Pacific,' *CNN*, March 10, 2016.
28 'Does ASEAN support U.S. military presence in South China Sea?' *Jakarta Post*, April 2, 2018.
29 Valencia, Mark J., 'Are Asean members still willing to support a provocative U.S. in the South China Sea?,' *South China Morning Post*, July 2, 2018.
30 'Philippines wary of US dragging it into "shooting war"', *Asia Times*, March 5, 2019.
31 'U.S. Military Claims it Can Destroy Beijing's Heavily Militarised South China Sea Island Bases – But Can It?,' *Military Watch Magazine*, June 2, 2018.
32 'China's Lethal New YJ-12 Anti Ship Missiles; Why their Deployment to the South China Sea Worries the Western Bloc,' *Military Watch Magazine*, May 6, 2018.
33 'Views from China's vice president,' *Washington Post*, March 8, 2012.
34 'Only countries in the region should define order in S. China Sea,' *Xinhua*, July 20, 2016.
35 Chomsky, Noam, *Who Rules the World?*, London, Hamish Hamilton, 2016 (pp. 82–83).
36 '"Hegemonic logic": China fumes after Pentagon calls it top target of U.S. "freedom of navigation" ops,' *RT*, April 26, 2016.
37 'U.S. Military Claims it Can Destroy Beijing's Heavily Militarised South China Sea Island Bases – But Can It?,' *Military Watch Magazine*, June 2, 2018.
38 Hammond, Philip, *Address to the Centre for a New American Security*, British Ministry of Defence, July 18, 2012.
39 'Unequal Treaty, Chinese History,' *Encyclopedia Britannica*.
40 Chomsky, Noam, *Who Rules the World?*, London, Hamish Hamilton, 2016 (p. 73).
41 Holehouse, Matthew, 'Britain will double personnel in Far East war games, David Cameron says,' *The Telegraph*, July 30, 2015.
42 Mitchell, Jon, 'Training of British troops on Okinawa bases may violate Japan-U.S. Security Treaty,' *Japan Times*, August 10, 2016.
43 McCurry, Justin, 'UK sends Typhoons to Japan for joint drills to strengthen security ties,' *The Guardian*, October 14, 2016.
44 Brunnstrom, David, 'British fighters to overfly South China Sea; carriers in the Pacific after 2020: envoy,' *Reuters*, December 2, 2016.
45 Doherty, Ben, 'Britain's new aircraft carriers to test Beijing in South China Sea,' *The Guardian*, July 27, 2017.
46 Roy, Ananya, 'South Korea, U.S. and UK to hold first joint military drill to counter North Korea threats,' *International Business Times*, September 29, 2016.

47 'UK Military Chiefs "See What Support" They Could Give U.S. in War With North Korea,' *Sputnik*, October 9, 2017.
48 Johnson, Jamie, 'Britain sends third warship to Asia Pacific to monitor North Korea,' *The Independent*, April 11, 2018.
49 Beale, Jonathan, 'Why is no-one talking about defence cuts?' *BBC*, April 24, 2015.
50 'British military funding crisis could see Royal Marines cut to pay for aircraft carriers,' *RT*, March 31, 2017.
51 Farmer, Ben, 'Forces braced for more cuts in defence cash squeeze,' *The Telegraph*, December 27, 2016.
52 Till, Geoffrey, 'Great Britain Gambles with the Royal Navy,' *Naval War College Review*, Volume 63, No. 1, Winter, Article 4, 2010.
53 Read, Carly, 'Britain does NOT rule the waves: Royal Navy fleet HALVED since 1990,' *Express*, June 21, 2018.
54 'Cuts have left the Navy "struggling to protect British citizens" with three quarters warships out of action,' *The Sun*, September 15, 2017.
55 Brown, Larisa, 'The £6 billion Royal Navy fleet that hardly ever went to sea: Warships that can't sail in the heat spent 80 per cent of the year in dock,' *The Daily Mail*, June 16, 2018.
56 'HMS Diamond aborts Gulf mission after breaking down,' *Sunday Times*, November 23, 2017.
57 'Cuts have left the Navy "struggling to protect British citizens" with three quarters warships out of action,' *The Sun*, September 15, 2017.
58 'Britain will have "3rd World" navy if budget is cut, says ex-first sea lord,' *RT*, September 18, 2017.
59 Forrest, Adam, 'Scallop war: UK will be unable to protect waters post-Brexit, former first sea lord warns,' *The Independent*, September 1, 2018.
60 'Royal Navy has "woefully low" total of ships, MoD made "extraordinary mistakes" – MPs,' *RT*, November 21, 2016.
61 'Crumbling military infrastructure threatens UK national security – MPs,' *RT*, November 15, 2016.
62 'Nearly a third of RAF's combat jets grounded by mechanical gremlins as 14 years of war take their toll,' *The Sun*, January 8, 2017.
63 'MoD's new jets and warships threatened by rising costs and falling pound warn MPs,' *The Telegraph*, April 25, 2017.
64 'Overstretched and Underfunded British Armed Forces Can't Afford Modernisation Program – Public Accounts Committee,' May 16, 2018.
65 IMF BoP IIP UK gross external debt NSA £m, *Office of National Statistics*, British Government.

66 Panda, Ankit, 'French Defence Minister to Urge EU South China Sea Patrols,' *The Diplomat*, June 6, 2016.
67 Paskal, Cleo, 'A French Pivot to Asia,' *The Diplomat*, May 1, 2017.
68 Kelly, Tim, and Kubo, Nobuhiro, 'French carrier to lead joint amphibious Pacific drill in show of force aimed at China,' *Reuters*, March 17, 2017.
69 'French amphibious carrier visits Japan ahead of Pacific show of power, Kubo, Nobuhiro,' *Reuters*, April 29, 2017.
70 'Just Business: China Encroaches on Former French Colonies in Africa,' *Sputnik*, May 20, 2015.
71 'France's Colonial Tax Still Enforced for Africa. "Bleeding Africa and Feeding France,"' *Centre for Research of Globalization*, January 14, 2015.
72 Marchesin, Philippe, Universite de Paris, *Mitterand l'Africain* (<http://www.politique-africaine.com/numeros/pdf/058005.pdf>).
73 Asher-Schapiro, Avi, 'Libyan Oil, Gold, and Qaddafi: The Strange Email Sidney Blumenthal Sent Hillary Clinton In 2011,' *Vice News*, January 12, 2016.
74 'South Korea Develops Plan to Annihilate Pyongyang in Case of War,' *Sputnik*, September 11, 2016.
75 'NATO's Stoltenberg says North Korea's "reckless behavior" requires global response,' *Reuters*, September 10, 2017.
76 Nagy, Tomas A., 'Thinking the Unthinkable: Central Europe at War With North Korea,' *The Diplomat*, March 12, 2018.
77 'S. Korea, U.S. will rehearse invasion of N. Korea in record-breaking joint military drills,' *RT*, February 22, 2016.
78 'Reckless game over the Korean Peninsula runs risk of real war,' *Global Times*, August 10, 2017.
79 'How China has Joined Russia in Drawing a Red Line to Prevent U.S. Military Intervention on the Korean Peninsula,' *Military Watch Magazine*, September 12, 2017.
80 'Escalation on Korean Peninsula Due to U.S. Military Buildup Unacceptable – Lavrov,' *Sputnik*, August 6, 2017.
81 'How to Interpret Russia's Growing Surface-to-Air Missile Deployments Near the North Korean Border,' *Military Watch Magazine*, August 11, 2017.
82 'Russian Senator Views Any U.S. Military Action in N Korea as a Security Threat,' *Sputnik*, September 27, 2017.
83 'How China has Joined Russia in Drawing a Red Line to Prevent U.S. Military Action on the Korean Peninsula,' *Military Watch Magazine*, September 12, 2017.
84 'Preventing War on the Korean Peninsula; China and Russia Launch Large Scale Military Exercises Near Korea Coinciding with U.S. Anti-Pyongyang Drills,' *Military Watch Magazine*, December 6, 2017.

85 Moorcraft, Paul, *Superpowers, Rogue States and Terrorism: Countering the Security Threats to the West*, Barnsley, Pen and Sword, 2017 (pp. 20–21).

86 Said, Edward W., *Orientalism*, London, Penguin, 1995 (Preface).

87 Pettus, Ashley, '10 Downing Street's Gulag,' *Harvard Magazine*, March 2005.

88 *New York Times*, October 15, 1900.

89 Hass, Richard N., 'What to Do with American Primacy,' *Foreign Affairs* 78/5, September-October 1999.

90 Ayson, Robert, *Asia's Security*, London, Palgrave MacMillan, 2015 (p. 35).

91 Frankopan, Peter, *The Silk Roads: A New History of the World*, London, Bloomsbury, 2015 (p. 258).

92 Andrade, Tonio, *The Gunpowder Age: China, Military Innovation, and the Rise of the West in World History*, Princeton, NJ, Princeton University Press, 2016 (pp. 302–303).

93 Gady, Franz-Stefan, 'This is How Europe Conquered Asia,' *The Diplomat*, August 3, 2017.

94 Narasimha, Roddam, *Rockets in Mysore and Britain, 1750–1850 A.D.*, Bangalore, National Aerospace Laboratories, 1985.

95 Durant III, Frederick C. and Fought, Stephen Oliver, and Guilmartin Jr., John F., 'Rocket and Missile System,' *Encyclopaedia Britannica.*

96 Hoffman, Philip T., 'How Europe Conquered the World,' *Foreign Affairs*, October 7, 2015.

97 Pagani, Catherine, 'Objects and the Press. Images of China in Nineteenth Century Britain,' in Codell, Julie F., *Imperial Co-Histories: National Identities and the British Colonial Press*, Madison, WI, Fairleigh Dickinson University Press, 2003 (p. 160).

98 Frankopan, Peter, *The Silk Roads: A New History of the World*, London, Bloomsbury, 2015 (p. 301).

99 Kelly, Robert, 'South Koreans are not Neo-cons,' *Asian Security Blog*, June 11, 2010.

100 Pagani, Catherine, *Objects and the Press. Images of China in Nineteenth Century Britain*, in Codell, Julie F., *Imperial Co-Histories: National Identities and the British Colonial Press*, Madison, WI, Fairleigh Dickinson University Press, 2003 (p. 160).

101 Frankopan, Peter, *The Silk Roads: A New History of the World*, London, Bloomsbury, 2015 (p. 301).

102 McKinney, Cynthia, 'Time to think of legacy? The Obama Doctrine,' *RT*, May 1, 2016.

103 'Commentary: Only countries in the region should define order in S. China Sea,' *Xinhua*, July 20, 2016.

104 Meher, Jagmohan, 'America's Afghanistan War: The Success that Failed,' New Delhi, Gyan Books, 2006 (p. 68, 69, 94).

105 Crile, George, 'Charlie Wilson's War: The Extraordinary Story of the Largest Covert Operation in History,' *Atlantic Monthly Press*, 2006 (p. 246, 285, 302).
106 Rashid, Ahmed, *Taliban: Militant Islam, Oil and Fundamentalism in Central Asia*, New Haven, CT, Yale University Press, 2001 (pp. 128–129).
107 'Al Qaeda's Origins and Links,' *BBC*, July 20, 2004.
108 Hoff, Brad, 'Hillary Emails Reveal True Motive for Libya Intervention,' *Foreign Policy Journal*, January 6, 2016.
109 Rosenburg, Matthew, 'C.I.A. Cash Ended Up in Coffers of Al Qaeda,' *New York Times*, March 4, 2015.
110 *Huffington Post*, May 21, 2016.
111 'U.S. lets militants train, mount attacks from its Syrian bases – chief of Russian General Staff,' *RT*, December 27, 2017.
112 'U.S. special ops forces & hardware spotted at ISIS positions north of Deir ez-Zor – Russian MoD,' *RT*, September 24, 2017.
113 'U.S. Support for Terrorists in Syria Main Obstacle of Defeating Them – Russian MoD,' *Sputnik*, October 4, 2017.
114 'Syrian regime forces enter buffer zone surrounding U.S. base,' *CNN*, October 4, 2017.
115 'Drones used by Syrian terrorists "require advanced training" – Russian MoD in response to US,' *Sputnik*, January 9, 2018.
116 'Inquiry Into Death of Russian Lt. Gen. Asapov Shows Data Leaks to Daesh – Source,' *Sputnik*, September 26, 2017.
117 'Iran accuses U.S. of alliance with ISIS, claims to have proof,' *RT*, June 11, 2017.
118 'No role for West and allies in Syria until they cut support to terrorists – Assad,' *RT*, August 21, 2017.
119 'West's shadow behind all terrorist groups, including Daesh – Erdogan,' *Sputnik*, October 8, 2017.
120 'U.S. Mission Suspends Visa Services in Turkey to "Reassess Commitment to Security,"' *Sputnik*, October 8, 2017.
121 '"I have confirmed evidence" Turkey's President Recep Tayyip Erdogan claims US-led coalition forces have supported ISIS,' *The Sun*, October 8, 2017.
122 U.S. Congresswoman Tulsi Gabbard Speaks on House Floor, September 13, 2018.
123 *H.R. 6504 – To prohibit the use of United States Government funds to provide assistance to Al Qaeda, Jabhat Fateh al-Sham, and the Islamic State of Iraq and the Levant (ISIL) and to countries supporting those organizations, and for other purposes*, 114th Congress, U.S. Congress, 2015–2016.
124 Carden, James, 'Why Does the U.S. Continue to Arm Terrorists in Syria?' *The Nation*, March 3, 2017.

125 'All Syrian Terrorist Groups Receive Weapons, Tasks From Abroad – Russian MoD,' *Sputnik*, March 24, 2018.

126 Lin, Christina, 'After Syria's partition, will Xinjiang be destabilized?' *Asia Times*, September 13, 2018.

127 Hubbard, Ben, 'In a Syria Refuge, Extremists Exert Greater Control,' *New York Times*, August 13, 2017.

128 Bandow, Doug, 'U.S. Should Stay Out Of Syria: "Safe Zones" Aren't Safe For Americans,' *Forbes*, February 1, 2017.

129 Johnson, Ian, 'Washington's Secret History with the Muslim Brotherhood,' *The New York Review of Books*, February 5, 2011.

130 'How We Trained Al Qaeda,' *Spectator*, 13 September 2003.

131 'Putin accuses U.S. of directly supporting Chechen militants,' *Press TV*, April 26, 2015.

132 *Congressional Record*, V. 151, PT. 17, U.S. Congress, October 7 to 26, 2005.

133 Ibid.

134 'We finally know what Hillary Clinton knew all along – U.S. allies Saudi Arabia and Qatar are funding Isis,' *The Independent*, October 14, 2016.

135 'Spread of Wahhabism was done at request of West during Cold War – Saudi crown prince,' *RT*, April 18, 2018.

136 *Congressional Record*, V. 151, PT. 17, U.S. Congress, October 7 to 26, 2005.

137 '"ISIS in Afghanistan is U.S. tool to cause trouble in the whole region" – ex-Afghan President Karzai to RT,' *RT*, October 19, 2017.

138 'U.S. Aircraft Evacuates Over 20 Daesh Commanders From Deir ez Zor – Source,' *Sputnik*, September 7, 2017.

139 '"ISIS in Afghanistan is U.S. tool to cause trouble in the whole region" – ex-Afghan President Karzai to RT,' *RT*, October 19, 2017.

140 'American political scientist: Western Intelligence used Azerbaijan to export terrorism into Russia,' *Panorama*, May 30, 2015.

141 Wu, Wendy, 'Rising tide of jihadists stopped trying to return to China, Chinese advisers say,' *South China Morning Post*, January 8, 2017.

142 Kang Lim, Benjamin, and Blanchard, Ben, 'Chinese suspects Tiananmen crash a suicide attack – sources,' *Reuters*, October 29, 2013.

143 Gramer, Robbie, 'The Islamic State Pledged to Attack China Next. Here's Why,' *Foreign Policy*, March 1, 2017.

144 'Dragon of the Mountains: China to Fully Fund Afghan Military Base,' *Sputnik*, January 11, 2018.

145 'Suicide Bomber Attacks Chinese Embassy in Kyrgyzstan,' *New York Times*, August 30, 2016.

146 'China Is Detaining Muslims in Vast Numbers. The Goal: "Transformation,"' *New York Times*, September 8, 2018.
147 Lin, Christina, 'Idlib militants eye China, Central Asia as next targets,' *Asia Times*, August 13, 2018.
148 Ibid.
149 '雪克来提·扎克尔：认真贯彻习近平总书记重要讲话精神 坚定不移推进社会稳定和长治久安,' *CPC News* (in Chinese), April 20, 2017.
150 'Crackdown in Xinjiang prevented another Syria or Libya, says China's state media,' *Straitstimes*, August 13, 2018.
151 Sengupta, Kim, 'Turkey and Saudi Arabia alarm the West by backing Islamist extremists the Americans had bombed in Syria,' *The Independent*, May 12, 2015.
152 'One 9/11 Tally: $3.3 Trillion – Interactive Feature,' *New York Times*, September 8, 2011.
153 Interview with Zbigniew Brzezinski, *Le Nouvel Observateur*, 1998.
154 'Daesh Militants Fleeing From Iraq, Syria Create New Threat in South-Eastern Asia,' *Sputnik*, October 4, 2017.
155 *The Military Balance*, Volume 118, International Institute for Strategic Studies, 2018 (Chapter 6, 'Asia').
156 Parameswaran, Prashanth, 'Singapore Warns of Islamic State Base in Southeast Asia,' *The Diplomat*, May 30, 2015.
157 Ibid.
158 Hariyadi, Mathias, 'Defense Minister Warns that Islamic State Terrorists Have Moved Into Indonesia from Philippines and Syria,' *Asia News*, May 17, 2018.
159 'Daesh Militants Moving to Central, South East Asia After Defeat in Syria, Iraq,' *Sputnik*, April 24, 2018.
160 Taylor, Adam, 'Bashar al-Assad says relations between Syria and China are "on the rise,"' *Washington Post*, April 12, 2017.
161 Bryne, Leo, 'North Korea Says it Wants to Help Syria Rebuild,' *NK News*, November 11, 2017.
162 Berlinger, Joshua, 'Report claims Rohingya militant group massacred nearly 100 Hindus,' *CNN*, May 26, 2018.
163 *Congressional Record*, V. 151, PT. 17, U.S. Congress, October 7–October 26, 2005.

CHAPTER 19

North Korea: Nuclear Weapons and Ideology

The surest deterrent to American action is a functioning nuclear arsenal.[1]
— Conclusion Reached in 2005 DoD Funded Study by the U.S. Army War College's Strategic Studies Institute and the U.S. Nonproliferation Policy Education Center.

History teaches that wars begin when governments believe the price of aggression is cheap.[2]
— U.S. President RONALD REAGAN on the need for a capable deterrent

Relations in a Post-Cold-War World: Threats of Invasion, the Axis of Evil and a Nuclear Program

Alongside the Korean War, the post-Cold War era has been the most influential era on modern North Korean ideology and on the conduct of the country's foreign policy. An understanding of the events that took place during this period are critical to understanding North Korea today, providing a background to its current antagonism with the Western Bloc and its investments in the development of nuclear and ballistic missile capabilities.

Although the Soviet Union was dissolved in December 1991, its presence as an international superpower capable of challenging the Western Bloc had by that time long since ceased to exist. From 1989 it was clear that the global balance of power had shifted and a unipolar Western led world order was emerging. The Soviet led Warsaw Pact military alliance had begun to disintegrate and the USSR had stagnated and been economically and militarily outmatched by the Western Bloc, with whom it sought compromise and from whom it sought aid. As the American *Foreign Affairs* journal stated in 1991: 'It has been assumed that the old bipolar world would beget a multipolar world … The immediate post-Cold War world is not multipolar. It is unipolar. The center of world power is an unchallenged superpower, the United States, attended by its Western allies.'[3]

Under this new world order several states lost both the military protection and economic benefits that relations with a superpower had granted them. As a result the United States, as a sole superpower, was able to undertake unilateral military actions across the world, including against former Soviet allies. According to Scott Silverstone, Associate Professor of International Relations at the United States' West Point Military Academy, preventative war, which had been rejected by all U.S. presidents throughout the Cold War as a sole pretext for military intervention, increasingly became an acceptable pretext by United States governments for military intervention from the early 1990s. While legal grounds for pre-emptive war, launching an attack preceding the expected initiation of conflict to gain an advantage, are already somewhat fragile, preventive war has little if any justification in international law and is considerably more aggressive still – involving initiating conflict to prevent a certain actor from attaining capabilities one deems undesirable. Conceptually the United States' grounds for waging wars had changed dramatically, and those termed 'rogue states,' even if not directly threatening the U.S. or its allies, could be targeted.[4,5,6] The threat to these states worsened when the Pentagon announced a shift in its nuclear deterrence strategy under which it rejected its no first use policy. The U.S. meanwhile rejected the Non-Proliferation Treaty linked negative security assurances banning the use of nuclear weapons against non-nuclear states which were parties to the treaty,[7,8] meaning that the United States reserved the right to launch nuclear strikes against any adversary – nuclear armed or otherwise.[9,10] A cornerstone of this new strategy relied on unpredictability regarding when and under what pretexts force, including nuclear force, may be used. U.S. planners avidly sought to avoid 'portray[ing] ourselves as too rational or cool-headed,' according to a critical 1990s STRATCOM report which emphasized the benefits of appearing an irrational superpower able to strike its enemies at will at any time, with a willingness to use nuclear weapons and ambiguity as to whether nuclear or conventional forces would be used to deal with American adversaries.[11,12]

As a result of the post-Cold War policy adopted by the United States the future survival of all states independent of the Western Bloc was in serious jeopardy. American leadership, from the president to its leading political strategists, was calling for a unilateral role for the United States in world affairs – the primary focus of which would be preserving American dominance.[13] In the 25 years between 1992 and 2017 the U.S. would launch 188 military interventions abroad, while during the entire Cold War from 1948 to 1991 they had launched just 46 such interventions – an increase of over 600 percent in the number of interventions per year.[14]

In the Middle East Ba'athist Iraq, a former Soviet client state, continued to act as though the Cold War status quo under which the USSR had somewhat checked the West's ability to act unilaterally against its allies still remained. Iraq's Western-aligned neighbor Kuwait was found to have been drilling for oil horizontally and extracting Iraqi oil illegally, which amounted to billions of dollars in annual revenues. Kuwait's oil policies were costing Iraq $7 billion annually,[15,16] and the country refused multiple Iraqi diplomatic overtures over several months and ignored threats of forceful retaliation to end what Baghdad perceived to be theft of its resources.[17] Iraq's response however came not in the form of limited military action, but with a full invasion of its neighbor and absorption of its entire territory in 1990. Iraq failed to realize its own vulnerability under the new world order, which cost the country dearly. It was ordered by United States not only to withdraw its military from Kuwait, but to comply with several further demands including ending its missile programs and curbing military research – or else face U.S. military intervention. While Iraq accepted the condition of withdrawal and a restoration of Kuwaiti sovereignty, the country refused these more extensive terms which were seen as a violation of its right to self-defense and an attempt to manipulate the regional balance of power further in the favor of American client states.[18] The United States could make these more extensive demands and back them by threats for two reasons. Firstly the USSR was no longer a force on the international stage which would protect its ally. Secondly Iraq had after several setbacks abandoned its nuclear program, and so could not deter military intervention against it by a superpower.

As it was, Iraq, an independent though reckless state at the time, had neither a powerful friend nor a nuclear deterrent, and with nothing to deter it the United States could commence military action against the small Middle Eastern nation. The Iraqi army, corrupt and poorly organized as it was, was quickly neutralized by America's military might,[19] while the country itself was devastated and its key civilian and military infrastructure was destroyed. Indeed, according to a report by the *Washington Post* in 1991, the purpose of the U.S. bombardment was to target living standards by destroying key infrastructure with precision guided weapons, such as oil refineries, electrical plants and transportation networks. Examples were the destruction of 80 percent of Iraq's power generation capabilities and the crippling of its sewage treatment system.[20] From an upper middle income country with living standards surpassing many Western nations, Iraq was reduced to the level of a third world country by the Western Bloc's bombing campaign and harsh sanctions over 12 years from 1991 to 2003. Living standards never recovered to pre-war levels and over 1 million of its population died as a result of war and subsequent sanctions.[21] According to U.S. statistics, by 1996 half a million Iraqi children had died as a result.[22,23,24] As Iraq's Foreign Minister and Prime Minister Tariq Aziz then lamented upon witnessing the devastation of his country: 'If we still had the Soviets as our patron, none of this would have happened.'[25]

While this went on, the world watched. North Korea particularly watched closely. The United States maintained its intent to reunify the Korea Peninsula under its influence by the toppling of the North Korean government, and it was only the military intervention of China and the strong presence of the Soviet Union which had prevented this outcome 40 years prior. Following the spectacle of the Gulf War and the demonstration of American military might against Iraq, the DPRK feared for its security – as many did. Its neighbor China responded by reorganizing and modernizing their own military, particularly their air defenses and fighter fleet, after seeing the American air fleet devastate the Iraqi military from the sky and go on to bombard its cities.[26] Generals of the People's Liberation Army also wrote to the Chinese leadership warning of the likelihood of U.S. military action against North Korea following their success in Iraq, recommending that Beijing take precautions against this as well including providing Pyongyang with military technical assistance.[27] The DPRK itself responded to the Iraqi demonstration by devoting significant resources to a nuclear program of it own.[28] They saw, as many analysts had during the Gulf War, that without a powerful military ally a nuclear weapon was the only sure deterrent an independent state had to protect its sovereignty and deter aggression.

North Korea's statements indicated that while in principle Pyongyang supported global nuclear disarmament after the Cold War ended it also felt significantly threatened by the United States which, while maintaining a significant and growing military presence on its borders and a vast nuclear arsenal of its own, never abandoned its goal of toppling the DPRK government. Charles Armstrong, Korean Studies Professor at Colombia University, noted on the persistent threats made against North Korea: 'The American security threat is no mere fiction from Pyongyang's perspective. No other country in the world has faced the threat of nuclear annihilation by the U.S. for nearly sixty years, as has North Korea; no country has been for so long the explicit target of a potential American attack.'[29] Therefore, while government sanctioned student festivals and events in Pyongyang calling for worldwide nuclear disarmament took place, the country was vulnerable without its own deterrent at such a critical time. The attention and resources the DPRK would devote to strengthening its defenses was directly proportional to the pressure and threats made against the state by the U.S.

From 1994 to 2002 the Asia-Pacific ceased to be a primary concern of U.S. foreign policy, which in that time focused increasingly on the Islamic world. The United States military and its European allies continued to blockade Iraq, enforce a no-fly zone and conduct regular airstrikes, operations which cost hundreds of millions of dollars annually. They were otherwise involved in conflicts in Yugoslavia, Haiti, Somalia, Sudan, Afghanistan and Yemen. In 2002 however the DPRK returned to the agenda when the United States labeled North Korea a member of the 'Axis of Evil,' a list of three states in which Washington openly sought regime change along with Iran and Iraq. Just weeks later U.S. President George W. Bush was seen at North Korea's border accompanied by military officials. Looking out over North Korea through military binoculars, he described looking at 'evil' and concluded: 'we are ready.'[30]

In 2003 Iraq, the state most harshly criticized by President Bush when he declared the 'Axis of Evil,' was invaded and the country's fragile government was toppled quickly with hardly any loss of American lives. The capital was occupied within two weeks and the president was later executed. Not only did the country, by the admission of its president, lack any weapons of mass destruction with which to deter and if necessary repel invasion,[31] but Iraq's military was, as neighboring Iran's military referred to it 'rotten.' Generals and soldiers alike were persuaded through bribery and other means to lay down their arms. The government of Saddam Hussein was highly corrupt and unpopular among the substantial religious and ethnic groups it had repressed – the Shiites, 60 percent of the population, and the Kurds, a further 15 percent. These weaknesses and failures were largely absent in Iran and the DPRK however, both of which maintained professional militaries, advanced weapons programs and lacked sizeable fifth columns.

In late 2003, emboldened following the apparent swift victory won in Iraq and the successful toppling of the Iraqi government, American officials again spoke of trying to topple the DPRK government. North Korea's leadership for its part appeared to have predicted that a successful campaign in Iraq would likely be followed by preparations for war against a second axis member, with state newspaper Rodong Sinmun stating just days before the attack on Baghdad was initiated: 'It is becoming certain that, in case the U.S. imperialists' invasion of Iraq is successful, they will wage a new war of aggression on the Korean Peninsula.'[32] The threats against North Korea's very right to exist were real enough. The Bush administration had repeatedly suggested that certain 'rogue states' could be legitimate targets of preemptive nuclear strikes. Following America's initial victories in Iraq, Defense Secretary Donald Rumsfeld stated that the DPRK government must draw the 'appropriate lesson.'[33] He went on to demand revisions in Operations Plan 5030, the United States' plan for war against North Korea. He also sought money from Congress for new bunker-busting nuclear weapons, an invaluable asset in a war against the dug in and highly fortified Korean military.[34] According to American insiders who read the plan, the strategy was to 'topple Kim [Jong Il]'s regime by destabilizing its military forces,' something which would have proven far more difficult than it did in Iraq.[35,36]

Should the United States have proceeded to launch a war against North Korea, the use of bunker busting tactical nuclear weapons would have been highly likely. There was a wide consensus among U.S. defense experts that North Korean weapons facilities were so deeply buried they would be all but immune to conventional attack – necessitating employment of bunker-busting nuclear weapons across much of the country to penetrate them.[37,38,39,40,41] Operations Plan 5030 was pushed 'by many of the same administration hard-liners who advocated regime change in Iraq.' Although very different, both were states which conducted foreign policy independently of the Western Bloc and were former Soviet allies which the United States wished to bring under its influence. Unnamed senior Bush administration officials considered elements of these plans to strike the DPRK 'so aggressive they could provoke a war.'[42,43]

Alongside Secretary Rumsfeld's threats came an American military escalation on the Korean peninsula targeting the DPRK. In 2003 the United States redeployed 24 of its nuclear capable heavy bombers to the Asia-Pacific within range of the DPRK, indicating that it may also send fighter escorts to support its reconnaissance missions which often infringed on North Korean airspace.[44] Reconnaissance flights near or even into the country's airspace also increased significantly. Such reconnaissance missions to gather data on potential targets would commonly precede a military strike.[45] For Pyongyang there remained a considerable chance that it would imminently be subjected to an American attack.[46]

As of 2002 the United States military's Nuclear Posture Review had required the Pentagon to draft contingency plans for the deployment of nuclear weapons against North Korea.[47] U.S. rhetoric meanwhile continued to escalate, and plans for war to 'tear this regime down' were strongly supported by such influential figures as Donald Rumsfeld, Paul Wolfowitz, John Bolton and Nicholas Eberstadt.[48] The U.S. Congressional Research Service's East Asia specialist Larry Niksch concluded at this time that 'regime change in North Korea is indeed the Bush administration's policy objective.' Niksch wrote that if sanctions against the DPRK and interdiction of its shipping did not produce the desired collapse of the government, Secretary Rumsfeld was considering 'a broader plan of massive strikes against multiple targets.'[49]

There were further extreme plans made for military action to be taken to overthrow the North Korean government and place the country under an American-led occupation. The highly influential New York based Council on Foreign Relations (CFR) published a 60-page report in 2009 projecting a full scale invasion of North Korea and deployment of a 'stabilization force' of an expected 460,000 occupying troops.[50] The influence of the CFR in the U.S. State Department was considerable, and Secretary of State Hillary Clinton referred to the relationship as follows: 'We get a lot of advice from the council ... [the council tells us] what we should be doing and how we should think about the future.'[51] Based on the influence of the CFR, the nature of their report, the United States' recent string of military interventions and the nature of the previous American military intervention in Korea, it was apparent that the country was seriously threatened.

It was clear that little had changed since the Cold War years and the Korean War, and that Washington was still intent on ousting the DPRK's government. As Professor Armstrong observed of the United States' approach to North Korea at this time and their unwillingness to negotiate: 'The rhetoric of the Bush administration ... seemed to suggest that 'rogue states' with weapons of mass destruction (WMD) were to be eliminated rather than bargained with. During the lead-up to war in Iraq, the general thrust of U.S. policy appeared to be "regime change" in Pyongyang, not diplomacy.'[52] He concluded that American attempts to negotiate with the DPRK were neither genuine nor realistic, stating: 'By 'diplomacy' the United States seemed to mean making unilateral demands on the North Koreans rather than anything resembling negotiation.'[53]

Though the Iraqi government had been swiftly toppled, the Iraq War continued as various factions, many formed by former members of the military or by Iranian aligned elements, waged an insurgency against and bogged down U.S. forces. This both kept the United States preoccupied in a quagmire in which casualties began to mount substantially, and slated the American public's taste for further wars in the near future. Plans for attacks on North Korea and other 'rogue states,' expected to be considerably more challenging still, had to be temporarily postponed. Significant threats by the US, which had proven itself multiple times to be capable of seeing them through in Iraq and Yugoslavia among several other former Soviet allies, but also in Korea where an estimated 20–30 percent of the population were killed in America's last war on the peninsula[54,55] led to a response. The DPRK realized what any rational state actor would. In a world of 'jungle laws' as they referred to it, with the United States, most often backed by Western partners or acting through NATO, acting as a global hegemon only a powerful deterrent could ensure the safety of the state and its people. This was all the more clear after 2003.[56] The DPRK Foreign Ministry stated in the wake of the Iraq War, referring to Iraq's nuclear disarmament preceding the U.S. military intervention and Korea's resulting need to develop a nuclear deterrent: 'The Iraqi war shows that to allow disarming through inspection does not help avert a war but rather sparks it.'[57]

Thomas Donnelly, member of the U.S. House of Representatives Committee on National Security, Strategic Communications Director at Lockheed Martin Corporation and former Deputy Executive Director of the Project for the New American Century (PNAC) himself commented on the importance of nuclear deterrence to the security of 'rogue states.' As director of PNAC, a neoconservative think tank with a key role in shaping the Bush administration's foreign policy[58,59] (of which Donald Rumsfeld, Deputy Defense Secretary Wolfowitz and Vice President Cheney were also members) with the stated goal of 'promoting American global leadership' and which strongly advocated for war against Iraq and other 'rogue states,'[60] he had key insight into the factors which would influence the United States' propensity to carry out strikes on the DPRK.

Donnelly stated in his highly influential PNAC paper *Rebuilding America's Defenses* published in 2000 that the DPRK's development of WMD and particularly a nuclear deterrent would be key to preventing the United States from launching military aggression against it: He reiterated this crucial point several times in his paper:

- 'The United States also must counteract the effects of the proliferation of ballistic missiles and weapons of mass destruction that may soon allow lesser states to deter U.S. military action by threatening U.S. allies and the American homeland itself. Of all the new and current missions for U.S. armed forces, this must have priority.'
- 'Weak states operating small arsenals of crude ballistic missiles, armed with basic nuclear warheads or other weapons of mass destruction, will be in a strong position to deter the United States from using conventional force.'

- 'When their missiles are tipped with warheads carrying nuclear, biological, or chemical weapons, even weak regional powers have a credible deterrent regardless of the balance of conventional forces.'
- 'In the post cold war era, America and its allies, rather than the Soviet Union, have become the primary objects of deterrence and it is states like Iraq, Iran and North Korea who most wish to develop deterrent capabilities. … 'weak states operating small arsenals of crude ballistic missiles, armed with basic nuclear warheads or other weapons of mass destruction, will be in a strong position to deter the United States from using conventional force, no matter the technological or other advantages we may enjoy..''[61]

The PNAC paper's statements were reiterated by Secretary of State Rumsfeld in 2001 when he described the goal of 'rogue states' acquiring deterrent capabilities as being: 'to deter us [the United States] from bringing our conventional or nuclear power to bear in a regional crisis.' Regarding the potential of WMDs to deter American military intervention he stated: '"asymmetric" approaches can limit our ability to apply military power.'[62] As the United States developed an increasingly assertive and interventionist foreign policy it was increasingly clear that the only way for those deemed 'rogue states,' governments which refused to become a part of the 'American century' and submit to the Western centric world order, to survive they would need to develop a nuclear deterrent.

The DPRK withdrew from the Treaty on the Non-Proliferation of Nuclear Weapons (NPT) in 2003. While signatories were prohibited under international law from developing nuclear weapons, as a non-signatory the DPRK could legally pursue a nuclear program just as India, Pakistan and Israel had done beforehand. Indeed, Article X of the treaty guarantees all states the right to withdraw with three months' notice if 'extraordinary events, related to the subject matter of this Treaty, have jeopardized the supreme interests of its country.' With the country's very right to exist under imminent threat, North Korea certainly qualified as a state whose supreme interests were threatened.

On the basis of a number of studies separately conducted by South Korean and Western experts, previously discussed in Chapter 10, which concluded that the United States was guilty of the crime of genocide against the Korean people during the Korean War, North Korea's nuclear program can be considered not only entirely legal – but also necessary to avert a second such attack by the U.S. and thereby prevent genocide. The DPRK proceeded to make very significant progress on their domestic nuclear program and soon after began a series of successful nuclear tests and concessive breakthroughs. The need for such defensive measures was reaffirmed several times after 2003, and the threat of military intervention was always imminent. Successful nuclear tests were conducted as follows:

- On October 9, 2006, 15 years after the first Gulf War, the DPRK announced that it conducted its first nuclear test. This was confirmed by seismic readings taken in neighboring countries. In January 2007 the North Korean government gave further confirmation that it had obtained nuclear weapons. According to several Western analysts the aim of the tests from their inception was to create a miniaturized nuclear warhead capable of being launched by missile – hence the low yield of just 0.7–2 kilotons of the first nuclear test.[63]
- In April 2009 the Director of the International Atomic Agency confirmed that North Korea had become a 'fully fledged nuclear power.' In May of the same year the country conducted a second nuclear test, with a yield many times that of the first.[64]
- In February 2013 North Korea conducted a third nuclear test, reportedly with a lighter warhead that delivered a far greater yield. The German Federal Institute for Geosciences and Natural Resources estimated the yield to be at 40 kilotons, several times greater than the previous test in 2009.[65]
- In January 2016 North Korea launched another nuclear test, which according to Pyongyang was a hydrogen bomb. In September that year the country launched another nuclear test and announced afterwards that it was capable of mounting nuclear warheads on ballistic missiles.[66]
- In September 2017 North Korea conducted its final nuclear test – a warhead with an estimated yield of up to 280 kilotons miniaturized sufficiently to allow it to deploy from an intercontinental range ballistic missile (ICBM).[67]The country in the same year completed three successful tests of the Hwasong-14 and Hwasong-15 ICBMs capable of striking the United States mainland,[68] as well as the Hwasong-12 intermediate range ballistic missile developed to target U.S. forwards bases on Guam. It proceeded the following year to demolish its nuclear testing site and declare a successful end to the program. 2017 thus marked the completion of the deterrence program.

Nuclear tests were from the beginning conducted with the intention of miniaturizing nuclear warheads while maximizing their payloads, a far more complex task than producing a large high yield weapon as the United States and USSR had done in the 1940s. With the sole target of a nuclear deterrent having always been the United States, and without bombers capable of feasibly reaching this target with a heavier warhead, developing a light warhead capable of being placed on a long-range missile was from the beginning the primary intent of the North Korean nuclear program. Following the first two nuclear tests North Korean Leader Kim Jong Un declared in 2012 that superiority in military technology was 'no longer monopolized by imperialists.' Referring to the country's experience during the Korean War, indicating the formative role it has played on the country's foreign policy ever since – its perceived need for a nuclear program included, Marshal Kim stated when later addressing a conference Korean War veterans: 'Our strength is not what it was in the 1950s, when we had to fight with rifles in our hands against the U.S. imperialists who were armed to the teeth. We now possess the strength with which to fight any form of warfare that may be chosen by the United States. We have the power to deter the United States from unleashing a nuclear war. Gone forever is the era when the United States blackmailed us with nuclear weapons.'[69]

Following the final test in September 2017, amid growing threats of military intervention by the United States, the Korean leader announced that the development of a nuclear deterrent was necessary to 'protect destiny and sovereignty from the long-standing nuclear threats of U.S. imperialists.'[70] The chances of the United States waging a war and using tactical nuclear weapons against North Korea were reduced substantially as their 'monopoly' on such force, referred to on several occasions by the DPRK leadership,[71] was ended and threat of nuclear retaliation increased – a form of nuclear parity. The country reiterated on several occasions that its nuclear weapons were aimed solely at the United States, and were not being aimed at neighboring U.S. allies such as Japan and South Korea. The focus on miniaturized warheads from the very beginning of testing lent credibility to these claims.[72]

The United States and its partners, including the European Union, Japan and South Korea, responded to North Korea's nuclear weapons development with condemnation and harsh economic sanctions. Military threats against the country increased alongside renewed and widespread calls for the imposition of regime change. This response was extensive and unique to the DPRK, considering that other aforementioned non-NPT states which have developed their own nuclear weapons have never been met with such reprisals. The inconsistency in the responses of the United States and its partners to nuclear development was attested to by Andrea Berger, senior research fellow and deputy director of the Proliferation and Nuclear Policy team at the British Royal United Services Institute. In her study she noted the conduct of the Western Bloc towards nuclear weapons states such as Pakistan, which she concluded were significant risks to global stability and alleged had ties to terrorist organizations, showed an immense discrepancy compared to their conduct towards North Korea – with Islamabad having continued to receive billions of dollars in American aid. The DPRK on the other hand, despite posing a far lesser threat to the international community as a whole, was sanctioned for developing the same weapons under similar circumstances (both were non-signatories of the NPT).[73]

The difference was that the North Korean deterrent, unlike those of Pakistan, Israel or India, served to limit the freedom of action of Western militaries and thus was a threat to Western interests – hence the double standards. As Vice Chairman of the Inter-Korea Historian Association, South Korean professor Jung Tae Hern, noted: 'in light of all these concerns, the U.S. appears to hold Pakistan at a much lower standard than it does North Korea. The disdain that the U.S. has shown North Korea over the past sixty years, some of which is based on false or unproven assumptions ... is not based solely on Pyongyang's nuclear threat since the U.S. continues to tolerate nuclear weapons of non-NPT members such as Pakistan, India an Israel.'[74] U.S. Congressman Ron Paul similarly concluded that North Korea was singled out by the United States and its partners for reprisals in a way that other nuclear states were not, stating: 'they get targeted. But nothing much is said about the nuclear armaments of Israel, Pakistan and India, and that is a significant event. And also the fact that our CIA watches everybody and ... they caught South Korea wanting to develop a nuclear weapon as well as Taiwan. So it's this inconsistency.'[75]

It appeared that the Western powers were capable of unilaterally determining the supposed legality and legitimacy of a country's nuclear weapons program, and the standards were very much based on how a country's nuclear development suited Western interests. Under the post-Cold War Western dominated world order only governments endorsed by the Western Bloc were allowed to arm themselves with capable asymmetric weapons. Development of such weapons in all non-Western aligned states from China[76] and the USSR to Syria and Iran, being deemed provocations threatening to 'upend the rules based international order' – in other words challenge the Western dominated world order.[77] While Indian nuclear missile tests aimed squarely at Chinese cities,[78] Pakistani tests of nuclear tipped cruise missiles aimed at the Indian coast[79] or even U.S. tactical nuclear weapons tests aimed at Russia and North Korea,[80] all drew little to no criticism – the fact that North Korea was developing asymmetric weapons to hold the Western Bloc and the military might of the United States in check in Asia made it unacceptable. As U.S. President Barack Obama stated in 2016 regarding his vision for the future of the Asia-Pacific region: 'America should write the rules. America should call the shots. Other countries should play by the rules that America and our partners set, and not the other way around.'[81] By developing a deterrent North Korea was setting its own rules and limiting American freedom to shape the future of the region and its peoples through force.

Existential Deterrence: The Exclusively Defensive Nature of North Korea's Nuclear Program

The DPRK claimed since the beginning of its nuclear program that its nuclear tests have been entirely defensive in nature – a measure critical to deterring aggression against it. The state run Korean Central News Agency (KCNA) stated to this effect: 'The [George W.] Bush administration's DPRK policy that stemmed from its ignorance of the DPRK resulted in making the DPRK a nuclear weapons state.'[82] It has been reiterated several times by the Foreign Ministry,[83] leadership[84,85] and state media[86] that American nuclear threats were a key motivation for the development of a nuclear deterrent. Considering both the circumstances under which North Korea carried out its first nuclear tests and the conclusions reached in PNAC's aforementioned study, which stated that 'the surest deterrent to American action is a functioning nuclear arsenal' among others to much the same effect,[87] Pyongyang's claims appear to be substantiated.

Russian nuclear weapons expert Vladimir Khrustalev, based on an extensive study of that the DPRK's nuclear program, was one of many analysts to conclude that their development was a defensive precaution which served, in the words of Defense Secretary Rumsfeld, 'to deter us [the United States] from bringing our conventional or nuclear power to bear in a regional crisis ... "asymmetric" approaches can limit our ability to apply military power.'[88] The analyst further noted that it was precisely for this reason that the development of a Korean deterrent was naturally strongly opposed by those with offensive designs against the country. As Khrustalev stated: 'Russia and China are not directly threatened by these missiles. Like any other means of nuclear deterrence, they threaten those who would attack the owner of nuclear weapons. It is obvious that it makes no sense for the DPRK to "go crazy" and press the red button for no reason. They could commit suicide in many other, simpler ways ... In this case, any scenario of attack on the DPRK makes no sense because the attacker would pay a price that would scare away anyone considering such attempts. In fact, it is a reproduction of the model, which was between the Soviet Union and the United States and which now exists between India and Pakistan.'[89]

Nuclear weapons and a strengthening of the DPRK's deterrence capability, far from being a danger or a destabilizing agent as the West has long claimed, will in fact help to protect peace on the Korean Peninsula and in East Asia. This is in much the same vein as Soviet, Israeli and Pakistani nuclear weapons arguably served to increase not only the security of these countries against hostile attack, but also reduced the likelihood of major wars in Europe, the Middle East and South Asia respectively. While the DPRK had always been under threat of a U.S. led Western invasion, the development of a nuclear deterrent reduced this threat significantly and has ensured that China, Japan and South Korea will not suffer from the fallout of a Western initiated war in their region. With a number of influential figures in the United States, from lawmakers,[90,91,92] congressmen[93] and military officials[94] to presidential national security advisors[95] and the chairman of the U.S. Joint Chiefs of Staff,[96] all having indicated a considerable degree of tolerance to collateral damage against targets in Japan and South Korea and thus supported the potential initiation of preventative military strikes against the DPRK, the country has had a strong incentive to develop a ballistic missile capable for delivering a nuclear warhead to the United States mainland and thus ensuring the viability of its deterrent. This has deterred American military action which would not only have devastated the DPRK itself, but which is expected to cause hundreds of thousands of casualties in neighboring countries as well.

North Korea is equally highly unlikely to attack any of its neighbors because this would in turn invite, in the words of U.S. President Donald Trump, 'fire and fury like the world has never seen'[97] and would be 'totally destroyed.'[98] Mutual vulnerability to one another's weapons of mass destruction guarantees the security of both states in much the same way as it prevented war from breaking out between the United States and the USSR for decades – making war on the Korean Peninsula far less likely than if one power maintained a monopoly on weapons of mass destruction.

President of the National Institute for Public Policy in the United States, Professor Keith Payne, noted in regards to nuclear deterrence: 'In contemporary cases, however, as in the past – if the complex variety of conditions necessary for deterrence to work are present and the challenger is risk – and cost-tolerant – then nuclear deterrence may be uniquely decisive in the challenger's decision making.'[99] While the United States has indicated that it may be somewhat risk averse to damage to its allies,[100,101,102,103,104] nuclear weapons and an ICBM under Pyongyang's command escalate the risks of aggression against the DPRK – thus eliminating American tolerance to the potential costs of war. As U.S. President Ronald Reagan stated during the Cold War: 'History teaches that wars begin when governments believe the price of aggression is cheap.'[105] By gaining the ability to strike the U.S. mainland and put American cities in the firing line, North Korea is innumerably increasing the 'price of aggression' and has thus made an American initiated war in East Asia considerably less likely.

Australian Professor Joseph M. Siracusa, a renowned expert on the history of nuclear weapons, noted that for the United States peace had meant U.S. military dominance, and the emergence of mutually assured destruction (MAD) and a balance of power threatened this concept of a hegemonic peace based on American primacy. He stated in the context of the Cold War: 'The idea of MAD did not sit well with American military chiefs preaching peace through strength. The "first principle of deterrence," General Thomas S. Powers wrote in 1965, was "to maintain a credible capability to achieve a military victory under any set of conditions or circumstances".'[106] American defense analysts and military planners were described by Siracusa as 'despising notions of parity and sufficiency.'[107] The idea that North Korea, a state of little over 20 million people, can effectively singlehandedly hold the U.S. military in check inevitably does not sit well in the United States considering its designs for absolute primacy.

Though the North Korean military has the capability to effectively deter an invasion by the overwhelming military forces of the United States and its partners, making a potential ground invasion an extremely costly affair, it does not have the capability to realistically achieve any meaningful military objectives by launching an offensive war. By virtue of its fortified missile sites, among the best hardened globally,[108] extensive underground military complexes and tunnel networks, which exceed those of any other country in the world, as well as basic militarily training for over a third of its population,[109] the DPRK's conventional forces can counter potential aggression against the country – so long as the United States does not deploy weapons of mass destruction to negate these defensive assets. North Korea's military is overwhelmingly tailored to fighting a defensive war, and while its Special Forces are equipped launch surgical counterstrikes against enemy targets these cannot bring about an occupation or any meaningful territorial gains. Invasion of a foreign country is not feasible, nor is it an objective of the country's armed forces. North Korea has nothing to realistically gain from an offensive war, but a great deal to lose including its sovereignty.

By contrast the forces of the United States and their partners possess overwhelming military forces which the American military leadership is near certain could occupy North Korea. While they project extremely heavy casualties,[110] military planners from Defense Secretary Ashton Carter to Chief of Staff General Mark Miley, ROK-U.S. Joint

Forces Commander General Sharp, House Armed Services Committee Chairman Mac Thornberry, and General Gary E. Luck, have stated they are confident that they can win an offensive war.[111,112,113,114,115] High profile papers by the Council on Foreign Relations laying out plans for an occupation of North Korea, and the South Korean government's somewhat premature allocation governorships for all the provinces of the north, demonstrates that governments in Seoul have long seen the downfall of the North Korean government and occupation of its territory as a very real possibility. One side is confident that they can win a war, while the other does all it can to deter attacks, knowing that it suffers a technological disadvantage in many of its conventional warfare capabilities and is severely limited in its ability to launch a meaningful offensive or hold ground beyond its borders.[116]

While North Korea's armed forces project for strikes on enemy targets to cause damage, a form of deterrence, the United States military projects for a full invasion and occupation, a feasible offensive war plan. White House strategy reviews project occupation and regime change,[117] as do numerous other American military plans.[118] North Korean missile strikes are never planned as part of a consequent occupation of the south, or any military action that could leave the state in a better position after a war than beforehand. As previously covered in Chapter 17, the U.S. military is heavily geared towards a power projection role and has invested heavily in assets key to launching attacks on and occupying overseas territories. North Korea's armed forces by contrast are heavily defensively oriented, with the KPA having invested very little in power projection capabilities and lacking the logistical assets needed to feasibly launch a long-term offensive beyond its borders. The key difference in military posturing between the two sides is that the United States believes that it can potentially invade and occupy the DPRK as it has done in other states across the world against which its rhetoric has been similar. The DPRK on the other hand aims to make a potential war as costly as possible for an invader by both strengthening its defensive capabilities and developing strike capabilities which can inflict maximum damage to its enemies. These are not war aims which will grant it territory or concessions, but rather sheer destruction for the sake of deterrence.

While both sides of the conflict possess weapons of mass destruction, their doctrines for the use of such weapons starkly differ. The United States' military doctrine for nuclear weapons, the *Doctrine for Joint Nuclear Operations*, states that the U.S. military commanders can use nuclear weapons to preempt an attack by a hostile party, including to destroy stockpiles of nuclear, biological or chemical weapons. Specifically mentioned are attacks on hardened installations which nuclear weapons would be required to penetrate – of which the DPRK in particular is known to have many.[119] North Korea, along with China and India are the only nuclear states which adhere to a no-first-use doctrine.[120,121,122]

The DPRK's nuclear strategic doctrine is classified as an existential strategy, used by small states which perceive threats to their sovereignty to deter military aggression or coercion. This is characterized as the least threatening and most defensively oriented of all nuclear weapons strategies, adhered to only by the DPRK and Israel. By contrast the United States' nuclear strategy is classified as a maximum deterrence strategy, under which not only can nuclear weapons be used to achieve military victory, but first strikes are also feasible. Nuclear weapons are used to attack enemy forces, and considered similar to conventional weapons under a maximum strategy. Nuclear weapons use can be limited and can be intended to win war. This is considered the most aggressive nuclear strategic doctrine. Under an existential strategy however nuclear weapons are used only to deter attack, and are considered distinct from conventional weapons. Their use cannot be a means to victory.[123]

American expert on Asian Security and Nuclear Weapons, Professor Susan Turner Haynes, described the United States' strategy of maximum deterrence as 'premised on the belief that it is possible to win a nuclear war. This belief derives from the base assumption that nuclear weapons are not qualitatively distinct from conventional weapons. Thus, according to adherents of maximum deterrence, war should be conducted similarly regardless of the weapons employed. Nuclear weapons present more risk but do not shift the entire calculus of war. Such a strategy requires what is known as a "first strike capability".'[124]

The United States has increasingly developed nuclear weapons with smaller yields capable of more precisely targeting enemy forces with 'limited' nuclear strikes. The focus on development of these 'tactical nuclear weapons' has been heralded by a number of analysts as a sign that the United States is increasingly willing to use nuclear weapons as a means to wage war rather than as an existential threat to prevent war. Former Vice Chairman of the U.S. Joint Chiefs of Staff and leading nuclear strategist General James E. Cartwright acknowledged in 2016 that 'what going smaller' by developing lower yield tactical nuclear weapons did was 'to make the weapon more thinkable.'[125] U.S. Air Force Chief of Staff General Norton Schwartz similarly stated that nuclear weapons with 'improved accuracy and lower yield is a desired military capability. Without a question'[126] which analysts believed strongly implied a role for nuclear weapons beyond deterrence.[127] Such a weapon would better suit a tactical nuclear strike on enemy forces rather than massive deterrence. The United States' Defense Science Board recommended in 2017 that the country take such options further, calling for 'a more flexible nuclear enterprise that could produce, if needed, a rapid, tailored nuclear option for limited use.'[128] The aforementioned bunker buster nuclear weapons designed to penetrate North Korean fortifications are a key example of this. These developments are wholly in line with the U.S. adherence to maximum deterrence, under which nuclear weapons can be used as a means to attain victory and limited use of nuclear weapons is an option. The contrast between the doctrines of the two nuclear powers therefore could not be greater, and North Korea's nuclear arsenal, as a result of the effective check it has put on the Western Bloc's ability to initiate a regional war and apply military force, is set to serve as an agent of regional stability in East Asia for years to come.

Nuclear Arms as a Deterrent Against Aggression: A Response to External Threats

North Korea has repeatedly claimed that its nuclear program was motivated by the threats made against it, citing Iraq and Libya as precedents showing that small independent states with inadequate defense capabilities could be and were often targeted by Western powers resulting in chaos and suffering for their respective populations.[129] If anything the DPRK is more threatened than these other 'rogue states' ever were, with calls from United States government for nuclear strikes to bring about regime change having been made.[130] Despite this and the well-known disastrous results of these American-led wars, North Korea's pursuit of nuclear weapon is still widely portrayed by the West as highly irrational – even illegal.

Seumas Milne, British journalist, political aide and party Executive Director of Strategy and Communications, wrote on Korea's nuclear program and its causes:

> Even the U.S. doesn't believe North Korea poses any threat of aggression against the South, home to nearly 30,000 American troops and covered by its nuclear umbrella. But the idea, much canvassed in recent days, that there is something irrational in North Korea's attempt to acquire nuclear weapons is clearly absurd. This is, after all, a state that has been targeted for regime change by the U.S. ever since the end of the Cold War ... In April 2003, North Korea drew the obvious conclusion from the U.S. and British aggression against Iraq. The war showed, it commented at the time, 'that to allow disarmament through inspection does not help avert a war, but rather sparks it.' Only 'a tremendous military deterrent force,' it stated with unavoidable logic, could prevent attacks on states the world's only superpower was determined to bring to heel. The lessons could not be clearer. Of Bush's 'axis' states, Iraq, which had no weapons of mass destruction, was invaded and occupied; North Korea, which already had some nuclear capacity, was left untouched and is most unlikely to be attacked in the future; while Iran, which has yet to develop a nuclear capability, is still threatened with aggression.[131]

Milne drew the same conclusion that many independent analysts have, that the DPRK among all states in the world is one of the most at risk of Western military intervention, and so has a right to develop nuclear weapons as a deterrent to aggression. He wrote: 'It's not just the breathtaking hypocrisy that underpins every Western pronouncement about the "threat to world peace" posed by the "illegal weapons" ... Or the double standards that underpin the nuclear indulgence of Israel, India and Pakistan ... So why North Korea, no longer even a signatory to the [nuclear non-proliferation] treaty and therefore not bound by its rules ... should treat them as a reason to disarm is a mystery.'[132]

Commenting on the prospects of North Korea unilaterally giving up its nuclear weapons and the rationality of Pyongyang's policy, Daniel R. Coats, the Trump Administration's Director of National Intelligence, noted that it was strongly against Korea's national security interests to disarm. He stated that the North Korean leadership 'has watched, I think, what has happened around the world relative to nations that possess nuclear capabilities and the leverage they have and seen that having the nuclear card in your pocket results in a lot of deterrence capability … The lessons that we learned out of Libya giving up its nukes … is, unfortunately: If you had nukes, never give them up. If you don't have them, get them.'[133] The Director's claims were strongly supported by North Korea's own Foreign Ministry, which stated regarding the valuable lessons learned from Tripoli's decision to terminate its deterrent force and its consequences: 'Libya's nuclear dismantlement much touted by the U.S. in the past turned out to be a mode of aggression by which the latter coaxed the former with such sweet words as "guarantee of security" and "improvement of relations" to disarm and then swallow it up by force.' The DPRK believed that in exchange for a lifting of sanctions and better relations Libya 'took the economic bait, foolishly disarmed themselves, and once they were defenseless, were mercilessly punished by the West.'[134]

Upon Libya's termination of its nuclear program and dismantlement of its ballistic missiles in 2003 U.S. President George W. Bush had pledged: 'leaders who abandon the pursuit of chemical, biological and nuclear weapons, and the means to deliver them, will find an open path to better relations with the United States and other free nations.' Libya was, according to the Bush administration, set to be 'a model for other countries.'[135] Following the Obama administration's decision to conduct an extensive bombing campaign to overthrow the Libyan government the country did serve as an example – one which alongside Iraq showed the price of giving up one's deterrence capabilities in exchange for security guarantees and promises of good relations from the United States and its European allies. The Western Bloc's efforts to instigate regime change, which according to leaked memos from U.S. Secretary of State Hillary Clinton were to protect their economic interests and gain access to Libyan oil,[136] led to a bombing campaign, support for a radical Islamist insurgency and brutal execution of its leader

– sodomy by a bayonet – in 2011.[137] This devastated the country – leading to its collapse into what former U.S. Ambassador to Libya John Graham called 'a completely failed state.'[138] Having previously enjoyed the highest living standards on the African continent, Libya entered an indefinite state of civil war where Western military powers have been able to operate freely,[139,140] has seen the rise of radical Islamist groups such as Islamic State, and has become a center for human trafficking and slave trading.[141,142]

The Economist, a staunch critic of the North Korean government, stated regarding Libya's example and its significance to North Korean policymaking: 'Mr. Kim [Jong Un] is behaving rationally. He watched Muammar Gaddafi of Libya give up his nuclear program in return for better relations with the West – and end up dead. He sees his nuclear arsenal as a guarantee that his regime, and he, will survive.'[143] In framing a selfish motive, the article notably failed to mention that it was not the Libyan leader and ruling elites, but the entire country, which suffered catastrophe,[144,145] and that a similarly bleak fate may well await the DPRK and its people should it leave itself vulnerable. Indeed, those who have suffered most in Libya have not been the Gaddafi era leadership, but the people themselves who have borne the brunt of resurgences in Islamic terrorism, human trafficking and slave trading in the aftermath of their government's fall.

This analysis was echoed by several other experts. Former U.S. President Jimmy Carter noted in October 2017 that North Korea's leadership were 'completely rational and dedicated to the preservation of their regime' and that there was 'no remaining chance that it [DPRK] will agree to a total denuclearization, as it has seen what happened in a denuclearized Libya and assessed the doubtful status of U.S. adherence to the Iran nuclear agreement.'[146] At a press conference in 2017 Russian President Vladimir Putin, elaborating on the reasons why the DPRK pursued and could not be pressed to give up its weapons program, recalled the catastrophic precedents set Iraq and Libya. He stated that the North Koreans 'would rather eat grass than give up their nuclear program unless they feel safe' – and that only 'the restoration of international law' under which the sovereignty of small states was protected could ever lead to a change in this.[147]

Azhdar Kurtov from the Russian Institute for Strategic Studies similarly stated that Pyongyang 'would not abandon its course because North

Korea's authorities have the vivid example of recent events in Libya and Iraq, where the U.S. violated international law and carried out a military intervention against sovereign states.' He concluded that a nuclear deterrent in the hands of Libya or Iraq would have prevented their destruction, and so it would be strongly in Pyongyang's interest to maintain such a deterrent.[148] Yale Political Science Professors and experts in nuclear policy Alexandre Debs and Nuno P. Monteiro reached similar conclusions in a study of North Korea's weapons program, noting the strong incentives the state had to acquire nuclear weapons in a U.S. dominated post-Cold War world.[149] *The Diplomat* published an article similarly arguing that North Korea's actions were largely influenced by the destruction wrought on close partner Serbia by the U.S. and its NATO allies in 1999, and that Korean weapons programs were an attempt to avoid a similar fate.[150]

Perhaps the best description of the motives for the nuclear program however was given by Daniel McAdams, Executive Director of the American right wing think tank, the Ron Paul Institute for Peace and Prosperity. Noting the precedents set by other targets of U.S. attacks, he stated: 'Look at the real world and what's happened to countries that have turned over their nukes. Look at Libya when it turned over its nuclear program, "regime change." Syria that didn't have a program, "regime change." [The United States has since demanded that the Syrian president be removed from power as a pretext to a cessation of hostilities with the country, against which it has conducted numerous illegal air and missile strikes.][151,152] Iran has ended their nuclear program and sent their enriched uranium to Russia, and what's happening with Iran?'[153]

What is clear is that the DPRK has had little choice but to continue to pursue a nuclear deterrent to ensure the defense of its people against persistent and uncompromising aggressive powers. Hostility towards North Korea will continue in exactly the same way should the country give up its nuclear program because its cause is unrelated to the nuclear issue. Abandoning nuclear weapons would leave the nation in greater danger of attack and 'regime change,' as it did in other states, which would destroy the lives of millions of Koreans.

Alongside North Korea's perceived need for a nuclear deterrent in light of the nature of the threats arrayed against it, development of a nuclear deterrent allows a nation which faces a threat of external aggression to reduce its conventional military spending and devote more resources to economic development. This strategy was previously employed in the USSR in the 1950s, which due to progress in its nuclear program was able to cut spending on its massive conventional forces which accounted for the vast majority of its defense budget. The release of these funds allowed the country to devote more attention to economic development and providing consumer goods.[154] The United States itself also relied on deployment of nuclear weapons to reduce expenditure on conventional forces and thereby reduce its spending deficit. In Korea the U.S. had deployed well over 300,000 military personnel in the aftermath of the Korean War while financially supporting a vast South Korean army of 720,000 men, over twice the size of that in the North,[155] which deployed 350,000. In 1956 President Eisenhower declared his intention to reduce the United States' substantial deficit by reducing this expenditure. Military leaders considered the deployment of nuclear weapons to the peninsula to be the only means of scaling down conventional forces and reducing military assistance to the ROK without leaving it vulnerable to attack.

The United States thus became the first party to nuclearize the Korean Peninsula, unilaterally withdrawing from article 13 (d) of the Korean War armistice agreement and deploying nuclear weapons to South Korea from January 1958.[156] Approximately 950 warheads were deployed,[157] and these nuclear forces were only withdrawn in 1992, at a time when technological advances meant that deployment of nuclear weapons on Korean soil were no longer necessary as nuclear submarines, nuclear tipped cruise and ballistic missiles and long-range bombers could cover the peninsula from elsewhere in the Pacific. This was the pretext given by the United States military for removal of these weapons, noting that nuclear bombers based on Guam, under two hours' flight from the Korean Peninsula, gave nuclear coverage of all of North Korea from the Yalu River to the DMZ.[158] If anything, these offshore nuclear assets are even more potent as deterrents as they are less vulnerable to preemptive destruction.

In May 2016 the DPRK reiterated its commitment to the new 'Byungjin' policy of prioritizing economic development and the development of defensive nuclear weapons simultaneously. That year the country proceeded to reduce its conventional military spending.[159] Nuclear weapons have continued to allow the DPRK to focus on economic development in a way that would otherwise not have been possible.[160] As former North Korean diplomat Kim Min Gyu, who defected in 2009, stated regarding the costs of the program: 'actually, what they spend isn't that much. Their workforce works for free and, except for a few key imported parts, they make everything else.'[161] What nuclear weapons offer therefore is, literally, more 'bang for the buck' than investment in conventional capabilities, making them key facilitators of security, lower military spending and a stronger economy. A stronger economy in turn will not only improve the lives of Korean citizens but also better ensure the country's security in the long run. Despite heightened tensions with the United States in 2017 and threats of war, North Korea was able to continue to reduce its conventional military expenditure as a result of its advancing nuclear deterrence capabilities. This has helped to lift the longtime economic burden of a sustaining massive conventional military, and was a major cause for the country's continued economic growth and stable living standards despite facing tightening Western drafted economic sanctions – globally unprecedented in their severity in recent history.[162,163,164] The country's ability to weather Western economic pressure has been particularly remarkable when compared to other targets of economic sanctions including Iran,[165] Iraq[166] and Russia[167] – the economies of which all quickly spiraled into decline in the face of far less severe forms of economic warfare. The DPRK's actions show that it is not only highly willing to reduce military expenditure should the threat against it be reduced, but also to reroute these resources to the economy.

Regarding the threats which have been arrayed against the DPRK since long before its first nuclear test, which continued and escalated throughout the development of the country's nuclear program, their severity alone can be seen as a sufficient incentive for the country to seek the development of nuclear arms. The United States military has frequently held massive military drills in South Korea, often several per year, which have rehearsed preemptive and at times even preventative strikes on the DPRK – followed by invasion and occupation of the country.[168,169] These drills involve tens of thousands of military personnel on the border of the DRPK, and by some estimates are the largest held anywhere in the world. The 2016 the

Key Resolve and Foal Eagle military exercises for example involved 90,000 South Korean soldiers and 15,000 U.S. troops. These drills have raised particular concern in North Korea because there is no peace agreement between the parties involved, with the United States unwilling to sign one. Under the fragile armistice that ended the Korean War, under which the Peninsula still remains technically at war, conflict could break out any time and any rehearsal of an attack could well be preparation for a real assault and a renewal of open hostilities.

A senior defense official in Seoul said in February 2016: 'This year's operations will involve recovering key facilities that are located deep within North Korea, all the way near its northern borders.' In the exercises, Operation 5015 would be rehearsed – entailing a nuclear first strike followed by killing the country's leadership and destroying all major military facilities. The United States and its allies would then proceed to invade and occupy the country.[170] Russian International Affairs Council expert and Leading Research Fellow at the Korean Studies Center at RAS Institute for Far Eastern Studies Konstantin Asmolov noted regarding the drills: 'it was openly admitted that the U.S. and South Korean forces would engage in sabotage at the nuclear sites. If North Korea announced a similar tactic, the Western media would already be filled with accusations that the DPRK was engaged in the international terrorism. In this case no one was alarmed by the creation of new raiding units acting under the preemptive strike strategy.'[171]

U.S. heavy bombers were also confirmed by the Pentagon to be carrying out simulated nuclear strikes on the DPRK from Guam, and considering the U.S. military's aforementioned doctrine for using nuclear weapons this presents an immediate and dire threat to North Korean security.[172] North Korea was previously vulnerable to U.S. strategic and tactical nuclear forces including nuclear powered warships, nuclear submarines[173] and nuclear capable B-52 and B-1B[174] and B-2 bombers staging military drills on its borders and stationed within range throughout the Pacific. This goes without mentioning the depleted uranium munitions deployed on platforms as small as Abrams tanks – highly poisonous weapons the status and legality of which remains contested, which were used extensively by U.S. forces in Yugoslavia,[175] Syria[176] and Iraq including in populated areas.[177]

Contamination from these weapons lasts indefinitely and has had devastating effects on the Serbian and Iraqi populations. Their use in a ground war in North Korea was almost certain.

The DPRK has continued to perceive drills projecting strikes on and an occupation of the country as potential preparations for a real invasion. Few countries are expected to or do tolerate such actions on their borders – with North Korea's response coming in the form of missile and nuclear testing – with ballistic missiles being the most effective means for North Korea to asymmetrically respond to the massed firepower displayed south of the 38th Parallel by the U.S. military and off the country's coasts – where the U.S. Navy has deployed aircraft carriers and nuclear submarines. North Korea has frequently launched nuclear and missile tests directly in response to these exercises, one example being in December 2017 when the country's two month pause in missile testing ended only with the U.S. announcement of the unscheduled Vigilant Ace military exercises.

The current stance of the DPRK regarding nuclear disarmament can be effectively summed up by a quote from U.S. President Theodore Roosevelt, who wrote regarding disarmament in November 1918: 'I am not willing to play the part which even Aesop held up to derision when he wrote of how the wolves and the sheep agreed to disarm, and how the sheep as a guarantee of good faith sent away the watchdogs, and were then forthwith eaten by the wolves.'[178] This seems to be the perception of the DPRK, with nuclear weapons representing the 'watchdogs' and the United states the 'wolves.' This belief that they are threatened by the United States is strengthened significantly by the memory of the Korean War and the millions of deaths and atrocities suffered by the Korean people.

As a North Korean friend told the writer when discussing the country's relations with the United States: 'it is because of this that we say the Americans do not act as people towards us. We say they are like wolves.' Indeed education in the DPRK, including textbooks for children, often describes the United States military as 'imperialist wolves.'[179] North Koreans' perceptions of the intentions of the United States are based primarily on their experience during the Korean War, perceptions which are reinforced by continuous U.S. military interventions across the world against sovereign states. It is based on this perception that the DPRK has sought a nuclear deterrent, to prevent the horrors of the Korean War from reoccurring. The DPRK will only give up its deterrent if its security can be guaranteed and military provocation ceases or to extend President Roosevelt's metaphor, the sheep will only disarm if they can be sure the wolves are away. To do otherwise would be, according to the DPRK's worldview, criminally irresponsible and putting the entire population at a terrible risk. Unilateral disarmament in the face of continued military posturing by the United States and its partners – who themselves threatened the country with nuclear arms of their own long before it had any nuclear capabilities – is therefore not an option for North Korea. As Han Song Ryol of the DPRK Foreign Ministry stated regarding the country's unwillingness to unilaterally disarm and its right a nuclear deterrent: 'It is the United States that caused this issue. They have to stop their military threats, sanctions and economic pressure. Without doing so, it's like they are telling us to reconcile while they are putting a gun to our forehead.'[180]

At One with the Past: The History of Western War Crimes and their Influence on Modern North Korean Thought

The DPRK today stands out for its continued adherence to anti-imperialist ideology and its opposition to what it perceives to be American imperialism. For the North Korean population perceptions of Western nations are primarily influenced not by the West's soft power and positive depictions of themselves through popular media, but rather by the state's anti-imperialist stances, the conduct of the Western Bloc's policy and the experiences of the Korean War. While elsewhere the United States may more readily be associated with its popular culture or with ideals of democracy and humanitarianism, in North Korea perceptions of the United States are shaped primarily by the government's perception of U.S. foreign policy, entailing war crimes and regular military interventions across the world with high human costs. North Korean children are taught about the war crimes of the United States in Korea, Vietnam and elsewhere as well as those of the Japanese Empire in Korea.[181] The North Korean government is almost entirely unique in its ability to shape its people's perceptions of the West, perceptions which elsewhere are shaped overwhelmingly by the West's own soft power through means such as entertainment and popular media.

A prime example of the DPRK's means of controlling the narrative regarding the nature of Western imperialism is through a very unique museum, The Museum of American War Atrocities in Sinchon. Here the war crimes committed by the United States and its partners during the Korean War are well documented and through artwork the crimes against North Koreans in areas occupied by U.S. soldiers during the war are graphically depicted. The museum contains testimonies of survivors and incriminating quotes from U.S. generals and other evidence of war crimes. It is located at the site of one of the many massacres which occurred during the war, and two storehouses used by the U.S. forces to perpetrate a massacre remain.

According to North Korean accounts, the evidence and remains found, and the testimonies of survivors, sadistic means of torture and killing were employed to kill and rape Korean people en masse. Several skulls of victims with nails hammered into their bodies can be seen, one of many ways the invading forces killed the Koreans under their power. Photographs of a large trench used to hide the bodies of the victims including babies and pregnant women can also be seen. These massacres were carried out to subdue the population for domination by the United States.

When visiting the museum in 2016, the writer asked the curator An Hyeon Hui how she felt the conduct of the United States in Korea compared to that of the Japanese Empire beforehand. She answered: 'despite almost 40 years of Japanese occupation, the atrocities of U.S. imperialists [in 3 years] are still greater.' Referring to the pictures of U.S. military exercises on the country's borders she said: 'The true nature of the U.S. will never change. They try now to occupy our country again. Our people do not want a war but if the U.S. provokes us again then our people will defeat them at once.' An Hyeon Hui presented various other pieces of evidence, including accounts written by international observers, photographs of the remains of the victims, often mutilated and pieces of jewelry and clothing from the victims' bodies. Crimes committed by occupation forces including dragging women down streets by hooks in their noses and jarring hot metal rods into their uteruses were also depicted. An said: 'The US, based on this, is talking about human rights in Korea.'

At first the writer was hesitant to believe these stories as they were told. Could the reality of war with the United States and Western powers truly be so horrific and could they be so inhuman in their treatment of Asian peoples? Considering the West's position as the world's center of power, and the immense soft power and cultural exports of Western nations, it would certainly be more comfortable to dismiss such claims. Though the claims made by the DPRK are dismissed as fabricated propaganda by a 'crazy dictatorship' by major media and scholarly sources in the West however, they are not only strongly supported by a wide range of highly reliable non-communist sources from the Korean War, from international and South Korean government commissions to highly respected journalists (as covered in Chapter 10), but are also highly in keeping with the historical conduct of Western powers in their interventions abroad. British torture camps in Kenya,[182,183] the genocidal and highly sadistic conduct towards the Australian aborigines[184] or the American genocide of their native peoples and the very similar and well documented crimes carried out in Japan and Vietnam within a decade of the Korean War, are but a few examples. It therefore seems wholly consistent and in keeping with the characteristics of these powers to carry out such actions against the Korean people. Further research based on Western and South Korean sources has not only fully verified North Korea's claims, but also shed light of further atrocities of a similar and at times more serious nature committed during the war both in South Korea and during the brief Western occupation of the north (as covered in Chapters 9 and 10).

While some North Korean depictions of the United States may be exaggerated or caricatured, based on the history of military interventions in the Asia-Pacific they may well be closer to the truth than the alternative Western depiction of a benevolent Western Bloc carrying Asia's best interests at heart and intervening only to democratize and protect its people. This alternative caricature of benevolence and good will, in total contrast to the lessons of history, is certainly how the Western Bloc has portrayed its intentions and justified its continued military deployments and interventions in the region. Reports of atrocities committed are glossed over either as propaganda – when this fails then as freak incidents committed by a few individuals, and can never be considered part of a consistent and longstanding trend towards atrocious conduct inherent to Western intervention in the Asia-Pacific region.

On May 24, 2016 the writer was able to meet Jeong Geun Seong, one of three survivors of the 1950 Sinchon massacre, and asked what happened to the people of Sinchon when under U.S. occupation. He was in his 70s at the time. Jeong Geun Seong continues to meet with visitors at the site of the massacre despite his old age. He says it is crucial that such facts are handed down to new generations. He said that the crimes of U.S. imperialists must never be forgotten, and asked that the writer help spread awareness of these crimes. South Korean sources and the Routledge Journal of Genocide Research (JGR) have confirmed that when Sinchon was under the control of U.S. forces approximately one quarter of its civilian population were massacred, 35,380 killings.[185] This estimate, given in a JGR paper published in 2004, was remarkably similar to that of North Korea which estimated 35,000 deaths during the Sinchon massacre,[186] verifying the DPRK's claims which had for so long been denied by the United States and widely dismissed as propaganda. The allegations made by Jeong and by the DPRK and the evidence presented are also highly consistent with the reports of several international observers in North Korea during the war – as previously covered in Chapter 10.

One reason for the Western Bloc's continued hostility towards the DPRK is that it is perhaps more than any other nation ideologically independent. North Korea continues to almost uniquely oppose the United States' regional initiatives and refuse to adopt their cultural, ideological and economic values. In 2014 the Museum of American War Atrocities was rebuilt on a greater scale. While other nations would find this distasteful and would fear defying the mainstream perception of civilized and ultimately good Western nations or risking worsening relations with the world's dominant powers, the DPRK has stood firm by the lessons of its history. They refuse to forget the crimes committed against Asian peoples out of simple convenience, and largely as a result suffer harsh consequences.

Ideologies which reject the status quo of Western dominance of the Asia-Pacific, be they nationalist, communist or pan-Asian, are severe threats to Western powers' control of the Asia-Pacific region. It is of paramount importance that such ideologies should be suppressed when they emerge, or else that states which adopt them should be isolated. Renowned American national security adviser, and former Secretary of State Henry Kissinger, one of the world's most influential foreign policy strategists, termed independent nationalism a 'virus' with the potential to 'spread contagion' to neighboring states. It was for this reason that the 'virus' of Vietnamese nationalism was so stringently opposed, lest it 'contaminate' the numerous American client states and allies throughout the region. This was a key motivator for the United States to launch a destructive war against the country, preventing it from exploring its potential or becoming a model for the rest of Asia.[187] The DPRK's nationalist ideology, which strongly rejects Western dominance and primacy based on its historical experiences, can potentially pose such a threat to Western dominance of the Asia-Pacific and beyond if not properly contained, demonized and economically restricted.

It is essential for the United States that North Korea's allegations regarding the nature of its intentions in Asia, the history of war crimes committed and what the U.S. and their Western partners have proven to be capable of are not taken seriously regionally or globally. Extensive demonization of the country is a key means by which to achieve this and prevent Korea's claims from being taken into consideration by foreign nations (as previously covered in Chapter 12). If for example Asian populations were aware of the reality of Western occupation as took place in Korea, the current balance of power in the Asia-Pacific region and views of Western powers as 'protectors' from China and North Korea and upholders of a 'rules based order' could well be very different.

In June 2016 the DPRK opened the National House of Class Education to educate its population on the 'History of Aggression' of foreign powers. The facility is intended particularly for younger North Koreans who, having not experienced the Korean War or Japanese occupation themselves, lack firsthand knowledge of the nature of foreign imperialism. North Korean media stated that the facility would help the people of the DPRK to clearly realize who its enemies are. Such a facility represents precisely the reason why North Korea poses a significant ideological threat, in that its population are uniquely well educated in the nature of the conduct of Western powers in Asia, in ways which other peoples who suffered similarly such as the Japanese and Filipinos are not. It is as a result of such education that an armed invasion of the DPRK would be nothing less than a total war against the entire population, unlike in other target states in which significant pro-Western fifth columns remain. To forget previous crimes and choose to ignore one's history and what it teaches regarding the intentions of states which have previously committed war crimes against one's nation is to leave oneself vulnerable to recurrences of the past. Only by being aware of reality of history can it be taken into account in the future, and so repetition of exploitation and crimes by the same perpetrators can be avoided. This is an underlying principle of the DPRK's ideology. As Kim Hyong Chol, the head of the National House of Class Education, said shortly after its opening in regard to its purpose: 'If we forget the history of aggression, it can be repeated. We need to teach a new generation not to forget it.'[188]

North Korea, its motivations and its ideology cannot be understood by the Western world because the West cannot come to terms with Korean War and their own atrocities which have shaped North Korea. Just as Holocaust has shaped the views of Jews and Russians, and so of modern Russia and Israel, towards the Third Reich, so have the crimes of the U.S. led coalition under the banner of the United Nations shaped North Korea's views of the Western-centric and American-led world order.

Just as Nazi Germany and their European allies killed up to 38 percent of the world's Jewish population, targeting them indiscriminately,[189] so too did the U.S. military and their own European allies indiscriminately target Korean civilians, cut off their food supplies, and kill up to 30 percent of the DPRK's population. Both were genocidal and intended to kill millions more, with Nazi Germany intending to kill and starve tens of millions of Russians[190] just as the United States sought to target the dams and rice fields feeding millions of North Koreans, which would have caused a widespread famine and killed many millions more had it not been for an emergency food aid program provided by the USSR and China. The Nazis burned their 'subhuman' victims en masse in concentration camps, while the U.S. Air Force doused Korean population centers with napalm and incendiaries. Both were found to have carried out medical experiments on their 'subhuman' prisoners.

As a result of the actions of Nazi Germany and its European allies, Holocaust memorials have been built from Israel to Berlin and are, rightly, seen as a commemoration of the suffering of the victims of European race war and brutality towards those perceived as subhuman. Education on the Holocaust is today seen as necessary to prevent such an incident from ever re-occurring, and a world Holocaust Memorial Day is commemorated every year. By contrast however North Korea's war memorials and education and commemoration are derided as propaganda and brainwashing in the West, not as a necessary step both to pay respect to the victims and to prevent such atrocities from re-occurring.

What is termed propaganda is also highly subjective and dependent on one's perspective. Holocaust memorials are certainly hardly termed 'Jewish propaganda' except by those who deny the Holocaust or else accuse the victims of manipulating their past for sympathy and political benefits. Equally, the West largely terms North Korean memorials of American atrocities such as those at Sinchon to be 'propaganda' because Western powers involved in the Korean War, while categorically refusing to launch any form of investigation into the killings of North Korean civilians – or even their massacres of South Korean civilians for that matter, do not accept any responsibility. A case has therefore emerged which closely reflects that of Holocaust deniers, where North Korea's commemoration of their history is deemed 'propaganda' which is exploited to indoctrinate its people and gain its leadership political benefits.

The reason for the vastly different portrayals and perceptions of genocides which took place under the Holocaust and the Korean War is that the West can and has come to terms with the crimes of the Third Reich, with which it today does not associate itself, but it fails to come to terms with the brutality and war crimes of the modern Western Bloc which emerged after 1945. As U.S. Senator John McCain, chairman of the Senate Armed Service Committee, stated at the Munich Security Conference in 2017: 'we cannot allow ourselves to question the rightness and goodness of the West.'[191] U.S. President George Bush previously stated in 1988 following the U.S. Navy's unprovoked downing of an Iranian civilian airliner over international waters in the Persian Gulf killing 290 passengers on board: 'I will never apologize for the United States – I don't care what the facts are.'[192] As the Western Bloc cannot perceive itself as anything other than an ultimate force for good in its recent history, it cannot understand why North Korea refuses to disarm in the face of American military drills on its border, adopt a Western economic and political system, and ultimately become part of the Western-centric world order. In the mindset of the West, North Korean grievances can never be acknowledged because they are so sure of the rightness of their causes and their history. As a result education regarding American war crimes will continue to be deemed 'propaganda,' defensive military drills will be deemed 'provocation' and pursuit of nuclear weapons to match those deployed by the United States throughout the Pacific will be considered unacceptable.

Notes

1 Sokolski, Henry and Clawson, Patrick, *Getting Ready for a Nuclear Ready Iran*, Carlisle, Pennsylvania, Strategic Studies Institute, U.S. Army War College, 2005. (p. 169).

2 Reagan, Ronald, *Address to the Nation and Other Countries on United States-Soviet Relations*, January 16, 1984.

3 *Foreign Affairs*, 69/5, Winter 1990/91, (p. 23).

4 Beinart, Peter, 'How America Shed the Taboo Against Preventative War,' *The Atlantic*, April 21, 2017.

5 Silverstone, Scott, *Preventative War and American Democracy*, Abingdon, Routledge, 2007.

6 Smith, Derek D., 'Deterring America: Rogue States and the Proliferation of Weapons of Mass Destruction,' Cambridge, Cambridge University Press, 2006 (pp. 116–120).

7 Hayes, Peter, *Pacific Powderkeg: American Nuclear Dilemmas in Korea*, Lexington, Mass, Lexington Books, 1991.

8 Cumings, Bruce, Korea's Place in the Sun, W. W. Norton and Company, New York, 1997 (p. 475).

9 Chomsky, Noam, *The New Military Humanism; Lessons From Kosovo*, London, Pluto Press, 1999 (Chapter 6, 'Why Force?').
10 *Defense Monitor*, Washington, DC, Center for Defense Information, 2000 (p. XXIX, 3).
11 *Essentials of Post-Cold War Deterrence*, Policy Subcommittee of the Strategic Advisory Group (SAG) of the United States Strategic Command, 1995.
12 Chomsky, Noam, *The New Military Humanism; Lessons From Kosovo*, London, Pluto Press, 1999 (pp. 145–146).
13 Miller, Eric A., and Yetiv, Steve A., 'The New World Order in Theory and Practice: The Bush Administration's Worldview in Transition,' *Presidential Studies Quarterly*, March 2001.
14 Duffy Toft, Monica, 'Why is America Addicted to Foreign Interventions?,' *The National Interest*, December 10, 2017.
15 Heikal, Mohamed, *Illusions of Triumph: An Arab View of the Gulf War*, New York, HarperCollins, 1993 (pp. 175–177).
16 Nixon, John, *Debriefing the President; The Interrogation of Saddam Hussein*, London, Bantam Press, 2016 (p. 112).
17 Heikal, Mohamed, *Illusions of Triumph: An Arab View of the Gulf War*, New York, HarperCollins, 1993 (p. 176, 178, 218).
18 Ibid. (p. 365).
19 *The Military Balance*, Volume 89, International Institute for Strategic Studies, 1989 (pp. 101–102).
20 Gellman, Barton, 'Allied Air War Struck Broadly in Iraq,' *Washington Post*, June 23, 1991.
21 'Iraq conflict has killed a million Iraqis,' *Reuters*, January 30, 2008.
22 'Sanctions Blamed for Deaths of Children,' *Lewiston Morning Tribune*, December 2, 1995.
23 Stahl, Lesley, 'Interview with Madeline Albright,' *60 Minutes*, May 12, 1996.
24 Gordon, Joy, *Invisible War*: The United States and the Iraq Sanctions, Cambridge, MS, Harvard University Press, 2010 (p. 87).
25 Friedman, Thomas, and Tyler, Patrick E., 'From the First, U.S. Resolve to Fight: The Path to War,' *New York Times*, March 3, 1991.
26 Heginbotham, Eric, *The U.S.-China Military Scorecard, Forces, Geography, and the Evolving Balance of Power 1996–2017*, Santa Monica, CA, RAND Corporation, 2015 (pp. 25–26).
27 Lam, Willy Wo-Lap, 'Iraq war hands lessons to China,' *CNN*, April 15, 2003.
28 Funabashi, Yoichi, 'The Peninsula Question: A Chronicle of the Second Korean Nuclear Crisis,' Washington, DC, Brookings Institution Press, 2007 (p. 126).

29 Armstrong, Charles, *Necessary Enemies: Anti-Americanism, Juche Ideology, and the Torturous Path to Normalization*, Washington D.C., US-Korea Institute at SAIS, Working Paper Series, WP 08-3, September 2008 (p. 4).
30 'Bush peers into "evil" North Korea,' *CNN*, February 20, 2002.
31 *Saddam Hussein Meeting with Ba'ath Party Members to Discuss the Results of the UN Inspectors' Mission to Look for WMDs*, Saddam Hussein's Iraq, Wilson Center Digital Archive, June 19, 1995.
32 *Rodong Sinmun*, March 28, 2003.
33 Ramesh, Randeep, 'The two faces of Rumsfeld,' *The Guardian*, May 9, 2003.
34 Pincus, Walter, 'Rumsfeld Seeks to Revive Burrowing Nuclear Bomb,' *Washington Post*, February 1, 2005.
35 Auster, Bruce B., and Whitelaw, Kevin, 'Upping the Ante for Kim Jong Il: Pentagon Plan 5030, A New Blueprint for Facing Down North Korea,' *U.S. News and World Report*, July 21, 2003.
36 O'Hanion, Machael E., 'North Korea Is No Iraq,' *Brookings Institute*, October 21, 2002.
37 Bennett, Bruce W., 'A surgical strike against North Korea? Not a viable option,' *Fox News*, July 14, 2017.
38 Smith, Derek D., 'Deterring America: Rogue States and the Proliferation of Weapons of Mass Destruction,' Cambridge, Cambridge University Press, 2006 (pp. 87, 108–109).
39 Woolf, Christopher, 'The only effective arms against North Korea's missile bunkers are nuclear weapons, says a top war planner,' *PRI*, August 10, 2017.
40 Sepp, Eric M., *Deeply Buried Facilities: Implications for Military Operations*, Occasional Paper No. 14, Maxwell Air Force Base, AL, Air War College, May 2000 (p. 5).
41 Levi, Michael A., *Fire in the Hole: Nuclear and Non-Nuclear Options for Counter-proliferation*, Working Paper No. 31, Washington, D.C., Carnegie Endowment for International Peace, November 2002 (p. 8).
42 Kim, Suk Hi, *The Survival of North Korea: Essays on Strategy, Economics and International Relations*, Jefferson, NC, McFarland, 2011 (pp. 49–50).
43 Park, Kyung Ae, *New Challenges of North Korean Foreign Policy*, London, Palgrave MacMillan, 2010 (p. 218).
44 'U.S. Repositioning Bombers Near North Korea,' *USA Today*, March 4, 2003.
45 'North Korea: Washington Flew 1,200 Spy Flights Over Country,' *Fox News*, July 25, 2004.
46 'North Korea Accuses U.S. of Spy Flights,' *Southern Illinoisan*, July 26, 2004.
47 Arkin, William M., 'Secret Plan Outlines the Unthinkable', *Los Angeles Times*, March 10, 2002.

48 Park, Kyung Ae, *New Challenges of North Korean Foreign Policy*, London, Palgrave MacMillan, 2010.

49 Ibid.

50 Stares, Paul B. and Wit, Joel S., 'Preparing for Sudden Change in North Korea,' Council Special Report No. 42, *Council on Foreign Relations Center for Preventative Action*, January 2009.

51 *A Conversation with U.S. Secretary of State Hillary Rodham Clinton*, Council on Foreign Relations, July 15, 2009.

52 Armstrong, Charles, *Necessary Enemies: Anti-Americanism, Juche Ideology, and the Torturous Path to Normalization*, Washington D.C., US-Korea Institute at SAIS, Working Paper Series, WP 08-3, September 2008 (p. 14).

53 Ibid. (p. 15).

54 Chossudovsky, Michel, 'KNOW THE FACTS: North Korea Lost Close to 30% of its Population as a result of the U.S. Bombings in the 1950s,' *Centre for Research on Globalization*, November 27, 2010.

55 Lindqvist, Sven, *A History of Bombing*, New York, The New Press, 2001 (p. 131).

56 'North Korea cites Muammar Gaddafi's "destruction" in nuclear test defence,' *Reuters*, January 9, 2016.

57 French, Howards W., 'A Nation At War: Nuclear Standoff; North Korea Says Its Arms Will Deter U.S. Attack,' *New York Times*, April 7, 2003.

58 Christie, Kenneth. *United State Foreign Policy and National Identity in the 21st Century*, Abingdon, Routledge, 2008 (p. 46).

59 Funabashi, Yichi, *The Peninsula Question: A Chronicle of the Second Korean Nuclear Crisis*, Washington, DC, Brookings Institution, 2007.

60 Project for a New American Century Letter to Bill Clinton, January 26, 1998 (<https://web.archive.org/web/20131021171040/http://www.newamerican-century.org/iraqclintonletter.htm>).

61 Donnelly Thomas, *Rebuilding America's Defenses*, A Report of The Project for the New American Century, September 2000 (pp. 6, 12, 51, 54).

62 *Memorandum from Secretary of Defense Donald Rumsfeld to Senior White House Officials, RE: Budget Issues, National Security Policy Issues, Post Cold War Threats*, The White House, February, 2001. (<https://archive.org/stream/GeorgeW.BushPresidentialPapers/GWB01_djvu.txt>).

63 Lewis, Jeffrey, 'The Game Is Over, and North Korea Has Won,' *Foreign Policy*, August 9, 2017.

64 Moore, Malcolm, 'North Korea now "fully fledged nuclear power,"' *The Telegraph*, April 24, 2009.

65 'How Powerful Was N. Korea's Nuke Test?' *The Chosunilbo*, February 14, 2013.

66 'Deadlier Than Nagasaki: North Korea's Nuke Test 30 Kilotonnes in Capacity,' *Sputnik*, September 9, 2016.

67 Warrick, Joby and Nakashima, Ellen, and Fifield, Anna, 'North Korea now making missile-ready nuclear weapons, U.S. analysts say,' *Washington Post*, August 8, 2017.

68 Panda, Ankit, 'US Intelligence: North Korea's ICBM Reentry Vehicles Are Likely Good Enough to Hit the Continental US,' *The Diplomat*, August 12, 2017.

69 Kim, Jong Un, *War Veterans Are Our Precious Revolutionary Forerunners Who Created the Indomitable Spirit of Defending the Country*, Congratulatory Speech Delivered at the Fourth National Conference of War Veterans, July 25, 2015.

70 'Kim Jong-un Says North Korean Nukes "Protecting Sovereignty" Aid U.S. "Threats,"' *Sputnik*, October 8, 2017.

71 Choe, Sang-Hun, 'North Korean Leader Stresses Need for Strong Military,' *New York Times*, April 15, 2012.

72 Lewis, Jeffrey, 'The Game Is Over, and North Korea Has Won,' *Foreign Policy*, August 9, 2017.

73 Berger, Andrea, 'Target Markets, North Korea's Military Customers in the Sanctions Era,' Abingdon, Routledge, 2016 (p. 302).

74 Han, Jongwoo, and Jung, Tae Hern, *Understanding North Korea: Indigenous Perspectives*, Lanham, MD, Lexington Books (p. 302).

75 Paul, Ronald, and McAdams, Daniel, *B-52s Over Korea … Protecting Our Homeland?*, Ron Paul Institute for Peace and Prosperity, Ron Paul Liberty Report, January 11, 2016 (00:07:20).

76 'China successfully tests nuclear-capable hypersonic missile – Pentagon sources,' *RT*, April 27, 2016.

77 Astrada, Marvin L., *American Power After 9/11*, London, Palgrave Macmillan, 2010 (p. 86).

78 Pandit, Rajat, 'Entire China could soon be within India's N-strike zone,' *Times of India*, January 19, 2018.

79 Panda, Ankit, 'Pakistan Conducts Second Test of Babur-3 Nuclear-Capable Submarine-Launched Cruise Missile,' *The Diplomat*, April 1, 2018.

80 'The U.S. Military's Development and Testing of the B61–12 Tactical Nuclear Bomb; Why it is Cause for Concern in Russia and North Korea,' *Military Watch Magazine*, August 30, 2017.

81 Obama, Barack, 'President Obama: The TPP would let America, not China, lead the way on global trade,' *Washington Post*, May 2, 2016.

82 'To React to Nuclear Weapons in Kind Is DPRK's Mode of Counteraction,' *Rodong Sinmun*, Korean Central News Agency, January 11, 2016.

83 'DPRK FM on Its Stand to Suspend Its Participation in Six-Party Talks for Indefinite Period,' *Korean Central News Agency*, February 10, 2005.

84 Kim, Jong Un, *Report to the Seventh Congress of the Workers' Party of Korea on the Work of the Central Committee*, June 20, 2016.
85 Kim, Jong Un, *War Veterans Are Our Precious Revolutionary Forerunners Who Created the Indomitable Spirit of Defending the Country*, Congratulatory Speech Delivered at the Fourth National Conference of War Veterans, July 25, 2015.
86 'DPRK Foreign Ministry's Spokesman Dismisses US Wrong Assertion,' *Korean Central News Agency*, October 3, 2006.
87 Donnelly Thomas, *Rebuilding America's Defenses, A Report of The Project for the New American Century*, September 2000 (pp. 6, 12, 51, 54).
88 *Memorandum from Secretary of Defense Donald Rumsfeld to Senior White House Officials, RE: Budget Issues, National Security Policy Issues, Post Cold War Threats*, The White House, February 2001.
89 'North Korea Reached "Point of No Return" in Obtaining Nuclear Technology,' *Sputnik*, September 9, 2016.
90 Friedman, Uri, 'Lindsey Graham Reveals the Dark Calculus of Striking North Korea,' *The Atlantic*, August 1, 2017.
91 McMahon, Patrick, 'Senator calls for "preemptive strike" on North Korea and offers a jaw-dropping justification for war,' *Rare News*, April 20, 2017.
92 Friedman, Uri, 'Lindsey Graham Reveals the Dark Calculus of Striking North Korea,' *The Atlantic*, August 1, 2017.
93 Brown, Daniel, 'Republican congressman says the U.S. should preemptively strike North Korea,' *Business Insider*, September 22, 2017.
94 Peters, Ralph, 'The moral answer to North Korea's threats, Take them out!' *New York Post*, September 4, 2017.
95 'Lt. Gen. H. R. McMaster on foreign policy; Sen. Schumer on President Trump's first 100 days,' *Fox News*, April 30, 2017.
96 Friedman, Uri, 'Lindsey Graham Reveals the Dark Calculus of Striking North Korea,' *The Atlantic*, August 1, 2017.
97 'Trump says North Korea will be met with "fire and fury" if it threatens U.S.,' *Reuters*, August 8, 2017.
98 'Read President Trump's Speech Threatening to "Totally Destroy" North Korea,' *Time*, September 19, 2017.
99 Payne, Keith B., *The Fallacies of Cold War Deterrence and a New Direction*, Lexington, University Press of Kentucky, 2001 (p. 53).
100 'Seoul warns Trump: U.S. must not strike North Korea without our consent,' *The Guardian*, November 15, 2017.
101 Brown, Daniel, 'Republican congressman says the U.S. should preemptively strike North Korea,' *Business Insider*, September 22, 2017.

102 Peters, Ralph, 'The moral answer to North Korea's threats, Take them out!' *New York Post*, September 4, 2017.

103 'Lt. Gen. H. R. McMaster on foreign policy; Sen. Schumer on President Trump's first 100 days,' *Fox News*, April 30, 2017.

104 Friedman, Uri, 'Lindsey Graham Reveals the Dark Calculus of Striking North Korea,' *The Atlantic*, August 1, 2017.

105 Reagan, Ronald, *Address to the Nation and Other Countries on United States-Soviet Relations*, January 16, 1984.

106 Siracusa, Joseph M., *Nuclear Weapons: A Very Short Introduction*, Oxford, Oxford University Press, 2008 (p. 67).

107 Ibid. (p. 69).

108 Kopp, Carlo, *Operation Odyssey Dawn – the collapse of Libya's relic air defense system*, in Defence Today, vol. 9, no. 1, 2011, Strike Publications (p. 14).

109 *The Military Balance*, Volume 114, International Institute for Strategic Studies, 2014 (pp. 254–257).

110 'North Korea: The War Game,' *The Atlantic*, July August 2005.

111 Thomas-Noone, Brendan, 'North Korea: War With U.S. Would Come With 'Intensity of Violence' We Haven't Seen In Decades,' The United States Studies Centre, University of Sydney, April 4, 2017.

112 Vandiver, John, 'Army chief Milley warns of tough choices ahead on North Korea,' *Stars and Stripes*, July 28, 2017.

113 'U.S. General Concerned by Threat to Seoul Posed by N. Korea's 800-Missile Arsenal,' *East-Asia-Intel.com*, October 17, 2008.

114 Yilek, Catlin, 'Mac Thornberry on war with North Korea, "We can win but it will be ugly,"' *The Washington Examiner*, November 7, 2017.

115 Debs, Alexandre, and P. Nuno, Monterio, *Nuclear Politics: The Strategic Causes of Proliferation*, Cambridge, Cambridge University Press, 2016 (p. 287).

116 Lankov, Andrei, *The Real North Korea; Life and Politics in the Failed Stalinist Utopia*, Oxford, Oxford University Press, 2015 (p. 175).

117 Lee, Carol E., and Gale, Alastair, 'White House Options on North Korea Include Use of Military Force,' *The Wall Street Journal*, March 1, 2017.

118 Stares, Paul B. and Wit, Joel S., 'Preparing for Sudden Change in North Korea,' Council Special Report No. 42, *Council on Foreign Relations Center for Preventative Action*, January 2009.

119 *Doctrine for Joint Nuclear Operations*, United States of America Department of the Army and United States Marine Corps Department of the Navy, Joint Publication (p. 3–12).

120 Talmadge, Eric, 'North Korea will not use its nuclear weapons first, Kim Jong-un tells Congress,' *The Independent*, May 8, 2016.

121 Yoshihara, Toshi, and Holmes, James R., *Strategy in the Second Nuclear Age, Power, Ambition and the Ultimate Weapon*, Washington, D.C., Georgetown University Press, 2012 (p. 92–94).
122 'DPRK Foreign Ministry Clarifies Stand'; 'DPRK Foreign Ministry Spokesman Totally Refutes UNSC "Resolution,"' Korean Central News Agency, October 17, 2005.
123 Turner Haynes, Susan, *Chinese Nuclear Proliferation: How Global Politics is Transforming China's Weapons Buildup and Modernization*, Lincoln, NE, Potomac Books, 2016 (pp. 14–15).
124 Ibid. (p. 39).
125 Broad, William J., and Sanger, David E., 'As U.S. Modernizes Nuclear Weapons, "Smaller" Leaves Some Uneasy,' *New York Times*, January 11, 2016.
126 Kristensen, Hans M., 'General Confirms Enhanced Targeting Capabilities of B61–12 Nuclear Bomb,' *Federation of American Scientists*, January 23, 2014.
127 E. Coyle, Philip, and McKeon, James, 'The Huge Risk of Small Nukes,' *Politico*, March 10, 2017.
128 Feinstein, Dianne, 'There's no such thing as a "limited" nuclear war,' *Washington Post*, March 3, 2017.
129 'North Korea cites Muammar Gaddafi's "destruction" in nuclear test defence,' *The Telegraph*, January 9, 2016.
130 Selden, Mark, and Y. So, Alvin, *War and State Terrorism: The United States, Japan, and the Asia-Pacific in the Long Twentieth Century*, Lanham, MD, Rowman & Littlefield, 2004 (Chapter 4, 'U.S. Air Power and Nuclear Strategy in Northeast Asia since 1945').
131 Milne, Seumus, *The Revenge of History*, London, Verso Books, 2012 (p. 185).
132 Ibid.
133 Schwarz, Jon, 'Trump Intel Chief: North Korea Learned From Libya War to 'Never' Give Up Nukes,' *The Intercept*, July 29, 2017.
134 Bandow, Doug, 'Thanks to Libya, North Korea Might Never Negotiate on Nuclear Weapons,' *The National Interest*, September 2, 2015.
135 Schwarz, Jon, 'Trump Intel Chief: North Korea Learned From Libya War to "Never" Give Up Nukes,' *The Intercept*, July 29, 2017.
136 Asher-Schapiro, Avi, 'Libyan Oil, Gold, and Qaddafi: The Strange Email Sidney Blumenthal Sent Hillary Clinton In 2011,' *Vice News*, January 12, 2016.
137 Walt, Vivienne, 'How Did Gaddafi Die? A Year Later, Unanswered Questions and Bad Blood,' *Time*, September 18, 2012.
138 '"Libya becoming completely failed state" – former U.S. Ambassador,' *RT*, May 30, 2017.
139 'U.S. ground troops are in Libya, Pentagon admits,' *RT*, August 12, 2016.

140 Schmitt, Eric, and Gordon, Michael R., 'U.S. Bombs ISIS Camps in Libya,' *New York Times*, January 10, 2017.
141 'African migrants raped & murdered after being sold in Libyan "slave markets" – UN,' *RT*, April 11, 2017.
142 Osborne, Samuel, 'Libya: African refugees being sold at "regular public slave auctions,"' *The Independent*, April 11, 2017.
143 'Handle With Extreme Care,' *The Economist*, April 22, 2017.
144 'African migrants raped & murdered after being sold in Libyan "slave markets" – UN,' *RT*, April 11, 2017.
145 Chivvis, Christopher S., and Martini, Jeffrey, 'Libya After Qaddafi; Lessons and Implications for the Future,' National Security and Research Division, *Rand Corporation*, 2014.
146 Carter, James Earl, 'Jimmy Carter: What I've learned from North Korea's leaders,' *Washington Post*, October 4, 2017.
147 'Vladimir Putin's news conference following BRICS Summit,' *President of Russia, Kremlin*, September 5, 2017.
148 'Will Rejecting China's Offer to Broker Peace in Korea Intensify the Standoff?', *Sputnik*, March 11, 2017.
149 Debs, Alexandre, and Monteiro, Nuno P., *Nuclear Politics: The Strategic Causes of Proliferation*, Cambridge, Cambridge University Press, 2016 (p. 294).
150 Ramani, Samuel, 'What North Korea Learned From the Kosovo War; NATO's intervention in Kosovo cemented North Korea's distrust of the U.S. and embrace of nuclear weapons,' *The Diplomat*, October 16, 2017.
151 Bolton, Alexander, 'McConnell: Assad must go,' *The Hill*, April 17, 2017.
152 '"No role for Assad": Tillerson's U-turn on Syria regime change,' *RT*, April 7, 2017.
153 Paul, Ronald, and McAdams, Daniel, *North Korea Nukes: A Case For Non-Intervention?*, Ron Paul Institute for Peace and Prosperity, Ron Paul Liberty Report, January 6, 2016.
154 Mathers, J., *The Russian Nuclear Shield from Stalin to Yeltsin: The Cold War and Beyond*, London, Palgrave Macmillan, 2000 (pp. 220–224).
155 *Progress Report Prepared by the Operations Coordinating Board*, Foreign Relations of the United States, 1955–1957, Korea, Volume XXIII, Part 2, United States of America Department of State, Office of the Historian, July 18, 1956.
156 Lee, Jae-Bong, 'U.S. Deployment of Nuclear Weapons in 1950s South Korea & North Korea's Nuclear Development: Toward Denuclearization of the Korean Peninsula,' *The Asia-Pacific Journal*, Volume 7, Issue 8, February 17, 2009.
157 Kristensen, Hans M., 'A History of U.S. Nuclear Weapons in South Korea,' *Federation of American Scientists*, September 28, 2005.
158 Rosenbaum, David E., 'U.S. to Pull A-Bombs From South Korea,' *New York Times*, October 20, 1991.

159 Ha-young, Choi, 'North Korea to decrease national defense proportion this year,' *NK News*, March 31, 2016.
160 Cordesman, Anthony H., and Colley, Steven, *Chinese Strategy and Military Modernization in 2015: A Comparative Analysis*, Washington, DC, Centre for Strategic and International Studies, 2016 (p. 377).
161 Pearson, James, and Park, Ju-min, 'North Korea overcomes poverty, sanctions with cut-price nukes,' *Reuters*, January 11, 2016.
162 Dorell, Oren, 'North Korean Economy Keeps Humming Despite Ever-Tighter Sanctions,' *USA Today*, November 25, 2017.
163 Lankov, Andrei, 'Sanctions working? Not yet ...,' *Korea Times*, May 29, 2016.
164 'North Korea 2016 economic growth at 17-year high despite sanctions – South Korea,' *Reuters*, July 21, 2017.
165 'How Sanctions Affect Iran's Economy,' *Council on Foreign Relations*, May 22, 2012.
166 Crossette, Barbara, 'Iraq Sanctions Kill Children, U.N. Reports,' *New York Times*, December 1, 1995.
167 *Russia Economic Report 34: Balancing Economic Adjustment and Transformation*, World Bank, September 30, 2015.
168 'S. Korea, U.S. will rehearse invasion of N. Korea in record-breaking joint military drills,' *RT*, February 22, 2016.
169 Ibid.
170 Ibid.
171 Asmolov, Konstantin, 'North Korea in New U.S. Subversion Plans,' *New Eastern Outlook*, November 10, 2015.
172 Gertz, Bill, 'U.S. B-52 bombers simulated raids over North Korea during military exercises,' *Washington Times*, March 19, 2013.
173 'Trump tells Duterte of two U.S. nuclear subs in Korean waters: NYT,' *Reuters*, May 24, 2017.
174 'U.S. military stokes N Korea flames with "secret nuclear silos" claim,' *RT*, November 16, 2017.
175 '"Up to 15 tons of depleted uranium used in 1999 Serbia bombing" – lead lawyer in suit against NATO,' *RT*, June 13, 2017.
176 Oakford, Samuel, 'The United States Used Depleted Uranium in Syria,' *Foreign Policy*, February 14, 2017.
177 Edwards, Rob, 'U.S. fired depleted uranium at civilian areas in 2003 Iraq war, report finds,' *The Guardian*, June 19, 2014.
178 Kissinger, Henry, *Diplomacy*, New York, Simon and Schuster, 1994.
179 Lankov, Andrei, *The Real North Korea; Life and Politics in the Failed Stalinist Utopia*, Oxford, Oxford University Press, 2015 (p. 63).

180 'North Korea not to surrender nuclear might under U.S. threats: Official,' *Press TV*, June 25, 2016.
181 Lankov, Andrei, *The Real North Korea; Life and Politics in the Failed Stalinist Utopia*, Oxford, Oxford University Press, 2015 (p. 63).
182 Pettus, Ashley, '10 Downing Street's Gulag,' *Harvard Magazine*, March 2005.
183 Parry, Mark, 'Uncovering the brutal truth about the British empire,' *The Guardian*, August 18, 2016.
184 'The Secret Country: The First Australians Fight Back,' British Central Independent Television, (Documentary), 1985.
185 Kim, Dong-Choon, 'Forgotten war, forgotten massacres – the Korean War (1950–1953) as licensed mass killings,' *Journal of Genocide Research*, vol. 6, issue 4, December 2004 (p. 536).
186 Figure given at Sinchon's Museum of American War Atrocities, Sinchon County, Democratic People's Republic of Korea.
187 Chomsky, Noam, *Who Rules the World?*, London, Hamish Hamilton, 2016 (p. 74, 156, 207).
188 'North Korea unveils study facility dedicated to anti-Japan, anti-U.S. education,' *Japan Times*, August 14, 2016.
189 *Jewish Population of Europe in 1933: Population Data By Country*, United States Holocaust Memorial Museum.
190 Cesarani, David, 'From Persecution to Genocide,' *BBC*, February 17, 2012.
191 Scott, Eugene, 'McCain warns of those who are "giving up on the West,"' *CNN*, February 18, 2017.
192 Bush, George H. W., *Ethnic Coalition Speech*, August 2, 1988.

Index

Lightning Source UK Ltd.
Milton Keynes UK
UKHW021833021120
372678UK00005B/251